THE MIDDLE EAST
1945–1950

SURVEY OF INTERNATIONAL AFFAIRS
1939–1946

EDITED BY

ARNOLD TOYNBEE

Director of Studies in the Royal Institute of International Affairs
Research Professor of International History
in the University of London
(Both on the Sir Daniel Stevenson Foundation)

EDITORIAL NOTE

Although this volume forms part of the war-time series of the *Survey of International Affairs* (1939–46), the author has, for the sake of continuity, also covered the post-war years 1947 to 1950. From 1951 onwards the subject of the Middle East is dealt with in the annual *Survey* volumes.

SURVEY OF INTERNATIONAL AFFAIRS

The Middle East 1945–1950

BY *Edward*

GEORGE KIRK

Issued under the auspices of the
Royal Institute of International Affairs

OXFORD UNIVERSITY PRESS

LONDON   NEW YORK   TORONTO

1954

Oxford University Press, Amen House, London E.C.4

GLASGOW NEW YORK TORONTO MELBOURNE WELLINGTON
BOMBAY CALCUTTA MADRAS KARACHI CAPE TOWN IBADAN

Geoffrey Cumberlege, Publisher to the University

PRINTED IN GREAT BRITAIN
AT THE UNIVERSITY PRESS, OXFORD
BY CHARLES BATEY, PRINTER TO THE UNIVERSITY

CONTENTS

MAPS

ABBREVIATIONS
USED IN THE TEXT AND FOOTNOTES

Ad hoc Committee	U.N. General Assembly, 2nd session, *Ad hoc* Committee on the Palestinian Question.
AKEL	*Anorthotikòn Kómma toû Ergazoménou Laoû*: Progressive Party of the Working People (in Cyprus).
Bashkirov	A. Bashkirov: *Rabochee i Profsoyuznoe Dvishenie v Irane* (Moscow, Profizdat, 1948).
C.H.P.	*Cumhuriyet Halk Partisi*: Republican People's Party (in Turkey).
Cmd. 6873	Great Britain, Colonial Office: *Palestine: Statement of Information relating to Acts of Violence*, Cmd. 6873 (London, H.M.S.O. [1946]).
Cmd. 7044	Great Britain, Foreign Office: *Proposals for the Future of Palestine, July 1946–February 1947*, Cmd. 7044 (London, H.M.S.O., 1947).
Cmd. 7179	Great Britain, Foreign Office: *Papers regarding the Negotiations for a Revision of the Anglo-Egyptian Treaty of 1936*, Cmd. 7179 (London, H.M.S.O., 1947).
European Recovery Program, Turkey	U.S.A., Economic Cooperation Administration: *European Recovery Program, Turkey Country Study* (Washington, U.S.G.P.O., 1949).
H.P.C.	*A History of the Peace Conference of Paris*, ed. H. W. V. Temperley. 6 vols. (London, Oxford University Press for British Institute of International Affairs, 1920–4).
Iskandarī	Iraj Iskandarī: 'Histoire du Parti Toudeh', *Moyen-Orient*, May 1950.
I.Z.L.	Irgun Zvai Leumi: National Military Organization (in Israel).
Problem of the Turkish Straits	U.S.A., Department of State: *The Problem of the Turkish Straits*, Publication 2752 (Washington, U.S.G.P.O., 1947).
UNSCOP	United Nations Special Committee on Palestine.

NOTE

British Parliamentary Debates (Hansard) are cited in the form suggested in the bound volumes of the Official Reports, preceded by the date (if not given in the text) and followed by the column number, e.g.

(for the House of Commons)
    24 November 1948, H.C.Deb. 5th ser., vol. 458, coll. 1238–9.

(for the House of Lords)
    13 April 1949, H.L.Deb. 5th ser., vol. 161, col. 1224.

Authorization has been obtained for all major quotations, and full reference to the book, the author, and the publisher has been given in each case in a footnote under the first mention of the work.

PART I

SYNTHESIS: THE INTERPLAY OF POLICIES
1945–1950

THE political atmosphere of the Middle East during the Second World War[1] may be compared with a gas under compression in a closed vessel. For the Allies the region was strategically important during the war, not merely or even primarily as a link in British imperial communications or as a source of oil supplies (which had been its significance between the two World Wars), but as the principal avenue (other than the dangerous Arctic sea-route) through which the United States and Britain had access to the Soviet Union. It was the supply of war material to the Soviet Union through Persia that brought United States troops into the Middle East for the first time since the young Republic's campaigns against the Barbary pirates at the beginning of the nineteenth century; it was through the Middle East that statesmen and soldiers from the West travelled on their difficult missions to Moscow; and it was at Tehrān that the 'Big Three' Allied leaders met for the first time in 1943. For the Governments and politically conscious classes of the Middle Eastern countries, however, the war supervened on the efforts which they had been making since the First World War or earlier to achieve their complete independence of Great Power influence and control; a control which, exercised primarily by imperial Britain and secondarily by France, had in 1919–20 been greatly intensified over the countries of the Fertile Crescent (hitherto subject to the Ottoman Empire) at the very time that it was already being challenged in Egypt, Turkey, and Persia. By 1939 the two last-named countries had for more than fifteen years been fully independent and sovereign; but the Turkish Republic nevertheless had difficulty in maintaining its non-belligerent status between the warring Powers in the Second World War, and Persia in 1941 temporarily lost her effective independence on account of the desire of Britain and the Soviet Union to establish communications across her territory. To the south, the independence of the Arabic-speaking states was in 1939 less complete than that of Turkey and Persia. Egypt and 'Irāq, who between the wars made the transition to sovereignty from their status of protectorate and mandated territory respectively, had been required by Britain to accept treaties of alliance with her; and the Levant States and Palestine were still under mandates. This unequal status was challenged, when opportunities presented themselves, during the Second World War itself. Britain used force, or the threat of force, in Egypt and

---

[1] See *Survey* for 1939–46: *The Middle East in the War.*

'Irāq respectively to secure the observance of her treaties of alliance against
attempts at collusion or reinsurance with the Axis on the part of militant
nationalists. In the Levant States the authority of the French mandate had
been undermined, first by France's capitulation to the Axis in 1940, but
more especially by the eviction of the Vichyist régime from the Levant by
the British and Free French a year later; and the nationalists took advantage of the marked differences between the British and Free French attitudes towards their demands to achieve almost complete independence
by the end of the war. In Palestine from 1942 onwards, while the intransigence of the most influential of the Arab politicians had manœuvred
them into an impotent exile, the Zionist movement was energetically bent
on achieving a sovereign status that would allow it complete control of
immigration, land-purchase, and settlement. In Persia, even while her
territory was occupied by the forces of the three principal Allies, the rejection of a Soviet demand for an oil concession in 1944 was accompanied by
envious references to the valuable concession held by the Anglo-Iranian
Oil Company.[1]

An American historian of the Middle East has observed that, as a by-
product of the war effort, Britain had unified most of the region politically
and economically as it had not been unified for centuries, and that the
British creation of the Arab News Agency and the Arabic broadcasting
station *ash-Sharq al-Adnā* were symbols of the process.[2] In many cases,
however, this unification was achieved against the wishes of local governments and nationalist movements; and their reaction against British
influence was therefore likely to be at least as strong at the end of the
Second World War as it had been in 1919–20. It had been Britain's
policy between the wars to safeguard her essential interests in the Middle
East by a series of balances and compromises effected with other foreign
interests such as those of France or those of United States oil companies,
or with the more moderate nationalists themselves. This policy would
continue to be pursued after 1945, but would call for all the greater finesse
because the great depletion of Britain's financial resources by the war had
lessened both her absolute power and her relative status as a world Power.
Britain had recognized with some reluctance during 1944[3] that the pre-
dominant interest in Sa'ūdī Arabia would henceforward belong to the
United States, who were operating an oil concession that had begun to

---

[1] See *Survey* for 1939–46: *The Middle East in the War*, p. 479. The Persian Government afterwards sought to recover sales tax on petroleum products used by the British forces in Persia
during the war. This point had apparently not been covered by any Anglo-Persian agreement
at the time, and the British Government afterwards contended that there 'could be no question'
of paying tax on products that had been used in Persia 'for the common allied cause and thus,
indirectly, for the defence of Persia' (*The Times* diplomatic correspondent, 9 September 1952).

[2] J. C. Hurewitz: 'Unity and Disunity in the Middle East', *International Conciliation*, May 1952,
pp. 222–4, 232.

[3] See *Survey* for 1939–46: *The Middle East in the War*, pp. 261–3.

approach in productivity that of the Anglo-Iranian Oil Company, and possessed an air-base at Dhahrān. The British war-time coalition Cabinet favoured, as an attempt to solve the Palestine question, the partition of that small country into a Zionist and an Arab state, and Churchill hoped to win the co-operation of the United States after the war in a joint policy towards Palestine.[1] The Foreign Office regarded the treaties of alliance with Egypt and 'Irāq (which had some ten years to run before their expiry) as models, no doubt capable of adjustment, for Britain's post-war relations with those countries and for France's relations with the Levant States; and it was hoped that the League of Arab States, whose formation in 1945 British policy had encouraged, would provide the political and social nexus of a system whose economic development might be furthered by some prolongation of the constructive work of the Anglo-American Middle East Supply Centre.[2] At the end of the war, however, the understanding between the Great Powers, on which the British concept of the post-war Middle East so largely depended, was rapidly breaking up; the British interventions of November 1943 and June 1945 in the Levant States, professedly to safeguard the general security of the Middle East region which was threatened by the clash between the nationalist insistence on independence and the unyielding conservatism of de Gaulle, furnished the nationalist forces everywhere with an example of the advantages of appealing from Herod to Caesar;[3] and nothing had yet been done to ease Britain's post-war relations with Egypt, the leading influence in the Arab League. In her two principal cities British headquarters and large numbers of troops were still installed, apparently for an indefinite time to come.[4]

Both in Egypt and by the Zionists the advent of the Labour Party to

---

[1] See below, pp. 191–2.

[2] See Guy Hunter: 'Economic Problems: The Middle East Supply Centre', in *Survey* for 1939–46: *The Middle East in the War*, p. 189. The British Middle East Office, which was created at the end of 1945 to carry on the advisory services of the Middle East Supply Centre in the field of economic development, was handicapped by post-war Britain's inability to provide any large-scale financial aid to the Middle East (Hurewitz, loc. cit. pp. 228–9; see also Great Britain, Central Office of Information: *Britain and Middle East Development* (London, 1951), pp. 43–45).

[3] *Hodie mihi, cras tibi* was the prophetic warning of France's Foreign Minister, Georges Bidault, in a debate in the Consultative Assembly (*Journal Officiel, Débats*, 16 June 1945, pp. 1114–18). In the following six years Britain in her turn was to experience frustration and bitterness when the United States, as the world's leading Power, intervened in Britain's entangled dealings with Palestine and Persia.

[4] The Anglo-Egyptian Treaty of 1936 had made provision for the withdrawal of the British garrisons from Cairo and Alexandria, and for the establishment of a limited garrison in the Canal Zone for which Egypt would provide the accommodation. The Egyptian Government had announced in June 1945 that they would not proceed with this, but would demand the complete withdrawal of British troops from Egyptian territory; and in August and September the Office of the British Minister Resident and the British Embassy seem to have disagreed on the desirability of announcing immediately the intention to withdraw from Cairo and Alexandria (see below, p. 116).

power in the British general election of June–July 1945 was heralded as portending a more accommodating policy than was to have been expected if a government led by Churchill had been returned. The Zionist movement, relying on recent endorsements of their claims by the British Labour Party, immediately pressed their maximum demands on the new Government; but British Middle East interests could not ignore the claim of the neighbouring Arab states to a voice on Palestine; and the Labour Government adopted their predecessors' policy of trying to lead the United States Government from the detachment expressed in admonitions concerning Britain's duties to association in working out and carrying through a Palestine settlement. The normal pace of diplomatic progress towards the setting up of the Anglo-American Committee of Inquiry on Palestine in November 1945 was, however, excruciating to the Zionists, who were insistent on having the 100,000 Jewish survivors in the Displaced Persons' camps of Germany and Austria admitted to Palestine before the winter, while legal immigration was virtually at an end owing to the exhaustion of the quota which the hated 1939 White Paper had imposed on the Zionist movement. Already in October 1945, therefore, a rhythmic antagonism—organized Zionist unauthorized immigration and British counter-measures against it, attacks by the Jewish Resistance Movement[1] on British installations and counter-operations by the British security forces—had been set in operation and (since the British Government dare not estrange the United States by employing the full rigour of military repression against the Jewish Resistance Movement) was to result inexorably in the erosion of the British mandate and the consequent breakdown of law and order in Palestine.

While the Zionists had to wait until November 1945 for an interim statement of British policy, the Egyptian Government did not receive an answer to their request for negotiations for a revised treaty until the end of January 1946—and that answer was non-committal. A major factor imposing caution on British policy at this time was the Soviet pressure on Turkey and Persia, which had begun before the end of the Second World War, and was to continue without intermission throughout 1946. The ultimate objective of the Soviet Government was doubtless to bring Greece,[2] Turkey, and Persia into that same satellite status to which they were reducing the countries of Eastern Europe and, just as the belt of pro-

---

[1] In this Resistance Movement the organizations which took their orders from a commander with a seat on the Jewish Agency Executive—namely the standing force called Palmaḥ and the territorial force called Haganah—were associated with the two organizations that were independent of the Agency and pledged to open warfare against British authority. These were the Irgun Zvai Leumi ('National Military Organization') and the 'Fighters for the Freedom of Israel', commonly known as the Stern Group after the name of their founder.

[2] For the role of Greece in the cold war, see *Survey* for 1947–8, pp. 177–83, and for 1949–50, pp. 120–6.

tective buffer territory beyond the Soviet Union's own frontiers had been thrust forward to the Elbe and the Adriatic, so in the Middle East they sought to screen the industrial regions of south Russia and Transcaucasia by a belt of protective buffer territory extending to the eastern Mediterranean and the Persian Gulf, as had been envisaged in Molotov's conversations with the Nazi leaders in November 1940.[1] Immediate objectives were the establishment of Soviet bases on the Black Sea Straits, the retrocession by Turkey of territory on the Transcaucasian frontier, and an oil concession in the five northern provinces of Persia. Owing to the determination of the Turkish Government and people to defend their sovereignty, the methods employed by the Soviet Government against Turkey were restricted to diplomatic pressure and intimidation; but they used the six months after the close of the Second World War, during which Allied military forces were authorized to remain in Persia, to set up under the protection of the Red Army Communist separatist régimes in the economically vital Persian province of Āzarbāijān and in the province of Persian Kurdistān, and to press the Persian Government to participate in a (nominally) joint Soviet-Persian oil company for the northern provinces. Although the war-time appointment of United States army officers as advisers to the Persian gendarmerie had been renewed in 1945, the unilateral decision of the United States Government to withdraw their troops from Persia four months in advance of the date stipulated by the Anglo-Soviet-Persian Treaty of 1942 had doubtless given an impression that the United States was not interested in Persia. It was the British Foreign Secretary, Ernest Bevin, rather than the United States Secretary of State, James Byrnes, who in December 1945 and January 1946 took the initiative in seeking an international investigation of the situation in Āzarbāijān. Not until March 1946, when the Soviet Government had declared their intention to maintain part of their force in north Persia after the date stipulated by international agreement, was the United States opposition to the Soviet pressure on Persia clearly demonstrated; and simultaneously the U.S.S. *Missouri*, one of the world's most powerful warships, was sent on a courtesy visit to Istanbul to emphasize United States interest in the independence and sovereignty of Turkey in resisting Soviet pressure.

Since, however, public opinion in the United States was not yet prepared for any commitment in a region where the nation's newly acquired interests, notably the oil of Sa'ūdī Arabia, were unfamiliar or even suspect to the public, the primary concern in countering the Soviet cold war pressure on the northern periphery of the Middle East continued during 1946 to lie with the British Government.[2] Had they been able to deal with

[1] See *Survey* for 1939–46: *The Middle East in the War*, p. 449.
[2] For an early attempt to prepare United States public opinion for the necessity of taking over some of Britain's responsibilities in the Middle East, see Halford L. Hoskins: 'The New Era of

the Palestine problem in isolation, they might well have considered, like the war-time coalition Cabinet, that the Zionist claim to statehood would be adequately met by a partition of Palestine, leaving the remainder to be combined with Transjordan; but amid the harassment of the Soviet cold war Britain needed at least the passive acquiescence of the neighbouring Arab states just as much as she had needed it from 1939 onwards. Pan-Arab feeling was not prepared to concede to the Zionists more than the status of a minority community in an Arab Palestine; there were threats of seeking the support of Moscow as some pan-Arab militants had sought that of the Nazis in 1940–1; and the lack of cohesion of the Arab League was not yet as apparent as it was to become in 1948. The majority of the Anglo-American Committee of Inquiry on Palestine evaded the surgical operation of partition by a more anodyne series of recommendations, and it could not be assumed that the United States would be willing to share in the task of maintaining law and order in Palestine which these recommendations or any other plan might entail. President Truman was not prepared to do anything besides facilitating the admission into Palestine of 100,000 Jews from Europe, and, as the Congressional election of November 1946 approached, his interventions in the Palestine question had at least the appearance of having been increasingly influenced by regard for the substantial Jewish vote in New York and other populous eastern States. The British Government had meanwhile been pressed by the Egyptian Government to concede in principle the complete withdrawal of British troops from Egypt as the price of negotiations for a new Anglo-Egyptian alliance, and the Security Council had requested Britain and France to withdraw their garrisons from Syria and Lebanon. Palestine was thus indicated as the principal future British base in the Middle East, and British policy, already stiffened as a result of Zionist acts of violence against British lives and property, underwent a further hardening. The Government made the admission of 100,000 Jews from Europe, as recommended by the Anglo-American Committee, conditional upon the disarming of the Jewish Resistance Movement. When the latter extended the scale of its acts of violence as a protest against the trend of British policy, the British Government allowed the army to round up compromised members of the Jewish Agency Executive and hundreds of identified members of the Resistance Movement. The killing of ninety-one persons (British, Arab, and Jewish) in the sabotage of the Palestine Government secretariat by one of the Zionist extremist organizations brought Anglo-Zionist relations to an unprecedented degree of tension; and it was at this stage that the British Government revived and published an old project for establishing Jewish and Arab autonomous provinces under a central British administra-

Power Politics' (Headline Series, no. 57, published by the Foreign Policy Association, New York, May–June 1946).

tion. This was rejected alike by President Truman and his advisers, by the Zionists, and by the Palestine Arabs, while the Arab states propounded an uncompromising set of proposals of their own. The shock of the British counter-measures against the Jewish Resistance Movement had, however, meanwhile caused the most responsible Zionist leaders to realize that the demand for the whole of Palestine, which had been their official policy since the Biltmore Declaration of 1942, would never be supported by the United States Government. They therefore produced proposals for a partition which would give them an independent state in two-thirds of the total area of Palestine, as compared with the Jewish province of about one-sixth of the total area envisaged by the British plan. The British Government now sought to reach a compromise with the Zionist leaders, but immediate policy on immigration remained an obstacle: the British Government had replied to an increased flow of organized unauthorized immigration to Palestine from Europe by forcibly diverting it to detention camps in Cyprus, and the Zionists would not agree to restrict this flow unless they obtained a substantial increase in the authorized immigration quota; but this the British had promised the Arab states that they would not concede during the present negotiations. The extremist organizations thereupon redoubled their militant attacks on British authority in Palestine, with such effect that at the end of January 1947 orders were issued for the evacuation of non-essential British civilians and the concentration of essential personnel in 'security zones' protected by troops and wired enclosures.

This 'policy of scuttle inevitably resulting in the loss of British prestige'[1] was the humiliating outcome of a situation in which the members of the Jewish extremist organizations enjoyed concealment and protection within their community, while the British security forces were denied recourse to any really drastic measures; for the Government had always to be considering the effect of their actions in Palestine on opinion in the United States, and for that matter in Britain, where opinion was divided and where the economic situation was precarious.[2] Britain's economy was tem-

---

[1] It was so described in a resolution passed by a meeting of British business men in Jerusalem (*The Times*, 1 February 1947).

[2] The maintenance of large forces overseas during the Second World War had caused Britain to contract heavy sterling debts to India and Egypt, and on a smaller scale to other Middle Eastern countries; and the severe strain imposed on her economy by the war had made it impracticable for her to pay off these debts in goods or convertible currency at the rate expected by the creditors. While in Britain it was argued that the amount of these debts had been artificially inflated during the war and should be scaled down to a more equitable level, the creditors argued that they required payment in full to develop their own economies. On both sides, moreover, the financial question acquired an emotional character, for Churchill, when Leader of the Opposition in 1951, revealed that his war-time coalition Cabinet had contemplated making counter-claims for Britain's part in defending these creditor countries from invasion, while they retorted that their exposure to Axis attack had been due precisely to their involuntary connexion with imperial Britain (see also below, pp. 136-7).

porarily paralysed in February 1947 by a coal shortage made worse by the most severe winter for sixty-six years; and simultaneously the Government made a series of radical decisions to reduce the burden of their overseas commitments. The Indian sub-continent was to receive its independence in the summer. The United States was informed that Britain would be unable after 31 March to continue the military and advisory aid which she had been giving since the war to Greece and Turkey in support of their independence against the Soviet cold war. British negotiations with Egypt for a revision of the Treaty of Alliance had already broken down over the status of the Anglo-Egyptian Sudan, which Egyptian public opinion had been led to regard as unanimously desirous of union with Egypt; and the Canal Zone remained the chief British military and air base when in August 1947 the Egyptian thesis, that the changed post-war circumstances had already nullified the Anglo-Egyptian Treaty before its expiry in 1956, failed to obtain a two-thirds' majority in the Security Council of the United Nations. Palestine had thus lost its major attraction as a British base, and the decision to relinquish the Mandate, which had not been entirely explicit when the British Government had referred the Palestine problem to the United Nations in February 1947, was announced in September, within a week of the announcement that the main military stores depot for the Middle East would be transferred from the Canal Zone to Kenya.

Meanwhile, the United States Government's decision, in March 1947, to take over and greatly expand the support that Britain had hitherto given to Greece and Turkey was a departure in United States foreign policy so radical as to earn it the unofficial name of the 'Truman Doctrine'. Despite opposition from traditional isolationists, from idealists who placed all their trust in the United Nations, and from those rootedly suspicious of becoming involved in British imperialism, the bill authorizing the necessary initial credits passed through both Houses of Congress with comfortable majorities. A military credit and the offer of a United States military mission were soon extended to Persia, where the pressure of the Soviet Government to obtain ratification of the oil agreement for north Persia, which they had imposed *vi et armis* in the previous year, had been circumvented by a subtle septuagenarian Persian Prime Minister supported by an energetic young United States Ambassador. The latter insisted that the Persian Parliament should freely decide on the merits of the draft Soviet-Persian oil agreement, while British policy was apprehensive that the slamming of a door on the Russians in north Persia might disturb the Anglo-Iranian Oil Company's operation of their concession in the south-west.[1]

Thus in the course of 1947 responsibility for underwriting the defence

[1] See below, p. 86.

of the northern periphery of the Middle East in the cold war had been effectively transferred from Britain to the United States. The Arabian-American Oil Company in Saʿūdī Arabia was rapidly expanding its production, and in December 1946 the Anglo-Iranian Oil Company, in which the British Government had a controlling interest, had conceded to two leading United States oil-distributing organizations the marketing for twenty years of 20 per cent. of its annual production.[1] When, however, the recommendations of the United Nations Special Committee on Palestine went before the General Assembly in September 1947 there was no harmonizing or reconciliation of British and United States policies. The responsibility for this lay with both Governments. The British Foreign Office still evidently laid most emphasis on the importance of seeking not to alienate from Britain the states of the Arab League; a revised treaty was now being negotiated with ʿIrāq which, Bevin hoped, would serve as a model for other Middle East defence arrangements.[2] The continuing tendency in Britain to depreciate the dynamic energy and determination of the Zionist movement was complicated by resentment (to which the Foreign Secretary had given personal expression)[3] at the success with which the Zionist 'activists' had subverted and paralysed the British mandatory authority. The Zionist movement had a great and widespread command of publicity, and it painted an invidious picture of Britain in Nazi colours as an 'occupying Power' against whom all methods of resistance were fair, while the Zionists (many of whom had played a conspicuous part in the 'underground' of Nazi-occupied Europe) were painted as the idealized Resistance Movement for which ambushes and bombs were liberating acts and any organized campaign of half-truth and innuendo no more than a smoke-screen of deception. The tolerance which the Governments of the United States and European countries showed to the very considerable financial and moral support given in those countries to the Zionist unauthorized immigration campaign and even to the

[1] Production in millions of metric tons:

	Arabian-American	Anglo-Iranian
1944	1·1	13·5
1945	2·9	17·1
1946	8·2	19·5
1947	12·3	20·5
1948	19·3	25·2
1949	23·5	27·2
1950	26·9	32·3

(United Nations, Department of Economic Affairs: *Review of Economic Conditions in the Middle East* (1951), p. 60, Table 24).

[2] 22 January 1948, H.C.Deb. 5th ser., vol. 446, col. 400. The revised treaty was signed in Britain by the ʿIrāqī Prime Minister and other Ministers, but was abortive on account of the immediate and violent demonstrations against it by the nationalists of Baghdād (see below, pp. 153–7).

[3] See below, p. 199, note 2.

militant extremists—the 'terrorists' of British parlance—added to the
British sense of frustrated irritation.[1] The inability to follow a line of
policy without regard to its possible effect in the United States led the
British authorities in Palestine into spasmodic and ineffectual gestures of
exasperation against the Zionists which merely added to their estrange-
ment. While, therefore, in the months preceding the termination of the
Mandate on 15 May 1948 the British attitude in Palestine became increasingly negative and self-centred, in the United States Government the
Departments of State and Defence continued to be concerned at the threat
that Arab hostility might interrupt the flow of Saʿūdī Arabian oil, which
was of increasing importance as an alternative source to the diminishing
reserves of the Western Hemisphere and was needed both by the United
States navy and to meet the expanding fuel needs of the European Recovery Programme.[2] The President seems, like many Americans, to have
had a disinterested personal sympathy with Jewish national aspirations in
Palestine, without, perhaps, being fully aware of the seriousness of the
difficulties arising from the existence and the national rights of the Palestinian Arabs; and the President was, no doubt, also moved, in the direction of his own personal inclinations, by the advice of the Democratic
Party managers, whose professional concern was with internal political
considerations: the Jewish vote and public opinion generally. Powerful
Presidential pressure was exerted at the critical moment to procure from
a hesitant United Nations Assembly the necessary two-thirds' majority
in favour of partitioning Palestine into the jigsaw of seven pieces (three
Jewish, three Arab, and one international) recommended by the Special
Committee. The unpractical character of the General Assembly debate
was demonstrated by its failure, despite admonitions from the British and
other delegations, to provide for keeping the peace between the rival
communities in Palestine, except for vague references to the formation of
an international volunteer force. The British Government (fully supported
by public opinion) had repeatedly said that their troops would not be
available for enforcing a policy on either community, to the annoyance of
the United States delegate who, for his part, put on record his pious hope

[1] Conversely, for some years after these events, some commentators in the United States
inferred disreputable motives for British policy. Thus J. C. Hurewitz states that until 1949 the
United Kingdom 'exploited' Arab resentment of American support for Israel, 'as a means of
ingratiating itself with the Arab League' ('Unity and Disunity in the Middle East', *International
Conciliation*, May 1952, p. 255); and James G. McDonald remarks that he and a number of other
Americans in the Middle East thought that the objective of 'generally having the Middle East
in a ferment of emotion directed away from Great Britain' was an 'important influence on
British policy' (*My Mission in Israel, 1948–1951* (London, Gollancz, 1951), p. 182).

[2] It had been postulated that Middle East oil production, which in 1947 amounted to 42
million tons, should be rather more than doubled by 1951, this representing an increase in its
share of world production from about 11 to 16 per cent. In fact, Middle East oil production
in 1951 attained the figure of 97·5 million tons, representing some 16·4 per cent. of world production.

that the boundaries between the Arab and Jewish states would be as friendly as the boundary between Canada and the United States.[1] This pattern of Anglo-American behaviour persisted when, from December 1947 onwards, Arab attacks on Jews and Jewish counter-action degenerated into a local war in which reinforcements from the Arab states came to the support of the Palestine Arabs, but the Zionists in April 1948 gained the upper hand, thanks to their superior cohesion and discipline in pursuit of their ideal of statehood. The British remained concerned primarily with extricating themselves from Palestine, professing a neutrality between the two warring communities which earned them the odium of both.[2] The soldiers and police, who during the past three years had suffered some hundreds of casualties at the hands of the Jewish 'terrorists' and had at the same time been prevented for political reasons from using their full force against their assailants, now showed a distinct tendency to discriminate against the Zionists;[3] and there was some circumstantial evidence that British deserters from the police were responsible for two major acts of revenge for Zionist terrorism that cost some fifty unoffending Jewish lives. United States policy, during this period of advancing anarchy in Palestine, wavered in an attempt to harmonize a number of diverse factors in the situation—notably the Arab threat to cease supplying oil from the Middle East, the 'Soviet menace',[4] the desire to avoid unnecessary bloodshed in Palestine, and the pro-Zionist pull of domestic politics—until, as the Mandate expired, the President finally decided on the immediate recognition of the State of Israel. The open warfare which now ensued in Palestine between Jews and Arabs caused acute tension between Britain and the United States. While the latter at the Security Council condemned the Arab states as aggressors and called for sanctions against them if they would not accept a truce, it remained British policy to induce the Arabs to accept a truce that would leave them in occupation of those parts of Palestine allotted to them by the General Assembly's resolution, but not further to antagonize them by threats of sanctions.[5] The fact that those

[1] See below, p. 250.

[2] A responsible Palestine Arab declared in 1953 that Britain should have collaborated with the United States in imposing the United Nations' partition resolution; and when the writer objected that the Arabs had at the time vehemently rejected the very suggestion of partition, he replied: 'Yes, but there is a *hadīth*: "Drag them into heaven, even with chains"!'

[3] 'The Jews claimed that they threw their weight on the Arab side, that they designed to hand over to the Arabs posts and camps, that they supplied them with arms, that they closed their eyes to Arab operations, and came down sharply on Jewish. There was exaggeration in this impression, but it was not without truth' (Harry Sacher: *Israel, the Establishment of a State* (London, Weidenfeld & Nicolson, 1952), p. 235).

[4] See Hal Lehrman, quoted below, p. 268. J. C. Hurewitz points out that from April 1948 onwards the Soviet bloc was systematically excluded from representation on the various United Nations commissions created to deal with the Palestine problem ('Unity and Disunity in the Middle East', *International Conciliation*, May 1952, pp. 253-4).

[5] See below, p. 273.

Arab states in alliance with Britain were still receiving arms from her, however, and that British officers serving in King 'Abdullāh's Arab Legion were taking part in the fighting was much more obviously compromising for Britain than the clandestine flow of arms, dollars, and volunteers from the United States to Israel was for the United States;[1] and there was a violent anti-British press and publicity campaign in the United States, which was again immersed in the excitement of an election year. The only beneficiary from this deplorable Anglo-American contretemps was the Soviet Government, who from May 1947 had temporarily suspended their hostility to Zionism for the purpose of bringing to an end the British mandate in Palestine and were now allowing their Czechoslovak satellite to sell aircraft and arms to Israel.

At the end of May 1948, however, British policy was adjusted to that of the United States. Both Governments combined to press the belligerents in Palestine to accept one month's truce during which they were not to receive reinforcements in men or materials from abroad; but, while British shipments of arms to the Arab states were now suspended for more than a year, the United States Government were less able or willing to check the flow of dollars to finance Israel's secret purchases of heavy arms overseas. The subsequent British attitude at the United Nations indicated that the Government favoured, if they did not inspire, the suggestions of the United Nations Mediator (Count Bernadotte of the Swedish royal family) for modifying the unrealistic territorial provisions of the General Assembly's resolution on partition to meet the present military situation in Palestine. These suggestions[2] envisaged the cession by Israel (in whole or part) of southern Palestine, which she planned to develop as an irrigated grain region and a source of minerals, in return for making permanent her recent military occupation of western Galilee; the British intention was evidently to preserve Arab control of southern Palestine, both as a potential military base and means of access between the Canal Zone and Jordan and because of the oil deposits which it might contain. By the time that the Mediator's recommendations went before the United Nations Assembly, however, Israel's acquisition of arms and the political squabbles among the Arab states had combined to give her military supremacy in Palestine; and, using Arab breaches of the truce as a pretext,[3] she had embarked on a series of local campaigns which by the end of 1948 were to place her in possession of substantial tracts of territory originally assigned to the Arabs,

---

[1] As a matter of fact, the number of volunteers for the Israeli forces from American Jewry seems to have been smaller than the number from British Jewry.

[2] Another suggestion by the Mediator, which contributed more than anything else to his murder in September by Israeli militant extremists, was that Jerusalem with its population of 100,000 Jews, whose precarious communications with the Israeli coastal belt had been maintained only with the greatest difficulty, should be included in the Arab territory.

[3] Breaches of the truce were being made on both sides at the time.

in addition to the whole of the territory assigned to Israel by the United Nations. In the meantime the British Government (who had not yet recognized Israel even *de facto*) made every diplomatic effort to check her successive advances at Arab expense, and were even ready to invoke the Anglo-Egyptian Treaty when Israeli troops engaged in expelling the Egyptian forces from Palestine penetrated into Egyptian territory; but the United States remained much more detached now that Israel was gaining the upper hand. The United States delegation at the United Nations mildly urged, but did nothing to enforce, a condition that if Israel occupied territories beyond the United Nations partition award she should offer to the Arabs an appropriate territorial exchange; and at the same time the United States warmly supported Israel's application for admission to the United Nations. Only when Israel's forces had crossed the Egyptian frontier and were reported to be threatening those of Transjordan did the United States read her a warning; and President Truman dissociated his Government from the British action in sending reconnaissance aircraft to observe the military situation on the Palestine-Egyptian frontier—an action as a result of which five British aircraft were shot down by the Israelis. The British parliamentary and public reaction to this humiliating experience, together with the opening of armistice negotiations between the Arab states and Israel, led to the relaxing of Bevin's uncompromising attitude towards Israel. The Jewish immigrants of military age whom the British Government had continued on their own initiative to detain in Cyprus were released, and Britain's *de facto* recognition of Israel was announced, but when in March 1949 Israeli patrols advanced to occupy the extreme southern outlet of Palestine on the Gulf of 'Aqaba, a British garrison recently established on Jordanian territory at 'Aqaba itself was reinforced. This garrison took no action, however, when the Israelis confined themselves to their side of the international frontier, and a British Government spokesman claimed that its presence had stabilized the situation and assisted the conclusion of an armistice between Israel and Jordan.

For the Arab states the war in Palestine had increased a sense of frustration that was to find concrete expression immediately in the murder of an Egyptian Prime Minister and the military overthrow of the political oligarchy that had claimed the credit of 'liberating' Syria from the French mandate in 1945. Ultimately, also, that frustration was to find an outlet in the murder of King 'Abdullāh of Jordan and in the Egyptian military coup that enforced the abdication of King Fārūq. Parallel with these internal convulsions of the Arab world, there went a strong revulsion from the West, particularly from Britain;[1] and Arab policy towards the West

---

[1] 'The prime causers of the disaster were the British. It was they who gave the Jews the Balfour Declaration in 1917 with its "national home", and then opened the doors to them. British

became one of obstinate non-co-operation. At the end of 1949 the United States and British Governments had decided that the *de facto* partition of the city of Jerusalem by the armed forces of Israel and Jordan had made impossible the attainment of the United Nations proposal of November 1947 to internationalize the Jerusalem area; and they supported a compromise proposal to confine the proposed international administration to the care of the Holy Places and the common interests of the city. Egypt and Syria, however, were able to express their simultaneous hostility towards the West, towards Israel, and towards 'Britain's vassal', Jordan, by inducing the Arab League states to vote with the Roman Catholic states and the Soviet bloc[1] in a curious combination that provided a two-thirds' majority for complete internationalization—though no one was now ready to enforce this upon Israel and Jordan. A joint declaration of the United States, British, and French Governments in May 1950, intended to stabilize the situation between Israel and the Arab states, was answered by the latter with restatements of the Arab point of view.

The urgent task which the United States assumed in Turkey under the Truman Doctrine was to increase the ability of the resolute, but materially obsolete, Turkish armed forces to resist possible Soviet aggression, and at the same time to prevent the financial burden from exhausting the still under-developed Turkish economy. The proposed solution, a large-scale modernization of the Turkish armed forces, inevitably involved the modernization of many branches of the general economy; and the strategic position of Turkey in the cold war was so important, and the response of the Turkish leaders so relatively encouraging (in contrast with the experience of the United States in nationalist China), that her aid to Turkey became a long-term commitment under the Mutual Security Act.

The situation in Persia, however, was far less propitious, and was to give rise in 1951 to another conflict of United States and British policies. No sooner had the immediate peril of Persia's coming under Soviet domination been averted, late in 1946, by a Soviet shift to a less aggressive policy than the Persian politicians formulated in outline an ambitious Seven-Year

---

protection and patronage enabled the Jews to make Palestine their home, and to multiply. Under the protection of British arms Jewish colonies were founded and extended, and Jewish immigration flourished. Under the wings of the British Mandate Jewish terrorism hatched and grew, and was trained by British hands until it became an organized military force. During all this the British prevented us from arming, and shut our eyes to the arming of the Jews, until the time came when they were strong enough to stand on their own feet. Then the British withdrew and announced their neutrality. Thus the British were the prime causers of the disaster, and on them lies its responsibility' (Musa Alami: 'The Lesson of Palestine', *Middle East Journal*, October 1949, iii. 373–4; this is to be regarded as a statement of relatively moderate Arab opinion).

[1] Jordan remained excluded from membership of the United Nations by the Soviet veto. In December 1948 the other Arab states had similarly combined with a number of other Asiatic and Latin American states and with the Soviet bloc to defeat a British proposal for the incorporation of Arab Palestine in the kingdom of Jordan (see below, p. 290).

Plan for the economic development of the country. It was reduced to more practical proportions by a United States firm of consultants in 1947, and was then estimated to cost $650 million, of which approximately equal parts would be furnished by royalties and other payments received from the Anglo-Iranian Oil Company, from Persian internal sources, and (it was hoped) by a loan from the International Bank. At this stage, however, the British Government's policy of dividend limitation automatically diminished the amount of Persia's oil royalties, and, though the Oil Company took the initiative in offering to negotiate a compensatory arrangement, politically conscious Persians, who were chronically dissatisfied that the exploitation of their country's most valuable natural asset should be in foreign hands, were reminded of the marked disparity between Persia's royalty receipts and the amount extracted from the Company by the British Government in taxation.[1] During protracted negotiations, punctuated by demonstrations against the Company by extreme nationalists and Communists, the Persian Government representatives invoked the example of the equal division of profits which the Venezuelan Government had recently obtained from a United States oil company engaged in production and refining; but the Persians not only ignored the fact that transport costs from Venezuela to the principal markets were less than from Persia, they also demanded that the equal division of profits should apply to all the world-wide ramifications of the Anglo-Iranian Oil Company's distributive and marketing business. A compromise was effected in July 1949 whereby Persia's royalties for 1948 and 1949 would be increased by 83 per cent., as compared with the existing agreement, with the prospect that the 1949 figure of £23 million would be further exceeded as a result of the expanding production of 1950 and the following years. The Persian Government were apathetic about the new agreement, however, and failed to secure its ratification by Parliament against the determined opposition of a small group of nationalists who were already making propaganda for the cancellation of the Anglo-Iranian Oil Company's concession. The situation was complicated by other unfavourable factors. There was a serious deterioration in the country's economy in 1949–50 owing to a combination of bad harvests with extravagant urban spending on imported semi-luxuries. The United States Government were unwilling to provide the $250 million loan solicited by the Shāh, on the ground that, until Persia's corrupt and inefficient administration was radically reformed, a foreign loan would be as thoroughly wasted there as in Kuomintang China. In 1949–50, moreover, there was a vigorous conflict

---

[1] In the years 1948 to 1950 inclusive the British Government took over £100 million in taxation, as against £38·7 million paid in royalties to the Persian Government (Dr. Laurence Lockhart: 'The Causes of the Anglo-Persian Oil Dispute', *Journal of the Royal Central Asian Society*, April 1953, xl. 145).

between the general oil interests of Britain and the United States;[1] and the director in Tehrān of the United States advisers on the Seven-Year Plan was a United States oil executive from the Persian Gulf who had publicly criticized what he regarded as the British failure to promote the economic development of the Middle East since the First World War. Little seems to have been done to create mutual understanding between the British engaged in oil production in Persia and the Americans at work on the Seven-Year Plan; and the Persians, who for over a century had maintained their independence by playing off the British and the Russians one against the other, now saw a prospect of enlisting United States sympathy against the obstinate refusal of the Anglo-Iranian Oil Company during 1950 to make concessions beyond the still unratified 'supplemental agreement' of 1949.

The consequences of this failure to harmonize British and United States attitudes towards Persia were not to become fully obvious until the summer of 1951, and therefore fall outside the chronological scope of this volume; but already the weakened position of Britain in the world had been appreciatively noted in an Egypt that was as intent as ever to free herself from the presence of British armed forces on Egyptian soil;[2] and, soon after the return of a Wafdist Government in the Egyptian general election of January 1950 had been followed by a resumption of Anglo-Egyptian defence conversations, the press was expressing the hope of appealing to the United States to extract concessions from the British.[3] Opponents of the much debated proposals for the union of the Syrian Republic with one of the Hāshimī kingdoms, 'Irāq or Jordan, were quick to represent such proposals as being encouraged by Britain (this on insufficient

---

[1] This arose from a combination of the urgent need of the sterling area to economize its dollar holdings, which produced the devaluation crisis of September 1949, with the rising production of British oil, notably in Persia. Although British oil production entailed an expenditure of gold or dollars (notably on royalties, United States technical equipment, &c.) its gross 'dollar element' was estimated for 1950 at only about 30 per cent., and its net 'dollar element' (allowing for prospective dollar earnings by British oil sales in North America) at only about 15 per cent., of the cost to the sterling area of a like amount of United States oil. In 1949, accordingly, the British Government took steps, throughout the sterling area and in countries such as Argentina and Denmark with whom they had bilateral trade agreements, to substitute the available quantities of British oil for previous imports of United States oil. There were strong protests by the United States oil companies affected, but a series of compromises was reached, and the world demand for oil was sharply stimulated by the outbreak of the Korean War and the rearmament programmes (see Horst Mendershausen: *Dollar Shortage and Oil Surplus in 1949–1950* (Princeton University Press: Essays in International Finance, no. 11, 1950)).

[2] 'Britain has lost her prestige in the world in general, and in Europe in particular. Her star has faded in the Far East. She has been forced to withdraw from India, Pakistan, Ceylon, and Palestine. She is today a third-class Power, behind the United States and Russia. She is a charge upon Washington for her economy, her military interests, her present, and her future' (the nationalist Fikrī Abāza in *al-Musawwar*, quoted by *Bourse Égyptienne*, 13 April 1951).

[3] 'Every time that Egypt says, "This is my right, the British are concerned only with their interests", the United States will say, "Right takes precedence over interests and advantage"' (*al-Ahrām*, quoted by *Bourse Égyptienne*, 10 June 1950).

evidence)[1] and opposed by the United States.[2] In Cyprus, likewise, the political leaders of the Greek-speaking majority who were intent on union with Greece were encouraged to hope for United States pressure on the British Government to grant their wishes.[3] The return of the British Labour Government with so precarious a majority in the general election of February 1950 no doubt affected both their prestige and authority in the Middle East and their resolution in formulating policy, particularly perhaps in grappling with the Persian oil deadlock before it passed beyond the range of rational politics. The United States Government were anxious not to appear as the supplanters of British influence in the Arab world, and their positive action at this stage was confined to offers of assistance with economic development, as proclaimed by President Truman in his inaugural address on 20 January 1949. In these countries, however, the prospective beneficiaries of 'Point Four' for a long time regarded it with an unwarranted degree of suspicion.[4] This attitude of negation, the outcome of the general reaction against imperialism and particularly of the sense of injustice and humiliation left by the disaster in Palestine, naturally found its strongest expression when the Arab states were invited to collaborate with the West in plans for joint defence against the possibility of a third world war. Political opinion was unanimous that Britain had made use of the Middle East in two world wars primarily for her imperial ends and with only perfunctory regard (with cynical disregard, according to the nationalists) for the interests of its inhabitants; and the desire to remain neutral, if possible, in a third conflict that would greatly surpass its predecessors in destructiveness was understandable. The desire for neutrality and the reaction against Anglo-American policy were ably exploited by Soviet propaganda as part of the 'Partisans of Peace' cam-

[1] 'The argument that King Abdullah has been induced by Great Britain to advocate Greater Syria seems to be unjustifiable in the light of Abdullah's correspondence with Britain on that scheme. In view of the strong opposition of Lebanon and Syria, might it not be also true that Abdullah has been restrained by Britain from pushing his plan against Arab opposition?' (Majid Khadduri: 'The Scheme of Fertile Crescent Unity', in *The Near East and the Great Powers*, ed. Richard N. Frye (Cambridge, Mass., Harvard University Press, 1951), p. 171).

[2] In quarters unfriendly to Britain the hints of an Anglo-American difference on this issue were magnified into facts; but cf. George Lenczowski: *The Middle East in World Affairs* (Ithaca, N.Y., Cornell University Press, 1952), p. 254: 'Although the American legation in Damascus maintained strict neutrality toward domestic Syrian developments, it was no secret that American policy gave high priority to cordial relations between the United States and Saudi Arabia on account of the American oil investments in the latter country. Ibn Saud stubbornly resisted the Greater Syrian scheme which would increase the strength of his rivals. . . . American policy, therefore, also favored the preservation of an independent Syria.'

[3] There had been leakages and inspired hints in 1944, 1946, and 1947 that the union of Cyprus with Greece was favoured in some quarters in the State Department (see below, pp. 172–3).

[4] See Arthur Z. Gardiner: 'Point Four and the Arab World, an American View', *Middle East Journal*, July 1950, iv. 298–9; and George Hakim: 'Point Four and the Middle East, a Middle East View', ibid. April 1950, iv. 183–95. The Arab League approved the principle of 'Point Four' in February 1951, and the member States soon signed acceptances.

paign;[1] and when, three weeks before the outbreak of the Korean War, the Chief of the British Imperial General Staff sought to discuss the defence of the Middle East with the Egyptian Prime Minister and Foreign Minister, his warnings that in the event of war a Soviet land force could reach Egypt in four months were countered by the observations that it was only as a British base that Egypt might become the object of aggression, that the risk of war had not increased since 1946 when Britain had offered to withdraw completely from Egypt, and that it would be very difficult to persuade the Egyptian people that a hypothetical Russian occupation would be worse than the existing British occupation.[2]

The decline of Britain's authority in the Middle East, which was inherent in her post-war condition but had been emphasized by the patent difference between American and British policy over the problem of Palestine, was now becoming sharply marked. The United States had found a reliable, if sometimes importunate, pivot of power in Turkey; but the Arab states and Persia were a 'power vacuum' in which a Muslim revival offered the only psychological resistance to the intrusion of Communism—and that resistance was an uncertain one, since Communists and Muslim revivalists tended to belong to the same stratum of the population and were ready to make common cause against Western 'imperialism'.[3] The Middle East as it was in the summer of 1950, at the outbreak of the Korean War, presented a spectacle not unlike that which Thomas Hardy portrayed in *The Dynasts* as his tragic imagination contemplated the drama of the Napoleonic struggle. The plight both of the Palestine Arab refugees and of the displaced Jews of many countries who were struggling to re-establish themselves in the Promised Land of Israel would amply evoke the compassion of his Spirit of the Pities. The Spirit Sinister would note with appreciation the part which terrorism had played in so many countries in breaking down political opposition or in making some public personality the bloody victim of the sense of frustration which had taken possession of whole groups and classes of society.[4] It was, however, to Hardy's Spirit Ironic that the Middle East offered the most varied material in this period of flux, as the institutions in which authority had recently resided were in

[1] See the article 'Préparatifs militaires et facteurs de paix', by Maxime Rodinson, editor of the Paris Communist organ *Moyen-Orient*, April 1950, pp. 4–5, 10.

[2] Egypt, Ministry of Foreign Affairs: *Records of Conversations, Notes and Papers exchanged between the Royal Egyptian Government and the United Kingdom Government, March 1950–November 1951* (Cairo, 1951), pp. 13–15, 21.

[3] See Mark Alexander, pseud.: 'Communist Strategy in the Middle East', *Twentieth Century*, November 1951, pp. 394–400, and 'The Near East's Communist-Fascist Front', *Commentary*, May 1952, pp. 456–62.

[4] For extreme nationalism as a 'blind and unconscious determination to wrest itself free from present political and economic frustration', see T. Cuyler Young: 'Nationalism in Iran', in *Nationalism in the Middle East: a series of addresses presented at the Sixth Annual Conference on Middle East Affairs, sponsored by the Middle East Institute* (Washington, Middle East Institute, 1952), p. 22.

manifest decay and the emergent institutions which now aspired to succeed them remained in a frail infancy. The Arab League, which was to
have been the unifying edifice that would repair the arbitrary partitioning
of the Arab world after the First World War, had itself split asunder
along the fault-lines of dynastic and personal rivalries;[1] the commissions
which it had created to promote co-operation in economic matters, communications, cultural matters, questions of nationality and passports,
social affairs, and public health had all been engulfed in the general obses-
sion with the political conflict. Arab resistance to Zionism, which had
refused even to discuss the partitioning of Palestine and indignantly
rejected the proposals which emerged from the United Nations in November 1947, was compelled little more than a year later to accept armistices
along demarcation lines far less favourable, and to invoke in vain those
same November 1947 proposals as the best which might now be hoped for.
Israel, for her part, had seen herself, before the struggle for independence
became acute, as a model socialist commonwealth in the Middle East and
an inspiration for her Arab neighbours; but in the event she was reduced,
by the necessity of attempting to fulfil so many purposes simultaneously,
to every kind of expedient that would attract the investments of foreign
capitalists and save her from economic paralysis. The Great Powers who
had created a United Nations Organization to banish war from the world
had proved impotent, chiefly on account of their conflicting aims and
divided counsels, to prevent the outbreak of a local war in 'a land no
bigger than Wales' (i.e. Palestine), or to do more than palliate the miseries
resulting from it, though they did succeed in bringing the fighting to a
stop within a month and, after it had broken out again, within a fortnight.
The British Labour Party, which in opposition had espoused all the Middle
Eastern critics of British imperialism from 1919 onwards, found amid the
responsibilities of office that it was defending the vestiges of an imperial
position against opposition within its own ranks; and that its well-inten-
tioned endeavours to solve a political problem on so comparatively small
a scale as that of Cyprus were frustrated both by the intransigence of local
nationalism and by the impact of strategic considerations arising out of
the cold war. Conversely, it was Churchill who took the lead in urging
the Government to abandon the Mandate for Palestine.[2] In Persia the
conflict between a nationalism, which took the minimum account of

[1] See A. D.: 'The Arab League, Development and Difficulties', *The World Today*, May 1951,
vii. 187–96.

[2] 'The one rightful, reasonable, simple, and compulsive lever . . . was and is a sincere readiness . . . to evacuate the country with which we have no connection or tradition and where we
have no sovereignty as in India and no treaty as in Egypt. . . . His Majesty's Government, by
their precipitate abandonment of their treaty rights in Egypt . . . are now forced to look for . . .
a jumping-off ground in Palestine in order to protect the Canal. . . . By this unwisdom they have
. . . greatly weakened our moral position in Palestine by stripping us of our disinterestedness in
that country' (1 August 1946, H.C.Deb. 5th ser., vol. 426, coll. 1255–6).

economic realities, and a great industrial organization, which its critics accused of having underestimated both the strength and the irrational character of that nationalism, was coming to a head in 1950. In general, American observers of the Middle East, by virtue of their comparative detachment from its problems, were more aware of the need for adjusting policies to the swiftly flowing nationalist currents than were the more directly involved British; but, while the latter tended to flinch from facing the awkward truth that their own effective power was declining, the effect of American interventions—in Palestine, in Persia, and later in Egypt—was to encourage Middle East nationalism in its repudiation of British authority[1] before the United States was ready to replace it (except in Greece and Turkey) by anything more substantial than offers of technical and financial aid[2]—aid that was received and absorbed without any sense of obligation in return; and the result was the expansion over almost the whole region of that 'power vacuum' which, in the circumstances of the cold war, threatened the Western conception of global security and was to lead in 1952 to a series of political upheavals throughout the Fertile Crescent.

[1] A judge of the United States Supreme Court, describing an unofficial journey through some Middle Eastern countries and India, could repeat the wildest allegations made to him in condemnation of British 'imperialism' without subjecting them to any judicial examination (William O. Douglas: *Strange Lands and Friendly People* (New York, Harper, 1951; London, Gollancz, 1952); see reviews in *International Affairs*, October 1952, xxviii. 549–50, and *Middle East Journal*, Spring 1952, vi. 252–3). Hans Kohn has pertinently remarked: 'We Americans should not think of national self-determination as a world panacea. . . . The world suffers from too much dynamism, not from too little; from too much fever, not from too little' ('General Characteristics of Nationalism in the Middle East', in Middle East Institute: *Nationalism in the Middle East*, pp. 66–67).

[2] George McGhee, Assistant Secretary of State for Near Eastern Affairs, was reported to have told a conference of United States diplomatic representatives in the Middle East in November 1949 that the United States would not promote any regional pact as long as there was no immediate prospect of Congress's approving large-scale expenditure there (McDonald: *My Mission in Israel, 1948–1951*, p. 182).

PART II

TURKEY, PERSIA, AND THE U.S.S.R.

(i) Turkey

(a) FROM 'WAR OF NERVES' TO 'TRUMAN DOCTRINE', 1945–7

A SECTION in a previous volume of this *Survey*[1] traced the course of Soviet-Turkish relations during the Second World War, and ended on the suspense which followed the Soviet Government's note to the Turkish Government on 19 March 1945, stating that the Turco-Soviet Treaty of Neutrality and Non-Aggression (which was approaching its term) was 'no longer in accord with the new situation' and needed 'serious improvement'. Some adjustment to post-war conditions was indeed natural; but in June the Soviet Government made it known[2] that if a new treaty were to be concluded they would require to be granted a base on the Black Sea Straits, which should be closed to the warships of all countries except Russia and Turkey, and the return of the districts of Kars and Ardahan that Russia had annexed to Transcaucasia in the war of 1877–8 and had re-ceded to Turkey in 1921.[3] Ankara Radio stated that the Soviet Government had also requested the formation of a more democratic and representative Turkish government,[4] and had held out as compensation for the retrocession of Kars and Ardahan that Turkey should recover from Syria the city and railway-junction of Aleppo.[5] Meanwhile, *Red Star*, the organ

[1] *Survey* for 1939–46: *The Middle East in the War*, pp. 443–66.

[2] Statements by Molotov to the Turkish Ambassador in Moscow, 7 June, and by the Soviet Ambassador in Turkey to the Turkish acting Foreign Minister, 22 June 1945; see Necmeddin Sadak (Turkish Foreign Minister, 1947–50): 'Turkey Faces the Soviets', *Foreign Affairs*, April 1949, xxvii. 458; *The Times*, 26 and 28 June 1945.

[3] Article 4, paragraph 2 of the Treaty of Brest-Litovsk, which Germany had imposed on the Soviet Government in March 1918, had provided for the evacuation of Russian troops from the districts of Kars, Ardahan, and Batum, and that Russia should not interfere in the reorganization of the relations of those districts with the neighbouring states, especially Turkey. When the Ottoman Empire broke up at the end of that year the ephemeral national republics of Armenia (Erivan) and Georgia had respectively occupied the districts of Kars and Ardahan; but in October 1920, when the resurgent Turkish nationalists and Soviet Russia both attacked the Armenian republic, Turkey reoccupied the Kars district, and in February 1921 demanded from Georgia the retrocession of Ardahan. The U.S.S.R., who was now reannexing the territories of the ephemeral national republics in Transcaucasia, recognized the Turkish possession of Kars and Ardahan by the Soviet-Turkish Treaty of 16 March 1921 (see *Survey* for 1920–3, pp. 361–72, and cf. Professor V. Khvostov: 'The Facts of the Case', *New Times*, 1 February 1946, pp. 24–25).

[4] The propaganda organs of the Soviet Union and their Balkan satellites forthwith directed a stream of attacks upon the Turkish political leaders and institutions, under the general label of 'Fascist' and 'reactionary'.

[5] When Eden visited Moscow in December 1941, Stalin had suggested to him that Turkey might possibly receive certain districts in north Syria, in return for concessions which Churchill,

of the Soviet army, had taken up the protestations of Turkish publicists that Turkey could not sacrifice her independence and honour for friendship with Russia and did not wish to become bolshevized like the Balkan countries, and accused them of exploiting differences between the Soviet Union and Britain and looking forward to a new war, with the menace: 'Such crazy opinions might have the most unpleasant consequences.'[1] On 10 July the Turkish Foreign Minister, Hasan Saka, broke his homeward journey from the San Francisco Conference to discuss the Soviet demands with Eden in London, and at a press conference on the following day pointed out that the Montreux Convention of 1936, on which the present régime of the Straits depended, was a multilateral agreement which could not therefore be revised by Turkey and the Soviet Union alone.[2] At the same time the Turkish official Anatolian News Agency denied 'reports circulating abroad' that Turkey had any designs for the recovery of the Aleppo district; but thereupon the Communist Parties of Syria and Lebanon announced their support of the Syrian national claims to recover the Sanjaq of Alexandretta (Hatay), which the French mandatory had ceded to Turkey in 1939.[3]

It was evident that the restrictions which Articles 19 and 20 of the Montreux Convention had imposed on the passage of the Straits in time of war could no longer be maintained against the Soviet Union. At the Potsdam Conference between Truman, Stalin, and Churchill, which opened on 17 July, Churchill took the initiative in stating that Britain would take part in a new agreement to ensure to the Soviet navy and merchant fleet the free use of the Straits; but, referring to the Soviet claims to a base on the Straits and to Kars and Ardahan, he urged that the Turks should not be 'unduly alarmed'. Stalin is reported to have replied that the first of these claims was a consequence of Turkey's being too weak to ensure the right of free passage effectively—a reference, no doubt, to the Soviet charge that the Turks had allowed Axis naval vessels to pass through the Straits during the war.[4] Truman coupled the question of the Straits with that of European inland international waterways such as the Danube, and presented a proposal for their free and unrestricted navigation; but Stalin refused to discuss this or allow any mention of it in the published communiqué;[5] and the three Governments could agree (in an article of the Protocol of

in his history of the war, does not specify (Winston S. Churchill: *The Second World War* (London Cassell, 1950), iii. 558; (Boston, Houghton Mifflin, 1950), iii. 628–9).

[1] See *Neue Zürcher Zeitung*, 29 June 1945, despatches from Moscow and Istanbul.

[2] *New York Times*, 12 July 1945.

[3] *Manchester Guardian*, 12 July, *Figaro*, 7 August 1945. For the cession of Hatay, see *Survey* for 1938, i. 479–92.

[4] See *Survey* for 1939–46: *The Middle East in the War*, p. 464.

[5] See James F. Byrnes: *Speaking Frankly* (New York, Harper; London, Heinemann; 1947), pp. 77–78; *Department of State Bulletin*, 12 August 1945, p. 212; Churchill: *The Sinews of Peace* (London, Cassell, 1948), p. 118, speech in New York, 15 March 1946.

the Conference which remained unpublished until 1947) only that the Montreux Convention should be revised 'as failing to meet present-day conditions', and that each of the three Governments and the Turkish Government should pursue direct conversations.[1]

It would appear that the claim which Stalin and Molotov advanced at Potsdam to recover the districts of Kars and Ardahan was based both on a return to the *status quo* before 1921 and on Russia's right to a more defensible frontier as the price of a new treaty with Turkey.[2] The claim was supported by Armenian communities in various countries, including the United States,[3] and their declarations for the restitution of Kars and Ardahan received generous Soviet publicity. Armenian church dignitaries from all over the world had been invited to Soviet Armenia in June 1945 to elect a Catholicos (Patriarch) of Etchmiadzin, an office which had lapsed under the Soviet régime; and a request by the new Catholicos 'that the lands forcibly seized by Turkey should be taken from her and returned to their rightful owners by being joined to Soviet Armenia' coincided with the publication on 2 December of a decision of the Council of the People's Commissars in Moscow that preparations were under way to receive expatriate Armenians who wished to return to Soviet Armenia.[4] When the Turkish Prime Minister sought to refute the Soviet Armenian claim to Kars and Ardahan by observing that there was 'not a single Armenian' living in those districts, a Soviet publicist retorted that there had been nearly 100,000 in the Kars region alone before the Turkish deportations during the First World War, and remarked self-righteously: 'Never before in the annals of international law has the wholesale massacre of the population of a locality been advanced as an argument in justification of the perpetrator's right to the territory of the massacred.'[5] As an historian had pointed out fourteen years earlier, however, 'the slaughter and obliteration of a great part of the Armenian nation' between 1914 and 1921 were the 'logical and morbid sequence' of a 'game of plots, incitements and solici-

[1] Great Britain, Foreign Office: *Protocol of the Proceedings of the Berlin Conference, Berlin, 2nd August, 1945*, Cmd. 7087 (London, H.M.S.O., 1947), article xvi.

[2] John C. Metcalfe (*New York Herald Tribune*, 10 October 1945) reported that Stalin had 'explained that Russia wanted Kars and Ardahan given back to [Soviet] Armenia, because Russia felt they rightfully belong to Armenia'; and W. E. D. Allen, who had travelled in and studied Transcaucasia, had remarked twenty years earlier, in connexion with the Caucasian campaigns of 1853–5, that Kars was 'an excellent advance base' for a Turkish offensive against Transcaucasia, but untenable for a Turkish army on the defensive (*Beled-es-Siba* (London, Macmillan, 1925), pp. 155–6). Byrnes's brief reference (op. cit. p. 77) lacks precision.

[3] See *New York Times*, 11 July and 7 August 1945.

[4] *New York Times*, 3 December, *The Times*, 4 December 1945, quoting *Soviet Monitor*. The enrolling of Armenians for repatriation at Soviet Consulates was actively pursued, and there was a considerable response, especially in the Middle Eastern countries where the Armenian refugee communities remained unassimilated and feared the rising nationalism of independent governments. *Moscow News* (16 July 1948) placed the total number of repatriates at 86,000.

[5] Khvostov, in *New Times*, 1 February 1946, pp. 24–25.

tations, of counter-plots and massacres', carried on between the Russian, Ottoman, and Persian Empires over the Christian and Muslim peoples of Caucasia since the end of the sixteenth century;[1] and a correspondent was afterwards to note that the number of Circassian Muslims massacred or deported, after their resistance to annexation by Russia had been finally broken in 1864, was about equal to the number of Armenians who had similarly suffered at the hands of the Turks fifty years later.[2]

On 2 November 1945 the United States Ambassador to Turkey delivered a note containing his Government's proposals on the Straits, which were designed to leave their sovereignty entirely in Turkish hands and at the same time to make substantial concessions, as compared with the Montreux Convention, to the Black Sea Powers. Their warships (like the merchant vessels of all nations) would be free to pass through the Straits at all times, instead of being restricted in time of war; and conversely, the warships of other Powers would be denied passage, except for an agreed limited tonnage in time of peace, or with the specific consent of the Black Sea Powers, or when acting under the authority of the United Nations.[3] The British Ambassador delivered a memorandum on 21 November supporting the United States proposals but commenting that revision of the Montreux Convention was not urgent.[4] The Turkish Prime Minister, Şükrü Saracoğlu, stated at a press conference on 5 December that his Government accepted the United States proposals as a basis for discussion, and would put forward their own proposals when all three interested Powers had made known their opinions; the participation of the United States in a conference to revise the Montreux Convention was 'not only desirable, but necessary'.[5] On 27 December The Times published a despatch from its correspondent in Turkey which may be regarded as semi-officially 'inspired'. It remarked that the United States proposal, that the warships of Black Sea Powers should be free to use the Straits 'at all times', would make Turkey's position 'untenable and even absurd' in the hypothetical case of her being at war with the Soviet Union; would the other signatory Powers be expected, in that case, to compel Turkey to keep the Straits open to Russian warships? Moreover, it was seriously doubted whether the United States proposals would satisfy the Soviet Government's thesis, which was that they could cover themselves against

---

[1] W. E. D. Allen: History of the Georgian People (London, Kegan Paul, Trench, Trubner, 1932), p. 164.

[2] The Economist, 5 October 1946, p. 547. It will be recalled that the Soviet Government had recently suppressed three autonomous republics in the Caucasus, and had deported their inhabitants to Siberia, for having sided with the German invaders in 1942.

[3] Text in U.S.A., Department of State: The Problem of the Turkish Straits, Publication 2752. Near Eastern Series 5 (Washington, U.S.G.P.O., 1947), p. 47. [This will be referred to hereafter as Problem of the Turkish Straits.]

[4] The Times, 26 November 1945.

[5] Monde and Neue Zürcher Zeitung, 7 December 1945.

the possibility of Turkish weakness or connivance with an aggressor against the Soviet Union only by acquiring a defensive base on the Straits, whether for permanent occupation or only in an emergency; 'but such a demand, no matter how mitigated the form of its presentation might be, would certainly be considered as infringing Turkish sovereign rights and would therefore be peremptorily rejected'.

The Turkish Government had recently been the object of sharp criticism, in Turkey itself as well as from the unfriendly propaganda of the Soviet bloc, for the restriction of democratic liberties which was a survival from Ottoman times that had not been completely eliminated under Atatürk's one-party régime, and which had perhaps inevitably been intensified through the exigencies of the Second World War.[1] Early in November 1945 the Turkish Government had abrogated the laws which severely limited the freedom of the press and of public assembly. This, however, had encouraged a number of new publications in Istanbul to adopt a line reminiscent of Soviet propaganda; one paper, for example, had demanded to know whether Turkey had become a British colony. The Government objected to this implied criticism of their policy of strengthening the Anglo-Turkish alliance of 1939, and continued to set much store on national unity as compared with the civil wars which threatened both Greece and Persia;[2] but to reintroduce the press laws would merely expose them to another broadside of Soviet anti-Turkish propaganda. Instead, therefore, a number of Deputies of the Turkish Parliament instigated the Istanbul university and high-school students to lead a demonstration on 4 December which attacked the offices and presses of the offending publications and two bookshops alleged to be pro-Soviet.[3]

An angry interchange of Soviet-Turkish notes and propaganda followed, an official Turkish assertion that the demonstration was 'spontaneously organized' by 'democratic' Turkish youth provoking a rejoinder from Moscow Radio which declared Turkey to be 'a faithful copy of the democracy of Himmler and Goebbels'.[4] A fortnight later (20 December, while the 'Big Three' Foreign Ministers were meeting in Moscow) the Moscow press and radio republished from a Tbilisi (Tiflis) newspaper a letter from

[1] See *The Times* Istanbul correspondent, 1 November 1945; Lewis V. Thomas and Richard N. Frye: *The United States and Turkey and Iran* (Cambridge, Mass., Harvard University Press, 1951), pp. 105–6; Bernard Lewis: 'Recent Developments in Turkey', *International Affairs*, July 1951, xxvii. 320.

[2] *Manchester Guardian*, Istanbul correspondent, 17 December 1945; for the Communist-inspired *coup d'état* in Persian Āzarbāijān at this date see below, pp. 58 seqq.

[3] The Minister of the Interior stated that 'police officers followed the demonstrators but did not intervene' (Ankara Radio, evening of 4 December), and the Prime Minister commented a week later that the demonstrators' purpose was 'to suppress unpatriotic activities' (*New York Times*, 13 December 1945). Lewis V. Thomas remarks that 'only a fraction' of the Turkish press 'has ever, by any stretch of imagination, faintly deserved the label pro-communist' (op. cit. p. 104, and cf. p. 111).

[4] Broadcast in Greek, 6 December 1945; texts of notes in *New York Times*, 17 December 1945.

two Georgian historians demanding the return to (Soviet) Georgia of the coastal region of north-east Anatolia as far west as Giresun, 180 miles from the present Soviet-Turkish frontier, and to a maximum depth of seventy miles inland—in other words, a substantial block of territory to the west of the districts of Kars and Ardahan that were already the subject of a Soviet claim. The letter claimed that 'in far antiquity the Georgian people lived, toiled, and struggled on this territory . . . creating new centres of civilization and government', and that the Ottoman Turkish conquest 'bringing only death and destruction' went back less than 500 years.[1] President Wilson's award of 22 November 1920 had proposed to include virtually the whole of the region now claimed, and much besides, in the abortive 'Greater Armenia';[2] but, whereas the Georgian princes had averted annexation by the Ottoman and Persian Empires and had preserved their Christianity (at least until their country's incorporation in the Soviet Union) by invoking the protection of Russia, the Laz peoples of the region now claimed by the Georgian professors had become converts to Islām as a consequence of the Ottoman conquest, and their feudal chieftains (derebeys) had been allowed a considerable measure of autonomy down to the nineteenth century.[3] As D. J. Dallin was to point out,[4] pseudo-historical claims of this type had hitherto been the objects of ridicule in the Soviet Union; but the assertion of the Turkish press that the whole nation was ready to 'plunge into fire' rather than cede 'the smallest portion' of territory was followed by the familiar exchange of insults, Red Star remarking that Turkey's 'warlike orators' had been silent when 'freedom-loving nations' had been fighting Hitler, and the Turkish Prime Minister, Saracoğlu, retorting in a broadcast that the two Georgian professors were either imbued with 'Hitlerian philosophy' or 'obsessed with a mania for shedding blood'.[5] It was doubtless not by chance that a leading article in the London Daily Worker of 12 January 1946, after repeating the observation that the Second World War had shown that Turkey was not fit to have control of the Straits, continued with the open menace:

Turkish reactionaries seem very fond of showing their muscles. They will perhaps soon learn that 1946 is not 1939 and that running with the hare and hunting with the hounds is an outmoded pastime.

---

[1] Text in New York Times, 21 December 1945.

[2] See A History of the Peace Conference of Paris, ed. H. W. V. Temperley (London, Oxford University Press for British Institute of International Affairs, 1924) [referred to hereafter as H.P.C.], vi. 83–84; United States, Armenian National Committee: The Frontier between Armenia and Turkey as decided by President Woodrow Wilson (c. 1945), with map.

[3] See Encyclopaedia of Islam, article 'Laz'.

[4] 'The Eastern Road to the Mediterranean', Free Europe, July 1946, xiii. 199.

[5] Manchester Guardian and New York Times, 28 December 1945, The Times, 7 January, New York Times, 13 January 1946.

This is to be a year of peacemaking and of the kind that will go straight to the very roots of war. Above all the Middle East must become a real stronghold of peace and democracy.

It was a measure of the rift between the Allies in the Second World War that now, only six months after the end of those hostilities, the Soviet efforts to transform Turkey into a 'stronghold of peace and democracy' after the Communist pattern should appear to the non-Communist world, and specifically to the Foreign Secretary in Britain's Labour Government, as a 'war of nerves . . . with press polemics on both sides'. Ernest Bevin assured the House of Commons on 21 February 1946 that he and his colleagues were anxious to keep in view the international aspect of the control of the Straits, since it did not contribute to world peace 'that one particular Power as against another should have bases in a particular spot';[1] but this cautious expression of opinion, and the views propounded in New York on 15 March by Winston Churchill (with that greater freedom enjoyed by the Leader of the Opposition),[2] were alike exposed to the retort that it was illogical for Britain to object to the Soviet desire to control the sole entrance to the landlocked Black Sea when Britain herself maintained a concentration of power at either end of that world thoroughfare, the Mediterranean, which was capable of closing it at will: 'This to Mr. Churchill appears to be part of the order of nature, whereas a Soviet fortress on the Straits means that the sun of Christian civilization is setting.'[3]

We have seen[4] that the United States note of 2 November 1945 had made proposals concerning the Straits which could be regarded as making Turkey's position untenable in the event of conflict with the Soviet Union. The United States Secretary of the Navy (James G. Forrestal) had, however, noted already on 24 June 1945 the Soviet aim 'to detach Turkey from the orbit of British influence';[5] the Soviet military and diplomatic pressure on Persia in the winter of 1945–6, and particularly the failure to withdraw the Red Army from Persian Āzarbāijān by the date (2 March 1946) on which the three Great Powers had previously agreed for the complete withdrawal of their forces from Persian soil,[6] had been an unmistakable danger-signal to public opinion in the United States; and on 5 March the Navy Department announced that the body of the Turkish Ambassador who had died in the United States sixteen months before would be repatriated in the U.S.S. *Missouri*, one of the world's most powerful battleships, whereas it was customary to assign a cruiser for this type of diplomatic courtesy. It later appeared that this decision was a compromise between the State Department's desire not to provoke the

[1] H.C.Deb. 5th ser., vol. 419, coll. 1355–6.   [2] Churchill: *The Sinews of Peace*, p. 118.
[3] *Daily Worker*, 19 March 1946.   [4] Above, p. 24.
[5] *The Forrestal Diaries*, ed. Walter Millis (New York, Viking Press, 1951), p. 71.
[6] See below, pp. 58–59 and 66–67.

Soviet Union[1] and the U.S. navy's wish to send a substantial force to cruise in the eastern Mediterranean,[2] a demonstration which the President had already approved. In fact, a publicist of the calibre of Walter Lippmann was still viewing the struggle for power in the Middle East as a 'British-Russian conflict' in which 'London, after all the fine rhetoric of the Labour party leaders, has a foreign policy which is not easily distinguishable from that of Palmerston at the time of the Crimean War'. He invited the Soviet leaders to study the American reaction to Churchill's Fulton speech: 'They will find that the American people have not accepted Mr. Churchill's proposal to enter into an anti-Soviet coalition ... a counsel of despair ... tantamount to confessing that the peace-making has failed.' Lippmann sought to define 'the outer limit of legitimate and acceptable Russian interest' in the Near and Middle East along a perimeter as extended as 'Trieste, Salonika and the Dodecanese[3] and the other Greek islands ... the Red Sea and ... the Persian Gulf'; but, he continued, the Russians should not attempt to magnify their legitimate interest in the Balkans, Turkey, and Persia into an exclusive interest. 'Here there will have to be collaboration, and respect for the principles and engagements they and we have jointly made, and then a settlement, or the consequences for all of us—for them and for ourselves—will be much worse than those who take a short view are likely to realize.' The cruise of the U.S.S. *Missouri* and an accompanying fleet would serve to make it 'unmistakably clear in Moscow just where we believe the outer limits of their expansion are'; and he remarked that while the American people, having emerged virtually unscathed from the Second World War, were not ready to admit failure in their attempts at peace-making, 'they are at the point where they admit the possibility of failure'.[4] This kind of reasoning was perhaps necessary to prepare responsible public opinion in the United States for the new obligation to maintain the balance of power in parts of the world hitherto remote from their thoughts, an obligation made imperative by the eclipse of British power and the rise of their own. Molotov and Vyshinsky, for their part, sought to avert an extension of the United

---

[1] Forrestal was afterwards told that Benjamin Cohen, Counsellor of the State Department, had favoured allowing the Russians a base on the Straits (*The Forrestal Diaries*, p. 181).

[2] Churchill, who had made his celebrated speech at Fulton, Missouri, on 5 March 1946, told Forrestal on the 10th that the entire force should sail into the Sea of Marmora (ibid. p. 145).

[3] Western strategists had been arguing that not merely bases on the Straits, but air superiority in the whole Aegean area, were now necessary to control communications between the Black Sea and the Aegean (see 'Russia, Turkey, and the Straits', *The World Today*, September 1946, ii. 400); and the Soviet Ambassador to Greece, Admiral Rodianov, had just suggested in the course of trade talks with the Greek Prime Minister that a Dodecanese port should be placed at the Russians' disposal for the refuelling and refitting of their merchant shipping trading with Greece (*Manchester Guardian*, 28 February, *Daily Herald* diplomatic correspondent, 1 March, *Sunday Times* diplomatic correspondent, 3 March, *Combat*, 3–4 March 1946 (citing as source the Greek Embassy in London)).

[4] *New York Herald Tribune*, 6 and 9 March 1946.

States' power and responsibility to the Middle East by accusing her, at a dinner which they gave for the United States delegation to the Paris conference that opened on 25 April, of seeking bases in Turkey, Egypt, and Persia.[1]

The relaxation of the Turkish press laws in November 1945 had been part of the outcome of a clash of personalities and principles within the Republican People's Party (*Cumhuriyet Halk Partisi*, hereafter abbreviated to C.H.P.), which at this time was still the only lawful political organization in Turkey. Opposition to President Inönü and the party leadership was led by Celal Bayar, who had been Prime Minister at the time of Atatürk's death in 1938. The grounds for opposition were various. The economic stringencies of the war had led to an increase of corruption and inefficiency which reflected on the men in power; and there was a growing feeling that some of the ideals of the Republic which had remained mere paper aspirations should now be applied, 'either as a matter of principle or else perhaps even as one of expediency, for Turkey was of course now anxious, consciously and unconsciously, further to approximate what she conceived to be the forms of the states who had come to be her only stay against Russia—Great Britain and the United States'.[2] The C.H.P. leadership had accepted the situation by abrogating in November 1945 the law proscribing any organized opposition, and in the following month the dissidents formally established a Democratic Party, pledged to a relaxation of government control over both the economic and the political life of Turkey.[3] The Government introduced in May 1946 legislation providing for the first time for direct and secret elections, as demanded by the Democrat opposition. The latter boycotted the municipal elections of 26 May, protesting that they had not been allowed sufficient time to build up their organization. The general election, which followed in July, was reported by an American observer to have been marked by 'some terrorism and coercion' (especially of peasant voters) by the Government party 'and then by great and widespread dishonesty in the compilation of returns', which gave the Democrats only 65 seats as against 396 for the Government—'a result which by no means reflected the total vote they would have polled in an honest court'.[4] The Democrats had had a useful opportunity to test their strength, however, and in cosmopolitan Istanbul,

[1] Byrnes: *Speaking Frankly*, p. 128.

[2] Thomas and Frye: *The United States and Turkey and Iran*, p. 103. See also Bernard Lewis: 'Recent Developments in Turkey', *International Affairs*, July 1951, xxvii. 321, for the part played in the formation of an opposition by Professor Fuad Köprülü, a distinguished historian who became Foreign Minister when the Democratic Party formed its first Government in 1950.

[3] See A. C. Edwards: 'The Impact of the War on Turkey', *International Affairs*, July 1946, xxii. 394, for a summary of the Democratic Party programme. Thomas (loc. cit.) points out that many liberally minded politicians chose to remain within the C.H.P. and to try to influence its development from within.

[4] Thomas and Frye, op. cit. p. 104.

still Turkey's intellectual metropolis, they had distinguished themselves by winning nineteen out of twenty-three seats, besides doing well in other important towns. The Government party evidently found it necessary to attempt to allay the widespread popular discontent at the high cost of living which persisted from the war and was aggravated by the heavy burden imposed on the national economy by the necessity of maintaining, on a footing of mobilization, an army estimated at 750,000 men to meet the threat of the Soviet cold war.[1] The Cabinet of Şükrü Saracoğlu was made the scapegoat for war-time sins of omission and commission, and only its Foreign Minister survived in the new Cabinet led by Recep Peker, a man noted for his uncompromising attitude towards the Soviet Union—an issue on which there was no difference whatever between Government and Opposition. The new Government sought to stimulate Turkish exports by a currency devaluation in September 1946, but this was of only temporary benefit.[2]

The Soviet cold war offensive against Turkey and Persia had given rise to attempts to create solidarity between Turkey and the Arab world. On 29 March Nūrī as-Saʿīd, the elder statesman of ʿIrāq, had negotiated a Treaty of Friendship and Good Neighbourliness with Turkey, which was, however, not ratified by the ʿIrāqī Parliament until June 1947.[3] On 28 November 1946 the Secretary-General of the Turkish Foreign Ministry was to visit ʿAmmān to convey his Government's congratulations to King ʿAbdullāh on the achievement of independence by the Hāshimī Kingdom of Jordan, and the King visited Turkey in January 1947 to conclude a Treaty of Friendship.[4] A state visit to Turkey by the Lebanese President in June 1946 was thought to have had the purpose of reconciling Turkey and Syria, estranged by the question of the Sanjaq of Alexandretta,[5] but the Syrian Government's jealousy of the Hāshimī states, ʿIrāq and Jordan, prevented any *rapprochement*.[6] With Egypt Turkish relations were strained on account of Turkish representations that it was inopportune for Egypt to demand the withdrawal of British troops from the Canal Zone. The Egyptian press retorted that, if a British garrison were strategically necessary, it had better be situated in Turkey rather than on the Canal: 'If we

---

[1] See below, p. 43, note 1. Soviet propaganda had continued its attacks on the 'reactionary' Turkish Government and its support for the Armenian claims. The Soviet Union was now supporting a 'democratic' government in Persian Kurdistān (see below, pp. 62–63); and on 15 June the trade-union newspaper *Trud* carried an article attacking Turkey for her treatment of her Kurdish minority of somewhat under 2 million. For reports on the situation of Kurds in Turkey see 'a correspondent recently in Turkey' in *The Economist*, 5 October 1946, p. 547, and Thomas and Frye, op. cit. pp. 79–80, 115.

[2] See ibid. pp. 109–10.

[3] See Majid Khadduri: *Independent Iraq* (London, Oxford University Press for Royal Institute of International Affairs, 1951), pp. 261–3, and below, pp. 150, note 1, 151; text in *Cahiers de l'Orient Contemporain*, 3me–4me trimestres 1947, xi–xii. 149–50.

[4] Text ibid. 1er–2me trimestres 1947, ix–x. 25–26.

[5] See above, p. 22 and note 3.   [6] See Khadduri, loc. cit.

are faced with the alternative, we would choose your having the Russians and our getting rid of the British'; and the influential Egyptian columnist 'Abd ul-Qādir al-Māzinī remarked that the proposed Middle East pact would make the Arab world a British and Turkish cat's-paw: 'We have nothing to gain by unnecessarily antagonizing Russia.'[1]

The Montreux Convention regulating the régime of the Straits was due for automatic renewal for five years on 9 November 1946 unless it were denounced by one of the signatories before 9 August. The Soviet Government had chosen this occasion to publish a selection of captured German Foreign Ministry documents dealing with German-Turkish relations during the war;[2] and on 8 August they delivered a note in which they renewed their complaint that the Turkish Government had failed to keep the Straits closed to Axis naval vessels during the war, adopted the United States proposals of 2 November 1945, insisted that responsibility for the control of the Straits lay with Turkey and the other Black Sea Powers, and concluded with the proposal that 'Turkey and the Soviet Union, as the Powers most interested in and capable of ensuring the freedom of merchant shipping and security in the Straits, shall jointly organize the defence of the Straits to prevent their use by other States for purposes hostile to the Black Sea Powers'.[3] The Communist *Humanité* justified the Russian claim on 15 August with the observation that south of the Straits lay seas dominated by Britain, whose proper interests were Atlantic but whose troops nevertheless were strung out all the way from Trieste, through Greece, to Palestine; and 'the Turkish pseudo-democracy, after having been during the entire war an instrument of German policy', was now becoming an instrument of British policy. It was to be expected, *L'Humanité* continued, that the 'imperialists' would now seek to refer the Straits question to some international assembly or conference which would pretend to impartiality while in fact the delegates would 'converse in the lobbies in English with the orchestra conductor from London'. A responsible British assessment of the position came on 19 August from the *Observer*'s diplomatic correspondent, who pointed out that Russia's encouragement of the autonomy of Persian Āzarbāijān[4] had the effect of turning Turkey's eastern flank, so that, if she now conceded bases on the Straits to Russia, she would be 'speedily reduced to vassalage, and, by the law of ninepins, Greece, Syria, and Iraq would immediately confront a similar situation'.

[1] Quoted by *Middle East Times* (Jerusalem, Zionist), 20 June 1946, and *Middle East Opinion* (Cairo, Arab League organ), 30 December 1946; see generally M. Colombe: 'La Turquie et les problèmes du Moyen-Orient', *Cahiers de l'Orient Contemporain*, 3ᵐᵉ–4ᵐᵉ trimestres 1947, xi–xii. 140–1.

[2] Afterwards translated from the Russian by Madeleine and Michel Eristov with the title *Documents secrets du Ministère des Affaires Étrangères d'Allemagne*, vol. i: Turquie (Paris, Éditions Paul Depont, 1946). For notice of their original publication see *Scotsman*, 13 August 1946.

[3] Text in *Soviet News*, 14 August 1946; *Problem of the Turkish States*, pp. 47–49.

[4] See below, pp. 58–59, and 67–68.

The correspondent compared the Anglo-Turkish alliance (which the new Turkish Prime Minister had just described as being the principal basis of Turkey's foreign policy)[1] with France's alliance with Czechoslovakia at the time of Hitler's war of nerves in 1938: as France could not then uphold Czechoslovak independence without British support, so now 'Britain cannot uphold Turkey's without the support of America. The question therefore hinges on whether the United States will regard the Straits as a vital interest.'[2]

On the same day, 19 August, the United States Government, who earlier had asked from Turkey only $4·5 million in cancellation of a Lend-lease account estimated at $140 million,[3] replied to the Soviet note with the observation that it contained no reference to the United Nations; the Security Council was competent to deal with an aggressive attack or threat of attack upon the Straits; and their normal custodianship should continue to be primarily the responsibility of Turkey.[4] A British note delivered on 21 August was similar in tenor,[5] and on the following day came the Turkish reply to the Soviet note, defending at some length Turkey's war-time control of Axis shipping using the Straits, and rejecting the Soviet demand for joint control as being incompatible with Turkey's 'inalienable rights of sovereignty', with her security 'which admits of no restriction', and with her role as a 'factor of equilibrium and liaison' in the Straits.[6]

Three days later, on 25 August, a Tass Agency despatch from Beirut reported that, according to 'local circles', the British had set up a military supply base in the Straits, exercised authority over the Turkish airfield at Yeşilköy near Istanbul, and had established and were directing anti-submarine radar stations in Thrace and on the Black Sea coast; the British Foreign Office confirmed that Turkey, like several other countries, had been supplied with radar equipment and technicians.[7] Moscow Radio on 1 September returned to the charge that Britain had established a supply base in the Straits, citing the number of naval vessels and aircraft and the quantity of anti-aircraft guns and radio and other equipment which Britain had supplied to Turkey during the present year,[8] and assert-

---

[1] *The Times*, 15 August 1946.   [2] *Observer*, 19 August 1946.
[3] *The Times*, 9 May, *New York Times*, 10 May 1946.
[4] Text in *Problem of the Turkish Straits*, pp. 49–50; see *The Forrestal Diaries*, p. 192.
[5] Text in *Problem of the Turkish Straits*, p. 50. Bevin stated on 22 October 1946 that, although the British Government had had some differences of opinion with the Turks during the war about their interpretation of the Montreux Convention, they considered that 'on the whole, its terms had been conscientiously observed' (H.C.Deb. 5th ser., vol. 427, col. 1495).
[6] Text in *Problem of the Turkish Straits*, pp. 50–55.
[7] *New York Times*, 25 August, *New York Herald Tribune*, 27 August 1946.
[8] Ibid. 2 September 1946; these figures were confirmed by the British Minister of State, 17 March 1947 (H.C.Deb. 5th ser., vol. 435, col. 20). The Tass Agency had already asserted that the United States was building airfields of international importance at Ankara, Istanbul,

ing that British experts were advising the Turks on the construction of coastal fortifications.[1] The Soviet military pressure on Turkey had meanwhile been intensified during the summer. There were reported to have been large-scale Soviet troop movements close to the Transcaucasian frontier at the time of the Turkish general election and again when the Soviet note of 8 August was presented; it was estimated in Washington that the Russians had 190,000 troops in Transcaucasia and 90,000 more in Bulgaria. A raiding party of 200 Soviet Armenians was afterwards stated to have penetrated into Turkish territory in the Kars-Ardahan area, perhaps in order to test the Turkish reaction; and according to allegedly reliable information this was not the only incident of the kind. The Soviet Black Sea fleet held manœuvres based on Poti, forty-five miles north of the Transcaucasian frontier, from mid-June to the end of August. The Turkish General Staff were led by these demonstrations to suspect that a real Soviet attack might be intended, and in September and October they held a general mobilization disguised as 'manœuvres', whereby they secretly withdrew their forces from the defensively untenable Kars position to the much stronger Pasînlar defile immediately east of Erzurum.[2] Meanwhile, Moscow Radio had commented critically on 28 August on the 'very big noise' which the Turkish and the 'reactionary' American press were making about the arrival in the Mediterranean of the U.S. aircraft-carrier *Franklin D. Roosevelt* and seven other vessels, and about the impending visit of two British destroyers to Istanbul.

It was with such 'war of nerves' preparation that a new Soviet note was presented to the Turkish Government on 24 September. It insisted on the essential contrast between the landlocked character of the Black Sea, the entrance to which was therefore of chief concern to the Powers on its shores, and such international sea-routes as the Straits of Gibraltar and the Suez Canal, which necessitated 'an international control with the participation of the Powers most concerned'—although this had not yet been realized. Turkey's 'indiscriminate' objections to the Soviet proposal for a joint custodianship over the Straits revealed

suspicions which are utterly groundless and, moreover, are incompatible with

Erzurum, &c., and had granted Turkey a loan of $4·5 million for this purpose (*Reynolds News*, 28 April 1946). Charges that United States specialists were actively assisting the Turks were repeated in the *New Times*, 1 January 1947, p. 15.

[1] Cf. *L'Humanité*, 22 October 1946: 'It is known . . . that the British control the airfields of Istanbul and Çanakkale and have radar bases on the whole Turkish coast. 5,000 British specialists are serving in the headquarters, service academies, air force, and navy of Turkey.'

[2] For the strategic value of Kars see above, p. 23, note 2; and of Erzurum, Lord Kinross: 'Where Russia and Turkey Meet', *Listener*, 6 March 1952, pp. 369–70. This secret withdrawal was afterwards disclosed to C. L. Sulzberger, who adds: 'The Soviet Union managed to infiltrate many agents into the evacuated area—mainly Azerbaijanis. Turkey has reestablished her strength in that region and cleaned up the suspects' (*New York Times*, 28 March 1950); see also *The Economist*, 3 January 1948, p. 21.

the dignity of the Soviet Union. . . . Should Turkey, after refusing to accept the proposals of the U.S.S.R., begin to take military measures in the Straits jointly with some non-Black Sea Powers, this of course would run directly counter to the interests of the security of the Black Sea Powers.[1]

The United States and British Governments replied to this with notes delivered on 9 October expressing the view that the direct conversations suggested by the Potsdam Conference had now fulfilled their purpose of exchanging views between the Soviet Union and Turkey, and that there was therefore no reason to continue them. The United States and British Governments remained ready to attend a conference of the signatories of the Montreux Convention to consider its revision.[2] The Turkish reply, delivered on 18 October, largely repeated the contentions of the Turkish note of 22 August, with a new reason for not admitting the question of the Straits to be the exclusive prerogative of the Black Sea Powers, namely that the Straits formed a link between 'two worlds'—the allusion was to the Soviet world north of the Black Sea and to the 'free' world of the Mediterranean and beyond—thus placing Turkey in 'a particularly delicate geographic situation'.[3] Before this note had been published, the *Pravda* commentator David Zaslavsky observed on 20 October: 'The product of Turkish diplomacy is only a copy of an Anglo-American original. . . . The translator from the American is becoming the leading force of Turkish diplomacy', which reflected 'all the niceties, or rather all the rudenesses, of American speech'.[4] It had, in fact, been announced on the previous day that the Export-Import Bank had approved a guarantee of $25 million to United States manufacturers, who themselves would be asked to extend a credit of perhaps an equal amount, in order to supply the Turkish Government with locomotives, rolling-stock, repair shops, and means of rehabilitating their state-owned industrial plant, which had suffered during the war by reason of the difficulty in obtaining spare parts from Germany whence much of it had originally come before 1939.[5]

In November reports of an increase in Bulgarian support for the Greek Communist guerrillas uncomfortably near Turkey's western frontier in Thrace[6] evidently provided the occasion for a new 'witch-hunt' for

---

[1] Text in *Soviet News*, 1 October 1946; cf. *Problem of the Turkish Straits*, pp. 55–58.

[2] Texts ibid. pp. 59–60. A further Soviet note, suggesting that the usefulness of direct conversations was not yet exhausted, was orally answered by the British Ambassador in Moscow with the observation that his Government believed that no further useful purpose could be served by continuing them (*The Times* diplomatic correspondent, 22 November, *New York Times*, 24 December 1946).

[3] Text in *Problem of the Turkish Straits*, pp. 60–68.

[4] Reported by *Soviet News*, 22 October 1946.

[5] *New York Times*, 20 October 1946. President Inönü had stated in April, during the visit of the U.S.S. *Missouri*, that Turkey hoped for a United States credit of 'several hundred million dollars' for this purpose (ibid. 12 April 1946).

[6] *The Times* Ankara correspondent, 26 November 1946.

Communism in Istanbul. That city, together with Thrace and the shores of the Straits, had been kept under martial law since the end of the Second World War, and when on 6 December the National Assembly voted to prolong this régime for a further six months the Democratic deputies opposed the resolution as 'a measure for the suppression of meetings and the suspension of newspapers'.[1] On 17 December, however, the officer in command of the local military district announced that severe measures had been taken to put an end to Communist-inspired activities which threatened to disturb the political and economic life of the country. Among the organizations suppressed were the Socialist Party of the Workers and Peasants (which had been legally formed during the last year by the Moscow-trained Dr. Şefik Hüsnü Değmertürk,[2] the original secretary-general of a Turkish Communist Party founded in 1920 but suppressed by Atatürk), the Socialist Party of Turkey led by Esad Adil Müstecabi, the Federation of Istanbul Workers' Trades Unions, and the Istanbul Workers' Club. Eight allegedly subversive publications were suspended and over seventy suspects arrested, of whom fifty-six were eventually brought to trial and forty-five received sentences ranging between one and five years, Şefik Hüsnü Değmertürk receiving the maximum while Esad Adil Müstecabi was among the eleven acquitted.[3] The United States commentator Stewart Alsop reported from Ankara that the Turkish estimates of Soviet expenditure on propaganda in Turkey varied from about $180,000 to five or six times that amount; and, even though these figures were probably exaggerated, 'competent observers' were satisfied that an attempt was being made, probably through Bulgaria, to exploit the prevailing economic discontent to win converts to Communism.[4] Moscow Radio made sarcastic comments on appeals in the Turkish press for 'harmony between capital and labour' which accompanied a new law of 20 February 1947 authorizing employees (but not civil servants) and employers to form unions, but forbidding both strikes and lock-outs and the organization of unions with a political programme.[5]

[1] *New York Times*, 6 December 1946.

[2] This surname, adopted under Atatürk's compulsory law of 1934 (*Oriente Moderno*, December 1934, pp. 577–9), may be translated 'the Turkish "common man"'; cf. the Persian Communists' choice of the derogatory title of 'Tūda', 'the masses'.

[3] *La République* (Istanbul), 15 July 1948. A Soviet writer, on the other hand, declared that 'thousands of progressive leaders and trade unionists' had been imprisoned. 'This rabid campaign against the democratic camp had been undertaken . . . on direct orders from Washington' (A. Kuzmina: 'Turkey's Foreign Policy', *New Times*, 14 April 1948, p. 9).

[4] *New York Herald Tribune*, 16 February 1947. About the time of the general election in July 1946 the Socialist Party had been suspended for sending greetings to the Social Democrats in Bulgaria, and a newspaper *Gerçek* (significantly synonymous with *Pravda*), which had recently appeared allegedly with a Russian subsidy, had been banned for 'provocative' writing (A. C. Sedgwick in *New York Times*, 27 July 1946).

[5] Article 5 laid down that such unions 'shall not, as such, engage in politics or political propaganda, or act as an instrument for the activities of any political organisation. The trade

Meanwhile, Britain's post-war Labour Government were trying to create a welfare state at home and reduce their imperial commitments at a time when the country's economic exhaustion due to the war was making itself increasingly felt. At the beginning of 1947 the country had run into a coal shortage which was made much worse by the severest winter experienced for sixty-six years, until it threatened to paralyse Britain's economic life. This 'winter crisis' reached its peak in February.[1] On the 14th of that month the harassed Government announced that the unresolved conflict in Palestine would be turned over to the arbitrament of the United Nations,[2] and on the 20th that the Indian sub-continent would be made ready to achieve its independence in the summer. Negotiations with Egypt for a revision of the 1936 Anglo-Egyptian Treaty had broken down in January;[3] and in a note dated 21 February the British Government informed the United States Department of State that from the end of the United Kingdom's financial year on 31 March they would be obliged to discontinue the financial, economic, and advisory assistance which they had been giving since the war to Greece and Turkey.[4] The American commentator Stewart Alsop had reported from Ankara on 19 February: 'The most optimistic estimate of Turkish resistance, in case of a Russian attack, is six months. Experts are more inclined to guess at between a month and six weeks.' At the same time, Alsop continued, the cost of keeping the Turkish army mobilized was 'bringing the specter of inflation and financial chaos constantly nearer. Here again there is no optimism among expert observers, but rather degrees of pessimism.'[5] On 12 March, accordingly, President Truman delivered to a joint meeting of the two Houses of Congress the address on the Mediterranean situation which went down to history as the Truman Doctrine, and in which he asked Congress for authority to furnish aid to Greece and Turkey to the amount of $400 million for the period ending 30 June 1948 and to supply those countries with skilled personnel and training facilities. Turkey's share was envisaged as $100 million, to be spent on modernizing her military equipment and transport system so as to make possible some degree of demobilization and thus relieve the national economy. As the Senate debate on the bill drew to its close the Republican Chairman of

unions shall be national organisations. They shall not carry on any activities which are unpatriotic or contrary to the national interest. With the consent of the Council of Ministers, a union may belong to any international organisation' (quoted by International Labour Office: *Labour Problems in Turkey* (Geneva, 1950), p. 174).

[1] See *Annual Register*, 1947, pp. 4-9.
[2] See below, p. 238.   [3] See below, p. 130.
[4] See statement by the Acting Secretary of State, Dean Acheson, 20 March 1947 (U.S.A., House of Representatives, Committee on Foreign Affairs: *Hearings . . . on H.R. 2616, a Bill to provide for Assistance to Greece and Turkey* [afterwards referred to as *Assistance to Greece and Turkey*] (Washington, U.S.G.P.O., 1947), pp. 1 and 7; *The Forrestal Diaries*, pp. 245-53.
[5] *New York Herald Tribune*, 19 February 1947.

the Committee on Foreign Relations, Senator Vandenberg, summed up the arguments in its favour as follows:

First. Heroic Greece, pleading for American aid, will almost inevitably become a totalitarian satellite within a few months if the bill shall fail. . . .

Second. Neighboring Turkey, the only independent country left on the immediate perimeter of Soviet Russia from the Baltic to the Black Sea, has been sturdily resisting a 'war of nerves'. If Greek independence fails, Turkey will be exposed upon every side. Her independence may well be the next sacrifice.

Third. From such key impulses, if the bill shall fail, we cannot ignore the probability of a Communist chain reaction from the Dardanelles to the China Sea and westward to the rims of the Atlantic. . . .

Fourth. America . . . cannot escape a primary self-interest that America shall not be stranded in a totalitarian world. . . .

Fifth. If we act, we 'hold the line' for the United Nations until such times as the United Nations can progressively take over these responsibilities—an evolution which we not only crave but openly invite. . . .[1]

Opposition in Congress came both from those idealists who feared that the United States was undertaking a commitment which was more properly that of the United Nations, and from those traditionally opposed to inheriting an 'imperialist' policy from Britain's failing hands.[2] The bill, however, passed the Senate on 22 April by 67 votes to 23 with five absentees, and the House of Representatives on 9 May by 287 votes to 107, with 37 not voting. Soviet and Communist propaganda had little new to say, except to suggest that United States oil monopolies were sponsoring the aid programme because of their desire to convert Greece and Turkey into bases 'for an offensive in the Middle East';[3] but one of Britain's leading Communist journalists wrote:

Supported by Messrs. Truman and Bevin, Turkey now totters to the front of the stage to take a bow before the astounded world as the defender of democracy and freedom. . . .

It is a land in which millions of peasants without land, and peasants with plots so small that they starve, toil to support a superstructure of immensely wealthy landowners, a brutally corrupt bureaucracy, an army of between 600,000 and 800,000 men, and a police apparatus as extensive, cruel and lawless as that of Franco Spain. . . .

They have nourished their scandalous Government and their monstrous plans of aggression on the anti-Soviet policies of London and Washington. Now the United States takes over the main burden of the upkeep of this dangerous gang.[4]

---

[1] *Congressional Record*, 22 April 1947, pp. 3772–3.
[2] See *Survey* for 1947–8, pp. 15–17.
[3] 'American Foreign Policy', *New Times*, 2 March 1947, p. 2; for a disclaimer by the Acting Secretary of State, Dean Acheson, see *Congressional Record*, 22 April 1947, p. 3780.
[4] Frank Pitcairn (pseud. of Claude Cockburn) in *Daily Worker*, 17 March 1947.

(b) From the Truman Doctrine to the Korean War, 1947–50

As the first step towards carrying into effect the Truman Doctrine, in so far as it concerned Turkey, a special service mission consisting of twelve United States army, six navy, and three air force officers and two State Department economists arrived in Turkey in May 1947 to confer with officers of the Turkish armed forces and civilian officials. The great degree of mechanization which the armed forces of the Great Powers had undergone in the last thirty years, and especially immediately before and during the Second World War, had left the Turkish armed forces far behind, so that relatively to those of the Great Powers they were weaker (despite what they had received from the West during and since the Second World War) than those of the Ottoman Empire in the First World War had been.[1] Moreover, much of their equipment was obsolescent and of heterogeneous origin, with the attendant difficulty of providing spare parts and ammunition. A thorough modernization of the armed forces was quite beyond the technical and financial means of the Turkish economy, still only in the early stages of industrialization; and Turkey was no exception to the rule that after a period of non-belligerence a country's most conservative element is to be found among the senior ranks of its armed forces. Turkey's higher staff officers had received their training from the Germans before 1914, and were inclined to underestimate their present deficiencies, reposing instead 'stupendous confidence'[2] in the traditional and well-tried courage of the Turkish soldier;[3] and while some were sublimely satisfied of Turkey's ability to produce for herself the latest ingenuities of mechanized warfare,[4] officers of more junior rank who were required to be initiated into these new mysteries were sometimes reluctant to submit to the indignity of becoming 'rude mechanicals'.[5]

[1] This widening gap between a country like Turkey and the technologically most advanced countries was general, not merely confined to the armed forces. Cf. Thomas and Frye: *The United States and Turkey and Iran*, p. 102: 'Was it not true that the Turkish blacksmiths of 1914 had been closer rivals to 1914 Pittsburgh than were the Turkish steel workers at Karabük to the technicians of Oak Ridge? Was it not true that all of Turkey's exertions to get enough New Turks to insure New Turkey's survival . . . represented in the end really only a net *loss*? . . . In terms of military power, the answer to these sharp-edged questions was very probably an unqualified "yes". Turkey of the late 1940's was farther from world-par than Turkey of the early 1920's had been.'

[2] Joseph G. Harrison in *Christian Science Monitor*, 26 February 1949.

[3] The Turkish private soldier could not be entrusted with tools, because his pay was so infinitesimal (the equivalent of $4 per year) that he could not be mulcted of the cost of even a hammer lost or damaged by his negligence, according to *U.S. News and World Report*, 12 May 1950, p. 21.

[4] A United States naval officer was told by Turkish naval friends of their determination to build an aircraft carrier. 'He finally got to visit the shipyard in which the Turks hoped to build the carrier, and gave it as his frank but not unfriendly opinion that the Turks would have a difficult job repairing an automobile there' (Joseph G. Harrison, loc. cit.).

[5] A friend of the writer, visiting a Turkish agricultural college some time before 1939, saw a gardener demonstrating the arts of pruning and grafting to a group of students. He then asked

This transitional condition between the slow-moving Ottoman past and Atatürk's dream of a modern secular state on the Western pattern was characteristic of the whole of the Turkish economy,[1] and the multifarious practical and psychological obstacles to be overcome soon made themselves apparent to the American advisers:

. . . But as American parties landed at Turkish ports, travelled on Turkish railways and roads, inspected Turkish farms, mines and factories, they learnt that the ports could not handle the material they proposed to send; that the road system would have to be rebuilt before a modern army could deploy; that there was no industry capable of sustaining the efficient war machine to be created. Gradually . . . the emphasis began to shift from guns and trucks to ports and roads. American delegations called at the Ministries of Public Works and Communications. They were told that the new five-year plan of industrialisation, only one of several big public projects, would alone increase road traffic by an estimated 500,000 tons p.a. But the latest road construction plan of the Ministry of Public Works showed that, even on paper, it would take 15 years at the planned annual expenditure rate of £140 million to construct and repair the 12,500 miles of highway required to raise the Turkish network to the average European level of 100 years ago. The Americans inspected ore mines—without smelting furnaces; new blast-furnaces—without coke ovens; potential oil fields— without wells. They carried off the impression of an undeveloped, inexpertly striving country, rich in economic potential and paper planning, but lacking capital, skilled labour and engineering, and, above all, economic common sense and organisation.[2]

A primary strategic axiom which presented itself was that in the event of war with Russia Turkey's ports in the Straits and the Aegean would be of little more value than those on the Black Sea, and that her most accessible port would therefore be Iskenderun (Alexandretta), 450 miles north-north-east of Port Said. Road and rail communications northwards from this port were, however, quite inadequate for modern military traffic (the poorness of communications had previously been an important factor of Turkish defensive strategy), and the Americans made preparations to build strategic roads, north-eastwards to Erzurum (the military base of eastern Anatolia for defence against invasion from Soviet Transcaucasia) and north-westwards to Ankara and Istanbul.[3] The traditional

if the students would practise this themselves, but was told with some warmth that it would be shameful (*ayip*, Arabic *'ayb*) for them to perform manual work.

[1] See Max Weston Thornburg, Graham Spry, and George Soule: *Turkey, an Economic Appraisal* (New York, Twentieth Century Fund, 1949), the result of an inquiry carried out in the summer of 1947 (see also the review in the *Middle East Journal*, October 1949, iv. 480–2). The section entitled 'An Economic Monstrosity' (pp. 108–9) provided a good example of the faulty planning which derived from the combination of idealism and inexperience which had 'concentrated too much on the fancy trappings of Westernization' (A. T. Steele in *New York Herald Tribune*, 19 November 1950).

[2] A correspondent in Ankara, *The Economist*, 3 January 1948, p. 21.

[3] See Robert W. Kerwin: 'The Turkish Roads Program', *Middle East Journal*, April 1950,

Turkish defences against Russian invasion were the lines of Çatalca in Thrace, thirty miles west of Istanbul, and the Pasînlar defile east of Erzurum;[1] but it would appear[2] that as a result of the Turkish military manœuvres of 1948 and early 1949 the United States military observers decided that these positions were unlikely to hold out for more than a very short time against a full-scale Soviet attack, and that the best that could be immediately hoped for was to hold with twelve to fifteen Turkish divisions the region south of the Taurus range, with Iskenderun as its supply-base, and to launch aerial attacks from this bridgehead upon the oilfields and industrial regions of South Russia.[3]

The American objective under the Truman Doctrine was to relieve the burden of the Turkish armed forces upon the national economy by reducing the number of men under arms by about 30 per cent., and at the same time to increase their fire-power and mobility by mechanizing these forces. While this programme was getting under way towards the end of 1947, however, the more general economic needs of Turkey urgently presented themselves. During the Second World War she had accumulated over $260 million in gold and dollars and approximately $65 million in unconvertible currencies, but had drawn heavily on these reserves after the war to make up her war-time accumulation of needs in capital and consumer goods. Thus her imports from the United States, which had stood at between $7 million and $14 million in 1936–9, had risen to about $81 million in 1947.[4] She counted on continuing to purchase from the United States to a much greater value than that of her possible sales to that country; and the prospective dollar gap could not be filled by private

---

iv. 196–208, for the economic implications of this programme, and for difficulties encountered. For a Communist view of its strategic significance see Samy el Basry: 'Les routes stratégiques du Moyen-Orient', *Moyen-Orient*, January 1951, pp. 8–9.

  [1] See above, p. 33.

  [2] See the article in the semi-official *Ulus*, 26 March 1949, quoted below, p. 51, and articles by Aslan Humbaraci in *New Statesman and Nation*, 4 June 1949, p. 579, *Tribune des Nations*, 10 June, *Monde*, 12 July 1949. This writer had been *New York Times* correspondent in Turkey since 1946, but resigned in the spring of 1949, ostensibly because he had been systematically subjected to censorship and 'intimidation', both Turkish and American, to prevent him from reporting objectively on the difficulties that had arisen between the Turkish armed forces and the United States missions (see text of his letter of resignation in *Armenian Affairs*, Winter 1949–50, i. 77–79). He then lived for a time in Prague, but later apparently revolted against conditions behind the Iron Curtain and found a refuge in Paris.

  [3] See Major George Fielding Eliot, writing after a visit to Turkey in May 1948 (*Hate, Hope, and High Explosives* (Indianopolis and New York, Bobbs-Merrill, 1948), p. 218). In fact, however, it was not until 1951 that the Turkish Government were willing to allow the United States the use of their air bases, partly for fear of provoking the Soviet Union and partly because they insisted in return on Turkey's admission to the North Atlantic Treaty Organization (see 'Bases and Treaties in the Middle East', *The Economist*, 3 March 1951, p. 491; D. J. K., 'Greece, Turkey, and N.A.T.O.', *The World Today*, April 1952, viii. 163; and below, p. 53).

  [4] U.S.A., Economic Cooperation Administration: *European Recovery Program, Turkey Country Study* (Washington, U.S.G.P.O., 1949), pp. 12, 14. [This is referred to hereafter as *European Recovery Program, Turkey*.]

American investment in Turkey, for American business men, with their shrewd sense for costs and efficiency, looked critically on the inefficient, state-monopoly structure of Turkish industry, producing goods at costs considerably above world prices for which internal markets were found only by the exclusion of competitive foreign products.[1] There was also the memory of Turkey's highly discriminatory capital levy of 1942–3. When such obstacles to foreign investment existed—and the suspicion of 'economic imperialism' inherent in Turkish nationalism was not easily overcome—it was a mere palliative to relax the ban which the Atatürk régime had imposed on a foreign company's transferring its capital or profits outside Turkey.[2]

The stated objective of the United States Government in furnishing Turkey with 'Marshall Aid' under the European Recovery Programme was that

Turkey is potentially a much larger producer of grain and other foodstuffs than it has been. An extension of the use of fertilizer, agricultural implements and machinery, the reclamation of land through drainage and irrigation, and the improvement of transportation within Turkey can be combined to increase output, eliminate waste, and improve distribution to a marked degree. These measures can raise the standard of living of the Turkish people from the low levels of the past, and at the same time make greater quantities of foodstuffs available for export to other ERP[3] countries. Exploitation of Turkey's mineral resources can provide Turkey with added exportable surpluses; at least one, chrome, is of vital interest to the United States for strategic purposes.[4] Economic development of this character can improve Turkey's internal and external economic position materially with reasonable prospects of achieving a new equilibrium at a higher level of national income.

With regard to agriculture, which supports three-fourths of the population, the great need of Turkey is for modern equipment and modern farming techniques in order to increase production from existing farm land and to put additional acreage under cultivation. The results should be substantial, for present

[1] See Elizabeth Monroe: 'Dollar Aid for Turkey', Scotsman, 21 January 1948; and for the historical reasons for Atatürk's policy of étatisme Ömer Celal Sarc: 'Economic Policy of the New Turkey', Middle East Journal, October 1948, ii. 430–46.

Much resentment was caused at one moment by the exclusion of Turkey's principal export commodity, tobacco, from the United States zone of Germany (for Germany had been Turkey's principal market for tobacco before the war). The Turks complained of discrimination in favour of Virginia tobacco; but it seemed that the exaggerated prices which they asked were partly responsible; cf. 'Le Plan Marshall et la question de nos tabacs', La République (Istanbul), 29 May 1948, with The Economist, 26 June 1948, p. 1053, and 24 July 1948, pp. 137–8. For the failure of the Peker Government's devaluation of the Turkish currency in September 1946 see above, p. 30.

[2] See New York Times, 26 May 1947. A special Economic Co-operation Agreement with the United States was signed in July 1948 and amended on 31 January 1950 (U.S.A., Department of State: Treaties and other International Acts Series, 1794 and 2037).

[3] European Recovery Programme.

[4] An account of the strategic importance of Turkey's chrome in the Second World War will be found in the Survey for 1939–46: Competitive War Effort.

equipment and methods are generally primitive and the rate of production is low in terms both of output per man and of output per acre. Important also to Turkey is the need to shift the emphasis in agricultural production; production of cereals, oil seeds, and industrial fibers can be increased. Additional and improved packing facilities for fruits and vegetables would enable both a greater domestic consumption and increased exports. The possibility of fish packaging for export, not as yet fully explored, offers possibilities.

In industry the greatest possibilities appear to be in the extraction of ores and minerals. Turkey is known to have considerable deposits of coal and lignite, although the quality has not been fully determined; in addition, there are substantial deposits of chrome and iron ore with possibilities of increased production of copper, manganese, and lead. With outside assistance, both in the form of credits and technical personnel, Turkey should be able greatly to increase activity in this economic sector.

Turkey is seeking to encourage leadership and managerial ability through education and by sending students and special groups abroad to increase the number of engineers, scientists, doctors, agronomists, and other professionally trained persons . . .[1] has utilized technical assistance from abroad in order to hasten the development of the country. There is every indication that the policy of increased education at home and utilization of foreign services will continue.[2]

Between the start of operations of the European Recovery Programme in April 1948 and the end of its financial year on 30 June 1950 Turkey accordingly received from this source $108 million in direct aid and the equivalent of $75 million in indirect aid—to be devoted mainly to the modernization of agriculture, coal-mining, and communications.[3] The value of military equipment supplied to Turkey in those two years was assessed at a nominal figure of about $200 million, although American military authorities declared that its actual value was greatly in excess of this amount.[4] The attitude of the Turkish Government to the measure of aid accorded to them has largely to be inferred from the comments of the Turkish press, but the amount of freedom which had so far been conceded

---

[1] One or more lines have been omitted at this point in the published text.

[2] *European Recovery Program, Turkey*, pp. 2–3.

[3] Alfred Michaelis: 'The Middle East Economy in 1950', *Middle East Journal*, Spring 1951, v. 225. The principal investment items for which the Turkish Government sought European Recovery Programme aid over the period 1948–53 were:

Agriculture and irrigation	$68·5 million
Equipment of the Zonguldak coal basin	41·9 „
Maritime services (operations)	40 „
Railways (operations)	30 „
Railway construction	19·6 „
Regional power stations	20·5 „

(*European Recovery Program, Turkey*, p. 37).

[4] See Turkey's Foreign Minister, Fuad Köprülü, quoted in *Cahiers de l'Orient Contemporain*, 1er semestre 1952, xxv. 31. Lewis V. Thomas recorded in December 1950 that some $700 million had been 'at least earmarked' for Turkey in both military and economic aid (Thomas and Frye: *The United States and Turkey and Iran*, p. 146).

to the press was probably not such as to admit of a complete divergence between press comment and the official attitude. In the press there was ever-renewed protest at the alleged inadequacy of the financial and military aid accorded to Turkey,[1] in comparison with the much larger sums bestowed upon the countries of Western Europe and even upon Greece, a country who (in Turkish eyes) had shown her impotence to settle accounts with her 20,000 Communist rebels, whereas Turkey, being virtually free from Communism,[2] was a valiant outpost of Western freedom against the Soviet menace.[3] It was asserted that in dealing with the United States Congress and people it was necessary to observe the Turkish proverb, 'The child that does not cry is not given the breast';[4] and American military aid was found wanting, not only quantitatively, but also because it did not comprise the very latest weapons, comparable with the best that the Soviet Union might use against Turkey.[5]

The United States advisers had to meet these problems of psychological adjustment with a great deal of patient understanding,[6] notably in the military sphere, where it was necessary to teach the English language to prospective Turkish instructors, to the number of some thousands, and train them in the rudiments of handling the variety of new mechanical apparatus and equipment; and always there was the Turks' impatience to acquire the most up-to-date equipment such as radar, as a matter of prestige and a symbol of their modernity, before there were enough

---

[1] The Turkish Government produced figures to show that, while proper development would enable Turkey to play 'a most important part' in European recovery, in her present under-developed state her level of food consumption was the lowest in Europe; and that, despite United States military aid, she was still spending 39 per cent. of her general budget on defence in 1949 (Turkish Government: *General Memorandum for O.E.E.C., Turkey: 1950–51 and 1951–52 Programmes* (Paris, Organisation for European Economic Co-operation, 1950, mimeographed), pp. 25–27, 54–62).

[2] It was thought unlikely that the Turkish Communist Party had more than 5,000 secret members, consisting essentially of 'Istanbul university students and disgruntled intellectuals' (C. L. Sulzberger in *New York Times*, 28 March 1950).

[3] See Abidin Dav'er, 'L'Amérique amie doit le comprendre!', *La République*, 15 July 1949, and 'La sécurité de l'Amérique et la Turquie', ibid. 1 August 1949; and cf. Thomas and Frye: *The United States and Turkey and Iran*, p. 128. It was reported that when in April 1948 Greece and Turkey had reaffirmed their pre-war friendship pact Ankara had pointedly declined the Greek suggestion of a military alliance (Homer Bigart in *New York Herald Tribune*, 15 April 1949).

[4] 'Ağlamayan çocuğa meme vermezler' (Abidin Dav'er in *La République*, 17 June 1949).

[5] 'The material that we are to receive . . . was produced in prototype seven or eight years ago, was turned out in great quantities during the last years of the war, and is now for the most part obsolete in the American armed forces; so that these $25 million which are allocated to us are, in effect, spent on producing new material for the American armed forces. . . . General MacBride may be satisfied with the aid furnished to us and with its continuing at the same slow pace. But we must tell the truth openly . . . and demonstrate the inadequacy of the American aid. We must insist on new arms and new material' (ibid. 26 July 1950).

[6] Lewis V. Thomas uttered a warning against 'the tendency of the American expert abroad to be fooled by his own expertism. When, for example, the American agricultural expert working in Turkey (not to mention the expert who has never worked in Turkey, or who has been there for only two weeks) asserts that "if we do X, Y will happen", his listener must at once find out

persons trained in its use.[1] At the very highest level the Americans had to press for a radical change in the status of the conservative Turkish General Staff. Field Marshal Fevzi Çakmak, Atatürk's devoted supporter in establishing the Turkish Republic a quarter of a century before, had then pledged the full support of the army to the new régime on condition that he, as Chief of the General Staff, should be responsible, not to the Cabinet, but directly to Atatürk as President of the Republic; and the result of this, until Çakmak's retirement in 1943, had been that he was left free from any civil control or interference. 'The army budget drawn up by the General Staff was sent to the Grand National Assembly for a vote of pure form. Never, during twenty years, did a member of Parliament dare to ask any question on the army budget.' After Çakmak's retirement, however, the Chief of the General Staff had been made answerable to the Prime Minister, and, when Parliament discussed the budget early in 1949, 'outspoken criticism on military matters was uttered for the first time, to the great embarrassment of the Government, no member of which was able to speak authoritatively on the subject. On the other hand, the American military aid ... made it desirable to concentrate military affairs under one responsible Government department.'[2] In June 1949, accordingly, the Assembly passed bills placing all national defence organizations under the authority of the Minister of National Defence, and creating a Supreme Council of National Defence to co-ordinate the country's resources in case of war; it included, besides the Prime Minister as chairman, the Minister of National Defence, the Chief of the General Staff, and heads of economic Ministries. 'Thus for the first time in Turkish history the armed forces of the country [were] placed under civil authority and control.'[3] This measure was followed, in October 1949, by the compulsory retirement of over 100 senior officers, in order to provide opportunities for younger men who were masters of the techniques recently taught them by the Americans.

In a wider field an American correspondent reported, perhaps a trifle optimistically:

Turkey's new confidence, due to its own increased security and to its firm belief

whether the meaning is (*a*) if X is done in Iowa (or Uganda, or wherever this man has worked), Y will happen, or whether he means (*b*) "we know upon the basis of adequate experience in Turkey that if we do X here, Y will happen here". It is only if he means (*b*) that that man is a true expert for Turkey.' (Thomas and Frye: *The United States and Turkey and Iran*, p. 149).

[1] Cf. in the economic field *European Recovery Program, Turkey*, p. 40: 'Since much of the equipment [sought by Turkey from the United States] . . . is intended for incorporation in the various capital projects planned by the Turkish Government, and since the development of these projects is presently behind schedule and ECA approval has not yet been given to most of them, the equipment will not actually be required, or purchased, in the volume initially forecast. . . . A serious deficiency in the economic development of Turkey has been the almost complete absence of cost accounting or of what may be termed "cost consciousness" ' (Robert W. Kerwin in *Middle East Journal*, April 1950, iv. 207).

[2] *The Times* Istanbul correspondent: 'Turkey in Transition', 17 August 1949.

[3] Ibid.

in American friendship, has resulted in a strengthening of democratic tendencies which even the official opposition parties[1] admit has given the 'new look' politically and from the standpoint of civil liberties.

Press laws are being revised to protect the legitimate right of newspapers to print criticism which stops short of treason. Election laws are being re-drafted to ensure free and democratic voting. And there has been an ascertainable drop in discrimination against racial minorities, mainly Greeks and Armenians.

Although these gains in civil rights were not the immediate aim of the United States in extending aid to Turkey, nevertheless they are the direct results of such aid and it is not too much to say that without it they would not have happened.[2]

In the summer of 1947 President Inönü sought to bring about a reconciliation, or at least a relaxation of mutual intolerance, between the Government party (C.H.P.) and the Democratic Opposition, but without success; and in July he obliquely announced his intention of relinquishing the position, which he had inherited from Atatürk, of being both leader of the C.H.P. and (*ex officio*, as it were) Head of the State, and of henceforward exercising his position as President of the Republic impartially. In September 1947 Cabinet resignations and the formation of a 'progressive' bloc of more than forty members, most of them young, within the parliamentary group of the C.H.P. forced the resignation of the conservative Prime Minister Recep Peker; and a new Government was formed by his Foreign Minister, Hasan Saka, who displaced some of the 'die-hard' members of Peker's Cabinet in favour of younger progressives.[3] In June 1948 parliamentary and press criticism of the economic policy of certain Ministers led to a reshuffle of the Saka Cabinet, which brought in more of the younger critics and now included four Ministers of under forty-five; but the Ministers concerned with the national economy continued to be harassed by the rising cost of living,[4] and the struggle between 'progressives' and diehard 'extremists'[5] within the C.H.P. went on unabated until Hasan Saka was forced to resign in January 1949, and a new Cabinet of predominantly progressive character, pledged to free elections and a free

---

[1] Besides the liberal Democratic Party, a Right-wing National Party had come into formal existence in July 1948, but secured only one seat and 240,000 votes in the 1950 election (see below, pp. 53–54).

[2] Joseph G. Harrison in *Christian Science Monitor*, 2 April 1949.

[3] See *The Times* correspondent in Turkey, 'Turkish Political Struggle: Cleavage in the Governing Party', 30 September 1947.

[4] The authorities' attempt to control the cost of living by fixing prices on a 'cost plus' basis had sometimes been ingeniously evaded by retailers conspiring to sell goods to the public only when such goods had travelled round the retailers' syndicate, each member of which in turn exacted the legally permitted percentage of profit (H. C. Hony: *Turkish-English Dictionary* (Oxford, Clarendon Press, 1947), p. 394, under the word 'zincirleme').

[5] The word adopted for 'extremist' was *ifratçi*, from the Arabic abstract noun *ifrat*, 'excess'. In Arabic, on the other hand, the usual word was *mutaṭarrif*, the participle of the derived verb *ṭarraf*, 'to walk on the side' (see *Oriente Moderno*, January–March 1948, p. 12; Bernard Lewis: *Handbook of Diplomatic and Political Arabic* (London, Luzac, 1947), p. 15).

press,[1] was formed by the Party's vice-president Şemsettin Günaltay. In June, however, the Minister of State for Economic Affairs resigned, apparently on account of criticism of his failure to extract a larger sum for Turkey from the European Recovery Programme; and the very low poll at the by-elections of October 1948, which the Opposition boycotted as part of its policy of protest against its exclusion from a share in supervising the conduct of elections, was an indication of the growing dissatisfaction, especially in the cities, with the C.H.P. régime.[2]

The Foreign Minister in Hasan Saka's Government, Necmeddin Sadak, had risen to that position from being a 'progressive' C.H.P. critic of Recep Peker's Government when editor of the newspaper *Akşam*. In an interview on 30 June 1948, while a United States naval squadron was visiting Istanbul, he declared that the Turkish Government, while being already 'more than allies' of the United States, 'would like to crystallize these relationships more formally and effectively through an alliance if this should prove legally possible from an American viewpoint'.[3] The U.S. Secretary of State, Marshall, however, commented at his press conference on 2 July that the United States was doing 'quite a bit' to help Turkey and had a deep interest in her maintaining a free and independent government; but a formal alliance would involve consideration of the United States' entire foreign policy and relations with 'practically every other nation'.[4] This gentle rebuff from Washington was followed by what seems to have been a somewhat clumsy overture to Turkey from the Soviet side. One United States journalist[5] had already seen in the appointment on 24 February 1948 of Alexander Lavrishchev as Soviet Ambassador to Turkey,[6] after that Embassy had been left in the hands of a chargé d'affaires for the past eighteen months, a Soviet attempt to exploit Turkish dissatisfaction with the scale of United States military and economic aid; but no visible impression was made on the Turks; and, at a reception at the Soviet Embassy on 17 November to celebrate the anniversary of the Russian Revolution, Lavrishchev perhaps attempted to embarrass the Turkish Prime Minister publicly. According to the most circumstantial account[7] of the incident, he insisted towards midnight on giving Hasan Saka 'one for the road' in vodka, and as he did so asked, in a voice that was overheard by a number of journalists and others: 'Who is it that

[1] See *Glasgow Herald*, 21 February 1949.

[2] See 'Turkey's Silver Jubilee', *The Economist*, 23 October 1948, p. 667. By-elections in Turkey were held, not as need arose, but at fixed intervals to fill the vacancies which had occurred since the last occasion.

[3] C. L. Sulzberger in *New York Times*, 1 July 1948.   [4] Ibid. 3 July 1948.

[5] A. C. Sedgwick, ibid. 9 April 1948.

[6] Lavrishchev had been Soviet Minister to Bulgaria, head of the Balkan Affairs department of the Foreign Ministry, and (in 1947) chief Soviet delegate to the United Nations Commission of Investigation concerning Greek Frontier Incidents.

[7] Alfio Russo in *Corriere della Sera*, 2 January 1949.

brought the Americans to Turkey? Do you recall the friendship between Russia and Turkey in the time of Atatürk and your War of Independence?' He continued, according to some accounts: 'You must know that in one day the Soviet army captured from the Germans double the number of tanks that the Americans have given you. We have common frontiers and common interests. Why do you allow strangers to come between us?' An 'inspired' Turkish version of the conversation made Hasan Saka reply with some vehemence that the responsibility lay with the Soviet Union for having threatened Turkey's independence and territorial integrity;[1] but some commentators thought that the alternative account, according to which he had made no answer to this undiplomatic *démarche*, was the more plausible.[2]

The toleration which the Soviet Government had extended during the Second World War to the Orthodox Church in Russia, with the revival of the Holy Synod for the purpose of electing a new Patriarch of Moscow, was used in order to attempt to increase the prestige of the Patriarchate of Moscow in the Orthodox Church outside Russia at the expense of the Oecumenical Patriarchate of Constantinople.[3] At the same time, however, the cold war seems to have been extended to the person and policy of the Oecumenical Patriarch himself. The election in 1946 of Maximos V, at the unusually early age of fifty-one, was said to have been favoured by the Soviet Government; but while they were afterwards disappointed by the 'strictly neutral' attitude which he sought to preserve, the Turkish Government (which in the early years of the Republic, after the repulse of the Greek invasion, had made things very difficult for the Patriarchate as the embodiment of Byzantine Hellenism)[4] were dissatisfied that he did not show himself more anti-Soviet; and the dual pressure upon him was the cause, if not the pretext, of a neurasthenia which was said in 1948 to have made his resignation essential.[5] When this resignation was, however, delayed, the Turkish periodical *Millet* warned the Holy Synod that if they did not cast ecclesiastical tradition aside and press the Patriarch to take this step, they would bring suspicion on themselves.[6] His resignation was eventually secured on 18 October 1948, and the Holy Synod of seventeen Metropolitans residing in Turkey proceeded to the election of his successor on 1 November. The candidate favoured by the Turkish Government was Archbishop Athenagoras of All the Americas, an outstanding personality

[1] *La République*, 23 and 24 November 1948, according to which Lavrishchev remarked that the 500 tanks and 500 aircraft which Turkey had received from the United States were scarcely enough for her military reviews.
[2] Russo, loc. cit.   [3] See *Survey for 1939–46: The Middle East in the War*, pp. 495–6.
[4] See *Survey* for 1925, ii. 266–72.
[5] See Constantine Argyris in *Christian Science Monitor*, 23 April 1948; *Bourse Égyptienne*, 21 July 1948, quoting the Turkish *Son Posta*; Marc Marceau in *Monde*, 24 November 1948.
[6] Quoted by *Bourse Égyptienne*, 7 October 1948.

who within the last twenty years had 'performed the seemingly impossible task of uniting the Orthodox communities in America'.[1] There was the formal difficulty that the Turkish Republic had hitherto required the Patriarch to be a Turkish subject,[2] and that Athenagoras had taken out United States citizenship in 1938; but he had been born in Epirus when that province was still part of the Ottoman Empire, and he duly received eleven of the Synod's votes, the other six being left blank. Turkish nationality was formally conferred on the new Patriarch, but he was reported to have remarked in Washington that this would be merely 'automatic' and that he would retain American citizenship in his heart.[3] On taking his departure from the United States he declared his certainty that that country would 'give to the world the spiritual and moral strength it needs in its struggle to maintain the sanctity of human freedom'; it was with regret that he left 'this blessed land', but he was taking to the Middle East 'a hope that the Four Freedoms you know here might become Four Freedoms for the world'; President Truman's inauguration speech, after his recent re-election as President, would 'pave the way for a new offensive against tyranny' and was 'a word of hope and encouragement for the world behind the iron curtain'.[4] His journey was made in an aircraft assigned to him by President Truman and manned by a crew of the United States air force. The countries of the Soviet bloc were not represented at his enthronement on 27 January 1949, but his first celebration, as Patriarch, of the Liturgy was attended by the Commander-in-Chief of the United States Atlantic and Mediterranean Fleets, as well as by the United States, British, and Greek Ambassadors.[5] In July 1949 he followed the example of the Pope in issuing a decree excommunicating all persons who supported Communism.

On 15 September 1948 the former Hungarian Prime Minister Ferencz Nagy, who had been living in the United States since his escape from Hungary a year before, arrived in Istanbul travelling with a United States passport and ostensibly as a correspondent for a United States magazine. The Turkish press reported, however, that his aim was to organize the anti-Communist refugees from the Balkan countries into a common front, and on 19 September Moscow Radio accused him of being 'inspired and encouraged by espionage organizations of the United States' to foment terrorist activities and sabotage behind the Iron Curtain. The Turkish

[1] Argyris, loc. cit.
[2] Under the *millet* system of the Ottoman Empire the Oecumenical Patriarch had, as a matter of course, been an Ottoman subject of the Orthodox *millet*.
[3] *New York Times*, 17 December 1948.
[4] Ibid. 24 January 1949.
[5] *Greek Bulletin* (London), 16 February 1949. For a 'Left-wing' version of these proceedings, see Aslan Humbaraci: 'Turkey in Balkan Politics', *New Central European Observer*, 28 May 1949, ii. 124–5.

Government immediately issued a communiqué stating that instructions had been given to expel any aliens who engaged in political activities directed against another state; and Nagy discreetly left for the west.[1] *Pravda* in April 1949 scented espionage also in the organizing, by a retired North Carolina missionary and a Fellow of the Royal Geographical Society of London respectively,[2] of expeditions to investigate a report[3] that high up on the slopes of the 16,900-foot Ağrî Dağ (the traditional Mount Ararat on Turkey's borders with the Soviet Union and Persia) a Kurd had discovered, after an unusually complete thaw of the snows, the 'petrified remains of what appeared to be a ship'. To the literal interpreter of the Old Testament this could be nothing else than Noah's Ark; and in what the *New York Herald Tribune* itself described as a 'somewhat eccentric expedition' and as 'this patently fantastic enterprise'[4] *Pravda*'s commentator suspected—perhaps not unreasonably—a 'Biblical masquerade' with intent of espionage. The organizer of the proposed British expedition (who was to be accompanied by a 19-year-old Dutch student) yielded to the Turkish Government's refusal to grant visas for a visit to this strategic area; but his American competitor was both more tenacious[5] and better provided with hard currency; and despite discouragement from the State Department Dr. E. Aaron Smith and four young assistants travelled by air to Turkey, overcame the misgivings of the Turkish authorities, and were given a Turkish escort to examine the slopes of the mountain—whence they soon returned exhausted, having discovered only that they had undertaken a task too great for their physical resources or mountaineering experience.

Meanwhile, there had been a grimmer incident in the chronicle of Soviet-Turkish relations. The wife of an official, of Muslim origin, in the Soviet Embassy in Ankara had allegedly sought refuge with the Turkish authorities when her husband was forcibly taken back to Russia; and in May 1949 the Turkish Ministry of the Interior refused to hand her over to the Soviet Embassy, which claimed to have a letter in which she asked for 'release' from 'detention' by the Turkish police.[6] On 31 May the Soviet Foreign Ministry informed the Turkish Ambassador in Moscow that a Turkish diplomatic courier, travelling alone by rail from Moscow to Ankara *via* Transcaucasia, had shot himself on the previous afternoon and died in hospital at Sochi, 150 miles on the Soviet side of the frontier.

---

[1] *La République*, 17 September, *New York Times*, 20 September 1948.
[2] The latter was said to have been, before the Second World War, assistant commercial attaché at the British Legation in Warsaw and communications officer at the British Embassy in Tehrān, although his name did not appear to figure in the *Foreign Office List* at that time.
[3] Associated Press correspondent at Istanbul, 13 November 1948.
[4] *New York Herald Tribune*, 14 April 1949.
[5] See *The Economist*, 6 August 1949, p. 291.
[6] *La République*, 29 May–2 June 1949.

This was a striking coincidence of events, to say the least; and Turkish scepticism concerning the cause of his death found expression in giving him a hero's funeral attended by nine senior generals.[1]

In December 1947 5,000 students of Ankara University, belonging to the National Students' League, had held a violent demonstration to demand the dismissal of three American-educated university teachers whom they accused of Communism, and had extorted a written note of resignation from the Rector of the University on the same charge, which in his case was apparently based on an article he had written twenty-five years before. When the case of the three suspect teachers came before the Inter-University Council, the representatives of the more mature University of Istanbul held that the charges against them had not been substantiated, while the minority representing Ankara University considered them guilty and allegedly tried to effect their suspension by administrative methods.[2] The land frontier with Bulgaria, although closely patrolled on both sides, offered opportunities for the passage of agents or escapers in both directions,[3] and in June 1949 the Turkish Government increased the penalties for subversive activities.[4] On the other hand, one of Turkey's leading anti-Communist editors began a campaign for reviewing the case of a celebrated poet, Nazim Hikmet, who in 1937 had been sentenced to twenty-eight years' imprisonment, allegedly as an avowed Communist whose writings were undermining the morale of the armed forces. Not only was his sentence manifestly excessive, but doubts were expressed about the validity of the law under which he had been convicted.[5] After

---

[1] *La République*, 3 and 4 June, *New York Times*, 14 June 1949.

[2] Nadir Nadi commented (*La République*, 25 February 1948): 'When Churchill fell from power in Britain and was replaced by the Labour Party, one of our distinguished writers of the Government party wrote in his paper: "We are farther to the Left than the British Labour Party, for we nationalized our mines and railways before they did." At one time it was fashionable to claim adherence to the "Left" and to aspire to nationalization, although certainly not in this ridiculous style. Then, with the coming of nylon stockings, a sort of individualism took possession of our social structure. It was as though we had shifted from one extreme to the other.'

[3] Turco-Bulgarian friction was also engendered by transgressions of their frontier in the air. On 9 February 1948 two Turkish Spitfires were shot down near the Bulgarian coast town of Sozopol, 35 miles north of the Turkish frontier, and at the end of June the passengers in a Bulgarian aircraft forcibly took possession of it and landed on Turkish territory, from where the Turkish Government refused to repatriate them against their wishes. For the Bulgarian Government's decision at the beginning of 1950 to expel a large part of the Turkish minority, see M. P.: 'The Expulsion of the Turkish Minority from Bulgaria', *The World Today*, January 1951, vii. 30–36.

[4] The law penalized membership of 'any association directed towards the domination of one social class by another or the suppression of a social class, or the overturning of the present social and economic order . . . or any association opposed to the republican régime or directed towards the suppression or weakening of national sentiments' (*Istanbul*, 10 June 1949, quoted by *Cahiers de l'Orient Contemporain*, 2me–3me trimestres 1949, xviii–xix. 167). Similarly, the Egyptian royal decree promulgated by Isma'il Sidqi's Government in July 1946 had penalized organizations 'which aim at giving predominance to one social class over another or the alteration of the economic or social structure of the State' (*Palestine Post*, 11 July 1946).

[5] *New York Times*, 2 October 1949.

nineteen days of hunger-strike he was amnestied and released on 15 July 1950, not before there had been a serious clash between his supporters and anti-Communist students.[1] He then escaped to the Soviet Union in June 1951.[2]

The preparations being made in the West at the beginning of 1949 for the conclusion of the North Atlantic Treaty naturally interested the Turkish and Greek Governments, as recipients of United States military aid. The Turkish Foreign Minister, Necmeddin Sadak, stated before leaving for London and Paris in February that, while there was no question of Turkey's adhering to the proposed Atlantic Treaty with its limited geographical range, she was interested in the creation of a Mediterranean security system embracing Turkey, Greece, Italy, France, and Britain, adding that Turkey's participation in the Palestine Conciliation Commission was an earnest of her desire to see a settlement of the Arab-Zionist conflict which had so envenomed the Middle East for more than a year.[3] The Greek Foreign Minister expressed a similar interest; and, after Sadak had had talks with Bevin and the French Foreign Minister, Robert Schuman, *The Times* commented sympathetically in a leading article on the Greek and Turkish Governments' natural wish to ensure that the new Treaty would not divert supplies and assistance from them.[4] However, the publication of the text of the North Atlantic Treaty, with its inclusion of Italy and the three northern departments of Algeria, provoked a bitter article on 26 March in *Ulus*, the official organ of the Government party, in which Peyami Safa declared: 'Since the security system organized by the West takes no note of our existence, we equally may ignore its existence. In this way our foreign policy acquires a suppleness and freedom which will allow us to adapt it to the understanding of our neighbours'; Turkey could escape being involved in a third world war if it broke out in some other part of the world; all that the United States promised her was a 'two-weeks' resistance' followed by 'years of occupation, during which Turkey will have to wait—at the peril of having half of her cities destroyed, half of her population exterminated, and the other half made Bolshevik— for the return of the Western Allies'.[5] Two days later, however, another

---

[1] *La République*, 16 May 1950. Lewis V. Thomas comments on such demonstrations: 'Does this mean that Turkey's university men . . . are going to approximate the chauvinist university mobs so characteristic of many countries in Europe . . . between the first two world wars? . . . There is no doubt that some of them may be going down that headstrong and disastrous path . . . as the tools of adults active behind the political scenes. . . . Turkey's well-wishers justly find more cause for fear in this problem than in any other single portent in the country today' (Thomas and Frye: *The United States and Turkey and Iran*, pp. 111–12).   [2] *Soviet News*, 6 July 1951.

[3] *The Times*, 10 February, *Bourse Égyptienne*, 14 February 1949; see also 'Projet de création d'un bloc oriental', *Cahiers de l'Orient Contemporain*, 1er trimestre 1949, xvii. 37–38. For the Palestine Conciliation Commission see below, p. 290.

[4] 'The Mediterranean', *The Times*, 23 February 1949.

[5] Quoted by *Cahiers de l'Orient Contemporain*, 2me–3me trimestres 1949, xviii–xix. 170–1, and by Aslan Humbaraci in *New York Times*, 28 March 1949.

article appeared in *Ulus* saying that the first one had been a personal expression of views only, and that the paper was not directly the organ of either the Government or the Foreign Ministry.[1] Observers doubted whether the original article could have been printed without official approval, but other Turkish newspapers were quick to dispel the suggestion of neutrality; and the Foreign Minister declared, before leaving for a visit to the United States, that 'no irresponsible opinions should be taken into consideration' with respect to Turkey's foreign policy, as defined by him in Parliament: 'If Turkey is attacked, she will defend herself with all the means in her power; if another country is attacked Turkey's attitude will depend on her contractual commitments.'[2] While in the United States he told the representative of the Munich organ of the United States Military Government in Germany, with an oblique reference to the rebuff which his request for a formal alliance had received from the American Secretary of State, Marshall, in the previous July,[3] that

it should be realized that Turkey and the United States have not yet entered into any written treaty relationship with one another. . . . The Turks are not 'pact-maniacs'; honourable persons are content to seal an agreement with a handshake; and so—for our own peace of mind—we do not stand on a formal contract. . . . I must say, however, that the Turkish people are concerned that Turkey has not been included in the Western European security system . . .

and he concluded that, although Turkey was 'thoroughly able to look after her own freedom and independence without taking part in a collective security system', she 'would nevertheless be incomparably better placed, both morally and materially, if a possible aggressor could be made formally aware that Turkey was supported by a mutual assistance pact with other free nations'.[4] Although Sadak took a reassuring message from President Truman back with him to Turkey, statements made by two Opposition senators in the United States in July (during the debate on the

[1] 'Mounting criticism obliged *Ulus* to ask the writer of the article for "clarification". . . . The writer claimed a misinterpretation of his views. His article . . . was the "result of national sorrow and resentment expressed by all our newspapers because of our being left out of the pact" and "not defense of a complete isolationist policy". He then shifted . . . to the defensive in "bitter complaint" that Turkey has been "condemned to isolationism" for which "our great friends in the West must take the moral responsibility"' (*Christian Science Monitor* special correspondent, 9 April 1949).
[2] *The Times*, 2 April 1949. The reference to contractual commitments involved only the pre-war friendship pacts with Greece, reaffirmed as valid on 5 April 1948, and the October 1939 mutual assistance pact with Britain and France, whose continuing validity those two Governments were to confirm in June 1949 (*La République*, 17 June 1949).
[3] See above, p. 46.
[4] *Die Neue Zeitung*, 21 April 1949. The Turkish desire to secure written guarantees was indeed such that some circles proposed to suppress from the 1939 Pact with Britain and France that clause by which Turkey had exempted herself from thereby becoming involved in war with Russia. (A fuller account will be found in the *Survey* for 1939–46: *Competitive War Effort* ; cf. *Monde*, 20 May, *La République*, 17 June 1949.)

North Atlantic Treaty) in favour of Turkey's admission to the Treaty Organization reawakened the latent dissatisfaction.[1] The admission of Turkey and Greece to the Council of Europe at its first meeting at the beginning of August[2] was, however, welcomed, although some Opposition critics in Ankara described it as a consolation prize;[3] and the resentment caused by Turkey's omission from the North Atlantic Treaty Organization temporarily subsided.[4] The visit paid to Istanbul and Izmir by a squadron of the United States Mediterranean Fleet at the beginning of March 1950 fortified Turkish confidence; but on 23 March the Foreign Minister, when about to leave for Rome to sign a treaty of friendship with Italy on the following day, once again emphasized the necessity of a Mediterranean alliance which 'must be based on the participation of the United States—and of course Turkey, with her key strategic position. Naturally, it also would include the United Kingdom and France.'[5] On 11 May, on the eve of a meeting of the United States, British, and French Foreign Ministers, the Turkish Government were reported to have asked for inclusion in the North Atlantic Treaty Organization, with the comment that the formation of an eastern Mediterranean defence pact could not be achieved while the Arab states were still technically at war with Israel, while the Arab League itself was so manifestly rent with discord, and while no acceptable replacement had been found for the Anglo-Egyptian Treaty of 1936.[6]

The landslide victory of the Democratic Party in the Turkish general

---

[1] *Congressional Record*, 18 July 1949, pp. 9624–5. 'The most important aspect of the question is that our American friends realize more and more every day that a strong Turkey is a vital necessity for the security of the United States herself. . . . Our attachment to the democratic front, by means of some pact or other, will be a guarantee of peace and, should war come, a guarantee of victory' (Abidin Dav'er in *La République*, 23 July 1949).

[2] *The Times* (leading article of 10 August 1949) expressed doubts about the appropriateness of Turkey's admission; see the rejoinder by Kasim Gülek, ibid. 18 August 1949.

[3] *New York Times* Istanbul correspondent, 7 August 1949. The Opposition parties' refusal, as part of their protest against the allegedly inequitable electoral system, to take part in delegations abroad was the cause of the Turkish delegation's now being composed entirely of members of the government C.H.P. (*The Times*, 12 August 1949).

While some members of the Council of Europe had asked whether Turkey, as an overwhelmingly Muslim country, could be described as 'sharing in the same heritage as her fellow members, and whether the species of government which has been the instrument of her progress altogether corresponds to the other members' interpretation of the rule of law' (*Manchester Guardian* Strasbourg correspondent, 10 August 1949), a Turkish leader-writer observed that 'secularism, liberty, and democracy' were the three principles of assimilation with Europe that Turkey must follow (Nadir Nadi in *La République*, 13 August 1949).

[4] Abidin Dav'er reported assurances he had received during a visit to London that Turkey had lost nothing and had incurred no new obligations in distant lands (ibid. 9 December 1949).

[5] Reported by C. L. Sulzberger in *New York Times*, 24 March 1950; see also Sadak's statement at a press conference on 7 April, quoted by *Oriente Moderno*, April–June 1950, pp. 67–68.

[6] See Abidin Dav'er: 'Pour la sécurité du Moyen-Orient', *La République*, 11 May 1950. Turkey had flouted the Arab League by becoming the first Muslim state to recognize Israel, in March 1949; diplomatic representatives were exchanged in December, and a trade agreement followed in July 1950.

election of 14 May 1950, displacing the C.H.P. after an unbroken reign of twenty-seven years since the foundation of the Turkish Republic, came as a great surprise to almost all foreign observers—who, while recognizing the 'mounting dissatisfaction of the Turkish people with a régime that has slowly "run down" after the tension of the heroic age',[1] could not believe that the administrative influence of the ruling party, so long established, would not again prevail, even in a genuinely free election.[2] It was natural that the Italian Communist *Unità* (21 May) should conclude that the United States had influenced the result in order to 'democratize the political façade' and bring in a party pledged to liberalize the state control of economic activity which had characterized the outgoing régime. A more objective, and infinitely better informed, student of Turkish affairs remarked, however:

There is no doubt that American pressure has been exerted rather strongly during the last three years in favour of private enterprise and against *étatisme*, and the moves of the C.H.P. Government in this direction are no doubt due in large measure to the terms of American loans and the advice of American advisors. But I know of no evidence supporting the theory of direct American action in favour of political change. The most that can be said is that they helped to create a favourable atmosphere.

He pointed out that the freedom of the election from influence by the Government party 'was not an isolated phenomenon, but the last of a series of steps towards democracy extending over five years', the freeing of the press being another example.

The rulers of Turkey are not likely to change their form of government in order to please a foreign State, nor are they naïve enough to believe that the extension or restriction of democratic liberties in Turkey would have much influence on a decision in Washington to help or to abandon them. But, as against a mere desire by the Government to please the West for mercenary reasons, there are many signs of a pro-Western and therefore pro-democratic orientation in Turkey generally. At the lowest level, it expresses itself in the prevalence of chewing-gum and leopard-skin shirts on the beaches of the Bosphorus and the streets of Istanbul; at the highest, in the study of the English and American languages, literature, and history in the university, the school and the home. . . . Many

---

[1] *The Times*, leading article, 16 May 1950. Philip Toynbee afterwards wrote that the C.H.P. 'had become corrupt, woodenly bureaucratic, complacent, and nepotistic. No one doubts that its earlier achievements as a party were gigantic . . . but in its last years of power the stature of the party had shrunk, its imagination had flagged, its energy had seeped away' (*Scotsman*, 11 November 1950).

[2] Egon Kaskeline was apparently alone in writing (*Christian Science Monitor*, 11 May 1950): 'Some observers even venture to forecast that the [C.H.P.] . . . will be ousted'; but Marc Marceau (*Monde*, 13 May) was expressing the general view in saying that the C.H.P. ought to win nearly 300 seats. In fact they secured only 69 as against 408 won by the Democrats and ten others. 53·6 per cent. of the voters supported the Democrats and 40·0 per cent. the Republicans; 88·9 per cent. of the electorate voted (*Manchester Guardian*, 23 May 1950).

different factors contribute to this growth of pro-Western feeling. On the one hand there is the replacement of Germany by the United States as the main bulwark, and therefore model, in resistance to the ancient Russian threat; on the other the inevitable attraction of a victorious cause and the resulting prestige attached to its institutions and habits. But that is by no means the whole story. In the schools and universities of the republic a new generation has grown up which, accepting the main objectives of the Kemalist revolution as already accomplished, is no longer satisfied with nationalism alone. For them, the liberal Western tradition has a profound attraction, and democracy is no mere question of temporary political alinements or changing fashions, but the best hope of achieving the cultural and political integration of Turkey, on a footing of equality and self-respect, in a free world.[1]

To sum up the lessons of these three years of United States aid to Turkey, at the moment when the outbreak of the Korean War was to heighten still further an international tension that was already threatening to discharge itself in another world conflict, both Americans and Turks had realized that the process of modernizing Turkey's military and economic apparatus would take 'far longer than originally anticipated',[2] and a United States naval commander was soon to express the view that

the period over which an aid program should be scheduled, and *planned*, is not two years—nor five—but a generation! This is the only way in which we may assist the Turk to alter progressively his traditional concepts and attain a characteristically modern point of view in relation to the technological world in which he lives. The trend has definitely been established. Time is required to make the change complete.[3]

At the same time, however, there had been a strong popular drive, to which both the C.H.P. and the new Government of the Democratic Party had to accede, to permit a substantial revival of the traditional practice of the Muslim religion, which had been 'disestablished', but not effectively stifled, by Atatürk's secular legislation. Atatürk had intended that the cult of Turkish nationalism should predominate over Islām in the collective and individual consciousness, but some sensitive Turkish educators had become aware that nationalism, however zealously propagated, left in the younger intelligentsia a spiritual and ethical void which might, for want of anything better, seek satisfaction in the pseudo-religion of Communism. However, those who in post-war Turkey were most enthusiastic to restore Islām to its former position were devotees who appeared, like the Bourbons, to have learnt nothing and forgotten nothing in the past thirty years; and well-qualified Western obser-

[1] Bernard Lewis: 'Recent Developments in Turkey', *International Affairs*, July 1951, xxvii. 322–3.
[2] C. L. Sulzberger in *New York Times*, 28 March 1950.
[3] Commander Harold G. Bowen, Jr.: 'Naval Aspects of the Mission to Turkey', *United States Naval Institute Proceedings*, October 1951, lxxvii. 1049.

vers[1] became concerned at the possibility of the movement's assuming a negatively reactionary character. The essence of Turkey's present standpoint in the world was, in fact, seized by Philip Toynbee, who pointed out that

Westernization has not yet touched the fundamental social structure . . . which remains obstinately Middle-Eastern. Compared to Egypt or Iran this is a mild variant of the pattern, but political changes have not yet changed the pattern. . . . Although one may say that Turkish political democracy is in some ways rather uneasily in advance of the country's social structure, that structure will not make Turkey a dubious military factor. The Turks will, if necessary, fight as hard and as long as they can, and if they are defeated it will not be because of any internal collapse or upheaval.[2]

(ii) Persia

(a) The Cold War, to the Repudiation of the Soviet Oil Demands, 1945-7

As the Second World War drew to a close, and while the British, Soviet, and United States forces were still in occupation of Persia, that country was already the scene of an internal conflict that dimly foreshadowed the war that was to break out in Korea five years later. The local antagonists in this conflict were, on the one hand, the revolutionary Tūda Party and its labour counterpart, the Central Council of United Trades Unions, both of which had become active during the war with the encouragement of the Soviet authorities, especially in their northern zone of occupation and in the capital; and, on the other hand, the forces at the command of the Persian propertied classes who dominated the Government and the administration.[3] Neither side showed any restraint in using violence and terrorism against its opponents. The organization and direction of the anti-Tūda forces was in the hands of the Chief of the General Staff, General Hasan

---

[1] See Bernard Lewis: 'Islamic Revival in Turkey', *International Affairs*, January 1952, xxviii. 38–48; Lewis V. Thomas: 'Recent Developments in Turkish Islam', *Middle East Journal*, Winter 1952, vi. 22–40. Emile Marmorstein, on the other hand, saw the situation more pregnantly: 'The peoples of the Middle East are troubled by new problems resulting from a combination of inter-dependent developments, the rise of nationalist movements, the introduction of new techniques, means of communication, and methods of administration, the spread of monopoly capitalism and the decay of traditional ways of life. They are looking for solutions which provide all the answers to all their questions as to why these things are happening to them and what they must do about them. Those who wish to adopt a positive attitude towards their world are forced to decide between the philosophy of national regeneration, the path of revolutionary Communism and devotion to the beliefs and practices of their ancestors.' In the so-called reactionary tendencies of the Turkish Islamic revivalists he saw the resurgence of a Church Militant against 'the eternal Amalek which they believe to be within us all' ('Religious Opposition to Nationalism in the Middle East', *International Affairs*, July 1952, xxviii. 357).

[2] *Scotsman*, 13 November 1950.

[3] See *Survey* for 1939–46: *The Middle East in the War*, pp. 28–29, 469 seqq.

Arfa', who, having a British wife, was a ready target for Tūda and Soviet propagandists;[1] nevertheless, as a result of systematic Soviet policy, by the summer of 1945 the Persian Government's authority in the Soviet-occupied northern provinces had been reduced virtually to zero. In that region the Tūda Party was in control of the chief towns, the communications, the police, and the prisons, in which they maltreated their political opponents in traditional style.[2] When the Persian Government sent a gendarmerie force to reassert their authority against the insurgent Tūda Party in the northern province of Māzandarān they were turned back by Soviet troops, while conversely Left-wing mutineers from the Persian army in Khurāsān were exceptionally allowed through a Soviet check-post to support the Tūda Party in rebellion in Gurgān province.[3]

The Anglo-Soviet-Persian Treaty of 1942 had provided that the Allied occupying forces should be withdrawn from Persia within six months of the cessation of the war. The British and United States Foreign Ministers at the Yalta Conference in February 1945 had suggested advancing the date as a gesture of goodwill towards Persia, but Molotov had said that his Government would require time to consider the proposal.[4] Agreement was reached, however, at the Potsdam Conference (17 July–2 August 1945) that the occupying forces should be immediately withdrawn from Tehrān, and that the further stages of the withdrawal should be considered by the three Foreign Ministers when they met in London in September.[5] The evacuation of the capital was duly reported complete before the end of September, although it was afterwards alleged that the Russians still had several thousand men there in civilian clothes. Meanwhile, the United States Government had unilaterally announced on 28 August that their troops would be withdrawn from Persia by 1 November, except for about 2,000 who would temporarily maintain and guard military installations. It followed from the date of the armistice with Japan that the subsequent six months' period within which the British and Soviet forces should be withdrawn from Persia would expire on 2 March 1946. When the three Foreign Ministers met in London in September 1945, Bevin suggested in

---

[1] See Iraj Iskandarī: 'Histoire du Parti Toudeh' [referred to hereafter as Iskandarī], *Moyen-Orient*, May 1950, pp. 8–9; A. Bashkirov: *Rabochee i Profsoyuznoe Dvishenie v Irane* (Moscow, Profizdat, 1948) [referred to hereafter as Bashkirov], pp. 50–51.

[2] E. P. Harries: *Trade Union Congress: World Federation of Trades Unions Delegation to Iran*: [Minority] *Report*, 29 May 1947 (typescript), p. 2 and appendix; L. P. Elwell-Sutton: 'Political Parties in Iran, 1941–1948', *Middle East Journal*, January 1949, iii. 57.

[3] See A. K. S. Lambton: 'Some of the Problems Facing Persia', *International Affairs*, April 1946, xxii. 261, 265; George Lenczowski: *Russia and the West in Iran, 1918–1948* (Ithaca, N.Y., Cornell University Press, 1949), pp. 239, 286–7; Communications from the Persian Foreign Ministry to the Soviet Embassy, published in U.N., Security Council: *Official Records*, 1st year, 1st series, supplement no. 1, pp. 61–73.

[4] *Survey* for 1939–46: *The Middle East in the War*, p. 481.

[5] Great Britain, Foreign Office: *Protocol of the Proceedings of the Berlin Conference*, Cmd. 7087, article xiv.

a letter to Molotov on the 19th that their two Governments should agree on the withdrawal of their respective forces from the whole of Persia by the middle of December, except that British forces might remain in the southern oilfield area, and Soviet forces in Āzarbāijān, until 2 March 1946. Molotov replied, however, with a stiff adherance to that stipulated date, observing only that, 'if necessary, the plan for the final withdrawal . . . could be discussed between us towards the end of the said period'; he saw no need for the three Foreign Ministers to discuss the question.[1]

The Persian Constitution, by this time nearly forty years old, had provided for the setting up of provincial councils,[2] but nothing had in fact been done. By the beginning of 1945, however, several Tūda newspapers had opened a campaign for provincial councils, the motive being revealed by their argument that, although the people of Āzarbāijān had 'shown that the reactionaries had very little influence over them' by returning Tūda members in the general election of 1943, the latter could not overcome the 'traitorous majority' in the central Parliament.[3] By midsummer the formation of an Āzarbāijān Committee for National Liberation had been reported; and, though this report was denied,[4] its substance was confirmed by the formation in that fertile and valuable province[5] in August of a 'Democratic' Party in which the local Tūda Party speedily incorporated itself. The pretext advanced by Tūda and Soviet propagandists[6] for this action was once again the repressive policy of the Persian Government in handling the Tūda agitation. The movement for autonomy drew strength from the facts that the province had felt the heavy hand of Rizā Shāh, prejudiced against Āzarbāijān because it had been the centre of support for the Qajar dynasty which he had overthrown in 1923–5, and that the central Government did not permit the official use of the local (Āzarī) dialect of Turkish.[7] Nevertheless, the 'Democrat'

---

[1] Bevin in the House of Commons, 10 October 1945 (H.C.Deb. 5th ser., vol. 411, coll. 245–7.)

[2] Article 29 of the Supplementary Fundamental Laws of 1907 (see Helen Miller Davis: *Constitutions, Electoral Laws, Treaties of States in the Near and Middle East* (Durham N.C., Duke University Press, 1947), p. 82); see also below, p. 64.

[3] *Shu'lavār*, 30 December 1944, *Azādagān*, 6 January, *Āzhīr*, 9 January 1945. For Tsarist Russia's *de facto* detachment of Āzarbāijān from Persia between 1909 and 1914, and for the Soviet authorities' connivance at the expression of separatist views there at the beginning of 1942, see *Survey* for 1939–46: *The Middle East in the War*, pp. 484–5, 29, 466.

[4] See Jon Kimche: *Seven Fallen Pillars* (London, Secker & Warburg, 1950), p. 115; Liberator (Kimche's pseudonym) in *Observer*, 1 and 15 July 1945; *Monde*, 17 July 1945.

[5] 'Its grain surplus supplies deficit areas elsewhere, notably in Teheran; fruit and leather are valuable exports, and together with poultry and dairy produce are also sent to other parts of the country. The Caspian provinces, some of the richest in Persia, producing rice and timber, and Khurasan, with its grain surplus and fruit (both in the Russian zone), are likely to be closely affected by the fate of Azarbaijan' (A. K. S. L.: 'The Azarbaijan Problem', *The World Today*, February 1946, ii. 56–57).

[6] Iskandarī (*Moyen-Orient*, May 1950, pp. 8–9); Bashkirov, pp. 54–61.

[7] James Aldridge, in a 700-page novel, *The Diplomat* (London, Bodley Head, 1949), attempted to portray the movement as 'genuine and . . . locally inspired', while 'the extent of Russian

leaders found it expedient to stiffen their local supporters by infiltrating 'numerous political prospectors' from Soviet Transcaucasia who could not be readily distinguished among the 'heterogeneous population and multiplicity of dialects' of Āzarbāijān.[1] The movement was led by Ja'far Pīshavārī, who had been Commissar of the Interior in the short-lived Soviet Republic in Gīlān province (1920–1) and subsequently a Comintern agent, had returned to Persia in 1936 ostensibly to escape the Soviet purge, had been imprisoned by the Government of Riẓā Shāh, and had emerged after the latter's abdication to edit the Tūda newspaper *Āzhīr*; he had been returned at the top of the poll for Tabrīz in the general election of 1943, but the Majlis (Parliament) had then rejected his credentials.[2] On 16 November all the elements who had rallied to the 'Democratic' Party, to which the Tass Agency had given generous publicity, came out in open rebellion, cutting off all communications between Tabrīz and Tehrān, and seizing during the next night the town and railway-junction of Miyāna, 100 miles south-east of Tabrīz. A merchant who arrived in Tehrān from Tabrīz two days later said that the rebels consisted mainly of Armenians and Red Army soldiers from the Baku area, wearing civilian clothes, while a Persian Government spokesman added that arms which were being distributed to them from Russian trucks had been identified as from the Persian army stocks confiscated by the Russians after their intervention in the summer of 1941. On 17 November the Persian Government asked the Soviet Embassy to inform their military authorities that a Persian armed force was being sent from the capital to Miyāna and Tabrīz;[3] but two infantry battalions that were the first to proceed were stopped by the Russians near Qazvīn. *Izvestia*[4] was at pains to inform its readers that the movement in Āzarbāijān was spontaneous and popular, but violently opposed by the local gendarmerie and 'reactionary big landlords'; the B.B.C., *Izvestia* continued, had falsely represented it as a separatist revolt with Russian connivance in order to divert attention from disorders in Palestine, Egypt, and Indonesia for which, 'as everyone knows', the British authorities were responsible.

The Persian Ambassador in Washington, the English-educated Husain 'Alā, made representations to the State Department, as a result of which

interference appeared to be negligible'. He made the novel's hero observe that 'there may be some Russian influence by indirect means, but I would suggest that it is less than our own influence in Iran which we exercise by direct control of ministers, political parties, state finances, and by petty bribery' (p. 606). By 1950 Aldridge had openly ranged himself on the Communist side over the question of Korea.

[1] *The Times* special correspondent in Persia, 26 January 1946.

[2] See Lenczowski: *Russia and the West in Iran*, p. 224; and, for other prominent members of the movement, Joseph and Stewart Alsop in *New York Herald Tribune*, 30 December 1946.

[3] Text of note in U.N., Security Council: *Official Records*, 1st year, 1st series, supplement no. 1, pp. 50–52.

[4] Quoted by *L'Humanité*, 21 November 1945.

the United States Government suggested to the Soviet Government on 24 November that immediate steps should be taken to complete the withdrawal of all Allied forces from Persia by 1 January; the United States note diplomatically suggested that the Soviet commanders who had turned back the Persian forces from the northern provinces might have been acting without instructions, and 'assumed' that the Soviet Government were issuing instructions to them in keeping with the declaration on Persian sovereignty which the Big Three had signed at the Tehrān Conference in 1943. The British Government delivered a similar note, but without this time proposing the withdrawal of troops in advance of the stipulated date of 2 March 1946.[1] The Soviet Government replied on 29 November that they saw no reason to reconsider the date of withdrawal, adding that they had

informed the Iranian Government that the dispatch of further Iranian forces to northern Iran could cause not the cessation but the increase of the disorders and likewise bloodshed, which would compel the Soviet Government to introduce into Iran further forces of its own for the purpose of preserving order and of insuring the security of the Soviet garrison.[2]

This professed concern for the security of the Soviet garrison in northern Persia, estimated at between 30,000 and 70,000 men, was considered 'as flattering to the Persian soldiery as insulting to the intelligence of those who know the Red Army'.[3]

It had meanwhile been reported from Moscow on 27 November that the Soviet Government had informed the Persian Government that they regarded with much sympathy the demands for autonomy proclaimed a week earlier by the 'All-Peoples' Assembly of Persian Āzarbāijān'.

Owing to the Russian ban on observers [a special correspondent of *The Times*

---

[1] Texts in U.N., Security Council: *Official Records*, 1st year, 1st series, supplement no. 1, pp. 53–55 (no. 7) and 56–57 (no. 10); for the Tehrān declaration see *Survey* for 1939–46: *The Middle East in the War*, p. 473.

On the publication of the United States note a Republican Congressman drew attention to a letter which he and another Congressman had sent to President Truman on their return from a visit to Persia in September. They had remarked on the recent reappointment for two years of United States army officers as advisers to the Persian gendarmerie, with the comment: 'We do not believe that our Government could look with favor upon a situation, for example, wherein Mexico might similarly contract with Russian army officers' (*Congressional Record*, 3 December 1945, pp. 11361–4, and 5 December 1945, pp. 11500–1). The New York *Daily Worker* (16 December 1945) accused Colonel Schwarzkopf, the chief United States adviser to the Persian gendarmerie, of 'crushing elementary democratic liberties of a people struggling against a semi-colonial feudal system bolstered by British and American oil trusts and airline monopolies', and the 'progressive' *New Republic* (31 December 1945, p. 888) commented: 'Our natural sympathy lies with the freedom-minded sharecroppers and intellectuals of the Tudeh Party, and even with the angry Azerbaijanis who call themselves "democrats".'

[2] U.N., Security Council: *Official Records*, 1st year, 1st series, supplement no. 1, pp. 57–58 (no. 11).

[3] *The Times* special correspondent in Persia, 26 January 1946; cf. Byrnes: *Speaking Frankly*, pp. 118–19.

reported], the gestation of this assembly could only be observed from afar; but sufficient facts are known. The movement was efficiently planned and executed, and bore all the marks of expert staging. The 'democrats' were well organized; their opponents were thoroughly cowed. The Persian Government forces in the region were powerless or were speedily rendered so. One or two military and gendarmerie posts showed fight, but most succumbed at once to Russian threat or blandishment, the men remaining passive in their barracks, many of the officers making for Teheran. The 'democrats' quickly disarmed the hated Persian gendarmerie. Their patrols controlled all communications, inquired into the business of travellers unless they had Russian passes and stopped all who did not answer 'democratic' questioning satisfactorily. A number of non-sympathizers were expelled from Azerbaijan and others fled. . . . There was practically no street-fighting and little looting. . . . It was, in fact, an almost bloodless revolution . . . [but], no matter how welcome the change may have been to the peoples of Azerbaijan, it was ludicrous to describe it as either 'popular' or 'spontaneous'. The presence of a strong hand guiding and restraining the whole movement could not be ignored. . . .

The . . . developments in Azerbaijan were watched in Teheran with anger and consternation, and the capital itself fell prey to alarm. It was . . . commonly believed that some 2,000 Russian officers and men, supported by another 1,000 importees from the north, remained in Teheran in plain clothes ready for any action that their commanders might contemplate. Russian arms were reported to have been distributed to certain elements in the population. The Red garrisons of Semnan to the east, estimated by the Persians at 20,000 men, and between Kazvin and Kerej [Karaj] to the west, stated to be another 10,000, were watched with apprehension. . . .

One of the first reactions of the Persian Government to events in the north was the convening of a Council of State, composed of five former Prime Ministers, to advise the Ministry. This was followed by instructions to provincial governors to carry out elections for provincial councils. . . . The establishment of these councils had repeatedly been urged upon the Persian Government by the British, but the Persians felt that British advice unbacked by pressure or threat could safely be ignored on the excuse that nothing could be done so long as foreign troops remained in the country.[1]

On 16 December, immediately before the meeting of the 'Big Three' Foreign Ministers in Moscow, it was announced that the small Persian army garrison in Tabrīz had surrendered to the 'Democrats'; and simultaneously, as a result of elections held in Āzarbāijān towards the end of November,[2] Moscow Radio announced the setting up of a 'National

[1] *The Times*, 26 and 28 January 1946.

[2] 'From a western point of view the elections were thoroughly unsatisfactory, though perhaps no more so than elections in the rest of Persia. The majority of the voters were described by eye-witnesses as factory-workers and "the scum of the towns". Few of the merchants or richer classes voted. Loads of voters were driven to the polls in American-built Red Army trucks driven by Soviet soldiers in uniform. Most voters were illiterate and their blank polling papers were filled in for them by the polling officers, though this would have equally been the procedure elsewhere in Persia. Only "democrat" candidates were allowed to receive votes. The results

Government of Persian Azarbaijan', led by Ja'far Pīshavārī. Its first proclamation declared private property to be inviolable; but, 'in order to
eliminate the ever-increasing unemployment in towns and villages, the
"Government" will divide among the peasants the State lands and the
lands of reactionaries who have fled from Azarbaijan and are instigating
propaganda against the autonomy of Azarbaijan'. The proclamation also
threatened with punishment as 'enemies of the people' 'all those who
threaten order and security by sabotage and harmful actions'; the National
Government recognized the Persian Central Government, and would
execute its orders in so far as they were not 'contradictory to the autonomy
of Persian Azarbaijan, the rights of the people, and the decisions of the
national *majlis* (Parliament) of Persian Azarbaijan'.[1]

In their promotion of autonomous movements against the central
Government the Russians had meanwhile turned also to the Kurdish inhabitants of the mountain region south-west of Āzarbāijān towards the
'Irāqī frontier, with whom they had already had a temporary liaison in
1942.[2] In 1944 the Soviet Consulate at Rizā'īya had resumed contacts
with the Kurdish nationalists there, and a Kurdistan-Soviet Society for
Cultural Relations was founded at Mahābād. To lead the Kurdish
nationalist movement the Russians had after some difficulty chosen Qādī[3]
Muhammad, hereditary judge and religious leader of Mahābād, a man
of 'strong and authoritarian character' who, after being 'hustled' off
with other notables to Baku for Soviet indoctrination in September 1945,
announced the formation of a Kurdish 'Democratic' Party and issued a
manifesto with aims resembling those of the Āzarbāijānī 'Democrats'. The
movement was opportunely reinforced in October by a band of 'Irāqī
Kurds of the Barzānī tribe under their leader, Mullā Mustafā. After a
protracted rebellion against the 'Irāqī Government, they had at length
been dislodged from their mountain stronghold and, having crossed the
frontier into Persia, were placed by Soviet officers under the orders of
Qādī Muhammad and there attracted other Kurdish refugees and adven-
turers from 'Irāq to a total of nearly 3,000 men, well equipped with British
arms which they had captured from the 'Irāqī army. The fall of Tabrīz to
the Āzarbāijānī 'Democrats' was the cue for Qādī Muhammad to proclaim
on 15 December a 'Kurdish People's Government', which controlled the

showed those overwhelming majorities . . . which are the hallmark of the supervised "free"
election' (*The Times*, 26 January 1946).
    [1] Ibid. 17 December 1945.
    [2] See *Survey* for 1939–46: *The Middle East in the War*, pp. 156, 466–7; and, on Kurdish national-
ism generally, W. G. Elphinston: 'The Kurdish Question', *International Affairs*, January 1946,
xxii. 91–103; Centre d'Études Kurdes: *Memorandum sur la situation des Kurdes et leurs revendications*
(Paris, 1948).
    [3] The Persian pronunciation of this Arabic word (= judge) is almost identical with that of
the Arabic *ghāzī* (victorious), and contemporary press reports often styled Qādī Muhammad
'ghazi' or 'qazi'.

area within a radius of about fifty miles of Mahābād. A 'national parliament' of thirteen members was formed, and on 22 January 1946 Qādī Muhammad was elected President. A number of men from the middle or upper classes were appointed 'cabinet ministers', and five tribal leaders received the rank of 'marshal' and were provided with Soviet senior officers' uniforms.[1]

At the opening of the Moscow Conference of Foreign Ministers on 19 December 1945, Stalin, at his first meeting with the United States Secretary of State, James Byrnes, emphasized the danger to the Baku oilfields of sabotage[2] directed from Persia, in whose Government, he said, no confidence could be placed. The withdrawal of the Soviet forces from Persia on the stipulated date in March would depend on the conduct of the Persian Government; and he reminded Byrnes that the Soviet-Persian Treaty of 1921 authorized the Soviet Government to send troops into Persia if there were a threat to Soviet security from a third party making use of Persia.[3] Stalin was non-committal to Byrnes, at their second meeting, on a proposal made by Bevin that the Big Three should send a joint commission to Persia to investigate the various aspects of the problem; but on the afternoon of Christmas Day Molotov privately told Byrnes that he thought Bevin's proposal was generally acceptable, to which Byrnes replied that he was 'particularly anxious' that the Persian question should not be raised at the impending first meeting of the United Nations. On that same evening Bevin accepted all of several amendments to his proposal put forward by Molotov, except one that left in doubt the stipulated date for the withdrawal of troops from Persia (Bevin's contention was that this date had been established by the Anglo-Soviet-Persian Treaty of 1942 and should not be changed).[4] When the three Foreign Ministers met again on the following afternoon it was evident that the Soviet attitude had hardened, for Molotov now said that the Persian question was not properly on their agenda and could not be considered.[5]

[1] Archie Roosevelt, Jr., 'The Kurdish Republic of Mahabad', *Middle East Journal*, July 1947, i. 247–57.

[2] For Stalin's repetition of this argument to the newly arrived United States Ambassador to Moscow on 4 April 1946 see Walter Bedell Smith: *Moscow Mission, 1946–1949* (London, Heinemann, 1950), p. 40.

[3] For the Soviet invocation of this Treaty to justify the intervention in Persia in August 1941 see *Survey* for 1939–46: *The Middle East in the War*, p. 135.

[4] See above, p. 57.

[5] Byrnes: *Speaking Frankly*, pp. 118–21; Bevin, in the House of Commons, 21 February 1946 (H.C.Deb. 5th ser., vol. 419, coll. 1357–8). On 24 April 1952, by way of clarifying a Presidential statement concerning United States policy over Persia in 1945–6, Byrnes said that on 19 December 1945 he had delivered a message to Stalin advising him 'that if the Soviet Union did not withdraw its troops from Persia, in accordance with its solemn promise made at Teheran in 1942 and if the Persian Government filed a protest in the United Nations, then the United States Government would support Persia in the United Nations' (*The Times*, 26 April 1952). The evidence previously published did not suggest that the United States Government had taken so firm a stand before March 1946; see below, pp. 66–67.

Between June and October 1945 the Persian Government had been led by a relatively strong man, Muhsin Sadr, who, because of his earlier career in the Ministry of Justice, was assailed by the Left-wing press as the 'murderer of the lovers of freedom . . . the famous butcher'. On his resignation, ascribed by the Tūda propagandist to 'the irresistible advance of the popular movement',[1] he had been succeeded as Prime Minister by the seventy-six-year-old Ibrāhīm Hakīmī. Since the Soviet Ambassador in Tehrān had been recalled to Moscow and the Embassy staff had ceased to have any dealings with the Persian Government, Hakīmī had not elicited any response when, on 14 December, he had informed the Soviet Government of his readiness to attend the Moscow Conference to discuss his country's problem[2] and, even before it became known that the 'Big Three' Foreign Ministers had failed to resolve that problem, Hakīmī's Government was tottering. On 1 December the Mayor of Tehrān had been dismissed, allegedly because of his connexion with the Irāda-yi Millī Party which had been formed a year earlier to combat the Soviet-inspired Tūda Party;[3] on 25 December the Minister of the Interior had been forced to resign, allegedly because he had not co-operated with pro-Soviet elements when he was Governor of Āzarbāijān; on the 31st came the resignation of a Minister without Portfolio who was regarded in Tehrān as strongly pro-British; and the following day saw the resignation of the Minister for Roads and Communications.[4] Hakīmī's Government nevertheless continued their study of Bevin's proposal, which the British and United States Ambassadors in Tehrān had renewed after the end of the Moscow Conference, for an Anglo-American-Soviet commission to study and advise the Persian Government on setting up provincial councils, to which the 'National Government of Āzarbāijān' might be assimilated. Opposition in the Persian Parliament, however, came from the Right as well as the Left—'as though Persia were being asked to do the allies a favour instead of being helped to escape from a situation that fills official circles here with alarm'[5]—and on 10 January 1946 the Government announced amid cheers their rejection of the proposal.

When the first session of the United Nations General Assembly was opening in London a week later, the Persian Ambassador to London, Saiyid Hasan Taqīzāda, who was leading the Persian delegation, asked both Bevin and Byrnes to advise him whether he should complain to the

[1] Iskandarī (*Moyen-Orient*, May 1950, pp. 8–9).

[2] Vyshinsky, however, afterwards contended before the Security Council that in a note of 1 December 1945 the Persian Government had declared that they were 'satisfied with the results of the negotiations of November 1945' with the Soviet Government (see U.N., Security Council, 28 and 29 January 1946: *Official Records*, 1st year, 1st series, no. 1, pp. 39–40, 49–51).

[3] See *Survey* for 1939–46: *The Middle East in the War*, p. 482.

[4] *New York Times*, 3 December 1945, 1 January 1946; *The Times*, 28 December 1945, 2 January 1946.

[5] *The Times* special correspondent in Persia, 28 January 1946.

Security Council of the Soviet interference in his country's affairs. The two Foreign Secretaries apparently pointed out to him the desirability that the Security Council at its present embryonic stage should be saddled with 'only the most urgent matters'. Nevertheless, the Persian complaint was formally lodged on 19 January; and the Soviet delegation, suspecting that the move had been inspired by Britain, retaliated two days later with a complaint against the presence of British troops in Greece, while the Ukrainian delegation lodged a similar complaint against the presence of British troops in Indonesia.[1] The Soviet reply to the Persian complaint, dated 24 January, argued that the question could and should be settled by means of bilateral negotiations, declaring at the same time that the events in Āzarbāijān had no connexion with the presence of Soviet troops, 'as the indisputable and entirely objective facts bear witness', but were exclusively Persian and internal—'the aspirations of the population' of northern Persia 'for national autonomy within the limits' of the Persian State, 'which is nothing unusual for a democratic State'; Vyshinsky's letter also observed, however, that 'the anti-democratic and pogrom activity, hostile to the Soviet Union, on the part of the reactionary forces' in Persia was creating 'a danger of organized hostile actions, diversions and so forth' for Soviet Āzarbāijān and Baku.[2] After making a detailed reply to this letter on the 26th, Taqīzāda presented to the Security Council on the 28th his Government's request that, until the withdrawal of Soviet troops from Persian territory was duly completed, Persian troops and officials should be allowed to carry out their normal functions without interference from the Soviet forces, and that the Council should recommend the withdrawal of all Soviet moral and material support from 'the rebels in Azerbaijan or dissident elements elsewhere'. Vyshinsky, with the support of the Polish delegation, insisted on his Government's readiness to continue bilateral negotiations with the Persian Government and opposed the retention of the question on the Security Council's agenda, but conceded on the 30th that the Council might ask for a progress report 'if, unexpectedly, owing to other circumstances or to the interference of some hotheads, no results are obtained'.[3]

---

[1] Byrnes: *Speaking Frankly*, p. 123; Bevin in the House of Commons, 21 February 1946 (H.C.Deb. 5th ser., vol. 419, coll. 1357–8). It is not clear on what evidence a writer in the Council on Foreign Relations' *The United States in World Affairs, 1945–1947* (New York and London, Harper, 1947), p. 89, based the assertion that the British tried to dissuade the Persians because they were 'not anxious for a public airing of their own policy' in Persia. Events were to show that neither the Soviet Government nor their Tūda instruments would attempt a public airing of grievances about Anglo-Persian relations. They tried instead to promote strikes in the Anglo-Iranian Oil Company's concession and to divert international attention to other sectors of the cold war.

[2] U.N., Security Council: *Official Records*, 1st year, 1st series, supplement no. 1, pp. 16–19.

[3] Ibid. p. 24; ibid. 1st year, 1st series, no. 1, p. 71. The reference to 'hot-heads' was perhaps directed at Bevin, who had taken the lead in wishing to keep the matter on the agenda.

While the Soviet delegation to the Security Council were thus playing for time, in Tehrān Hakīmī's Government had at last fallen on 20 January; and on the 26th the Majlis elected as Prime Minister—but only by a margin of one vote, fifty-two against fifty-one—Ahmad Qavām us-Saltana, a seventy-year-old landowner from the Caspian province of Gīlān, who, since his term as Prime Minister in 1942-3,[1] had entered into a tactical association with the Tūda Party and had used his local influence in their favour in the 1943 elections. He brought to the handling of affairs an assuredness and energy which many Persian politicians lacked; and, though he now claimed in an interview to have no bias for or against any foreign nation but to be concerned only with serving Persia, he had been hailed in Persia for some two months as the one man capable of negotiating with the Russians.[2] He received a friendly reply from Stalin to messages which he sent to the Big Three on assuming office,[3] and on 18 February left in a Soviet aircraft to lead a Persian mission to Moscow. Two days before his departure he had dismissed General Arfa', assailed by the Left-wing press as 'Fascist' and 'pro-British reactionary', from his post as Chief of the General Staff, and at the last moment three intended members of the mission were left behind, allegedly because they were not welcome in Moscow. The mission's departure coincided with a violent campaign in the Left-wing press against the alleged British arming of the south Persian tribes,[4] against the British Ambassador, and against the Anglo-Iranian Oil Company, which was accused of maintaining 'appalling conditions' for its workers, although in truth, despite an acute housing problem resulting from the war-time scarcity of materials, their conditions were better than those of any other industrial workers in Persia.

Meanwhile, the United States forces had been withdrawn from Persia by 1 January, and on 23 February the General Officer Commanding the British forces in Persia and 'Irāq stated that only 600 British troops now remained in Persia and that these would duly leave on the stipulated date, 2 March. On 1 March, however, Moscow Radio announced that the Persian Prime Minister had been informed in Moscow four days before that the Soviet forces would be withdrawn, 'with effect from 2 March', from the north-eastern provinces 'where the situation is relatively quiet', but that 'the Soviet forces in other parts of Persia will remain there pending clarification of the situation'.[5] In Tehrān all ninety-six of the deputies

---

[1] See *Survey* for 1939-46: *The Middle East in the War*, pp. 154, 156.
[2] See *New York Times*, 27 January, *Observer* 'Profile', 24 March 1946.
[3] *The Times*, 5 February 1946.
[4] This charge had already been levelled a year before; see *Survey* for 1939-46: *The Middle East in the War*, pp. 481-2, and A correspondent lately in Persia, *The Times*, 6 April 1946.
[5] *The Times*, 2 March 1946. In *L'Humanité* (3/4 and 5 March 1946) M. Magnien dutifully argued that Qavām us-Saltana's Government was 'not yet absolutely secure against a coup d'état' by a 'reactionary feudal conspiracy' which, he declared, was both provoking disorders in the north and intriguing with the southern tribes whom the British were allegedly arming. 'It

present in the Majlis (the Tūda fraction absenting themselves) cheered a speaker who called for a vigorous protest against this announcement, and in Moscow the Persian Prime Minister sent Molotov a letter of protest.[1] The United States Government, who had not hitherto taken the lead in the dispute over Persia, were now roused to action. They stated in a note to Moscow dated 6 March that they could not remain indifferent to this decision to retain Soviet troops after the date stipulated by the 1942 treaty; and on the 12th the State Department announced that they had received reports that 'during the last week additional Soviet armed forces and heavy military combat equipment have been moving southward from the direction of the Soviet frontier through Tabrīz toward Teheran and to-ward the western border of Iran'.[2] A statement by the Tass Agency that this report did not correspond with the facts was broadcast from Moscow on the 14th; but according to Lenczowski, who was able to draw on United States official sources, the United States air attaché in Persia observed Soviet Sherman tanks only twenty-five miles west of Tehrān:

During the Iranian New Year's holiday of March 21–27 an armed coup by the Tudeh and the Soviet agents was generally expected in the capital. Yet it never materialized. Diplomatic observers ascribed Soviet hesitation at this juncture to the stiffening of the American attitude as evidenced by immediate publicity given the Russian troop movements by the State Department and, on the other hand, by the determined measures taken by the gendarmerie adviser, Colonel Schwarzkopf, to protect the capital.[3]

The British Foreign Office also had not failed to press, through its Moscow Embassy, for an explanation of the continued presence of the Soviet forces in Persia.

Meanwhile, Qavām us-Saltana had arrived back from Moscow on 10 March, and on the 12th had addressed the Majlis, which was meeting for the last time before its statutory dissolution for a general election.[4] On the following day he told press correspondents that his negotiations in Moscow had produced no result. The Soviet Government had been un-

can be said with certainty that the British have not much to lose by evacuating their *regular* troops from Persia, since they possess a very strong contingent of mercenaries. . . . Is not Great Britain maintaining troops in Syria, Lebanon, Palestine, Cyprus, Egypt, Greece, and North Italy against the wishes of the peoples of these countries, to say nothing of Libya and Tripolitania, Gibraltar, and Malta? . . . What treaty permits the British troops to interfere in Greek affairs? By what right are the armed forces of the fascist Anders, under British authority, brought into the Slovene territory of the Julian March? What are British troops doing in the Netherlands East Indies?'
   [1] Husain 'Alā to the U.N. Security Council, 27 March 1946: *Official Records*, 1st year, 1st series, no. 2, pp. 65–66.
   [2] *New York Times*, 8 and 13 March 1946.
   [3] Lenczowski: *Russia and the West in Iran*, p. 298.
   [4] The Right Wing had wished to table a bill prolonging its mandate until the Soviet evacua-tion should have been completed, but for several days a Tūda-organized mob had prevented a quorum from meeting (*New York Times*, 7 and 13 March 1946).

able to accept his main and pressing demand for the withdrawal of their troops, and he had been unable to agree to their demands, which were subsequently stated to be as follows:

1. USSR troops to remain in some parts of Iran for an indefinite period.
2. The Iranian Government to recognize the internal autonomy of Azarbaijan. In the event of the Iranian Government's acquiescence in this request, the USSR Government offered to take steps to arrange that:
   (a) The Prime Minister of Azarbaijan, in relation to the central Government, would bear the designation of Governor General;
   (b) Azarbaijan would have no Ministry of War or Ministry of Foreign Affairs;
   (c) Thirty per cent of Azarbaijan revenue would be paid to the Iranian central Government;
   (d) All correspondence with the central Government would be in Persian.
3. The USSR Government to abandon its demand for an oil concession; instead, an Iranian-USSR joint stock company should be established in which fifty-one per cent of the shares would be owned by the USSR and forty-nine per cent by Iran.[1]

Qavām said that he hoped for new negotiations about the Soviet troops when the newly appointed Soviet Ambassador arrived in Tehrān in a few days' time, and when they had been withdrawn he would open negotiations with the Āzarbāijān 'Government' and consider an oil agreement with Russia; but only the Majlis could agree to these, and by a recent law there could be no elections for a new Majlis until all foreign troops had been withdrawn.[2] On 14 March a State Department official announced that, if the Soviet-Persian differences were not settled before the Security Council met on the 25th and the Persian Government did not themselves raise the matter, then the United States would do so.[3] The State Department understood that the Soviet chargé d'affaires had warned the Persian Premier that his Government would regard a Persian appeal to the Security Council as an 'unfriendly act', and the United States Ambassador in Tehrān thereupon confirmed that his own Government would take the matter up if the Persians did not. There was a difference of opinion in the Persian Cabinet on the tactics to be employed; but on the 18th the Persian Ambassador to the United States, Husain 'Alā, brought the dispute

---

[1] Husain 'Alā, 27 March 1946: U.N., Security Council: *Official Records*, 1st year, 1st series, no. 2, pp. 64–65. Meanwhile, *Izvestia* was reminding its readers of the extravagant claims which the Persian representatives at the Versailles Conference in 1919 had put forward to territories annexed by Tsarist Russia in the nineteenth century (see *H.P.C.*, vi. 211), and declared that the Persian 'ruling clique' still hoped to secure these territorial claims by embroiling the Soviet Union with some other Powers (reported by *The Times*, 15 March 1946).

[2] *The Times* diplomatic correspondent, 14 and 25 March 1946.

[3] *New York Times*, 15 March 1946. See Byrnes: *Speaking Frankly*, p. 126, for Molotov's bitter complaint to him on the United States attitude when they met again in Paris in April.

to the notice of the Security Council. On the following day Vyshinsky's understudy, Andrei A. Gromyko, informed the Secretary-General of the United Nations that the Persian move was unexpected, since negotiations between the two Governments were in progress, and his Government accordingly asked that consideration by the Security Council should be postponed until 10 April.[1] On 20 March the new Soviet Ambassador, Ivan V. Sadchikov, arrived in Tehrān and was reported to have given the Prime Minister a message from Stalin; simultaneously, Saiyid Ziyā ud-Dīn Tabātabā'ī, who had for three years been assailed by the Tūda as one of their most formidable opponents, was taken into 'preventive' custody.[2] On the 23rd the Prime Minister told a press conference that it was possible that as a result of direct negotiations the Soviet troops might begin to withdraw before the Security Council met in two days' time; meanwhile, he had instructed Husain 'Alā to 'avoid any statements and actions likely to lead to further misunderstandings', which was taken to be a rebuke for 'Alā's letter of the 20th objecting to the Soviet request for delay in the Security Council proceedings.[3] On the 24th the Soviet Ambassador called on Qavām and handed him three memoranda, one announcing that the evacuation of the Red Army would begin that day and last five to six weeks, one relating to the proposed joint Soviet-Persian oil company, and one suggesting a form of autonomous government for Āzarbāijān. On that same evening Moscow Radio broadcast a statement that the evacuation had begun 'according to the agreement made with the Persian Government', but according to the Persian account of the proceedings Qavām had objected to the condition, verbally notified to him by the Soviet Ambassador, 'that no unforeseen circumstances should occur'.[4]

The consideration of the Persian complaint by the Security Council was now skilfully used by Qavām as a lever for extracting better terms from the Soviet Government. When the Council began on 26 March to consider its agenda, Gromyko contended that the Persian complaint should not be included, as the evacuation of the Soviet troops had already begun.

[1] U.N., Security Council: *Official Records*, 1st year, 1st series, supplement no. 2, pp. 43–45.

[2] See *Survey* for 1939–46: *The Middle East in the War*, pp. 472–3. He was released on 17 March 1947. General Arfa', the former Chief of Staff, was arrested on 8 April, a Government spokesman (apparently Muzaffar Fīrūz, on whom see below, p. 78, note 4) stating that reports and documents proved that he had been plotting against the safety of the state and arming robber bands for his private guerrillas (*The Times* and *New York Times*, 10–11 April 1946; and see above, p. 66). He was released from close imprisonment on 30 October.

[3] U.N., Security Council, loc. cit. According to Lenczowski, 'the instructions given by Qavām during this nerve-racking period were largely conditioned by his alternating conversations with the Soviet and the American Ambassadors in Teheran. Unfortunately for Iran, the American Ambassador, Mr. Murray, was at this juncture confined to bed at his doctor's orders. As a result, the Soviet Ambassador's calls on the Premier were more frequent and his insistence on a solution satisfactory to Moscow stronger' (Lenczowski: *Russia and the West in Iran*, p. 299).

[4] Text of the Moscow broadcast in *The Times*, 25 March 1946; cf. Husain 'Alā, 3 April 1946: U.N., Security Council: *Official Records*, 1st year, 1st series, no. 2, pp. 85–86.

Defeated on this procedural point after a lengthy discussion, he then asked again for postponement until 10 April, asserting that an understanding between the Soviet and Persian Governments had already been reached, and warned the delegates that his Government were not prepared to take part in discussing the question at the Council before that date. Defeated again on this point, on which only the Polish delegate supported him, he angrily left the Council chamber on 28 March, leaving the Persian representative to state that, while he was aware of the reports that the Soviet withdrawal had begun, he knew of 'no agreement or understanding, secret or otherwise', between the two Governments concerning any of the matters in dispute. On the 29th, in the continued absence of the Soviet delegation, it was unanimously agreed that the two Governments should be asked to report by 3 April on the progress of their negotiations, and particularly whether or not the reported withdrawal of troops was being made conditional on their reaching an agreement.

The Soviet Embassy in Tehrān now appears to have endeavoured to secure Husain 'Alā's replacement as Persia's delegate at the Security Council,[1] but on 1 April the Council's president received a communication from Qavām confirming 'Alā's accreditation. On the 3rd 'Alā told the Council, in reply to a message from Gromyko reiterating that an agreement had been reached between the two Governments on the withdrawal of the Soviet troops, that his latest information from his Government, dated 1 April, did not confirm this: Qavām had commented on the Soviet proposals of 24 March that he could not accept the imposing of any conditions for the complete withdrawal of the Soviet forces from the whole of Persia; that the status of Āzarbāijān was an internal matter with which his Government would deal; and that the proposal for a joint Soviet-Persian oil company was a matter for submission to the next Parliament, after the withdrawal of the Soviet troops should have made it possible to hold lawful elections. Husain 'Alā went on to say (doubtless on instructions from Tehrān) that if the Soviet delegate would withdraw the condition about 'unforeseen circumstances' attached to the withdrawal of the Soviet troops, and would assure the Council that their unconditional withdrawal would be completed by 6 May, he would not ask the Council to consider the matter further at present, provided that it remained on the agenda. The Council accordingly agreed to defer further proceedings until 6 May,[2] and

[1] This is an inference from a statement made on 31 March by the Persian Director of Propaganda, Prince Muzaffar Fīrūz. His father—Prince Fīrūz, Nusrat ud-Dawla—was a scion of the former Qājar dynasty who had actively opposed British policy in Persia immediately after the First World War and had subsequently died in prison under Rizā Shāh (see the Hon. J. M. Balfour: *Recent Happenings in Persia* (Edinburgh and London, Blackwood, 1922), pp. 123–4, 156, 218, 227, 254–5, 276, 280; Lenczowski: *Russia and the West in Iran*, p. 231).

[2] The London *Daily Worker* commented (5 April 1946): 'The adventure of the anti-Soviet cohorts at U.N.O. has for the time being petered out. . . . The United Nations Organization . . . can flourish only on the basis of equal rights and equal respect for the rights of every nation.'

in the early morning of 5 April the Persian Cabinet formally approved an agreement with the Soviet Government on the following bases:

1. Persian territory was to be evacuated completely within six weeks of 24 March.
2. A project for a joint oil company with a duration of fifty years, for the first half of which Russia would hold fifty-one, and Persia forty-nine per cent. of the shares,[1] was to be submitted to the Persian Parliament within seven months of 24 March.
3. Āzarbāijān was to be recognized as being an internal problem, with which the Persian Government would deal benevolently and with consideration for the need for reforms under the existing laws.

On 22 April Tehrān Radio broadcast the central Government's proposals for Āzarbāijān:

It stated that the heads of departments . . . would be selected by the provincial council and confirmed by the central Government. A Governor-General would be appointed by the central Government in agreement with the provincial council. The commandant of the gendarmerie would be appointed by the central Government. The official language would be Persian. . . . The activities of democratic political organizations and workers' unions in Azerbaijan would be free. . . . No action would be taken against the people or workers of Azerbaijan in respect of any part taken by them in the 'democratic' movement. A Bill would be submitted to the next *Majlis* to increase the number of deputies from Azerbaijan to correspond with the real population of that province.[2]

An Āzarbāijānī mission, wearing the uniforms of their 'National Army', arrived in Tehrān on the 28th. They were led by Ja'far Pīshavārī, and included Sādiq Pādigān, the Russian-born chairman of the central committee of the 'Democratic' party; the governor of the Khamsa province (south-east of Āzarbāijān; capital, Zinjān), which the 'Democrats' with Red Army connivance had overrun during the winter; and a representa-

[1] For the text of the draft oil agreement see *Soviet News*, 13 September 1947. On paper it seemed considerably more favourable to Persia than the Anglo-Iranian Oil Company's concession (as *Pravda* asserted on 24 August 1947), but the Persians' experience of the Soviet-Persian Caspian Fisheries Company, set up by an agreement of 1 October 1927 for twenty-five years, and nominally giving the Persian Government a half-share of the capital and half the seats on the board of directors, had not been encouraging. 'The convention sets up no authority to cast the deciding vote when the board is evenly divided; but in practice the Soviets insist that the three Persian members shall be "friendly". Persians and Russians are supposed to alternate in the position of manager; but in 1941, when the Persian turn came, the Russians refused to permit Persian direction of the company. When on rare occasions the directors get into a deadlock the Russian manager proceeds to follow the views of the Russian members of the board and refers objections to the Soviet Embassy at Teheran' (Arthur C. Millspaugh: *Americans in Persia* (Washington, Brookings Institution, 1946), p. 175; cf. E. P. Harries: *World Federation of Trades Unions Delegation to Iran*: [Minority] *Report*, 1947, Appendix, p. 2; Édouard Sablier in *Monde*, 12 August, M. Philips Price, M.P., in *Manchester Guardian*, 25 October, Elizabeth Monroe in *Observer*, 2 November 1947).
[2] *The Times*, 23 April 1946.

tive of the 'Kurdish Republic'. The negotiations were protracted and on 3 May Tabrīz Radio, which had all along been displaying a defiant attitude towards Tehrān, announced that a twenty-years' treaty between the 'National Governments' of Āzarbāijān and Kurdistān had been signed on 23 April.[1]

On 6 May Husain 'Alā informed the Security Council that official investigations by his Government had shown that the evacuation of the north-eastern and Caspian provinces by Soviet troops was complete.[2] His Government had been informed 'through other sources' that the evacuation of Āzarbāijān would be completed before 7 May; but, because of the interferences previously complained of, Persian Government officials had exercised no effective authority in the province since 7 November 1945 and had therefore been unable to verify these reports by direct observation; they would report to the Council as soon as they were able to ascertain the true state of affairs. They were accordingly asked (the Soviet delegation again resentfully absenting itself[3]) to make a further report by 20 May. On the 11th Tabrīz Radio announced that the negotiations with the central Government had broken down: 'The Āzarbāijān nation will not submit to the tyranny of the central Government. . . . The Āzarbāijān national army is now ready to fight against the enemies of freedom.' According to the Persian Premier, the deadlock had arisen over the demand of the 'Democrats' that they, and not the central Government, should appoint the provincial governor and the commanders of the army and the gendarmerie (with the approval of Tehrān), and that they should be free to distribute state land among the peasants. The delegates had returned to Tabrīz for further instructions and the talks would be continued later. On the evening of the 19th, however, Tabrīz Radio announced in several languages: 'Bloodshed has started. At 5 p.m. the news was received that Government armies had taken up the offensive. A state of war has been proclaimed. Be ready to fight. Stand firm. Defend your freedom. Fight without ceasing to the last drop of blood.' It stated further that all large towns had been placed under martial law, and that military governors

---

[1] Text in Archie Roosevelt, Jr.: 'The Kurdish Republic of Mahabad', *Middle East Journal*, July 1947, i. 258–9.

[2] The Soviet forces were reported to have 'not only lived on the country but stripped it of real property ranging from its forests to the very doors and windows of its barracks' (A special correspondent, *The Economist*, 29 March 1947, p. 460).

[3] A majority on the Security Council, led by the United States and Britain, had on 15 and 23 April ruled that the Persian case should remain on the agenda until 6 May, despite the Persian Government's withdrawal of their complaint on 15 April in 'complete confidence in the word and pledge of the U.S.S.R. Government'. This had led Gromyko to protest with injured innocence 'that certain States consider Iran as a sort of pawn, which may be moved in any direction, depending upon circumstances and upon the political game which is being played at the moment. . . . Efforts to use Iran as small change in the bargaining game of international politics can serve no good purpose' (U.N., Security Council: *Official Records*, 1st year, 1st series, no. 2, pp. 140, 203).

had been appointed for the province and the chief towns.[1] On the following day the Persian delegate to the Security Council made the report for which he had been asked a fortnight earlier: his Government were still being prevented from exercising effective authority in Āzarbāijān and particularly from investigating reports that Soviet troops in civilian clothes had been left there and Soviet military equipment placed at the disposal of the autonomists. He added, however, that a commission of investigation had been appointed and was now stated to be in Tabrīz; and on the following day he reported information from his Government that the commission, after a week's careful investigation of Tabrīz and seven other towns, had found 'no trace whatever of USSR troops, equipment or means of transport. . . . According to trustworthy local people, who were questioned in all these places, USSR troops evacuated Azarbaijan on 6 May. (Signed) Ghavam es-Sultaneh.'[2]

Shortly before this the Tabrīz 'Government' had withdrawn its proclamation of martial law, with the announcement that 'peaceful methods prevail'. In Tehrān the Minister for War informed the Cabinet that it was believed that a local commander had been bribed to begin the attack that had alarmed the Tabrīz 'Government',[3] and on the following day Tabrīz Radio announced that the area of the recent fighting would be inspected by two missions, from Tabrīz and Tehrān respectively. The Persian Embassy in Washington stated on 29 May that their Government had instructed Husain 'Alā not to make any further statements to the Security Council about the Soviet-Persian dispute.[4] The tone of Tabrīz Radio now became conciliatory, and on 11 June Muzaffar Fīrūz led a central Government mission to Tabrīz to 'work out full details for accepting the province back into the Government'. Received by a guard of honour and led through cheering crowds to the autonomous Government's headquarters, he needed only two days to reach agreement on a programme not very different from that proposed by Qavām us-Saltana on 22 April. The Āzarbāijān 'parliament' would become a provincial council with the right to retain three-quarters of the provincial revenues; the central Government would appoint a Governor-General chosen from a panel of nominees of the provincial council;[5] a joint commission would determine the future of the 'national army'; Āzarī (the Turkish of Āzarbāijān) or, where appropriate, Kurdish would be taught in the primary schools alongside Persian.[6] The explana-

[1] New York Times, 20 May 1946.

[2] U.N., Security Council: Official Records, 1st year, 1st series, supplement no. 2, pp. 52–54. Simultaneously Muzaffar Fīrūz stated in Tehrān that Husain 'Alā's first report had been 'his own personal views, not the view of the Persian Government'.

[3] New York Times, 22 May 1946.   [4] Ibid. 30 May 1946.

[5] Lenczowski: Russia and the West in Iran, p. 290. Its choice fell on the Minister of the Interior of the Tabrīz Government, Dr. Salāmullāh Jāvīd, a Communist of long standing and Russian education who had been recently engaged in building up the secret police.

[6] New York Times, 15 June 1946.

tion of these devious manœuvres that had taken place between Tehrān and Tabrīz was obviously the consideration that the ratification of the Soviet-Persian oil agreement by the Majlis depended on the holding of elections, which Qavām us-Saltana had made dependent in their turn on the submission (at least nominally) of the Tabrīz 'Government'; and it was safe to assume that pressure from Moscow lay behind the accommodating attitude that Tabrīz had adopted, when once Tehrān had confirmed the final departure of the Soviet troops and the accusing voice of Husain 'Alā had been silenced at the Security Council.

On 2 June a Moscow radio commentator was reported to have said: 'The attitude of the Soviet Union towards Persia is one of such friendship as has seldom been found in all history between a great State and a comparatively small one', and to have gone on to criticize conditions in the Anglo-Iranian Oil Company's concession in the south-west Persian province of Khūzistān, where the British authorities were accused of obstructing the Tūda-dominated trade union and all 'democratic' parties and organizations.[1] In fact, as early as 1942–3 the Tūda party had sent agents to Khūzistān with orders to stir up dissatisfaction among the workers in the oilfields and in the great refinery at Ābādān. These agents (many of whom came from Āzarbāijān) had strict instructions to act discreetly, however, and not to cause any major upheaval as long as the war continued, so as not to jeopardize the flow across Persia of the war material that Russia urgently needed and the Western Allies were supplying, including aviation spirit from the Ābādān refinery; but the agents had been told to arrange for large-scale disturbances to occur in Khūzistān as soon as possible after the end of the war, when the Allied supplies of material to Russia would have ceased.[2]

The plan for fomenting trouble in the Anglo-Iranian Oil Company's field of operations had been very carefully worked out. The place chosen for the first outbreak was the comparatively new Āghā Jārī oilfield, about ninety miles east of Ābādān. Intensive development in that field had entailed a large increase in the labour force, and the war had limited the ability of the Company to provide its workers there with adequate amenities to offset the particularly airless and dusty local conditions. The consequent discontent was readily exploited by the Tūda agitators, who succeeded in bringing about a strike on 10 May 1946. It lasted for three weeks, and was settled by the Company's granting a very substantial wage increase with full pay during the strike, and undertaking to furnish extensive new amenities and social services in all the oilfields. The strike at Āghā Jārī had immediate repercussions in the other oilfields and at

[1] Quoted in *Scotsman*, 3 June 1946.
[2] See Dr. Laurence Lockhart: 'The Causes of the Anglo-Persian Oil Dispute', *Journal of the Royal Central Asian Society*, April 1953, xl. 142–3.

Ābādān, where the ground had been carefully prepared by Tūda agents. The most serious disturbances occurred at Ābādān in mid-July, after the proclamation of a general strike. The Tūda agents from north Persia had skilfully worked upon the latent animosity between the local Arabs and the Persian element of the population,[1] with the result that many people lost their lives in bloody clashes. The situation would have become even more menacing had not the Persian Government, belatedly realizing the danger, declared martial law. The Persian military and police forces thereupon intervened and soon restored order; the strikers, however, refused to return to work. On 16 July Muzaffar Fīrūz arrived from Tehrān at the head of a government commission, and persuaded the strikers to return to work by promising them wage increases and other advantages, and also releasing on bail five of the Tūda leaders whom the local Persian military governor had arrested. Afterwards, in order to appease the Tūda representatives who were taken into the Persian Cabinet, this governor was court-martialled for the steps that he had taken to restore order during the strike.

Meanwhile, in the chief towns of Persia thousands of opportunists had been enrolling themselves as trade unionists or members of the Tūda as being evidently the party of the future, while in the country districts the Tūda claimed with considerable exaggeration the formation of peasants' unions everywhere and 'veritable peasants' revolts' in some favoured areas, with refusals to pay rents, looting of the landlords' granaries, and seizure of their land.[2] On 1 August Qavām formed a new Cabinet in which Muzaffar Fīrūz, that 'ally of the Tūda party', became Vice-Premier and Minister of Labour and Propaganda; Īraj Iskandarī was appointed Minister of Commerce and Industry; and the portfolios of Education and

---

[1] Arabs constituted a majority of the inhabitants of the Khūzistān plain and Persians detested its torrid climate. The Arab chiefs, who had been autonomous until the rise to power of Rizā Shāh (see *Survey* for 1925, i. 539–43), complained of discrimination by Persian administrators.

The Tūda propagandist Iskandarī falsely imputed the blame for these disorders to the incitement of the Arabs by alleged agents of the Oil Company, and in his 'Histoire du parti Toudeh' (*Moyen-Orient*, July 1950, pp. 8–9) gave a most tendentious account of the events at Ābādān. In fact, the Soviet Consulate at Ahvāz had played a prominent part in organizing the disturbances at Ābādān, and it was perhaps significant that the Soviet Consul had paid an official visit to the Refinery immediately before the trouble broke out.

Simultaneously there was a violent clash at Kirkūk, 350 miles away, between the 'Irāqī police and workers of the 'Irāq Petroleum Company who had been on strike since 3 July, allegedly incited by Left-wing agitators from Baghdād (see Robert Stephens in *Scotsman*, 18 November 1946). The more violent of the clandestine propaganda distributed in this strike was said to be almost identical in content with that simultaneously distributed at Ābādān.

[2] Iskandarī (*Moyen-Orient*, June 1950, pp. 9–10); but cf. Gideon Hadary, 'The Agrarian Reform Problem in Iran', *Middle East Journal*, Spring 1951, v. 194: 'Despite the overwhelming predominance of the peasant population and the agricultural character of the Iranian economy, rural dwellers accounted for a small fraction of the total Tudeh membership at the height of its strength'. Iskandarī repeated the party-line statement that on May-day 1946 over 700,000 persons in thirty towns marched behind the standards of the Tūda party and its trade unions; cf. Bashkirov, p. 70.

Health went to two of his Tūda colleagues. Significantly, however, Qavām retained for himself the key portfolios of the Interior and Foreign Affairs. *The Times* diplomatic correspondent commented on 3 August that British employees of the Anglo-Iranian Oil Company were still dissatisfied with the Persian Government's provisions for the maintenance of law and order; the British Admiralty had on 17 July ordered three warships to 'Irāqī territorial waters in the Shatt ul-'Arab off Ābādān, as was permitted under the Anglo-'Irāqī Treaty of 1930; and on 2 August the Government of India (then still under British control) announced: 'In order that they may be at hand for the protection, should circumstances demand it, ot Indian, British, and Arab lives, and in order to safeguard Indian and British interests in South Persia,[1] troops are being sent from India to Basra.' A spokesman of the India Office in London stated that no question arose of the troops' entering Persian territory, except in a grave emergency.[2] On the following day the Persian Government issued a statement criticizing the British action, on the ground that they were fully capable of managing their internal affairs without outside interference. The Persian Left-wing press leapt into action, Tūda's organ *Rahbar* denouncing the British move as 'unsuitable for a world of peace and democracy', and asking: 'Has Mr. Attlee's and Mr. Bevin's Government been brought into power by that group of British individuals who wear a crown of oil on their heads and sit on a throne constructed from the pounded bones of the colonies?'[3] On the 6th the British Foreign Office stated:

The Persian oil industry provides a field for the continuance of fruitful co-operation between Great Britain and Persia to the benefit of both. His Majesty's Government intend to play their part in any direction in which their help can be of value and are confident that the Anglo-Iranian Oil Company will cooperate with the Persian Government to the fullest extent. It is, however, the responsibility of the Persian Government to ensure that such conditions of security prevail in the country as will enable Persian oil to play its full part in Persian and world economy.[4]

The Persian Foreign Ministry announced on the 8th that they had asked for the recall to India of the brigade group that had now arrived at Basra, and had protested against the tone of B.B.C. and New Delhi broadcasts; but the general attitude of the Persian note was described as 'not un-

---

[1] Many hundreds of Indians were employed in the oilfields.

[2] *The Times* and *New York Times*, 3 August 1946. An official 'Irāqī communiqué of 4 August stated that the 'Irāqī Government had approved a British intention to send replacements for British troops stationed at the airfield of Shu'aiba near Basra whom it had been decided to withdraw (*New York Times* and *Daily Telegraph*, 5 August 1946).

[3] Quoted by *The Times*, 5 August 1946.

[4] Ibid. 7 August 1946. It had been reported that already after the three weeks' strike in June the British Government had drawn the Persian Government's attention to the importance of maintaining law and order in the oilfields (*Daily Telegraph*, 6 July).

friendly'.[1] A conciliatory British reply on the 15th welcomed the Persian Government's quick and successful efforts to restore order and security in the oilfields, and denied reports that the troops recently brought to Basra had instructions to enter Persia in any eventuality.

While he was still manœuvring for the withdrawal of the Soviet troops from north Persia, Qavām us-Saltana had been severe with his critics and opponents on the Right Wing;[2] but when once the Soviet withdrawal was complete, and the 'agreement' with Āzarbāijān had been concluded on 13 June, he allowed only a fortnight to elapse before announcing, on the 29th, the foundation of a 'Persian Democratic Party' whose real purpose, while ostensibly working for good relations with all three Great Powers and for internal reform, was to counteract the influence of the Tūda and secure a majority for Qavām in the forthcoming elections.[3] In the three weeks' lull which followed the oilfields crisis Qavām went quietly ahead with his plans; but on 8 September it was announced that the indefatigable Muzaffar Fīrūz had unearthed at Isfahān an anti-Government plot, led by the chiefs of the Bakhtiyārī tribe 'with foreign help' for the purpose of provoking internal chaos and setting up a 'reactionary, feudal, tribal government'.[4] On the 20th a rising of the Qashqā'ī and other tribes in Fars province[5] was reported, and three days later the provincial governor arrived in Tehrān with a list of demands which the tribal leaders and urban personalities opposed to the Tūda had drawn up at Shīrāz, the provincial capital. They called for the resignation of the entire Cabinet,

[1] The Communist Party of Great Britain stated on 9 August: 'After all the slander campaign which was engineered by western reactionaries at the time of the United Nations Council, to accuse the Soviet Union of pressure on Persia, it is now British policy which is openly using methods of military coercion to interfere in Persian internal politics. . . . The dispatch of troops as well as the dispatch of a cruiser to Persian [sic] waters is intended to coerce the workers employed by the Anglo-Persian Oil Company who have been striking to improve their miserable conditions. It follows immediately on the inclusion of members of the Tudeh Party, the popular democratic party of the Persian people, in the Persian Government. This interference is the most shameless aggressive imperialism on behalf of big oil monopolies against the freedom of a small country' (Daily Worker, 10 August 1946).

[2] See above, pp. 68–69. He had said in a broadcast on 18 May: 'Let these traitors and evilwishers know that I am fully aware of their instigations and treachery, and will eradicate them just as a gardener must destroy the pests which are ruining his flower-garden.'

[3] The Tūda propagandist Iskandarī referred to Court intrigues to create antagonism between Qavām and the Tūda, and saw in the support which Qavām's party now received from landowning and commercial interests 'proof of the complicity of the two imperialisms, British and American' (Moyen-Orient, July 1950, p. 9).

[4] Cf. M. Sergeyev's attack on the tribal leaders: 'In Southern Iran', New Times, 15 February 1946, pp. 20–24.

[5] That they could attempt such a thing was due, not to the hypothetical supply of arms by the British, but to their natural propensity to acquire arms, in which they had been greatly assisted by the abandoning of large quantities by the Persian army when it disintegrated after the Anglo-Soviet intervention in August 1941. For the smuggling of arms in this region before 1914, especially through Masqat, cf. Sir Arnold Wilson: The Persian Gulf (London, Oxford University Press, 1928), p. 270; Philip Graves: Life of Sir Percy Cox (London, Hutchinson, [1942]), pp. 141–3, 160–3.

except for Qavām himself; the release of the Bakhtiyārī chiefs whom Fīrūz had arrested; and the same degree of provincial autonomy that had been granted to Āzarbāijān in June. The British Foreign Office denied reports emanating from Tehrān and Moscow that British ships in the Gulf were supplying the rebels with arms and ammunition.[1] Just when the head of the Middle Eastern department of the Soviet Foreign Ministry arrived in Tehrān on a visit, the Persian Ambassador in London asked the Foreign Office to investigate an accusation by Moscow Radio that the British Consuls-General at Ahvāz and Isfahān had incited the southern tribes to rebel; and, despite the Foreign Office's categorical denial of their complicity, the Persian Government persisted for a time in their request for the removal of these two officials.[2] The rebellion continued to spread, the stronghold of Kāzirūn and the port of Bushire being lost to the Government, who were forced to reopen negotiations with the tribal leaders and eventually to concede most of their demands. 'In such a situation', the Tūda propagandist afterwards wrote, 'the Tūda party's collaboration with Qavām no longer had any meaning. On 16 October, in accordance with the decision of the Party's Central Committee, the three Tūda Ministers refused to take part in the work of the Cabinet.'[3] Qavām re-formed his Cabinet on the 19th, dropping the three Tūda Ministers and also Muzaffar Fīrūz, whom he appropriately appointed Ambassador to Moscow.[4] In

---

[1] *New York Times*, 24 September 1946; contrast the London *Daily Worker* diplomatic correspondent, same date: 'Long and carefully laid British plans to detach the oilfields from Persia and incorporate them in Iraq appear to be maturing. The tribesmen who have seized ports on the Persian Gulf are well armed, and it was not their own government which provided them with sub-machine guns, rifles and ammunition. . . . It is known that representatives of these tribes have recently made visits to Basra, where British H.Q. is situated. . . . An atmosphere of tension is being deliberately built up—just the atmosphere in which it will be possible for the British to carry out their threat to send troops across the frontier to "protect British lives and property".'

[2] *The Times* diplomatic correspondent, 30 September, *Daily Telegraph*, 2 October, Joseph and Stewart Alsop in *New York Herald Tribune*, 2 October 1946.

The Tūda propagandist afterwards alleged that at the end of August the Persian Government had come into possession of a document revealing a secret conference of Bakhtiyārī and Qashqā'ī chiefs and British agents 'in the presence of Trott, the British Consul-General at Isfahān' (Iskandarī (*Moyen-Orient*, September 1950, p. 4); but Trott was in fact Consul-General at Ahvāz: see *Foreign Office List*). The document in question was probably identical with 'a photograph of a British Consul at Shiraz receiving some captured German arms from a tribal chief', which was found by a member of the Tūda Party and 'taken to be a picture of the Consul doling out British arms' (Christopher Sykes, letter to *New Statesman and Nation*, 14 October 1950, p. 362; for the surrender of a party of German agents by the Qashqā'ī in 1944, see *Survey* for 1939–46: *The Middle East in the War*, p. 157, note 1). The British Consul-General at Isfahān left Persia on 4 October to take up a new appointment, 'the arrangements for which had been made before the trouble in Persia started' (*Daily Telegraph*, 5 October 1946), and the Persian Government's request for Trott's removal was dropped.

[3] Iskandarī (*Moyen-Orient*, October–November 1950, pp. 13–14).

[4] In August 1947 the Persian Government relieved Fīrūz of this appointment and the Public Prosecutor indicted him on charges reported to include treason and embezzlement. It was stated in Moscow that he had left that city by air for Tehrān on 14 September; but instead he made for Geneva and Paris, where he published a manifesto calling on Persian 'progressives'

Tehrān it was 'reliably' reported that the Cabinet crisis had arisen over Qavām's dismissal of the Tūda governors of Tehrān, Isfahān, and Kermānshāh, in which connexion (it was 'authentically' added in Washington) he had defied a warning by the Soviet Ambassador that such an action was an affront to the U.S.S.R.; he had been strongly encouraged by the young Shāh, who in turn was given 'intimations of support' from the United States and British Embassies.[1]

In retrospective 'self-criticism' it seemed to the Tūda propagandist that his party had 'allowed itself to be misled by the illusion that Qavām was bound by his undertaking in the Soviet-Persian Agreement of 4 April to hold an election as soon as possible, and had over-estimated the personal differences separating Qavām and the Shāh'; the 'Persian democratic movement' now had to face 'an increasingly ferocious repression' as an essential part of Qavām's preparation of the elections.[2] Meanwhile, the date of 24 November, by which Qavām had undertaken in April to submit the draft Soviet-Persian oil agreement to the Majlis for ratification,[3] was rapidly approaching. One of the purposes of the visit to Tehrān of the head of the Middle Eastern department of the Soviet Foreign Ministry at the end of September had presumably been to hasten this, and on 6 October it had been officially announced that the Shāh had signed the decree for the elections. There was still considerable discussion about when they should begin, however, the Left Wing dutifully calling for speed, the conservatives urging postponement on account of the unsettled conditions in the provinces; and while the official discrimination and repression had already cost the Tūda a considerable amount of its influence, the centre and Right-wing newspapers had (with official sanction) begun to express their views with a frankness that would not have been possible a few weeks earlier.

On 4 November the Prime Minister announced that the elections would begin on 7 December, and on 21 November he further stated that 'in order to ensure freedom of voting and to suppress possible disturbances' they would be held under the supervision of government forces throughout the country.[4] Two days later, after a conference between the Shāh, the Prime Minister, and the army commanders, the 'Democrat' Governor-General of Āzarbāijān was informed that this decree would apply to his province also. Its relations with the central Government had improved but little, in spite of the June 'agreement', and government troops had just encountered 'Democrat' resistance in reoccupying Zinjān, the capital of

to rouse themselves to action (*New York Times*, 20 September 1947; *Cahiers de l'Orient Contemporain*, 3ᵐᵉ–4ᵐᵉ trimestres 1947, xi–xii. 213; Bedell Smith: *Moscow Mission*, p. 96).

[1] Robert Stephens in *Observer*, 20 October 1946; Peter Whitney in *Scotsman*, 24 October 1946.

[2] Iskandarī, loc. cit.   [3] See above, p. 71.

[4] *Manchester Guardian*, 3 October, *The Times*, 7 and 24 October, 5 and 23 November 1946.

Khamsa province which the 'Democrats' had agreed to evacuate by 14 November.[1] Amid violent protests from Tabrīz, the United States Ambassador, George V. Allen,[2] announced on the 27th:

It is the well-known policy of the American Government to favour the maintenance of Persian sovereignty and territorial integrity. This principle is embodied in the United Nations Charter.

The intention of the Persian Government to send its security forces into all parts of Persia, including any areas where such forces are not at present in control, for the maintenance of order during the elections, seems to me an entirely normal and proper decision.[3]

On the same day, it was reported, the Soviet Ambassador left his sick-bed to protest to the Shāh and the Prime Minister against the Government's 'unfriendly policy'; the Soviet Union could not 'look with favour on bloodshed in Azarbaijan'. He reminded the Premier of the still-pending oil agreement;[4] but Qavām's action had adroitly posed the Soviet Union with two mutually exclusive alternatives: either having a Majlis elected as a preliminary to the submission of the oil agreement for ratification, or to maintain the Communist régime in Āzarbāijān at the price of an indefinite postponement of ratification. To combine both alternatives it would be necessary to invade Persia again, or at least to threaten an invasion;[5] and Russia's foreign policy in general had recently become more conciliatory, a change which was plausibly ascribed both to the resistance which the United States and Britain had shown to her aggressive demonstrations since the end of the war and to the acute internal difficulties arising from the reconstruction of her war-ravaged economy.[6] Meanwhile, as the Persian Government troops continued their advance from Zinjān (amid accusations from Tabrīz Radio that 'Qavām is repeating the atrocities of the German and Japanese Fascists'), Qavām rejected a suggestion by the Āzarbāijān provincial council that the central Government should content themselves with sending inspectors and press correspondents to watch the conduct of the elections by the provincial authorities, and proclaimed on 3 December that the opening of the elections was postponed until the 11th. In reply Tabrīz Radio announced that the provincial 'Government' had distributed arms to all workers, members of the 'national militia', and youth associations and, alleging that the central Government's troops had crossed the provincial boundary, made the rousing declaration:

[1] *The Times*, 25 November 1946.

[2] Appointed in April 1946 at the age of forty-three, having been previously Deputy Director at the Office of Near Eastern and African Affairs in the State Department.

[3] *Daily Telegraph*, 28 November 1946. This attitude was confirmed by the U.S. Acting Secretary of State, Dean Acheson (*New York Times*, 11 December 1946).

[4] *New York Times*, 29 November 1946; cf. Husain 'Alā's letter to the Security Council (U.N., Security Council, S/204, 5 December 1946).

[5] Cf. Lenczowski: *Russia and the West in Iran*, p. 307.

[6] Cf. 'So Poor—and So Plentiful', *The Economist*, 15 March 1947, pp. 380–1.

'After all our efforts and bloodshed for the creation of our republic, we will defend it to the last drop of blood. We are all willing to carry out the orders of our leaders, who will lead us against those foreign secret forces which are supporting Falangist Spain, and whose blind tool the Tehran Government has become.'[1] But it was vain for Pīshavārī to shout: 'Let the great revolution, which will free the people from its oppressors, rise in full strength.' Qavām was said to have taken the precaution in mid-November of ordering the arrest of 100 leading Tūda members in Tehrān; the only sympathetic reaction to the threatened 'people's democracy' came from Zīrāb, a mining town in Māzandarān province, and the *putsch* which the Tūda Party attempted there was quickly suppressed.[2] While central government aircraft scattered leaflets exhorting the people of Āzarbāijān to overthrow the 'Democratic' régime, a note assured the Soviet Embassy that the intended action was merely for the purpose of supervising the elections, and was in no way directed against Soviet interests. It was observed in Moscow that the Soviet press was commenting on the Āzarbāijān crisis as a purely internal Persian matter, 'with a certain air of detachment'.[3] The government troops crossed the provincial border on the 10th, meeting with only slight resistance from the 'ill-equipped and undisciplined' opposing forces, and after entering Miyāna on the following day received news of the capitulation of the 'Democrats'.[4] Resistance now petered out, except from isolated groups of enthusiasts, and the government troops entered Tabrīz on the afternoon of the 13th. Again in retrospective 'self-criticism', the Tūda propagandist sought to explain the 'Democrat' collapse on the grounds that 'the militant peasants were so dispersed and unorganized that their indispensable alliance with the working class could not yet be realized, while the working class itself . . . did not yet have the necessary cohesion and political training to play effectively its role of leader in the revolutionary movement'. The Provincial Assembly, he continued, had on 12 December reached the 'grave decision', dictated by 'extremely rigorous revolutionary logic' and derived from an 'exact analysis of the international situation', to abandon armed resistance: for it would have been followed by a direct intervention of the imperialist Powers in south-west Persia, 'bringing the war to the immediate frontiers of the Soviet Union and constituting a grave danger for world peace and

---

[1] *The Times*, 4 and 5 December 1946; for the Tūda's organization in Tehrān of a demonstration against the Spanish régime in the previous July see below, p. 84.

[2] Lenczowski: *Russia and the West in Iran*, p. 308; *New York Times*, 8 and 9 December, *The Times*, 28 December 1946.

[3] Alexander Werth in *Manchester Guardian*, 10 December 1946.

[4] Quarters 'in very close touch with the Shāh' stated that at this very time the Soviet Ambassador was asking him to stop the advance, since it 'would provoke disturbances which the Soviet Union could not accept without reservations for the security of her borders'. The Shāh was able to reply that there was no danger of disturbances, since Tabrīz had welcomed the government troops and the civil war had ended (*New York Times*, 14 December 1946).

security'. He admitted, however, that the withdrawal of the 'popular' forces immediately became a 'disorganized rout'.[1] While Pīshavārī and other 'Democrat' leaders made good their escape to the Soviet Union,[2] some hundreds of their luckless followers were hunted down and slaughtered in the days that elapsed between the capitulation and the 'restoration of order' by the government forces.

Three United States and British press correspondents who had already arrived in Tabrīz on 12 December reported that the government forces were received with enthusiasm.[3] A year later, a 'progressive' foreign observer reported that the 'Democrat' régime had initiated more reforms in one year than Tabrīz had ever known—founding a maternity hospital, a university, and a radio station, diminishing crime and molestation by efficient policing, enforcing the labour law, fighting the opium traffic, starting (though not carrying very far) a land reform, and dismissing redundant civil servants. Nevertheless, he heard 'harsh words, even from its friends, of the abuses of its power and of the terror it had fostered. It had frightened merchants away from the city, and business had slumped heavily.' Moreover, the 'Democrats' had 'utterly failed' to win support for separatism among the mass of the population, or to awaken the 'decisive or enthusiastic support' of the peasantry.

By collecting the landlord's share of the crop, they kept alive the suspicion that landlordism had not vanished. The Azerbaijani peasants drew no distinction between the landlord's agent and the representative of the Tabriz Government. While they were promised land, and in some parts of the province had actually received grants, they were still under obligation to pay tribute to outsiders. . . . Pledges of ultimate complete land reforms and of the importation of machinery and livestock . . . had fallen on ears that were becoming increasingly deaf to eloquent rhetoric.[4]

The Persian central authorities now set themselves to eradicate all traces of the autonomist régimes in Āzarbāijān and Kurdistān. In the former province the students were reported to have 'spontaneously' destroyed the textbooks in the local Turkish dialect with which the 'Democrat' régime had provided them, and Persian became once again the language of Tabrīz Radio and the local press. The central government troops, on arriving at Mahābād, had arrested most of the leaders of the

---

[1] Iskandarī (*Moyen-Orient*, October–November 1950, pp. 13–14, and January 1951, pp. 12–13).

[2] It was afterwards reported in Tehrān that, after a Persian Government request for Pīshavārī's extradition, news was received from Soviet sources that he had been killed in a car accident at Baku (*New York Times*, 20 September 1947).

[3] Ibid. 14 December 1946.

[4] Maurice Hindus: *In Search of a Future* (London, Gollancz, 1949), pp. 92–94: the writer had visited Persia, including Āzarbāijān, in the summer of 1947. See also the report by Joseph and Stewart Alsop in *New York Herald Tribune*, 30 December 1946.

autonomist Kurdish Republic, and a number of them, including Qādī Muhammad himself and two of his kinsmen, were later tried by military court and publicly hanged, while Mullā Mustafā and about a thousand of his Barzānī followers succeeded in crossing the frontier into Soviet Āzarbāijān. The Persian authorities prohibited teaching in the Kurdish language, closed the Kurdish printing-press, and publicly burnt all the Kurdish books they could find.[1] Meanwhile, in Tehrān the witch-hunt against the Tūda party was in full hue and cry. On 13 December a mob of Āzarbāijānī expatriates, exultant at the capitulation of the 'Democrats' in that province and unhindered by the Tehrān police, destroyed the party headquarters; their newspapers *Rahbar* and *Zafar* had been suppressed, and their clubs attacked and closed, allegedly by a uniformed force called the 'Liberation Guard'; and it was said that workers in government factories were threatened with dismissal unless they tore up their Tūda union cards and joined the new union sponsored by Qavām's party.[2] Within the Tūda itself, the Central Committee delegated its powers to a provisional executive committee which on 5 January 1947 issued a manifesto denouncing 'past errors', condemning the Āzarbāijānī movement, appointing a committee to purge the party of undesirables, and declaring that its political attitude was intended to 'conform with the democratic principles applied in Great Britain, the United States, and Sweden'.[3] This seems to have been purely an expedient, however, for six months later a French journalist reported that, while he found the leaders of the new executive committee 'decent, intelligent, and in more than one respect likeable personalities' with a better reputation for financial honesty than those in power in Persia,

like the European models that they diligently imitate, they have an unfortunate tendency to distort every truth which would not harmonize with their views. They watch the course of events in the light of a dogmatism that perverts its meaning for them, and makes them the tools—more or less consciously—of the masters whom they claim as their inspiration. In Persian eyes they are deliberately playing Russia's game, most commonly to the detriment of national interests.[4]

In a country so vast, thinly populated, and ill-administered as Persia

---

[1] Archie Roosevelt, Jr.: 'The Kurdish republic of Mahabad', *Middle East Journal*, July 1947, i. 266–8; James de Coquet in *Figaro*, 30–31 March, Édouard Sablier in *Monde*, 14 August, *The Times*, 24 October 1947.

[2] *New York Times*, 14, 17, and 21 December 1946; Andrew Roth: 'Backstage in the Persian Theater', *Nation*, 3 May 1947, p. 516.

[3] See *Bourse Égyptienne*, 6 January, *The Times*, 10 January 1947; Iskandarī (*Moyen-Orient*, January 1951, pp. 12–13).

[4] Édouard Sablier in *Monde*, 15–16 August 1947. The Tūda Party newspaper *Mardum* ('the people') which was now their principal organ (*Rahbar* having been discontinued as hopelessly compromised) was described as 'merely a pallid edition of *Pravda*' (*The Times* Tehrān correspondent, 24 October 1947).

elections were normally protracted over weeks or even months, and on this occasion the precariousness of government control in Āzarbāijān and Fars provinces were the cause of, or the pretext for, even more than the usual delay. Meanwhile, in December 1946 the United States Government had agreed in principle to sell to the Persian army and gendarmerie (Brigadier-General Schwarzkopf was at this time still serving as the gendarmerie's adviser) 'reasonable quantities of military supplies for the purpose of maintaining internal security'.[1] On 26 December 1946 an agreement was announced, whereby a large part (reported to be 20 per cent.) of the output of the Anglo-Iranian Oil Company would for twenty years be made available to two leading American oil-distributing organizations for supplying the Eastern Hemisphere, which had before the war been supplied mainly from Western Hemisphere oil resources which it was now desired to conserve.[2] In February 1947 it was announced that a United States engineering and construction company (Morrison-Knudsen) had been engaged by the Persian Government to study the country's possibilities of development under a seven-year plan, and that when it had reported it was proposed to seek a loan, probably of $250 million, from the International Bank.[3] After the enunciation of the Truman Doctrine by which the United States took over the obligation previously borne by Britain to provide economic and military aid to Greece and Turkey, threatened respectively by Communist revolution and Soviet aggression,[4] the State Department created a new Division for Greek, Turkish, and Iranian Affairs.[5]

Meanwhile the World Federation of Trades Unions, which was passing increasingly under Communist control, had been taking a close interest in Persian Left-wing politics. Its secretary-general, Louis Saillant (who was on the Left Wing himself),[6] invited by the Persian Government to see for himself the growth of the Persian trade union movement, had addressed mass demonstrations organized in Tehrān by the Tūda in July 1946 against the Franco régime in Spain.[7] On 18 December 1946, on the instance of Rizā Rūstā, the Moscow-trained Communist president of the

---

[1] New York Times, 11 April 1947.
[2] Petroleum Press Service, January 1947, xiv. 9–11; Survey for 1939–46: The Middle East in the War, p. 363.
[3] Financial Times, 12 February 1947; Stewart Alsop in New York Herald Tribune, 12 March 1947, and see below, pp. 92–93 and 98–99.
[4] See above, p. 36.
[5] Lenczowski: Russia and the West in Iran, p. 311.
[6] 'A non-Communist labor leader before the war, Saillant had become one of the leading men of the underground in France; whether he ever joined the Communist Party is unknown, but the fact remains that his former friends in the trade union movement describe him as a "traitor" and that he has followed in all important issues the line of the Communist Party' (Adolf Sturmthal, 'Crisis in the International Labor Movement', American Perspective, May 1949, p. 93).
[7] The Times, 22 July 1946; Bashkirov, pp. 70, 72–73.

Central Council of United Persian Trades Unions, a W.F.T.U. delegation headed by Saillant had demanded of the Persian Ambassador in Paris that his Government should restore the freedom of action of the Tūda-dominated unions,[1] and permission was obtained for a W.F.T.U. delegation to visit Persia. It was led by the Lebanese Communist trade union leader Mustafā al-ʿArīs,[2] and had Russian, British, and French members. Shortly before its arrival in Persia in February 1947 an anti-Communist faction within the Persian trade union movement was reported to have marched on the union headquarters and thrown out Rizā Rūstā, who was later arrested on a charge of seditious and fraudulent activities, notably of having sought to arrange that trade union advisers whom the W.F.T.U. were to send to Persia should be strong Communists. On the initiative of al-ʿArīs and its Russian member, the W.F.T.U. delegation produced a report which in its first draft defended the Tūda-dominated union against the Government charge that it had planned revolution, stating instead that it had acted only in the service of the working classes and against Fascism, as witness the great demonstration against the Franco régime in the previous July: 'If the Persian Government persists in its policy, and if this unnatural situation in Persia, which resembles more the countries under the domination of the Hitler regime, continues, then the Delegation suggests that the case of the workers' unions of Persia should be discussed by U.N.O.' At the end of a somewhat stormy session, however, the British delegate (E. P. Harries, secretary of the Organization Department of the Trades Union Congress) withdrew and drafted a minority report, as a result of which his two Communist colleagues (the Frenchman having apparently dropped out) drastically revised their report. Harries signed this because he accepted its recommendations, although he still disagreed with a great deal of the report itself: in his view, the imprisoned trade unionists about whom his Communist fellow delegates made so great an outcry had taken part in an unsuccessful civil revolt, and 'any Government faced with this situation' would have dealt similarly with them.[3] The delegation's *Report on the Trade Union Situation in Iran* was presented to the Executive Committee of the W.F.T.U. meeting in Prague in June; and on the 8th Louis Saillant delivered to the Persian Minister there a resolution of the executive committee condemning the 'anti-democratic measures taken by the Persian Government against free and democratic unions

---

[1] *New York Herald Tribune*, London *Daily Worker*, 19 December 1946; Bashkirov, pp. 92–93.

[2] Born about 1911, employed in a printing office 1923, became a member of the Communist party 1934, Lebanese delegate to the Seventh Congress of the Comintern, Moscow, 1935 (U.S.A., House of Representatives, Committee on Foreign Affairs: *The Strategy and Tactics of World Communism*, Supplement iv, 'Five Hundred Leading Communists' (House Document No. 707, 1948), p. 87).

[3] See E. P. Harries: *World Federation of Trades Unions Delegation to Iran*: [Minority] *Report*, 1947, Appendix, for the Communists' refusal to hear evidence from those who had suffered at the hands of the Tūda in their heyday.

and their members' and threatening to bring the case before the United Nations.[1]

On 19 June the Persian Cabinet resigned and enabled Qavām to form a new Government with several members who were described as 'very friendly towards the western Governments', including three graduates of the American College of Tehrān. This reorganization of the Government coincided with the United States grant of a military credit of $25 million on 20 June.[2] As the procedure for assembling the Majlis (the elections having at last ended), electing its officers, and examining the credentials of its members, took its leisurely course through the hot summer days, the Soviet press and radio made strong attacks on 'Persian reactionaries', 'stranglers of the working class', and 'intriguers of the Anglo-Iranian Oil Company'; and on 12 August the Soviet Ambassador handed to Qavām us-Saltana a draft treaty on the lines of the oil agreement of April 1946. Six days later Qavām was reported to have told him that he disliked the terms of the agreement and could not force the Majlis to ratify it,[3] whereupon the Soviet Ambassador on 28 August handed him a note drawing attention to his Government's 'violation' of the agreement and describing their action as 'a return to the policy of hostility and discrimination against the Soviet Union pursued under the Government of Rizā Shāh, and under the Governments of Sā'id, Sadr, and Hakīmī which succeeded it'.[4]

Once the Soviet Government's failure to withdraw their troops from Persia by the stipulated date had aligned the United States Government with the British Government in resisting the Soviet cold war in this sector, there was for eighteen months no apparent divergence between British and United States policy over Persia; but a divergence was now to appear which was fraught with important consequences for future years. The British Government, according to 'well-informed quarters' in London, were apprehensive that, if the Persian Government were encouraged to reject outright the Soviet demand for the joint development of the oil resources of northern Persia, their latent nationalism might be tempted to challenge the Anglo-Iranian concession in the south;[5] and in the first

---

[1] *New York Times*, 8 June 1947, and cf. *The Times* Tehrān correspondent, 11 July 1947. For an interview with the Soviet member of the delegation see *Soviet News*, 21 May 1947, and cf. Bashkirov, pp. 92–97.

[2] *New York Times*, 22 June, *Christian Science Monitor*, 24 June 1947.

[3] Qavām had already stated on 12 June: 'The circumstances in which we signed the agreement have indisputably changed. . . . We cannot impose our will . . . on representatives elected by universal suffrage and enjoying full freedom of thought and opinion, for if we did we should risk seeing the very principle of the agreement rejected by Parliament. The two parties must therefore take account of these conditions and find an understanding by which the Bill laid before the Chamber will be presentable and acceptable to Parliament and public opinion' (Édouard Sablier in *Monde*, 14 June 1947).

[4] Text in *Soviet News*, 10 September 1947; cf. a minatory article in *Pravda*, reproduced ibid. 26 August 1947.

[5] *New York Times*, 13 September 1947.

week of September the British Ambassador handed Qavām a note which recommended that

the Persian Government might be well advised to leave the door open for further discussions. . . . The Persian Government should not give a blank refusal and leave the matter at that. If they could not accept the Soviet draft treaty—because it was based on a provisional agreement made at a time of acute pressure and because it was put forward as a demand—they might leave opportunity for revised and fairer terms to be presented.[1]

The delivery of this note created an immediate and widespread suspicion in Tehrān that Britain and the Soviet Union, and perhaps the United States, had reached an agreement at Persia's expense; the British Ambassador now went on leave and did not return to Persia until the beginning of November;[2] unlike Britain, the United States Government had no preoccupations arising from a direct stake in Persian oil; and on 11 September their Ambassador in Tehrān made a statement to the Persian-American Cultural Relations Society which Persian opinion was bound to interpret as full encouragement to reject the Soviet proposals outright:

Certain rumors and allegations have appeared concerning the attitude of the United States in this matter, and I have been asked to state my Government's position.

The American Government has frequently made known its respect for Iran's sovereignty. An important aspect of sovereignty is the full right of any country to accept or reject proposals for the development of its resources.

Iran's resources belong to Iran. Iran can give them away free of charge, or refuse to dispose of them at any price, if it so desires.

The United States has no proper concern with proposals of a commercial or any other nature made to Iran by any foreign government, as long as those proposals are advanced solely on their merits, to stand or fall on their value to Iran.

However, we and every other nation of the world do become concerned when such proposals are accompanied by threats of bitter enmity[3] or by statements that it would be dangerous for Iran to refuse.

The United States is firm in its conviction that any proposals made by one sovereign government to another should not be accompanied by threats or

---

[1] *The Times* diplomatic correspondent, 15 September 1947. A leading article in *The Times* of 25 November observed that 'the terms of the 1946 agreement are by no means bad from the Persian point of view; and, on the assumption that oil exists in the northern provinces, the arrangement proposed for sharing it between the Soviet Union and Persia are reasonably equitable. . . . However . . . the original refusal of the Soviet Government . . . to withdraw its troops until the arrangement had been signed . . . invested the whole transaction from the beginning with a flavour of duress, which has strengthened a long-standing Persian fear of the extension of Russian influence.'

[2] *Scotsman*, 1 November 1947.

[3] Associates of Qavām had stated on the previous day that the Soviet Ambassador had warned him that Russia would consider Persia a 'bitter blood-enemy' if the Majlis did not ratify the Agreement (*New York Herald Tribune*, 11 September 1947).

intimidation. When such methods are used in an effort to gain acceptance, doubt is cast on the value of the proposals themselves. . . .

The United States has dedicated its full energy and resources to freeing the peoples of the world from the fear of aggression. Our determination to follow this policy is as strong as regards Iran as it is anywhere else in the world. Patriotic Iranians, when considering matters affecting their national interest, may therefore rest assured that the American people will support fully their freedom to make their own choice.[1]

The Soviet Ambassador handed Qavām on 15 September a second note couched in 'extremely severe' terms demanding that 'delaying tactics' should be abandoned; the Soviet press and radio kept up a 'violent campaign of abuse and misrepresentation directed against both the Shah and the Persian Government';[2] and at last on 22 October, after Qavām had given Parliament a lengthy account of his negotiations with the Soviet Government, the president of the Persian Foreign Affairs Commission moved the following resolution, which was adopted by 102 votes against 2:

1. The Premier's negotiations for an oil agreement with the U.S.S.R. were null and void, but he would be exempted from the penalties provided by the law of 2 December 1944 against any minister who should negotiate oil concessions with foreigners.

2. Persia would explore her oil resources during the next five years and exploit them with her own capital. Should it be found necessary to engage foreign experts, they would be drawn from 'completely neutral' countries.

3. If Persian enterprise discovered oil, the Government might negotiate its sale to the U.S.S.R., the Majlis being kept informed throughout.

4. Persia would not grant concessions to foreign Powers, or take foreigners into partnership in any oil company.

5. 'In all cases where the rights of the Iranian nation . . . have been impaired, particularly in regard to the Southern oil, the Government is required to enter into such negotiations and take such measures as are necessary to regain the national rights and inform the Majlis of the results.'[3]

Future events were to give significance to this last clause, with its oblique reference to the Anglo-Iranian concession; and four years later the extreme nationalist Husain Fātimī was reported as saying that he had begun a press campaign to nationalize the Anglo-Iranian Oil Company 'immediately after the Egyptian Government's appeal to the Security Council against Britain', i.e. in the second half of 1947.[4]

[1] New York Herald Tribune and New York Times, 12 September 1947.
[2] The Times, 19 September and (leading article) 25 November 1947.
[3] New York Times and Combat, 23 October 1947; text of clause 5 in Oil Forum, April 1952, special 'insert' (A. H. T. Chisholm: 'Anglo-Iranian answers Iran with Facts'), p. xiii. For the law of 2 December 1944 see Survey for 1939–46: The Middle East in the War, p. 479.
[4] Bourse Égyptienne, 28 June 1951, reporting the Tehrān correspondent of the Cairo Ākhir Sa'a; cf. L. Lockhart, in Journal of the Royal Central Asian Society, April 1953, xl. 144.

The nationalist fervour of the Persian Parliament had been so inflamed that Qavām became alarmed for his authority over it; he had received from the Soviet Ambassador on 20 November a third note charging his Government with the responsibility of having 'treacherously violated its undertakings' in a manner 'incompatible with normal relations between two states';[1] and on 1 December, after summoning a secret session of Parliament and failing to obtain a quorum,[2] he broadcast to the nation a warning that Persia should remain neutral between the two Great Power blocs.[3] While he had refused the Soviet demand to exploit the oil resources in the north, he claimed to have also 'pursued the case of the Anglo-Iranian Oil Company' and would 'persist as long as necessary to secure satisfaction for the Persian nation'; he had, furthermore, entered into negotiations to assert Persia's sovereignty over the oil-producing Arab island of Bahrain in the Persian Gulf, which he described as 'an inseparable part of Persia' and to which Rizā Shāh's Government had repeatedly advanced claims based on Persia's past greatness two centuries before.[4] This appeal to nationalist sentiment did not save Qavām, however; he had not consulted his Cabinet colleagues before making the broadcast, and all but three of them tendered their resignations. When on 10 December his request to Parliament for a vote of confidence received only 46 votes against 39 with 27 abstentions, he resigned, and after being temporarily placed under arrest was allowed at the end of the month to leave for Europe for medical reasons. Meanwhile, on 22 December the Majlis elected as his successor Ibrāhīm Hakīmī, who had been displaced from the premiership by Qavām in January 1946 when the Soviet pressure on Persia was at its height. On the same day the United Nations released the information that the United States and Persia had on 6 October signed an agreement for sending a United States military mission to raise the efficiency of the Persian army. The agreement was to be valid for eighteen months, with the possibility of its extension, and as long as it remained in force the Persian Government were not to engage any other foreigners for duties connected with the Persian army, except with the agreement of the United States.[5]

[1] Text in *Soviet News*, 22 November 1947.

[2] For the frequent abuse of the article in the Constitution requiring an abnormally large quorum see *Survey* for 1939–46: *The Middle East in the War*, p. 479, note 2.

[3] The semi-official newspaper *Ittilāʿāt* had written on 14 August: 'Though Iran, unlike Turkey, has not yet joined the anti-Soviet front, nevertheless Iran, Turkey, and Iraq stand together in view of their proximity to the Soviet frontiers' (quoted by *Soviet News*, 26 August 1947).

[4] *The Times*, 3 December 1947. See Majid Khadduri: 'Iran's Claim to the Sovereignty of Bahrain', *American Journal of International Law*, October 1951, xlv. 631–47; *Cahiers de l'Orient Contemporain*, 1ᵉʳ trimestre 1948, xiii. 54, and 2ᵐᵉ–3ᵐᵉ trimestres 1948, xiv–xv. 172; *Survey* for 1934, p. 224, and for 1936, p. 227.

[5] *United Nations Treaty Series*, vol. xi, no. 171, pp. 303–23; *New York Herald Tribune*, 23 December 1947.

(b) The Frustration of Western Aid, to the Rejection of the Anglo-Iranian Supplemental Oil Agreement, 1948-50

'Plus les nations sentent leur infériorité, plus elles suspectent toute
aide qu'on leur offre.'[1]

On 31 January 1948, while the Persian Parliament was considering the purchase of $10 million worth of United States surplus war material out of the $25 million credit recently granted to Persia for this purpose,[2] the Soviet Government delivered a note protesting against the activity of the recently appointed United States military mission which, they said, was not only re-equipping the Persian army and planning the reorganization of the Persian arsenals, but was organizing the construction at Qum (400 miles from Russia's Caucasian oilfields) of a large airfield, 'apparently not intended for Iranian aircraft', and of underground petrol stores in southern Persia, building fortifications along the Soviet frontier, and planning airfields and carrying out air photography in the same region. The note ended with the warning that 'all the facts mentioned are incompatible with the state of good-neighbourly relations proclaimed in the Soviet-Iranian Treaty of . . . 1921, and . . . the Soviet Government expects the Iranian Government to take without delay the necessary measures to eliminate the existing abnormal situation'.[3] The intention of this note was 'obviously . . . to exert the strongest pressure'[4] on the Persian Government to abandon their reliance on the United States. The Persian Government and the United States Ambassador in Tehrān issued categorical denials of the specific Soviet charges,[5] and the Persian reply of 4 February advanced counter-charges of the Soviet protection extended to the Āzarbāijānī and Kurdish 'traitors' who had escaped to the Soviet Union a year before,[6] and of the provocation constantly offered by the Persian-language broadcasts from Baku. The threatening tone of the Soviet note did not prevent the Persian Parliament from approving on 17 February, with only six dissentient votes and ten abstentions after a stormy debate, the purchase of the $10 million worth of arms from the United States; but it was char-

[1] J.-F. Köver: 'L'Incendie couve en Iran', *Revue Politique et Parlementaire*, April 1948, p. 71.
[2] See above, p. 86.
[3] Text in *Soviet News*, 3 February 1948. For Stalin's reference, in conversation with the United States Secretary of State in December 1945, to the authority given to the Soviet Union by the 1921 treaty to send troops into Persia if there were a threat to her security from a third party in Persia, see above, p. 63. A Soviet note of 14 May 1950 again referred to the treaty when protesting against the contemplated Persian employment of United States experts to make aerial surveys in connexion with oil prospecting in the provinces bordering on the Soviet Union (text in *Soviet News*, 16 May 1950).
[4] *The Times* diplomatic correspondent, 4 February 1948.
[5] The Qum airfield, for example, was said to be merely a small civil landing-ground, and the United States military mission to consist of only thirty officers.
[6] See above, p. 82.

acteristic that they refused to provide funds for the shipment and insurance of the arms, so that their forwarding was delayed;[1] and Reuter's correspondent reported the sentiment in Tehrān political quarters that

if the United States wants to make their country another Greece or another Turkey, and if Congress thinks that Persia might become the first battlefield in the next war, then . . . the U.S. should equip the Persian army free of charge.

. . . The Americans should offer Persia a substantial loan on favourable terms to be used on constructive work for the benefit of Persia. The country . . . does not wish to become a battlefield or a security zone for Russia or the United States, or for any other foreign power, and would find it too much to have to pay for being used by the Great Powers as a 'scapegoat for their mammoth interests'.[2]

On 18 March Moscow Radio broadcast a talk by one Professor Steinberg accusing the United States of 'trying to get hold of northern Iranian oil and to make Iran into a second Greece', warning the Persian Prime Minister that he was 'playing with fire', and declaring that 'Russia cannot permit the existence of a government on her border that is trying to change Iran into a military base for attacking Russia'. The Persian Government protested that the motive for their recent dealings with the United States was only to safeguard their national interests and independence;[3] but the Soviet Government replied with a note dated 24 March which recalled the consequences in the summer of 1941 of the then Persian Government's attempt to deny the activities of Nazi agents in Persia; it repeated that the United States had now been given 'a monopoly right to put American military advisers in key positions', and rejected the Persian protest against the granting of asylum in the Soviet Union to Persians 'persecuted by the Iranian Government for their democratic convictions and for defending the cause of democracy and progress'.[4] The Persian Government retorted on 1 April that they considered it 'unnecessary to give further details or explanations' of the employment of the United States advisers, and countered with a catalogue of Persia's grievances against the Soviet Union since the end of the war: the harbouring in Russia of 'criminals, thieves, and brigands' under the name of democratic lovers of freedom was 'regrettable and contrary to the basis of friendship and good neighbourly relations' and especially to the Soviet-Persian Pacts of 1921 and 1927.[5] On 7 April the Soviet Government delivered a further note in Tehrān rejecting the Persian protest against the Moscow broadcast of 18 March on the ground that the speaker was a private citizen and

---

[1] Sam Pope Brewer in *New York Times*, 29 April 1948.
[2] *Glasgow Herald*, 16 March 1948. For the desire already expressed for a 'substantial loan' from the United States see above, p. 84, and below, pp. 92–93 and 98–99.
[3] *New York Times*, 30 March 1948.
[4] Text of note in *Soviet News*, 5 April 1948.
[5] Text in *Oriente Moderno*, April–June 1948, pp. 91–93.

therefore 'perfectly free to express his views at any time, at any place, on any subject'. 'On the other hand', it continued, 'the Soviet Government protests strongly against the slanderous Persian press campaign against the Soviet Government and also against the publication of anti-Soviet cartoons and other caricatures by the Persian press.'[1] There were rumours in Tehrān of what might be Soviet preparations for breaking off diplomatic relations or even war,[2] and the Soviet Ambassador in Tehrān was reported to have treated another member of the diplomatic corps to a 'tirade' in which he threatened a Soviet invasion of Persia at an early date; but, it was commented, 'most of the experts believe that this Soviet bluster is mere war-of-nerves stuff, intended for the present only to promote the chaos and insecurity the Kremlin desires everywhere'.[3]

This proved to be so, although the Soviet propaganda campaign continued and even increased in the winter of 1948–9.[4] Meanwhile, the Government of Ibrāhīm Hakīmī had been increasingly criticized in the Persian Parliament for their alleged encroachments on the sovereign powers of that irresponsible body. On 9 July 1948 Parliament refused him a vote of confidence, and a new Government was formed by his Minister of the Interior, 'Abd ul-Husain Hazhīr. An agreement was signed in Washington on 29 July adding to the original armaments credit of $10 million a further $16 million for repairing, packing, and shipping the armaments purchased by Persia. The State Department had previously announced that none of these 'were of a character which would be used for offensive action against a foreign power';[5] but in the following weeks the Soviet Ambassador and military attaché in Tehrān again expressed their apprehension that the United States intended to use Persia as a base for attacking the Soviet Union; the Soviet army began to hold manœuvres near the Persian frontier and minor frontier incidents incurred; and about the same time normal Soviet trade with Persia was virtually suspended.[6]

In 1947 the Morrison-Knudsen International Company of the United States, whose advice had been sought by Qavām us-Saltana's Government, had made recommendations for a seven-year development plan for Persia on a more modest and practical scale than the 'extremely ambitious project' originally put forward by Qavām's Government, which had envisaged an expenditure of no less than $1,840 million, or ten times Persia's current

---

[1] *Manchester Guardian*, 9 April 1948.

[2] *New York Times*, 5 April, *Christian Science Monitor*, 12 April 1948.

[3] Joseph Alsop in *New York Herald Tribune*, 23 April 1948, pointing out that there had been a similarly calculated Soviet diplomatic outburst directed against Norway and Denmark shortly before the Communist *coup d'état* in Czechoslovakia in February.

[4] *Manchester Guardian* diplomatic correspondent, 5 March 1949.

[5] United States officials placed the initial cost of the armaments to be supplied under this agreement at $120 million (*New York Herald Tribune*, 29 May 1948). They did not begin to arrive in Persia until the beginning of 1949 (*New York Times*, 10 February and 29 March 1949).

[6] C. L. Sulzberger, ibid. 25 October 1948.

annual revenue.[1] Qavām had applied to the International Bank for a loan of $250 million to assist with the financing of this plan: but Dr. A. C. Millspaugh, who had been the United States adviser to the Persian Ministry of Finance from 1943 to 1945, had issued public warnings against it,[2] and the Persians were invited to submit projects demonstrably within their means. Hazhīr's Government, with the encouragement of Max W. Thornburg, a former executive of the Standard Oil Company of California (one of the participants in the oil production in Saʿūdī Arabia and Bahrain) and 'an old Middle East hand',[3] accordingly approached Overseas Consultants, Inc., a consortium of engineering, management, and business-appraisal firms in the United States, with an invitation to draw up a seven-year plan to cost $650 million;[4] and, before the consortium had begun its investigations, its president had described the undertaking to the press as 'a recovery program in which American taxpayers will not have to foot the bill'. About $390 million, he said, would be provided in Persian currency, and $260 million would be required in dollars or other foreign currency; the royalties paid by the Anglo-Iranian Oil Company, then running at $35–40 million per annum, would play a 'vital part' in providing this, and there would probably also be an application to the World Bank for a loan.[5]

We have seen, however, that in 1944 and again in October 1947 envious eyes had been turned in the Persian Parliament towards the Anglo-Iranian Oil Company's concession;[6] and the announcement on 1 June 1948 of the Company's dividend for the year 1947 precipitated a Persian demand for a larger return from the exploitation of the country's most valuable natural asset. The Company's net profit after taxation had risen

---

[1] See 'Le Plan septennal iranien et ses rapports avec l'économie iranienne', *Études et Conjoncture, Économie Mondiale*, January–February 1950, v. 76–77, 90; and cf. 'U.S. Engineers in Iran', *Fortune*, February 1950, p. 73: 'The first approach of the government was to drag down off the shelf every piece of public works proposed within the memory of the oldest living bureaucrats in Tehran. It made quite a list . . . much of it incapable of adding a single calorie to the intake of the Persian peasant.'

[2] 'The result of a development loan now would be to involve the [Persian] Government more heavily in enterprises which it is incompetent to maintain and to operate. The Iranian tax system, while bearing heavily on the poor, fails to meet the demands of a needlessly expanding army and a wasteful, politics-ridden bureaucracy. The budget, if one can call it such, has shown a sizable deficit for the last six years. Accounting and auditing are hopelessly in arrears' (quoted by *Christian Science Monitor*, 10 February 1948; cf. a Persian, Heshmat Ala'i: 'How Not to Develop a Backward Country', *Fortune*, August 1948, pp. 76 seqq.). For Millspaugh's disillusionment with Persia see his *Americans in Persia* (1946), and a letter to *Fortune*, September 1948, p. 40.

[3] *Fortune*, Feburary 1950, p. 131; cf. *New York Herald Tribune*, 20 March and 17 April 1949. For Thornburg's decided views of the 'failure of the British to parallel political with economic development' in the Middle East since the First World War see his article in *Review of Middle East Oil* (London, *Petroleum Times*, 1948), p. 99.

[4] *Fortune*, loc. cit. and p. 132.

[5] *New York Times*, 20 October 1948.

[6] See *Survey* for 1939–46: *The Middle East in the War*, p. 479, and above, p. 88; see also *Survey* for 1934, pp. 224–47, for the dispute with Riżā Shāh in 1932–3.

from £9·6 in 1946 to a new record of £18·6 million. The dividend, however, remained at the same rate as in the previous year in accordance with the British Labour Government's policy of dividend limitation, and this had the automatic effect of limiting a portion of the royalty immediately payable to the Persian Government[1] since, by Article 10 of the 1933 Convention,[2] that Government received annually, besides a royalty on the tonnage of oil produced, 20 per cent. of the dividend paid to the ordinary shareholders in excess of a small stated minimum.[3] The total amount received by the Persian Government for royalty and taxation in 1947 thus totalled £7·1 million, as compared with 'not far short of £20 millions' taken by the British Government in their 'dual role of majority shareholder and taxgatherer'.[4] The Company, realizing that the Persian Government would be dissatisfied by this position, offered to consider how the consequences of dividend limitation might be rectified, and sent a delegation to Tehrān in August 1948 for this purpose.[5] On 6 November, however, Hazhīr's Government resigned after receiving a poor response to their demand for a vote of confidence; and the new Prime Minister, Muhammad Sā'id Marāgha'ī, who as Prime Minister in 1944 had resisted the Soviet demand for an oil concession in north Persia,[6] said on 10 January 1949 that his Government required a larger share in the profits of the Anglo-Iranian Oil Company, whose wealth did not 'accord with the poverty of the nation'.[7] On 3 February 2,000 students, comprising both Communists of the Tūda Party and nationalist and religious extremists (who during the last two years had been reaping the reward of supporting the Government against the Tūda in 1946), demonstrated outside the Parliament building with banners demanding the cancellation of the Company's concession and the suppression of the British-owned Imperial

---

[1] A commentator in the *Financial Times*, 23 September 1948, estimated that dividend limitation had reduced Persia's royalty receipts for 1947 by about one-seventh.

[2] Published in *League of Nations Official Journal*, December 1933, pp. 1653–60, and republished in Great Britain, Foreign Office: *Correspondence between the . . . U.K. and the Persian Government and Related Documents concerning the Oil Industry in Persia, February 1951 to September 1951*, Cmd. 8425 (London, H.M.S.O., 1951), pp. 9–19.

[3] The Persian Government were also credited with 20 per cent. of the sum paid to reserves by the Company, but this 20 per cent. was not payable to Persia until the expiry of the Concession in 1993.

[4] Statement by the Company's Chairman at the annual general meeting (*Financial Times*, 1 July 1948) and comment ibid. 21 June 1948.

[5] The British Chancellor of the Exchequer stated on 25 January 1949 that the Government, although majority shareholders in the Company, did not propose to interfere with the directors in their negotiations with the Persian Government (H.C.Deb. 5th ser., vol. 460, col. 748); but three years later the Foreign Under-Secretary in the Labour Government of 1950–1 admitted that the Persian 'revolt' against the Company 'might have been anticipated and perhaps action could have been taken earlier' (Ernest Davies: 'Labour's Foreign Policy', *Political Quarterly*, April–June 1952, xxiii. 129).

[6] See *Survey* for 1939–46: *The Middle East in the War*, pp. 475 seqq.

[7] *The Times*, 11 January 1949.

Bank of Iran.[1] The Government were thought to be in danger of a vote of censure; but the excitement was diverted when on the following day the Shāh received two bullet wounds from a would-be assassin.[2] The police directed their reprisals not only against the Tūda Party[3] but also against two extreme Right-wing organizations. One of these was the 'National Front' led by the old and ill but redoubtable Dr. Muhammad Musaddiq, who both in 1944 and in 1947, when opposing the Soviet demand for an oil concession in north Persia, had attacked the existing Anglo-Iranian concession in the south also;[4] the other was the Fidā'iyān-i Islām ('Devotees of Islām') inspired by the religious leader Saiyid Abū'l Qāsim Kāshānī, an inveterate adversary of the British, who was among those now arrested.[5]

Negotiations with the Oil Company were resumed on 9 February, but

[1] The Bank's sixty-year concession had expired on 30 January. As a condition of allowing it to continue as a bank of deposit dealing in foreign exchange (under the new name of 'The British Bank of Iran and the Middle East', the Persian Government objecting to the word 'imperial' and the Bank registering the fact that its interests in neighbouring countries now surpassed those in Persia itself), the Persian Government now imposed the condition that 55 per cent. of its public deposits, and those of other foreign banks, should be placed with the state bank (Bank Millī-yi Īrān) free of interest, a restriction which the Bank's chairman described as 'without precedent in its severity' (Annual Statement, *The Times*, 6 July 1949). This was no doubt one reason why members of the British Conservative opposition objected to the payment of £8·2 million in transferable sterling to Persia in settlement of the balance due to the Persian Railways for carrying British military war-time traffic (10 November 1949, H.C.Deb. 5th ser., vol. 469, coll. 1601–2).

[2] While the police produced documentary 'proof' that the Shāh's assailant (whom they had beaten to death) was a member of the Tūda Party, the Associated Press representative in Tehrān afterwards reported that the weight of evidence was against this (*New York Herald Tribune*, 24 May, *Christian Science Monitor*, 7 June 1950). Left-wing and radical sources (*Soviet News*, 15 February 1949; Andrew Roth in *The Hindu*, 19 July 1950) connected him with the religious-fanatical Fidā'iyān-i Islām (see above). It was this organization that murdered 'Abd ul-Husain Hazhīr in November 1949 for his alleged flagrant interference in the elections (see T. Cuyler Young: 'The Race between Russia and Reform in Iran', *Foreign Affairs*, January 1950, xxviii. 282, and 'The Social Support of Current Iranian Policy', *Middle East Journal*, Spring 1952, vi. 142–3); and in March 1952 they murdered the moderate Prime Minister, 'Alī Razmārā.

[3] It was now that the Tūda Party's secretary, Īraj Iskandarī, escaped to Paris (Sam Waagenaar in *Tribune des Nations*, 18 November 1949), and began to write his tendentious history of the party for the Communist periodical *Moyen-Orient*.

[4] See *Survey* for 1939–46: *The Middle East in the War*, p. 479. The Tehrān correspondent of *The Times* remarked with prophetic discernment: 'If ardent love could make Persia strong and prosperous without the help of knowledge, sagacity, or diligence, Dr. Mosaddeq would be an ideal Prime Minister' (22 November 1949); cf. L. Lockhart (*Journal of the Royal Central Asian Society*, April 1953, xl. 143), who remarks that when Musaddiq led the opposition to the Soviet demand for an oil concession in 1944 he had 'the sympathy and support of Great Britain and the United States'.

[5] Kāshānī, who had spent his youth in the Shī'ī town of Najaf in 'Irāq, had taken part in the anti-British rising of 1920, for which the British had interned him on a torrid island in the Persian Gulf (see *Oriente Moderno*, April–July 1951, p. 92, and *Observer* 'Profile', 14 September 1952, and cf. P. W. Ireland: *Iraq, a Study in Political Development* (London, Cape, 1937), pp. 264–5) Kāshānī and Dr. Musaddiq's son-in-law had been among those Persian notables whom the British had interned during the Second World War for their connexion with the German agent, Franz Mayr (see *Survey* for 1939–46: *The Middle East in the War*, pp. 156–7).

were suspended again for three weeks in March to enable its representatives to return to London for consultations. The Company's chairman,
Sir William Fraser, himself visited Tehrān at the end of April, but the talks
were again suspended a fortnight later: it appeared that, while the Company was offering a 50 per cent. increase in the tonnage royalty, the Persian
Government were holding out for considerably more. They observed that
in 1943 the Venezuelan Government had obtained a new agreement giving them a half-share in the profits of the Creole Petroleum Company, a
subsidiary of the Standard Oil Company of New Jersey; they knew that
the Sa'ūdī Arabian Government were already pressing the Arabian-
American Oil Company for a new agreement on these terms; and, claiming that the growth of the Anglo-Iranian Oil Company to its present
commanding size and wealth was a direct consequence of its 'unjust enrich-
ment' at the expense of Persia, they asked for a half-share of the profits
earned by the Anglo-Iranian group, not merely in Persia but throughout
the world.[1] The Company's reply was that, while it was prepared to
concede to the Persian Government a half-share of its profits in Persia
only, 'no oil company, if it wished to remain in business, could agree to
operate on a 50:50 basis unless the profits to be shared were limited to
those arising from the country of operation';[2] it was also remarked that the
operations of the Creole Petroleum Company in Venezuela did not extend
to distribution and marketing, like those of the Anglo-Iranian Oil Company, and that Venezuelan oil had to bear lower transport costs than
Persian oil.[3] While some Persian deputies called for the difference to be
referred to the International Court or the United Nations, already some of
Dr. Musaddiq's supporters, with influential press backing, were demanding the cancellation of the Company's concession.[4] The Company denied
the subsequent Persian allegation that pressure was brought to bear on
the Persian Government to sign the Supplemental Agreement of 17 July
1949. By this agreement the tonnage royalty was increased from 4s. to 6s.
gold per ton, and the dividend limitation difficulty was to be circumvented
as follows: the sum paid to reserve in any given year was to be notionally
augmented to neutralize the impact of British taxation upon it, and the
Persian Government were to receive 20 per cent. of this augmented sum
immediately, instead of having to wait for the expiry of the concession in

---

[1] 'Iran Presents Its Case for Nationalization', by 'A Persian Government Official', *Oil Forum*,
March 1952, pp. 87–89.
[2] 'Anglo-Iranian Answers with Facts', ibid. April 1952, special 'insert', p. xiii.
[3] See United Nations, Department of Economic Affairs: *Review of Economic Conditions in the
Middle East* (1951), p. 27.
[4] *The Times*, 10 June and 22 November 1949. The Company's annual report for 1948,
published at this moment, showed British taxation (£28·3 million) as more than double the
royalty payable to Persia (£13·5 million) under the terms of the 1933 convention which was now
being revised.

1993.[1] The effect of these readjustments, which were made retrospective
to cover the year 1948, was that Persia's royalties for that and the following
year would together amount to £41·6 million, compared with £22·7
million under the 1933 agreement,[2] and that she might expect a propor-
tionate increase in 1950 and the following years. The Persian Finance
Minister made a 'dutiful but unenthusiastic' attempt to advocate before
Parliament the ratification of this new agreement which he himself had
concluded; but Dr. Musaddiq's ambitious supporter Husain Makkī, taking
advantage of the apathy of the moderates, talked out the bill almost single-
handed until Parliament was dissolved on 28 July for a statutory general
election,[3] the Prime Minister promising that he would try to negotiate
with the Company a more profitable agreement before the new Parliament
assembled.[4] There were, however, no new developments during the long-
drawn-out procedure of the Persian general election, though it was significant that four of Dr. Musaddiq's supporters were returned at the head of
the poll in Tehrān. The Company made financial advances to the Persian
Government totalling £14 million against their expectation of royalties;[5]
but a *New York Times* correspondent in Tehrān reported that Persian newspaper editors and political gossip (not content with accusing the Oil
Company of starting a typhoid epidemic to divert attention from itself)[6]
were insinuating that the United States was on Persia's side in the oil
dispute, on the grounds that 'the United States hopes for great advantages
from the realization of the Seven Year Plan . . . and that there is accordingly a clash between British oil interests and United States Seven Year
Plan interests'.[7]

While this correspondent added that responsible British and Americans
were leaving inquiring Persians in no doubt of their countries' solidarity,
the charge was subsequently made in the United States that

the British stood aloof from and even derided the postwar attempt of the U.S. to
help Iran stabilize her economy and raise her miserable standard of living. . . .
The U.S. State Department, to be sure, did not officially approach the British
with a well-worked-out scheme for a joint assault on Iranian misery. But this

[1] For examples of the application of this principle, see Great Britain, Foreign Office: *Correspondence . . . concerning the Oil Industry in Persia*, Cmd. 8425, p. 22.
[2] Anglo-Iranian Oil Company, Chairman's Statement for the year ended 31 December
1949 (*The Times*, 3 July 1950).
[3] A Persian Government official afterwards implied that the Company had 'carefully timed'
the signature of the agreement to coincide with the dissolution of the Persian Parliament, 'thus
permitting that body only a few days to discuss and ratify it'. The Company's spokesman retorted that the closing stages of the negotiations had been much delayed by the Persian Government's representatives (see *Oil Forum*, March 1952, p. 89, and April 1952, special 'insert'.
p. xiii).
[4] *Financial Times*, 29 July 1949.   [5] Ibid. 12 September 1950.
[6] *Fortune*, March 1951, p. 166.
[7] Albion Ross in *New York Times*, 23 February 1950; cf. an editorial in *Monde*, 2/3 January
1949, and see above, p. 93.

did not entitle the British to act as if their best interests lay in aiding and abetting the ineptness of the Americans.[1]

Overseas Consultants, Inc., had now established in Tehrān a staff of a dozen men led by Max W. Thornburg to advise the all-Persian Supreme Planning Board on the execution of the Seven-Year Plan, now embodied in a 1,500-page report,[2] and the Persian Parliament had adopted proposals for financing it, as follows:[3]

Income	$ million	Expenditure	$ million
Royalties and payments from the Anglo-Iranian Oil Company	242	Agriculture and irrigation	201
		Transport and communications	115
Sale of government property	31	Mines and industries	112
Private capital, minimum of	31	Initial capital of a Persian oil company	31
Loan by the Bank Millī	139	Posts and telegraphs	22
International Bank loan, maximum of	208	Housing	46
		Water and electricity supply	31
		Public health	31
		Technical education	31
		Sundries	31
	651		651

The Governor of the Bank Millī,[4] who was a member of the Supreme Planning Board, held that no loan from the International Bank would be necessary for the first two years, during which the Plan could be financed by the oil royalties (the British Treasury was furnishing the Persian Government with sterling convertible into hard currencies for the purchase of goods not reasonably available in the sterling area), by internal loans, and by halving the existing exceptionally good 100 per cent. cover of the Persian currency by gold and securities. Many Persians of the propertied class, including the Shāh, were unwilling to lower the currency cover, however;[5] and it was admitted in advance that a loan from the International Bank was one of the objectives of the Shāh[6] in visiting the United

[1] *Fortune*, March 1951, pp. 166, 168.

[2] Thornburg appeared to be much more optimistic about the Plan's prospects than were Persian observers, according to Sam Waagenaar: 'Planification des mirages', *Tribune des Nations*, 11 November 1949.

[3] *Études et Conjoncture, Économie Mondiale*, January–February 1950, v. 78–79.

[4] This was Abū'l Hasan Ibtihāj, 'a shrewd and energetic man who impressed Western businessmen as one of their own' (*Fortune*, August 1950, p. 73). Millspaugh, who during the war had found him 'a vigorous administrator, a good technical banker, and an honest, courageous man', nevertheless remarked: 'He expressed a vehement nationalism; and took no pains to conceal his belief that he was equal or superior in ability to Americans. One soon took note or heard of his nervousness, his incredibly hot temper, his inclination to ride rough-shod over opposition, and his dictatorial propensities' (*Americans in Persia*, p. 95, and cf. pp. 127–8).

[5] See T. Cuyler Young: 'The Race between Russia and Reform in Iran', *Foreign Affairs*, January 1950, xxviii. 287.

[6] The Shāh had taken advantage of the attempt on his life in February 1949 to wrest from

States in November.[1] In a press interview in New York the Shāh assessed
Persia's dollar needs at the conventional figure of $250 million and referred
to her need for larger quantities of modern arms;[2] the Export-Import
Bank had already furnished a loan of $35 million; and the official com-
muniqué at the end of the Shāh's visit stated that the United States would
support Persian applications to the International Bank for 'economically
justifiable' loans for furthering the Seven-Year Plan.[3] But what *was*
economically justifiable in a country administered with the incompetence
and corruption of Persia? The United States Ambassador, John C. Wiley
(1948–50), was reported to have 'made it plain that American aid would
be forthcoming provided the Iranians set up a reform Government with
a sound plan for putting the country on the road to a higher living standard';[4] but there were 'definite indications' of a tendency in the State
Department to compare Persia with Kuomintang China; and the expression 'pouring money down a rat-hole' was 'perfectly familiar' in
Tehrān.[5]

Parliament an increase of his constitutional powers. Observing that Parliament had obstruc-
tively abused the powers over the executive conferred on it by the Constitution, the Shāh
obtained the creation of a Senate, half of whose members were to be nominated by the Crown,
and the Crown's right to dissolve either or both Chambers at will (see 'Recent Constitutional
Changes in Iran', *Journal of the Royal Central Asian Society*, July–October 1949, xxxvi. 265–6;
Cahiers de l'Orient Contemporain, 1er trimestre 1949, xvii. 57, and 2me–3me trimestres 1949, xviii–
xix. 173–4; and, for the increased powers conferred on the 'Irāqī Crown in 1943, Khadduri:
Independent Iraq, pp. 206–16).

Some Persians believed that the British Government, during the Shāh's visit to Britain in
July 1948, had supplied him with legal advice in connexion with the projected increase of royal
authority; and this was taken as another example of British interference in Persia's internal
affairs.

[1] It was reported from Washington that 'although State Department officials are inclined to
stress the "good will" aspects of the Shāh's visit, Iranian diplomatic representatives do not
hesitate to call attention to their country's military and economic condition' (Walter H.
Waggoner in *New York Times*, and cf. Homer Bigart in *New York Herald Tribune*, both 13 November 1949). In the spring Egon Kaskeline (*Christian Science Monitor*, 18 March 1949) had commented: 'Iran's financial needs are perhaps one reason why Iranian leaders are not reluctant
to emphasize the Russian danger for all it is worth at this particular moment.' Soviet propaganda
had been intensified as a result of the outlawing of the Tūda Party after the attempt on the
Shāh, and of the beginning of United States armaments deliveries (see above, pp. 92, 95),
and a number of frontier incidents had caused some alarm.

[2] The Shāh, like some Turkish circles, was 'known to be annoyed' because the arms which the
United States was prepared to supply did not include her latest jet fighter aircraft (*Christian
Science Monitor* Tehrān correspondent, 25 June 1949). An agreement was signed on 23 May
1950 for the supply of United States arms to Persia under the Mutual Defence Assistance Programme, to the value of $10–15 million.

[3] *New York Times*, 31 December 1949. Frequent Persian claims to preferential financial
treatment as a result of the Three-Power declaration issued after the Tehrān Conference in
1943 were not justified by the text of that declaration, which stated only that Persia's economic
problems at the end of the war 'should receive full consideration along with those of the other
members of the United Nations' (*Documents on American Foreign Relations, July 1943–June 1944*
(Boston, World Peace Foundation, 1945), p. 236).

[4] *Fortune*, March 1951, p. 168.

[5] Albion Ross, reporting to *New York Times*, 14 February 1950, from Tehrān.

Between the announcement in early August 1949 of the Shāh's intention to visit the United States and his departure there had been a significant *détente* in Soviet-Persian relations. The protection which the Persian authorities had given to a Soviet officer and two soldiers who had deserted across the frontier in July had been followed by Soviet reprisals in the form of kidnapping Persian soldiers in the frontier region,[1] but a party of eleven soldiers thus seized was repatriated on 25 September. On 7 August the Persian Prime Minister had complained that the United States had treated a Persian appeal for the gift of 200,000 tons of wheat, to relieve the effects of a succession of bad harvests, 'purely as a business proposition, not as an economic or political question as we expected'; consignments of American wheat, when eventually purchased, arrived in poor condition, and Persian inefficiency allowed more to deteriorate in the port of Khurramshahr.[2] On 5 October, however, Persia succeeded in buying 100,000 tons of wheat from the Soviet Union. The Soviet Government agreed to the appointment of a Persian director to the Soviet-Persian Caspian Fisheries, which the Russians had treated since their establishment in 1927 as a virtual monopoly, but whose charter was due for renewal in 1952;[3] and Soviet frontier officials were reported to have received instructions to be more 'friendly and cooperative'.[4]

'For many months, the State Department had considered that conditions in Iran were stable and the country need not be a source of major worry to American strategists'; but about the beginning of 1950 'a series of alarming reports began pouring in' from the Ambassador in Tehrān, who represented to Washington that $100–200 million was urgently needed as a tonic to the Persian economy.[5] In July 1950 a British authority, in a public assessment of 'Some Economic Problems of Persia',[6] expressed the view that the 'enormous capital outlay' involved in the building of the Trans-Iranian Railway between the two World Wars had started a wave of inflation which, exaggerated by the Second World War and the Allies' expenditure in Persia, was 'an ever-present menace' to the country's economy. An 'enormous spending power' had been created for which there was no corresponding increase in consumer goods, and the purchasing power of the currency had steadily declined.[7] The new industries

---

[1] See *The Times*, 15 and 28 August 1949.

[2] *New York Times*, 8 and 9 August 1949, 4 April 1950.

[3] See above, p. 71, note 1; *Daily Telegraph*, 18 August 1950.

[4] C. L. Sulzberger in *New York Times*, 29 November 1949.

[5] John M. Hightower in *Christian Science Monitor*, 17 April 1950; cf. *Fortune*, March 1951, p. 168.

[6] i.e. Edward Sykes in *Journal of the Royal Central Asian Society*, July–October 1950, xxxvii. 262–72; cf. T. Cuyler Young: 'The Race between Russia and Reform in Iran', *Foreign Affairs*, January 1950, xxviii. 284–5; *Fortune*, February 1950, pp. 132, 134.

[7] The cost of living, already enormously inflated when compared with the pre-war level, had increased by an additional 15–20 per cent. during 1949 (*Christian Science Monitor*, 9 March 1950); this was probably due largely to the harvest failure of the previous season.

promoted by Rizā Shāh, at a time when agriculture was being neglected, had attracted many thousands from the villages. 'The countryside has lost much labour which it can ill afford, and, on the other hand, the city populations have become swollen beyond their capacity to give productive employment, and insoluble problems of housing and health have been created'.[1] The United States participation in the Seven-Year Plan had fostered the idea that the Persians themselves 'could sit back and watch the dollars perform miracles'[2]. Meanwhile, there had been an orgy of wasteful expenditure by the well-to-do minority: '... A plenitude of flashy American cars, expensive mansions, well-dressed people and shop windows richly stocked with luxury goods from the factories of America and Europe'.[3] Imports could invariably undersell, often by wide margins, the products of Persia's inefficient industries, especially those run by the State, and in Isfahān and other manufacturing towns factories were closing or going on short time, with a consequent increase in popular support for the Communists and in demonstrations by unemployed workers. In Āzarbāijān, which had suffered severely from the recent bad harvests, the provincial administration, restored at the end of 1946, was reliably reported to be merely the corrupt instrument of the absentee landlords, and a risk was felt that the peasantry might welcome the return of the Communist régime.[4] The details of the Seven-Year Plan, quite apart from its basic failure to elicit a handsome dollar loan, were attracting criticism from Persian quarters that were far from disinterested. The prime emphasis of the Plan, as we have seen, was on the modernization of agriculture; the Shāh had made known his wish to distribute Crown lands (much of them confiscated by his arbitrary father) to landless peasants and to promote agricultural co-operatives; and the present Government had a proposal for limiting the size of landed estates. However,

manure and tractors are not spectacular, many small dams have less publicity value than one large one, and the results of agricultural education make themselves felt only slowly. Many influential Persians on the other hand are in a hurry to have something to show, a factory or an oil well, and some might prefer even a factory which did not work to an agricultural reform which did, and which in doing so threatened to lessen their own influence. . . .

Meanwhile the volume of imports is likely to increase . . . while exports . . .

[1] Sykes, loc. cit. pp. 265–6. Reuter's Tehrān correspondent, Leopold Herman, pointed out that the population of Tehrān had doubled in eight years to a figure of 1·2 million (*The Hindu*, 2 January 1950).

[2] Sykes, loc. cit. p. 267. It was this kind of observation which no doubt prompted the American charge that the British regarded the Plan as 'visionary' (*Fortune*, March 1951, p. 170).

[3] A. T. Steele in *New York Herald Tribune*, 10 December 1950.

[4] *New York Times*, 15 and 28 February 1950. Philip Toynbee, on the other hand, while confirming the corruption and extortion, commented: 'Among these peasants of Northern Persia there is clearly a brutish incredulity in the face of cheerful promises, based on an age-old experience' (*Observer*, 26 November 1950, and cf. above, p. 82).

continue to decrease. Some exporters think that only a large devaluation of the rial could restore their trade. Devaluation, however . . . would not be popular, and even if it were to restore prosperity to the Isfahan cotton mills it would affront the national pride.

It is this national pride which lies at the root of opposition to the supplementary agreement with the Anglo-Iranian Oil Company. British people argue . . . that the oil company has brought great economic advantages to Persia and that the agreement is a generous one, but their arguments are largely wasted against the feeling of Persians that Abadan, their second greatest industrial city, is built in a foreign style, is filled with foreign institutions, echoes with a foreign language, and is wholly dependent on a single industry controlled and, in its higher posts, mainly staffed by foreigners. Even those Persians who are fully convinced of the advantages Persia derives from the oil company's concession do not like to dwell on them, for they cannot wholly conquer their own distaste.

This is a strong emotion which ought to be respected. Ultimately it is based on a half-conscious recollection of Persian history, its compact civilization, its individuality, now more or less imperilled by the infiltrations of the west and of Russia. It affects that large part of the nation which, like similar classes in other nations, has no great aptitude for coherent thought and yet is far from foolish.[1]

Faced with this economic deterioration, the Government of Muhammad Sā'id Marāgha'ī resigned, after a number of re-shuffles, on 19 March 1950. The problem of aid to Persia was discussed at conferences of the United States diplomatic representatives in the Middle East at Istanbul in November 1949 and in Cairo in March 1950; but the State Department made it clear that such aid would be conditional on the establishment in Tehrān of a government pledged to reform the administration; and at the end of May the sixty-eight-year-old Henry F. Grady, who had won a reputation as a 'trouble-shooter' when combating Communism as Ambassador to Greece during the past two years, was appointed Ambassador in Tehrān, 'to act as a watchdog' with eight economic experts to assist him.[2] The Shāh responded by appointing as Prime Minister on 26 June (the day after the outbreak of the Korean War) the Chief of the General Staff, General 'Alī Razmārā, who had distinguished himself in the suppression of the Āzarbāijān autonomist movement in December 1946 and won a reputation as an efficient organizer.[3] It was afterwards reported[4] that the outgoing United States Ambassador had let it be known to the Persian

---

[1] *The Times* Tehrān correspondent, 30 January 1950; cf. Leopold Herman in *The Hindu*, 2 January 1950; C. L. Sulzberger in *New York Times*, 4 April 1950; 'Iran presents its Case for Nationalization', *Oil Forum*, March 1952.

[2] Albion Ross in *New York Times*, 27 June and 5 September 1950.

[3] The new Government was violently assailed by Dr. Musaddiq as a 'dictatorship', and he also denounced the United States as being 'the dupe of British policy' in her policy towards Persia (*Cahiers de l'Orient Contemporain*, 2me semestre 1950, xxii. 226).

[4] *Fortune*, March 1951, p. 168.

Government that he had advised Washington that at least $100 million would be needed to get them 'off to a good start'; and they confronted Grady with the contention that the United States 'had already promised them' that mystical sum of $250 million which, as we have seen, had been their target for the last three years.[1] It was not until October that the Export-Import Bank advanced a loan of $25 million for the purchase of agricultural and road-building machinery. Grady failed to persuade Washington to indicate to the Persian Government that this sum might be increased to $100 million for 'properly accredited projects . . . basic, grassroots aid';[2] and the 'Point Four' Programme, from which the Persian Government had in 1949 solicited $129 million as their 'immediate urgent minimum need',[3] allocated half-a-million dollars for improving health, agriculture, and education.

Meanwhile, the Seven-Year Plan had run into political difficulties. In the approved programme, as we have seen,[4] 30 per cent. of the entire expenditure was to be devoted to agriculture and irrigation; but the allocation for the first year gave only 5 per cent. to this purpose, as against 15 per cent. to liquidating the debts of the Industrial and Mining Bank set up by Riẓā Shāh to finance state industries, while other sums were allotted to 'more spectacular (and graft-ridden) projects'[5] such as new railways and the founding of a Persian oil company to exploit the resources of the whole of Persia except the Anglo-Iranian concession. In retrospect, with the Arabian-American Oil Company (Aramco) about to conclude a profit-sharing agreement with the Saʿūdī Arabian Government at the end of the year,[6] the Anglo-Iranian Oil Company seem to have been short-sightedly stiff in their negotiations with Razmārā;[7] and the uncertainty

---

[1] See above, pp. 84, 98–99. Grady remarked that the origin of the figure 'has always been something of a mystery' ('What Went Wrong in Iran?', *Saturday Evening Post*, 5 January 1952, p. 57).

[2] Ibid. Grady makes no mention of the Persian administrative chaos which was the reason for Washington's misgivings.

[3] The Persian Foreign Minister, quoted in *New York Times*, 8 August 1949.

[4] See above, p. 98.

[5] *Fortune*, March 1951, p. 170; cf. 'Can Persia Plan?'; *The Economist*, 6 May 1950, p. 983; M. Philips Price, M.P., in *Manchester Guardian*, 9 October 1950, and *Journal of the Royal Central Asian Society*, April–July 1951, xxxviii. 105; Georgiana G. Stevens, 'Reform and Power Politics in Iran', *Foreign Policy Reports*, 15 February 1951, p. 219.

[6] While a Persian Government official afterwards asserted that 'in mid-1950 it became known that Aramco was inclined to agree', the Anglo-Iranian Oil Company maintained that 'it was not until the end of 1950 that the likelihood of this Agreement became known. The Aramco did not inform A.I.O.C. beforehand' (*Oil Forum*, March 1952, p. 89, and April 1952, special 'insert', p. xiv).

[7] On coming to power Razmārā requested, as political concessions which might induce Parliament to ratify the Supplemental Agreement, that the Company should allow the Government a larger control over the measurement of the Company's oil exports; should give the Government all surplus natural gas and reduce the price of petrol sold to Persia; and should accelerate its programme of substituting Persian for foreign employees. The Company replied that the Government already had the right to measure oil exports and that they were prepared

about the future size of the oil royalties combined with the misgivings of
United States bankers to prevent the financing of the Seven-Year Plan.
Parliamentary opposition brought to a standstill a purge of dishonest or
incompetent officials initiated by the Razmārā Government;[1] and the
Soviet Government took advantage of Persian dissatisfaction with both
Britain and the United States to offer a new trade agreement. This was
signed on 4 November 1950 amid the 'extravagant congratulations' of
'almost the whole Teheran press, from the ultra-conservative to the frankly
fellow-travelling';[2] and at the end of the year, after a Persian parliamentary commission dominated by Dr. Musaddiq had unanimously rejected
the Supplemental Oil Agreement and had debated nationalization as an
alternative to it,[3] Overseas Consultants, Inc., withdrew from the Seven-
Year Plan. An American authority on Persia had already commented,
one year before, that Persia had

a record of paying high prices for advice and then disregarding it, and it is well
to be aware that personnel problems will become acute. It is difficult to retain
high caliber advisers and to maintain morale when disinterested advice is
constantly disregarded.

. . . The landed and mercantile classes are likely to perceive in the plan a
threat to their present supremacy . . . and it is altogether probable that among
these privileged classes there will be many who will strive to sabotage the whole
effort. These supporters of the status quo will be abetted by the conservative
clerics who fear this program of industrialization and modernization as a threat
to the Islamic religion, way of life and social structure.[4]

And now the once optimistic Max Weston Thornburg, after an allusion to
the revenues 'justly due' from the oil company, complained that

the plan was doomed from the start when politicians moved in and took over.
Important appointments were made on the basis of political and personal interests instead of competence and experience. Utilization of the money available

to pay for any independent firm of inspectors chosen by the Government to make regular checks;
they made concessions on the second point (cf. *Oil Forum*, April 1952, p. xix); and they agreed
to pursue the programme of introducing Persian employees 'in so far as this was consistent with
maintaining the highest degree of efficiency and economy in the administration and operation
of the Company'. For the new United States Ambassador's criticisms of the Company's attitude
see Henry F. Grady: 'Oil and the Middle East', *Foreign Policy Bulletin*, 15 December 1951, pp.
1–2; 'Tensions in the Middle East with Particular Reference to Iran', *Proceedings of the Academy
of Political Science*, January 1952, xxiv. 558; 'What Went Wrong in Iran?', *Saturday Evening Post*,
5 January 1952, pp. 30, 56–58.
    [1] See *Cahiers de l'Orient Contemporain*, 2me semestre 1950, xxii. 227.
    [2] Philip Toynbee: 'The Weakest Frontier', *Observer*, 4 February 1951.
    [3] For the extent to which Musaddiq was influenced by motives of internal politics see L. Lock-
hart in *Journal of the Royal Central Asian Society*, April 1953, xl. 145–6.
    [4] T. Cuyler Young: 'The Race between Russia and Reform in Iran', *Foreign Affairs*, January
1950, xxviii. 286, 288. The extremist religious leader Kāshānī was reported to have denounced
the Plan as a 'godless enterprise' (*Christian Science Monitor*, 12 January 1951).

was determined by personal and political interests. In the absence of modern accounting methods it is impossible to know what really happened to the money.[1]

[1] *New York Times*, 9 January 1951; and cf. Thornburg's warning statement of 5 April 1950 (France, Présidence du Conseil: *Notes et Études Documentaires*, no. 1,363 (5 August 1950), 'L'Économie de l'Iran', pp. 26–27).

PART III

THE ARAB COUNTRIES AND THE WESTERN POWERS

(i) The End of European Ascendancy in the Levant States

DE GAULLE's intransigence, which had been mainly responsible for the Syrian crisis of May 1945 and for the consequent British intervention between the French forces and the Syrian Government,[1] had had the effects of making a final end of French authority in the Levant (though, for the present, French forces remained in certain cantonments in Syria, and at large in Lebanon), and of straining Anglo-French relations in that region apparently to breaking-point. The Syrian and Lebanese Governments, meanwhile, were now anxious to obtain the final withdrawal of the foreign troops. It was reported from Paris on 14 October 1945 that intermittent negotiations had been going on for an adjustment of Anglo-French relations in the Levant, but that the French Government were still hoping that Britain would help them to obtain treaties comparable with her own pre-war treaties with Egypt and 'Irāq, even including the concession of air-bases.[2] The French were so far out of touch with the realities that the Syrian Government's closing of the French schools, which were attended by some 46,000 pupils, came as a surprise which evoked a protest from the French Government and polemics from the French press.[3] On 24 October the Syrian Premier, Sa'dullāh al-Jābirī, made it clear at a press conference that it was the French troops whose withdrawal his Government primarily desired: the position of the British troops, on the other hand, was (he said) comparable with that of the Allied forces in liberated Europe, and they would be withdrawn as soon as 'the strategic reasons for their presence had disappeared'. A few days later President Shukrī al-Quwwatlī told a press correspondent that 'unless the French leave Syria and Lebanon there will be bloodshed again. How can the British

[1] See *Survey* for 1939–46: *The Middle East in the War*, pp. 293–304.
[2] Dana Adams Schmidt in *New York Times*, 15 October 1945.
[3] The French claimed that the right to maintain these schools rested upon an Agreement with the Ottoman Empire of 18 December 1913. The Syrian Government now insisted that they should submit to the Ministry of Education particulars of their sources of income, their staff, and curriculum, admit government inspectors, and devote a minimum amount of time to the teaching of Arabic, &c. When the French Délégué sought to make these requirements the subject of negotiation the Syrian Premier was reported to have stated at a press conference that the question was bound up with others, notably the withdrawal of the French troops, &c. (cf. *Monde*, 4/5 November, *Aube*, 6 November 1945; Sirri Kaltakji, Syrian press attaché at Washington, letter to *New York Herald Tribune*, 16 December 1945; *Journal Officiel, Débats*, 18 January 1946, p. 89).

expect me to have faith in the French when their agents and their gold undermine my authority and they scatter leaflets over my country boasting that they will return?'[1]

In this inauspicious atmosphere a draft agreement was negotiated between Bevin and the French Foreign Minister, Bidault, and their respective Ambassadors, and on 13 December they exchanged letters which confirmed that

British and French military experts will meet at Beirut on December 21, 1945, to draw up the details of a programme for evacuation by stages, with a corresponding regrouping of forces. One of the objects of this discussion will be to fix a very early date on which the withdrawal will begin.

It is understood that the evacuation of Syria shall be carried out *pari passu*, in such a way as to be completed at the same time by the British and French forces. The programme of evacuation will be drawn up in such a way that it will ensure the maintenance in the Levant of sufficient forces to guarantee security, until such time as the United Nations Organization has decided on the organization of collective security in this zone. Until these arrangements have been carried out the French Government will retain forces regrouped in the Lebanon.

His Majesty's Government in the United Kingdom and the French Government will inform the Lebanese and Syrian Governments of the details of the evacuation, and will invite those Governments to appoint as soon as possible representatives empowered to discuss the dispositions to be jointly agreed upon as a result of these decisions.[2]

Sir Alexander Cadogan told the United Nations Security Council on 15 February 1946 that 'the local Governments asked for an assurance that British troops would not withdraw from the Levant so long as other foreign troops remained, an assurance which, in the circumstances, His Majesty's Government gave, the more so as in our view it was in line with the spirit of the Agreement'.[3] When the military experts began their discussion, however, the French held to their interpretation that, 'while the French troops still in Syria were to be regrouped in cantonments in the Lebanon, the British troops there would be evacuated to 'Irāq, Transjordan, or Palestine', so that the French troops in the Levant 'would not be placed in numerical inferiority . . . pending the decisions of Uno regarding the future security of the Levant'; the British military authorities, on the other hand, appeared to propose that the British troops in Syria should also be regrouped in the Levant, where they would far outnumber the French. 'In that case', the Paris correspondent of *The Times* commented, 'nothing would have been done for French prestige . . . and the value of

[1] *Figaro*, 26 October, *Monde*, 27 October 1946; Richard Wyndham in *News of the World*, 4 November 1946.
[2] Text in *The Times*, 22 December, *Monde*, 23–24 December 1945.
[3] U.N., Security Council: *Official Records*, 1st year, 1st series, no. 1, p. 295.

the agreements, particularly that which deals with the harmonization of policies, for the preservation of common interests, would be almost negligible.'[1] On 26 December, however, the Lebanese Legation in Paris stated:

Lebanon, enjoying the same rights as all the member States of the United Nations Organization, demands the total and simultaneous withdrawal of all the foreign troops stationed on her territory. She intends to maintain friendly relations with all the states of the world in the framework of her obligations and rights as a member of the United Nations and the Arab League, and refuses to be a bridgehead directed against the independence of the Arab countries.[2]

The Lebanese Prime Minister, Sāmī as-Sulh, a cousin of Riyād as-Sulh who had led the nationalist 'revolt' against the French in the autumn of 1943,[3] stated on the 28th that the Lebanese delegation to the United Nations General Assembly, meeting in London in January, had been empowered to raise the question of the Anglo-French occupation of their country.[4] *The Times* diplomatic correspondent admitted on the 28th that the wording of the Agreement of 13 December 'if anything . . . supports the French contention'; but, it was stated, 'it was made clear to the French Government during the discussions that the Lebanese objected to the presence in their country of French troops only, and that the British Government had accordingly promised to retain some troops there as well until the final withdrawal of both'.[5]

On 31 December the rising tension in the Levant was heightened by the disembarkation at Beirut of between 150 and 210 French troops, ostensibly as replacements for a larger number of men, which aroused memories of the troop arrivals which had provoked the crisis of the previous May; and simultaneously General Oliva-Roget, who had been responsible for the shelling of Damascus during that crisis,[6] arrived at Mizza airfield outside that city. It was explained later that he was bound for Beirut, to collect the effects he had had to leave behind on his hasty enforced departure in the previous June; but the rumours to which this coincidence gave rise (notably that the newly arrived troops were Senegalese) brought out the nationalist students (who had already been demonstrating against the Anglo-French Agreement) and others in a general strike in Damascus,

---

[1] *The Times*, 27 December 1945. The British forces in the Levant were estimated at 25,000–30,000, as against French forces numbering some 8,000, of whom half were a remnant of the locally recruited Troupes Spéciales (see *Survey* for 1939–46: *The Middle East in the War*, pp. 286–8, 303) who had elected to remain under the French colours (*Scotsman*, 18 December, *Combat*, 27 December 1945).

[2] *Combat*, 27 December 1945.

[3] *Survey* for 1939–46: *The Middle East in the War*, pp. 275 seqq.

[4] *New York Times*, 29 December 1945, report from Beirut.

[5] *Scotsman*, London correspondent, 31 December 1945.

[6] *Survey* for 1939–46: *The Middle East in the War*, pp. 298–300.

Aleppo, and Beirut.[1] In the following days it was confirmed that the Soviet Minister in Beirut, Daniel Solod, had verbally expressed to the Lebanese Foreign Minister his Government's disapproval of the Anglo-French Agreement, and it was also stated that the United States equally disapproved.[2] While the deadlock between the French and British Governments over the interpretation of their 'agreement' continued, the Syrian and Lebanese Governments presented them on 10 January with a joint note demanding the 'speedy and complete removal' of their forces, and on 4 February delivered a letter to the Secretary-General of the United Nations, asking him 'to bring this dispute to the attention of the Security Council and to request it to adopt a decision recommending the total and simultaneous evacuation of the foreign troops from the territories of Syria and Lebanon'.[3] When the discussion of the complaint opened on 15 February, after the Lebanese and Syrian delegates had stated their case, the French Foreign Minister, Bidault, claimed that

France has not wavered in her policy of bringing the two States . . . to full independence. . . . The Agreement of 13 December is not interpreted by the signatories as implying any intention to maintain troops in the Levant indefinitely in the absence of a decision on the part of the Security Council. My Government is prepared to examine the question with the Syrian and Lebanese Governments with a view to settling with them the details of this solution. I therefore ask the representatives of the United Nations, in view of the efforts which have been made to bring about the independence of Syria and Lebanon, to place their trust in France to ensure, in conjunction with Great Britain, the solution of this problem.[4]

After Sir Alexander Cadogan had briefly explained the British position and Stettinius had expressed 'the hope . . . that the desires of the Syrian and Lebanese Governments that the foreign troops in their territory should depart at the earliest practicable moment shall be met by means of a mutually satisfactory agreement', Vyshinsky critically examined Bidault's offer 'to examine the question' with the two Governments 'with a view to settling the details with them'. Was not this an echo, he asked, of General Beynet's memorandum to the two Governments of 18 May 1945, with its

---

[1] Clifton Daniel, reporting from Damascus in *New York Times*, 2 and 3 January 1946.

[2] 'Liberator' (Jon Kimche) in *Observer*, 6 and 13 January 1946; cf. *Monde*, 13–14 January 1946. The Soviet Government had already raised the question of the future of the Levant States at the Potsdam Conference (Fleet Admiral W. D. Leahy: *I Was There* (London, Gollancz, 1950), pp. 464, 499).

[3] U.N., Security Council: *Official Records*, 1st year, 1st series, Supplement no. 1, pp. 82–83; cf. U.N., General Assembly: *Official Records*, 1st session, 1st part, pp. 248, 255 (19 January 1946). In Paris the de Gaullist *Pays* remarked: 'There are heavy odds that Soviet policy is, to say the least, not a stranger to this latest resolution', and the Right-wing *Époque* described the note as 'the latest amplification of Vyshinsky's diversionist manœuvre' (Reuter, reported by the *Star*, 6 February 1946).

[4] U.N., Security Council: *Official Records*, 1st year, 1st series, no. 1, pp. 290–4.

unacceptable conditions of the maintenance of French cultural, economic, and strategic privileges?[1] The Anglo-French Agreement of 13 December was likewise a violation of the sovereignty and independence of the two states. As for the claim that the foreign troops were necessary 'to guarantee security', 'it will appear that British troops were concentrated there to prevent disorders resulting from the presence of French troops, while French troops were being kept there because the British troops would not leave'. On the following day the Lebanese and Syrian delegates asked what negotiations, as implied by Bidault's remarks, were necessary in connexion with the proposed evacuation. Bidault replied:

Either there is a dispute, in which case we are required under Article 33 of the Charter to negotiate with a view to seeking a solution of the dispute; or else, if there are no negotiations and if there is a refusal to negotiate, the assumption must be that there is no dispute. . . .

As I see it, what has been happening at this table in the last few hours is this: although there is no dispute on fundamentals, an attempt is being made to secure, in addition to full satisfaction, something resembling a vote of censure against France. . . . France would not under any circumstances be prepared to accept such a stigma.

The Lebanese delegate rejoined:

Mr. Bidault said that France could not evade the responsibilities for security conferred upon her under the League of Nations mandate[2]. . . . We no longer recognize anybody's right to argue on the basis of that mandate, and in particular we resent any attempt to claim privileges under the mandate.

. . . We are not seeking to censure France; what we do wish and ask for are clear provisions, because the main cause of our former difficulties was just the obscurity of our relations, of the requests which were made to us, and of the basis on which we were asked to negotiate.

The Syrian delegate added, rather more bluntly: 'The Syrian Government is not asking to enter into negotiations on any subject under the pressure of armed forces in its territory. It is obliged to say that, because of the last experience it had, it is afraid that such things may be repeated.' After further discussion the Lebanese delegate said that he would be prepared to accept the following resolution, proposed by Stettinius, provided that the italicized words were included:

The Security Council . . .
Expresses its confidence that the foreign troops in Syria and Lebanon will be

[1] *Survey* for 1939–46: *The Middle East in the War*, p. 295.

[2] Bidault had said: 'France was given a mandate by the former international organization; that is to say, she was given certain responsibilities. When France . . . decided, in the middle of the war, to proclaim the independence of Syria and Lebanon . . . we were confronted with a vacuum. . . . In order to fill this gap, the Agreement of 13 December 1945 proposed a system of collective security.'

withdrawn as soon as practicable, and that *technical* negotiations *exclusively* to that end will be undertaken by the parties without delay; and requests the parties to inform it of the results of the negotiations, *as well as of the final date of withdrawal*.

When Bevin objected that these amendments were not practical, because 'there are other matters which have to be settled, some of them quite vital . . . as my Syrian and Lebanese friends know', the Lebanese delegate replied: 'It would be a dangerous thing for us, as we saw on 18 May 1945, if we were offered a simultaneous discussion on cultural questions and on strategic bases; that would be entirely unacceptable.' After further discussion he defined his position more clearly:

The ways and means of the withdrawal, its technical aspect, and the time-limit, those matters we shall be very happy to discuss. But I must say once again that anything extraneous to the withdrawal of troops is ruled out of the discussion. We are prepared to have discussions on any subject, whether economic, cultural or social; we shall pass all conventions as soon as we have reached agreement, but we definitely cannot agree that the political conditions inserted in the Agreement of 13 December should continue to be relied upon.

The Syrian delegate was even more precise:

I express the views of my Government when I say that, for the time being, it prefers that no other subject should be opened for negotiation with France as long as troops are in our country. When the troops have gone, we shall be able to express our desire to open negotiations on any matter on which we may be asked to negotiate, and we shall achieve results which will enable good relations to be maintained.

After a number of resolutions, including a Soviet amendment which recommended the British and French Governments to withdraw their troops immediately, had failed to get the necessary seven votes, the original unamended United States resolution received that number of votes but was vetoed by Vyshinsky 'because the amendments which would have enabled me to vote for it have not been accepted'. The resolution was therefore lost, but the French and British Foreign Ministers announced their willingness to carry out the majority decision as expressed in the vote.[1]

Meanwhile, de Gaulle's resignation of the French premiership on 20 January was believed to have eased the relations between the French and British Governments,[2] though official French opinion continued to hope that the Security Council would see fit to charge France with the eventual construction of a collective security system in the Levant.[3] Anglo-French military conversations on the withdrawal began in Paris

[1] U.N., Security Council: *Official Records*, 1st year, 1st series, no. 1, pp. 271–368.
[2] Cf. *Neue Zürcher Zeitung* London correspondent, 19 February 1946.
[3] *The Times* Paris correspondent, 1 March 1946.

on 1 March and resulted within three days in an agreement for the simultaneous withdrawal of their forces from Syria, to begin on 11 March and be completed by 30 April.[1] On 9 March, while it was stated that the British would have left Lebanon by 30 June and the command and the bulk of the French troops would have moved to Tripoli by 31 August, a French Foreign Office spokesman announced that their evacuation might not be completed until 1 April 1947.

The Foreign Office spokesman insisted at great length and with a wealth of detail that the year's delay resulted entirely from technical details of transporting troops and material. He admitted that there were only 8,000 French troops in Lebanon, but cited what he insisted were extensive installations that must be dismantled and salvaged by the French.

He referred to the aviation workshops at Rayak as one of these installations. He also referred to the engineering and tank and armored car parks at Beirut, although it had been said earlier that the largest part of the material in Lebanon was completely obsolete.

The spokesman said that the date of April 1 next year could be considered as the very outside date when all the French and their equipment would be out of Lebanon. This date, he said, might be replaced by a much earlier one if the Lebanese cooperated effectively by furnishing laborers and administrators for the evacuation project.

He conceded that the British had opposed the April 1 date advanced by the French, but said they had promised, nevertheless, to aid with shipping. The French, he said, were prepared to open discussions with the Lebanese with a view to reconciling them to the year's delay after the conferences here had given every indication of an earlier evacuation date.

The spokesman said the French did not desire to remain in Lebanon one week longer than was necessary and would be out sooner than the date stipulated if they had near-by territory, such as British Palestine, now so convenient for the evacuation of the British forces. . . . Beirut was 3,000 kilometers from Marseille, with attendant transportation difficulties.[2]

The Lebanese Government were not satisfied with this proposal, and after further discussion between their representatives and the French it was agreed that the French troops would leave the country by 31 August, but that a mission of thirty French officers and 300 technicians would stay to supervise the evacuation of the remainder of the material by 31 December.[3] A national holiday was held in Syria on 17 April to mark the completion of the withdrawal of the foreign troops from that country; but French suspicions that Great Britain was trying to replace France in the Levant States persisted, and found some grounds in the activities of certain British business men there.[4] The British Government declined a Syrian request

---

[1] *The Times*, 5 March 1946.   [2] *New York Times* Paris correspondent, 10 March 1946.
[3] Texts in *Monde*, 26 March 1946.
[4] Contrast Brigadier J. G. Frere: 'Britain and Syria', *Spectator*, 19 April 1946, pp. 393–4, with Pertinax, pseud., in *New York Times*, 27 May 1946.

for a British military mission to continue the training of the Syrian army, and though a Brigadier Fox later undertook this somewhat thankless task[1] he did not remain very long.

On 2 July G.H.Q. Middle East announced that, except for a small liquidation staff which left on 30 September, British troops had completed their evacuation of Lebanon, and on 31 August a similar announcement was made in respect of the French troops, with the exception of their liquidation staff. A correspondent wrote: 'The departure of French troops has ... begun to bring the French position in the Levant into its proper perspective. In Syria there is still uncompromising bitterness against the French ... but in the Lebanon, now that the French are no longer to be feared, they are free to be admired again.'[2] The British sold to the Lebanese Government the Tripoli–Rās un-Naqūra railway, which the Middle East Forces had constructed during the war, for 5 million Lebanese pounds, or one-tenth of the sum they originally asked;[3] but there remained the much larger question of the French Government's properties in Lebanon.[4] The Lebanese Government were aggrieved that the French Custodian of Enemy Properties, when requested by the Lebanese Government in January 1946 to transfer these (Italian) properties to them, had instead handed them over directly to the Italian Vice-Consul in Jerusalem, and that the French wished to maintain the French magistrates temporarily in the Mixed Courts.[5] There remained the question of French Government property in Lebanon, on which the Lebanese Foreign Minister said in an interview with a French journalist that France ought to hand over the airfield at Rayāq and an ordnance depot.[6] The French attitude, on the other hand, was that any transfer of property 'must be made by agreement and at a reasonable price approved by the French Parliament. . . . The mandate over the Levant States has cost France enough in disappointments for us to ask that its liquidation should not add a new burden to our budget.'[7]

Since Lebanon had achieved her independence her Government had expressed their disapproval of the Consular Masses which for several centuries the Maronite Church had been in the habit of celebrating in the presence of the French diplomatic or consular representatives. The Government now considered that the ceremony was a survival from a past that had been left behind, and expressed the wish that the Maronite

---

[1] *New York Times*, 21 March, *Reynolds News*, 13 October 1946.

[2] Robert Stephens in *Scotsman*, 21 October 1946.

[3] É. Sablier in *Monde*, 8 November 1946.

[4] Cf. Maurice Ferro: 'Que doit faire l'État de ses propriétés libanaises?', ibid. 26 September 1946.

[5] Cf. Great Britain, Foreign Office: *Exchange of Notes between the United Kingdom and Syria concerning the Settlement of Pending Cases before the Syrian Courts*, Cmd. 7140 (London, H.M.S.O., 1947).

[6] Maurice Ferro in *Monde*, 29 November 1946.

[7] Editorial, ibid. 6 December 1946.

Church (which represented less than 30 per cent. of the Lebanese population)[1] should discontinue the tradition. The Maronite Archbishop of
Beirut, Mgr. Ignatius Mubārak, was ready to do so at Easter 1947, but
was disavowed by the Maronite Patriarch, Mgr. Antūn 'Arīda, who had
consistently expressed the view that 'since Lebanon is the Christians' only
refuge in the Levant, her independence must be specially protected by
France' against Syrian Muslim encroachment.[2] As a compromise it was
agreed that the Consular Mass should be celebrated, not as formerly in
Beirut at the Maronite Cathedral, but at the Patriarchal residence at
Bukarkī (Bkerké).[3]

It had been suggested in France that an agreement on the outstanding
questions might be deferred until after the forthcoming elections, due in
1947, had given Lebanon a government 'deriving from a freer poll than
that of 1943';[4] but in fact the elections of 25 May 1947 'were generally
regarded as an extravagant farce. Even Government supporters agree on
this, though they argue that the gerrymandering was unnecessary, since
the government candidates would in any case have won fairly easily'.[5]
After this defeat of the friends of France financial negotiations were begun
on 1 October in Paris between representatives of France, Lebanon, and
Syria. The Syro-Lebanese note issue, now standing at the equivalent of
23,000 million francs, was managed by the French-controlled Banque de
Syrie et du Liban against assets held in Paris. The French offered to
transfer 7,000 million francs in merchandise or European currencies within
the next two years, to transfer French properties in the Levant whose
value they estimated at 2,000 million francs, and to guarantee the remainder for ten years against the devaluation of the franc. The Lebanese
Government accepted this offer, but the Syrians maintained that in Janu-

---

[1] About 37 per cent. in all belonged to Churches in communion with Rome, and followed the
Maronite lead in their relations with France (cf. Pierre Rondot: *Les Institutions politiques du Liban*
(Paris, Institut d'Études de l'Orient Contemporain, 1947), p. 29).

[2] Cf. the anti-Muslim sentiments ascribed to Mgr. Mubārak in an interview with Gerold
Frank (*Palestine Post* (Zionist), 21 March 1946): 'I am very much in favour of Zionism because
I have the good of Palestine at heart. If you wish to follow the desires of Muslim Arabs, they
want to dominate the country and to cast the Christians out. I tell you frankly that if you oppose
Zionism in Palestine it means returning the people to the domination of savagery. . . . We realize
that here is a struggle between civilization and regression, and that the Jews represent civilization.
We Christian Lebanese prefer civilization to regression. . . . The Jews in Palestine and the
Christians in Palestine can work together. If the Arab Muslims would wish to assist it would
be magnificent, but unfortunately they are opposed to everything meaning progress'; cf. Lorna
Lindsley's report of another interview with the Archbishop, reporting him as saying: 'We wish
more Jews would come to Lebanon, we need them' ('Lebanon Looks to the West', ibid. 17 May
1946).

[3] *Bourse Égyptienne*, 16 April 1947.

[4] Maurice Ferro in *Monde*, 26 September 1946.

[5] Kevin Hyland: 'Middle East "Switzerland"', *Scotsman*, 30 September 1947; cf. Clifton
Daniel, reporting from Beirut, *New York Times*, 26 May 1947. The pro-French 'National
Lebanese Bloc Party' published a *Black Book of the Lebanese Elections* (New York, Phoenicia Press,
1947).

ary 1944 General Catroux had pledged France to protect the Syro-Lebanese currency against devaluation at all times.

They balked at the value the French placed on their property, maintaining that much of it had been sold under duress during the mandate period. They protested against France's charging them for part of the expenses of the Troupes Spéciales maintained here during the mandate. And they were angered by what they said were efforts by the French to use the situation to revive their trade and cultural interests.[1]

The Syrian Government accordingly on 31 January 1948 declared their independence of the franc bloc, while an agreement between France and Lebanon was signed on 7 February, in which the French made concessions to the Lebanese, notably in undertaking to take a large proportion of Lebanese exports in order to close the extremely adverse balance of trade with France.

The Syrian and Lebanese Governments had been all the more inclined to part company on this question of their relations with France because they had failed to agree on the apportioning between them of the economic 'Common Interests' which were a legacy of the mandatory period, and notably on customs policy.[2] Thus the war-time coalition of the Syrian and Lebanese politicians to secure their independence of the French had soon yielded to the stresses of political and economic particularism; and, though France's influence in Muslim Syria continued to stand at a minimum, at least until the overthrow of the National Bloc Government in March 1949, her influence amid 'the cosmopolitan luxury and ease of Beirut' and among the Christians of Lebanon generally was 'steadily reaffirmed' in a variety of ways.[3] During the brief Syrian dictatorship of Husnī az-Za'īm (30 March–14 August 1949) French influence in Syria notably increased,[4] and, when az-Za'īm was put to death by a rival military junta, the usually responsible *Monde* did not scruple on 16 August 1949 to impute the responsibility for his judicial murder to 'the clan Sterling, Frere, Spears, Glubb, and Company for whom a genuinely national regime in Syria was an anomaly that had to be removed'. It was hoped, however, that the declaration of a common Middle East policy by the British, French, and United States Governments on 25 May 1950[5] had finally laid the ghost of this historical rivalry.

---

[1] Dana Adams Schmidt in *New York Times*, 1 February 1948.

[2] Cf. 'Pour une refonte de nos rapports économiques avec la Syrie en 1948', *Le Commerce du Levant*, 14 January 1948.

[3] *The Economist* Cairo correspondent, 24 June 1950, p. 1391.

[4] See Alford Carleton: 'The Syrian Coups d'État of 1949', *Middle East Journal*, January 1950, iv. 7–8.

[5] See below, pp. 312–13.

(ii) Anglo-Egyptian Relations

(a) THE BACKGROUND TO NEGOTIATIONS, 1945–6

We have seen in a previous volume of this series that, while in the last half-year of the Second World War Egyptian political opinion was pressing for a complete ending of Egyptian dependence on Britain through the withdrawal of British troops and authority from both Egypt and the Anglo-Egyptian Sudan,[1] British policy apparently remained static, either because (as at the close of the First World War) it was preoccupied with more pressing problems in other parts of the world, or because Churchill personally still tended to think of Egypt in terms of the former British protectorate.[2] The removal of the British war-time headquarters and large garrisons from Egypt's two principal cities, Cairo and Alexandria, is said to have been a matter of contention between the Foreign Office and the British military authorities;[3] and, while Lord Altrincham, who as Sir Edward Grigg had been British Minister Resident in the Middle East until 12 August 1945, afterwards declared that early in September he had advised the new British Labour Government to announce such a withdrawal immediately and to put it into effect as expeditiously as conditions allowed,[4] it was stated that the British Embassy in Cairo advised against such a gesture. A subsequent article in the *Round Table*[5] asserted that at the end of the war Egypt 'was in a mood to respond generously to generous treatment' and to offer Britain 'the willing co-operation of a grateful Egypt'; but this seems an improbable outcome of seventy years of disillusioning by unhappy Anglo-Egyptian relations. There were indications that the advent of the Labour Government to power in Britain may have been too eagerly interpreted in Egypt as the sign of a readiness to yield, and in the existing Egyptian mood of making maximum demands the British officials in Cairo may have felt it their duty to apply the brake rather than the accelerator. The Embassy asked the Egyptian Prime Minister, Mahmūd an-Nuqrāshī, in the autumn of 1945 not to call at that time for negotiations for a revision of the Anglo-Egyptian Treaty of 1936; but Nuqrāshī was already under increasing pressure for immediate action. The powerful Wafd Party, which had been thrust into opposition in October 1944 and kept there as a result of the election of January 1945,[6]

---

[1] See *Survey* for 1939–46: *The Middle East in the War*, pp. 267–8.

[2] Ibid. pp. 197, note 3, 260.

[3] For the reluctance of the military authorities, even after the conclusion of the Anglo-Egyptian Treaty of 1936, to withdraw the garrison from Cairo see Sir David Kelly: *The Ruling Few* (London, Hollis & Carter, 1952), pp. 261–2.

[4] See *Sunday Times*, 19 May 1946; 21 May 1946, H.L.Deb. 5th ser., vol. 141, coll. 348–9; 30 July 1951, H.C.Deb. 5th ser., vol. 491, col. 1049.

[5] 'Anglo-Egyptian Relations', *Round Table*, March 1951, p. 115.

[6] See *Survey* for 1939–46: *The Middle East in the War*, p. 263, note 4.

would lose no opportunity to make trouble for the Government; the extremist groups were by definition anti-British; and the cry for immediate treaty revision was upheld by a section of Nuqrāshī's Cabinet, led by the Finance Minister, Makram ʿUbaid. An Egyptian note was accordingly delivered on 20 December 1945 which argued that the restrictions on Egyptian sovereignty maintained by the 1936 treaty were of a transitory character arising out of a past international crisis; Egypt's war-time collaboration had surely dispelled the British mistrust which had not yet entirely disappeared in 1936; and Egypt would 'shrink from no sacrifice in order, in the immediate future, to place her military potential in a state enabling her to repel aggression pending the arrival of the reinforcements of her allies and of the United Nations'. For the British Foreign Office, on the other hand, aggression was not a future hypothesis but a present menace, in the form of the recent proclamation of a Communist govern-ment in Persian Āzarbāijān[1] and the Soviet pressure on Turkey;[2] and they answered the Egyptian note on 27 January 1946 with the observation that, while the British Ambassador would be instructed to open preliminary conversations intended to place Anglo-Egyptian relations 'on a footing of full and free partnership, as between equals', 'the essential soundness of the fundamental principles' underlying the 1936 treaty had been demon-strated by the Second World War.[3]

From the opening of their post-war relationship, therefore, the Egyptian and British Governments were operating (as a subsequent leading article in *The Times* was to express it) on different wave-lengths: the Egyptians were concerned with questions of national prestige and aspiration to the exclusion of the realities of regional power-politics, while the British were concerned with the new Soviet threat to the Middle East *status quo*. Since this serious threat had arisen at a time when the sapping of Britain's strength by the war was making itself increasingly felt, the British were in-clined to give first consideration to the Russian menace in dealing with the problems of Egyptian or Zionist nationalism, and therefore to temporize over these local problems. Against this British temporizing, and against the Egyptian Government for its apparent acquiescence in it, demon-strations were already being organized in Cairo and Alexandria. The demonstrators were drawn from the less responsible members of the too numerous student body, organized by the Wafd or belonging to such extremist associations as the Ikhwān al-Muslimūn (the Muslim Brother-hood) or Misr al-Fatāh (Young Egypt), and from an urban proletariat whose enrolment in trade unions had recently been undertaken by leaders who themselves were subject to Communist influence, notably by virtue of their representation at the Paris conference of the World Federation of

[1] See above, pp. 58–60.   [2] See above, pp. 21–27.
[3] Texts of the Egyptian and British notes in *The Times*, 31 January 1946.

Trades Unions in September 1945.[1] After this conference a significantly named Workers' Committee of National Liberation had been formed in Egypt, and this had then established contact with the extremist student leaders and established a 'National Committee of Workers and Students' whose leading figure, Mustafā Mūsā, was afterwards to become a Left-wing Wafdist deputy. The reopening of the Fu'ād I University in Cairo on 9 February 1946 was the signal for rioting[2] by students and workers in Cairo, Alexandria, and other towns, with demands for the dismissal of the Government. It was afterwards stated that at this point the British Ambassador, Lord Killearn (who had on four occasions between 1940 and 1944 exerted his influence upon King Fārūq to obtain or retain an Egyptian Government amenable to British policy),[3] informed the King of the British Government's doubts of Nuqrāshī's ability to maintain order for the negotiation of a revised treaty. At all events, Nuqrāshī resigned on 13 February,[4] and the King entrusted the formation of a new Government to the wealthy and politically independent Ismā'īl Sidqī, who had established a reputation as a strong Prime Minister in 1930–3. In calling upon him, however, Fārūq had spoken of the popular desire for demonstrations as 'a healthy manifestation of the people's ambition to realize their just claims',[5] and Sidqī had accordingly removed the ban on demonstrations which Nuqrāshī had recently imposed. The 'National Committee of Workers and Students' responded by holding on 21 February a general strike in which they called on their followers to avoid disturbances or destruction of property but to show Britain and the world 'that Egypt is ready for a struggle which will end only when the sixty-five-years' occupation is terminated'. Extensive burning and looting of British property in Cairo accompanied the strike, however, and when further demonstrations were held in Alexandria on 4 March to commemorate the 'evacuation martyrs' a mob set fire to a British military police outpost and stoned to death two of its five occupants. These incidents were followed by public

[1] See Dr. Zaki Badaoui: *Les Problèmes du travail et les organisations ouvrières en Égypte* (Alexandria, Société de Publications Égyptiennes, 1948), pp. 153–4, 168–70; William J. Handley: 'The Labor Movement in Egypt', *Middle East Journal*, July 1949, iii. 283–5.

[2] A correspondent afterwards referred to the 'students and schoolchildren whose knowledge of international affairs matches their immaturity, the "two-piastre boys" who are a kind of stage army of paid supporters, the idlers and hooligans hoping for opportunities to create disorder and then loot' ('Anglo-Egyptian Relations', *Round Table*, March 1951, p. 114).

[3] See *Survey* for 1939–46: *The Middle East in the War*, pp. 39, 208–10, 259.

[4] Nuqrāshī afterwards accused the British Government, before the Security Council, of bringing about the dismissal of an Egyptian Cabinet 'in 1945'. The British delegate referred to the matter as an oral communication by the Ambassador to King Fārūq 'about current difficulties between the United Kingdom and Egypt. . . . The Ambassador's representations did not lead to the dismissal of the Egyptian Cabinet' (11 and 13 August 1947, U.N., Security Council: *Official Records*, 2nd year, no 73, p. 1866; no. 75, p. 1953).

[5] Quoted by the Secretary for the Dominions in the House of Lords, 26 February 1946 (H.L.Deb. 5th ser., vol. 139, col. 873).

exchanges in which the British and Egyptian Governments each tried to place upon the other's nationals the responsibility for the violence and loss of life which had occurred; and the world Communist press made capital out of the situation.

(b) Negotiations in Cairo and London, 1946

It was amid the continuation of these disorders, manifesting themselves in bomb outrages against British troops and civilians, that Sidqī sought to form a delegation composed of all parties, as in 1935, for negotiations with Britain. The Wafd, however, made their participation conditional on their having majority representation, with their leader, Mustafā an-Nahhās, as chairman of the delegation, and on a guarantee of new elections. Sidqī thereupon excluded the Wafd from a delegation, otherwise representative of all parties and leading personalities, which he succeeded in forming on 8 March, and made a further show of firmness by suppressing three Wafdist newspapers and ordering the arrest of the leader and four other members of the terrorist Misr al-Fatāh organization. According to the autobiography which Sidqī subsequently published,[1] the failure of the British Government to announce promptly the names of their delegation caused much surprise in Egyptian political circles, and it was not until 30 March that the new British Ambassador (Sir Ronald Campbell, who had succeeded Lord Killearn a month before) stated in reply to Sidqī's inquiry that he himself was to lead a delegation composed of senior military experts and Embassy officials. Sidqī argued very strongly that the members of the Egyptian delegation were among the most distinguished figures in Egyptian political life and expected to negotiate with British personalities of the same order; and, he added: 'People in Egypt believe, and will not forget, that the policy adopted during the last decade and especially during the war—a policy which did not leave a good impression—was planned and executed by the very Embassy officials whom you now wish to have as your political assistants.'[2] On 2 April, accordingly, the British Foreign Secretary announced that he would lead the delegation, although the earlier part of the discussions would be entrusted to the Secretary for Air, Lord Stansgate, and the British Ambassador; Sir Kinahan Cornwallis, British Ambassador to 'Irāq in 1941–5 and at this time head of the Middle East secretariat of the Foreign Office, would be the chief political adviser, and the three Commanders-in-Chief in the Middle East would be the military advisers. The appointment of Lord Stansgate was publicly welcomed by Sidqī with the remark that 'as Mr. Wedgwood Benn, he defended

---

[1] *Mudhākarātī* (Cairo, Dār ul-Hilāl, 1950; in Arabic). The short passages quoted in translation from this work have been furnished by Mr. Emile Marmorstein, who is engaged in making a complete translation.

[2] Ibid. pp. 61–62.

the Egyptian cause in and out of Parliament just after World War One, when few other Britons spoke favourably on behalf of my country. Thus Wedgwood Benn's name is always remembered as a ray of hope in Egypt.'[1]

When the delegation arrived in Cairo on 15 April, the first thing which it heard from Sidqī, according to Lord Stansgate's subsequent account, was: 'You can have no agreement with Egypt except on the basis of evacuation.' The British military advisers, however, sought to awaken the Egyptian delegation to the threat to the security of the whole Middle East inherent in the Soviet cold war pressure on Persia, Turkey, and Greece; they emphasized the vital importance, as a base for the defence of the Middle East, of the military installations and communications of Lower Egypt, with its abundant supply of skilled, semi-skilled, and unskilled labour which had proved so serviceable in two world wars; they urged the Egyptians to think of the defence of the region as a whole, not of the narrower interests of the Nile Valley, and, since Egypt's unaided resources were inadequate for this wider concept, to accept British technical specialists in civilian clothes in peace-time, with the maintenance of a regional headquarters in the Canal Zone.[2] The vision of the Egyptian delegation, however, tended to be restricted to the narrow confines of their Nile Valley, and the desire to put an end to the British occupation excluded any wider considerations. Moreover, the continuing student demonstrations and bomb outrages, and the ever present risk of assassination, were deterrents to any divergence from the basic Egyptian demands; and on 7 May the British Government sought to break the deadlock by offering

the withdrawal of all British . . . forces from Egyptian territory, and to settle in negotiation the stages and date of completion of this withdrawal, and the arrangements to be made by the Egyptian Government to make possible mutual assistance in time of war or imminent threat of war in accordance with the alliance.[3]

This offer was debated twice in the Commons, and once in the Lords, in the course of the next seventeen days. While some supporters of the Government who had served in the Middle East during the war argued that the Canal could be equally well defended from bases not on Egyptian territory, Opposition speakers pointed to the impermanence of Britain's tenure of both the obvious alternatives, namely Palestine and Cyrenaica,

[1] *The Times*, 22 April 1946. British Conservative circles were correspondingly critical of Lord Stansgate's appointment.

[2] Lord Stansgate afterwards asserted: 'Had we been able on our arrival to announce that in future British troops would only be in Egypt by Egyptian consent, we could have had a treaty in a month' ('The Egyptian Point of View', in the *Listener*, 25 January 1951, p. 127); but he said nothing at this point about the Sudan question, which was just as important to the Egyptian nationalists; see below, pp. 125-7.

[3] The Prime Minister, H.C.Deb. 5th ser., vol. 422, coll. 781-2.

and the inadequacy of Cyprus. Churchill and Eden, with the experience born of the Egyptian Government's hesitation in the crisis of June 1940[1] (although they did not refer directly to this incident), gave a warning of the danger of relying solely on a British right to reoccupy installations in a time of possible future international emergency:

The Great Power with whom we shall be in dispute would, of course, say to the Egyptian Government: 'We should regard any movement into the Canal zone of British Forces as an unfriendly act.' Can anyone suppose that the Egyptian Government, confronted with this situation and not desiring anyhow to have British troops or Air Forces in the Canal zone, will not refuse permission for us to re-enter? . . .

Can one imagine the British Government in such a situation, when the dread issue of peace or war in a renewed world struggle may be hanging in the balance, forcing the issue? . . . It is a positive act, an act which will be widely regarded and denounced as an act of aggression, as an act destroying the last hopes of peace.[2]

Herbert Morrison inadvertently let slip that the Government had acceded 'reluctantly' to the Egyptian request for an offer of withdrawal as a preliminary to a study of the future of the Anglo-Egyptian alliance and military aid; the Prime Minister said: 'If the whole matter breaks down, there is still, of course, the Treaty'; and Bevin wound up the series of debates by giving the assurance:

There must not be a vacuum. If the Egyptian Government try to force a situation in which there is a vacuum—meaning that we have gone and that there is nothing there for security instead, regional defence or other organization—to that I can never agree. But I have offered . . . a new basis of approach, in which I believe. Perhaps partnership is the wrong term, but it is a joint effort for mutual defence not only in the interests of Great Britain and her Commonwealth, but in the interests ultimately of the contribution to what I hope will yet become a United Nations defence for the security of the world.[3]

Meanwhile, the whole of the Egyptian press, with the exception of the Sa'dist *ad-Dastūr*, had commented unfavourably on the British offer. The Wafdist Opposition condemned the principle of the Anglo-Egyptian alliance as such, and others expressed suspicion of the condition that Britain must have facilities in Egypt in case of war or the threat of war. On 21 May Britain presented to the Egyptian Government what Nuqrāshī subsequently described to the Security Council as 'a draft of a treaty of alliance, together with a draft of a military treaty which incorporated in substance the burdensome and objectionable military conditions imposed in the 1936 Treaty'.[4] The writer of the article in the *Round Table* already

---

[1] *Survey* for 1939–46: *The Middle East in the War*, p. 39.
[2] Churchill, 24 May 1946, H.C.Deb. 5th ser., vol. 423, coll. 774–5.
[3] H.C.Deb. 5th ser., vol. 423, col. 788.
[4] U.N., Security Council, 5 August 1947 (*Official Records*, 2nd year, no. 70, p. 1747).

quoted remarked that the Egyptian delegation soon saw, and saw with resentment, that the Foreign Office were 'treating Egypt as a slippery customer who had to be made to sign an absolutely watertight bond. . . . More caution could not have been taken in dealing with a defeated enemy.'[1] The recollection of the attempts made in June 1940 and February 1942[2] to evade Egypt's responsibilities under the treaty was, no doubt, still fresh in the minds of the Foreign Office, and they may well have felt that it was unsafe to leave too much to future Egyptian goodwill in view of the cold war that was already being waged on the northern fringes of the Middle East.

Meanwhile, the tactical coalition between the Wafd and both the extreme nationalists and the Communists[3] continued its active opposition both to the Anglo-Egyptian alliance and to Sidqī personally, successfully exploiting the social unrest which had been growing as a consequence of the cessation of the war-time demand for labour, now aggravated by the beginning of the withdrawal of British troops. It was already estimated that there were at least 200,000 unemployed, while those in work, having been organized in embryonic trade unions during the war, refused to recognize the present decline in the demand for labour and not only tried to enforce a forty-hour week by stay-in strikes but also demanded that employers should be compelled to maintain production regardless of fluctuations in the demand for their goods. The Communist-inspired Workers' Committee of National Liberation had renamed itself the Workers' Congress and ambitiously claimed to have federated the entire trade union movement. Amid strikes of state telegraph workers, government engineers, and teachers, and the threat of a general strike, the Government on 9 July approved a bill imposing heavy penalties for strikes by state employees; and, since the Wafd and Makrams' Kutla party had called for a general strike on the 11th (the anniversary of the Royal Navy's destruction of the Alexandria forts in 1882, which had been the overture to the British occupation), there were large-scale police raids on the premises of Wafdists and suspected Communists. Eleven ostensibly educational, scientific, and cultural organizations were closed down. Among those arrested were an Italo-Egyptian Jew who maintained a

[1] *Round Table*, March 1951, p. 115. Some British observers thought that the Liberal and Sa'dist, and some of the independent, members of the Egyptian delegation were ready to collaborate with Britain, though not on Britain's terms, and that their position *vis-à-vis* their extreme colleagues and the Wafdist Opposition was made untenable by the attitude of the Foreign Office and its military advisers.

[2] See *Survey* for 1939–46: *The Middle East in the War*, pp. 39, 208–10.

[3] A writer in the Paris Communist *Humanité* of 23 July 1946 wrote approvingly of 'relatively progressive and nationalist forces, such as the Wafd'. In their flirtations at various times with Communist influences for the purpose of bringing pressure on Britain or (if the Wafd were in opposition) on the Egyptian Government of the day, the Wafdist leaders were manifestly playing with fire.

bookshop in a fashionable Cairo square for the display and sale of Marxist literature; a well-known Coptic writer of the radical school, Salāma Mūsā; and the Muslim editor of the Wafdist newspaper al-Wafd al-Misrī, whom a government organ described as 'an agent of the Third International who had been seeking a *rapprochement* between it and the Wafd'. His newspaper was suspended, as also were seven 'progressive' periodicals. The estimated number of those arrested rose to 220; and, although by November nearly all of them had been released without being formally charged, the 'cultural' organizations had been allowed to reopen, and the editor of al-Wafd al-Misrī was back at his desk, the incident gave the Communist *Humanité* the opportunity to indite an article under the title: 'Fascism in Egypt: Under Bevin's Flail.'

The three months of June, July, and August passed in Anglo-Egyptian negotiations amid the summer heat, interspersed with the exchange of formal notes and consultations with London. The Egyptian delegation was kept rigidly to its original demands by the stiffness of three or four of its members, among whom Makram rendered himself conspicuous by publicly announcing his determination to abide by those demands,[1] while the British delegation continued to propose compromises between their own original standpoint and that of the Egyptians. Thus, while the Egyptians insisted on the complete withdrawal of the British troops within a year (which was probably a physical impossibility on account of the extensiveness of their technical installations), and the British originally proposed a maximum of five years 'to avert the danger of a "defensive vacuum" between the departure of the last British forces and the Egyptian assumption of their commitments',[2] a British offer in mid-August proposed to strike the average at three years. Again, the Egyptians wished to limit the *casus foederis* of their joint defence obligations to an act of aggression committed against Egypt or one of her immediate neighbours, while the British sought to extend it to those countries on the fringe of the Middle East that were most threatened by the Soviet cold war—Persia, Turkey, and Greece; the British mid-August offer proposed a new concession to Egyptian fears, namely that in the case of those remoter countries not immediately bordering on Egypt her obligation should be restricted to 'consultation on the action to be taken'.

The small body of political opinion that was now emerging in the Anglo-Egyptian Sudan[3] contained an important element that hoped to achieve self-government with the help of Egypt and was therefore anxious that any Anglo-Egyptian agreement that resulted from the present negotiations

[1] In a press interview he attacked the proposed Joint Defence Board as 'certainly some sort of masked protectorate . . . practically an Anglo-Egyptian Control Board, or rather a joint Ministry of National Defence' (al-Ahrām, 17 July 1946).
[2] The Alexandria correspondent of the *Daily Telegraph* and the *Scotsman*, 5 August 1946.
[3] See *Survey* for 1939–46: *The Middle East in the War*, pp. 260–2.

should not fail to include provisions for the Sudan's future. A delegation, representing both this element and the rival group which traditionally mistrusted Egypt,[1] had therefore been sent to Cairo with compromise proposals for the setting up of a Sudanese democratic government which would be free to choose the form both of their country's future union with Egypt and of its alliance with Britain. The delegation had, however, split again into its two components when Egyptian politicians of all parties had insisted on its accepting the permanent union of the Sudan with Egypt under the Egyptian Crown; and those favouring independence of Egypt had returned to Khartūm.[2] The Egyptians repeated this claim to the British negotiators, who were bound by their Government's pledge that the Sudanese should be constitutionally consulted before any change was made in their country's status.[3] The British therefore suggested in mid-August that the question should be made the subject of separate negotiations, divorced from the defence of Egypt.

It was reported that the Egyptian Ambassador in London was told that the mid-August proposals represented Britain's final offer, and that both Sidqī and King Fārūq were prepared to accept it as such. The intransigent section of the Egyptian delegation led by Makram, refused, however, to be moved, and

consistently exploited their official knowledge of the negotiations to publicize confidential discussions and secret documents in an endeavour to prove that they are more patriotic than their colleagues. . . . The climax came . . . when a complete text of the latest Egyptian reply to the British proposals was published in an Arabic weekly paper before it was communicated to the British delegation, while concerted efforts were made to invest the document with the uncompromising finality of an ultimatum.[4]

---

[1] The 'great divide' in modern Sudanese history was the claim of Muhammad Ahmad of Dongola in 1881 to be the long-expected Mahdī whose appearance (according to popular Muslim tradition) was to usher in the millennium, and his consequent revolt against the oppressive and corrupt misgovernment of the agents of the Khedive of Egypt. While the tribesmen of the western Sudan rallied to his banner, those of the eastern provinces who belonged to the already existing Khatmīya sect opposed him, and their leaders found refuge in Egypt from his conquering hordes. The continuing rivalry between the Mahdīya and Khatmīya sects, which from c. 1920 onwards were led respectively by the two 'grand old men' of the Sudan—Sir Saiyid 'Abd ur-Rahmān al-Mahdī (the posthumous son of the Mahdī) and Sir Saiyid 'Alī al-Mirghānī —provided rallying points for the two opposed groups of Sudanese 'intellectuals' who had split during the Second World War on the question of whether to rely on the British or on Egypt for support on the road to Sudanese self-government (see Mekki Abbas: The Sudan Question (London, Faber & Faber, 1952), pp. 108–10, 130–2).   [2] Ibid. pp. 110–11, 133.
[3] Bevin in the House of Commons, 26 March 1946, H.C.Deb. 5th ser., vol. 421, col. 217. Lord Stansgate afterwards declared that for the Egyptians the 'whole issue' was prejudiced by Bevin's reference to Sudanese self-government 'as a first step towards eventual independence' (Listener, 25 January 1951, p. 127). Mekki Abbas remarks that 'the sentiments of the British officials in the Sudan Government were with the independence groups' and 'were implicit in a secret directive circulated by the Civil Secretary . . . to all senior British officials' in 1945 (The Sudan Question, p. 133; cf. A special correspondent lately in the Sudan, The Times, 16 May 1952).
[4] The Times Alexandria correspondent, 30 September, and leading article, 1 October 1946.

Sidqī accordingly resigned his premiership on 28 September; but, after the King's uncle, Sharīf Sabrī, had unsuccessfully attempted to form an all-party Cabinet embracing the Wafd together with Liberals and Sa'dists, the King again turned to Sidqī on 2 October. Meanwhile Lord Stansgate and the British Ambassador had gone to London for consultations, and Sidqī proposed to the British Foreign Office that he should follow them 'to explain personally to Mr. Bevin the national ideals inspiring his Government's policy, and to assure himself that the British Foreign Secretary is fully informed of the reasons for the Egyptian attitude'. Thereupon there were more hostile demonstrations of students and workers.

Sidqī and his Foreign Minister, the Sa'dist Ibrāhīm 'Abd ul-Hādī, had five meetings with Bevin in London between 17 and 25 October, as a result of which they initialed a new draft treaty.[1] Britain undertook to evacuate Cairo, Alexandria, and the Delta by 31 March 1947, and the rest of Egyptian territory by 1 September 1949. Egypt, in return, agreed to take action in the event of aggression 'against countries adjacent to Egypt', while the Joint Defence Board would examine the repercussions of

all events which may threaten the security of the Middle East, and shall make . . . suitable recommendations to the two Governments, who, in the case of events threatening the security of any one of the neighbouring countries of Egypt, will consult together in order to take in agreement such measures as may be recognised as necessary.[2]

There remained the difficult problem of reconciling the Egyptian claim for sovereignty over the Sudan with the pledge that Bevin had given in March for the consultation of the Sudanese.[3] Bevin afterwards stated that, in negotiating with Sidqī a protocol on the Sudan to be annexed to their draft treaty, he had felt justified in admitting a reference to

the existence of a symbolic dynastic union between Egypt and the Sudan, provided always that no change was introduced in the existing system of administration, whereby the Sudan is administered by the Governor-General under the powers conferred on him by the 1899 Agreements, as confirmed and interpreted by the Anglo-Egyptian Treaty of 1936; and provided that no change took place in the arrangements under which the defence of the Sudan is assured.

According to Bevin, Sidqī admitted that nothing in the proposed protocol could prejudice the right of the Sudanese to achieve their independence,

---

[1] Great Britain, Foreign Office: *Papers regarding the Negotiations for a Revision of the Anglo-Egyptian Treaty of 1936*, Cmd. 7179 (London, H.M.S.O., 1947) [referred to hereafter as Cmd. 7179].

[2] Ibid. p. 3. A British authority previously cited 'did not think that the defence clause adequately protected our interests, and was glad when it all came to nothing'.

[3] See above, p. 124 and note 3.

but argued that this was a universal principle, not a matter for incorporation in the draft treaty.[1]

The result of this attempt to combine the Egyptian and the British theses on the Sudan in a single compromise formula[2] was no more successful than the attempt (which it so closely resembled) of the Oecumenical Council of Chalcedon in A.D. 451 to reconcile the Orthodox and the (Egyptian and Syrian) Monophysite views on the Incarnation.[3] Sidqī had secured the key-phrase 'unity . . . under the common Crown' and was probably trusting to the interplay of Egyptian intransigence with the British habit of compromise to cut its own course through the British phraseology that followed those key-words. At all events, on his return to Cairo on 26 October, he made a statement to an Egyptian journalist which was reported as follows: 'I said last month that I should bring the Sudan to Egypt, and I say now that I have succeeded, that it has definitely been decided to achieve unity between Egypt and the Sudan under the Egyptian Crown.'[4] The British Prime Minister on the 28th 'regretted' this report, which seemed to him 'partial and misleading'.[5] On the following day Egyptian official sources released a paraphrase of the Sudan protocol which, while probably not departing deliberately from the still unpublished authentic English text, seems to have been slightly coloured in a sense favourable to the Egyptian thesis. These Egyptian publications gave rise to such anxiety among the supporters of independence in the Sudan that nothing would convince them that the dynastic union with Egypt proposed by the Bevin-Sidqī protocol would be symbolic only and dependent upon the consent of the Sudanese. Mekkī 'Abbās, who was a member of the Advisory Council for the Northern Sudan which had been

[1] Bevin, 27 January 1947, H.C.Deb. 5th ser., vol. 432, coll. 617–18. When, however, his alleged admission had been divulged by the Governor-General of the Sudan, Sidqī had issued on 8 December 1945 a communiqué denying that he had agreed in London to recognize the Sudan's right to eventual secession from the Egyptian Crown. His resignation followed immediately; see below, p. 128.

[2] 'The policy which the High Contracting Parties undertake to follow in the Sudan, within the framework of the unity between the Sudan and Egypt under the common Crown of Egypt will have for its essential objectives to assure the well-being of the Sudanese, the development of their interests and their active preparation for self-government and consequently the exercise of the right to choose the future status of the Sudan. Until the High Contracting Parties can in full common agreement realise this latter objective after consultation with the Sudanese, the Agreement of 1899 will continue.' (Cmd. 7179, p. 4).

[3] ' . . . in two natures, uncommingled, unchangeable, indivisible, inseparable; the differences between the two natures not removed by reason of their union, but rather the characteristics of each found united together in one Person and one Hypostasis.'

[4] *Observer* diplomatic correspondent, 27 October 1946. The *Round Table* article previously quoted (March 1951, p. 115) contained the following apology for Sidqī: 'An old, sick, and exhausted man . . . made an incautious and probably misreported statement . . . as he stumbled from his aircraft late in the night. . . . As this writer well knows, had Sidky Pasha been asked to modify his alleged statement before official notice was taken of it, he would have done so and all might have been well.' Sidqī's autobiography is not revealing on the point.

[5] H.C.Deb. 5th ser., vol. 428, coll. 295–6.

created in 1944,[1] attended meetings of the Council at which the Governor-General (Major-General Sir Hubert Huddleston, who had spent most of his military career in the Sudan and had been appointed Governor-General in 1940 when an Italian invasion from East Africa seemed imminent) and the Civil Secretary 'laboured in vain to convince the councillors that no change in the *status quo* was contemplated'. The Independence Front and the pro-Egyptian 'National Front' held rival demonstrations in the twin cities Khartūm and Umm Darmān (Omdurman), largely for the purpose of showing off their respective strengths, and the introduction of supporters from the provinces by both parties created a risk of serious disorders.[2] The Governor-General, summoned to London, acquainted the Foreign Secretary with the situation.

It was now no secret that seven out of the twelve members of the Egyptian delegation were opposed to all three of the main clauses—dealing with evacuation, joint defence, and the Sudan—in the draft which Sidqī had brought back from London. On 26 November, accordingly, King Fārūq (who, it was reported, had made no secret of his conviction that the conclusion of a treaty acceptable to both countries was in the interest of both)[3] dissolved the delegation. Sidqī obtained a vote of confidence from 159 of the 264 deputies who constituted the Chamber, while the remainder absented themselves or refrained from voting; but he was immediately confronted by a new outbreak of street demonstrations instigated by the Wafd, which led him to ban a proposed Wafdist political rally and to hint that they were receiving material aid from Soviet sources. This the Wafdist *al-Balāgh* denied, but only to add: 'We want the friendship of Russia and other Communist countries, in order to have their support when we submit our case to the Security Council.'[4]

When defending his policy to the press on 28 November Sidqī was reported[5] to have said that there was little hope of persuading the British to accept the full sovereignty of Egypt over the Sudan which, the Egyptian public now believed, was her right. On 6 December Bevin, after his consultations with the Governor-General of the Sudan, was stated to have sent Sidqī a draft 'letter of interpretation' to be affixed to the treaty, in which Sidqī was asked to agree that the draft protocol 'amounts to an affirmation of the existing status' of the Sudan and 'in no way affects the right of the United Kingdom to secure the defence of the Sudan'.[6] This Sidqī

---

[1] See *Survey* for 1939–46: *The Middle East in the War*, p. 260. From the start the pro-Egyptian parties had boycotted it.

[2] Mekki Abbas: *The Sudan Question*, pp. 118, 134. In some British quarters in Cairo that were anxious for an Anglo-Egyptian settlement, however, the Sudan Government's attitude was considered unnecessarily alarmist.

[3] *The Times*, leading article, 29 November 1946.   [4] Cf. Sidqī: *Mudhākarātī*, p. 126.

[5] *New York Times* Cairo correspondent, 29 November 1946.

[6] Quoted by Nuqrāshī to the Security Council, 11 August 1947 (*Official Records*, 2nd year, no. 73, p. 1871).

could not do; and on the following day the Governor-General, now back
in Khartūm, stated that the British Prime Minister had authorized him
to give the following assurance to the Sudanese people:

His Majesty's Government are . . . determined that nothing shall be permitted
to deflect the Sudan Government, whose constitution and powers remain un-
altered by the recent conversations, from the task to which that Government
have applied themselves—the preparation of the Sudanese for self-government
and for the task of choosing freely what their future status is to be.[1]

It was officially added in London:

The Governor-General's statement was necessitated by the situation created
in the Sudan itself by earlier and partial disclosures in Egypt of the Sidky-
Bevin conversations. . . . Continued silence by the Sudan Government in the
face of one-sided interpretation, which aroused the feelings of a large section of
the Sudanese people, would have resulted in serious unrest, if not worse.

. . . All the British Government are endeavouring to do is to establish that,
when the time is ripe for the Sudanese to choose their future, they shall be
free to say if they so desire that they choose the status of an independent State.
Clearly this is only one of the choices open to them. For example, they may
choose union with Egypt.

But it would be manifestly impossible for any British Government to acquiesce
in an interpretation of a treaty with Egypt . . . which denies one of the fundamental rights of free people—a right which Egypt has never ceased to claim for
herself.[2]

Sidqī thereupon issued a communiqué denying that he had agreed in
London to recognize the Sudan's right to secede from the Egyptian Crown,
and resigned on 9 December, ostensibly on medical advice.

He had, indeed, done as much as any Egyptian could to reconcile the
Egyptian and British theses; but the clash of British and Egyptian desiderata
over the three vital issues—evacuation, joint defence, and the Sudan—had
been too much for him.[3] The Egyptians' fundamental anxiety over the

---

[1] *Daily Telegraph*, 9 December 1946. The Sudan Government later ignored an Egyptian
request to publish the official text of a speech which the Governor-General made at al-'Ubaiyad
(el-Obeid), one of the centres of support for Sudanese independence, on 22 December. The
version published in the Cairo press, which the Sudan Government criticized as inaccurate,
reported him as expressing his personal dislike of the 'nominal and symbolic' Egyptian sovereignty over the Sudan which the Bevin-Sidqī protocol had conceded; and as saying: 'The Sudan
Government will actively pursue a policy that will allow the Sudan to become independent when
she is prepared for it', and that meanwhile Egyptian officials and propaganda in the Sudan
would not be allowed to increase.

[2] *The Times*, 10 December 1946.

[3] In his autobiography Sidqī asserted that the Bevin-Sidqī plan fully satisfied Egypt's demands
for the withdrawal of British troops from Egypt and for sovereignty over the Sudan. He attributed his failure to the intrigues of his Egyptian opponents in the field of party politics, to Soviet
attempts to prevent any agreement, and to the opposition to a compromise solution shown by
the British Conservative Party and by some officials of the Foreign Office and the Sudan Government (*Mudhākarātī*, pp. 126, 131).

prospect of a self-governing Sudan was that it would be in a position to curtail Egypt's vital share of the Nile waters; but this point was rarely ventilated in the Egyptian press at this stage; greater play was made with dubious appeals to history and pseudo-anthropological arguments. Thus in March 1947 *as-Siyāsa*, a government organ, declared that

the people of the Nile Valley are all Hamites. As for language, everyone knows that the Sudanese speak Arabic. Those among them who do not know this language speak a primitive dialect which is not even reckoned as one of the forms of human speech. As soon as they become educated they learn Arabic. . . . The Sudanese have known a religion other than Islām only since the entry of Christian missionaries patronized by the imperialists . . .

and a correspondent in *al-Ahrām* boldly asserted: 'The non-Arab tribes are also of Egyptian origin. They are descended, in fact, from the ancient Egyptians, as Egyptologists have established. It is true that among the Sudanese there are some non-Muslims; but it is no less true that these non-Muslims are for the most part idolaters, whose worship is that of their ancestors, the ancient Egyptians.'[1]

A new government of Sa'dists and Liberals was formed by Nuqrāshī, whose sincere advocacy of Egyptian nationalist interests was not tempered, as Sidqī's was, by a wider awareness of the general problems of the post-war world. Nuqrāshī declared to the Chamber on 16 December 1946:

In affirming the permanent unity of Egypt and the Sudan under the Egyptian Crown we simply expressed the unanimous will and wishes of the inhabitants of this Valley. . . . When I state that the unity of Egypt and the Sudan under the Egyptian Crown is a permanent unity, I hope that the whole world will understand that I am expressing the opinion of all Egyptians and all Sudanese. . . . There is therefore no ground to suspect that we wish to colonize the Sudan, as the desire to dominate cannot exist between brothers.[2]

The decision of the Sudan Government to appoint a Sudanese as Grand Qādī of the Sudan, in place of an Egyptian whose term of appointment was now coming to an end, caused further annoyance in Egypt, where it was contended that the appointment should be made by the King of

---

[1] Reported by *Bourse Égyptienne*, 13 and 14 March 1947. The eminent authority Professor C. G. Seligman had, however, written: 'Chronological factors forbid us to believe that the Divine Kings of the [southern] Sudan are directly due to Egyptian influence; rather must we regard them as examples of an old and widespread Hamitic belief, though there has become attached to them through [ancient] Egyptian influence a number of specifically Egyptian rites' (*Egypt and Negro Africa, a Study in Divine Kingship* (London, Routledge, 1934), p. 60).

[2] A Cairo periodical that went so far as to admit the existence in the Sudan of an opposition to union with Egypt dismissed it as consisting of 'the comparatively small number of the members of the family of Sir Abdel Rahman el-Mahdi, the supporters of the idea of Mahdism, mostly in the western provinces, and a group of opportunists who hope to secure material advantages', while the supporters of unity consisted of 'the enlightened classes opposed to reactionary imperialism, and the great number of the religious adherents of El Sayed Ali el Mirghani' (quoted by the special correspondent of *The Times* in the Sudan, 24 January 1947).

Egypt on the recommendation of the *'ulamā* of al-Azhar. Conversations in the first half of January 1947 between Nuqrāshī and the British Ambassador on the Sudan question failed, in Bevin's words,

to reach anything in the nature of an agreed interpretation, whether in the form of an exchange of letters, or of agreed statements to be made by the spokesmen of both sides, or even of agreed statements in which the difference separating the parties would be honestly declared in the hope that it could be composed later. . . . I have offered every guarantee for the safeguard of Egyptian interests in the Sudan—for no one realises more clearly than His Majesty's Government how vital, for instance, is Egyptian interest in the waters of the Nile—I have offered to sign the treaty of mutual assistance and the evacuation protocol . . . and to discuss the Sudan question *de novo* at a conference with ourselves, the Egyptians and the Sudanese. To all these proposals I have received either an uncompromising negative, or proposals which would involve my re-entering negotiations committed to the thesis that the right of the Sudanese to self-determination must be subject to permanent union between Egypt and the Sudan.[1]

On 26 January Nuqrāshī confirmed earlier reports that his Government would take the whole question of Egypt and the Sudan to the United Nations; and on the following day Bevin, after giving the House of Commons his account of the negotiations, stated that the British Government would hold to the 1936 treaty (implying the maintenance of their forces in the Canal Zone) until they could deal with 'a more fully representative Egyptian Government', with which negotiations would 'avoid being the subject of Egyptian party politics'.

(c) EGYPT'S APPEAL TO THE SECURITY COUNCIL, 1947

Nuqrāshī's Government spent the whole of February in trying to broaden the basis of their popular support, and to decide whether to take Egypt's case to the Security Council, the General Assembly, or the International Court of Justice. Sidqī openly, and others privately, urged the resumption of direct negotiations with Britain, and it was confirmed on 24 February that the Syrian and Lebanese Governments had offered themselves as mediators; but on 2 March the Egyptian Government announced that they would dispense with the services of the British Military Mission at the end of the year,[2] and on the following day proclaimed their decision to appeal to the Security Council. Amid rumours of further attempts at mediation by the United States and other Governments, the evacuation of British troops from the Delta to the Canal Zone was completed on 31 March. On the 24th, during the Moscow Conference of

---

[1] 27 January 1947, H.C.Deb. 5th ser., vol. 432, coll. 619–20.

[2] All British police officers (including the commandants of the Cairo, Alexandria, and Suez Canal police) had been retired in 1946, as the result of a decision taken by Nuqrāshī's Government at the end of the war (see *The Times*, 23 August 1945).

Foreign Ministers, Stalin and Bevin were afterwards reported to have discussed Egypt's complaints against Britain among other Middle Eastern matters which they had examined in a review of the Anglo-Soviet alliance of 1942: according to a British Government spokesman, Stalin had appeared 'generally to appreciate Britain's position in the Middle East and Egypt' and had assured Bevin that Russia would remain neutral in the Anglo-Egyptian dispute. The Tass agency later denied this report, but admitted that Anglo-Egyptian relations concerned those two countries only, 'and that the U.S.S.R., in conformity with its invariable policy of non-interference, did not intend to interfere in this matter'.[1]

On 16 May Bevin declared that there would be 'no attempt to appease the Egyptian Government at the expense of the Sudanese people. . . . Whether they take this to the Security Council or elsewhere, we cannot go any further [than] the offer we have made',[2] a statement that finally killed the Egyptian hope of some new British concession. However, inter-party dissension,[3] the misgivings of Egyptian diplomats abroad, and calculations as to which state would hold the presidency of the Security Council from month to month, delayed the presentation of the Egyptian complaint, and it was not finally lodged until 11 July. It declared the presence of British troops on Egyptian territory without Egypt's free consent to be 'an offence to its dignity, a hindrance to its normal development, as well as an infringement of the fundamental principle of sovereign equality, and . . . therefore contrary to the letter and spirit of the United Nations Charter, and to the resolution adopted unanimously by the General Assembly on 14 December 1946'.[4] The British Government's 'unwarranted' military occupation of Egypt, it said, had enabled them since 1899

to force upon Egypt their partnership in the administration of the Sudan and subsequently to assume exclusive authority therein. Taking advantage of this

---

[1] *Bourse Égyptienne*, 2 May 1947, reporting *al-Ahrām; New York Times*, 8 May, *Soviet News*, 15 May 1947. Already on 27 January the Tass agency had denied Egyptian press reports that Molotov had recently told the Egyptian Minister in Moscow that his Government were prepared to support Egypt on the Sudan question at the United Nations (ibid. 29 January 1947). Soviet policy was at this time still seeking to conciliate Britain as a means of separating her from the United States; for Bevin's expression of some optimism at the end of the Moscow Conference see *Survey* for 1947–8, p. 236.

[2] H.C.Deb. 5th ser., vol. 437, col. 1963.

[3] Just as it had done a year before, the Wafd made its participation in the delegation to Lake Success conditional on its having majority representation and the chairmanship, and the guarantee of a general election after the delegation's return to Egypt. Makram and his Kutla Party also could not be reconciled with Nuqrāshī on this issue.

[4] This had recommended members to undertake 'the withdrawal without delay of their armed forces stationed in the territories of Members without their consent freely and publicly expressed in treaties or agreements consistent with the Charter and not contradicting international agreements' (*Resolutions adopted by the General Assembly during the second part of the First Session*, no. 41 (i)).

situation, they have adopted a policy designed to sever the Sudan from Egypt; discrediting Egypt and the Egyptians; creating discord between them and the Sudanese, and dissension among the Sudanese themselves; instigating and encouraging artificial separatist movements. By this policy the Government of the United Kingdom have endeavoured, and are endeavouring, to impair the unity of the Nile valley, notwithstanding that this unity is urged by the common interest and aspirations of its people.[1]

The exordium of Nuqrāshī's appeal to the Security Council on 5 August was telling,[2] but he was on weaker ground when he descended to particulars. After taking the Council through a rapid survey of Anglo-Egyptian relations since 1882 as seen through Egyptian eyes, he went on to argue:

No one can seriously claim that the restrictions on Egyptian sovereignty embodied in the 1936 Treaty were intended to continue after the war. The war was the implicit term to these restrictions, and the 1936 Treaty has now outlived its purpose. . . . Today, Egypt's relationship with the United Kingdom can no longer be charted by the provisions of the 1936 Treaty. It must be governed by international law and by the Charter of the United Nations. . . .

In this high forum, I shall not argue the juridical position of the 1936 Treaty, but my country has no hesitation in placing its reliance on the Charter.

He then gave the Council another historical review of conditions in the Sudan after its conquest by Muhammad 'Alī in 1821:

Egyptian rule opened the Sudan to modern civilization. The chaos and anarchy which had existed were replaced by order and prosperity. . . . Such was the picture when the United Kingdom directed its covetous gaze to the valley of the Nile! . . . A religious revolt, led by a chief who called himself El-Mahdi, supplied it with the needed opportunity. . . . When energetic action could have quelled the budding rebellion, the United Kingdom prevented such action by every conceivable means. It forced the disbandment of the Egyptian army in Egypt, the destruction of its ammunition, and the complete withdrawal of the Egyptians from the Sudan.

After declaring that the British in the Sudan discriminated politically and economically against Egypt, and kept the country 'backward and divided',[3] he complained:

In recent years, a malevolent propaganda has pictured the unity of the Nile

---

[1] U.N., Security Council: *Official Records*, 2nd year, no. 59, pp. 1343-5.

[2] 'Against this historic background of Anglo-Egyptian relations, an alliance of this sort is but another form of subordination. It masks a relationship which is both unbalanced and undignified. It ties Egypt to British economy; its subjects Egypt to the vagaries of British diplomacy; and it imprisons Egypt within the orbit of British imperial power' (ibid. p. 1756).

[3] The sale of an *ad hoc* publication by the Sudan Government, entitled *The Sudan: a Record of Progress, 1898-1947*, had just been banned in Egypt because it gave a 'picture of the Sudan different from that in the minds of the Egyptian public' (*The Times* Cairo correspondent, 5 August 1947).

valley as a concept of 'Egyptian imperialism'—as if it were imperialistic for us to desire union with our fellow-countrymen, for us to seek to preserve the bonds which nature and history have forged for linking the Sudan with other parts of Egypt as one and the same entity.[1]

For Britain Sir Alexander Cadogan pointed out that the 1936 treaty could legally be revised before its expiry in 1956 only by the consent of both parties. The Egyptian argument that the removal of the Axis threat to peace had altered the circumstances of the treaty was an invocation of the *rebus sic stantibus*[2] doctrine which would find no support in any international tribunal. As for the assertion that the presence of British troops in Egypt was contrary to the United Nations Charter, the wording of the resolution of 14 December 1946 which Egypt had invoked had made an exception for the presence of armed forces by consent 'freely and publicly expressed in treaties . . . consistent with the Charter'. He demonstrated by a series of quotations that the treaty had in 1936 been almost unanimously welcomed in Egypt; and the rule *pacta sunt servanda* was a primary principle of international law. His Government had met 'in the most sympathetic manner' the Egyptian request for a revision of the treaty and had offered to withdraw the British forces from Egypt on reasonable conditions; the Bevin-Sidqī agreement had failed to come into force 'for only one reason, namely, that Egypt was not prepared to accord in the future to the Sudanese people the right of self-determination which it had claimed for Arabs elsewhere'.[3]

On 11 August, when the Security Council continued its hearing of the question, Nuqrāshī was called upon first and described Cadogan's speech on the 5th as 'an unrestrained apology for nineteenth-century Imperialism'. Cadogan, in his reply, declared again that Britain was holding to the 1936 treaty only because Egypt had rejected the Bevin-Sidqī draft on account of the Sudan protocol.

Nokrashy Pasha [he said] replies that the Security Council must not be 'stimied by the legal rights of the parties'. The Council must act in the same way, 'treaty or no treaty'. It must put aside treaty rights whenever the party to a given treaty says that it dislikes its obligations enough to be ready to allow its people to create a menace to the peace rather than accept them. Egyptian politicians have been stirring up feeling against the Treaty with the deliberate intention of gaining their wishes. It is they who are creating the threat to the peace if there is any.[4]

The debate being now thrown open to general discussion, the represen-

---

[1] U.N., Security Council: *Official Records*, 2nd year, no. 70, pp. 1753–65.

[2] This is the doctrine that the validity of a treaty is confined to the period during which the circumstances obtain which existed at the time of its signature. The contrary, and generally accepted, principle that treaties must be observed during the period for which they were made is summed up in the formula *pacta sunt servanda*.

[3] U.N., Security Council: *Official Records*, 2nd year, no. 70, pp. 1767–84.

[4] 13 August 1947 (ibid. no. 75, p. 1955).

tative of Poland expressed the view that the Council could not be bound
by the legal aspect of the question solely: a treaty which had 'outlived its
purpose and exhausted its objectives' stood in the way of 'the justified
national aspiration' and sovereignty of a member state. Poland would
support Egypt's demand for the 'immediate, complete, and unconditional'
withdrawal of British troops from Egypt and the Sudan, but could suggest
no solution at the present moment for the problem of the 'development of
self-government and free political institutions' which should be the United
Nations' primary objective in the Sudan. The Russian delegate, Gromyko,
expressed the same views. The Brazilian delegate submitted a draft resolution on 20 August, recommending the two parties 'to resume direct negotiations and, should such negotiations fail, to seek a solution of the dispute
by other peaceful means of their own choice'. The Chinese (Nationalist)
delegate proposed to add to its preamble a paragraph noting that Britain
had already partially withdrawn her troops from Egypt and was ready to
negotiate on the completion of the evacuation; and he added: 'I cannot
see how this Council can be a party to any arrangement which would
deprive the Sudanese people of this right of self-determination, which is
the foundation of the Charter of the United Nations.' The United States,
French, and Belgian delegates supported the Brazilian proposal, the last-
named suggesting that a requirement expressed by Cadogan should be
met by referring the question of the 1936 treaty's validity to the International Court.

Nuqrāshī, however, rejected the Brazilian resolution as an 'evasion' of
the Council's 'primary responsibility': Egypt could not admit Britain's
claim to any special consideration based on the 'initial vice' of her 'invasion' in 1882. He likewise rejected an Australian amendment to provide
for consultation with the Sudanese in so far as their future was affected:
the Egyptian Government, Nuqrāshī insisted, would 'work out the future
of the Sudan in consultation, not with the British, not with the Sudanese
while they are hampered by the British occupation, but with the Sudanese
acting of their own free will. The United Kingdom has no place in the
matter, and we shall not discuss it with that country.' His rhetorical
assertion: 'We shall not forsake the Sudanese. We shall do everything in
our power to protect them from a foreign, alien imperialism, from losing
their identity in a vast conglomeration of subject peoples. . . . We shall not
barter away the future of the Sudanese people', did nothing to remove
the unfavourable impression on the Council that (as Cadogan emphasized)
'the Sudan's full right of self-determination . . . is not, apparently, admitted by the Egyptian Government'. France's relations with Egypt had
recently been strained by the latter's sending an auxiliary cruiser to
Tunisia, without French authorization, with grain to relieve a famine,
and by her giving sanctuary to the Moroccan Muhammad 'Abd ul-Karīm

(Abdel Krim) who had escaped to Egyptian soil from the ship which was taking him to France after more than twenty years' exile. The French delegate accordingly compared Nuqrāshī's repudiation of the 1936 treaty with the repudiations practised by the Nazis before the war: 'Every Hitlerite aggression was preceded by a declaration announcing that the treaty signed a few years or a few months before . . . was now useless, an anachronism, and contrary to the trend of historic development.' To this, Nuqrāshī's reply was: 'No legal instrument will hold back the tide of history. Already, in the brief span of eleven years, the Treaty of 1936 has lost its viability. Events have robbed it of any effective voice. It stalks today as a phantom; it persists only as a relic of bygone buccaneer days, which the world is trying to forget.'[1]

When the Brazilian resolution was put to the vote, it unexpectedly failed by one vote to obtain the necessary seven supporters: Poland voted against, and those abstaining (the U.S.S.R., the United Kingdom, and Syria) were joined by Colombia, whose delegate had considered the Brazilian resolution too broad and vague and had announced his intention to submit a new proposal[2] after a vote had been taken. Only five supporters were forthcoming for this Colombian proposal, however; only four for an Australian amendment expressing confidence that the renewal of negotiations would result in an early evacuation 'and also in the settlement of the other issues in dispute'; and only two for a Chinese resolution to which Cadogan objected because it seemed to give priority to evacuation over the other questions. Since there was no other proposal on the table, the Council adjourned on 10 September leaving on its agenda the Egyptian question still unsolved.

The rejection of the Egyptian Government's fundamental claim that its signature to an agreement should be binding only *rebus sic stantibus* came as a shock to the Egyptian public, and the reaction in some quarters was irresponsible. The Brazilian Legation in Cairo received a letter from 'The Egyptian Terrorist Society' demanding payment of £5 million as reparation for Brazil's 'impertinence' in moving her resolution at the Security Council, and on the night of 28–29 August two small bombs were exploded outside the Legation, but without doing any damage. Chinese and Belgian residents also received threatening letters; and, while the Soviet Union was hailed as Egypt's friend, the Cairo correspondent of *The Times* reported on 5 November 1947:

---

[1] U.N., Security Council: *Official Records*, 2nd year, no. 86 (28 August 1947), pp. 2290, 2292.
[2] This called on the two parties to resume direct negotiations with a view (*a*) to completing at the earliest possible date the evacuation of all British military, naval, and air forces from Egyptian territory, subject to mutual assistance being provided for in order to safeguard in time of war or imminent threat of war the liberty and security of navigation of the Suez Canal; and (*b*) to terminating the joint administration of the Sudan with due regard to the principle of self-determination of peoples and their right to self-government.

One widely circulated newspaper has said that the British are not unlikely to stage outrages against foreigners here in order to justify a reoccupation of the Egyptian cities. Another publication . . . has accused them of having plotted the communal massacres in India. . . . Forged documents have been published in an attempt to discredit the British authorities here. . . .[1] When cholera broke out near Cairo last month, several leading papers immediately attributed its origin to the British camps in the Canal Zone, although not a single case had occurred there.[2]

(d) ANGLO-EGYPTIAN FINANCIAL NEGOTIATIONS, 1947

Meanwhile, in February 1947, preliminary negotiations between British and Egyptian representatives had begun over the question of Egypt's sterling balances. These had accrued to Egyptian banks during the war, when Egypt was largely prevented from spending sterling owing to the lack of goods to be obtained from Britain, and when on the other hand the British armed forces in Egypt and the Sudan were requiring large sums in Egyptian currency to pay for local labour, services, and supplies. At the end of the war, accordingly, Egypt had been left 'rich in sterling but impoverished in regard to all types of supplies . . . and, though the supply of consumer goods came forward fairly quickly, the deficiency in capital goods continued for many years after the war'.[3] Egyptian opinion was therefore unanimous in wishing to extract the full value in goods of these sterling assets, which amounted in all to nearly £E 450 million[4] according to a census made by the Ministry of Finance in 1946. The British Government released scarce currencies to Egypt, as a member of the sterling area, to a value of £E 30·44 million for the period between 1 January 1945 and 15 July 1947, when, according to the provisions of the Anglo-American Financial Agreement of 1945, all newly accruing sterling credits were to become freely convertible into other currencies. In the course of post-war Britain's effort to place her exports where they would earn her scarce currencies or purchase raw materials, an imperialist prejudice developed against 'unrequited' exports to former 'colonial' countries, such as Egypt and especially India, that had accumulated large sterling credits during the war. It was argued that the volume of these credits had been unrealistically swollen by the excessive inflation which their Governments had

[1] Investigations in 1951 indicated the existence of a gang which had for some years apparently been producing forged documents, purporting to be foreign diplomatic and military reports and plans, and publishing them for the purpose of damaging Anglo-Egyptian relations and discrediting Egyptian politicians; see *The Times* Cairo correspondent, 9 and 11 June 1951.

[2] This charge was repeated in a dissertation by a press attaché of the Egyptian Embassy in Paris; see Moustapha el-Hefnaoui: *Les Problèmes contemporains posés par le Canal de Suez* (Paris, Imprimerie Guillemot et de Lamothe, 1951), p. 93.

[3] Royal Institute of International Affairs: *Great Britain and Egypt, 1914–1951*; Information Papers no. 19 (London, R.I.I.A., 1952), p. 158.

[4] £1 Egyptian = £1·025 sterling.

allowed to occur during the war, and that they should now be scaled down to a more reasonable figure;[1] the Governments in question, on the other hand, maintained that in their present genuine need for capital and consumer goods they should not be penalized for an inflation largely due to the war-time combination of Britain's demand for their currencies with her inability to supply goods. A more radical British argument was advanced by Winston Churchill as Leader of the Opposition. Churchill contended that there should be set against these sterling assets a 'counter-charge' for Britain's having saved the creditor countries during the war from 'all the horrors and indignities of invasion and subjugation'. He declared that he had ventilated this idea among his colleagues of the war-time Coalition Government;[2] but for obvious reasons no such counter-claim had been lodged at the time with the Governments of countries in which sterling credits were accumulating; and these assets were in fact held by banks and commercial companies to a much larger extent than by the respective Governments.

When formal negotiations opened in London on 6 June 1947 the Chancellor of the Exchequer himself, according to his subsequent statement to the House of Commons, 'urged the Egyptian representatives to make proposals for the cancellation, in whole or in part, of this war debt arising out of our war effort, so costly both in blood and treasure, in defence of Egypt'.[3] The Egyptian delegation put in a counter-claim for an allocation of gold for four to five years to cover the banknote issue, for the transfer of British shares in the Suez Canal Company and other Egyptian concerns on the analogy of the recent transfer of British assets in Argentina, and for a guarantee against the devaluation of sterling.[4] Hard bargaining followed, and the Egyptian delegation postponed their intended date of departure, until on 30 June an agreement was reached whereby, in return for the 'freezing' of the bulk of Egypt's sterling assets (whose total was now computed at £356 million) in a 'No. 2 account', where they could be invested or reinvested but not otherwise drawn upon, Britain would make freely available for payments in any currency area a No. 1 account credited as follows:

(i) The volume of confirmed Egyptian credits on banks in the United Kingdom, estimated at about £22 million;

[1] See *Financial Times*, 20 March 1947.

[2] 13 December 1945, H.C.Deb. 5th ser., vol. 417, coll. 720–1; cf. 20 March 1951, vol. 485, col. 2377; 30 July 1951, vol. 491, coll. 1067–8.

[3] Hugh Dalton, 3 July 1947. Oliver Stanley offered the support of the Conservative Opposition in resisting an Egyptian claim 'which we believe to be wholly unjustified' (H.C.Deb. 5th ser., vol. 439, coll. 1518–21).

[4] The Under-Secretary of the Egyptian Ministry of Finance, reported by *Financial Times*, 7 July 1947. The analogy of Argentina had been cited by his Minister in an interview with *Bourse Égyptienne*, 7 May 1947.

  (ii) £8 million, as the release for the second half of 1947;

  (iii) £12 million as a working balance out of which any temporary shortage in Egypt's means of payment might be met;

  (iv) All future Egyptian earnings of sterling.[1]

The chairman of the Egyptian delegation announced that, as from 15 July, when new earnings of sterling were to become freely convertible, Egypt would cease to be a member of the sterling area. This financial tie with Britain had in fact become vexatious in Egyptian eyes at a date when Egypt was about to ask the Security Council to decree the nullity of the Anglo-Egyptian Alliance; and it was felt that, once free of the sterling area, Egypt would have a better chance of securing a loan from the United States, who had in March come to the help of Greece and Turkey under the Truman Doctrine.[2]

Within six weeks of 15 July, however, the heavy drain which convertibility imposed on British holdings of gold and dollars compelled the British Government to suspend the free convertibility of the No. 1 accounts of Egypt and other sterling creditors, and to limit their use to the sterling area and the transferable sterling accounts of other countries. There were strong protests from the Egyptian Government, since in fact Egypt had not during the six weeks' interval converted into dollars an excessive proportion of her No. 1 account; but the British Government remained immovable; and Egypt had to be content with a new agreement of 5 January 1948, whereby Britain made the following concessions:

  (i) A dollar allocation of the value of £6¼ million;

  (ii) Egypt's additional subscriptions in gold to the International Monetary Fund and Bank, amounting to approximately $4 million.

  (iii) The transfer for the year 1948 of £21 million to the now restricted No. 1 account, and a further transfer of £11 million for the working balance.[3]

(e) Constitutional Developments in the Anglo-Egyptian Sudan, 1947–8

It will be recalled that the Advisory Council for the Northern Sudan, established in 1944, had been consistently boycotted by the pro-Egyptian parties, but welcomed by the Independence Front, which hoped to achieve self-government by collaboration with the present British-controlled Sudan Government.[4] The Independence Front, however, regarded the Advisory

---

[1] Great Britain, Foreign Office: *Financial Agreement between the U.K. and Egypt, London, 30th June, 1947*, Cmd. 7163 (London, H.M.S.O., 1947).

[2] In April the Egyptian Government had, officially or semi-officially, sought a fifteen-year loan of $88 million in the United States, but without success (see *Bourse Égyptienne*, 17 April, 3, 5, 8, and 10 May 1947).

[3] Great Britain, Foreign Office: *Financial Agreement between the U.K. and Egypt, Cairo, 5th January, 1948*, Cmd. 7305 (London, H.M.S.O., 1948).

[4] See above, p. 124, note 3.

Council as only a stepping-stone towards their goal. The Governor-General, acceding to their requests, had set up in 1946 an administration conference, with a large Sudanese majority, to consider what further constitutional progress was desirable, and on 29 July 1947, only a week before the Egyptian complaint against Britain came before the Security Council, Sir Robert Howe[1] endorsed this conference's recommendations that the Advisory Council should be superseded by a Legislative Assembly representative of the whole country (including the south, still largely pagan and non-Arabic-speaking) and having a large elected majority; from this Assembly six Sudanese Under-Secretaries should be appointed to serve on the Governor-General's Executive Council, which would consist in all of twelve members, the other six being the Civil, Legal, and Financial Secretaries, the Commander-in-Chief, and two nominees of the Governor-General. These recommendations were duly presented to the British and Egyptian Governments. The former accepted them, but on 25 November the latter put forward the following counter-proposals: Egypt should be represented on the Executive Council; full electoral rights should be given immediately to the whole population, instead of the limited franchise which had been recommended as more suited to a population which in many parts of the country was still largely illiterate; the wide powers reserved to the Governor-General should be drastically curtailed, and those of the Legislative Assembly extended, although a right of veto should be reserved for the Egyptian Government.[2] *The Times* commented on 9 January 1948:

These Egyptian proposals seem to represent an attempt to outbid Britain for the support of those Sudanese who are eager to obtain a share of immediate political power, but it is by no means certain that they are conceived in the best interests of the country as a whole; until the tribal areas in the south gain some experience of representative institutions, the men who must speak for them cannot be properly chosen by a purely electoral system and may be best selected by impartial officials. Even so the suggestions for giving increased power to the proposed legislative assembly deserve examination, provided that the members of the assembly are in fact representative of the country as a whole and not merely of the urban educated classes. Both Britain and the Sudan have to be convinced that Egypt is in earnest in the desire to associate the Sudanese people as a whole with the responsibility of administration.

In January 1948 the British Government proposed to the Egyptian

---

[1] Sir Hubert Huddleston had retired on 15 March 1947 on account of his age and prolonged service, and the Egyptian Government had accepted as his successor the British Government's nominee Sir Robert Howe, who had been for the past two years the Foreign Secretary's principal adviser on Middle Eastern affairs.

[2] The Governor-General's reserved powers were described by *The Times* (4 March 1948) as 'a familiar balancing factor in the transition from colonial rule to self-government'; *al-Ahrām*, on the other hand, published a satirical article entitled 'His Majesty Robert Howe I, King of the Northern Sudan, the Southern Sudan, and the Bahr ul-Ghazal'.

Government the appointment of British and Egyptian non-official authorities on constitutional practice to study the Sudan Government's proposals in consultation with that Government's technical experts, taking into consideration also the opinion of representative Sudanese. The Egyptian press, however, greeted the publication of this proposal with such headlines as 'Plot to Establish Dictatorship in the Sudan', and on 1 March the Egyptian Cabinet unanimously rejected it.[1] On 9 March it was reported that the Advisory Council for the Northern Sudan, having debated the draft ordinance for a Legislative Assembly and an Executive Council, had unanimously[2] recommended that the Government should put the legislation into effect as soon as possible.

Early in May the Egyptian Government received new proposals from the British Government which they found satisfactory, and on 10 May an Anglo-Egyptian committee was set up, under the headship of the Egyptian Foreign Minister (Ahmad Muhammad Khashaba) and the British Ambassador, to examine the question of constitutional reform in the Sudan. In three weeks they reached agreement on the following points:

(1) An Anglo-Egyptian Sudanese committee to supervise the progress of the Sudanese towards self-government.

(2) An Anglo-Egyptian committee to supervise the elections to the Legislative Assembly.

(3) The nomination to the Executive Council of two Egyptians from among the Egyptian officials serving in the Sudan.

(4) The attendance of the Senior Staff Officer of the Egyptian forces in the Sudan at all meetings of the Executive Council at which defence matters were being discussed.

(5) The continuance of the present administrative system for three years, subject to renewal.[3]

Khashaba submitted this draft agreement to the Foreign Affairs Commission of the Egyptian Senate on 4 June, explaining somewhat apologetically that the Government had agreed to his taking part in the conversations only in order to give effect to the expressed wish of the Sudanese to have a practical share in the administration of their country; the conversations had not dealt with any of the fundamentals of the Sudan problem. The

---

[1] Text of Egyptian note in *Cahiers de l'Orient Contemporain*, 1er trimestre 1948, xiii. 9–11.

[2] While, on account of the boycott of the Advisory Council by the pro-Egyptian parties, most of its members belonged to the Independence Front, it was stated that at least three of Saiyid 'Ali al-Mirghani's supporters were members of the Council and voted for the reforms ('A Vital Month in the Sudan', *African World*, April 1948, p. 25).

[3] Statement by the British Under-Secretary for Foreign Affairs, 14 June 1948 (H.C.Deb. 5th ser., vol. 452, coll. 19–21); *The Times* Cairo correspondent, 7 June 1948.

The Egyptian Government had asked for 'representation on the Executive Council on a basis of parity with the British, so that when the transitional period had elapsed the Sudanese would be in a position to assume full control of their own affairs under the common Egyptian Crown and the unity of the Nile Valley' (text in *Bourse Égyptienne*, 6 July 1948).

Foreign Affairs Commission did not accept this submission, but unanimously rejected the proposed plan on the grounds that the two Egyptian officials to be nominated to the Executive Council should hold ministerial posts and that two places for Egyptians on the Council were in any case inadequate.[1]

On 14 June the British Government announced that, despite this Egyptian rejection, 'they could no longer stand in the way of the Governor-General doing as he thinks fit' regarding the promulgation of the Ordinance on the constitutional reforms;[2] and the Ordinance was duly promulgated five days later, the Egyptian Prime Minister having meanwhile obtained from the Senate a delay of three weeks before the Foreign Affairs Commission's report was considered.

The Ordinance made the following provisions:

(1) A Legislative Assembly of 65 elected members, not more than 10 nominated members, and a number of *ex officio* members, i.e. members of the Executive Council and Under-Secretaries not already members of the Assembly. Of the 65 elected members, 10 would be directly elected in Khartoum, Omdurman, and other towns; 42 would be chosen by indirect election in the less advanced parts of the Northern Sudan; and 13 would be elected by the Provincial Councils of the three southern provinces.

(2) A Leader, elected by the Assembly, would become in effect Prime Minister. His views would be taken into consideration by the Governor-General in appointing other Sudanese Ministers and not more than twelve Sudanese Under-Secretaries.

(3) The Executive Council would have between 12 and 18 members, not less than half of them Sudanese, including:
  (a) The Leader of the Assembly, and other Ministers and Under-Secretaries.
  (b) Not more than four *ex officio* members appointed by the Governor-General from the Civil, Financial, and Legal Secretaries and the Commander-in-Chief.
  (c) Not more than three persons appointed by the Governor-General at his discretion.

(4) The following extensive powers were retained by the Governor-General:
  (a) To dismiss Ministers or Under-Secretaries and appoint others in their place.
  (b) To veto decisions of the Executive Council, 'should it be necessary . . . for the good government of the Sudan'.
  (c) To dissolve the Assembly and direct fresh elections to be held.
  (d) To veto the Assembly's choice of Speaker.
  (e) To legislate by Ordinance, if a Bill prepared by the Executive Council were rejected by the Assembly.
  (f) To define what were reserved matters on which the Assembly might

not legislate—viz., the Constitution, the Condominium, foreign relations, and Sudanese nationality.

(g) To define what were special matters on which the Assembly might not legislate without the consent of the Executive Council—viz., defence, currency, and the status of religious or racial minorities.[1]

A responsible Sudanese comment on the Constitution was that, however irksome the retention of the Governor-General's veto powers was to Sudanese nationalism, it was a direct consequence of the Condominium Agreement of 1899, and was tempered in fact by the provision that these powers would be exercised only after reference to the British and Egyptian Governments. The delay in promulgating the Constitution which had arisen from the Egyptian counter-proposals of November 1947 had had the advantage of effecting an increase in the powers of the Assembly and of ensuring that the Sudanese members of the Executive Council should be responsible Ministers and not, as originally proposed, merely Under-Secretaries.[2]

The Egyptian press now castigated the Sudan Government's plan to extend the participation of Sudanese in the Government as an 'imperialistic scheme',[3] and the pro-Egyptian parties in the Sudan ordered their followers to boycott the elections for the Legislative Assembly.[4] *Al-Ahrām*, however, was sceptical about the optimistic prophecies that the boycott campaign would prevent the elections from taking place; arguments (it remarked) that elections held in such circumstances would be invalid would have no practical value.[5] On the polling day, 15 November 1948, disturbances were organized by the pro-Egyptian parties, as a result of which ten people were killed and more than 100 injured.[6] In the ten urban constituencies where polling was by direct election it was estimated that only 18 per cent. of the electorate had voted, and most of the seats were won by members of the Independence Front; but how far this low poll was due to the boycott by the pro-Egyptian parties, and how far to the general political immaturity of a large part of the electorate, is not clear,

[1] Based on M. F. A. Keen's *An Account of the Constitution of the Sudan* (Khartoum, McCorquodale [1951]).

[2] Mekki Abbas: *The Sudan Question*, pp. 138–40.

[3] *Egyptian Gazette*, 20 August 1948, quoting *Sawt ul-Umma*.

[4] Mekki Abbas (op. cit. pp. 138–9) makes the distinction, however, that, whereas the Ashiqqā Party (for which see below, p. 143, note 1) refused to acknowledge any Assembly formed by the existing British régime in the Sudan, the supporters of Saiyid 'Alī al-Mirghanī and the Unionist Party declared their willingness to take part in the elections if the powers of the Assembly were increased and the electoral law amended.

[5] Quoted by *Bourse Égyptienne*, 28 October 1948.

[6] When officials of the pro-Egyptian parties were charged with fomenting these disorders, seven Egyptian lawyers, including Makram, wished to undertake their legal defence in Khartūm but were excluded by the Sudan Government on the grounds that members of the Sudan Bar were perfectly qualified to act for the accused. The seven lawyers, trying to enter the Sudan by air without permits, were compelled to land at Wādī Halfa and were sent back to Cairo.

since, as Ernest Bevin was afterwards to point out, in the Egyptian general election of 1950 'only some 15 per cent. of the Cairo electorate was understood to have used its vote'. Whereas the Egyptian Government claimed two years later that the most important and numerous religious sects in the Sudan supported the 'unity of the Nile Valley', and that the elections for the Graduates' Congress and the municipal elections were in effect votes in favour of it, the British Government declared that 'the Graduates' Congress did not even represent the majority of the Sudanese intelligentsia, and in recent years . . . had come under the domination of an extremist clique which represented only a very small proportion of the Sudanese people'; that the municipal elections were not decisive since 'the Unionists were in the minority in Khartoum and had a majority of only one in Omdurman'; and that they were led to believe 'that those Sudanese who professed to favour union with Egypt were not more than about one-fifth of the total population of the country'.[1] It did not follow, however, that the remaining four-fifths would be of one mind in expressing their wishes, and the majority of these unlettered villagers and tribesmen would, unless influenced, fall into the 'don't know' category familiar to the professional samplers of 'public opinion'.

(f) Interlude: the Palestine War and its Aftermath, 1948–9

Before the Security Council had ended its inconclusive debate on the Egyptian complaint against Britain, the United Nations Special Committee on Palestine had already on 1 September 1947 published its recommendation of the partition of that country between a Jewish and an Arab state.[2] In the course of the protracted debate on these recommendations by the United Nations General Assembly, the Egyptian Senator Amīn Yūsuf, a former Minister to Washington who claimed to have 'sincerely and often successfully worked for close understanding between Egypt and Britain',[3] urged the British Government, in a letter to *The Times*, 'to outline a policy in Palestine which will convince the Arabs that Britain is still their friend'; British troops should 'immediately' be withdrawn from the Canal Zone, and 'it should be realized that at least 90 per cent. of the Sudanese favour the union between Egypt and the Sudan'.[4]

---

[1] Great Britain, Foreign Office: *Anglo-Egyptian Conversations on the Defence of the Suez Canal and on the Sudan, December 1950–November 1951*, Cmd. 8419 (London, H.M.S.O., 1951), pp. 17, 20–21. The 'extremist clique' referred to above was the Ashiqqā Party, nominally led by a Sudanese said to have left teaching for active politics because his claim for preferential treatment in the matter of official accommodation had been refused (Muhammad Hasanain Haikal, in *Ākhir Sa'a*, quoted by *Bourse Égyptienne*, 28 November 1951); but the party was in fact financed and directed from Cairo. According to an Egyptian writer, it claimed to represent 'about 88 per cent.' of the Sudanese population (Rashid al-Barawi: 'Egypt and the Sudan', *India Quarterly*, October 1951, vol. 7, p. 361).   [2] See below, pp. 245–6.

[3] He was the author of *Independent Egypt* (London, Murray, 1940).

[4] *The Times*, 21 November 1947.

It has been alleged, especially since the enforced abdication of King Fārūq in July 1952, that the King compelled Egypt to take part in the war against Israel despite the misgivings of the Government, led by Nuqrāshī, and of the Egyptian army. It might have been logical for Egypt, when once committed, to concentrate on the war with Israel, and to seek a reconciliation, however temporary, with a British Government who were prepared to strain their relations with the United States in the pursuit of an understanding with the Arab belligerents.[1] Since the breakdown of negotiations with Britain, however, Egypt had been using the Arab League (which she influenced through its Egyptian secretary-general, 'Abd ur-Rahmān 'Azzām, and through the fact that Egypt provided 42 per cent. of the funds of its secretariat) as an instrument of her anti-British policy. The war fever which the Zionists' progress towards independence had stimulated in the Arab cities did not greatly discriminate between Jews and other foreigners;[2] and Nuqrāshī's weak coalition Government of Sa'dists and Liberals dared not risk offending nationalist sentiments by any visible *détente* with Britain. We have seen that the draft agreement on the Sudan, which an Anglo-Egyptian committee reached in May 1948, was rejected by the Egyptian Senate;[3] and, once the supply of British arms to the Arab states had been suspended by the application of the first truce in Palestine,[4] the advantages to Egypt of a *rapprochement* with Britain were further diminished. The antagonism between Egypt and King 'Abdullāh of Jordan, which was allowed to interfere so seriously with the Arab conduct of the war against Israel,[5] was due not only to 'Abdullāh's ambitions for a Greater Syria but also to the Egyptians' partiality towards the Muftī of Jerusalem, Britain's enemy, as against 'Abdullāh, Britain's ally.[6] When finally the victorious Israelis crossed the Egyptian frontier and the British Government took action to restrain them, the Egyptian Government (disorganized, it is true, as a result of the political murder of Nuqrāshī, the Prime Minister, by extremists one week before) preferred to negotiate an armistice with Israel rather than invoke the support of the British garrison in the Canal Zone under the Anglo-Egyptian Treaty;[7] for it was possible to represent the armistice as the free act of an Egypt abandoned by her

[1] See below, pp. 272–5. The extreme nationalist Fathī Ridwān, who became Minister of State for propaganda in the Egyptian Government of September 1952, is reported to have asserted, however, that when in 1947–8 Egypt and 'Irāq refused to make new treaties of alliance with Britain 'the Foreign Office incited the United States to intervene in the Middle East for the purpose of provoking a Jew-Arab conflict', and that thus Egypt and the other Arab states were launched unprepared into the Palestine War (Édouard Sablier in the *Monde*, 16 September 1952).   [2] See below, p. 292.
[3] See above, pp. 140–1.   [4] See below, pp. 275–6.   [5] See below, pp. 270, 280–1, 286.
[6] When on 1 December 1948 'Abdullāh had himself proclaimed 'King of All Palestine' by a congress of Palestine Arabs at Jericho (see below, p. 290), the Cairo newspaper *Akhbār ul-Yawm* remarked bitterly: 'As if we had made so many sacrifices for Palestine to become a British base with an Arab title, a British colony under an Arab crown' (quoted by *Bourse Égyptienne*, 6 December 1948).   [7] See below, pp. 292–3.

Arab allies,[1] whereas the British garrison and the treaty were the obnoxious symbols of the incompleteness of Egyptian independence.

Nevertheless, the end of the war with Israel made it possible for the Egyptian Government to deal realistically with certain practical questions.[2] The Ministry of Public Works, with the collaboration of Egyptian and British scientists, had completed a survey of the entire Nile basin and had published its findings in 1948. First place among its recommendations for further irrigation works was given to the construction of a dam and hydro-electric works at Owen Falls in Uganda, a few miles below the point at which the infant Nile leaves Lake Victoria. The agreement of the Egyptian and British Governments that this work should begin, at an estimated cost to Egypt and Uganda of £4½ and £7½ million respectively, was announced in May 1949.[3] Its conception was but part of a much larger scheme, for whose completion twenty-five years were estimated to be necessary, for converting Lakes Victoria and Albert into storage reservoirs and cutting a by-pass canal through the Sudd swamps of the southern Sudan, and so allowing the flow of water to the lower Nile to be equalized, not merely between seasons, but between years of abundance and years of deficiency over a long period.[4]

Another achievement at this time was the conclusion on 7 March 1949 of a new agreement between the Egyptian Government and the Suez Canal Company. Egypt's original financial interest in the Canal had lapsed when the Khedive Ismā'īl had been compelled by his impending bankruptcy to sell his 44 per cent. share of the capital to the British Government in 1875, and when the bankrupt Egyptian Government had likewise ceded to the French Crédit Foncier in 1880 their right to 15 per cent. of the annual net profits of the Canal Company. In August 1937, however, an agreement had been concluded whereby the Company had granted to Egypt two places among the thirty-two members of its board of directors, an annual royalty of £E 300,000, and the admission of Egyptians to employment in a proportion which by 1958 was to attain 33 per cent.[5] An

[1] 'Egypt alone has been completely faithful to the League. . . . She is alone on the battlefield, carrying the whole burden, the victim of foreign intrigue and domestic differences' (the government newspaper al-'Assās, quoted by The Times Cairo correspondent, 5 January 1949).

[2] The execution of the project to build a great hydro-electric power station at the Aswan Dam, which was launched in 1946 and was intended to be completed by 1951, was fatally delayed by the disturbed political conditions during the following years. By July 1951, when the whole question was referred back to the Finance Committee, the rise in world costs of materials had raised the estimated cost of the work from the original estimate of £E 10·5 million to £E 24·6 million; and little had in fact been done.

[3] Bevin in the House of Commons, 19 May 1949 (H.C.Deb. 5th ser., vol. 465, coll. 617–21). For a progress report, see Great Britain, Central Office of Information, Reference Division: Commonwealth Affairs, 13 April 1951, section 4 (i), pp. 35–36.

[4] See H. E. Hurst: The Nile (London, Constable, 1952), pp. 281–322.

[5] Journal officiel égyptien, no. 73, 9 August 1937; see also Moustapha el-Hefnaoui: Les Problèmes contemporains posés par le Canal de Suez, p. 254.

Egyptian company law of July 1947 required companies established in Egypt, and the branches or agencies in Egypt of companies established abroad, to allot within three years 40 per cent. of their directorships to Egyptians, and to employ Egyptians to the proportion of 70 per cent. among their clerical and technical employees and of 90 per cent. among their labourers. The Canal Company argued that, because of their international responsibilities, this company law ought not to be applied to them; but the Egyptian Government insisted on their point, and the Company had to take into account that in twenty years, namely in 1968, their concession was due to revert to Egypt. It was accordingly agreed that two existing French vacancies on the board of directors should be transferred to Egypt, who would also receive the next British vacancy, and two further vacancies within the next fifteen years, a total of seven seats in all; her annual royalty would be converted into a 7 per cent. share of the gross profits, with an annual minimum of £E 350,000; the increase in the proportion of Egyptians employed by the Company would be applied more gradually, so as not to impair the efficient working of the Canal; 95 per cent. of the labour to be employed on a new by-pass in the Canal was to be Egyptian; and Egypt would benefit from the concession of transit *gratis* to vessels of under 300 tons. The bill ratifying this agreement was attacked in the Senate by the Wafdist Opposition, but it was carried by sixty-one votes against forty.[1]

The fundamental Anglo-Egyptian question of the defence of Egypt was not so readily to be resolved, however. The lesson which the Egyptian Government drew from the defeat of their armed forces by Israel was that expenditure on them should be greatly increased, to a figure of £52 million in a total budget of £193 million for the following year; and the president of the Chamber (a prominent member of the Sa'dist Party, and therefore presumably representing Government views) declared that the Egyptian forces had shown that they were able to fill any vacuum left by the withdrawal of British troops from Egypt.[2] The Chief of the Imperial General Staff (Field-Marshal Sir William Slim), who visited Egypt in March 1949 'as the result of an Egyptian approach', and Sir William Strang (Permanent Under-Secretary for Foreign Affairs), who followed him, repeated the British arguments for a joint defence pact. Technical discussions in the summer and autumn of 1949 worked out an air defence scheme for Egypt, providing for a force of twenty squadrons at the outbreak of war and for appropriate airfields and communications, radar, an observer

---

[1] See el-Hefnaoui, op. cit. pp. 257–77; and for the text of the agreement ibid. pp. 364–86.

[2] *Al-'Assās*, quoted by *Egyptian Gazette*, 30 May 1949. This was in answer to a statement by the veteran Ismā'īl Sidqī pointing out that Egypt was technically outclassed by Israel, and that Egypt should associate herself with the Atlantic Pact, 'the Powers whose interests coincide with ours, and who can help us in the realization of our aspirations' (letter to *al-Ahrām*, quoted by *Bourse Égyptienne*, 28 May 1949).

corps, anti-aircraft, and civil air defence; but, while the British envisaged this scheme on a joint Anglo-Egyptian basis, the Egyptian Government 'lacked sufficient support to commit themselves', and their spokesmen in the technical discussions maintained the Egyptian thesis that the existing British fighter strength of five squadrons should be withdrawn in peace-time from Egypt to the British bases in Cyprus, Malta, Cyrenaica, Jordan, and 'Irāq, and that the Egyptian air force should be equipped by Britain to take their place.[1] A general election in Egypt was constitutionally necessary in or before January 1950; and it was probably hoped on the British side that this would produce (to quote Bevin's words in 1947)[2] 'a more fully representative Egyptian Government' with which negotia-tions might 'avoid being the subject of Egyptian party politics', as they always were when the Wafd Party was in opposition. The return of the Wafd to power as a result of this general election opened a new phase of Anglo-Egyptian relations, whose unpropitious course is treated in the *Survey of International Affairs* for 1951.

(iii) Anglo-'Irāqī Relations

In October 1941, four months after the collapse of the short-lived anti-British *putsch* in 'Irāq,[3] Nūrī as-Saʻīd, who among that country's politicians was the warmest supporter of the alliance with Britain, had taken over the premiership and had retained it without a break (though with a number of Cabinet re-shuffles) until the beginning of June 1944, when he had resigned, ostensibly for reasons of health.[4] During this tenure of office, exceptionally long for 'Irāq (whose political life, especially since 1933, had been volatile),[5] he had worked in close collaboration with the British Ambassador, Sir Kinahan Cornwallis, who had had a long experience as a British adviser in 'Irāq. The chief problems had been the maintaining of essential supplies and the attempt to keep inflation within reasonable limits amid the war-time difficulties,[6] and tribal revolt among the Kurds of northern 'Irāq. Meanwhile political effervescence in the towns had been kept within prudent bounds by the collaboration of the 'Irāqī and British security authorities, a vigilant press censorship, and the presence of British ground forces since May 1941.

---

[1] See Great Britain, Foreign Office: *Anglo-Egyptian Conversations on the Defence of the Suez Canal and on the Sudan, December 1950–November 1951*, Cmd. 8419, p. 3; Egypt, Ministry of Foreign Affairs: *Records of Conversations, Notes and Papers exchanged between the Royal Egyptian Government and the United Kingdom Government (March 1950–November 1951)*, pp. 44–47, 54–55.

[2] 27 January 1947, H.C.Deb. 5th ser., vol. 432, col. 620; see above, p. 130.

[3] *Survey* for 1939–46: *The Middle East in the War*, pp. 56–78.

[4] *The Times*, 5 June 1944.

[5] Khadduri: *Independent Iraq*, chapters iii–ix.

[6] Cf. A. R. Prest: *War Economics of Primary Producing Countries* (Cambridge University Press, 1948), pp. 199–200.

One of the early acts of the new Government which succeeded to Nūrī was to establish diplomatic relations with the Soviet Union (10 September 1944), following the example set by the Wafd Government in Egypt a year before. One week earlier than this act, a new daily newspaper, *ash-Sha'b* (*The People*), had begun publication in Baghdād, and on 15 September it advocated the formation of a political party[1] to work for the realization of 'Irāq's national aims, since (it said) unless the people took part in the national struggle the declarations and promises of the Allies, although made with the best intentions, would remain merely paper promises. The relaxation of the press censorship became evident a month later upon the celebration of the anniversary of the Russian Revolution. In a five-column article *ash-Sha'b* declared that the Revolution had created powerful allies for the Arabs against imperialists and exploiters; it was a mistake to suppose that, because their nation was small and weak, they must therefore prefer one master to another; they must aim at delivering themselves from every master; it was not necessary to imitate the October Revolution, but rather to study it in order to benefit from the experience of the Russian peoples in their own national struggle. A monthly periodical, *ar-Rābita*, praised the Soviet Union for having abandoned the concessions in neighbouring countries (notably Persia) which she had inherited from her Tsarist predecessors,[2] and regretted the false ideas about the Soviet Union that had been formed in Arab minds, largely (it said) because of misleading information from British and United States sources. Greater publicity than hitherto began to be given to the speeches of Deputies opposing the Government: for example, a statement by Mahmūd Ramīz in January 1945 calling for the removal of every form of foreign control, in which he reminded the House that he was one among many who demanded a revision of the Anglo-'Irāqī Treaty of 1930, which was valid for another ten years. On 10 February 1945 *al-'Alam al-'Arabī* asked how 'Irāq would fare at the peace conference: the Great Powers were working to organize the political and economic future of the world, but 'Irāq wished to complete her national sovereignty and remove the last vestige of imperfection in her independence.

Such was the very natural state of mind of the politically conscious minority at the end of the war in Europe. Soon after that date the Prime

[1] While 'Irāq had known during her twenty years of constitutional life far more than her share of violent political faction, this had turned upon the rivalries of personalities, as in most other Middle Eastern countries. The only really distinctive programme had been that of the 'progressive' Ahālī group, influenced both by Western reformism and by Marxism; but this group, which had hoped to be a beneficiary of Bakr Sidqī's military dictatorship in 1936, had been thrust into the background even before his overthrow in 1937 (see Khadduri: *Independent Iraq*, pp. 104–7, 118–20).

[2] At this very time, however, the Soviet Government were vigorously pressing claims, which had come down from the Tsarist régime, for an oil concession embracing the whole of Persia's five northern provinces (*Survey* for 1939–46: *The Middle East in the War*, p. 475 and note 4).

Minister, Hamdī al-Pachachī, outlined to a British press correspondent four points which his Government were discussing with the British Embassy, and of which only one required any actual amendment of the treaty, while the rest were a matter for mutual arrangement.[1] Early in July the 'Irāqī Legation in Cairo denied current reports that negotiations for a modification of the treaty were in progress, and remarked that this would be premature while Britain was still at war with Japan.[2] On 13 July, however, the Amīr 'Abd ul-Ilāh, Regent since 1939 for the boy-king Faisal II, stated in London that during his present visit to England he would discuss changes to bring the treaty into accord with post-war conditions; certain clauses would have to be altered, while maintaining the Anglo-'Irāqī alliance.[3] Interviewed in December, the Regent and Prime Minister again referred, with some difference of emphasis, to a note exchanged at the time of the conclusion of the 1930 treaty concerning the priority to be given to Britain in 'Irāq's engagement of foreign experts.[4] On 30 January 1946 Hamdī al-Pachachī's Government resigned, having failed to satisfy the demand of the younger 'intelligentsia' (encouraged by the success of the British Labour Party in the 1945 general election) for the removal of censorship and security regulations and the freedom to form political parties, a demand which the Regent, newly returned from a visit to the United States, had publicly supported in a speech in December 1945. After twenty-five days without a government a more liberal Cabinet was formed by the elder statesman Tawfīq as-Suwaidī, who set up a committee to study the revision of the Anglo-'Irāqī Treaty.[5] On 20 April five new parties, on both the Right and the Left Wings and representing in the main the younger generation,[6] were

[1]   (i) The 'Irāqī Legation in London, and certain foreign Legations in Baghdād, to be raised to the status of Embassies.
      (ii) 'Irāq to have more freedom in the choice of foreign experts.
      (iii) Britain to agree to raise the standard of the 'Irāqī army.
      (iv) Britain to assist in the development of irrigation, agriculture, and transport (Richard Wyndham, *News of the World*, 1 July 1945).

[2] A. C. Sedgwick in *New York Times*, 7 July 1945.

[3] *Manchester Guardian*, 14 July 1945.

[4] 'The 'Irāq Government will normally engage British subjects when in need of the services of foreign officials. . . . This shall not prejudice the freedom of the 'Iraq Government to engage non-British foreign officials for posts for which suitable British subjects are not available' (Great Britain, Colonial Office: *Treaty of Alliance between the United Kingdom and 'Iraq, Baghdad, 30th June 1930, together with Notes exchanged*, Cmd. 3627 (London, H.M.S.O., 1930), p. 10, Note III); cf. Clifton Daniel in *New York Times*, 19 and 20 December 1945.

[5] In the last few days of this Government's life the Committee hurriedly reported that the Anglo-'Irāqī Alliance was no longer necessary in view of the establishment of the United Nations Organization, and that the 1930 treaty should therefore be replaced by a simple treaty of friendship. It may be doubted whether it would have reported in this sense had al-Suwaidī not known that his Government was about to fall; the publication of the report was well calculated to embarrass his successor.

[6] See Khadduri: *Independent Iraq*, pp. 217–18, 265–6. The nationalists of the Istiqlāl (independence) Party had been encouraged by the escape from Europe to Sa'ūdī Arabia in June

officially recognized and allowed to publish newspapers and pamphlets and to organize on a national basis. However, as-Suwaidī's Government soon lost favour in influential political quarters[1] and was forced to resign on 30 May, being succeeded by a Government led by the Mayor of Baghdād, Arshad al-'Umarī, professedly as a neutral who would conduct the general election that was constitutionally due within the next year. Meanwhile, however, the political situation in both 'Irāq and Persia was becoming more tense. On the publication of the Anglo-American Inquiry Committee's report on Palestine on 1 May, the five 'Irāqī political parties were stated to have appealed to the Soviet Minister in Baghdād for help in having the Palestine problem referred to the Security Council; and on 28 June there were disturbances lasting five hours in Baghdād when 3,000 workers and students marched through the city repeating this demand and also demanding the immediate withdrawal of British troops from 'Irāq. The Government responded by warning and then suspending offending newspapers.[2] In July Baghdād Communists exploited a strike for higher wages and better housing on the part of the 'Irāq Petroleum Company's workers in the Kirkuk oilfield; this strike coincided in date with the general strike of the Anglo-Iranian Oil Company's workers at the great Ābādān refinery, which was manifestly Communist-directed; and the 'Irāqī Government incurred further odium when the police fired on the Kirkuk strikers and killed between five and eight of them. The agitation reached its height when the 'Irāqī Government endorsed the British Government's sending of an Indian brigade-group to Basra for the purpose of ensuring the security of the Anglo-Iranian oilfield on the Persian side of the Shatt ul-'Arab.[3] On 4 September the Ministry of the Interior opened proceedings against the Baghdād Left-wing newspapers *ash-Sha'b* and *Sawt ul-Ahālī* for publishing allegedly inaccurate reports on the Kirkuk strike,[4] and banned the admission of the Soviet publications *New Times*

1945 of the political leader of the 1941 *putsch*, Rashīd 'Alī al-Gīlānī. He was reported to have travelled, after Germany's collapse, from Austria to Brussels, Paris, Marseilles, and then by sea to Beirut, allegedly disguised as a stoker in a French ship. The Muftī of Jerusalem, his associate in political intrigue and subsequent exile in the Axis camp, was also in the hands of the French authorities (cf. 24 October 1945, H.C.Deb. 5th ser., vol. 414, coll. 1987–8 and 2005; *Neue Zürcher Zeitung*, 18 October, *New York Times*, 28 October 1945). It was, however, formally denied that the French authorities had ever had the slightest responsibility for Rashīd 'Alī's movements; he had not crossed France during his flight; there was no evidence that he had passed through Beirut; and he had not found refuge in a French ship (*Figaro*, 30 October 1945).

[1] They probably felt that it was relaxing the war-time security measures too quickly; and Nūrī, who was in Ankara negotiating a treaty with Turkey and paid little attention to instructions from Baghdād, had his differences with the Government (Khadduri: *Independent Iraq*, pp. 262, 266). For the treaty with Turkey see below, p. 151.

[2] Khadduri, op. cit. p. 267; *Palestine Post*, 19 May, *The Times*, 29 June 1946.

[3] See above, p. 76; Khadduri, op. cit. pp. 274–5.

[4] Cf. the decidedly *ex parte* complaint of an editor of *Sawt ul-Ahālī* and vice-chairman of the 'left-of-centre' National Democratic Party, Muhammad Hadīd: 'Conditions in Iraq', *New Statesman and Nation*, 14 September 1946, pp. 186–7.

and *Soviet Weekly*, the London *Daily Worker* and the Communist *Labour Monthly*, and several other publications of similar tendency.[1]

As a result of al-'Umarī's energetic reaction to this Left-wing agitation, there could no longer be any claim to impartiality if the impending elections were held under his premiership.[2] As had become almost traditional when the situation was thought to be getting out of hand, therefore, Nūrī (whose Treaty of Friendship with Turkey had been initialed on 29 March),[3] formed on 21 November 1946 a new Cabinet which he was at pains to make as representative as possible, including in it members of groups usually opposed to him, among them the National Democratic Party, although the latter subsequently resigned because they could not agree on what constituted free elections in a semi-tribal society like that of 'Irāq. The boycott of the elections by the three diminutive but noisy Left-wing parties—ash-Sha'b (the People), al-Ittihād al-Watanī (National Unity), and at-Taharrur al-Watanī (National Liberation)—though publicized by the Tass Agency[4] as a reflection on political conditions in 'Irāq, was in reality an enforced move on their part, since they had no prospect of winning a single seat, however free the elections.

The Chamber returned by the elections consisted largely, as usual, of non-party men (45 per cent. on this occasion). Meanwhile, in January 1947 the police had arrested the leading members of the underground Communist Party of 'Irāq, the dissident 'Communist League' (Rābitat ush-Shuyū'īyīn), and the 'fellow-travelling' National Liberation Party, and seized a mass of revealing documents.[5] The situation was at last ripe for the presentation to Parliament for ratification, at the end of May, of Nūrī's draft treaty with Turkey. It was violently attacked by the newspapers of the Left-wing Sha'b and Ittihād al-Watanī Parties, who declared that 'Irāq was being bound to a country controlled by 'imperialism', and described the treaty as a British attempt to undermine the Arab

[1] The *Daily Worker* (5 September 1946) protested against this 'general offensive against the democratic movement in Iraq which has been proceeding for several months with the full knowledge of the British'.

[2] Cf. Khadduri, op. cit. pp. 267–8, for the Regent's disapproval on his return from a visit to England.

[3] Text in *Cahiers de l'Orient Contemporain*, 3me–4me trimestres, 1947, xi–xii. 149–50; cf. Khadduri, op. cit. pp. 261–2. The motive for this treaty was mutual assistance in the Soviet cold war against Turkey and Persia (cf. above, p. 30).

On 27 September the British Government had agreed to abandon their former insistence on the precedence of the British Ambassador over the representatives of all other Powers, and to raise the 'Irāqī Legation in London to an Embassy (Great Britain, Foreign Office: *Exchange of Notes between the U.K. and Iraq respecting the Status of the Iraqi Diplomatic Mission in London and the Precedence of H.M. Ambassador at Bagdad, Bagdad, 2nd August 1946*, Cmd. 6918 (London, H.M.S.O., 1946)). The Amīr Zaid, half-brother of King Faisal I, became the first 'Irāqī Ambassador.

[4] Cf. *Soviet Monitor*, 30 December 1946.

[5] These documents were subsequently printed in six volumes under the title *Secret Compilation regarding the Secret Iraqi Communist Party* (Baghdad, Government Press, 1950; in Arabic).

League, while parliamentary opponents of the Government[1] denounced it as part of an international plan to foment another world war, committing 'Irāq to support Turkey if the latter found herself at war with Syria, the U.S.S.R., Bulgaria, or Greece.[2] Goaded by these attacks, the Government instituted criminal proceedings against the leaders of the Sha'b and Ittihād al-Watanī Parties. On 24 June the court which had been trying the Communists arrested in January sentenced ten of the accused to fifteen years' imprisonment, and awarded death sentences (commuted on 14 July to imprisonment for life) to the three party leaders.

As a member of the sterling area 'Irāq had received from Britain allocations of scarce currencies amounting to some £9·074 million in the two and a half years preceding 15 July 1947,[3] when in accordance with the Anglo-American Financial Agreement of 1945 all newly acquired sterling was to become freely convertible into other currencies. Negotiations on the future of 'Irāq's sterling balances, which as a result of British war-time spending were estimated at between £60 and £75 million, had been opened by Sir Wilfred Eady of the British Treasury in Baghdād on 5 March 1947, and were resumed in London on 18 June by an 'Irāqī delegation headed by the Foreign Minister, Muhammad Fādil al-Jamālī. His Government were anxious to obtain the maximum amount of free currency for the development of irrigated agriculture along lines recently recommended by an irrigation development commission under a British

[1] Sālih Jabr had become Prime Minister after the elections, Nūrī taking the Presidency of the Senate. A sympathetic British press correspondent had remarked that several of the leading members of the youthful parties that were so vehemently attacking British 'imperialism' had graduated from British universities, where they had acquired Left-wing British ideas on social and economic questions; see also Jon Kimche: 'Iraq Breaks with Britain', *Nineteenth Century and After*, June 1948, p. 307, and *Tribune*, 23 April 1948, p. 9.

[2] Khadduri: *Independent Iraq*, pp. 262–3; *Bourse Égyptienne*, 29 May and 5 June 1947. *Pravda* of 21 April 1947 had quoted the Sha'b newspaper *al-Watan* as saying: 'The 'Irāqī people does not wish to assume obligations binding it to the reactionary Turks, slaves to the interests of Anglo-American imperialism. . . . The 'Irāqī people do not wish to be the centre of a British policy which aims at forcing the 'Irāqīs over the precipice of the Sa'dābād Pact and other imperialist projects that are full of mortal dangers' (*Oriente Moderno*, 1947, p. 107). Commentators had seen in the Turco-'Irāqī Treaty, a Turco-Transjordanian Treaty of Friendship of 11 January 1947, and an 'Irāqī-Transjordanian Treaty of Alliance of 15 April, an attempt to resurrect the quadripartite Sa'dābād Pact of 1937 (Marcel Colombe: 'La Turquie et les problèmes du Moyen-Orient', *Cahiers de l'Orient Contemporain*, 3me-4me trimestres, 1947, xi–xii. 138–41; cf. *Survey* for 1936, pp. 793–801, and *Survey* for 1939–46: *The Middle East in the War*, pp. 489–90). From the self-centred standpoint of Egypt in her relations with Britain at this time it was declared: 'It is the aim of British politicians to form an Eastern Bloc which would include Turkey, 'Irāq, and Transjordan. . . . We have heard that the formation of this Eastern Bloc would be directed against Communism and Russia. . . . We must say that Britain is tired of the Arab League and now aims at dividing the Arab countries. She is trying to annex what she can to Turkey, Persia, or Afghanistan . . .' (Ibrāhīm 'Abd ul-Qādir al-Māzinī, in *al-Balāgh*, quoted by *Egyptian Gazette*, 20 June 1947).

[3] Great Britain, Foreign Office: *Exchange of Notes between the U.K. and Iraq concerning the Prolongation of Existing Arrangements regarding Iraqi Foreign Exchange Requirements, Bagdad, 10th/22nd February, 1947*, Cmd. 7110 (London, H.M.S.O., 1947).

chairman.[1] After protracted negotiation an agreement was signed on 13 August, whereby Britain would release some £11–12 million in convertible currencies immediately and an additional £15 million over a period of five years.[2] *The Times* commented in its City Notes (21 August):

This appears on the face of it to be almost quixotic generosity in view of the foreign exchange position in which this country now finds itself.[3] The answer to that is no doubt that ... Iraq would face an economic crisis if substantial amounts were not released. .... For many reasons a crisis in Iraq would be unwelcome.

One of these reasons was the political pressure to which, as we have seen, the 'Irāqī Government were being subjected by the Opposition parties. Another was that negotiations for a revision of the Anglo-'Irāqī Treaty were at last about to begin, Sālih Jabr having stated on 10 April that this was the basis of his policy. The withdrawal of the British army formations that had been stationed in 'Irāq since 1941 had been completed by 26 October, and only the two small R.A.F. detachments at the bases of Habbānīya and Shu'aiba, for whose presence in time of peace the treaty of 1930 had provided, now remained.[4] By 6 January 1948 the conduct of the negotiations through diplomatic channels had been taken so far that Sālih Jabr, Nūrī, and the Defence Minister (Shākir al-Wadī), together with the independent Tawfīq as-Suwaidī, arrived in London to conclude them, while Fādil al-Jamālī had already been there for three weeks on his way home from the United Nations General Assembly. As Sālih Jabr and the British Foreign Secretary, Bevin, initialed a new draft treaty on the 10th, in Baghdād the Acting Premier, Jamāl Bābān, issued a statement that Britain had agreed to 'Irāq's 'national demands', relinquishing Britain's partial control of the State Railways[5] and the port of Basra, and handing back the two treaty bases; to this the 'Parliamentary Constitutional Front', a temporary coalition of the nationalist opposition parties, rejoined: 'The old treaty and the new are basically the same, especially with regard to Anglo-'Irāqī co-operation in defence matters, military guidance, and the training of the 'Irāqī Army, which the nation opposes.'[6] Since the 'Irāqī statesmen were visiting British naval installations and

[1] 'Irāqī Government, [Haigh] Irrigation Development Commission: *Report on the Control of the Rivers of Iraq and the Utilization of their Waters* (1949); cf. 'A Plan for Iraq', *The Times*, 25 June 1947.

[2] Great Britain, Foreign Office: *Financial Agreement between the U.K. and Iraq, London, 13th August, 1947*, Cmd. 7201 (London, H.M.S.O., 1947).

[3] On that very day, in fact, the heavy international run on sterling compelled the British Government to suspend convertibility indefinitely. A supplementary agreement with 'Irāq was accordingly necessary (Great Britain, Foreign Office: *Financial Agreement between the U.K. and Iraq Supplementary to the Agreement of 13th August, 1947, Bagdad, 7th November 1947*, Cmd. 7269 (London, H.M.S.O., 1947)).

[4] *The Times*, 17 April and 27 October 1947.

[5] Great Britain, Foreign Office: *Agreement between the U.K. and Iraq regarding the Railway System of Iraq ... Bagdad, March 31st 1936*, Cmd. 5282 (London, H.M.S.O., 1936).

[6] *Manchester Guardian*, 12 January 1948.

Bevin was convalescing in the Isle of Wight, it was at Portsmouth that the new treaty was signed on 15 January, the two delegations afterwards celebrating the occasion by lunching together aboard H.M.S. *Victory* 'which won her imperishable fame in an older fight for the defence of liberty against aggression'.[1] The new treaty proposed to continue the close Anglo-'Irāqī alliance established by the treaty of 1930 and repeated the clause precluding the adoption by either party of a foreign policy inconsistent with that alliance. As in the abortive negotiations with Egypt in 1946,[2] the British Government sought to concede the semblance of parity in the alliance by proposing to replace the British Military Mission by the immediate establishment of an Anglo-'Irāqī joint defence board, with equal numbers of members drawn from the competent military representatives of the two Governments, whose functions would include:

(a) The formulation of agreed plans in the strategic interests common to both countries;

(b) Immediate consultation in the event of a threat of war;

(c) The co-ordination of measures to enable the forces of either party to fulfil their obligations under the treaty;

(d) Consultation regarding the training of the 'Irāqī forces and the provision of equipment for them;

(e) Arrangements for joint air training operations.

In the event of war or a threat of war involving either party, 'Irāq would invite Britain to send the necessary forces of all arms into 'Irāq and would furnish all facilities and assistance, including communications through the country. Operational units of the R.A.F. would continue to have free access to the two air-bases at Habbānīya and Shu'aiba, until such time as peace treaties had entered into force with all ex-enemy countries and the Allied forces had been withdrawn from their territories; subsequently 'Irāq might invite R.A.F. units to use the bases on the advice of the Joint Defence Board in the light of the circumstances then prevailing. Britain would provide the technical staff, installations, and equipment to maintain the two bases at the necessary state of operational efficiency at all times, whether of peace or of war. 'Irāq would continue to choose her foreign military instructors from among British subjects and to send her personnel for advanced military training to establishments within the British Commonwealth, though without being precluded from sending them elsewhere if the instruction required were not available within the Commonwealth; the armament and essential equipment of the 'Irāqī forces would continue to be of the British type. The clause in the 1930 treaty permitting British naval vessels to visit the Shatt ul-'Arab was maintained. The treaty was to remain in force for twenty years, and its revision might be requested by either party after fifteen years, such

[1] *The Times*, leading article, 16 January 1948.   [2] See above, pp. 119–30.

revision to provide for continued alliance and co-operation. In an exchange of letters annexed to the treaty the British Government undertook to provide experts or technically qualified officials to assist 'Irāq in carrying out extensive plans of economic and social development.[1] At the signing ceremony Bevin said that this treaty 'was the beginning of a new series of treaties, regularizing and expressing the friendship between this country and the Arab world. Great Britain prized that friendship and he was sure the Arab world equally valued it.' In reply, Sālih Jabr said

they were signing a treaty which was an expression of their mutual desire and determination to live as free and equal allies and friends. It put the traditional friendship of their two peoples on a new, firm, and solid basis. This treaty would help them to work together for international peace and prosperity.[2]

Comments from overseas were, however, less favourable. The *Monde* (17 January) remarked: 'The letter is changed, the spirit remains.' The *Hindu* (17 January) remarked that except for some British concessions to nationalist sentiment

there is no difference between the old and the new treaties and the two countries are bound as closely as ever in the event of war. We do not see what innovations there are in the new treaty to suggest that it is the model or the foundation-stone for a Middle East defence system. Iraq's weaker status is evident not only in the defence arrangements but in the continuance of the foreign oil monopolies. A real regional system for the Middle East, working under the aegis of the United Nations, will only come when the economic independence of the Arab countries is assured.

In Baghdād the moderate press, 'though not enthusiastic for the joint defence plan', pointed out the necessity of support from a Great Power in view of Soviet pressure in the Middle East, and accepted the plan as the best possible. Newspapers supporting the Government reserved their comment; but the Istiqlāl Party—which was described by British observers as being 'undoubtedly the spiritual—and probably the actual—descendant of the pro-Nazi movement led by Rashid Ali that culminated in the 1941 revolt',[3] and which was excited by the conflict between Arabs and Zionists

---

[1] Text in Great Britain, Foreign Office: *Treaty of Alliance between the U.K. and Iraq, Portsmouth, 15th January, 1948*, Cmd. 7309 (London, H.M.S.O., 1948).

[2] *The Times*, 16 January 1948.

[3] *The Times* Baghdād correspondent, 20 January 1948; cf. Khadduri, p. 217. Some hundreds of Rashid 'Ali's followers, who had been interned by the restored 'Irāqī Government after the collapse of his *putsch*, had been released in 1946–7. 'So far ... from having lost face through their incarceration, the internees were now able to pose as victims of imperialist oppression and to enjoy considerable popularity. A measure of the Government's change of heart in such matters is the fact that previous officials were not only reinstated, but given full pay for their period of confinement and permitted to treat it as contributory to their promotion and pensions. ... The effect of their reappearance in public life might have been foreseen. Many were instructors in institutions of higher education. Others resumed an independent career in politics, editing newspapers and broadcasting. Their principal object became the exploitation of student patriotism

in Palestine that was now growing in violence every day[1]—naturally came out strongly against the treaty; the opposition Liberal and National Democratic Parties,[2] who complained that the 1947 election had not represented the true opinion of the people, had declared that they would not accept any treaty signed by the present Government; and the Communists were still active underground.[3] Incited by these forces, there had been demonstrations against the negotiations almost daily in Baghdād since 3 January,[4] and after the publication of the treaty in the press on the 16th the students of the various colleges proclaimed a three-day general strike. On the 20th and 21st there were clashes between the police and some 6,000 rioters, who stoned or set fire to British and United States offices and repelled by sheer numbers the initial efforts of the police to quell them; some seven police and four civilians were reported killed, and hundreds injured.[5] In the evening of the 21st the Regent summoned a meeting of those members of the Cabinet who were not in England and other political leaders, comprising former Premiers, the Vice-President of the Senate, the President of the Chamber of Deputies, members of the Senate and Chamber, and representatives of the political parties. It was stated in a communiqué

that they had unanimously decided that the Anglo-Iraqi treaty signed at Portsmouth does not realize the country's aspirations and is not a beneficial instrument to consolidate the bonds of friendship between the two countries. As the Council of Ministers has not approved the ratification of the treaty, the Regent promises the Iraqi peoples that no treaty will be ratified that does not assure the rights of the country and the national aspirations.[6]

On the following day Sālih Jabr issued a statement in England in which he said: 'On our return to Iraq we shall explain the intentions of the new treaty to the Parliament and people. We are confident that it will be

and the economic complaints of industrial workers' (George Pigott: 'Iraqi Relapse', *The Spectator*, 25 June 1948, p. 761).

[1] See below, pp. 251 seqq.

[2] A spokesman of the latter party declared that any treaty which 'Irāq concluded with Britain would have to conform with the spirit of the United Nations Charter by recognizing the equality of the two contracting parties. 'Britain can no longer regard 'Irāq as one of the countries within her sphere of influence, but must accept her as a completely independent and sovereign state, free to follow her own will' (quoted in 'Aperçu sur l'évolution politique de l'Iraq' (France, Présidence du Conseil: *Notes et Études Documentaires*, no. 1,501, 7 July 1951, pp. 11–12, note 77)).

[3] *The Times* Baghdād correspondent, 20 January 1948. An article in the Communist *Moyen-Orient* (February 1950, pp. 6–7) afterwards boasted that 'in the forefront of this movement, acting as a General Staff of the 'Irāqī rising, a Committee of Co-operation (*lajnat ut-ta'āwun*), formed on the initiative of the 'Irāqī Communist Party and composed of representatives of the National Liberation Party, the Kurdish Democratic Party, the Sha'b Party . . . independent elements, and Communists, assured the unity of the national forces in the struggle for independence'; but cf. below, p. 158.

[4] Khadduri, *Independent Iraq*, p. 270.

[5] *New York Times* Baghdād correspondent, 21–22 January 1948.

[6] *The Times*, 22 January 1948.

found that the national aspirations of the country are fully realized in this treaty and that the overwhelming majority of the country will support it.' In the House of Commons that afternoon Bevin said: 'There must have been some misunderstanding in Baghdad, but the Iraqi delegates should be able to remove it upon their return.'[1] Instead, however, the demonstrations broke out with redoubled fury after Sālih Jabr's return to Baghdād on the 26th, and on the following day some thirty persons were reported killed and 300 injured in street battles with the police. As had so often happened in the Middle East when the police had had to deal severely with the unrestrained mob violence of political demonstrations, they were now left in the lurch by the politicians: the Minister of Justice, the President of the Chamber of Deputies, and about thirty deputies resigned.[2] On the evening of the 27th the Regent announced the resignation of Sālih Jabr's Cabinet, and broadcast an appeal for good order to save the country from bloodshed. 100,000 people attended the funeral on the 28th of fifteen students killed in the demonstrations:

A six-mile procession was led by political and religious leaders and the coffins were covered with huge flags and bore large letters written in the blood of the victims. Thousands of people brandished swords, knives, and revolvers, and carried banners inscribed with 'Victims for freedom and independence', 'You died so that the 'Iraqi people could live', and 'We want the heads of Salih Jabr, Nuri as-Said, and their henchmen'. Demonstrators again marched through the city . . . praising the Regent . . . for his 'wisdom against traitors and imperialist slaves'. Headlines in the evening papers include, 'Thirty years' enslavement destroyed in three days', 'Our blood washes out traitor Salih Jabr's signature'.[3]

The ex-Premier slipped away to the Hilla *liwā* where, as a member of the Shī'ī sect, he enjoyed powerful tribal support; and an 'eminently safe' Cabinet came into power with the principal task of appeasing the demonstrators and restoring some semblance of order. Police officials who were held responsible for the casualties suffered by the demonstrators were punished, while the latter were for some time left unmolested to exert their nationalist pressure on the Government.[4]

One of the causes of the popular outcry against the treaty was the manner in which the negotiations had been conducted. Sālih Jabr was 'intensively secretive by nature', and afterwards admitted that 'he had left instructions that no Arab version of the treaty was to be published until his return from London, in order that he might have the opportunity

---

[1] Ibid. 23 January 1948; 22 January 1948, H.C.Deb. 5th ser., vol. 446, col. 400.
[2] Khadduri: *Independent Iraq*, p. 272.
[3] *Manchester Guardian*, 29 January 1948.
[4] Prospective visits by the King and Prime Minister of Jordan apparently came under the nationalist ban, on the ground that they were too well disposed to Britain; see Kimche: *Seven Fallen Pillars*, pp. 89–90, and the same writer's 'Iraq Breaks with Britain', *Nineteenth Century and After*, June 1948, p. 303, and *Tribune*, 16 April 1948, p. 9.

to put it clearly to Parliament and the nation'.[1] He had apparently not allowed for unofficial disclosures of the terms, or for the extent to which, after nearly a year in office, he had lost the confidence of the Regent, of the 'Irāqī army, which objected to his interference with a commission which had been sent to Britain to purchase military equipment and transport, and of the urban population, which was suffering much hardship from a bread shortage, the result of a combination of a bad harvest with the exportation of wheat by rich landowners.[2] Although the Regent had been extremely nervous about the general situation in the country at the end of December 1947, he was almost certainly unprepared for the demonstration of popular discontent that followed the publication of the treaty. Almost every politician in Baghdād had joined in this demonstration, out of ill will towards Sālih Jabr, the Istiqlāl militants taking the lead, while the role of the Communists had been substantially diminished by the repression of the last year. On the British side, the Ambassador, Sir Francis Stonehewer-Bird, who had a long experience in the Arab world, had been forced by a serious illness to leave in July, and the negotiations had perforce passed out of his hands.

The violence of the nationalist opposition to the proposed revision of the alliance with Britain did not result, however, in 'Irāq's permanent relapse into a sudden isolation, as had been forecast by some reporters.[3] Instead, the defeat of the Arab armies in the war against Israel in 1948 seems to have made the effective shapers of policy in Baghdād feel that a return to more moderate counsels was expedient. In January 1949 the elder statesman Nūrī as-Sa'īd had returned to the centre of the political stage and continued to dominate 'Irāqī policy for the next three years, except for a short period from December 1949 to February 1950. No attempt was made to renew negotiations for a revision of the British alliance; but despite the harassing tactics of the Opposition the Government could take up the report of an irrigation development commission which had been set up in 1946 under the leadership of F. F. Haigh, a former official of the Indian Service of Engineers, to survey the country's requirements in flood control and water storage, irrigation, and land-drainage.[4] In 1950 the Government of Tawfīq as-Suwaidī set up a Development Board with six executive members whose appointments were intended to be non-political; and, despite Opposition criticism of the employment of non-'Irāqīs, a former financial secretary of the Government of the Anglo-Egyptian Sudan was appointed as member for financial and economic affairs and secretary-general, and an American specialist in irrigation was also

---

[1] *Scotsman* Baghdād correspondent, 6 February, *The Times*, 19 February 1948.
[2] See George Pigott: 'Iraqi Relapse', *Spectator*, 25 June 1948, p. 761.
[3] e.g. Jon Kimche: 'Iraq Breaks with Britain', *Nineteenth Century and After*, June 1948.
[4] See 'Irāqī Government, [Haigh] Irrigation Development Commission: *Report on the Control of the Rivers of Iraq and the Utilization of their Waters* (1949).

appointed, both to serve under an 'Irāqī deputy president; the other three members were 'Irāqīs. The Haigh Commission had presented, besides a long-term plan of development at an estimated cost of some £88 million, a ten-year plan of flood control, irrigation, and development at an estimated cost of some £20 million. The increased oil royalties resulting from the expanded production of the 'Irāq Petroleum Company, when its new pipe-line to the Mediterranean at Bāniyās should be completed, were expected to finance this scheme; and the International Bank of Reconstruction and Development granted in June 1950 a loan of $12·8 million to meet the foreign exchange costs of constructing a large reservoir in the Wadi Tharthār, a dry valley lying to the west of the middle Tigris,[1] for the purposes of flood prevention and eventual irrigation.

(iv) The British Régime in Cyprus

(a) THE BACKGROUND, 1931–45

The hearts of the Cypriots, whose origin is obscure and whose history is the history of others, yearn for a Mother Greece who never bore them and for a Greek past which was never theirs. . . . In character and appearance they have more in common with the stolid Anatolians, across the water. Indeed, when the Greeks first arrived to colonize parts of Cyprus they found an indigenous population, probably of Asia Minor stock. But since the days of Byzantium the Cypriots have been Greek by language, religion and culture. After the collapse of the Empire they made no attempt to resist Latin and Moslem conquests. But their conquerors never absorbed them. Beneath their acceptance of foreign domination, a certain obstinate sense of Greekness survived.[2]

The claim to political unity (*Enosis*) with the modern Greek state was voiced by the spokesmen of that 80 per cent. of the population of Cyprus that were Greek-speaking[3] and belonged to the Orthodox and Apostolic Church.[4] The British Government, who had occupied Cyprus under an agreement with the Ottoman Empire in 1878, had been unwilling to grant this demand, primarily for reasons of imperial strategy and secondarily out of consideration for the objections of the Turkish-speaking and Muslim minority, which amounted to 19 per cent. of the population.[5] The political

---

[1] See International Bank for Reconstruction and Development: *The Economic Development of Iraq* (Baltimore, Johns Hopkins University Press, 1952).

[2] Patrick Balfour: *The Orphaned Realm* (London, Percival Marshall, 1951), pp. 25, 207–8.

[3] For statistics, see Great Britain, Colonial Office: *Annual Report on Cyprus for 1950* (London, H.M.S.O., 1951), p. 10.

[4] The Cypriot Church had been, since early days, an autocephalous member of the group of churches belonging to the Orthodox communion.

[5] See *Survey* for 1931, p. 360. A special correspondent in Cyprus regarded the consideration for the Turkish minority as 'rather overworked'; the latter were inclined to produce 'the rather specious argument that, because of the geographical position of Cyprus, the Greek Cypriots are really a minority in a Turkish and Muslim world' (*The Times*, 30 May 1952).

discontent of the Greek-speaking majority had expressed itself in October 1931 in riots in which Government House was burnt to the ground,[1] after which Letters Patent had been issued depriving Cyprus of its Legislative Council,[2] abolishing popular election to the District and Municipal Councils, suspending all clubs and organizations, prohibiting the unauthorized flying of flags and the holding of meetings of more than five persons except with the permission of the local Commissioner, and imposing a press and film censorship.[3] The Governor and Commander-in-Chief ruled bureaucratically, with the advice of an Executive Council of four official and two non-official members, 'one Moslem and the other non-Moslem', i.e. Greek; and since 1933 there had been an Advisory Council of four official and ten non-official members appointed by the Governor, which (it was officially stated) 'has no legislative powers but is consulted by Government on legislative and other measures, and so functions as a means whereby persons fitted by character and attainments for the task may formally advise Government on the Colony's requirements'.[4] The island was reported in 1939 to be 'not unprosperous', though there was still a great deal of rural poverty and indebtedness, deriving from the uncertainty of the island's rainfall and water supplies.[5] Government revenues, which had reached the figure of £757,000 in 1929, the last year before the world economic crisis, had risen to £1·02 million in 1938; these had been years of steady, if unspectacular, economic development. A trade union movement had come into being towards the end of 1937, and hours of work had been reduced and wages raised as a result.

Such material benefits, however, did not at all console the politically conscious section among the Greek majority of the Cypriots for the denial to them of the political liberty which had been enjoyed by their fellow Greeks in Greece since 1829, and which, since the First World War, had been gained progressively by neighbouring Middle Eastern peoples, including some that were politically much less mature than the Cypriots were.

[1] See *Survey* for 1931, pp. 354–94.

[2] This essay in self-government had not been very successful. B. J. Surridge, in his *Survey of Rural Life in Cyprus* (1930), had noted that 'only eighteen per cent. of the peasant proprietors were not in debt. . . . The peasant was the slave of the money-lender, obliged to buy seeds and stock from him at the highest price and to sell produce to him at the lowest' (quoted by W. L. Burn: 'The Future of Cyprus', *Fortnightly Review*, June 1947, p. 410), and the Governor had found in 1926 that four out of the twelve representatives of the Greek-speaking majority on the Council (who consisted of eight lawyers, a bishop, a merchant, and a farmer) were engaged in money-lending (Fabian Colonial Bureau: *Strategic Colonies and their Future* (London, Fabian Publications and Gollancz, 1945), p. 32).

[3] The censorship was applied with apparent impartiality to the Turkish-speaking minority as well as to the politically dissatisfied 'Greeks'; thus the film of Atatürk's funeral had been banned (*The Times*, 3 May 1939).

[4] Colonial Office, Annual Reports: *Cyprus*, 1938, pp. 9–10.

[5] 'At the outbreak of the war . . . chronic indebtedness and the stranglehold of the money-lender were a millstone round the farmer's neck' (Sir Charles Woolley, Governor of Cyprus, reported by *The Times*, 22 May 1945).

One of their spokesmen made an unfavourable comparison between the 'British dictatorship' in Cyprus since 1931 and even the 'worst excesses' of the Metaxas dictatorship in Greece; he admitted that a Committee for Cyprus Autonomy, which had been formed in 1937 in London ('the only practicable place where political questions affecting Cyprus could be raised without fear of persecution'), had succeeded, by ventilating such questions in the British press and Parliament, in drawing attention to the 'most odious aspects' of the régime and effecting 'a certain relaxation of repression'; but, he complained, the Colonial Office had remained 'blissfully disinterested' in the Committee's presentation in 1939 of a document embodying the 'fundamental constitutional demands' of 200 persons and organizations in Cyprus.[1] As against this viewpoint, the seriousness of the Cypriot demand for political liberty and for union with Greece were called in question by Sir Richmond Palmer, who was Governor from 1933 to 1939.[2]

Similar doubts were expressed by the British Colonial Secretary, Malcolm MacDonald, in answer to a series of critical oral questions in the House of Commons on 5 July 1939:

There has of late been a certain amount of discussion in Cyprus regarding constitutional reform. One of the principal means by which an agitation has been conducted has been the circulation amongst the people of petitions asking for changes in the Constitution. The methods by which those responsible have sought to obtain signatures have not in all cases been proper. Thus the Acting-Governor has represented that petitions have been placed in front of villagers by persons upon whose favour they are dependent,[3] and that signatures have been obtained by false suggestions. It was stated, for instance, that a measure of self-government was to be granted to the islanders in the near future; and suggested that those who refused to sign would suffer when self-government came. . . .

I am satisfied that the great majority of the people of Cyprus are not discontented under the present administration. The policy of the administration is to work in the direction of more representative government; but this process cannot be hurried, and in my view it must proceed first through a gradual increase of responsibility in local government.[4]

---

[1] Doros Alastos: *Cyprus, Past and . . . Future* (London, Committee for Cyprus Affairs [1943]), pp. 44, 60–61.

[2] See Sir Richmond Palmer: 'Cyprus', *Journal of the Royal Central Asian Society*, October 1939, xxvi. 606–7, 617. In the course of two articles critical of the Cyprus Government Arthur Merton had written (*Daily Telegraph*, 29 December 1938): 'The Government's determination to retain control of the Press is justified in the light of my experience of the Cyprus papers of 1931. Regulations should, however, be susceptible of intelligent interpretation. The control will have to be drastically overhauled.'

[3] W. L. Burn (*Fortnightly Review*, July 1939, p. 85) spoke of the complicated 'web of fear and dissimulation which indebtedness has woven in almost every Cyprus village'. There was also the powerful and pervasive influence of the Church, whose clergy were the mainspring of the Enosist movement.

[4] H.C.Deb. 5th ser., vol 349, coll. 1283–5.

The attitude of the Cypriots to the Second World War was, as the above-quoted Cypriot writer admitted, at first apathetic.

Nobody could tell them what the aims were of the British Government. As a political part of the British Empire they were declared belligerent and invited to join the army as volunteers. But the Colonial Office did not make any move which at least might have led them to expect that their conditions of life would have been improved, or a modicum of freedom granted them. Therefore it was the grim march of events that made the Cypriots adopt a definite attitude towards the war.[1]

A combatant force, the Cyprus Regiment, was established in February 1940—'but it attracted few recruits'. It was the entry of Italy into the war, and especially her invasion of Greece in October 1940 that 'brought the war home' to the Greek-speaking Cypriots. Six thousand Cypriots were said to have taken part among the British forces in the Greek campaign, and by October 1941 some 19,000 were serving in the forces, over 5,000 of them abroad. It was chiefly the workers and peasants who volunteered.

On 25 November 1942 the British Colonial Secretary announced that steps were being taken to hold municipal elections in Cyprus as the first step towards the restoration of representative government.[2] Meanwhile, a 'Progressive Party of the Working People' (*Anorthotikòn Kómma toû Ergazoménou Laoû*, commonly abbreviated to AKEL) had received authorization to constitute itself, but had failed to obtain permission to hold a meeting to celebrate the 1942 anniversary of the Soviet Revolution.[3] In December workmen employed by the Government on defence and other work in the capital (Nicosia) held a ten-day strike for higher wages since, despite substantial government subsidies and attempts to control supplies and prices and combat profiteering and the black market, the cost-of-

---

[1] Alastos: *Cyprus Past and . . . Future*, pp. 61–62.

[2] 'The administration began to sense the difficulties under which the Cypriots were labouring, taking part as they were in the gigantic battle for freedom and themselves being politically strait-jacketed by authoritarianism; [so] that it began to mend its ways. The entry of the Soviet Union into the war, [and] the declarations of the Atlantic Charter, gave a new impetus to the forces of progress' (ibid. pp. 66–67; cf. *Daily Telegraph*, 21 October 1941; L. S. Amery in *Sunday Times*, 6 April 1947).

[3] See 25 November 1942, H.C.Deb. 5th ser., vol. 385, coll. 742–3; *Daily Worker*, 27 November 1942. Alastos (op. cit. p. 67) contended that AKEL performed 'similar functions to those of the British Labour Party . . . it is a Labour Party operating in a predominantly peasant country'; but according to Martin Ebon (*World Communism Today* (New York and Toronto, Whittlesey House, 1948), pp. 423–4), the title represented by the initials AKEL had been adopted in 1934 by the Cyprus Communist Party. The party supported the recruiting campaign for the 'war against Fascism', but was afterwards alleged by a British observer to have infiltrated some 'one hundred of its most highly trained propagandists and agitators . . . by twos and threes into selected units' (Beverley Nichols in *Daily Telegraph*, 30 July 1946, after a visit to Cyprus). Evidently a great deal turned on what the political complexion of AKEL really was, and in the nature of the case it was difficult to obtain exact and conclusive evidence of their affiliation to Communist organizations outside the island.

living index had risen to 246 (August 1939 = 100);[1] on the other hand there was no lack of employment owing to defence works and copious military spending, which was enabling the peasantry at last to shake off their burden of debt.[2] In connexion with this strike of December 1942 seven trade unionists were sent to prison for having threatened the life of a 'black-leg'.[3]

While the municipal elections of 21 March 1943 returned a middle-class Enosist mayor in the capital, AKEL candidates were successful in the ports of Famagusta and Limassol. The new mayor in the latter town was a former printer, Ploutis Servas, who had spent the years 1929–34 in Moscow and had afterwards been deported from Greece.[4] A protest against the high cost of living soon followed. A one-day general strike on 27 August 1943 was threatened by the trade unions, which were closely associated with AKEL, but it was called off as a result of an official warning that it would be illegal.[5] A one-day general strike proclaimed for 25 October had, however, some success in urban areas; and at Limassol two municipal councillors, who had previous convictions for seditious conspiracy, and three others were sentenced to terms of imprisonment, while thirty other persons, including Servas, were fined for holding a procession without official permission, contrary to the legislation of 1932.[6] About this time the Cyprus Government invited the trade unions to provide representatives on all advisory committees appointed to deal with the cost of living, but the

[1] 'This was hotly controverted by local newspapers as not really representative of the true state of affairs. . . . For a long time the government was strangely reluctant to establish control—much less rationing—of even the really essential commodities, and allowed the situation to get almost out of control before they intervened. There were scandals in connection with the distribution of certain articles, such as petrol' (Fabian Colonial Bureau: *Strategic Colonies and their Future*, p. 33).

The Cyprus Government's Department of Labour's *Annual Report* for 1943 admitted that 'clothing had become increasingly scarce and, as there was plenty of money in circulation, prices soared. . . . Those who had to supplement the Government issue with purchases on the free market [*sic*] had to pay seven times the pre-war price or more. . . . All classes of the community were unwilling to restrict their purchases to what was available' (pp. 1–2, paras. 2 and 8).

[2] The Governor stated on 21 May 1945 that a Debt Settlement Board had reviewed the debts of 14,000 farmers amounting to £1·3 million. They had been cancelled or reduced, either amicably between the parties or by order of the Board, and interest had been reduced to 5 per cent. (*The Times*, 22 May 1945).

[3] The case was brought up in the Parliament at Westminster; see 3 February 1943, H.C.Deb. 5th ser., vol. 386, coll. 888–9; 3 March 1943, vol. 387, coll. 536–7; 31 March 1943, H.L.Deb. 5th ser., vol. 126, coll. 1028, 1042; Alastos, op. cit. pp. 69–72.

[4] 'The District Commissioner was on genial terms with Mr. Servas, and told me that he was not at all a bad fellow. . . . Grizzled and shock-headed, with a lazy, cynical charm, he talked with a sweet Liberal reasonableness which might reflect either his genuine personal convictions or the latest tactical directive from Moscow' (Balfour: *The Orphaned Realm*, p. 189; cf. L. Marsland Gander in *Daily Telegraph*, 21 October 1943, Richard Capell, ibid. 14 April 1944, Beverley Nichols, ibid. 30 July 1946).

[5] *Daily Telegraph*, 27 August, *Daily Worker*, 2 September 1943.

[6] The prison sentences were remitted by the Supreme Court (see the British Colonial Secretary, 3 November 1943, H.C.Deb. 5th ser., vol. 393, coll. 649–51; *Daily Worker*, 7 and 20 December 1943).

unions, as also the municipalities of Limassol and Famagusta, where AKEL was in office, refused to co-operate unless the Government agreed in advance to accept the committees' findings—a step which the British Colonial Secretary declined to take, on the ground that it 'would be manifestly inconsistent with the responsibilities of the Government to the community'. The same two municipalities also declined to co-operate in a scheme to control the marketing of perishable produce, which had received the support of the producers, on the argument that popularly elected bodies should be given greater control.[1] On 1 March 1944 1,800 Government labourers and craftsmen, mainly employed on military work, struck for an increase in wages, but returned to work on the 25th on an assurance of an official inquiry into their grievances.[2] About the same time, during a strike at a Limassol factory, hand-grenades were thrown at the houses of various persons: the Government decided early in April to call up a number of special constables to assist the regular police to keep order, but were confronted with a demand by trade unionists among the special constables that equal numbers should be chosen from the different political parties; and, when this and other requests were refused, the retort was absenteeism.[3]

Meanwhile the Enosists represented in the middle-class political parties had not been silent or inactive (for example, they denounced remarks made in the course of a House of Lords debate on 31 March 1943);[4] and when on 21 July 1944 it was announced that the Permanent Under-Secretary for the Colonies, Sir Cosmo Parkinson, would shortly visit Cyprus, the acting head (locum tenens) of the autocephalous Church of Cyprus[5] tried to persuade the National Party (the middle-class Enosists),

[1] 1 December 1943, H.C.Deb. 5th ser., vol. 394, coll. 385–6; 26 January 1944, ibid. vol. 396, coll. 676–8.

[2] 20 March 1944, ibid. vol. 398, coll. 1420–5; Manchester Guardian, 14 March, Daily Worker, 18 and 19 March, Reynolds News, 26 March 1944.

[3] 3 May 1944, H.C.Deb. 5th ser., vol. 399, coll. 1312–14.

[4] A Labour peer, Lord Farringdon, had averred that Greece 'is not truly the mother country of the Cypriots and . . . is also a country from which they could obtain no possible advantages'; while in reply the Under-Secretary for the Colonies had spoken of the two pitfalls in dealing with colonial questions, the one being complacency, and the other 'too readily believing that a very limited number of agitators, not perhaps very responsible persons, really represent the aspirations of a nation rightly striving to be free' (H.L.Deb. 5th ser., vol. 126, coll. 1023–45; cf. The Times, 7 April, Manchester Guardian, 12, 13, 24 April and 29 May 1944).

[5] The Bishops of Kyrenia and Kition had been sentenced to deportation for life for the leading part that they had played in the agitation that had caused the riots of 1931 (Survey for 1931, pp. 382–7). Laws enacted in 1937 had provided that the Archbishop of Cyprus must be a Cypriot, must be approved by the Governor, and must not have been deported or convicted for sedition. The Church of Cyprus had maintained that these laws conflicted with its constitution and that because of the deportations there was no quorum of bishops to fill the vacancy in the Archiepiscopal See that had existed since 1933; and it continued to be administered by the remaining Bishop, Leontios of Paphos, as locum tenens (Arthur Merton in Daily Telegraph, 29 December 1938; 16 February 1944, H.C.Deb. 5th ser., vol. 397, coll. 161–2; Manchester Guardian, 22 December 1943, 22 February 1944); but see below, pp. 174–5.

the peasants, and organized labour to agree on a joint memorandum to be presented to him. Immediately on Parkinson's arrival he received telegrams from the political organizations asking for *Enosis* after the liberation of Greece, for the immediate abolition for all 'illiberal' laws and orders, and for the granting of freedom of speech, of the press, and of assembly. On 19 August some seventy-five persons, including the mayor of Limassol, Servas, and the trade union leader Andreas Ziartides, were fined or bound over for holding unauthorized processions at Larnaca and Nicosia respectively. At his first press conference on the 22nd Parkinson told editors of Greek-language newspapers that he was not authorized to discuss in any way the separation of Cyprus from the British Empire. AKEL, the trade union committee, and the shopkeepers' union thereupon proclaimed a general strike on the 28th 'as a day of expression of the people's national feelings', and they informed Parkinson 'that they were willing to meet him if the illiberal orders adopted by the Government during his stay in Cyprus were abolished'. He left, however, on 3 September without meeting the AKEL and trade union representatives.[1] In December, when the British forces in Greece intervened to prevent the Communist attempt at a *putsch* in that country, Servas cabled a protest to the *Daily Worker*, and manifestoes denouncing British 'imperialism' were posted up at Nicosia.[2] Later, the two municipalities where AKEL was in office were prohibited from sending donations of £500 each to the Greek Relief Fund, since the Municipal Corporations Law required municipal revenue to be devoted exclusively to municipal purposes, though the British authorities admitted that in the past municipal councils had made a few small grants for charitable purposes which had inadvertently contravened this law.[3] Meanwhile, the conflict between Right and Left in Greece was bringing into the open the latent conflict between the middle-class Enosists and AKEL in Cyprus.[4] During the celebration of Greek Independence Day, 25 March 1945 (for which the Government had granted all applications for meetings and processions), a dispute broke out at the village of Lefkoniko between the Right and Left-wing parties, and one of them (evidently AKEL)[5] formed a procession for which no permit had been sought or issued. According to an official statement,

[1] 4 October 1944, H.C.Deb. 5th ser., vol. 403, coll. 919–21; according to which Servas had been permitted to hold his meeting on an understanding, which was broken, that no procession would follow it. Cf. Committee for Cyprus Affairs: *National Rehabilitation for Cyprus*, a pamphlet [1944].   [2] *Daily Worker*, 9 December, *Daily Telegraph*, 15 December 1944.
[3] 11 April 1945, H.C.Deb. 5th ser., vol. 409, col. 1832.
[4] 'In every city and village, chalked up on the walls of the streets and the cafés, you see the word Enosis . . . and usually underneath that word, the three letters E.A.M. . . . the organization of the Greek Communists' (Beverley Nichols in *Daily Telegraph*, 30 July 1946).
[5] 'Much more could be written about AKEL—its elaborate system of spies; its gradual, insistent infiltration into the rural communities by means of the shepherds—who are, as a rule, the potential toughs and gangsters of the districts' (ibid.).

a Cypriot police sergeant, fearing a more serious clash between the parties, intervened and repeatedly called on the procession to disperse. The demonstrators failed to do so and the police sergeant eventually called on two Cypriot police constables, who had joined him, to open fire, with the result that a man and a boy were killed and 14 other persons injured.

A commission of inquiry was set up, and, during the three days that elapsed between the incident and its first sitting, restrictions were placed on the publication of reports and comments (since statements greatly exaggerating the casualties were being circulated), though it was made clear that these restrictions would be removed when the hearings began. Nevertheless, the newspaper editors and the trade unions of printers and newsvendors decided unanimously not to publish the issue of 28 March as a protest. In Great Britain M.P.s belonging to the Labour Party, including the future Colonial Secretary, Arthur Creech Jones, criticized the police action in strong terms,[1] and a *Manchester Guardian* editorial (27 April) declared: 'The Cyprus Government had given a fresh grievance to a people already desperately prone to discover grievances against British rule.'

(b) THE LABOUR GOVERNMENT AND CONSTITUTIONALISM, 1945–8

The British Fabian Society's study *Strategic Colonies and their Future*, which has already been quoted in this section, appeared in October 1945, about the time at which a general election in Great Britain brought the Labour Party into office. The line taken at this time in regard to Cyprus by one of the organs of the British Labour Movement is therefore of considerable historical interest.

It would be foolish [the study concluded] to underrate the present agitation for severance from Britain and unity with Greece. The strength of Greek nationalist sentiment in Cyprus is a very real factor in the situation. The problem is an emotional one. It is useless to point out to the Cypriot how advantageous it will be to him to remain in the Empire. He may well ask what is the ground for believing that Britain, after her record of neglect, will do better in the future. Even if it were possible, intellectually, to convince him, as soon as he was with his own compatriots the intellectual consent would be submerged by the emotional urge.

But while emotion cannot be ignored, it is not necessarily wisest to give in to it. Submission to this agitation and the granting of immediate self-government may strengthen certain anti-social influences and reactionary interests. It may delay the development of local government and political responsibility, and eventually act to the detriment of the real social and economic interests of the ordinary people. As Cyprus is not self-supporting and will have to lean for

---

[1] 18 April and 16 May 1945, H.C.Deb. 5th ser., vol. 410, coll. 192–4, 2460–1; cf. *Daily Worker*, 31 March, 6 April 1945.

protection and security on a larger state, the best chance of economic recovery and a higher standard of living may, in spite of suspicion, rather lie in association with Britain which is now actively pursuing schemes of economic, political and educational development, and has already given an earnest in other territories of a new, progressive orientation in her colonial policy.[1]

There was an unconfirmed report that, perhaps under some suasion from the United States, the new British Government were 'close to' ceding Cyprus to Greece in September, but 'changed their minds for strategic reasons and fears of a Left-Wing Government in Athens'.[2] On 10 October, however, the Colonial Secretary, George Hall, made it evident that, for the time at any rate, the Labour Government were not intending to grant the Cypriot demand for union with Greece. He stated that the Government's policy for Cyprus was

to develop representative institutions in the sphere of local administration . . . before extending them to the central machinery of government. In accordance with this policy elected municipal councils were restored in 1943, and some months ago proposals for the extension to rural areas of a similar system of local administration through elected councils were made public. I am hopeful that these councils will prove so successful as to make it possible to contemplate the institution of a Legislative Council with unofficial elected representatives as early as possible.[3]

At this very time, Cypriot soldiers on home leave were demonstrating against being called upon for a further period of overseas service and were demanding their early demobilization. When Indian troops were called to the Famagusta transit camp on 8 October to get two reluctant Cypriot companies aboard a transport shots were fired which killed one Cypriot and wounded two. A military Court of Inquiry reported that the casualties were caused by soft-nosed bullets, and that the Indian troops were not armed with this type of ammunition, and the inference was that the shots had come from persons in the crowd that had gathered. These findings were, however, 'repudiated', as a British newspaper expressed it, 'by that section of the local press which had prejudged the issue'.[4] On the previous 20 July charges of seditious conspiracy had been brought against the

---

[1] Fabian Colonial Bureau: *Strategic Colonies*, p. 36. It had already remarked that 'at the present time . . . the tragic condition of Greece holds out little hope that union with Greece would solve the problem of raising the standard of living in Cyprus for some years to come' (ibid. pp. 34–35).

[2] C. L. Sulzberger in *New York Times*, 7 July 1946. When the same correspondent had earlier described an official United States plan for South-East Europe which included the union of Cyprus with Greece, the U.S. Secretary of State, Stettinius, said that Sulzberger 'had apparently seen some departmental study paper that was private and not final' (ibid. 1 January, *The Times* and *Daily Telegraph*, 3 January 1945); cf. below, pp. 172–3.

[3] H.C.Deb. 5th ser., vol. 414, col. 218.

[4] *The Times*, 9 October, *New York Herald Tribune*, 10 October 1945; 23 October 1945, H.C.Deb. 5th ser., vol. 414, coll. 1862–3; 31 October 1945, ibid. vol. 415, col. 574.

eighteen members of the Pan-Cyprian Trades Union Committee, which (unlike the 122 legally recognized unions) was not itself a registered union, though it was claimed for it that it had been brought into existence by a meeting of 435 delegates representing 13,500 trade unionists in September 1944, and that the Government had given facilities to its delegate to attend the World Trades Union Conference held in London in February 1945, and the Paris Conference of the World Federation of Trades Unions in October. According to Creech Jones, however (a critic of the previous Government's Cyprus policy who was now Under-Secretary for the Colonies),

it was revealed to the authorities in Cyprus that there was a quantity of seditious and inflammatory written material which was being circulated, secretly and illegally, by the persons who were charged in this case, and that the documents included directions for inciting the people to seditious activities. . . . The charges were, briefly, the encouragement by propaganda of the overthrow of the Con-stitution of Cyprus by revolution, the overthrow by violence of the established Government of Cyprus, and the overthrow by violence of organized government, and that there was seditious intention to excite disaffection and to procure the alteration of the law otherwise than by lawful means.[1]

The trial before the Nicosia assize court[2] began on 17 December and ended on 21 January 1946 with sentences of eighteen months' imprison-ment for twelve of the accused and one year for the remainder. The defence claimed that much of the propaganda to which the prosecution took exception was 'quotations from Marxist classics—such as Stalin's *Marxism and the National and Colonial Question* . . . and his *Leninism*'. The Cyprus Solicitor-General was reported to have said in the course of the trial that the possession of Marxist books and the propagation of Marxist theory were crimes under Cyprus law; but the British Secretary of State for the Dominions subsequently explained that 'the intention was to convey that Marxist literature as interpreted by the accused, and propa-ganda in their documents, constituted an offence'. After a request for leave to appeal had been refused, the case was raised in the British House of Commons by L. J. Solley (a lawyer who was to be expelled from the Labour Party in 1949 for his Communist sympathies). Solley represented that the law under which the accused had been sentenced was 'Fascist and anti-working-class in its character', that they were merely 'engaged in publicising the classic works of Socialism', and that 'it will be difficult to imagine any honest, patriotic Cypriot not feeling hatred against the foreign Government under which he has had to suffer all his life, and, indeed, it would be difficult to imagine why he would not seek to overthrow that

---

[1] 5 March 1946, H.C.Deb. 5th ser., vol. 420, col. 304.
[2] The court consisted of three judges sitting without a jury. The British institution of the jury had not been introduced into Cyprus by the British administration in the island.

Government with any means at his disposal.'[1] A writer who evidently had some personal acquaintance with the island remarked about this time:

It is a natural reaction of the Administration, always prone, in any case, to regard the *status quo* as sacrosanct, to argue that the granting of a liberal constitution to Cyprus would be worse than useless because, leaving aside minor arguments, the Cypriots would immediately sabotage the new constitution in an endeavour to achieve and as a means of expressing their undying desire for union with Greece. The Administration is therefore tempted to argue that it is a waste of time even thinking of being liberal towards the Cypriots and is much more practical periodically to imprison or even shoot a few Cypriots in the course of maintaining British rule.[2]

Municipal elections held on 26 May 1946 were fought between the Right-wing 'National Front' and the Left-wing 'National Co-operation Front', whose nucleus was AKEL. The latter not only retained their hold on Limassol and Famagusta, but won Nicosia and all but two of the principal towns.[3] The British Government's decision in August to transfer to a detention camp near Famagusta the Jewish refugees from Europe now arriving illegally in Palestine in considerable numbers[4] evoked an immediate declaration from the AKEL Mayor of Famagusta that the people were being led 'to suspect an attempt to weaken the Greek majority by an influx of foreigners'; and after it had been officially stated that the refugees would not be allowed to become residents of Cyprus, the Mayor of Limassol submitted to the Governor a demand that their transfer to Cyprus should be stopped nevertheless, since it was alleged that their provisioning was leading to a shortage of supplies and an increase of prices, and that this was causing a considerable hardening of Cypriot opinion.[5]

During this summer of 1946 there had been unofficial reports that, as a result of the undertaking to withdraw all British troops from Egypt on condition that that country would make adequate joint defence arrangements with Britain,[6] a new British military and air base would be established in Cyprus. At the same time the British Government attempted to liberalize the political régime and develop the island's economy. On

---

[1] 30 January and 6 February 1946, H.C.Deb. 5th ser., vol. 418, *written answers*, coll. 228–9, 392–3; 5 March 1946, vol. 420, coll. 298–306; 29 July 1946, H.L.Deb. 5th ser., vol. 142, coll. 1113–14; cf. *Daily Worker*, 11 and 22 January, 6 and 7 March, *Reynolds News*, 13 January *Manchester Guardian*, 22 July 1946, quoting an article in *Pravda*.

[2] Percy Arnold: 'The Cyprus Dilemma', *Contemporary Review*, August 1946, p. 80.

[3] *The Economist*, 28 October 1946, p. 656.

[4] See below, p. 227, note 2.

[5] *New York Times*, 11 August and 8 September 1946. The Zionists had naturally done their utmost to foment Cypriot opposition; cf. Barnett Litvinoff in *Zionist Review*, 16 August 1946, p. 4: 'The food problem . . . will be so enormously affected by this sudden increase in population that unless the British Government take full responsibility for their victualling (and in present times this is by no means assured) Cyprus is liable to become a huge concentration-camp, with all the disorders attendant upon hunger.'

[6] See above, p. 120.

5 October it was announced that Lord Winster, hitherto Minister of Civil Aviation in the Labour Government, would shortly go out as Governor;[1] on the 18th the twelve convicted trade union leaders who had received the longer sentences were, as an act of clemency, released with their six comrades who had completed their shorter sentences. They at once made speeches reaffirming their intention to carry on the struggle for the national cause.[2] On the 23rd Creech Jones, who had now become Colonial Secretary, stated that the Government had reviewed their policy

with a view to seeking opportunities to establish a more liberal and progressive regime in the internal affairs of the island. . . . I propose to invite the Governor, Sir Charles Woolley . . . to call together a Consultative Assembly, drawn from representative elements in the island, to consider the framing of proposals for constitutional reform, including the re-establishment of a Central Legislature. . . .

His Majesty's Government are also determined to press on with vigour the programme of economic development and social welfare, which has been successfully initiated during recent years. . . . A systematic and detailed plan of development covering the next 10 years . . . is being published in Cyprus to-day. This plan deals with every aspect of the island's life and economy—agriculture and irrigation, the forests, medical and education services, the expansion of the ports, the provision of tourist facilities and so on.[3]

There are two further matters on which I can also announce decisions. The first relates to the situation at present existing in the Church of Cyprus, of which the Archiepiscopal See has now been vacant for many years. There seems little doubt that the three local laws enacted in 1937 with the object of controlling certain aspects of the election of a new Archbishop[4] have impeded the settlement of this problem. . . . His Majesty's Government have now decided that they should be repealed as soon as practicable. . . .

Finally, the Government consider that the time has now come to permit the return to Cyprus of those persons who were deported from the Island for their part in the disturbances of 1931.[5]

---

[1] As Commander R. Fletcher, M.P., he had in 1939, at the meeting of the Royal Central Asian Society addressed by the then retiring Governor Sir Richmond Palmer, criticized recent policy in Cyprus 'in some respects', and said: 'Unless Cyprus is to be under an authoritarian form of government for ever, the question arises as to when we are to make a start, and whether the old Constitution or some amended form of it is to be set up' (*Journal of the Royal Central Asian Society*, October 1939, xxvi. 614–15).

[2] *The Times*, 19 October 1946.

[3] From 1941 until March 1946 the British Government had made free grants to Cyprus under the Colonial Development and Welfare Act totalling £600,000 for the above purposes, and a further allocation of £1·75 million had now been made. The development plan was estimated to cost £6 million, while the cost of a separate scheme to provide the whole island with electric light was estimated at £3·35 million; priority was to be given to schemes costing about £4 million. It was hoped to raise revenue and local loans, since bank deposits amounted to £11·5 million (Cyprus Government: *A Ten-Year Programme of Development for Cyprus*, 1946, p. ii).

[4] See above, p. 164, note 5.

[5] H.C.Deb. 5th ser., vol. 427, *written answers*, coll. 396–7.

Admirable as Lord Winster found the new statement of policy to be, he afterwards claimed to have urged that its announcement should not be made until after he had arrived in Cyprus as the new Governor and could in person make a simultaneous offer of the reforms to the people.[1] Creech Jones, on the other hand, held that it was essential to announce the Government's intentions immediately, in the hope of rallying liberal opinion, the moderate trade unionists, and the countryside in their support. In the event Lord Winster did not arrive until March 1947, on account of his failure to obtain in London certain assurances on policy; and immediately after Creech Jones's statement the Ethnarchic Council (an unofficial Enosist body over which the locum tenens presided as Ethnarch or 'leader of the nation') had cabled to the British Government rejecting 'categorically and with indignation any solution of the Cyprus question not granting national liberty by union with Greece', while the Greek parties urged the formation of a united front to continue the struggle for *Enosis*. The *Manchester Guardian* had since 1931 consistently criticized the official British policy in Cyprus; but an editorial of 26 October 1946, which welcomed Creech Jones's statement as 'belated reparation' for the years of 'constitutional gloom', concluded by expressing regret that the immediate response had been only a repetition of the Enosist claims. The Liberal newspaper agreed with the Labour Government in holding that these ought not to be conceded. 'Along that path lie deadlock and frustration, because for an unforeseeable time to come no move in that direction can be made. We have not beckoned Cyprus out of the twilight in order to watch her plunge into a deeper and more hopeless darkness.'

At the end of December a 'national delegation', led by the locum tenens and consisting of the chairman of the Chamber of Commerce (representing the Right-wing 'National Front'), the Mayor of Nicosia, Klerides (representing the Left-wing 'National Co-operation Front'), and a secretary, arrived in London to put their case for union with Greece. They travelled by way of Athens, where they received expressions of deep sympathy from the public and the whole of the press. While British Liberal sympathizers expressed doubts whether union was really desirable at this moment when Greece's internal politics were in such turmoil,[2] the delegation submitted to the British Colonial Secretary on 7 February 1947 a memorandum in which they claimed that the island and its people were in religion, language, tradition, and national conscience 'staunchly and immutably' Greek, and therefore rejected the constitutional reforms and economic scheme which he had announced three months before; the rights of the

---

[1] See Lord Winster: 'Administrative Problems in Cyprus', *United Empire*, July–August 1949, xl. 179, and article in the *Daily Telegraph*, 28 April 1949. *The Economist* had commented (26 October 1946, p. 655) that Creech Jones's statement was weak in presentation, and in failing to capture the Cypriot imagination.

[2] *Manchester Guardian* London correspondent, 22 January 1947.

Turkish minority would be fully safeguarded, and arrangements could no doubt be made with the Greek Government to ensure British defence interests in the eastern Mediterranean.[1]

Meanwhile, the parties of the Turkish minority, looking as ever to the British connexion to preserve their position, had telegraphed to the British Government protesting against the pretension of the Ethnarchic Council and the delegation to speak for all the people in Cyprus; and while the Turkish organizations urged their members to give the new Governor a welcome on his now expected arrival, the Ethnarchic Council and their political parties instructed the Greek majority to boycott him.[2] A new development occurred when on 28 February the Chamber of Deputies in Greece unanimously approved a resolution confiding 'the sacred national demand for the union of Cyprus with Greece' to friendly discussions between the Greek and British Governments.[3] While agitation in Cyprus continued from both Right and Left—the Pan-Cyprian Trades Union Committee allegedly calling on 9 March for a 'mass mobilization against the foreign occupation'[4]—there was a leakage in Washington on the 21st from an 'unofficial background document' presented confidentially by the State Department to members of the House of Representatives Foreign Affairs Committee in order to promote the Truman Doctrine for aid to Greece and Turkey:[5] the document declared *inter alia* that the United

[1] *The Times*, 8 February 1947. The secretary to the delegation afterwards claimed, apparently without foundation, that Creech Jones had undertaken to put their proposals before the Cabinet. Creech Jones told the House of Commons that he had reminded them of a statement he had made in the House on 11 December 1946 (in reply to a question by the Communist member, Piratin) that the Government did not contemplate any change in the status of the island (*Manchester Guardian*, 27 February, *The Times*, 28 February 1947; 12 March 1947, H.C.Deb. 5th ser., vol. 434, coll. 1318–19).

[2] *The Times*, 17 February 1947. A correspondent afterwards stated that the initiative in the boycott came from AKEL, 'fearing the possibility that the Right might come to terms with the British either on autonomy or future promises of some sort of Greek citizenship. . . . There is every indication that a number of Right-wing leaders were opposed to the idea . . . but a polite reception by the Right, in the face of abstention from the Left, would have resulted in accusations of fawning to the British or of scheming for autonomy. Either would have meant a serious loss of popular support' (*The Economist*, 26 July 1947, p. 159).

[3] Text in *Greek Bulletin*, issued by the Greek Information Office, London, 3 March 1947. In November 1941 the Premier of the Greek Government in Exile was reported to have made a statement visualizing the union of Cyprus with Greece after the war, and in 1944 his successor Papandreou was said to have raised the question in discussions with Churchill in Italy (*Daily Telegraph*, 5 December 1941; *Yorkshire Post*, 20 September 1944).

The Hon. Steven Runciman (representative of the British Council in Greece, 1945–7) afterwards said: 'In Greece itself the Greeks were not very enthusiastic about their Cypriot brethren. They usually told one that the Cypriots were the Irish of Greece. But still every Greek did feel that Cyprus was being kept from him. Cyprus was to the Greeks a *terra irredenta* and though they were on the whole too fond of the British to make much of it, that feeling did obtain. On the other hand, if the Greek Government were suddenly to be given a present of Cyprus he thought it would be highly embarrassed. Greece was a poor country and in a very difficult situation, and the island would be a financial and administrative liability' (*United Empire*, July–August 1949, xl. 182).

[4] Reuter, Kyrenia, reported by *Neue Zürcher Zeitung*, 11 March 1947.   [5] Cf. above, p. 36.

States Government favoured the union of Cyprus with Greece, provided that that was acceptable to the Greek and British Governments.[1] British official sources were reported to have expressed surprise and concern at this disclosure at so delicate a time, and the State Department withdrew this and other passages of the document, explaining that they had been issued in error from a preparatory study, there having been insufficient time for adequate revision owing to Congress's demand for information.[2]

Immediately after this, on 27 March 1947, Lord Winster at last arrived to take up his post as Governor. Many of the Greeks of the capital had kept the Greek flags flying that they had displayed for Greek Independence Day two days earlier, and it was left for the British officials and members of the Turkish minority to welcome the new Governor. On the following day the Greek notables who had been invited to a reception to meet him absented themselves, with the exception of government officials, on the instructions of the Ethnarchic Council, which had already sent the new Governor a memorandum in which it spoke of an enslaved people struggling for self-determination: among the absentees were the locum tenens, the Bishop of Kyrenia (newly returned from his fifteen years' exile), the mayor of Nicosia, Klerides, and four members of the Advisory Council. The Governor could hardly be expected to tolerate the subservience to the Ethnarchic Council of members of his Advisory Council, and two days later the four offenders were informed that their services were no longer required and that they would not be received at the forthcoming meeting of the Council to which they had accepted invitations. After this inauspicious beginning the Governor issued on 4 April a message to the people of Cyprus calling attention to the Colonial Secretary's reaffirmation on 11 December 1946 of

the policy of successive British Governments that Cyprus shall remain under British sovereignty as a valued and trusted partner sharing in the common strength of the British Commonwealth. There is no change in that policy, which goes hand in hand with the programme of development and the intention

---

[1] James Reston in *New York Times*, 22 March, *New York Herald Tribune*, 24 March 1947. 'The million Greeks in America are just as anxious to see Cyprus restored to the motherland as are the Greeks in Europe or the Greek Cypriots themselves. Under the race-conscious and powerful Greek-American society, the A.H.E.P.A., they have used their influence in keeping the subject constantly in the minds of the American public' (Thomas Anthem: 'The Cyprus Farce', *Contemporary Review*, June 1947, p. 338).

Visiting the island unofficially about this time the British elder statesman L. S. Amery revived a suggestion which he had originally studied when Colonial Secretary (1924–9), but evoked no practical response: 'Any Cypriot should, after a minimum period of residence in Greece, be entitled to enjoy all the rights and privileges of a Greek citizen without forfeiting his status as a British subject outside Greece. Conversely, any Greek citizen settling in Cyprus should, without loss of his citizenship, similarly become entitled to all the rights and privileges of a British subject in Cyprus—and possibly, after a longer period of domicile, to those of a British subject outside of Cyprus as well' (*Sunday Times*, 6 April 1947).

[2] *The Times* and *Daily Telegraph*, 25 March 1947.

of establishing a liberal and progressive régime in the internal affairs of the island and of promoting its prosperity. . . . The road lies clear for a new start. . . . Let us from the outset go forward together in friendship in pursuit of the aims I set before you.[1]

At this late stage it was hardly to be expected that there would be any response from the Enosists;[2] and on 26 April the Colonial Secretary of the Cyprus Government[3] warned newspaper editors that while the right to criticize the Government, however trenchantly, would be maintained and respected, the Government could no longer ignore the use of the press for campaigns or propaganda in the nature of incitement to disorder or subversive of the machinery of government; certain newspapers had shown 'a fantastic irresponsibility in the dissemination of reports varying from cunning distortion of the truth to deliberate lies', with the object of bringing the Government of Cyprus into disrepute and contempt; and, where the press was so used, he would have no hesitation in using his powers to suspend or suppress a newspaper.[4]

It had been decided, Lord Winster wrote afterwards,

to allow the archiepiscopal elections to be held before summoning the Consultative Assembly. It was a foregone conclusion that an archbishop would prove hostile to [the] Government; so that, in the spirit which once led an English commander to allow the enemy to fire first, we were agreeing to bring a powerful opponent into the field before we proceeded with our plans.[5]

The locum tenens repeatedly declared to his Greek supporters, and gave a pledge, that he would not accept nomination as Archbishop. On 27 April he resigned all his offices, announced his intention of retiring to a monastery on Mount Athos, and was reported to have said that he had been accused of dividing the people instead of uniting them, adding cryptically: 'All those interested are great persons; they are dictators. Great Powers dominate the Near East and the Mediterranean. They want to impose their own order of things, and for national reasons our nation needs those Powers.' On the following day, however, he yielded to the persuasion of

---

[1] *The Times*, 7 April 1947.

[2] The Right and Left Wings were estranged from one another at this time by the refusal of the AKEL Mayors of Limassol and Famagusta to lower the Greek flag to half-mast for the funeral of King George II of Greece, as requested by the Enosist authorities; a large crowd stormed Limassol Town Hall on 6 April (*Daily Telegraph*, 7 April 1947).

[3] The chief official of the Cyprus Government after the Governor—to be distinguished, of course, from the Colonial Secretary in London.

[4] *The Times*, 28 April 1947. The British Colonial Secretary confirmed that the warning had been issued after consultation with himself. It was piquant to find Anthony Eden, during whose party's long tenure of office from 1931 to 1945 the Cyprus Government had frequently had recourse to the Press Laws, asking from the Opposition for 'an assurance that there will be no prolongation of this state of affairs, and that he [the Colonial Secretary] will consult with the Governor as to when full freedom can be restored' (7 May 1947, H.C.Deb. 5th ser., vol. 437, coll. 409–11).

[5] *Daily Telegraph*, 28 April 1949.

the representative of the Oecumenical Patriarch of Constantinople, who had come to complete the quorum of bishops, and withdrew his resignation; he now had the support of the parties of the Left, notably AKEL;[1] and at the primary election on 4 May, which passed off quietly apart from stabbing affrays in some villages, his supporters won an overwhelming victory. The electoral college so chosen duly gave him, on 20 June, fifty-eight votes out of seventy-five. He again refused to accept election, but again yielded to the urgent appeal of the Patriarchal representative. The aged Bishop of Kyrenia, a pillar of the Right Wing, thereupon shouted: 'I will not enthrone you; I will not recognize you', but he also was eventually persuaded to withdraw his opposition, so that the electoral synod was able to announce that Bishop Leontios of Paphos had been unanimously elected Archbishop, and the Bishop of Kyrenia officiated at his enthronement. Despite the support he had received from the Left, he immediately signalized his appointment by rejecting an invitation from the Patriarch of Moscow (an office re-created by the Soviet Government in 1943 in rivalry to the Oecumenical Patriarchate of Constantinople)[2] that he or his delegate should represent the Church of Cyprus at a forthcoming conference of all the Orthodox Churches in Moscow; it was, he said, the prerogative of the Oecumenical Patriarch to convene such a conference.[3] The Cyprus Government were reliably reported to be 'not unduly perturbed' by the result of the election, and on 9 July the Governor issued a proclamation announcing that nominations were being invited for a Consultative Assembly to make recommendations to him on the form of constitution to be established in order to secure the participation of the people of Cyprus in the direction of the internal affairs of the island, due regard being paid to the interests of minorities. Among those invited were Greek- and Turkish-speaking nominees of the municipal councils, the Bar, the medical association, the association of industrialists, the chamber of commerce, the farmers' association, secondary-school teachers, the press, the 'pan-Cyprian' trade unions, the newer Cyprus Workers' Confederation,[4] the Turkish farmers' union, and the Turkish trade unions. The Archbishop immediately issued a statement that the Governor's proclamation was

---

[1] He had 'unusual influence' with AKEL, according to Charles G. Curran (*Spectator*, 20 August 1948, p. 234); but Lord Winster was hardly justified in describing him as 'a man of the extreme Left' (*United Empire*, July–August 1949, xl. 179).

[2] Cf. above, p. 47.

[3] *The Times*, 29 and 30 April, 6 May, 28 June 1947.

[4] This had been founded at Limassol in order to be free of Left-wing influence, but was from the start accused by its older 'pan-Cyprian' rival of being a 'company-union' (Cyprus Government, Department of Labour: *Annual Report*, 1943, p. 3, paragraph 13), while the Colonial Under-Secretary in the British Labour Government was to describe it as 'sponsored by Right-wing parties' (17 November 1948, H.C.Deb. 5th ser., vol. 458, coll. 363–4). At the end of 1946 it had only 9 per cent. of the membership of the more leftward union (Great Britain, Colonial Office, Annual Reports: *Cyprus, 1947*, p. 8); cf. below, p. 182.

'hostile to the people of Cyprus, and we shall do all in our power to thwart its objectives'; and in a counter-proclamation, which was published in all the Greek newspapers and read from all Orthodox pulpits, he declared that Britain was offering the Cypriots 'a knife with which to cut in pieces their own national rights, for the people are asked to endorse the perpetuation of their enslavement'; the composition of the proposed Consultative Assembly, he said, was based on 'anti-democratic and fascist prototypes', and dealt a mortal blow to democratic conceptions; the people would be united in continuing their lawful struggle for *Enosis*, and would seal their ears to the Governor's proclamation.[1] This was Archbishop Leontios's last political act, however, for on 26 July he died of typhus, following chronic diabetes.[2] 'It was then decided', wrote Lord Winster afterwards, 'to allow another archbishop to be elected before we modestly proceeded with our own plans.'[3] At the primary election on 5 October the Right secured forty delegates supporting the aged Bishop of Kyrenia, while the Bishop of Derkon (who had been the Patriarchal representative at the election of Archbishop Leontios) had the support of twenty-six delegates from the Left.

From the time the second Archbishop was elected [said Lord Winster afterwards] he used every power the Church possessed to proclaim a boycott of everything that H.M. Government was offering and to preach a doctrine of subversion and disobedience. That was what the Secretary of State got for his offer to restore the ecclesiastical hierarchy of the island. He got an uncompromising opposition to British rule, the Archbishop using every influence he had to defeat the aims and objects of the British Government.

As for the development programme, there again we met with a complete blank refusal to co-operate in any way whatever. Whatever plan we proposed for the development of their industries and so on we could find no help or support for it. There was no co-operation whatsoever.[4]

Meanwhile, towards the end of August the Governor, 'in view of widespread rumours', had denied any suggestion that the British Government were entertaining the idea of ceding Cyprus to Greece. 'No agreement between the British and Greek Governments concerning the union of Cyprus with Greece exists in any form whatsoever', he said. 'Further, no such agreement is in course of negotiation or is contemplated. Statements

---

[1] *The Times*, 25 June, 10, 11, and 14 July 1947. In view of this uncompromising attitude of the Church, it is difficult to accept the charge of C. L. Sulzberger (a consistent propagandist for *Enosis*) that 'the Colonial Office . . . has shown a tendency to regard the threat of the Enosis movement as more menacing than the growth of Communism. . . . As a result Communism has been permitted to spread while Greek nationalism has been held in check' (*New York Times*, 17 May 1949, from Paris).

[2] *The Times* Nicosia correspondent wrote (28 July 1947) that the news of his death was received with 'profound sympathy' by the British community, 'who differed with his political views but respected him as a sincere priest and a true Christian'.

[3] *Daily Telegraph*, 28 April 1949.   [4] *United Empire*, July–August 1949, xl. 179.

or rumours to the contrary are untrue and entirely without foundation'.[1]
At last the Government were ready to issue invitations to the Consultative
Assembly, on as impartial and representative a basis as was possible in an
island where the elective principle, as demonstrated in the municipal
elections, was open to so many abuses.[2] The intention was to have an
Assembly of forty members, but because of the boycott imposed by the
Church it never numbered more than eighteen, consisting of eight Left-
wing Greeks, six Turks, two non-party Greeks, and one Maronite, with
the Chief Justice, Sir Edward Jackson, who had taken part in framing the
Constitutions of Malta and Ceylon, as chairman.[3] The eight Left-wing
Greeks, asked by the Colonial Secretary of the Cyprus Government
whether they intended to co-operate with the Assembly within its terms of
reference, assured him that they did; but, when the Assembly met in
November 1947, the Left-wing members immediately asked if they might
discuss self-government,[4] and insisted, against the advice of the British
chairman, on sending a memorial to Creech Jones requesting a Constitution similar to that of Malta or Ceylon, with a Legislature consisting
entirely of elected members and the Governor's powers restricted to defence, external affairs, and the special interests of minorities. When no
reply was received, a deputation consisting of the mayor of Limassol,
Servas, the mayor of Nicosia, Klerides,[5] and the secretary of the Cyprus
Communist Party visited London to press the claim. On the advice of
Lord Winster and of Colonial Office officials, Creech Jones refused to
receive the deputation officially, but gave way to the suggestion of a number of Labour M.P.s to meet it in a 'short informal talk' in which the
Constitution was not discussed.[6] This talk probably had the effect, however, of destroying any remaining hopes of a successful outcome of the
Consultative Assembly; for, on the deputation's return to Cyprus, Servas
'allowed it to become known that . . . he had received powerful unofficial
support and that self-government was on the way'.[7]

---

[1] *The Times*, 27 August 1947.

[2] See Lord Winster, loc. cit. and *Daily Telegraph*, 28 April 1949.

[3] See *The Economist* special correspondent, 29 May 1948, p. 884.

[4] The Communist-minded 'Pan-Cyprian' Federation of Labour had agreed at its annual
conference in May that the achievement of union with Greece was remote as long as Greece
was ruled by a 'Fascist monarchy' (*Daily Worker*, 26 May 1947). The change of policy was
doubtless due both to the possibility of exploiting the opportunities presented by the creation of
the Consultative Assembly, and to the fact that the régime in Greece had been strengthened by
the granting of United States aid under the Truman Doctrine.

[5] Two years later Klerides, having been defeated in the municipal elections of May 1949,
broke with the extreme Left and was reported to be organizing a centre Socialist party, which
earned him the title of 'collaborationist' from both Left and Right (*Cyprus Mail*, 30 October–
30 November 1949).

[6] Creech Jones, 26 April 1948, H.C.Deb. 5th ser., vol. 450, coll. 377–8; cf. *Daily Worker*, 31
January, Atticus, pseud., in *Sunday Times*, 21 March 1948.

[7] Lord Winster, loc. cit.

(c) THE COLD WAR REACHES CYPRUS, 1948–9

On 13 January 1948 the workers of the American-owned Cyprus Mines Corporation at Mavrovouni had gone on strike when their demand for a forty-hour week and higher wages had been rejected. The Corporation tried to recruit non-union workers; and when twelve of these had reported on 3 March,

a crowd of about 1,000 persons . . . assembled . . . with sticks and stones. One police sergeant and five constables, all unarmed, warned the crowd to disperse but they refused. Two police inspectors and additional men were sent for and the final reinforcement brought two rifles. The inspectors again ordered the crowd to disperse, without effect. When the 12 prospective employees left . . . the crowd assaulted them and the police with stones. An inspector gave a further warning, telling the crowd that unless they dispersed he would open fire. The crowd succeeded in knocking down the unarmed police sergeant and were kicking and beating him. Upon this, fire was opened and 15 rounds were fired . . . mainly directed against those who were attacking the sergeant, who was later admitted to hospital with a broken arm and head injuries. Four members of the crowd were wounded by the police, three being minor casualties and only one serious. . . . The police behaved with restraint in a difficult situation.[1]

On the 8th the police again opened fire on a crowd that was trying to stop the unloading of equipment for the Corporation from a United States merchant ship. The Pan-Cyprian Trades Union Federation had proclaimed a twenty-four hour general strike throughout the island on the previous day, and as the miners' strike dragged on into May it was claimed that 'every organized worker in Cyprus' was giving a day's wages to the strike fund and that contributions were being received from Cypriots all over the world.[2] The attitude of the Communist trade union leaders was probably hardened by the fact that the British were constructing air-base installations equipped with radar in Cyprus, and transferring to the island from Palestine (where the Mandate was due to expire on 15 May) a considerable number of troops, the Middle East radio-monitoring service, and the Arabic broadcasting station *ash-Sharq al-Adnā*,[3] while the United States

---

[1] Under-Secretary for the Colonies, 10 March 1948, H.C.Deb. 5th ser., vol. 448, coll. 1231–2. A member of the Parliament at Westminster, D. N. Pritt, declared that the strike was *inter alia* a demand for trade union recognition which the Corporation had refused; but the Under-Secretary denied this.

[2] *Daily Worker*, 6 May 1948. The strike ended ten days later with small wage increases for certain categories of workers, and a reconstitution of the trade union so that only employees of the Cyprus Mines Corporation could belong to it and so that it should be free from outside interference and political control (*The Times*, 18 May).

[3] In answer to questions on the transfer of *ash-Sharq al-Adnā* to Cyprus in March, the British Foreign and Colonial Secretaries declared that it was operated by a 'group of Arabs and of British persons interested in Arab affairs' (16 and 23 June 1948, H.C.Deb. 5th ser., vol. 452, coll. 409–10, 1342).

(whose association in these strategic developments was to become evident later) opened a consulate in Cyprus for the first time since the island had passed under British occupation in 1878.[1]

Meanwhile the British Government, urged by the Cyprus Government to counter the requests of the Left-wing Greeks in the Consultative Assembly by producing their own concrete idea of a suitable Constitution, had taken as their starting-point a tentative outline which Sir Edward Jackson had already laid before the Assembly on 7 November 1947. Some months elapsed, however, before the Cabinet could find the 'right formula', and it was not until 7 May 1948 that the Governor, who in the previous month had flown to London for consultations for the third time during his thirteen months of office, received from the Colonial Secretary a despatch on the Cyprus Constitution, for further discussion by the Assembly. It proposed that the Legislature should consist of four official members (the Colonial Secretary, Attorney-General, Treasurer, and Senior Commissioner), and twenty-two members elected by universal adult male suffrage (to be extended to women if the Consultative Assembly wished); of these, eighteen were to be elected on a general register, and four on a Turkish communal register. The Legislature would be able to question the four official members, and the only absolute limitation on its legislative competence would be on its power to discuss the status of Cyprus within the British Commonwealth. However, it must also obtain the Governor's consent before introducing a money bill or resolution, or a bill which in the opinion of the Governor affected defence, external affairs, or the special rights of minorities, or which amended the Constitution. Furthermore, the Governor would retain 'the usual reserve legislative powers' to 'hold back for signification of the Royal pleasure' (i.e. to veto) bills passed by the Legislature, especially those concerned with the reserved subjects detailed above; and to declare valid any bill or motion which the Legislature had rejected or passed in an unacceptable form, if he considered it necessary in the interests of public order, good faith, or good government. These provisions, it was added,

are not intended to circumscribe the freedom of the Legislature unnecessarily; and occasions on which it might be necessary to invoke some of them, in particular the 'reserve power', should be very rare. These provisions should, therefore, be regarded only as safeguards which His Majesty's Government consider necessary and not as evidence of any desire on the part of His Majesty's Government to interfere with the freedom of action of Legislature in the normal domestic affairs of the Island.

It was further proposed that three Greek and one Turkish elected member

---

[1] Sam Pope Brewer in *New York Times*, 7 March, C. L. Sulzberger, ibid. 12 July 1948. Immediately before 1878 the two brothers Cesnola had held appointments in Cyprus as United States Consul and Vice-Consul respectively, to facilitate their archaeological work.

should be appointed to the Governor's Executive Council, at present composed almost entirely of officials, and should be associated with specific
departments of government—becoming, as it were, Under-Secretaries, as
in the new constitutional proposals for the Anglo-Egyptian Sudan.[1]

The Colonial Secretary's despatch contained the warning that the
Government 'would be unable to give their approval to a Constitution
which fundamentally exceeded these proposals in the direction of full self-
government'; but during the months of waiting moderate opinion in
Cyprus had become discouraged, and now remained aloof while the
Church and the Communists proclaimed their opposition. The Archbishop
issued a declaration describing the proposals as 'wholly unacceptable',
urging the people to adhere to the principle '*Enosis* and only *Enosis*' and to
boycott a general election, and accusing the British of 'fostering Communism' by their dealings with the Left-wing Greeks in the Consultative
Assembly.[2] These also were instructed by a meeting of the 'Popular Front'
(as it now called itself) not to accept the British proposals, as they were
'not in the interests of the people'. At a meeting of the Consultative
Assembly on 20–21 May they duly voted against the proposals and withdrew from the Assembly, which was accordingly adjourned *sine die*.

On 27 July 1948, while the Governor was again in London discussing
the next step to be taken, King Paul of Greece was interviewed by C. L.
Sulzberger, and said in reply to a question:

Greece certainly desires and will continue to desire the union of Cyprus to the
rest of Greece. It is difficult to understand why this has not yet been effected.
The argument that this might interfere with British security positions is not
valid. Were Cyprus to be given to Greece, as the vast majority of its population
desires, this would in no way interfere with any military or other bases Britain
has established there. Furthermore, if it could be arranged under the United
Nations, Greece would be prepared to offer further base facilities to Britain or
the United States in Crete or elsewhere.[3]

While the British chargé d'affaires in Athens delivered an *aide-mémoire*
stating that in his Government's opinion 'any encouragement of agitation
in favour of the union of Cyprus with Greece would not be in the best
interests of either Great Britain or Greece', and the Greek Liberal (Opposition) newspapers *Bema* and *Eleuthería* took the King to task for his incursion into politics,[4] 1,500 employees of the Anglo-American asbestos mines

[1] Great Britain, Colonial Office: *Cyprus Constitution*, Col. No. 227 (London, H.M.S.O., 1948),
p. 5.

[2] Fitzhugh Turner in *New York Herald Tribune*, 13 May 1948; *The Times*, 12, 15, 18 May 1948.

[3] *New York Times*, 28 July 1948.

[4] 22 September 1948, H.C.Deb. 5th ser., vol. 456, *written answers*, col. *120*. While the Greek
Foreign Minister stated that the King had been 'inaccurately reported', the Premier said that
he had 'merely repeated the national feelings already expressed in Parliament' (*Daily Telegraph*,
2 August, *The Times*, 4 August 1948).

at Amiandos proclaimed a general strike on 2 August to enforce their wage
and other claims, and occupied the underground and surface workings,
from which police baton charges failed to dislodge them. When the news
reached Nicosia large crowds marched in protest to the Secretariat, shout-
ing for self-government and against 'anti-working-class government' and
making the Communist salute with the clenched fist; twenty-seven persons, including ten trade union and AKEL leaders, were charged with
taking part in this unauthorized demonstration. On 12 August the
Governor told the Turkish and independent remnant of the Consultative
Assembly that, in view of the action of the Left-wing Greek members in
voting against the British Government's constitutional proposals and
leaving the Assembly, it was now dissolved. The proposals could be taken
up again 'if at any time responsible and fully representative political
leaders' came forward to ask that they, or comparable proposals, might
be re-examined.

Once again . . . I must repeat that no change in the sovereignty of the island is
intended. I am authorized to state categorically that there is no substance in
any rumours that negotiations are intended between Great Britain and Greece
on the subject. . . . Anything to the contrary which you may hear in the future
here or elsewhere designed to make you believe that the question is still open or
that negotiations are contemplated is untrue, and put about solely with a view
to deceive and mislead you on a question on which His Majesty's Government
have decided their policy. . . .

His Majesty's Government join with you in regretting the irresponsible nature
of the opposition which has led to a temporary breakdown. You yourselves
have by your actions shown that leaders exist in Cyprus who are prepared to
come forward and to put the good of the island before petty intrigues or policies
which take no account of the realities of the situation.[1]

The *Manchester Guardian* commented editorially (14 August):

These proposals . . . would have given the Cypriot leaders invaluable experience
in political responsibility, beyond anything known in the island for centuries,
and a firm platform from which to make the next step upwards towards
autonomy. That they have not been grasped and turned to good account is a
sign of the unreal and irresponsible atmosphere of Cypriot politics. These have
been dominated for so long by the barren issue of 'Enosis' . . . that when a chance

---

[1] *The Times*, 13 August 1948. Lord Winster afterwards remarked that the opposition to the
British constitutional proposals had been led by the mayors of the four principal towns: 'It was
brought to my notice that not one of those towns had a fire brigade which could be called a
fire brigade in any sense of the word, and had a big fire broken out in any of those towns the
town would have been burned down. I felt that it was a little early for people who could not
even run a fire brigade to claim self-government. I am speaking seriously about this. So serious
was the matter that I had to remove the fire brigades from the municipalities and entrust them
to the police force. When we talk about self-government, those are matters which have to be
borne in mind, and people must realise their responsibility for allowing themselves to be guided
and helped along the road to self-government' (13 April 1949, H.L.Deb. 5th ser., vol. 161, col.
1224).

of real advance is presented, it is spurned because it does not satisfy the slogans of pan-Hellenism.

Immediately upon the Governor's statement, the Left-wing Federation of Labour organized mass meetings of protest against the 'so-called Labour Government in London', and on 13 August 15,000 workers took part in a twenty-four hour general strike of protest on the constitutional issue and in support of the Amiandos strike, which came to an end on the 30th. Meanwhile, however, the Federation of Labour had called another strike in the building trades. When the breakaway Cyprus Workers' Federation refused to join the strike, the AKEL-led strikers began to blow up buildings under construction and throw grenades at their opponents. The Under-Secretary for the Colonies stated in the House of Commons on 17 November: 'Since 1st June there have been 29 incidents in which dynamite has been used and 74 cases of assault, malicious injuries and arson, credibly related to conflicts between rival trade unions. Of the complainants in recorded cases, 120 belong to the Right-Wing and nine to the Left-Wing'.[1] The police believed that a United States radio station for the monitoring of Soviet and Cominform broadcasts, which was being transferred from Egypt to Cyprus and whose buildings were now under construction, was a particular target for sabotage. A special correspondent wrote from Nicosia on 17 October:

... It is now obvious that the Cypriot Left wing is simply carrying out orders that are but one facet of Moscow's anti-western activity in the area. ... The Left, which controls a majority of the political groups that pass under the name of trade unions, has money enough to finance lengthy strikes. It is believed that some, at least, of this came in the form of smuggled gold sovereigns from a Red fountainhead located in Beirut. ...[2]

Support for this cold war interpretation of events was given by articles contributed to the London *Daily Worker* (13 September 1948, 24 February 1949) by the secretary of the Committee for Cyprus Affairs, Evdoros Ioannides, who asserted that the people of Cyprus had 'reacted with the utmost determination', by means of demonstrations and strikes, against both the threat of dictatorship and the turning of Cyprus into an 'anti-

[1] H.C.Deb. 5th ser., vol. 458, col. 363.
[2] *The Economist*, 23 October 1948, p. 666; cf. Sam Pope Brewer in *New York Times*, 4 January 1949 and Jean Wolf in *Bourse Égyptienne*, 11 June 1948; 'From time to time Yugoslav or Bulgar ships call at Famagusta. Frequently on such occasions meetings take place ashore or aboard between the ship's officers and some island agitator well known for his subversive activities. ... Quite recently one of these ships called at Limassol. On the eve of her departure one of her crew got drunk and took one of his drinking companions into his confidence. The latter, an agent of the Intelligence Service, immediately reported to the authorities. A general search of the suspect ship was organized and, while the Customs had found nothing in the course of their routine superficial inspection, the Military Police discovered a false hull containing printing material, thousands of Greek-language pamphlets ready for distribution, and gold sovereigns together with thousands of genuine sterling notes. A number of the crew had false papers.'

Soviet imperialist base'. He referred to the building of camps large enough for the training of 100,000 troops, the improvement of harbours, the landing of squadrons of fighter aircraft and of United States aircraft, and to the installation of the United States radio monitoring service. 'The strengthening of the working-class movement and the national liberation movement for the ending of imperialist rule' had alarmed both the Government and the Cypriot Right Wing, which, the writer declared, had employed *agents provocateurs* to dynamite buildings in order to discredit AKEL.

The agitation culminated in an AKEL demonstration at Nicosia on 31 October in answer to a Nationalist rally held two weeks earlier. Twenty-five thousand people were estimated to be present, hundreds of lorries brought in villagers, one party marched 100 miles carrying banners inscribed 'We do not want a British or American war-base in Cyprus', the Mayor of Limassol made a speech, and a collection was taken for the Greek Communist rebel leader, Markos. On 11 November the Governor again arrived in London for consultations with the Colonial Secretary, and simultaneously *The Times* Nicosia correspondent rejected, as grossly exaggerated, reports that had been cabled abroad that Cyprus was in a state of anarchy, with the result that insurance rates against civil commotion had been increased fivefold. The laws making the holding of meetings and demonstrations in Cyprus subject to administrative approval had not been stringently applied while the Labour Government had been making its effort to secure the Cypriots' co-operation in a programme of progressively giving Cyprus self-government, short of liberty to secede from the British Empire. But these laws remained on the statute book; and, on representations from Lord Winster, the Government at Westminster now approved a return to a stricter application of them.[1] On 10 November the AKEL Mayor of Famagusta, Adamantos, was fined £100 for making a political speech when he had been authorized to speak only on the builders' strike, and another labour leader was fined £50 for putting up loud speakers to relay the offending speech without authorization; on 26 November the Mayor of Limassol, Servas, was sent to prison for three months, and thirty-one other members of AKEL for one to two months, for taking part in an unauthorized procession at Limassol to demand a general election.[2] The Communists complained that 127 persons received

---

[1] This approval was coupled with the Colonial Secretary's 'regretful' acceptance of Lord Winster's wish 'to seek release' from the Governorship, 'solely on the grounds that, efforts to secure acceptance of the Constitution . . . having proved unavailing, the primary purpose for which he undertook that appointment . . . no longer existed' (Colonial Office statement, *Observer*, 14 November 1948). See also *The Times*, 15 November 1948; Creech Jones, 1 December 1948, H.C.Deb. 5th ser., vol. 458, *written answers*, col. *174*; Lord Winster (*United Empire*, July–August 1949, xl. 181).

[2] Adamantos and Servas had respectively nine and eight previous convictions for such offences

short prison sentences and several hundreds fines in this reassertion of authority.[1] The Government's action was reported to have had the effect of discouraging many of the more casual adherents—estimated at up to 40,000—to a Communist hard core which was not thought to number more than 3,000–5,000.[2]

Meanwhile, AKEL's secretary-general, Fifis Ioannou, and the trade union leader Ziartides were reported to have conferred during the winter with the Cominform leaders in Prague and Bucharest.[3] The triennial municipal elections were due to take place in May 1949; at the beginning of March an AKEL party statement announced that serious faults had been committed by party leaders, and that 'self-criticism revealed that the majority of the Central Committee consisted of elements with petty bourgeois tendencies which have no place in the AKEL leadership'. The Central Committee and Politburo had accordingly resigned to facilitate changes in the leadership, and Ioannou had been replaced as Secretary-General by E. Papaioannou, who had been active in Cypriot affairs in Britain during the war. The purpose of these changes may have been to complete a reorientation of the party line from a demand for 'self-government', which had failed to obtain the desired constitutional concessions from the British Government, back to a demand for *Enosis*, in order to compete with the Right Wing in the coming elections.[4] On 21 March a district court sentenced Minos Perdios, editor of the AKEL newspaper *Néos Demokrátes*, to three months' imprisonment, with a fine of £50, for alleging a government conspiracy to prepare false electoral lists.[5] On the 29th the

(Creech Jones, 24 November and 8 December 1948, H.C.Deb. 5th ser., vol. 458, col. 1238; vol. 459, col. 358). For Patrick Balfour's impressions of Adamantos, see *The Orphaned Realm*, pp. 189–90).

[1] Evdoros Ioannides in the *Daily Worker*, 24 February 1949.

[2] *New York Times* Nicosia correspondent, 4 January 1949.

[3] C. L. Sulzberger in *New York Times*, 17 May 1949.

[4] *Daily Telegraph* and *Daily Worker*, 9 March, C. L. Sulzberger in *New York Times*, 17 May 1949. The shift had been foreshadowed, soon after the Governor's dissolution of the Consultative Assembly, by a memorial addressed to him by the seven Left-wing Cypriot political leaders formerly on that body (the mayors of the five chief towns and the two representatives of the Federation of Labour) referring to the 'national claim' and calling for a plebiscite on union with Greece (*The Times*, 13 September 1948; Platts-Mills, 23 September 1948, H.C.Deb. 5th ser., vol. 456, *written answers*, col. *174*). A correspondent of *The Economist* (18 September 1948, p. 459) had observed that this had been done 'with a view to catching some *enosist* votes at the municipal elections. . . . The Right has clearly gained ground of late, thanks to better organisation in Church political circles as well as to a general fall in Russian stock since the Czech coup and the Tito incident. Unless the Left stirs its stumps it cannot hope to repeat its success at the last municipal elections. . . . Adoption of the catchy *enosis* slogan is the start of its election campaign'; cf. a correspondent in *Tribune*, 31 December 1948, p. 10.

[5] Ziartides was reported to have said in London on 21 December 1948 that the Government had just enacted a law restricting the municipal vote to those who had lived at least two years in the same town, and conferring the responsibility for preparing the electoral lists on Right-wing headmen (*Daily Worker*, 22 December 1948). The reference was to the Municipal Corporations (Amendment) Law, 'amending extensively the principal Law in the light of past experience, and particularly providing for new regulations for the preparation of electoral lists by *mukhtars*

Cyprus Government *Gazette* published an amendment to the Criminal Code, raising from six months' to five years' imprisonment the maximum penalty for the publication of words or documents with seditious intent. Then on 12 April the judge revising the electoral lists at Limassol ordered the names of the mayor, Servas, and a municipal councillor to be struck off, on the ground that their recent terms of imprisonment in Nicosia prison had interrupted their local residence.[1]

The elections were held in different municipalities on four successive Sundays, 8–29 May 1949. On the first day AKEL won seven out of the eight seats at Morphou, the largest rural municipality, but the returns on the 15th showed a swing in favour of the Right-wing candidates. This was maintained when the larger towns polled on the 22nd: AKEL retained control of the ports of Limassol, Famagusta, and Larnaka by narrow majorities, but the Nationalists won back the capital, Nicosia, amid outbreaks of violence 'every few minutes' between the two rival groups, as a result of which one man was killed, several injured, and 170 arrested.[2] The final result showed the Nationalists in possession of eleven out of the fifteen municipalities, having polled in the aggregate some 60 per cent. of the votes.[3]

The newspapers recorded an incident in Larnaca. The Left Wing mayor refused to supply the Right Wing stadium with the municipal water-cart. So the Right Wing municipality of Nicosia lent its water-cart, which drove down in

---

and *azas* [village headmen and councils] and for their revision by a revising judge specially nominated by the Chief Justice from amongst the members of a district court' (Government of Cyprus: *Legislation during 1948*, Sessional Paper no. 4 of 1939, p. 4, no. 34). The British Colonial Secretary explained that the purpose of the two-years'-residence rule 'was to exclude from the municipal electoral registers casual labourers and villagers who come into towns for work over short periods and have no permanent interest in municipal affairs' (27 January 1949, H.C.Deb. 5th ser., vol. 460, *written answers*, coll. *181–2*).

[1] Challenged on this point, the British Under-Secretary of State for the Colonies said that the Municipal Corporations (Amendment) Law contained 'no reference to voluntary removal, and the question at issue was whether a period of imprisonment counted as "temporary absence" within the meaning of the law. The revising judge, following the principle laid down in previous judgments in similar cases, ruled that it did not. . . . This is a judicial matter in which my Right Honourable Friend cannot properly intervene' (5 May 1949, H.C.Deb. 5th ser., vol. 464, *written answers*, col. *69*). On 12 May a Nicosia court sentenced Servas to pay £1,000 libel damages for publishing an article calling an Executive Councillor a 'malicious collaborationist with the Government' (*Daily Worker*, 13 May 1949).

[2] Those arrested were 'youths, some with cuts over their foreheads, who jumped out [of the police vans], chattering and looking pleased with themselves, to crowd into the cells'. 'The Left-Wing gang were boys, too young to vote, in coloured shirts, with badges and the latest plastic belts. I looked towards their hip-pockets for weapons. From each protruded, not a truncheon or a revolver, but a coloured pocket-comb. For this, after all, was Cyprus' (Patrick Balfour: *The Orphaned Realm*, pp. 195–6; the entire chapter, pp. 183–97, is a brilant picture of Cypriot politics).

[3] A victory parade organized by AKEL had to be cancelled, and the party's new secretary-general was reduced to declaring that to have retained the three seaports and 40 per cent. of the aggregate poll 'under conditions of Right-wing terror' showed that the party had actually gained supporters since the 1946 elections (*Néos Demokrátes*, reported by *Cyprus Mail*, 28 May 1949).

triumph, watered the stadium, then proceeded, with a cavalcade of supporters, through the streets of Larnaca, watering them profusely all the way.

For the mountain of conflicting world ideologies had begotten a municipal mouse. The political exuberance of the Cypriots flowed back into the humdrum channels of town drains and village water-supplies. It had still no wider outlet than local government. Cyprus still elected no representative assembly, no legislative council, to deal with the island's more vital affairs.[1]

The Administration had made substantial progress in the spheres of agricultural development, forest conservation, and public health, notably in the virtual eradication of malaria, which had formerly made serious inroads on the islanders' vitality;[2] but in the political field there had been no advance towards an understanding between the Greek community in Cyprus and the British Government. If there was a body of opinion in the Greek community that would have welcomed a compromise, it lacked the will to express its views publicly; the Nationalists remained as uncompromising as ever in their claim for *Enosis*;[3] AKEL had not succeeded in taking advantage of the British constitutional proposals to win their way into power. It was necessary for them to outbid the Nationalists by demanding full self-government immediately; and in so doing they were demanding more than the British Labour Government, despite their long record of support for self-government in British colonial territories, were willing to concede in Cyprus. The reason was not, of course, that any British Government really thought that the Cypriots were politically less mature than, say, the Burmans (not to speak of the Sudanese or the Libyans). They refused the Cypriots what they had given to the Burmans because they realized that, if the Cypriots were to attain all the rights inherent in dominion status, they would avail themselves like the Burmans of the right to secede from the British Empire, and both parties in Great Britain at this time were determined to retain Cyprus within the British Empire for strategic reasons. By 1948, as a result of the rejection by Egypt and 'Irāq of British proposals for joint arrangements for regional defence in the cold war, and of the collapse of British authority in Palestine, Cyprus had reacquired the strategic significance which had attracted the interest of Disraeli in 1878 but which had been superseded by the British occupation of Egypt in 1882.[4] The violence of the attack by the Cyprus

---

[1] Balfour: *The Orphaned Realm*, p. 197.

[2] See 'Agriculture in Cyprus, Review of Ten Years' Progress', *Commonwealth Survey*, 11 June 1949, pp. 33–36; 'Forestry in Cyprus', ibid. 12 November 1949, pp. 41–42; M. Aziz: 'Eradication of Malaria in Cyprus', *Corona*, March 1950, ii. 102–4; Balfour, op. cit. pp. 200–1; *The Times* special correspondent in Cyprus, 29 May 1952.

[3] Without ever reinforcing their 'rhetorical and emotional' appeal by 'a single material or economic argument', according to Lord Winster in the *Daily Telegraph*, 28 April 1949, and *United Empire*, July–August 1949, xl. 180; cf. Balfour, op. cit. pp. 207–10.

[4] Cf. ibid. p. 206.

Communists and their followers, in the second half of 1948, on the Anglo-American arrangements to establish military installations in Cyprus[1] showed that they, on their side, were aware of the strategic motive behind the British opposition to their political demands; and differences of opinion (or at least of timing) over the same issue, between the Labour Government in London and the Governor of Cyprus, whom they themselves had appointed, appear to have been one of the causes of Lord Winster's resignation and the choice of a civil servant as his successor.[2] It is the more noteworthy that the violence of the Communists should have defeated its own purposes, as it had done, by provoking the Church of Cyprus and the middle-class Nationalists into organizing their own supporters and inflicting a setback on the Communists in the municipal elections of May 1949.

(v) The British Régime in Palestine, 1945–8

(a) The Mandatory Power and the Jewish Resistance Movement, August to October 1945

The tension in Palestine which, after rising for thirty years, culminated in the explosion of 1948 was partly due to the unfortunate ambiguity of the diplomatic instruments under which Palestine was administered during that period. The Balfour Declaration and the Mandate promised 'the establishment in Palestine of a national home for the Jewish people' without prejudice to 'the civil and religious rights of existing non-Jewish communities', and a lawyer could argue that these two provisions were not incompatible with one another. But this juridical point was academic in face of the psychological inevitability that these formulae would arouse, in both Zionist and Arab minds and hearts, expectations which certainly could not be reconciled. The Mandate was of the 'A' class, applying to 'certain communities belonging to the Turkish Empire' which had 'reached a stage of development where their existence as independent nations' could 'be provisionally recognized'; and, considering that the Palestinian Arabs constituted the overwhelming majority of the population of Palestine at the time, they not unnaturally regarded the Mandate as a recognition of their title to become—as other ex-Ottoman Arabs did eventually become

---

[1] At the height of the Communist agitation, student opinion in Turkey and the Opposition press there had taken up the support of the Turkish minority in Cyprus and argued that, if British rule were to be terminated, the island ought to revert to Turkey (*New York Times*, 12, 26, and 31 December 1948; Laurence S. Moore in *Christian Science Monitor*, 5 January 1949).

[2] The new Governor, Sir Andrew Wright, had seen twenty years' service in Cyprus before becoming successively Colonial Secretary, Trinidad, and Governor of Gambia. AKEL regarded his appointment as 'an indication of the disposition of imperialism to clamp a new dictatorship on the people of Cyprus and complete the work of turning the island into an imperialist war base' (*The Times* Nicosia correspondent, 11 May 1949).

in 'Irāq, Syria, Lebanon, and Jordan—a fully self-governing Arab people, notwithstanding the provision, likewise contained in the Palestine mandate, for the establishment, in Palestine, of a national home for the Jews. At the same time, it was also not unnatural that the Zionists—notwithstanding the stipulations in the Mandate for securing the rights of the non-Jewish inhabitants of Palestine—should have interpreted 'the establishment in Palestine of a national home for the Jewish people' as 'recognizing Palestine as the National Home of the Jewish people', which was what they had asked for in 1917 but had not, in fact, been granted.[1]

The Palestine White Paper of May 1939 had placed strict limitations upon the further expansion of the Jewish National Home, with the primary object of preventing the security of Britain's strategic bases in the Middle East from being undermined in the then impending war by the active and concerted hostility of pan-Arab nationalism, which could have had the most serious consequences for the entire war effort. This object the White Paper largely achieved;[2] but in limiting future Jewish immigration for a period of five years to a total of 75,000 it barred from Palestine an undefinable number[3] who might otherwise have escaped from Europe, and so included them among the 4 to 6 millions of Hitler's Jewish victims. By the end of the war in Europe, therefore, the Zionists' impatience of the White Paper on political and ideological grounds had been immensely heightened by the addition of the distinct, and more urgent, considerations arising from their wish to provide homes in Palestine for the survivors of continental European Jewry.

Their sense of extreme urgency[4] had been accentuated by the contacts which they had recently established with the Jewish survivors in the concentration camps or at large in those parts of Europe newly liberated from the Nazis. For most of these survivors, estimated to number $1\frac{1}{4}$–$1\frac{1}{2}$ million, there seemed no future in the countries where they had been subjected to such appalling inhumanities; nor (even if the Zionist Movement had been prepared, in the new circumstances, to reverse the fateful decision, made in 1905, when they had declined an offer from Great Britain of a national home for Jewry in East Africa) did any other overseas haven now offer itself on any considerable scale. By far the greatest potential asylum for European Jews was the United States, and on 22 December 1945 President Truman issued a statement announcing a policy of expediting the admis-

---

[1] Chaim Weizmann: *Trial and Error* (New York, Harper, 1949), p. 203. Weizmann, president of the World Zionist Movement and of the Jewish Agency for Palestine, was himself to admit at the World Zionist Congress in December 1946 that there was 'a vast difference between one interpretation and the other' (*New Judaea*, December 1946–January 1947, p. 66).

[2] See *Survey* for 1939–46: *The Middle East in the War*, p. 10.

[3] 'Hundreds of thousands', in the view of Sydney Silverman, M.P. (1 August 1946, H.C.Deb. 5th ser., vol. 426, col. 1263).

[4] 'Divine impatience' was the phrase used by Rabbi Stephen Wise at a World Zionist Conference in August 1945 (*Zionist Review*, 3 August 1945, supplement, p. 4).

sion into the United States of displaced persons and refugees from Europe, and a corresponding directive to government agencies concerned, setting up an inter-departmental committee to put this policy into effect. This executive action was, of course, subject to the existing United States immigration legislation, and a year later, on 19 December 1946, the President announced that, by 21 October, only 4,767 persons had been admitted under these executive arrangements. Thereafter, an amendment of the existing legislation was put in train; but the consequent Displaced Persons Act, providing for the entry into the United States, without regard to immigration quotas, of 202,000 displaced persons over a period of two years, did not become law till June 1948, that is to say, not until one month after the termination of the British mandate for Palestine and the proclamation of the establishment of the State of Israel. These measures were not exclusively for the benefit of Jewish displaced persons; and any considerable increase in the Jewish community in the United States seems not to have been favoured even by the Jewish community itself; for it already numbered over 5 millions, and its concentration in the large cities of the United States had already given rise to a serious degree of anti-Semitism which the community was anxious not to exacerbate.[1] Besides the humanitarian reasons for pressing for immediate large-scale immigration into Palestine, there was also the consideration that time might not be on the Zionist side. As Weizmann told a World Zionist Conference in London in August 1945, 'in the Middle East new facts are being created which are calculated to prejudge the issue'.[2] Chief among these was the formation, in March 1945, of the League of Arab States as a loose confederation which, somewhat to the embarrassment of its British sponsors, was pledged by its Charter to resist the Zionist political objectives in Palestine.[3] These political objectives had found extreme expression under the stress of the Second World War and the Nazi extermination policy, when the World Zionist Movement and the Zionist governing institutions of Palestine Jewry had overwhelmingly adopted the 'Biltmore Programme' of 1942. They had then demanded the establishment of the whole of the Palestinian territory under mandate as a Jewish state, as the only means of

[1] When Britain's Foreign Secretary, Ernest Bevin, at the Labour Party conference at Whitsun 1946 (see below, p. 217) declared that the reason for United States pressure for the admission of Jews into Palestine was 'because they did not want them in New York', a United States Jewish correspondent admitted that his remark 'contained some uncomfortable grains of truth. Many of the most enthusiastic Congressional supporters of Jewish immigration into Palestine were equally enthusiastic advocates of limiting immigration into the United States. Even American Jewish organizations hesitated at the thought of asking for the liberalization of this country's immigration laws—because they knew, or thought they knew, that any change in those laws would be sure to be for the worse' (Maurice J. Goldbloom, 'The Month in History', *Commentary*, July 1946, p.60); cf. Sidney Hertzberg, ibid. February 1946, p. 48; Richard Crossman: *Palestine Mission* (London, Hamish Hamilton [1947]), pp. 53–55.

[2] *Zionist Review*, 10 August 1945, p. 4.

[3] See *Survey* for 1939–46: *The Middle East in the War*, p. 342 and note 1.

assuring that total freedom in the crucial matters of immigration and land-purchase which had not been attainable under the Mandate owing to Britain's need, as a power with vital interests in the Middle East, to study the claims of pan-Arab, as well as Zionist, opinion.[1]

Already on 22 May 1945, only a fortnight after VE-Day, the Jewish Agency had served on the British Government a series of requests which Lord Samuel afterwards described in the House of Lords as 'a disastrous political blunder',[2] involving as they did the Government's acceptance of the extreme Biltmore Programme:

(a) That an immediate decision be announced to establish Palestine as a Jewish State;

(b) That the Jewish Agency be invested with all necessary authority to enable as many Jews as it finds possible to come to Palestine and settle there, and to develop, fully and speedily, all the resources of the country—especially land and power resources;

(c) That an international loan and other help be given for the transfer of the first million of Jews to Palestine, and for the economic development of the country.[3]

While Churchill had replied that the Palestine question must await study by the Great Powers at the peace conference, the signal victory of the Labour Party in the British General Election released, despite the cautious attitude of the Hebrew press in Palestine, 'a wave of limitless optimism' among the Jewish community there;[4] and indeed resolutions of the Labour Party, during its long years in opposition, had consistently whetted the Zionists' hopes and had in 1944 even gone beyond their expressed claims for a free hand in Palestine.[5]

---

[1] See *Survey* for 1939–46: *The Middle East in the War*, pp. 21–23.

[2] 23 April 1947, H.L.Deb. 5th ser., vol. 147, col. 80.

[3] These requests were confirmed by the World Zionist Conference held in London in August 1945 (*Zionist Review*, 17 August 1945, pp. 6–7), and, in view of this, there would appear to be no basis for a Zionist historian's subsequent contention that the Biltmore Programme 'had never been officially adopted by the Zionist movement' (Sacher: *Israel, the Establishment of a State*, p. 67).

[4] Daphne Trevor: *Under the White Paper* (Jerusalem, the Jerusalem Press, 1948), pp. 145–6; this book was afterwards advertised in a list of documentary publications by the Jewish Agency.

[5] See *Survey* for 1939–46: *The Middle East in the War*, p. 316, and 'British Labour's Pledge', *Zionist Review*, 28 September 1945, pp. 4–5. Harry Sacher (op. cit. p. 29) quotes Hugh Dalton's speech to the Labour Party annual conference at Whitsun 1945, in which he advocated Jewish immigration into Palestine 'without the present limitations' so as to establish 'a happy, a free, and a prosperous Jewish State in Palestine'. These words ought, however, to be read in conjunction with the following italicized passage, taken from a corrected galley-proof of Dalton's speech: *'This is not a matter which should be regarded as one for which the British Government alone should take responsibility. If we are to get an agreed settlement, if it is to stand firm and unshaken by changes from year to year, it is indispensable that it should be backed and supported by the American and Soviet Governments as well as by the British Government'*, &c.

The *Zionist Review* (3 August 1945, p. 5) listed the names of ninety Labour Members of the new Parliament who had 'put on record their support for the Zionist cause'. Twenty-eight 'sons of Jews on both sides' were returned to Parliament, of whom twenty-six belonged to the Labour

One week after the announcement of the election result, a World Zionist Conference opened in London on 1 August, and Dr. Weizmann expressed the belief that co-operation with the British Government, by which he had tried to steer Zionist policy since the days of the Balfour Declaration, would have a better chance with Labour at the helm, especially as the Opposition also was being led by an old friend of Zionism in the person of Churchill.[1] The Chairman of the Jewish Agency Executive and popular leader of Palestine Jewry, David Ben Gurion, on the other hand,[2] warned his hearers against undue optimism; the acid test would be the new Government's action over the White Paper, and he called for 'passive and active resistance to the implementation of the White Paper policy in its present form or in any modified shape'.[3] The president of the Zionist Organization of America, the Rabbi Abba Hillel Silver,[4] declared that 'the personal diplomatic approach of yesterday' (as employed by Weizmann)[5] was 'totally inadequate today'; it might be 'the height of statesmanship to be unstatesmanlike', to prepare the Jewish masses for any emergency and maintain their fighting spirit; they must never again confuse Zionism and the objective of the Jewish state with mere immigration and 'refugeeism'.[6] The head of the Jewish Agency's political department, Moshe Shertok (afterwards Sharett), admitted that at present there was no prospect of reaching an agreement with the Arabs on the basis of the Zionist programme, and the Agency was at pains to argue that while those primarily concerned with the Palestine question were the Great Powers, world Jewry, and the Palestine Arabs, the remainder of the Arab world had no status in the matter other than that pertaining to members of the United Nations.[7]

Thus, immediately upon the end of the war the Zionists had presented the British Government with a series of radical demands without any public word of caution from their 'moderate' elder statesmen. A year later, Churchill said in the House of Commons that had he been returned

Party and one was a Communist. Nineteen were sitting for the first time, and it was stated that almost all were 'first-generation English Jews', i.e. the sons of immigrants (*Jewish Yearbook* for 1947, pp. 319–20; Mark Raven, pseud.: 'British Jewry in Heavy Weather', *Commentary*, May 1947, p. 453).

[1] *Zionist Review*, 3 August 1945, supplement, p. 4.

[2] For the ascendancy which Ben Gurion had gained over Weizmann in Palestine during the War, see *Survey* for 1939–46: *The Middle East in the War*, p. 311.

[3] *Zionist Review*, 10 August 1945, p. 4, 17 August 1945, p. 3. Ben Gurion had declared on two occasions during a recent visit to the United States that, if the British Government intended to maintain and enforce the White Paper, they would have to use 'bloody terror', 'constant and brutal force' (ibid. 29 June 1945, p. 3, 13 July 1945, p. 2).

[4] See *Survey* for 1939–46: *The Middle East in the War*, pp. 315–16.

[5] For Weizmann's negotiations with Roosevelt and Churchill see ibid. pp. 312–14.

[6] *Zionist Review*, 10 August 1945, p. 6.

[7] Ibid. p. 10, 24 August 1945, p. 3. The Arab states were, however, assured that they would find the Jewish state a 'faithful ally' for their 'underpopulated and underdeveloped territories' (ibid. 17 August 1945, pp. 6–7).

to power at the general election, he had intended 'to put it to our friends in America, from the very beginning of the post-war discussions, that either they should come in and help us in this Zionist problem . . . on even terms, share and share alike, or that we should resign our Mandate'; the 'whole weight of the Zionist policy', which 'went beyond anything that was agreed to by the Mandatory Power', was an 'unfair burden' for Britain while Arabs and Muslims, 'so important for our Empire, were alarmed and estranged, and while the United States . . . and other countries sat on the sidelines and criticized our shortcomings with all the freedom of perfect detachment'.[1] At the Potsdam Conference, therefore, Churchill and (after the change of government consequent upon the result of the general election) the new Prime Minister, Attlee, discussed the Palestine question with President Truman in the hope of achieving a common Anglo-American policy, but to no purpose, for United States public opinion was at this time all in favour of 'bringing the boys home' and against any new overseas commitments. The British Labour Government, confronted by the active propaganda emanating both from the Zionists and from the pan-Arab politicians (who were insisting on adherence to the letter of the 1939 White Paper and threatening to take violent measures if there were any yielding to the Zionist demands),[2] set up a Cabinet sub-committee to study the problem, and were embarrassed by the visible gulf between their party commitments to Zionism before assuming the responsibilities of office and the advice now tendered by their permanent officials specializing in Middle Eastern affairs. The decline in Britain's material power as a result of the war had increased the importance for her of maintaining good relations in the strategic region of the Middle East, that 3,000-mile-wide bloc from Tripolitania to the mouth of the Persian Gulf, in the central third of which—from Egypt to 'Irāq inclusive—the politically conscious opinion of the Muslim Arab majority was as sensitive as ever on the subject of Palestine.[3]

It will be recalled that Ben Gurion had said at the London Zionist Conference that the 'acid test' of the new Government would be their action with regard to the 1939 White Paper; and the limit of 75,000 additional immigrants imposed by that document was now within a few thousand of being reached. Within ten days of the Labour Government's taking office, a Zionist deputation (led by Ben Gurion) repeated to the

---

[1] 1 August 1946, H.C.Deb. 5th ser., vol. 426, coll. 1250–3.

[2] Cf. J. C. Hurewitz: *The Struggle for Palestine* (New York, Norton, 1950), pp. 228–9, 231.

[3] Jon Kimche reported that Bevin and Sir Stafford Cripps, who were the two leading members of the Cabinet sub-committee, 'went back to the Cabinet . . . indignant. . . . They felt strongly that they had been the victims of an over-facile approach by their Zionist friends' (*Seven Fallen Pillars*, p. 142, based upon an article 'British Labor's Turnabout on Zionism', in *Commentary*, December 1947, p. 512). Cf. R. H. S. Crossman in *New Statesman and Nation*, 10 February 1951, p. 48.

new Colonial Secretary (George, afterwards 1st Viscount, Hall) a request
which had been made to the Churchill Government in mid-June, for the
immediate grant of 100,000 immigration certificates to satisfy the most
urgent requirements for settling the Jewish survivors found in the concentration camps,[1] and also an immediate declaration that Palestine should
become a Jewish state.[2] Richard Crossman, a member of the Labour
Party who took an active interest in the Palestine question and whose
sympathies were on the Zionist side, afterwards commented that this was
a 'disastrous interview'.[3] The Colonial Office replied on 25 August with
an offer which seems to have been intended primarily to provide the
Government with a breathing-space: it suggested that the certificates remaining unused from the White Paper quota, amounting to some 2,000,
should first be allotted, and perhaps held out the prospect of seeking Arab
agreement to a continuation of immigration at the monthly rate of 1,500—
a 50 per cent. increase on the quota proposed by the Royal Commission of
1937 in case its primary recommendation of partition were not accepted.[4]
This offer was summarily rejected by the Jewish Agency as totally inadequate.[5] Meanwhile, President Truman had been subjected to strong and
concerted pressure to give his support to the exorbitant demands that were
now being made by the Zionist movement. The Governors of thirty-eight
out of the forty-eight States of the Union had recently supported a petition
asking him to take steps for the opening of the doors of Palestine to Jewish
mass immigration and colonization, and for the establishment of Jewish
independence by converting Palestine into a Jewish State 'at the earliest
possible moment';[6] and on 31 August he passed on to Attlee the recommendation of his nominee to the Inter-Governmental Committee on
Refugees that the Jewish refugees in Germany should be granted 100,000

---

[1] See Hurewitz: *The Struggle for Palestine*, p. 225. There were 98,000 Jews in the assembly
centres in Germany and Austria when the Anglo-American Committee of Inquiry visited them
in February 1946. Weizmann had told the 1944 conference of the Zionist Federation of Great
Britain that they could in certain conditions admit 100,000 people a year to Palestine, and this
was part of the policy which he had formulated when visiting Palestine in 1944–5 (see *Survey*
for 1939–46: *The Middle East in the War*, p. 326; below, pp. 207–8, 214).

[2] 1 August 1946, H.C.Deb. 5th ser., vol. 426, col. 1314.

[3] Crossman: *Palestine Mission*, p. 201. 'Not a request for . . . consideration by His Majesty's
Government . . . but a demand', said Lord Hall later; 'the attitude . . . was different from anything which I had ever before experienced' (23 April 1947, H.C.Deb. 5th ser., vol. 147, coll.
107–8).

[4] The moderate Moshe Smilansky afterwards wrote that 'it seemed almost certain' that the
British Government were prepared to increase the quota to 2,500 per month, 'and that it was
also willing to instruct local authorities to relax the restrictions on Jewish purchases of land'
('Construction, not "War" ', *Commentary*, December 1946, p. 533).

[5] Weizmann: *Trial and Error*, p. 440. He told an emergency conference of the Zionist Federation of Great Britain that the Agency had 'informed the Government that they could have no
dealings with them on the basis of the White Paper, which they had always held to be immoral
and illegal' (*Zionist Review*, 28 September 1945, p. 3).

[6] Ibid. 13 July 1945, p. 2.

immigration certificates to Palestine, the President commenting that the main solution of their problem appeared to lie in 'the quick evacuation of as many as possible . . . to Palestine. If it is to be effective, such action should not be long delayed.'[1] To this the British Prime Minister was understood to have replied in September that any radical change of immigration policy in the Zionists' favour depended on the United States being ready to take a share in the maintenance of security in Palestine, a condition which the President had rejected when it had been proposed to him at Potsdam.

'Resistance', 'battle', 'offensive', and 'struggle' had been key-words in the World Zionist Conference in August; and while the United States and British Governments, with their very different interests and exposed to very different influences, were thus nervously fingering the two separate, though interrelated, problems of European Jewish homelessness and the future of Palestine in its Middle East setting, a number of impatient 'activists' on the staff of the Jewish Agency had begun to conspire, for the purpose of forcing the British Government's hesitant hand, with those very extremist organizations 'dissident' from the Agency's authority[2] whose murderous activities the Agency had so strongly denounced less than a year before, and who had recently been carrying into effect their threat that 'VE-Day for the British is D-Day for us'.[3] In August thirty-seven-year-old Dr. Moshe Sneh[4] (who had gone to Palestine from Poland as recently as 1940 and had soon achieved a leading place in the General Zionist Party organization) had been co-opted to the Jewish Agency Executive[5] and had become commander of the chief Zionist underground paramilitary organization, the Haganah, which was believed to have some 60,000 members equipped and trained primarily for the self-defence of the settlements.[6]

---

[1] Text in New York Times, 14 November 1945. According to the ex-Under Secretary of State, Sumner Welles, the President's Democratic Party advisers had informed him that the Republican presidential candidate, Governor Dewey of New York State (with its concentration of 2·2 million members of Jewish religious congregations, to say nothing of non-practising Jews who might still feel and act as Jews politically), intended to take up the refugees' cause in public (Sumner Welles: We Need Not Fail (Boston, Houghton Mifflin, 1948), p. 32); cf. below, p. 229, note 4.

[2] These were the Irgun Zvai Leumi ('National Military Organization', commonly abbreviated to Irgun or I.Z.L.) with an estimated active strength of 1,000 and a reserve of 4,000, and its offshoot the Stern Group ('Fighters for the Freedom of Israel'), estimated at 150–200 dangerous fanatics. Cf. Survey for 1939–4: The Middle East in the War, pp. 321–4; Palestine Government: A Survey of Palestine . . . (Palestine Government Printer, 1946), ii. 601–6.

[3] See Major R. D. Wilson: Cordon and Search, With 6th Airborne Division in Palestine, 1945–1948 (Aldershot, Gale & Polden, 1949), p. 48.

[4] Described as 'brilliant and biting' by Samuel Rolbant, in the New Statesman and Nation, 18 August 1951, p. 176; cf. Palestine Affairs, November 1946, p. 8.

[5] As specialist in 'security matters', according to Zionist Review, 31 August 1945, p. 4.

[6] For the history of the Haganah cf. Palestine Government: Survey of Palestine, ii. 600–1; Survey for 1939–46: The Middle East in the War, pp. 247, 307. Harry Levin, himself a member of Haganah, afterwards wrote of 'the elaborate forms of conspiracy that are so much part of its underground structure: its leaders, known only to the few, moving about as farmers from the

Already at the World Zionist Conference Sneh had said that the Zionists 'had to devise new methods to resist the entire policy of the White Paper. They had to act as if the document did not exist. They had to defy its regulations, which did not mean terror.'[1] On his return to Palestine, however, while the negotiations which the Agency leaders (Weizmann, Ben Gurion, and Shertok) were pursuing in London were making no headway with the British Government, Sneh and the leaders of the two terrorist organizations[2] were coming to an agreement whereby the Haganah and they might co-operate under Haganah direction in offensive operations against British installations; and on 23 September Sneh dispatched to the Agency's London office a cipher telegram which was one, but by no means the first, of a series that was intercepted and read by the British authorities.[3] Sneh's suggestion that the militant organizations should cause 'one serious incident', to be publicized as 'a warning and an indication of much more serious incidents that would threaten the safety of all British interests in the country' if the Government did not grant the Zionist requests, evidently marked a new stage in the progressive recourse to organized violence by members of the Palestinian Jewish community. The British Foreign Secretary, Bevin, who had been made responsible for Palestine policy in its broad Middle East setting, had been conferring with the British diplomatic representatives from the Middle East, before receiving both Weizmann and the Secretary-General of the Arab League, 'Abd ur-Rahmān 'Azzām. According to Weizmann,[4] Bevin's 'opening remarks' at

settlements engaged on special duties, as members of innocuous public institutions or committees; the Government clerks, engineers, policemen who are also officers of Haganah; the labour organizers, teachers, taxi-drivers and its other contact men. . . .

'The other day Z., now Operational Chief in Jerusalem, told me of his early days in Haganah, 20 years ago. . . . Had British police penetrated their hide-outs they would have found only groups of students with their tutors, armed with an innocent story and piles of books to substantiate it' (Harry Levin: *Jerusalem Embattled* (London, Gollancz, 1950), pp. 73–74).

[1] *Zionist Review*, 10 August 1945, p. 6.

[2] These young conspirators, the leaders of the Haganah (Moshe Sneh), the I.Z.L. (Menachem Begin), and the Stern Group (Nathan Friedman-Yellin), had all been at Warsaw University together, where they were fellow-residents of the Jewish Academicians' House (see Menachem Begin: *The Revolt* (London, W. H. Allen [1951]), pp. 183–5, 199). They thus represented the next generation of East European Jewish 'activism' after that of Ben Gurion and Shertok, and were able temporarily to bridge the gap of ideological mistrust that separated the Socialists of the Haganah from the Right-wing I.Z.L.

[3] For examples, see Great Britain, Colonial Office: *Palestine: Statement of Information relating to Acts of Violence*, Cmd. 6873 (London, H.M.S.O. [1946]) [referred to hereafter as Cmd. 6873]. The Colonial Secretary declined a request for publication of *all* the evidence in the Government's possession concerning the relations between the Jewish Agency and the terrorists (3 March 1947, H.C.Deb. 5th ser., vol. 434, col. 36).

The Agency challenged the Government to prove that the Agency was responsible for the composition, authorization, or dispatch of the telegrams published in Cmd. 6873, and Ben Gurion's comment was: 'I don't say all these documents are forged, but such cases are known in history' (*The Times*, 26 July 1946, *Zionist Review*, 2 August 1946, p. 8). Begin, on the other hand, unreservedly admits their authenticity (*The Revolt*, pp. 183–5).

[4] Weizmann: *Trial and Error*, p. 440.

their meeting on 5 October included the words, 'Are you trying to force my hand? If you want a fight you can have it.' If these words were spoken, it may be presumed that they were expressions of Bevin's reaction to the evidence in Sneh's intercepted telegram that at least one member of the Agency Executive was prepared to make use of terrorism for coercing the British Government.[1]

The 'activists' within the Jewish Agency were, to be sure, expressing the pent-up impatience of the Jewish community in Palestine, of whom probably a majority either had to mourn relatives and friends who had perished under the Nazis or had renewed contact with survivors whom they wished to bring to safety. As the weeks passed while the British Government were anxiously seeking United States co-operation in finding some compromise between the exorbitant demands of the Zionists and the Arab refusal to admit any relaxation of the White Paper restrictions, the match was laid to the tinder of a Zionist 'resistance movement' of the type which the Allies (especially Britain) had enthusiastically fostered in Europe for the harassing of the Nazis. On 4 October the Agency leaders in Palestine called for a half-day general strike to take place four days later as a mass demonstration of protest against the continuation of the White Paper policy, and on the same day the Haganah's illegal mobile radio transmitter *Qol Yisrael* (Voice of Israel), which had been silent since the outbreak of war in 1939, again began to operate as 'the broadcasting station of the Jewish Resistance Movement'.[2] At the same time the Zionist official organizations, whose connexions with the Jewish survivors in Europe were now well established through the Jewish Brigade and the relief organizations such as UNRRA and the American Jewish 'Joint Distribution Committee',[3] had actively resumed the smuggling of illegal immigrants into Palestine, both by sea and over the northern land frontier, where a clash occurred on 6 October between the Trans-Jordan Frontier Force, searching for a party of illegal immigrants, and the inhabitants of neighbouring Jewish settlements who were harbouring them.[4] On the 10th the Palmaḥ,[5] the permanently mobilized wing of the Haganah, raided

---

[1] The relations between the Haganah and the terrorists were discussed by Richard Crossman in a speech in the House of Commons (31 July 1946, H.C.Deb. 5th ser., vol. 426, coll. 1008–13); by a *New Judaea* editorial, March–April 1948, p. 83; and by Sacher: *Israel, the Establishment of a State*, p. 188. For the Haganah's attempt to avoid loss of life, except in self-defence, see below, p. 202, note 1.

[2] Moshe Sneh (Cmd. 6873, telegrams nos. 6 and 7); cf. *Zionist Review*, 20 September 1946, p. 2.

[3] Cf. Crossman: *Palestine Mission*, pp. 86–87. 8,000 Jewish refugees had passed through the Jewish Brigade lines in Italy *en route* for Palestine in seven weeks in June and July 1945, according to Bernard Casper: *With the Jewish Brigade* (London, Goldston, 1947), pp. 70–90.

[4] Trevor: *Under the White Paper*, pp. 136–7. For the organization of this overland smuggling of immigrants, as seen by a British field security N.C.O., cf. Richard Pearse: *Three Years in the Levant* (London, Macmillan, 1949), pp. 190–5, 210–22.

[5] The final 'ḥ' was not silent like the final 'h' in Haganah but sharply aspirated, though

the Palestine Government's clearance camp for immigrants at Athlit, south of Haifa, and released 208 detained illegal immigrants who were immediately absorbed by the Jewish settlements and provided with forged identity papers. On the 12th the High Commissioner for Palestine, Lord Gort, received three of the Zionist leaders, including the Canadian-born Bernard Joseph,[1] who in the continued absence in London of Shertok was acting as head of the Agency's political department. Already on the 10th Bernard Joseph had reported to the London office of the Agency a divergence of views within the Agency Executive on how far the challenge to British authority was to be carried; and on the day on which he saw the High Commissioner a reply in pre-arranged code was sent to him from London in Shertok's name, conveying Ben Gurion's approval of 'isolated actions' without becoming involved in a general conflict with the British.[2]

Meanwhile, in anticipation of disorder, the British forces in Palestine were being reinforced, notably by the arrival of the 6th Airborne Division, which had distinguished itself in the Western European campaign of 1944–5;[3] the British navy and the R.A.F. were patrolling the coast to intercept illegal immigrant ships; and there was active recruiting for the British cadre of the Palestine Police. October passed without the impatiently awaited statement of British policy, although at the end of the month there were reports of the prospect of setting up a joint Anglo-American committee to investigate the Palestine problem.[4] On the night of 31 October–1 November the Jewish Resistance Movement struck its warning blow. The Palmaḥ sank three small naval craft which had been used for the interception of illegal immigrants and sabotaged the tracks of Palestine Railways in fifty localities; the I.Z.L. (Irgun Zvai Leumi) attacked Lydda railway station, causing some damage and casualties, and the Stern Group carried out an attack on the Haifa oil refineries in which one man was killed. On 1 November the Jewish Agency reported this concerted action to their London office, in the continued absence abroad

distinct from the guttural 'kh'; the conventional English rendering 'Palmach' was phonetically ambiguous. The word was an abbreviation of the Hebrew *plugoth ha-maḥatz*, 'spearhead detachments'. They were estimated to be about 2,000 strong.

[1] He adopted the name Dov Yosef after the achievement of Israel's independence.

[2] Cmd. 6873, telegrams nos. 2 and 3; cf. *Zionist Review*, Jerusalem correspondent, 26 October 1945, p. 8.

[3] According to its historian, however, every effort was to be made to prevent the Division becoming involved in internal security duties (Wilson: *Cordon and Search*, p. 4).

[4] It was afterwards reported that the announcement of the decision to set up such a committee was delayed 'presumably to avoid hurting the Democratic ticket' in municipal elections in New York City (Sidney Hertzberg, 'The Month in History', *Commentary*, January 1946, p. 39).

Earlier, it had been reported that the British Government had contemplated referring the Palestine question to the United Nations Organization at this early moment in its career, but had changed their plans when the London meeting of the 'Big Three' Foreign Ministers had confirmed the desire of the Soviet Government to extend their interests to the Mediterranean (*New York Times*, 24 September and 7 October 1945).

of Ben Gurion and Shertok. They boasted that 'the activities have made a great impression in the country. The authorities are bewildered'; the Haganah's clandestine radio *Qol Yisrael* proclaimed that 'the nights of heroism since Athlit are an expression of our strength and decision'; and the Stern Group's illicit publication declared: 'For the first time the attack was co-ordinated and concentrated. The Jewish Resistance Movement has embraced all the Jewish resistance forces, with a view to their being guided by a single authority which would control the common fight.' An editorial in the *Palestine Post* declared that 'external factors, which . . . threaten the existence of the Jew in the land promised to him as his National Home, will be opposed by the people who consider that a fight for their very lives has been forced upon them'; and the *Zionist Review*'s Jerusalem correspondent added bluntly: 'Even if Jews cannot and do not want to enter into an armed struggle against the British Empire, they must demonstrate that an anti-Zionist policy, too, will be difficult to apply, and that it will involve a higher cost even than a pro-Zionist policy.'[1]

(b) THE ANGLO-AMERICAN COMMITTEE OF INQUIRY, AND ITS STILL-BORN REPORT, NOVEMBER 1945 TO MAY 1946

The British authorities in Palestine did not immediately proceed against the authors of these acts of defiance, for on 13 November Bevin was at last able to announce that the United States Government had accepted an invitation to co-operate in a joint Anglo-American Committee of Inquiry. Bevin also announced the Committee's terms of reference, by which it was

'(1) To examine political, economic and social conditions in Palestine as they bear upon the problem of Jewish immigration and settlement therein. . . .

(2) To examine the position of the Jews in those countries in Europe where they have been the victims of Nazi and Fascist persecution. . . .'[2]

---

[1] Cmd. 6873, telegrams nos. 4 and 5, and p. 6; *Palestine Post*, 2 November, *Zionist Review*, 16 November 1945, p. 6. The secret telegrams revealed, however, a continued conflict of opinion within the Zionist leadership about the 'activist' policy. On 2 November, the anniversary of the Balfour Declaration, mobs in several Egyptian towns attacked Jews and other foreigners and did considerable damage to property. The campaign of violence spread to Libyan Tripoli, where the British military authorities were taken by surprise, and over 100 native Jews were massacred by Muslims between 4 and 7 November.

[2] 13 November 1945, H.C.Deb. 5th ser., vol. 415, col. 1929. President Truman afterwards tried in vain, through the chairman of the Senate Foreign Relations Committee, to deter Congress from passing a joint resolution, of the kind which the Executive had succeeded in stifling in 1944, favouring the free immigration of Jews into Palestine 'so that they may freely proceed with the upbuilding of Palestine as the Jewish national home and, in association with all elements of the population, establish Palestine as a democratic commonwealth in which all men, regardless of race or creed, shall have equal rights' (*Congressional Record*, 17 December 1945, pp. 12138–43, 12165–89; cf. *Survey* for 1939–46: *The Middle East in the War*, pp. 315, 318, 319).

The terms of reference placed equal emphasis on the European and the Palestinian aspects of the question; but in his accompanying statement Bevin said that, amid the recent demands for large-scale Jewish immigration into Palestine, the Government could not accept the view that Jews would not again be able to live without suffering discrimination in those European countries in which they had become the victims of the Nazis; while Palestine might contribute to the problem of the European Jews, it did not by itself provide sufficient opportunity for grappling with that whole problem; the Government had a dual obligation to Jews and Arabs, between whom there was a conflict of claims liable to cause disturbance in a much wider field; any sharp change of policy without adequate consultation 'would probably cause serious reactions throughout the Middle East and would arouse widespread anxiety in India', i.e. among its Muslim minority of 90 millions who had not yet become the separate state of Pakistan. The Government would not allow the Palestine problem to be settled by violent conflict: while awaiting the interim recommendations of the Committee, they would (as the definitive quota of 75,000 Jewish immigrants provided by the 1939 White Paper was now virtually filled) seek Arab consent to an agreement which would permit Jewish immigration to continue at the existing monthly rate. Bevin ended his statement to the House by appealing to both pro-Zionist and pro-Arab questioners not to pursue racial antagonisms, adding: 'I will stake my political future on solving this problem, but not in the limited sphere presented to me now.' Questioned afterwards by press correspondents about the Zionist projects for increasing the capacity of Palestine to absorb immigrants by the intensive development of its natural resources,[1] he was reported to have said that they seemed to him to combine 80 per cent. of propaganda with 20 per cent. of fact, but the experts must pass judgement. He made another remark which was afterwards to be constantly quoted against him out of its context: 'I am very anxious that Jews shall not in Europe over-emphasize their racial position. The keynote of the statement I made in the House is that I want the suppression of racial warfare, and therefore if the Jews, with all their sufferings, want to get too much at the head of the queue,[2]

---

[1] An economic study financed by United States Jews had estimated 'the central range of net immigration possibilities for the next decade as falling between about 685,000 and 1,250,000', of whom 90 per cent. would be Jews (Robert R. Nathan, Oscar Gass, and Daniel Creamer: *Palestine Problem and Promise* (Washington, Public Affairs Press for the American Palestine Institute, 1946), p. 399).

[2] Bevin's blunt phraseology and particularly his later undisguised resentment of the influence of United States Zionists on the Palestine problem (see especially his address to the 1946 Labour Party conference, *Zionist Review*, 21 June 1946, p. 3, and his remarks in the House of Commons, 25 February 1947, H.C.Deb. 5th ser., vol. 433, col. 1907) helped to incur for him the Zionist charge of being 'anti-Semitic' and even the 'heir to Hitler's mantle' (Frank E. Manuel: *The Realities of American-Palestine Relations* (Washington, Public Affairs Press, 1949), p. 331, and cf. McDonald: *My Mission in Israel*, pp. 22–24). One attempt to find some other explanation for

you have the danger of another anti-Semitic reaction through it all.' He ended by warning the armed Jewish organizations that their attacks had only prejudiced their case, and he urged them and the Arabs to surrender their arms.[1]

The British Government had clearly decided that the Palestine question must be viewed within the framework of British interests in the Middle East as a whole, and the initial sympathy with Zionism with which some members of the Cabinet were credited must have been strained by the Jewish Agency's recourse to 'activism' in order to express the impatience of the Jewish community in Palestine. In the United States Bevin's statement attracted a flood of criticism from a wide range of Jewish organizations, from the organs of publicity, and from a variety of politicians. At a press conference Senator Taft (a strong Republican contender for the Presidency) and the Democratic acting-President of the Senate supported the co-chairman of the American Political Action Committee for Palestine, an organization which was suspected of being associated with the terrorist Stern Group; a Zionist rally in New York City was said to have attracted 150,000 of the city's 2 million Jews, and it was reported that many of their leaders not only publicly approved the 'activism' in Palestine but accused the British Government of fomenting the anti-Jewish riots that had occurred in Arab countries.[2] In Palestine the Haganah's clandestine transmitter *Qol Yisrael* broadcast on 14 November an appeal for active resistance:

What Hitler did in his murderous blitz against the Jewish people is now being repeated in the form of slow, grinding political policy by the democracies. We are being condemned to live in an intolerable ghetto so as not to deprive Europe of its Jewish talents. The new proposals are anti-Jewish and inhuman. This land is ours to work in, to build, to create, and to defend. . . . We call on you to rise against this conspiracy and to fight the evil decrees of the new democratic policy with all our strength. On this day we repeat again our oath to defend all that is precious to us with all our might.[3]

In view of such incitements it was hardly surprising that a twelve-hour protest strike proclaimed by the Jewish National Council (Vaad Leumi)

his attitude was to suggest that as a trade union leader he had had to contend with 'a handful of Communists who happened to be Jews, or Jews who happened to be Communists' (Kimche: *Seven Fallen Pillars*, p. 143, a passage originally published by him in *Commentary*, December 1947, p. 512; see also Bevin himself, 25 February 1947, H.C.Deb. 5th ser., vol. 433, col. 1910, and Politicus, pseud., *Zionist Review*, 7 March 1947, p. 6). Much more probable, however, is Richard Crossman's subsequent conclusion that Bevin's principal motive was 'not some psychological quirk or streak of anti-Semitism, but incessant preoccupation with the . . . Middle Eastern base' (*New Statesman and Nation*, 10 February 1951, p. 148).

  [1] 13 November 1945, H.C.Deb. 5th ser., vol. 415, coll. 1927–35; *The Times* and *New York Times*, 14 November 1945.

  [2] See above, p. 198, note 1. See also *The Economist*, 24 November 1945, p. 751, 8 December 1945, p. 828; Sidney Hertzberg: 'The Month in History', *Commentary*, January 1946, pp. 37–38.

  [3] *Manchester Guardian*, 15 November 1945.

for that day was made the occasion for a disorderly minority in Tel Aviv and Jerusalem to set fire to government buildings, loot British shops, and stone the troops and police, with the result that Tel Aviv was placed under military occupation for five days. A United States Jewish journalist, who had arrived in Palestine early in November and was an eye-witness of the Tel Aviv disorders, described how much of the damage was done by gangs of Jewish adolescents; he heard a British officer order his men to direct their fire on the adults who were inciting them, but reported that twenty children aged under sixteen were wounded among the total Jewish casualties of six killed and some sixty wounded during these five days.[1] The historian of the Airborne Division remarked that as a result of the 'firm handling' by the troops mass disorders on this scale were never repeated in Tel Aviv;[2] and, on the day (18 November) on which the Mayor of Tel Aviv complained to the Chief Secretary of the Palestine Government that prompter police action could have prevented the loss of life, the joint secretary of the British section of the Jewish Agency was telling the Board of Deputies of British Jews[3] that they must warn the Government that, if they intended permanently to limit Palestine Jewry to a minority within the country, they would have to 'exterminate every Jew in Palestine'.[4]

The Agency's immediate activity remained the promoting of illegal immigration, for which it commanded virtually the unanimous support of Palestine Jewry, including even those moderates like Dr. Judah Magnes who most consistently opposed its political aims.[5] An American Jewish press correspondent who had counselled restraint until the Anglo-American Committee had made its recommendations reported that he had received the reply: 'Six million Jews died in Europe while we waited for the democratic Powers to act. Thousands more of the remnant will die if we sit here with hands folded during the winter while they investigate again.'[6] The driving power that impelled the organizers of illegal immigration was, indeed, the human need of the Jews in the displaced persons' camps in Germany to find a new home, which was tragically at variance with the

[1] Meyer Levin: 'The Battle of the Children', *Commentary*, January 1946, pp. 25–27; cf. Trevor: *Under the White Paper*, pp. 161–3.

[2] Wilson: *Cordon and Search*, p. 29. Six years later, when there had been violent demonstrations against the Israel Government, its semi-official organ, the *Jerusalem Post*, observed that the last thirty years had clearly taught the Zionists that 'those elements which are prepared to use violence to achieve their own ends and break the laws of the State for political purposes can be suppressed only if the necessary force is used against them unhesitatingly at the time of their first attempts at intimidation' (quoted by *The Times*, 9 January 1952).

[3] The Board of Deputies was a venerable institution of which the Zionists had gained control in 1943 'by infiltrating methods that aroused widespread hostility at the time', according to Alan A. Schper: 'London: British Jewry Post-War', *Commentary*, August 1946, p. 163.

[4] *Zionist Review*, 23 November 1945, pp. 4 and 9.

[5] See *Survey* for 1939–46: *The Middle East in the War*, p. 248, note 2.

[6] I. F. Stone in *The Nation*, 22 December 1945, p. 678.

mandatory Power's anxiety to prevent the conflict between Jews and Arabs in Palestine from getting out of hand. On the night of 24–25 November, two nights after an illegal immigrant ship had been intercepted offshore some twelve miles north of Tel Aviv, two coastguard stations equipped for such interception were blown up by members of Palmah,[1] who returned the fire of the police in the stations. Police-dogs followed scents from the coastguard stations to four Jewish settlements, round which British troops threw cordons with the intention of searching for the saboteurs. The local Zionist authorities, however—acting on the presumption that the intention of the troops was to search for illegal immigrants, of whom some 200 were estimated to have escaped from the ship before its interception—roused the surrounding settlements, and some 10,000 well-organized Jews armed with clubs and stones converged to prevent the searches.[2] Their stubborn resistance cost them at least six killed and forty-two injured, while the principal result of the searches was the finding in one settlement of more than 175 lb. of explosive. The Jewish Agency cabled to the United States a 'solemn protest' which alleged that 'British troops and police forcibly entered three peaceful Jewish agricultural settlements, wantonly beat hundreds of men and women, shot and killed four persons, and wounded many others without reason or provocation'.[3]

[1] Wilson: *Cordon and Search*, p. 30; the Haganah's radio *Qol Yisrael* ascribed the operation to the Jewish Resistance Movement. A Haganah 'underground' publication of 22 January 1946 was to declare that in these operations to assist illegal immigration or attack the installations designed to prevent it they would try to avoid loss of life, either to themselves or their opponents, except in self-defence (quoted by Shlomo Katz, 'Understanding Jewish Resistance in Palestine', *Commentary*, July 1946, pp. 47–48); cf. Begin: *The Revolt*, pp. 213–14, for the Haganah 'philosophy' of resistance.

[2] Cf. Wilson, op. cit. p. 33; also Trevor: *Under the White Paper*, pp. 164–71. The general principles of such Haganah operations were described as follows: 'While armed units of Hagana protected the landing of Jewish immigrants, masses of the Jewish population would create a diversion by milling around and blocking possible police reinforcements at the strategic points: on other occasions they would mingle with the new arrivals, thus preventing their identification and arrest; long-time residents in Palestine would refuse to show their identification papers and therefore be arrested: the time wasted by the police in identifying them gave the newly landed immigrants an opportunity to find refuge; in agricultural settlements the entire population would impede the entry of British forces and refuse to be identified—on several occasions they locked arms and lay down on the ground, compelling the British to force each one individually away from the group and into the barbed wire enclosures where they were searched' (Shlomo Katz, loc. cit.). The casualties incurred by such resistance were invariably made the subject of atrocity propaganda throughout the Jewish world.

[3] *New York Herald Tribune*, 28 November 1945. It became the regular propaganda technique of the Zionists to equate the British security forces with their former Nazi persecutors; cf. the *Qol Yisrael* broadcast of 29 June 1946: '. . . the unclean sons of Titus . . . the Nazi-British regime' (quoted by Begin: *The Revolt*, p. 205). The historian of the 6th Airborne Division, who reported that when troops were searching settlements the children were lined up and encouraged by the adults to indulge in 'a vulgar form of spitting drill', commented: 'It was certainly not in the interest of the soldiers deliberately to stir up hatred. . . . But expressions such as "Gestapo" and "English bastards", spat out with such venom, could hardly be ignored indefinitely, and without doubt were sometimes answered in kind' (Wilson, op. cit. pp. 59–60). Conversely Meyer Levin (*Commentary*, January 1946, pp. 25–27) wrote of the endless 'murderous conversations'

Again, while the security forces were celebrating Christmas, a party of 250 illegal immigrants was landed north of Haifa and absorbed in neighbouring settlements in an operation worked out in considerable detail by the Haganah, which by this time had appointed public relations officers like any regular force and had established a regular liaison with Reuter's correspondent, a naturalized British subject of Jewish origin whom they conducted to the scene of the operation.[1] The understanding between the Haganah and the 'dissident' terrorist organizations did not preclude independent activity by the latter; for after a period of quiet, probably in response to the announcement of the names of the members of the Anglo-American Committee of Inquiry, the I.Z.L. (as a reprisal for the continued deportation of suspected terrorists to a British detention camp in Eritrea) made destructive sabotage attacks on 27 December on two police headquarters, at Jerusalem and on the Jaffa–Tel Aviv border, and raided a military arms store in Tel Aviv, killing in all nine members of the security forces. According to the later testimony of the I.Z.L. leader, the Haganah chiefs had given in advance their 'unofficial' approval of these I.Z.L. attacks;[2] but Ben Gurion and Shertok, summoned by the High Commissioner,[3] were stated in an Agency communiqué to have 'completely dissociated the Zionist movement' from these acts and to have deplored the loss of life, adding, however: 'To our deep regret our ability to co-operate in combating these excesses has been rendered futile by the British Government's present policy in Palestine. Any appeals to Jews to obey the law would fall on deaf ears at a time when the Palestine Government itself consistently violated the fundamental law of the country of which it was the mandatory Power.'[4]

The Zionists were intensely alive to the efficacy of well-timed propaganda, especially in the United States, where the action of highly organized

about, and vilification of, the Jews by the British troops and police during the Tel Aviv operation of November 1945; and cf. subsequently Richard M. Graves: *Experiment in Anarchy* (London, Gollancz, 1949), p. 147, diary entry of 24 February 1948.

[1] Kimche: *Seven Fallen Pillars*, pp. 161–7.

[2] 'They would try, they said, to prevent denunciation of the operations in the Press' (Begin: *The Revolt*, p. 198). Begin adds that the joint Haganah–I.Z.L. conferences were usually held once a fortnight during this period (ibid. p. 188).

[3] Lord Gort had resigned at the beginning of November and died not long afterwards. He was succeeded by Lieut.-General Sir Alan Cunningham, who remained High Commissioner until the end of the Mandate. A responsible source has commented to the writer that the contrast between the two régimes was typified by Gort's habit of walking through the streets of Jerusalem whereas his successor (admittedly in worsening conditions) went about in a bullet-proof car with an armoured-car escort.

[4] *Manchester Guardian*, 29 December 1945. The sole remaining representative of non-Zionist Jewry on the Agency Executive, in sending Weizmann his resignation on 24 December, had stated: 'The majority of my colleagues . . . and men like Dr. Silver had either been led by the *Stimmung* of the masses instead of influencing them, or are responsible for creating or inciting the destructive political attitude of the masses instead of directing them in a statesmanlike way' (Dr. Werner Senator, text in *Commentary*, October 1946, pp. 384–6).

'pressure groups' had for long been a potent factor in politics;[1] and, on more than one critical occasion during this chapter of history, Zionist propaganda resorted to a method which the targets of it might justly resent. At the most effective moment some incident, comparatively unimportant in itself, would suddenly be taken up, echoed and distorted through scores of publicity channels, and would then be allowed to drop when it had served its purpose. Thus, immediately before the opening meeting in Washington of the Anglo-American Committee of Inquiry, a storm of violent Zionist indignation was aroused at some impromptu remarks made at a Frankfurt press conference by the British head of UNRRA in Germany, Lieut.-General Sir Frederick Morgan. No official verbatim report of these remarks was apparently published, but according to the Associated Press Morgan said that

thousands of Polish Jews were coming into the United States zone from the east ... with a 'well organized, positive plan to get out of Europe'. He believed that an unknown secret Jewish organization was behind the infiltration. . . . The problem of Palestine was closely linked with the movement. . . . He was not convinced by 'all the talk about pogroms within Poland'. . . . Jews arriving in Berlin in trainloads from Lodz and other Polish centres were 'well-dressed, well-fed, rosy cheeked, and have plenty of money. . . . They certainly do not look like persecuted people. . . . The persons coming in tell the same monotonous story about pogroms.'[2]

Two years later Zionist writers were to make no secret of the fact that the movement of Jews through Central Europe *en route* clandestinely to Palestine had been organized by the Haganah;[3] but at this moment Weizmann, who was in the United States, denounced Morgan's statement as 'palpably anti-Semitic'; the president of the United States section of the World Jewish Congress, Rabbi Stephen Wise, declared that it not only savoured of Nazism at its worst but was reminiscent of the forged 'Protocols of the Elders of Zion'; the film-actor Eddie Cantor took a two-column advertisement in the *New York Times* to denounce Morgan under the caption 'I Thought Hitler Was DEAD'; and the radio commentator Walter Winchell declared that the General 'must be repudiated by His Majesty's Government and stripped of his uniform before decent Americans can again

[1] Cf. Edward Hallett Carr: *The New Society* (London, Macmillan, 1951), pp. 74–75.

[2] Quoted by Sidney Hertzberg: 'The Month in History', *Commentary*, February 1946, pp. 44–45, with the comment: 'It had never been suggested that these Jews were fleeing poverty and famine. They were, or thought they were, running away to save their lives or their sanity. And while the anti-Jewish manifestations in Poland had not assumed the proportions of mass murder, there were easily understandable reasons both physical and psychological why the most urgent thing in the life of a still dazed surviving Polish Jew would be to become an expatriate.' For the later exodus of Jewish 'entrepreneurs and middlemen' from Communist Rumania cf. the pro-Zionist Jorge García-Granados: *The Birth of Israel* (New York, Knopf, 1948), p. 226.

[3] See Mark Wischnitzer: *To Dwell in Safety* (Philadelphia, Jewish Publication Society of America, 1948), pp. 278–9; Trevor: *Under the White Paper*, p. 143; Crossman: *Palestine Mission*, pp. 91–95, with the comment: 'What the General had said was a great deal less than the truth.'

commiserate with England'.[1] Not to be outdone by this outcry in the United States, the London political secretary of the World Jewish Congress declared: 'General Morgan's allegation of a secret Jewish force inside Europe aiming at a mass exodus to Palestine is not only fantastically untrue, but is clearly designed to prejudge the findings of the Anglo-American Committee of Inquiry.'[2] This imputation was unproven and unconvincing, and, like all such allegations, it could only recoil on the heads of those who made it.[3]

Of the six United States and six British members of the Anglo-American Committee of Inquiry, the three who afterwards published personal accounts to supplement the Committee's official report and the records of its public sessions all came to be identified with the Zionist cause. The *Palestine Mission* of Richard H. S. Crossman, a member of the Labour Party who had given up a university career in order to devote himself to politics and had entered Parliament in 1945, was particularly valuable for its extracts from the diary which he kept while the Committee was active and for the candour and penetration with which he analysed his own changing reactions.[4] Bartley C. Crum, author of *Behind the Silken Curtain*, was a San Francisco corporation lawyer, a 'fighting liberal' whose unvarying and uncritical sympathy for Zionism, and mistrust of British 'imperialism' and the allegedly pro-British manœuvres of the State Department, made him a less reliable reporter than Crossman.[5] Dr. James G. McDonald had in 1935 resigned his post as League of Nations High Commissioner for Refugees from Germany as a protest against international vacillation in dealing with the problem; he had afterwards given himself wholeheartedly to the Zionist cause;[6] and President Truman was to choose him in 1948 as the first United States diplomatic envoy to

[1] Quoted by Hertzberg, loc. cit.; cf. *The Forrestal Diaries*, pp. 544, 546–7.

[2] *Manchester Guardian*, 3 January 1946.

[3] An American Gentile commentator warned the Zionist movement that 'hysterical screaming at every turn of events is not the way to make friends and influence people' (George Fielding Eliot, quoted by Hertzberg, loc. cit. p. 47). General Morgan's superiors in UNRRA immediately called for his resignation, which he refused to give; and at the end of January, after meetings in Washington with the Director-General, Herbert Lehmann (sometime Governor of New York State), he expressed his 'deepest regret' for any misunderstanding caused by his statement, and was confirmed in his appointment, only to be removed (in a different connexion) in the following August by the then Director-General (Fiorello La Guardia, sometime Mayor of New York City).

[4] While treating the Zionist claims with some reserve during the greater part of the Committee's activities, Crossman had made a number of friends among Jewish intellectuals during visits to Germany before 1933, and he had seen the horrors of the Dachau concentration camp after the liberation (*Palestine Mission*, pp. 15–16, 18–22).

[5] In the preface of *Behind the Silken Curtain* (New York, Simon & Schuster, 1947), Crum was 'proud' to assert that 'this is in no sense a disinterested book', and he acknowledged 'a deep debt of gratitude above all to Gerold Frank', an American Zionist writer, 'for his brilliant assistance' in its preparation (pp. vi–vii). He claimed to have learnt at the outset of State Department opposition to President Truman's choice of him as a member of the Committee (ibid. p. 4).

[6] The Jewish Agency had published his appeals *Palestine to the Rescue* and *Where Can the Refugees Go?* (London, 1943 and 1945 respectively).

Israel. The other British members of the Committee (in which the British group was led by Sir John Singleton, a High Court Judge) were men who, whatever their political allegiance, were generally sceptical of ideologies and likely to favour a compromise that would not seriously disturb the British position in the Middle East;[1] and it was significant that one of the two secretaries appointed by the Foreign Office was Harold Beeley, whose assessment of the pre-war development of the Palestine problem in an earlier volume of the *Survey of International Affairs* had incurred vigorous Zionist criticism.[2] Singleton's co-chairman, and leader of the United States contingent, was Judge Hutcheson of the Federal Circuit Court, an unconventional Texan who in the course of his career had shown himself sympathetic to aliens in difficulties, and described himself as an 'Old Testament Christian'; some, at least, of his colleagues were instinctively critical of British 'imperialism', and a United States Jewish reporter found generally much that was good to be said of the President's choice of the United States members.[3]

While one of the United States members, William Phillips, had been President Roosevelt's special representative in India during the war, there was none with previous experience of the Arab world; and when the United States team proposed that the inquiry should open in Washington, their British counterparts felt some 'annoyance and suspicion' that they were to be subjected from the outset to the 'full blast' of Zionist propaganda. According to Crossman, however, the more objective-minded of the United States members of the Committee were shocked by the 'totalitarian claims' advanced by the American Zionists.[4] Crum afterwards recorded his dismay on being (as he reports) warned, in Washington and during the Committee's transatlantic voyage, by representatives of the State Department and by Harold Beeley of the British Foreign Office, that the Committee would not be able to consider the associated problems of Palestine and the Jewish refugees in a vacuum devoid of power politics, but that, on the contrary, the decision which the Committee would reach would have to be carried out in a region which was already the seat of a Great Power conflict.[5] In fact, the shock of the Soviet-organized 'Demo-

---

[1] Crossman noted in his diary, on the day on which the party arrived in New York: 'We have a feeling that the whole idea of a Jewish national home is a *dead end* out of which Britain must be extricated ... that Arab independence in the end must be granted' (*Palestine Mission*, pp. 25–26, italics in the original).

[2] See L. B. Namier: *Conflicts* (London, Macmillan, 1942), pp. 109–19, part of a reprint of a review of the *Survey* for 1938, vol. i. Professor Harold Laski was to take up the attack on Beeley: see *Zionist Review*, 1 October 1948, pp. 3–4.

[3] I. F. Stone in *The Nation*, 22 December 1945, p. 678. For brief assessments of the personalities of the Committee members, see Crossman, op. cit. pp. 23–25, 29–31; Crum, op. cit. pp. 3–11.

[4] See Crossman, op. cit. pp. 22, 47 (diary-entry of 13 January 1946).

[5] See Crum, op. cit. pp. 7–8, 31, 33, 35–36; and cf. Crossman, op. cit. pp. 49–56, a section entitled 'American Power-politics'.

crat' *coup d'état* in Persian Āzarbāijān was only a month old at this time, and the Soviet propaganda machine was waging a 'war of nerves' against both the Turkish Government and the Anglo-Iranian Oil Company.[1]

While Arab and pro-Arab spokesmen overstated their case in Washington and London no less than did the Zionists, Crossman emerged from the London hearings (25 January–1 February 1946) with a 'peculiar exasperation', which he attributed to his colleagues also, at the double claim to be both Jews and at the same time members of some Gentile nation,[2] and at the 'double loyalty'—'to their home country and to their national home'—of those Zionists who did not go to Palestine yet expected both the concession of Palestine to Jewry as a National Home and simultaneously the 'recognition of a separate and exclusive Jewish community within each democratic state'.[3] The Committee's next move was bound to have a considerable effect on their feelings and outlook and was therefore open to criticism if it was not in accordance with the Committee's terms of reference. In giving a list of the Committee's tasks, these terms of reference had mentioned the examination of the 'political, economic, and social conditions of Palestine as they bear upon the problem of Jewish immigration and settlement' *before* the examination of the position of the Jewish refugees in Europe; and it was to be presumed that the terms had been carefully drawn up with the intention that they should be followed exactly. By changing the sequence of their instructions and visiting Europe at this stage the Committee were exposing themselves to the tremendous emotional impact of the homelessness of the Jewish refugees in advance of their visit to Palestine and the Middle East.[4] They found the Jewish survivors in the assembly centres of Germany and Austria, amounting to almost exactly 100,000 persons, living in relatively good physical conditions but suffering progressive demoralization from their continued detention in these lands where they had endured and witnessed such unprecedented horrors. The Zionist ideal was the one positive source of organization and self-discipline that countered this demoralization; and while virtually all the survivors were above all anxious to start a new life in some new environment, for about 70 per cent. of them, and these mainly vigorous young people who had survived the concentration camps, no haven other than Eretz Yisrael (Palestine) was thinkable.[5] The Committee's terms

---

[1] See above, pp. 21–27 and 58–61.   [2] Crossman: *Palestine Mission*, pp. 73–74.

[3] Ibid. p. 76. In this passage, Crossman mentions two other classes of Jews: the outright assimilationists and the nationally conscious Jews who went to Palestine. But he points out that the Jews who supported the National Home, financially and morally, while continuing to live elsewhere 'make up the bulk of the Zionist movement, and also of World Jewry outside the U.S.S.R.'.

[4] The United Nations Special Committee on Palestine in 1947, on the other hand, deferred its visit to the European refugees until after its hearings in Palestine and the Arab states.

[5] See Crossman, op. cit. pp. 85–86, 90–91; and cf. Crum: *Behind the Silken Curtain*, pp. 79–127.

of reference allowed it to issue an interim report and recommendations, and the impressionable Crum proposed that it should, without more ado, recommend the admission of these 100,000 Jews into Palestine;[1] but the majority of the Committee objected that to accept this round number, before even setting foot in Palestine and studying the local situation, would give the Arabs a legitimate grievance. Most of the British members, indeed, wished to call attention immediately to the infiltration of Jews from Eastern Europe,[2] which was adding to the pressure for immigration to Palestine, and two British members, including the British co-chairman, wished to draw the attention of the two Governments to the anomaly that while this infiltration from Eastern Europe was being encouraged in the United States zone of Germany, the policy in the British zone was to prevent it. Crum felt so strongly about his demand for an immediate recommendation on immigration that he threatened to resign from the Committee, but was mollified by a message from President Truman requesting that there should be no interim report or recommendations.[3]

In Cairo the Committee heard an intransigent expression of the views of the Arab League that the Zionists had no rights in Palestine beyond those of a minority within an independent Arab state;[4] and it travelled on to Jerusalem on 6 March. Meanwhile, on 17 January Bevin had told the United Nations General Assembly of his Government's intention to establish and recognize Trans-Jordan in the near future as a sovereign independent state. This was a logical step forward from the special status conferred on Trans-Jordan by Article 25 of the Palestine mandate, from the invocation of that article by the British Government in 1922 to exclude Trans-Jordan from those provisions in the Mandate which promoted a Jewish national home in Palestine, and from subsequent Anglo-Transjordan agreements moving in the general direction of the country's self-government;[5] and the Trusteeship Committee of the General Assembly

---

[1] Crum had just incurred a rebuke for giving an unauthorized press interview, independently of the rest of the Committee, on his impressions of the refugees' condition. He afterwards asserted (op. cit. pp. 121, 127-8) that his proposal for an immediate recommendation to admit them to Palestine had the support of the British member who had visited the German camps with him, and of Crossman; but Crossman (op. cit. p. 105) seems to imply the contrary.

[2] For the controversy whether these persons were in fact in danger see above, p. 204 and note 2. Local clashes between Poles and Jews culminated in a pogrom, of which the source of instigation is obscure, at Kielce on 5 July 1946, in which thirty-six Jews were reported killed.

[3] Crum, op. cit. pp. 128-9; Crossman, op. cit. pp. 105-6.

[4] For the Arab League's attempts to establish a common front, among the Palestine Arabs, between the supporters and the opponents of the Muftī cf. Hurewitz: *The Struggle for Palestine*, pp. 233-5, 239-40.

[5] See *Survey* for 1925, i. 361-3; Great Britain, Foreign Office: *Agreement between His Majesty and the Amir of Trans-Jordan, Jerusalem, February 20, 1928*, Cmd. 3488 (London, H.M.S.O., 1935); *Agreement between the United Kingdom and Trans-Jordan, supplementary* [to the foregoing], *Jerusalem, June 2, 1934*, Cmd. 4999 (London, H.M.S.O., 1935); King Abdullah of Transjordan: *Memoirs* (London, Cape, 1950), pp. 220-1.

had accordingly accepted the British proposal.[1] The Zionists, on the other hand, had never admitted the exclusion of Trans-Jordan from the area within which they might establish their national home; indeed, in their terminology, the river Jordan was not a boundary of Palestine but merely divided 'Eastern Palestine' from 'Western Palestine';[2] and they now protested vigorously against the proposal to make Trans-Jordan independent.[3]

The quota of 75,000 Jewish immigrants permitted under the 1939 White Paper being by this time exhausted, the High Commissioner on instructions from London had sought the agreement of the Palestine Arab political leaders to continue immigration at the current rate of 1,500 monthly until the Anglo-American Committee should have made its recommendations. A boycott of Zionist goods proclaimed by the Arab League had, however, come into effect at the beginning of the year,[4] and the Palestine Arab leaders refused any concession in the vital matter of immigration. Meanwhile, the Jewish terrorist organizations, allegedly with the connivance of the Haganah,[5] had continued their sabotage in protest against the interception of illegal immigrants. The Palestine Government accordingly promulgated on 28 January additional defence regulations providing death as the maximum penalty for taking part in a terrorist attack or for 'being a member of any group or body of persons of whom any one or more members have been committing an offence against this regulation', or for the illegal possession or manufacture of firearms, ammunition, bombs, incendiaries, or explosives: the High Commissioner was empowered to

---

[1] United Nations, General Assembly: *Official Records*, 1st session, 1st part, plenary meetings, pp. 167, 591. Trans-Jordan accordingly became independent on 22 March 1946; see Great Britain, Foreign Office: *Treaty of Alliance between the United Kingdom and Trans-Jordan, London, 22nd March, 1946*, Cmd. 6916 (London, H.M.S.O., 1946).

[2] See Moshe Sneh: 'What are the Facts?', *Zionist Review*, 15 February 1946, supplement, p. i.

[3] 'We have always looked forward to arrangements that would make Jewish settlement in Trans-Jordan feasible and permit joint development with Palestine, which the Jewish Agency could initiate and implement together with the Arabs of Trans-Jordan. This would at the same time make it possible for Jewish settlement to be fostered and to improve the conditions of the inhabitants. We saw in the continued maintenance of the joint Mandate an open door for such joint development. We have never excluded from our consideration those great, desolate and uncultivated stretches of land across the river which are capable of settlement and development' (Shertok, 24 January 1946, cited in *Palestine Post*, 25 January 1946). The Revisionist Party and the I.Z.L. continued to demand the outright annexation of Trans-Jordan: and Sam Pope Brewer of the *New York Times* wrote: 'No Jewish leader interviewed by this writer in Palestine, except the late Dr. Judah L. Magnes, ever strongly criticized that ambition' (*Middle East Journal*, Winter 1951, v. 114, reviewing Kenneth W. Bilby's *New Star in the Near East*).

[4] The *Zionist Review* (4 January 1946, p. 1) described the boycott as 'nationalism run mad' and the Palestine Government was denounced for not declaring it illegal. During its first three months Palestinian exports to the boycotting countries were reduced to 31 per cent. of their value in the first quarter of 1945, but a black market began to operate in Jewish products that were still difficult to obtain from the West, and Arab 'notables' still sometimes availed themselves of the skilled services of Zionist doctors and hospitals.

[5] See Begin: *The Revolt*, pp. 196-8.

deport or exclude any person from Palestine while the regulation remained in force. To balance this, however, the High Commissioner announced on the 30th that the monthly rate of immigration would remain provisionally at 1,500. The Jewish community on the following day held a protest strike against the continued restrictions on their freedom of immigration and land purchase, and resolved that they would not rest until the White Paper restrictions had been removed 'and the gates of Palestine opened for the remnant of Israel'. The Jewish Agency continued to accept each monthly quota as it became due, however, and in this way 21,000 immigrants (or 1·1 per cent. of the existing population) entered Palestine legally during the next troubled year.[1] The Palestine Arabs, for their part, held a protest strike on 2 February against this departure from the strict letter of the White Paper which, although most of them had rejected it as inadequate at the time of its promulgation,[2] had by the passage of time and the change of circumstances been transformed into the palladium of their aspirations for independence. They also were given a consolation, however, in the permission to return to Palestine extended to the exiled Muftī's relative Jamāl al-Husainī, who had been captured after the 'Irāqī *putsch* of 1941 and interned in Rhodesia.[3]

An announcement that the British military authorities intended to employ German prisoners of war to labour on military installations in south Palestine was violently attacked by the Zionists, probably because they regarded these installations as a reinforcement of British authority. While, however, the executive council of the Zionist Federation of Great Britain protested that 'any importation into Palestine of Germans for whatever purpose' was 'an outrageous provocation and . . . an act likely to disturb the peace of the country',[4] that 'peace' was already being disturbed by a renewal of Haganah collusion with the terrorists in joint attacks on military installations that were used to combat illegal immigration. On 20 February the Palmaḥ blew up the radar station at Haifa, wounding eight R.A.F. personnel, and two days later carried out co-ordinated attacks on three camps of the Palestine Mobile Force, a specialized formation of the Palestine Police, while on the 25th the I.Z.L. and Stern Group destroyed or damaged fifteen aircraft[5] on three airfields, at an estimated cost to Britain of £750,000. The Haganah, in pamphlets and broadcasts over its

---

[1] Bevin in the House of Commons, 18 February 1947, H.C.Deb. 5th ser., vol. 433, col. 986. Although the Zionists denounced the quota as a 'trickle', it may be noted that in the United States the ratio of annual immigration to total population had only exceptionally exceeded 1 per cent. before 1914, and had never come near that figure since that time (see William S. Bernard: *American Immigration Policy* (New York, Harper, 1950), p. 158, table 37).

[2] Cf. *Survey* for 1938, i. 465–6.

[3] For the Arab political situation at this stage see Hurewitz: *The Struggle for Palestine*, pp. 239–42.

[4] *Zionist Review*, 1 March 1946, p. 1; cf. Trevor: *Under the White Paper*, p. 189.

[5] 'Dozens', according to Begin: *The Revolt*, p. 93.

'underground' radio, boasted of the part played in these operations by the Jewish Resistance Movement.[1]

Despite this attitude of defiance to the Palestine Government, Ben Gurion, who (as was afterwards asserted and not denied, so far as the present writer knows)[2] 'had been responsible for Haganah and national defence for a long time', showed at his first appearance before the Anglo-American Committee in Jerusalem on 11 March an apparent lack of candour which evoked an adverse comment in Crossman's diary,[3] and led to Ben Gurion's being recalled at the last hearing in Jerusalem on 26 March before the Anglo-American Committee of Inquiry for a judicial questioning by the British co-chairman. The verbatim report of the proceedings on this occasion needs no comment:

Singleton: . . . Hagana, is that under the Jewish Agency?

Ben Gurion: I haven't spoken of it. Hagana is a Hebrew word which means defence.

Q. It is a body of some sort?

A. I think there are many bodies of defence in Palestine.

Q. Don't let it be a matter of imagination. We have heard in this hall of some body which is some sort of a military organization, bearing the name of Hagana. Is that under the Jewish Agency?

A. I don't think there is such an organization bearing that name. I think it's merely [that] in Hebrew the word Hagana means defence. There are certainly defence organizations of Jews in Palestine, I believe in each place. In every Jewish community I am sure there is such an organization.

Q. Is the organization under the Jewish Agency?

A. No, it is under the Jews in Palestine. . . . The Jewish Agency is engaged very much—it is a question of defence and security, and it applies from time to time to the Government to strengthen the security in the colonies and settlements and cities. . . .

Q. . . . Then the Hagana is not under some form of control by the Jewish Agency, is it?

A. No, the Agency is not engaged in any illegal or any secret activity.

Q. I did not ask you that. I asked you just this question: is or is not the Hagana under some form of control by the Jewish Agency?

[1] Cmd. 6873, p. 7, and cf. Trevor, op. cit. pp. 179, 186–7. In order apparently to counter 'wide public criticism' of the Haganah over the loss of four young members of Palmaḥ killed during the attack on one Palestine Mobile Force camp, they were given a public funeral by the Jewish Agency and the entire Hebrew press published their obituary notices (Begin: *The Revolt*, pp. 192–3; cf. *Zionist Review*, 1 March 1946, p. 1).

[2] L. Avigdor: 'The Drama of "Independence Day" ', *Zionist Review*, 29 April 1949, p. 4.

[3] 'He seems to want to have it both ways, to remain within the letter of the law as chairman of the Agency, and to tolerate terror as a method of bringing pressure on the Administration. . . . The Irish leaders made up their minds and went underground: they openly declared war on Great Britain. I wonder whether Ben Gurion wouldn't be wiser to do the same or to accept the lead of Weizmann and the moderates who really and genuinely regard the use of force as a mistake' (Crossman: *Palestine Mission*, p. 139; cf. Arthur Koestler: *Promise and Fulfilment: Palestine 1917–1949* (London, Macmillan, 1949), pp. 137–8, for the discrediting of the Zionist movement by this 'double-faced policy').

A. I can tell you about the Agency but not about the Hagana. I represent the Jewish Agency here and not the Hagana, and I can answer about the Agency. The Agency has nothing to do with any illegal or any secret activity of Jews which is in this country, and therefore it can have nothing to do with any secret organization.

Q. Mr. Ben Gurion, you must know that that is not an answer to my question . . . Is the Hagana under some form of control by the Jewish Agency?

A. There is no organization of such a kind under the control of the Jewish Agency, as far as I know.

Q. Have you answered my question?

A. Yes, Sir.

Q. Then are you saying that the Hagana is not under some form of control by the Jewish Agency?

A. . . . It is not controlled by the Jewish Agency.

Q. Who pays the cost of it?

A. I do not know, Sir. The Jews in Palestine.

Q. Is it done through the Jewish Agency?

A. No, Sir. I told you, no.

Q. Is there anything in your accounts showing expenditure on defence organization?

A. Yes, many things.[1]

Q. Very well, I may take it that the Jewish Agency has nothing to do with the Hagana?

A. No, Sir, that is a secret organization. With defence, yes. The word 'Hagana' has a double meaning. The word 'Hagana' means defence, but when you use 'Hagana' it is a proper name of a secret organization. With defence we have to do; with an organization which is called Hagana, no.

Q. Will you take it that I asked the question of you in the widest possible sense. Has the Jewish Agency anything to do with the Hagana?

A. I told you, no; with defence, yes, because Hagana means also defence.[2]

None but the familiar arguments were advanced in Jerusalem by either the Zionist or the Arab spokesmen; for the personality of the absent Muftī, and that of his returned henchman Jamāl al-Husainī, were potent to intimidate any possible Arab dissenter, and among the Jewish community it was afterwards stated that 'strict orders were issued that no one was to testify . . . along any but "official" lines'.[3] In the other Arab states in which

---

[1] It was afterwards disclosed that during the thirty years of the Mandate the Jewish Foundation Fund, the main financial instrument of the Agency (Israel Cohen: *The Zionist Movement* (London, Muller, 1945), p. 179), spent some £27 million on defence, disguised as 'national organization' (M. Eskolsky: 'Foundation Fund of Statehood', *Israel and Middle East*, June–July 1950, p. 101.)

[2] *Public Hearings before the Anglo-American Committee of Inquiry*, Jerusalem, 26 March 1946 (mimeographed), pp. 12–14. An eye-witness, reporting the scene for a generally pro-Zionist weekly, observed how 'throughout the whole drama, Moshe Shertok sat just behind the witness, looking pale; and every now and then plucking at Ben Gurion's sleeve and whispering in his ear' (*Middle East Times* (Jerusalem), 28 March 1946).

[3] Moshe Smilansky (a prominent member of the small Ihud group that openly favoured a

sections of the Committee held hearings, representatives of the local Jewish communities were marshalled before them, in a procedure reminiscent of the totalitarian states, to testify submissively that they were satisfied with their present status and had no wish to migrate to Palestine.[1] When the Committee drew up its report at Lausanne, Crossman and Crum were apparently alone in favouring the partition of Palestine into a Jewish state in the potentially fertile lowlands and an Arab state in the high-lands:[2] but the majority of the Committee, having regard to the economic interdependence of the two politically rival communities[3] (and also, no doubt, to the Soviet pressure on the northern edge of the Middle East) clung to the hope, against all the experience of the previous ten years, that somehow the two communities might be induced to live together in peace, if a greater measure of co-operation could be secured from the United States in ensuring that the militants did not receive financial and material support from abroad.[4] The Committee recalled that the British partition commission of 1938 had had great difficulty in determining an equitable demarcation line between the two geographically entangled communities, and that the very idea of partition was repugnant to the Palestine Arabs and the Arab states, while the Zionists would be likely to reject any parti-tion which did not give them substantial new areas for settlement. With these facts in mind, British official opinion did, in fact, shrink from the idea of trying to impose a partition without United States backing, since it was anxious to avoid a disturbance of the Arab states' relations with Britain at a time when the Soviet Government were actively engaged in a 'war of nerves' to reduce Turkey and Persia to satellite status,[5] and when the demand for the complete evacuation of British troops from the Levant States and Egypt made the continued possession of a base in Palestine a matter of strategic importance.[6] The two advocates of partition finally

measure of compromise with the Arabs), 'The Anglo-American Report Points the Way', *Commentary*, July 1946, p. 5; cf. *Survey* for 1939–46: *The Middle East in the War*, p. 248, n. 2. The Ihud's leader, Dr. Judah L. Magnes, did appear before the Committee with more moderate pro-posals, which were reported to have made a great impression on the Committee and to have had considerable influence on their recommendations. The evidence given by Dr. Magnes and by Martin Buber has been published in Judah Magnes and Martin Buber: *Arab-Jewish Unity* (London, Gollancz, 1947).

[1] See Crum: *Behind the Silken Curtain*, pp. 238–49.

[2] See Crossman: *Palestine Mission*, pp. 176–9.

[3] This economic interdependence was the basis both of the British federal proposals of 1946–7 and of the United Nations plan for 'partition with economic union' in 1947 (see below, pp. 223–4, 245–6).

[4] A British suggestion of joint Anglo-American responsibility for maintaining order in Pales-tine while the Committee's recommendations were being carried out found no favour with the United States members, and was withdrawn (see Crossman: op. cit. pp. 185–6; McDonald: *My Mission in Israel*, p. 22).

[5] See Hurewitz: *The Struggle for Palestine*, pp. 246–7.

[6] See above, pp. 106–11 and 119–20. The need to reduce Britain's huge war-time bases in Egypt and to evacuate the Levant States was perhaps as important a factor as the maintenance of order

yielded to the majority, and the report was unanimously signed on 19 April for publication on the night of 30 April–1 May. While its appreciations of the various aspects of the Palestine problem contained much sound observation, notably on the precariousness of the Zionist economy, its recommendations were clearly an attempt to give some satisfaction to all parties by a balanced juxtaposition of their proposals for a 'solution' of the problem. They recommended the immediate issue of 100,000 immigration certificates for Jewish refugees, but rejected the idea of either a Jewish or an Arab state in favour of a trusteeship; they called for assistance to Jewish immigration and the abolition of the restrictions on Jewish land purchase, but also the lifting of the statutory ban on the employment of non-Jewish labour on enterprises financed by Jewish national funds; they encouraged economic and educational development, but observed that the ambitious Zionist project for the utilization of the Jordan waters for large-scale irrigation required the willing co-operation of adjacent Arab states. Finally, on British insistence,[1] they recommended that it should be made clear

beyond all doubt to both Jews and Arabs that any attempt from either side, by threats of violence, by terrorism, or by the organization or use of illegal armies to prevent its execution, will be resolutely suppressed.

Furthermore . . . the Jewish Agency should at once resume active cooperation with the Mandatory in the suppression of terrorism and of illegal immigration, and in the maintenance of that law and order throughout Palestine which is essential for the good of all, including the new immigrants.[2]

The view held by Crossman and the United States members of the Committee was that 'an attempt to disarm the Jews by force would only strengthen the position of the terrorists and involve a far larger military commitment than the rapid and decisive implementation of the report'; but implementation coupled with the refusal of the United States to share the responsibility would have involved the British Government (as Crossman admitted) in reviewing afresh their whole Middle Eastern policy, at this critical moment in the Soviet 'war of nerves' on the northern flank

in Palestine in raising the British garrison of that country to nearly 100,000 men, and thereby providing a multiplicity of static targets for the guerrilla attacks to which they were exposed.

[1] According to Crum (*Behind the Silken Curtain*, p. 279) the British members, except Crossman, were moved chiefly by the British casualties at the hands of the terrorists; and Sir John Singleton and others argued that the ending of this lawless campaign, of which the Haganah and the Jewish Agency were accomplices, should be a condition of allowing further Jewish immigration.

[2] U.S. Department of State: *Anglo-American Committee of Inquiry: Report* (Washington, U.S.G.P.O., 1946), p. 12. Crossman had noted in his diary on 23 March 1946 that some members of the Palestine Administration wished to see further Jewish immigration made conditional upon the reorganization of the Jewish Agency and the disarming of the Haganah (*Palestine Mission*, p. 166, and cf. p. 196). Crum ascribed such views to British members of the Committee while they were crossing the Atlantic in January (*Behind the Silken Curtain*, p. 43); but Crum's testimony is perhaps not to be taken so seriously as Crossman's.

of the Middle East and while an attempt was being made to negotiate a new treaty with Egypt. Crossman's estimate—that the Jewish community would, 'the moment its wrongs were righted', suppress the terrorists and co-operate loyally—probably took insufficient account of the intransigence of the Zionist demands and the impossibility of satisfying them without the risk of precipitating a pro-Soviet reaction on the part of likewise intransigent political forces in the Arab countries. Bevin, 'despite urgent requests', would not discuss the matter with Crossman and one of his British colleagues during the coming months; the Cabinet, according to Crossman, considered the Anglo-American Committee's report only when it had been critically analysed by a committee of military and civilian officials;[1] and while these deliberations were still in progress a terrorist attack on a military car park in Tel Aviv on 25 April, in which seven British soldiers were caught unprepared and killed, hardened British opinion against the Zionists.[2] Furthermore, Crossman admitted the 'lamentable' effects in Britain of the letter which President Truman issued with the publication of the Anglo-American Committee's report on 30 April; this letter welcomed as 'immediate objectives' all the Committee's recommendations that favoured the Zionists, but dismissed the other recommendations as 'questions of long-range political policies and questions of international law which require careful study and which I will take under advisement'.[3] Ernest Bevin's biographer records that Truman's letter threw Bevin into 'one of the blackest rages I ever saw him in'.[4] He sent an immediate protest to Washington, and Crossman observed that Attlee's reaction also, in a statement to the House of Commons on 1 May, was 'extremely sharp'. The Prime Minister 'very properly'[5] deprecated the President's selective attitude towards the Committee's

[1] Crossman, op. cit. pp. 199–201. In addressing the Fabian Society in 1951 he put it that the Government had 'permitted its Socialism to be overruled by expert advice. . . . It was a clear case where principle was overruled by the false advocates of expediency' (R. H. S. Crossman and Kenneth Younger: *Socialist Foreign Policy*, Fabian Tract no. 287 (London, Fabian International Bureau, 1951), p. 3.) Crossman's conviction 'that the Jews had set going revolutionary forces in the Middle East which, in the long run, would benefit the Arabs' (*Palestine Mission*, pp. 176–7) did not, of course, provide any solution for the difficulties of British authorities responsible for dealing with the immediate problems of the Middle East 'cold war'.

[2] The Divisional Commander replied to a message of regret from the Mayor of Tel Aviv: 'I hold the [Jewish] community to blame. There is no doubt whatsoever in my mind that many members either knew of this project or could have given some warning before it happened. Further, I am quite certain that if you, as representative of the community of Tel Aviv, chose to do so you could produce sufficient information to lead to the arrest of the criminals.' British troops took the law into their own hands and attacked some innocent Jews the following night (Wilson: *Cordon and Search*, pp. 47–48). This was apparently the first case of unauthorized British reprisals for Jewish terrorism, though such reprisals had been not uncommon against the Arabs during *their* rebellion in 1938–9.

[3] United States, 79th Congress, 2nd session, Senate Document no. 182, p. iii.

[4] Francis Williams: *Ernest Bevin, Portrait of a Great Englishman* (London, Hutchinson, 1952), p. 260.

[5] Crossman, op. cit. pp. 197–9.

recommendations; he wished to know to what extent the United States would share in the additional military and financial responsibilities of implementing them; and he declared that the Government could not admit so large a body of immigrants as the 100,000 originally proposed by Weizmann, underwritten by President Truman, and adopted by the Committee, unless and until the 'illegal armies' in Palestine had been disbanded and their arms surrendered. Jews and Arabs in Palestine alike must disarm immediately, and it was essential that the Jewish Agency should 'take a positive part' in the suppression of the recent violent attacks on British installations and lives.[1]

Pro-Zionist circles strongly criticized the British Government for thus linking the issue of the proposed 100,000 immigration certificates with the disarmament of the Zionist illegal organizations, since (they argued) the Committee's Report had not made the one recommendation dependent on the other in this way. It must, however, be recalled that the Government, unlike their critics and the Committee, were fully aware through the intercepted secret telegrams of the regular collusion which still continued between the Jewish Agency Executive and the terrorists who had just committed the 'cold-blooded murder' of 25 April; and they were therefore not disposed to draw the distinctions, drawn by Crossman and others who were concerned to put the Zionist case, between the different ethics of revolt observed by the Haganah and the 'dissidents' respectively, or to credit the Haganah with the single-minded intention of keeping the terrorists within some bounds. The Haganah's 'underground' radio *Qol Yisrael* on 3 May accused the Government, by their linking of immigration with disarmament, of 'merely hedging and endeavouring to evade the carrying out of the operative recommendation of the . . . Report'; on the 7th the Haganah command informed the I.Z.L. leader that Zionist influence was being exerted in the United States to have pressure brought upon the British Government to withdraw their insistence on the disbandment of the illegal organizations;[2] and on the 12th, when the British Government had conditionally offered to the Egyptian Government the complete withdrawal of the British forces from that country,[3] *Qol Yisrael* made a defiant broadcast authorized by Shertok. In this the Jewish Resistance Movement warned the British Government against their 'dangerous manœuvre . . . based on an erroneous assumption' that they could replace Egypt by Palestine as their military base in the Middle East without fulfilling their mandatory responsibilities as these were now being interpreted by political Zionism. If the British Government continued to vacillate even over the 'tepid conclusions' of the Anglo-American Committee, and particularly over admitting the 100,000 immigrants, the

---

[1] 1 May 1946, H.C.Deb. 5th ser., vol. 422, coll. 195-7.   [2] Begin: *The Revolt*, p. 202.
[3] See above, p. 120.

Jewish Resistance Movement would 'make every effort to hinder the transfer of British bases to Palestine and to prevent their establishment in the country'.[1]

The British Foreign Office announced on 15 May that their decisions on the Anglo-American Committee's recommendations must await the completion of consultations with the United States Government and with Arab and Jewish leaders. Meanwhile, in the United States the Acting Secretary of State, Dean Acheson, had assured representatives of the Arab states on the 10th that in accordance with Roosevelt's promise to Ibn Sa'ūd in 1945[2] the Government would consult both Arabs and Jews before making any decision on Palestine; and on the 20th the State Department invited both parties to present their views within a month, Dean Acheson remarking that the Anglo-American Committee had been advisory only, and that consequently its recommendations were not binding. A meeting of Zionist leaders in Washington declared itself 'outraged' by the delay: their spokesman commented bitterly that the State Department's general attitude 'was more in line with the British point of view than with that of the President';[3] and the *Zionist Review*'s Jerusalem correspondent reported:

It is difficult to consider the latest developments calmly and dispassionately. Despite all efforts to maintain an even temper, the blood persists in coursing through one's veins with unwonted rapidity, and the very ink in one's pen turns an angry red when it is put to paper. It is not too much to say that the Yishuv is seething at the decision to consult the Arab countries.

If there is any danger to Middle East security, it is more likely to come from the Jews than from the Arabs. . . . To many members of the Yishuv, and to the younger ones in particular, the logic of events is inescapable: once again the Arabs, by means of empty threats, have wrung concessions from Britain. Why, then, not try the effect of threats backed by force, with a few more acts of sabotage to show that we mean business?[4]

(c) TRIALS OF STRENGTH AND UNSUCCESSFUL EFFORTS AT COMPROMISE, JUNE 1946 TO MARCH 1947

At this time the British Government came under criticism at the Labour Party's annual Whitsun conference for their attitude to the Anglo-American Committee's report. The criticism came notably from the party's political philosopher and chairman, Professor Harold Laski, who, while admitting that the situation in Palestine was too complex for the 'formula' of a Jewish state to be acceptable, asked that neither 'Arab blackmail' nor

---

[1] Cmd. 6873, pp. 8–9; cf. Sacher: *Israel, the Establishment of a State*, p. 190.

[2] See *Survey* for 1939–46: *The Middle East in the War*, p. 327.

[3] Benjamin Schwadran in *Palestine Affairs*, June 1946, p. 2; see also Sidney Hertzberg, 'The Month in History', *Commentary*, June 1946, p. 67.

[4] 'An Angry Community', *Zionist Review*, 31 May 1946, p. 5.

Britain's Middle East strategy should be allowed to make the 100,000 Jewish refugees in Europe 'the victims of hesitation and timidity in Downing Street. . . . A British statesman who sacrifices the Jews who escaped from the tortures of Hitlerism to the Arab leaders does not understand the elementary principles of the socialist hypothesis.'[1] To such appeals to Socialist principles Bevin replied on 12 June in his pragmatic if sometimes barely coherent manner.[2] He declared that the proposed admission of 100,000 Jews immediately would necessitate sending another division of British troops to Palestine and the expenditure of £200 million,[3] which the Chancellor of the Exchequer agreed to be impossible. The Government had therefore suggested to the United States Government the appointment of a joint committee of experts to consider the practical problems involved: 'finance, military matters, transport, housing, and what is probably the most vexed problem of all, the land problem'; and President Truman had on the previous day appointed a Cabinet committee to study a British questionnaire on these points.

An editorial in the *Zionist Review* of 21 June asked: 'Is Mr. Bevin so sure that it will cost him less—from the military point of view—to keep the Jews out of Palestine than to admit them?' This was a declaration of war after the event, for during the evening of the 16th the Palmaḥ had destroyed or damaged four road bridges, four railway bridges, and the Allenby Bridge across the Jordan, while on the following evening the Stern Group had attacked the Haifa railway workshops.[4] This renewal of collusive activity by the Jewish Resistance Movement[5] decided the British Govern-

[1] *Zionist Review*, 14 June 1946, p. 2.

[2] Official text ibid. 21 June 1946, p. 3, and *Arab News Bulletin*, 28 June 1946.

[3] Bevin doubtless meant to convey that the Arab reaction to large-scale Jewish immigration might involve Britain in heavy expenditure in maintaining order (cf. Attlee, addressing the House of Commons, 1 July 1946, H.C.Deb. 5th ser., vol. 424, col. 1911); but the figure of £200 million seemed inordinately large. The Zionists afterwards wrote ironically of a 'trivial miscalculation' on Bevin's part, referring only to the cost of transporting the immigrants, which they estimated at £2 million (see Pendennis, pseud., in the *Observer*, 12 June 1949, and cf. a letter from Ben Gurion to *The Times*, 20 June 1946); but one of Bevin's clearer assertions was that 'it is not merely taking the people and putting them there'.

[4] Cmd. 6873, pp. 8–9. On the evening of 15 June, one day before the attacks on the bridges, *Qol Yisrael* claimed in a broadcast that the Haganah had acquired 'a highly secret military document containing the plan of the Palestine authorities for the liquidation of the Haganah and cleaning up the Jewish community, together with appropriate operation orders'. It then gave what purported to be the contents of this 'infamous document' (see texts in *Zionist Review*, 21 June 1946, p. 7; Trevor: *Under the White Paper*, p. 211, note 14), but these were a string of generalizations such as might readily have been fabricated from the knowledge which the Haganah had acquired during the Second World War of British staff procedure, to say nothing of their penetration of all departments of British activity in Palestine (see Wilson: *Cordon and Search*, p. 36). Such stolen documents as the Zionists subsequently published were of a relatively low grade, however, and not comparable with this alleged 'highly secret' plan (see American Christian Palestine Committee: *The Arab War Effort: a Documented Account* (New York, 1947); *The British Record on Partition as Revealed by British Military Intelligence and Other Official Sources* (New York, supplement to *The Nation*, 8 May 1948)).

[5] On 18 June also the I.Z.L. kidnapped six British officers as hostages for two members of that

ment to take the step for which the military authorities had been pressing,[1] namely to authorize the High Commissioner to proceed against those known to be involved in these acts of violence. Among those arrested in the military operation which began on 29 June were such prominent members of the Jewish Agency as Shertok and Bernard Joseph (but not Ben Gurion, who was still in Europe), and the Chairman of the Vaad Leumi, David Remez. The Jewish Agency building in Jerusalem was occupied for a short time to allow documents to be seized, and buildings were occupied in Tel Aviv which the illegal organizations were believed to use as headquarters. Finally, the British troops had instructions to arrest as many members as possible of Palmah. Two years later, a Palmah battalion-commander admitted that the British 'knew just where to look and whom to arrest. . . . Most of our top commanders were warned in time, but 200 of our officers were caught and thrown into jail';[2] in all, 2,700 persons were arrested, of whom some 700 were detained after questioning.[3] It was not expected when the operation began that any thorough arms searches would be possible;[4] but a week's search of the settlement of Yagur, near Haifa (which a Palmah battalion-commander afterwards admitted to have been one of their chief arms stores[5]) revealed thirty-three caches of arms concealed beneath the floors of childrens' nurseries, cowsheds, &c., and containing 10 machine-guns, 325 rifles, 96 mortars, 800 lb. of explosives, 425,000 rounds of small-arms ammunition, &c. Later, between 28 August and 2 September, British troops searched Dorot and Ruhama, two settlements in south Palestine founded during the Second World War and used by the Haganah as reception points for consignments of stolen British arms smuggled in from Egypt. 'It was hoped that by demonstrating that we were in a position to cripple them by arms seizures as and when we chose', wrote Major Wilson, 'a steadying influence might be exerted. These hopes were well founded,

organization who were under sentence of death for terrorist activities. One of the officers escaped, and the rest were eventually released, two before and the others after the death sentences on the two terrorists had been commuted (see Begin: *The Revolt*, pp. 245–50; Wilson: *Cordon and Search*, pp. 55–56).

[1] Ibid. pp. 47–48.

[2] Lawrence Lader: 'The Spirit of the Palmach', *New Republic*, 15 November 1948, p. 14; cf. Trevor: *Under the White Paper*, p. 216. The I.Z.L. leader, who was no friend of the Palmah, wrote appreciatively that 'every communal village in which a Palmach unit was "secretly" stationed was well-known to the British military intelligence. . . . The blow to the Palmach was tremendous' (Begin: *The Revolt*, p. 204). The British Government seem afterwards to have been embarrassed by the implication that the operation was directed more against the Palmah than the 'dissident' terrorists, who were more successful in maintaining their secrecy (see Hurewitz: *The Struggle for Palestine*, p. 355, note 15.)

[3] Ibid. pp. 254–5, with the suggestion that the British military action was restrained by consideration for the fate of the vital United States loan to Britain, which the House of Representatives was about to debate and against which some Zionist voices were now raised.

[4] Wilson, op. cit. p. 57.

[5] Lader, loc. cit.

and during the next two years the Haganah repeatedly revealed by their actions that they were very conscious of this chink in their armour.'[1]

The Zionists' anger at this frontal attack by the British, whom for a year they had been trying to coerce into surrender to their uncompromising demands, were expressed in comments that were not justified by the facts. Weizmann himself contrasted the detention of Shertok, who had 'raised an army of 25,000 Jewish Palestinians to fight shoulder to shoulder with Britain in World War II', with the present position of the Muftī of Jerusalem, 'a war criminal and sworn enemy of Britain', who on 29 May had evaded his partial surveillance as a political refugee near Paris and had travelled under an assumed name with a Syrian passport in a United States aircraft to Cairo where, Weizmann said, he now 'sat in a palace'— as if he had effected this escape by British favour.[2] In Britain Zionist propaganda represented the round-up of the Palmaḥ as directed against Jewish trade unionists and the socialist and co-operative settlements, and Crossman declared in the House of Commons that the army had arrested 'the whole of . . . the political Left . . . in the belief that they are the leaders of the resistance movement'.[3] There was a sheer misrepresentation of the truth in a statement, issued by settlements in the Beisan area, which declared that 'children, old people, men and women, also pregnant women, sick and crippled people, were savagely beaten with rifle-butts, prodded with bayonets, trodden underfoot, and kicked into unconsciousness. . . . Scores were left unconscious with broken limbs.'[4] Nevertheless, a chronicler acceptable to the Jewish Agency[5] was afterwards to admit that over the whole country 'at the end of the first day's operations, one British

---

[1] Wilson: *Cordon and Search*, p. 79; but cf. Hurewitz: *The Struggle for Palestine*, p. 255. The metal containers for concealed arms were buried under a depth of 4½–5 feet of earth to avoid discovery by electrically operated mine detectors, but were discovered by specially trained dogs. Zionist atrocity propaganda, which had declared that the British had made 'another Lidice' of Yagur (see Maurice J. Goldbloom in *Commentary*, August 1946, p. 143), again denounced the 'acts of wanton destruction' to 'peaceful agricultural settlements' occasioned by these later searches; but it was never explained how search for caches so cunningly concealed could be made without damage. Zionist charges of looting by the troops were also constant, and no doubt had some foundation in fact. 'But looting was neither general nor frequent' and in many cases, when towns were searched, looting was 'proved in the end to be the work of the less scrupulous members of the Jewish community', according to Wilson (op. cit. p. 62).

[2] Weizmann, quoted by Hurewitz, op. cit. p. 256. For an account of the Mufti's escape see *New York Times*, 9 June, *The Times*, 10 and 13 June 1946; and cf. *Survey* for 1939–46: *The Middle East in the War*, p. 158, note 5. The Haganah had asserted that one of the motives for their sabotage operations of 16 June had been 'to protest against the "laxity" that resulted in the Muftī's return' (Shlomo Katz in *Commentary*, July 1946, p. 49) but their broadcast of 18 June had contained no reference to it (see Cmd. 6873, pp. 8–9).

[3] *Zionist Review*, 5 July 1946, p. 1; 1 July 1946, H.C.Deb. 5th ser., vol. 424, col. 1873. More than two years later the arrested members of Palmaḥ were similarly referred to by Crossman as being 'for the most part good, sound trade unionists' (26 January 1949, ibid. vol. 460, col. 982).

[4] *Zionist Review*, 12 July 1946, pp. 10–11.   [5] See above, p. 190, note 4.

soldier had been killed and four Jews. . . . No more people were killed after the first day. . . . Of the scores of injured (eighty according to the official communiqué)—the settlers' accounts added up to a much higher total—only one man . . . was in hospital for a considerable period'.[1]

President Truman had deferred to British insistence that the Anglo-American Committee's report must be studied as a whole, and dispatched to London the 'alternates' of his Cabinet committee on Palestine, under Ambassador Henry F. Grady, to seek an understanding with British specialists on Palestine. Meanwhile, the I.Z.L. and Haganah commanders, realizing that the self-confidence of considerable sections of the Jewish community had been severely shaken by the British large-scale arrests of 20 June, decided that their morale 'could be restored only by a successful counter-attack'.[2] Already in the spring the I.Z.L. had conceived the plan of blowing up the Palestine Government's headquarters, which shared with the military headquarters the east wing and the upper floors of the King David Hotel in Jerusalem, while the lower floors were used normally as a hotel. The Haganah commanders, to whom the plan had been duly propounded, had not objected to it in principle, but at the time had considered it premature. After the British round-up of 29 June, however, they immediately sanctioned it as a reprisal,[3] to be executed after office hours to avoid loss of life.[4] Two or three times in the following weeks they apparently asked for a postponement of the proposed date,[5] and the I.Z.L. finally decided to act alone at midday on 22 July. Milk-churns filled with explosives were driven in a truck manned by terrorists dressed as Arabs to the (apparently unguarded) kitchen entrance of the hotel, and rolled

[1] Trevor: *Under the White Paper*, pp. 221–3. After a military search of Tel Aviv from 30 July to 2 August the Jerusalem correspondent of the *Zionist Review* (16 August 1946, p. 6) wrote: 'The behaviour of the troops—as on the occasion of the searches in the settlements on the 29th June and subsequently—was on the whole restrained. Regrettable incidents did occur, especially in the poorer sections of the city; but they do not provide sufficient material for any general charges of brutality. . . . The behaviour of the troops is, if anything, to be commended.'

[2] Begin: *The Revolt*, p. 217.

[3] A Jewish Agency official afterwards stated that during the months in which, after the Stern Group's murder of Lord Moyne in November 1944, the Agency were giving the British some assistance against the terrorists (see *Survey* for 1939–46: *The Middle East in the War*, pp. 325–6), the Agency had on several occasions warned the authorities to be on their guard against extremist attempts to blow up the King David Hotel (T. Kollek in *New Statesman and Nation*, 10 August 1946, p. 99; cf. 31 July and 1 August 1946, H.C.Deb. 5th ser., vol. 426, coll. 1009–10, 1315).

[4] Sacher: *Israel, the Establishment of a State*, p. 191.

[5] It is alleged that Weizmann had been incensed that the Haganah attack on the bridges on 16 June had been made without advance information to him (apparently as a result of a hitch in communications), and after the British counteraction of 29 June he had threatened to resign his presidency of the Zionist organization unless Haganah attacks were suspended until after the forthcoming World Zionist Congress and unless Moshe Sneh were removed from the command of the Haganah. The resignation of the latter, who had evaded the British round-up, was announced on 21 July, one day before the King David outrage (see Begin: *The Revolt*, pp. 209–10; Kimche: *Seven Fallen Pillars*, pp. 157, 182; *Manchester Guardian* Jerusalem correspondent, 22 July 1946).

along a basement passage to the basement of the east wing: the kitchen staff were held up and a British officer who inconveniently appeared was shot. The terrorists made their escape under cover of a harmless 'cracker-bomb' and instructed a female accomplice to telephone a warning to the hotel management to evacuate the building, with other warnings to the office of the Zionist *Palestine Post* and to the French Consulate which were close to the hotel.[1] The time-fuse had been prepared to detonate the 500 lb. of T.N.T. and gelignite after half an hour. The explosion caused the collapse of the entire southern half of the east wing, killing 91 British, Arabs, and Jews, and wounding 45 others.

On the evening after this outrage the Haganah high command ordered a compliant attitude towards the British authorities, 'to demonstrate the opposition of the Jews to what occurred at Jerusalem';[2] as on previous occasions of the kind, the Agency and Vaad Leumi issued a perfunctory call to the Jewish community 'to rise against these abominable outrages'; but in the meantime the new Haganah commander apparently resumed the collusion with the terrorist leaders exactly where Moshe Sneh had left it. 'It seems to me', wrote the I.Z.L. leader, 'their relations with us were probably never more close than in the period following' the King David outrage; 'we continued for a long time to prepare co-ordinated plans'.[3] Meanwhile the Agency and a number of the manifold channels of Zionist propaganda did, once again, what they had done with General Morgan's press interview in January.[4] They now found another opportune means of diverting attention from the Zionist campaign of terrorism, in an order which the General Officer Commanding in Palestine (Lieut.-General Sir Evelyn Barker) issued for restricted circulation within his Command, ordering the stopping of all social contacts between the troops and the Jewish community. It was couched in the following terms:

The Jewish community of Palestine cannot be absolved of responsibility for a

[1] In timing these warnings the terrorists had not apparently made sufficient allowance for the isolation of the Government offices from the hotel premises; and the shooting of the British officer seems to have confused the hotel management. The Government's Public Information Officer afterwards denied that anyone in the Secretariat 'in an official position, with any power to take action' had received a warning (*Palestine Post*, 25 September 1946); but a story had been put in circulation that the warning had been received and disregarded by a senior official, and this untruth was not entirely scotched when the Chief Secretary brought a successful libel action against an American Zionist who had named him in this connexion (see *Evening Standard*, 12 April 1949; Begin: *The Revolt*, pp. 221-2; Sacher: *Israel, the Establishment of a State*, p. 191).

[2] See Wilson: *Cordon and Search*, p. 70, note.

[3] Begin: *The Revolt*, p. 226. Since the British military authorities knew that the I.Z.L. operated from headquarters in Tel Aviv, that city was cordoned and searched from 30 July to 2 August, but without capturing the terrorist leaders (cf. ibid. pp. 227-30). A quantity of arms, together with equipment for forging Government bearer bonds and £50,000 worth of forged bonds, was found in the basement of the Great Synagogue, and a larger quantity of arms was found in three caches built into the fabric of the basement of a school (Wilson, op. cit. pp. 67-73; Trevor: *Under the White Paper*, p. 232, note 29).

[4] See above, p. 204.

long series of outrages culminating in the blowing up of a large part of the
Government offices in the King David hotel, causing grievous loss of life.
Without the support, actual or passive, of the general Jewish public the terrorist
gangs who actually carry out these criminal acts would soon be unearthed, and
in this measure the Jews in the country are accomplices and bear a share of the
guilt.

I am determined that they shall suffer punishment and be made aware of the
contempt and loathing with which we regard their conduct. . . .

I appreciate that these measures will inflict some hardship on the troops, yet
I am certain that if my reasons are fully explained to them they will understand
their propriety and will be punishing the Jews in a way the race dislikes as much
as any—by striking at their pockets and showing our contempt for them.[1]

The text of this order promptly found its way into Zionist hands, and
Hebrew translations were posted up all over the three principal cities of
Palestine, while it was given publicity abroad[2] by a Jewish journalist, Jon
Kimche. When, in the course of a House of Commons debate on Palestine
on 31 July, questions were asked about General Barker's order, the British
Government felt that they must dissociate themselves from its actual terms,
though they were 'satisfied that the instructions . . . were justified' and
made 'all allowances for the provocation to which our Forces are exposed';[3]
and the order was withdrawn on 9 August.

As the British Prime Minister was attending the Paris Peace Conference
and Bevin was having one of the bouts of illness which were increasingly
to incapacitate him in the following years, it fell to Herbert Morrison,
Lord President of the Council, to announce the present state of Government policy.[4] He said that the British and United States 'expert delegations' had made 'unanimous recommendations on both sides', first to
attempt to resettle a substantial number of the European displaced persons
in Europe or overseas, and in Palestine to establish Arab and Jewish
provinces enjoying a large measure of autonomy under a central Government. For this purpose the country would be divided into a Jewish and an
Arab province,[5] of which the former would 'include the great bulk of the
land on which Jews have already settled and a considerable area between
and around the settlements' and the latter would be 'almost wholly Arab

---

[1] *The Times*, 29 July 1946.

[2] Kimche: *Seven Fallen Pillars*, p. 176.

[3] Herbert Morrison, H.C.Deb. 5th ser., vol. 426, col. 959. An editorial in the Labour Party
organ *Daily Herald*, on the other hand, had declared on 30 July: 'If General Barker really wrote
this letter, then it seems to us that he has demonstrated overwhelmingly his unfitness for his
command.' For the Opposition the former Colonial Secretary, Oliver Stanley, agreed with the
Government that strain of the kind occasioned by the King David outrage might well excuse
'a certain bitterness of words' (H.C.Deb. 5th ser., vol. 426, col. 975).

[4] See Great Britain, Foreign Office: *Proposals for the Future of Palestine, July 1946–February
1947*, Cmd. 7044 (London, H.M.S.O., 1947), pp. 3–8. [This will be referred to hereafter as
Cmd. 7044.]

[5] See map A at end of volume.

in respect both of land and of population'; the central Government would continue to administer directly the Jerusalem district including Bethlehem, and the 'triangle of waste land in the south of Palestine beyond the present limits of cultivation'. The Jewish and Arab provinces would be internally self-governing, while the central Government would retain exclusive authority for defence, foreign relations, customs and excise, and initially for the administration of law and order also. The High Commissioner would appoint the councils of ministers of the Jewish and Arab provinces after consultation with their elected legislatures, and would exercise his right to veto bills passed by those legislatures only if they were inconsistent with the prescribed safeguards for internal harmony and the rights of minorities. The Jewish province would have the right to admit immigrants up to the limits of its economic absorptive capacity (final control resting with the central Government), and it was hoped to admit 100,000 Jews from Europe within twelve months of the plan's taking effect; but the Arab province would have full power to exclude Jewish immigrants. Subject to the consent of the Trans-Jordan Government, the common water resources should be surveyed as soon as possible with a view to the large-scale economic development of both Palestine and Trans-Jordan. When the debate continued in the House of Commons on the following day, Sir Stafford Cripps explained that the Government intended to discuss this Provincial Autonomy Plan in London with 'representative Jews from various countries, as well as in Palestine' though without 'side-tracking the Jewish Agency'; and with 'Arabs in Palestine as well as the Arab States',[1] though without inviting the Muftī from his new haven in Cairo.[2]

In the course of the debate it had immediately become clear that this Provincial Autonomy Plan was no new creation of the British and United States consultants, but a plan that had been worked out at the Colonial Office under the war-time Coalition Government as an alternative, in

---

[1] By the terms of the Jewish Agency's revised constitution of 1930, by which it secured the financial support of Jewry in the United States, each of its organs, including its Executive, was to be composed equally of Zionists and non-Zionists; but the latter had been gradually squeezed out, the last of them on the Executive resigning in December 1945 as a protest against the collusion with the terrorists (see above, p. 203, note 4, and Albert M. Hyamson: *Palestine under the Mandate* (London, Methuen, 1950), p. 116). In 1947 the Colonial Office was to point out that the present composition of the Jewish Agency 'did not conform with the arrangements accepted in 1930', and asked it to take 'urgent steps . . . to render its composition irreproachable on constitutional grounds' (*Zionist Review*, 6 June 1947, p. 2). Since it was very questionable whether the Arab Higher Committee could claim to be representative of the Palestine Arabs (see Hurewitz: *The Struggle for Palestine*, pp. 250–3), the British Government had some reason for inviting Jews and Palestine Arabs from outside the two 'official' organizations. In the event, however, no independent person or organization from either community was prepared to come forward in defiance of the refusal of both the Zionist and the Palestine Arab official organizations to take part in the proposed conference.

[2] See above, p. 220.

case a final definite scheme of partition (which Oliver Stanley, the Colonial Secretary at that time, and many of his colleagues had considered practicable and which had been 'accepted as practicable by many people who were authorities on Palestine') proved unacceptable. Stanley now added that he had always regarded the Provincial Autonomy Plan as a second best. Furthermore, a very similar set of proposals had been submitted to the Anglo-American Committee of Inquiry in January and rejected by it 'because it did not appear to have the merits of finality'.[1] For the first time the Labour Government's handling of the Palestine problem received severe treatment from other quarters of the House than their own small pro-Zionist wing. Oliver Stanley criticized them for having allowed the time and effort expended by the Anglo-American Committee to be spent to no purpose, when the present plan had been at the Colonial Office all the time; but the Government might have replied that the wear and tear of one year's troubled administration of Palestine would not be a heavy price to pay if (though it was a large if) the United States Government could be at length induced to share the responsibility for a solution. Perhaps the most radical suggestion came from Churchill. He urged that the Government should say 'that if the United States will not come and share the burden of the Zionist cause, as defined or as agreed, we should now give notice that we will return our Mandate to U.N.O. and that we will evacuate Palestine within a specified period'.[2] Nearly two years later a Conservative member was to declare that the Government did not at the time follow this advice of Churchill 'because of a combination of obstinacy and of misplaced optimism, and the refusal . . . to believe that the Socialist Party could fail to secure agreement between Jew and Arab';[3] but while the first part of this charge may have been partially justified it was less than the whole truth. August 1946 was no time for any British Government to take an irrevocable step with regard to the Palestine mandate while both the treaty negotiations with Egypt and the question whether Persia could be saved from sinking to the status of a Soviet satellite[4] were still delicately poised in the balance; whereas by the following year, as we shall see, the element of uncertainty had been temporarily removed from both these important factors in the general Middle Eastern situation, and the British Government had, to that extent at least, become freer agents in their choice of policy in Palestine.

Before Churchill made his speech it had already become apparent that

---

[1] Stanley, H.C.Deb. 5th ser., vol. 426, coll. 984–5; R. E. Manningham-Buller (a member of the Anglo-American Committee) and Crossman, ibid. coll. 1024–5; cf. Crossman: *Palestine Mission*, p. 67.

[2] 1 August 1946, H.C.Deb. 5th ser., vol. 426, col. 1256.

[3] R. E. Manningham-Buller, 10 March 1948, ibid. vol. 448, col. 1348.

[4] See above, pp. 123 and 75–77; and cf. Jon Kimche: 'British Labor's Turn-about on Palestine', *Commentary*, December 1947, p. 515.

the Government's hopes of obtaining United States acceptance of the Provincial Autonomy Plan (afterwards to be distinguished as the Grady–Morrison, or Morrison–Grady Plan) were unlikely to be fulfilled.[1] Nor was this surprising; for, quite apart from the traditional reluctance of the United States Government and people to assume overseas commitments in time of peace, the present moment, with a hard-fought Congressional election due in November, was no time for expecting the Democratic Party to do anything other than compete with the Republican Opposition in courting the favour of the powerful Zionist pressure group.[2] Already, before the contents of the Provincial Autonomy Plan had been published, James G. McDonald, one of the two convinced supporters of Zionism among the United States members of the Anglo-American Committee of Inquiry, had persuaded two pro-Zionist senators to join him in protesting to President Truman against the new plan. The President received them with such coldness that he would not allow McDonald to read a short memorandum expressing his views; but Jews among his Democratic Party advisers appear to have warned the President of the likely effect on the 'Jewish vote' in the forthcoming election if his Government continued to support the new plan.[3] In his indecision he reconvened the six United States members of the Anglo-American Committee to discuss the new plan with his Cabinet committee 'alternates' newly returned from London, under the chairmanship of the Under Secretary of State, Dean Acheson; the former group not unnaturally regarded the plan as a radical departure from their own earlier recommendations and unanimously recommended its rejection. The President thereupon abandoned it, against the advice of the Secretary of State, and the United States was not represented at the forthcoming London conference convened by the British Government to discuss the plan.[4]

[1] Cf. Cripps, 1 August 1946, H.C.Deb. 5th ser., vol. 426, coll. 1242–3.

[2] Already at the end of 1945 Zionist leaders in the United States were reported to be using statistical evidence to argue that the 'Jewish vote' had been a factor in securing Roosevelt's success in the 1944 Presidential election (see Sidney Hertzberg: 'The Month in History', *Commentary*, January 1946, p. 39); and it was alleged that in 1947 the Democratic National Committee received a 'substantial part' of its funds from Jewish sources that wished to influence the Government over Palestine (*The Forrestal Diaries*, p. 345). United States contributions, which were exempt from income tax, to the Zionist national funds and institutions had risen as follows:

Average of the years 1939–44	£million 1·537
Jewish year 1944–5	3·989
Jewish year 1945–6	5·768

('Jewish National Finances', *Bulletin of the Economic Research Institute of the Jewish Agency*, 2nd issue of 1947, pp. 66, 68).

[3] See *The Forrestal Diaries*, pp. 346–7. Rabbi Silver was to tell the World Zionist Congress in December: 'The decisive role which the American Zionists played in having this scheme rejected by the American Government is well known' (*New Judaea*, December 1946–January 1947, p. 41).

[4] See *The Forrestal Diaries*, pp. 346–7; McDonald: *My Mission in Israel*, p. 10; *New York Times*, 8 August 1946.

Meanwhile, the Jewish Agency Executive, meeting in Paris so. as to include Ben Gurion who was still on the Palestine Government's list for detention with his other 'activist' colleagues, had on 5 August announced its rejection of the Provincial Autonomy Plan; but it was evident that although, before the King David outrage, a propagandist for the Jewish Resistance Movement had threatened a 'noticeable intensification of the struggle' if the British did not surrender over the immigration and land-purchase issues,[1] the firmer counter-measures taken by the British military authorities in Palestine had shaken the confidence of the Agency Executive.[2] It now belatedly undertook a withdrawal from the extreme political demands of the Biltmore Programme, which the Zionist leaders had still presented as their official policy to the Anglo-American Committee. They now drew up in Paris a plan for the establishment of 'a viable Jewish State in an adequate area of Palestine',[3] which should comprise, in addition to the area proposed in the Provincial Autonomy Plan, the whole of Galilee (as proposed by the Royal Commission in 1937) and also the whole of the Negev or southern Palestine; the Arabs would be left with the high-lands from the Vale of Jezreel to a southerly limit midway between Hebron and Beersheba, with a corridor to the Mediterranean at Jaffa.[4] The plan was flown to Washington for submission to President Truman, and on 15 August Weizmann and two United States members of the Agency Executive proposed it to the British Colonial Secretary as a basis for nego-tiation.[5] However, no agreement on procedure leading to the Agency's

[1] Shlomo Katz: 'Understanding Jewish Resistance in Palestine', *Commentary*, July 1946, p. 49.

[2] The British action of 29 June had 'put an end to the theory of *lō yaezu* ("they won't dare") . . . preached in Palestine for many years by some Labour leaders, among them the late Berl Katznelson and Ben Gurion' (Robert Weltsch: 'The End of the Biltmore Road', ibid. February 1947, p. 106). Shlomo Katz (loc. cit. p. 50) had also asserted that the British could not afford to take more vigorous action against illegal immigration than to detain new arrivals in Palestine until their turn came under the monthly quota. 7,200 illegal immigrants had, however, arrived by sea during the months of May to July and more were expected; and the British Government accordingly announced that they would henceforth be transferred to Cyprus to await their ad-mission to Palestine (*The Times*, 9, 10, and 13 August 1946). Two transport ships in Haifa harbour were sabotaged and the would-be immigrants offered violent resistance; but the Zionist institutions' threats of non-co-operation with the Palestine Government were empty, because their political co-operation was already virtually non-existent and economic non-co-operation would have rebounded upon the Jewish community (see Trevor: *Under the White Paper*, p. 247).

[3] Harry Sacher implies that they had already been prepared to accept the partitioning of Palestine at the hands of the Anglo-American Committee, and states that they would have accepted the Committee's report 'in principle', since it 'opened out possibilities of unlimited immigration and development' (*Israel, the Establishment of a State*, p. 189).

[4] *New York Times*, 14 August 1946, and see map B at end of volume. On 6 October eleven Jewish settlements were simultaneously established in the comparatively well-watered and cultivable north-west of the Negev (*Zionist Review*, 11 October 1946, p. 5; 29 August 1947, p. 8).

[5] The defenders of this change of Zionist policy were to argue at the World Zionist Congress in December that 'the Executive had no alternative at a time when there was an absolute dead-lock, when there was no contact with the Government, and the Palestine leaders were in jail. Had the offer not been made, America would have washed her hands of the whole troublesome

official participation in the proposed London conference on Palestine was reached. The British Government insisted on the Provincial Autonomy Plan being the first item on the agenda, leaving the Jewish and Arab delegations full liberty to propose modifications; while the Agency demanded full freedom to designate its own delegates 'including any who are now detained or are subject to detention',[1] and to issue, in consultation with the British Government, the invitations to all the members of the Jewish delegation, which would include representatives of important bodies and organizations other than the Agency.[2]

The Palestine Arab Higher Committee likewise refused to send a delegation except as the exclusive representatives of the Palestine Arabs; and the conference, which opened on 10 September, was therefore attended only by representatives of the Arab states and the Arab League secretariat. Their proposal was for the transfer of authority in Palestine to a unitary state governed by representatives of all communities popularly elected in their respective numerical proportions. Citizenship would be restricted to those born citizens of either the Ottoman Empire or mandatory Palestine, or those who had acquired Palestine citizenship by naturalization before the issue of the 1939 White Paper, or those who had subsequently acquired it and also had had ten years' permanent residence, or who might subsequently acquire it on the same terms. *In no case, however, should the number of Jewish representatives in the Legislature exceed one-third of the total.* The existing land transfer restrictions should be maintained, and future Jewish immigration be entirely prohibited, unless and until a majority of the Arab members of the Legislature voted otherwise. Hebrew would be a second official language in districts where Jews were in an absolute majority, and the Jewish community and other bodies might maintain private schools and universities, subject to the compulsory teaching of Arabic and to government control 'for the purpose of maintaining educational standards and preventing subversive teaching, with the object of creating common allegiance'. These rights guaranteed to the Jewish community might not be altered without the consent of a majority of the Jewish members of the Legislature.[3] On this note the conference was

problem' (Dr. Nahum Goldmann in *Zionist Review*, 20 December 1946, pp. 6–7; cf. Rabbi Silver in *New Judaea*, December 1946–January 1947, p. 61).

[1] British sympathizers with Zionism had tried to persuade the Government that 'such men as Shertok and Remez should be released since they were willing and eager to assist in capturing the Irgun leaders' (Crossman: *Palestine Mission*, p. 205). To judge from their later conduct, however, it seems probable that they would have made any such collaboration conditional on a Government surrender over immigration (cf. below, p. 238, note 3).

[2] Text of letters exchanged in *Zionist Review*, 13 September 1946, pp. 4–5.

[3] Text in Cmd. 7044, pp. 9–11. The Egyptian Prime Minister told the United Nations Mediator for Palestine in May 1948 that he 'expected' that in the unitary state which remained the Arab League's policy for Palestine the Jewish minority 'would be free to purchase land, develop industry and carry on commerce throughout the whole of Palestine and not solely in the Jewish area. If, however, the money for the purchase of land for the Jews were to be supplied

adjourned for two to three months until after the United States elections and the meetings of the United Nations General Assembly and the Council of Foreign Ministers.

Meanwhile, when in September the terrorist organizations resumed their campaign of violence the Agency condemned them; and the Haganah, though it did not resume co-operation with the Government against them, issued a pamphlet accusing them of maintaining themselves by 'gangster-ism, smuggling, large-scale drug traffic, armed robbery, organising the black market, and thefts'.[1] On 1 October the British Foreign and Colonial Secretaries had a preliminary exchange of views with Weizmann and his Agency colleagues at which Bevin advanced the idea (as already pro-pounded by Crossman in the House of Commons)[2] of an interim arrange-ment for trusteeship for a period of three, five, or ten years, leading ultimately to self-government. The Government were clearly as anxious as the Agency Executive to bridge the gap between them. On 4 October, as part of a Cabinet reshuffle, Creech Jones, whose personal sympathies had been on the Zionist side,[3] was promoted to the Colonial Secretaryship from being Under-Secretary; and the conversations with the Agency representatives continued notwithstanding the publication of a new state-ment by President Truman[4] which threatened to cut the ground from

from outside for the purpose, the Arabs, in self-protection, might have to take measures to limit the right of land purchase by Jews' (Count Folke Bernadotte: *To Jerusalem* (London, Hodder & Stoughton, 1951), pp. 26–27).

[1] Quoted by Sacher: *Israel, the Establishment of a State*, p. 192. Cf. *Zionist Review*, 20 September 1946, p. 2; 27 September, p. 3.

[2] 31 July 1946, H.C.Deb. 5th ser., vol. 426, col. 1018.

[3] It should not, however, be assumed that he was accurately reported in the words attributed to him as having been spoken at a Zionist meeting in New York City in 1945, before the British general election placed his party in power: 'It will be for us in London to carry on our work in Parliament and elsewhere so that . . . the White Paper policy is reversed, so that the Jews can be sure that at last their National Home is being established firmly and securely and they can realize their own Commonwealth' (quoted by Rabbi Silver, 5 March 1948: U.N., Security Council: *Official Records*, 3rd year, nos. 36–51, p. 18).

[4] On 4 October (the eve of the Jewish Day of Atonement) Truman yielded to Zionist elec-tioneering pressure by issuing a statement supporting the Jewish Agency's new policy of 'a viable Jewish State, in control of its own immigration and economic policies, in an adequate area of Palestine' with the immediate issue of 100,000 immigration certificates as a 'solution of the Palestine problem' (text in *Zionist Review*, 11 October 1946, p. 3, and see *New Judaea*, December 1946–January 1947, p. 61, speech of Rabbi Silver to the World Zionist Congress; cf. *The Forrestal Diaries*, p. 309).

Jon Kimche (in *Commentary*, December 1947, p. 516) confirmed Bevin's assertion that when Truman made this statement the talks with the Agency Executive had 'raised high hopes inside the British Government that a settlement was at last possible'; Bevin, warned in advance of the statement, had begged that it should not be issued, but was told that in that case the Republican Party leader, Governor Dewey of New York State with its $2\frac{1}{2}$ million Jews, would issue a com-petitive statement as part of the Congressional election campaign (Bevin in the House of Com-mons, 25 February 1947, H.C.Deb. 5th ser., vol. 433, coll. 1907–8; cf. Sidney Hertzberg: 'The Month in History', *Commentary*, November 1946, pp. 452–7). Attlee was reported to have pro-tested strongly against the President's statement and to have said that there would be no change in immigration policy until the constitutional issue had been settled; and when Truman repeated

under the British negotiators' feet. Military searches of Jewish settlements ceased, and, on the other hand, arrests were made on 21 October at
the Haifa office of the Arab boycott committee whose agents had been
holding up and confiscating Jewish goods in transit. On the following day
it was announced that General Barker, whose unmeasured expression of
anger at the King David outrage had not been forgotten, would shortly
be promoted to a home command.[1] On the 29th the Inner Zionist Council, meeting in London, passed a series of resolutions which, while they
refused to consider any proposals limiting the right of all Jews to enter
Palestine in any circumstances or to bargain over the release of their
leaders who had now been detained for four months, condemned terrorism
and called on the Jewish community to deny all assistance to those per-
petrating it.[2] The new Colonial Secretary thereupon announced on
5 November that the Government had concurred in the release of the
Jewish leaders and others detained in the June round-up.[3] Later in the
month it was announced that 2,800 of the illegal immigrants detained in
Cyprus would be admitted to Palestine as part of the November–January
quotas, though meanwhile new illegal arrivals continued to be sent to
Cyprus.[4] On the 20th it was learned that Jewish shopkeepers and others
who had been evicted to provide accommodation for the government
departments displaced by the King David outrage[5] would receive compensation from the Government, and that recruiting for the Jewish Settlement Police, which had been suspended since the operation against the
Palmah (of which the Settlement Police formed the core), would be
resumed. In the words of a chronicler acceptable to the Jewish Agency,

his request for increased immigration into Palestine Attlee replied with a recital of Truman's
embarrassing interventions in the problem, according to *Palestine Affairs* (prepared by the
American Zionist Emergency Council), December 1946, p. 1.

[1] Since this 'gentlemanly stellenbosching' did not take effect for a further four months, the
Zionists did not consider it a 'strikingly handsome gesture' to repair their injured dignity (Trevor:
Under the White Paper, pp. 271–2).

[2] Ibid. p. 274.

[3] At the same time a number of Arab extremists were released from detention or amnestied
and allowed to return to Palestine (H.C.Deb. 5th ser., vol. 428, coll. 1226–30).

[4] For the new policy of transferring illegal immigrants to Cyprus see above, p. 227, note 2.
The Government had on 15 October rejected an Agency request for an increase in the immigration quota 'as a gesture towards the improvement of relations', stating that they had promised
the Arabs that there would be no changes of policy while the London Conference stood adjourned
(Benjamin Shwadran in *Palestine Affairs*, December 1946, p. 4); and a subsequent government
communiqué expressed regret at being 'compelled' by illegal immigration to continue the transfers
to Cyprus. The *Zionist Review* afterwards (4 April 1947, p. 6) boasted that in fourteen months
twenty-four ships, 'bought, manned, and piloted by Hagana members', had brought into
Palestine waters some 23,500 illegal immigrants, and an anonymous commentator remarked that
'the tribulations . . . of the 20,000 refugees now in detention-camps in Cyprus are the natural
result of Haganah's forceful unauthorized immigration policy' (Palestinius, pseud.: 'Palestine's
Mood after UNSCOP', *Commentary*, October 1947, p. 342).

[5] The block of buildings thus commandeered by the Administration and made defensible was
officially called the Jerusalem Fortress, and nicknamed by the Jews 'Bevingrad'.

these gestures, 'half-hearted as they were, did succeed in relieving tension.
. . . If there was no refreshing sense of a new start, no renewal of real confidence, there was at least a feeling that a breathing-space had been
afforded.'[1]

The Zionist Movement throughout the world was now holding elections
for delegates to the 22nd World Zionist Congress, the first to be held since
the outbreak of the Second World War; and the Jewish Agency leaders
needed such a breathing-space to enable them to organize support for their
recent change of policy, namely their readiness (since the whole of Palestine was not attainable)[2] to accept a Jewish State in part of Palestine only.
When the Congress opened at Basle in Switzerland on 9 December it was
evident, however, that the more militant wing of the movement might be
expected to present a strong front.[3] Weizmann was elected president of
the Congress by a bare 51 per cent. of the delegates; and after he, in his
presidential address, and Ben Gurion had commended the Executive's
partition plan,[4] they were accused by the uncompromising vice-president
of the Zionist Organization of America, Dr. Emanuel Neumann, of having
abandoned the Biltmore Resolution, reaffirmed at the London conference
of August 1945,[5] demanding a Jewish State in an 'undivided and undimin-
ished' Palestine. Dr. Nahum Goldmann, one of the two United States
members of the Executive who had taken the new plan to Washington and
had accompanied Weizmann in presenting it to the British Colonial
Secretary on 15 August, replied that the movement must be ready for
'tragic concessions in order to break the present political deadlock', to
get rid of foreign rule and open the gates to large-scale immigration; the
Biltmore Programme of 1942, with its demand for the whole of mandatory
Palestine, had been based on the assumption that millions of Jews would
be transferred to Palestine immediately after the war; but that had not
happened, and it was a delusion to suppose that the United States would
quarrel with Britain seriously over Zionist claims to Palestine.[6] Rabbi

---

[1] Trevor: *Under the White Paper*, p. 278.

[2] Self-government was necessary to 'accumulate strength through immigration, settlement,
and construction', and so ensure peace with their Arab neighbours (Eliezer Kaplan, treasurer
of the Agency Executive in *Zionist Review*, 15 November 1946, p. 5; cf. Ben Gurion, ibid. 29
November 1946, p. 4).

[3] The Revisionists, who claimed the whole of Palestine and Trans-Jordan and whose militant
arm was the I.Z.L., as the Haganah was the Agency's, had won 10·6 per cent. of the seats
throughout the world movement, and 14 per cent. of the seats for Palestine (see *Supplementary
Memorandum of the Government of Palestine . . . to the United Nations Special Committee* (Jerusalem,
1947), p. 20).

[4] The plan claimed about 65 per cent. of the area of mandatory Palestine. Ben Gurion commended it as aiming at 'fructifying over three-quarters of western Palestine—at present uncultivated desert', according to *Zionist Review*, 13 December 1946, p. 7.

[5] See above, pp. 190–1.

[6] The Secretary of State had recently announced in Washington that, if both Zionists and
Arabs would take part in the resumed London conference, the United States Government
would send an observer.

Silver once more denounced what he described as the 'organized conspiracy' of the British Government to deny the Zionists' 'rights' in Palestine; expressed a fear that the Executive's partition plan would weaken their bargaining power at the London conference; and opposed the movement's attending it. The political debate was closed by Weizmann, who recalled how his hopes in 1944 of obtaining a Jewish state 'perhaps in a substantial part of Palestine' from the Churchill Government had been shattered by the Stern Group's murder of Lord Moyne,[1] 'the greatest disaster which had overtaken us in the last few years'. Pursuing a line of argument already levelled by Ben Gurion against Rabbi Silver and Emanuel Neumann, Weizmann declared that the new settlements in south Palestine[2] counted for more than a hundred speeches about resistance, 'especially when the speeches are made in Washington and New York, while it is intended that the resistance shall take place in Jerusalem or Tel Aviv. . . . Moral, financial, and political support is precious little when you send others . . . to pit themselves against British guns and tanks'—a frontal attack on the United States militants which apparently earned the venerable president the retort of 'Demagogue' from Emanuel Neumann. Weizmann concluded with a warning against short cuts, and especially against terrorism, 'a cancer in the body-politic of Palestinian Jewry':

We often have quoted to us the example of Ireland, of the Boers, and of other national revolutionary movements. But one thing is forgotten. . . . If you have lost your faith that better times may come, and wish to secure your redemption through means . . . which do not accord with Jewish morale, with Jewish ethics or Jewish history, I say to you that you are worshipping false gods. . . . Go and re-read Isaiah, Jeremiah, and Ezekiel, and test that which we do and wish to do in the light of the teachings of our great prophets and wise men. They knew the nature and character of the Jewish people. 'Zion will be redeemed through righteousness'—and not by any other means.[3]

In the words of a contemporary chronicler,[4] the Congress

was a confused and confusing spectacle, and the votes on the various resolutions at the end defied the analysis of outsiders and often of the voters themselves; but . . . though some groups voted against propositions they supported and were manœuvred into putting into office leaders they detested, though the Congress and its committees were swept by doctrinaire storms and riddled with personal rivalries . . . the results by and large reflected very exactly the situation of the Zionist Movement and the frustration of its policies.

The coalition of Ben Gurion's Mapai (Labour) Party with Weizmann's supporters among the middle-class General Zionists sponsored a resolution empowering the Executive to decide for or against participation in the

---

[1] *Survey* for 1939–46: *The Middle East in the War*, pp. 323–4.   [2] See above, p. 227, note 4.
[3] *New Judaea*, December 1946–January 1947, pp. 65–67.
[4] Trevor: *Under the White Paper*, p. 293.

resumed London conference if the conditions of free immigration, large-scale settlement, and the establishment of a Jewish state in part of Palestine were conceded; but this resolution was defeated early on 24 December, securing only 154 votes against 171 in favour of a more restrictive resolution supported by Rabbi Silver's followers from the United States, the Revisionists, the religious Mizrahi Party that demanded the whole of Palestine, and the Left-wing parties who were opposed to partition since their ideal was a Jew-Arab socialist state in the whole of Palestine. In view of this rejection of his policy of gradualism, Weizmann withdrew his candidature for the Presidency of the Agency, with the result that this office remained unfilled, since his personal pre-eminence was still such that there was no one to replace him. A new Executive was elected with some stiffening from Rabbi Silver's party.

The Congress's ban on participation in the London conference did not, however, prevent Ben Gurion and other Agency leaders from making preliminary soundings with Creech Jones who, according to one account, suggested that, if Palestine could have three months free of terrorism or illegal immigration, the British Government might then be disposed to be generous. The difficulty, from the Zionist point of view, was that 'it was the ban on immigration that set the scene for terrorism'.[1] Terrorism had, in fact, been intensified after the Inner Zionist Council's condemnation of it on 29 October, but there had been a 'precarious truce' during the Zionist Congress, apparently as a result of Haganah pressure; during the entire year 28 Palestine police had been killed, 45 members of the British armed forces killed and 93 wounded, and 300 civilians of all Palestinian communities killed (including the King David Hotel victims) or wounded, without a single direct culprit of these crimes being convicted.[2] The primary cause of the terrorists' immunity was the non-co-operation of the Jewish community with the British authorities, and this derived partly from the fear of reprisals at the hands of the terrorists and from the traditional Jewish desire to avoid contacts with alien officials, but also perhaps partly from a certain pride in Jewish feats of daring, even when these took the perverse form of acts of terrorism, as well as from a belief that their kinsmen who had perished under Hitler would be alive in Palestine if the British had not kept them out of the country.[3] Meanwhile, the routine procedure of the British military courts in dealing with apprehended members of the terrorist organizations was being answered by bold reprisals on the part of the I.Z.L.,[4] and these in their turn were believed to be leading the British

[1] Ibid. p. 299.

[2] Ibid. pp. 289–90, 292; 22 and 31 January 1947, H.C.Deb. 5th ser., vol. 432, coll. 197 and 1336.

[3] See Shlomo Katz: 'Curfew in Jerusalem', *Commentary*, December 1946, pp. 530–1.

[4] The I.Z.L. was said to have increased its membership during the past year, largely by recruitment from the Haganah, from about 5,000 to something like 10,000, plus several thousand

military authorities once more to demand a freer hand with counter-measures. On 29 December, after the execution of a sentence of caning on a youthful extremist for his part in an armed robbery of a bank, the I.Z.L. seized and flogged a British officer and three sergeants.[1] During the High Commissioner's absence in London for consultations, the Chief Secretary (Sir Henry Gurney, who had recently succeeded Sir John Shaw) remitted another sentence of caning which had been confirmed by the G.O.C.,[2] and on 21 January 1947 an amendment to the Defence Regulations was announced reducing from eighteen to sixteen years the maximum age of youths liable to caning.[3] Meanwhile, after a meeting between Ben Gurion and the High Commissioner on the latter's return from London, the Vaad Leumi had passed on 20 January a resolution which declared its abhorrence of murder as a means of political resistance but affirmed its support of the political struggle and repudiated any idea of active opposition to the terrorists: 'We are not courting civil war, nor do we wish to provoke internecine warfare, and there is no reason for any contest within while fighting for our rights without.'[4]

No death sentence against the terrorists had been executed in Palestine since the outbreak of Jewish terrorism in 1942, although in 1946 nineteen such sentences had been imposed and then been commuted to imprisonment for life;[5] but on 24 January 1947 General Barker confirmed the death sentence on Dov Grüner for his part in an attack on a police post in which a policeman had been killed.[6] The I.Z.L. riposted by abducting

passive sympathizers (*Zionist Review* Jerusalem correspondent, 30 May 1947, p. 4; cf. Crossman, 31 January 1947, H.C.Deb. 5th ser., vol. 432, coll. 1322–4). It received the bulk of its financial backing from the United States, where the press gave free publicity to the military training of young Jewish extremists of both sexes in New York City (cf. Sidney Hertzberg: 'The Month in History', *Commentary*, April 1946, p. 66), and the *New York Herald Tribune* printed as a full-page advertisement on 15 May 1947 a scurrilously eulogistic 'Letter to the Terrorists of Palestine', signed by a film-scenario writer (Ben Hecht) who was co-chairman of the extremist American League for a Free Palestine. In the House of Lords on 23 April 1947 Lord Hall referred to a report indicating that already since the beginning of that year $25–30 million had been collected in the United States for illegal Jewish purposes, including illegal immigration (H.L.Deb. 5th ser., vol. 147, col. 114).

[1] 'For seventy generations, in seventy lands, we had suffered the lashes of our oppressors. . . . Was an oppressor now to whip us in our own country?' (Begin: *The Revolt*, pp. 231–2).

[2] Begin declares that the British had vainly tried to induce the young culprit in question to claim that he was physically unfit to receive the caning (ibid. p. 234).

[3] 'This is the road of abject defeat', Churchill commented in the House of Commons on 31 January (H.C.Deb. 5th ser., vol. 432, col. 1345).

[4] *Zionist Review*, 31 January 1947, p. 2. The temporary head of the Agency's political department, Mrs. Golda Meyerson, likewise warned the terrorists but added: 'It is by no means our intention to make our position even more difficult by starting internecine warfare. We have made it clear to the Government on more than one occasion that we could use moral pressure. . . . It was impossible for us to take police duties on ourselves without having State or police authority' (*New York Times*, 3 February 1947).

[5] Wilson: *Cordon and Search*, p. 89.

[6] Ibid. p. 120. It had become clear that neither the terrorists nor the official Zionist Movement were going to respond to clemency; but Daphne Trevor saw in the confirmation of the

as hostages on 26 and 27 January a British judge from the Tel Aviv district court and a British civilian. The High Commissioner issued an ultimatum announcing that unless they were released unharmed within forty-eight hours the Tel Aviv area would be placed under the orders of a military commander. On 28 and 29 January it was intimated that Grüner's lawyer was lodging an application to appeal to the Privy Council against the sentence; the G.O.C. granted a stay of execution, although Grüner had refused to sign the appeal; and the two hostages were released. At this time the British Government were being harassed at home by the combined pressure of Britain's post-war financial weakness and a serious shortage in fuel production that was aggravated by the most severe winter for sixty-six years.[1] Their reaction to the danger that British women and children in Palestine might be kidnapped and held as hostages was, on 31 January, to order their evacuation and that of certain other civilians, in order that the Government and armed forces might not be hampered in their task; and on 4 February it was disclosed that essential British personnel remaining in the three principal cities would be concentrated in a number of enclosed and guarded zones, where 2,300 Jews and eighty Arabs were evicted from their homes to make room for them.[2] On the previous day the Chief Secretary had followed up a series of invitations to the Jewish Agency to co-operate in preventing terrorism[3] (which had invariably been refused or evaded) with a request that it should 'state categorically at once whether the Agency and the Vaad Leumi are prepared within seven days to lend their aid to the Government by co-operating with the police and armed forces in locating and bringing to justice members of terrorist groups'.[4] Despite rumours among the Zionists that a declaration of martial law was impending,[5] the Agency on 10 February returned a flat refusal to the Chief Secretary's request:

sentence, not the truth that British patience was exhausted, but 'a superb piece of timing calculated to sabotage at a stroke the efforts of months on the part of the High Commissioner and Jewish leaders' (*Under the White Paper*, p. 301).

[1] See *Annual Register* for 1947, pp. 5–6.

[2] The Colonial Secretary stated that no Arabs were being evicted in Jerusalem (3 April 1947, H.C.Deb. 5th ser., vol. 435, *written answers*, col. *380*); but this did not deter Lord Strabolgi from painting a verbal picture of 'the vast procession of Jews and Arabs who were being evicted from those areas of Jerusalem . . . jointly marching in protest' (23 April 1947, H.L.Deb. 5th ser., vol. 147, col. 87).

[3] Golda Meyerson, reported by *New York Times*, 3 February 1947.

[4] Since Golda Meyerson had said: 'What they expect of us is that we shall all become informers. . . . We cannot make out of 600,000 Jews informers, each one watching his neighbour or friend' (ibid.), the Chief Secretary's note continued: 'What is being demanded is recognition of the ordinary legal and moral duty to co-operate against crime which belongs to citizens and institutions of any civilized State, and it can in no way be associated with the terms "informer" and "spy" ' (*The Times*, 4 February 1947).

[5] The High Commissioner, however, informed Agency representatives on 9 February that martial law was not being contemplated at present, although in the situation created by the terrorists preparations had to be made for all eventualities.

The community . . . cannot be called upon to place itself at the disposal of the Government for fighting the evil consequences of a policy which is that of the Government's own making and which the Yishuv regards as a menace to its existence. Any appeal to the community, as suggested by the Government, would not only be ineffective but likely to cause harm rather than good.[1]

Meanwhile, representatives of the Arab states, this time including the Palestine Arabs also, had resumed their conference with the British Government in London on 27 January, and the Jewish Agency Executive had separately begun informal talks with the British Foreign and Colonial Secretaries on the 29th. In these discussions Bevin is reported to have revealed the Government's intention to refer the Palestine question to the United Nations if agreement were not reached. The Zionist leaders seem not to have liked this prospect, and they offered, if Britain would concede under the Mandate their standing demands for immigration 'up to the full extent of the country's economic absorptive capacity' and the unrestricted purchase of land, 'to forgo mention of a Jewish State as the goal, and to leave the outcome to time'.[2] If, however, Britain sought an immediate solution, they would repeat their request for a viable Jewish state in an adequate part of Palestine. Creech Jones, with the support of the majority of the British Cabinet, was reported[3] to have advocated that an offer of partition should be made, since the Zionist and Arab claims were clearly irreconcilable; but the Government's legal advisers stated that an attempt to impose partition on either party would not be consistent with the terms of the Mandate; and in the uncompromising mood of the Arabs[4] the Foreign Office apparently felt that Britain might become involved in a serious conflict with them.[5] It was therefore agreed that Bevin should make one final compromise offer, for a continuation of British administration for five years with the declared object of preparing the country for independence; the central Government would transfer a large range of its powers to the local administrations of the Jewish and Arab areas,[6] and the High Commissioner would endeavour to form an advisory council from representatives of these local administrations and of labour and other organized interests; Jewish immigration would be at a monthly rate of 4,000 for the next two years, guaranteeing the entry of approximately 100,000 persons, and would thereafter be determined by the High Com-

---

[1] *New York Times*, 11 February 1947.

[2] See Sacher: *Israel, the Establishment of a State*, p. 72; and cf. *Zionist Review*, 7 March 1947, pp. 8–9.

[3] *Observer* political correspondent, 2 February 1947.

[4] The Arab delegates refused even to discuss 'any scheme for partition or any scheme which might lead to it, and any form of continuous immigration' (communiqué in *The Times*, 5 February 1947).

[5] Creech Jones, 25 February 1947, H.C.Deb. 5th ser., vol. 433, col. 2004.

[6] Creech Jones implied (ibid. col. 2005) that the Jewish area would be about the same as that proposed in the Provincial Autonomy Plan.

missioner in consultation with his advisory council, with reference to a United Nations arbitration tribunal in case of disagreement;[1] the local Jewish and Arab administrations would have control over land transfers in their respective areas; at the end of four years an elected constituent assembly would be invited to set up an independent state with the approval of a majority of both its Jewish and its Arab members—failing which, the United Nations Trusteeship Council would be asked to advise on future procedure.[2]

This offer was made on 7 February and was rejected by both sides, Shertok complaining that 'the area allotted to the Jews was inadequate, since it hemmed them in without room for further expansion' and repeating the demand for 'the establishment of an adequate Jewish area with full control of immigration . . . and eventual recognition of Jewish independence in at least part of Palestine',[3] while the leaders of each of the Arab delegations re-emphasized their rejection of any proposal involving any form of partition or Jewish immigration. The deadlock was thus complete, and on 14 February Bevin announced that the Government had decided to refer the whole problem to the United Nations, without themselves recommending any particular solution.[4] When on the 25th the House of Commons debated the new situation, Oliver Stanley for the Opposition and Crossman from the other side both criticized the Government for not having recognized the irreconcilability of the Zionist and Arab demands many months earlier, in time to submit the problem to the United Nations at the General Assembly of September 1946; and they urged that, failing United Nations agreement on some policy that Britain could support, she should surrender the Mandate by a stated date and leave the United Nations to frame a policy. Daniel L. Lipson, a Jewish independent Member of the Parliament at Westminster who had been consistently critical of political Zionism, appealed to the Government and the Arabs to permit immigration at the monthly rate of 4,000, as provided in the rejected British proposal of 7 February, until the case went before the United Nations;[5] but the Foreign Office view, as afterwards expressed, was that the Government were responsible not only for the maintenance of law and order, for which immigration policy was of 'cardinal importance',

[1] Bevin on 25 February expressed the belief that the Arabs 'could be persuaded to agree' to immigration on these terms (H.C.Deb. 5th ser., vol. 433, col. 1909).

[2] See Cmd. 7044.

[3] *Zionist Review*, 14 February 1947, p. 3.

[4] Cf., however, Creech Jones's statement that the Government were not going to the United Nations to surrender the Mandate but to ask their advice as to how it could be administered and, if that were impossible in its present form, how it could be amended (25 February 1947, H.C.Deb. 5th ser., vol. 433, col. 2007).

[5] The Zionists in Palestine afterwards alleged that the High Commissioner had supported this appeal and had offered his resignation when the Government did not accede to it, according to Harry Levin: *Jerusalem Embattled* (London, Gollancz, 1950), p. 43.

but also for ensuring that nothing should be done to prejudice the eventual decision of the United Nations.[1]

The I.Z.L. terrorists now redoubled their efforts[2] to coerce the British Government into relaxing the immigration restrictions. On the afternoon of 1 March they destroyed the Goldsmith Officers' Club in Jerusalem with explosives; on the same day a number of vehicles were wrecked in a car park at Haifa, and minor outrages were committed elsewhere, the total casualties being eighteen killed and twenty-five injured, of whom a number were civilians. The High Commissioner thereupon decided to place under statutory martial law those Jewish areas from which it was well known that most of the terrorist operations were conducted: these were a strip of territory three to four miles wide extending from Tel Aviv seven miles eastwards to Petah Tiqvah, and a Jewish semi-slum area in Jerusalem; within these narrow limits lived some 240,000 Jews, or more than one-third of the entire community. The effect of this decision was to suspend the normal civil government, including civil courts of law, in these areas, and involved the closing of banks and the control of movements of persons and vehicles into and out of the specified areas by order of a military commander.[3] The ban was maintained until 17 March, when it was officially announced that seventy-eight persons had been arrested for their complicity with the terrorists, whose activities nevertheless continued unabated; that there had been 'instances' in the Jewish community of a willingness to assist the authorities;[4] and that it was 'not desired to extend indefinitely the loss, unemployment, and dislocation in the economic situation'. A Zionist correspondent admitted that the ban had been removed 'just as its effects were threatening to become really serious', the direct losses being estimated as £200,000, and the terrorists were left with 'a feeling of real triumph'.[5] A series of editorials in the moderate newspaper *ha-Aretz* (11–23 March 1947) blamed the Agency Executive's adherence to the Biltmore Programme and the slogan of 'activism' for encouraging

[1] *The Times*, 22 August 1947. Contrast the argument of the veteran British Zionist, Harry Sacher (*Zionist Review*, 7 March 1947, p. 9), that the Government should 'encourage the expansion by immigration and creative effort necessary to enable the Jews to take over their responsibilities when the British administration withdraws'.

[2] See Begin: *The Revolt*, p. 319.

[3] See Trevor: *Under the White Paper*, pp. 318–19, note 77. A communiqué accompanying the proclamation pointed out that there had been forty-eight terrorist outrages since the Government had appealed in vain to the Agency and the Vaad Leumi a month earlier to co-operate against the terrorists. The Agency issued a counter-statement making its co-operation conditional upon the concession of an increased immigration quota, and adding: 'The Government is now retaliating against the Yishuv as a whole for the crimes of a few desperate gunmen, and is seeking by the imposition of martial law . . . to punish an entire community' (*Zionist Review*, 7 March 1947, p. 2).

[4] When, however, the Government wished to circulate photographs and descriptions of ten 'wanted' terrorists in the hope of obtaining information, the Hebrew press refused to print them (Trevor, op. cit. pp. 324–5).

[5] *Zionist Review* Jerusalem correspondent, 4 April 1947, p. 4; Begin: *The Revolt*, p. 323.

and raising the prestige of the terrorist extremists, and urged that a new Executive led by Dr. Weizmann should make one more attempt to find a basis for negotiations with the British Government before the matter was taken to the United Nations. A ten-day meeting of the Executive was followed by a denial of any split among the Zionist leadership, however,[1] and Ben Gurion made a speech to the Vaad Leumi in which he denounced British policy in the most uncompromising terms.[2]

(d) Investigation and Debate by the United Nations, April to November 1947

On 2 April the British delegation to the United Nations requested the Secretary-General to summon a special session of the General Assembly to set up a special committee which would study the Palestine question and report to the regular session of the Assembly in September; and in the course of the special session of the Assembly Sir Alexander Cadogan stated the British view that Britain 'should not have the sole responsibility for enforcing a solution which is not accepted by both parties and which we cannot reconcile with our conscience'.[3] The Assembly set up a Special Committee of representatives of eleven states,[4] selected on a regional basis and (against Soviet wishes) excluding the five permanent members of the Security Council, and invested with 'the widest powers . . . to investigate all questions and issues relevant to the problem of Palestine', to 'conduct investigations in Palestine and wherever it may deem useful', and to report to the Secretary-General not later than 1 September. The policy of the Soviet bloc during this special session was to work for the ending of the British connexion with Palestine: the delegations of the Soviet and of three of its satellite states supported an amendment unsuccessfully moved by

[1] *Zionist Review*, 28 March 1947, pp. 3–4; but see ibid. 14 March 1947, p. 5, and 21 March 1947, p. 1, for expressions of uneasiness about the possible effect of the terrorist campaign and the imposition of martial law upon the less resolute elements in the Jewish community.

[2] 'Its intention was to liquidate the Jews as a people, and to recognise only the existence of individual Jews who could serve as objects either of pogroms or of pity. . . . The present British Government has no interest in reaching a settlement which would remove the differences between Jews and Arabs; it was more desirable for them, for reasons not connected either with Jews or with Arabs, that such differences should persist. . . . Many journalists have expressed astonishment that the Palestine police make no serious efforts to root out the terrorist gangs. . . . Some openly assert that there are contacts between the police and the terrorists. Without suggesting any motive, it is clear that the present regime derived concrete advantages from terrorism' (ibid. 11 April 1947, p. 3). Similarly, Jorge García-Granados, the most pro-Zionist member of the United Nations Special Committee that arrived in Palestine in June 1947, was told by a [Zionist] friend that the British deliberately allowed the terrorist campaign to continue 'so as to profit from the unrest in the country' (*The Birth of Israel*, p. 117).

[3] 9 May 1947, United Nations: *Official Records of the 1st special session of the General Assembly*, iii. 184. This was neither the first nor the last time that this British view was declared, and it surely deserved more consideration than it ever received.

[4] The eleven states were Austria, Canada, Czechoslovakia, Guatemala, unpartitioned India, the Netherlands, Persia, Peru, Sweden, Uruguay, and Yugoslavia.

the Arab states to place the termination of the Mandate and the declaration of the independence of Palestine on the agenda of the special session; and in his final speech Gromyko spoke in favour of the partition of Palestine between the Zionists and the Arabs if a single independent state were unattainable.[1]

In the meantime relations between the Jewish community in Palestine and the British had continued to deteriorate. On the Jewish side the terrorist campaign was unremitting; on the British side there was some increase in the number of assaults by troops and police on Jews in Jerusalem;[2] the hanging of Dov Grüner and three other terrorists on 16 April infuriated the Zionists, who had come to expect the commutation of death sentences for these political crimes;[3] and when, after the General Assembly's special session, the Secretary-General of the United Nations, at British request, invited all member states to do all in their power to discourage illegal immigration into Palestine while the Special Committee carried out its investigation,[4] the Jewish Agency denounced the British action as 'a devious and improper stratagem', and the Secretary-General's compliance with it as improper likewise.[5]

The United Nations Special Committee on Palestine (UNSCOP) included an outspoken sympathizer with Zionism in the Guatemalan member, Jorge García-Granados, and he had the support of the representatives of Uruguay, a country with a well-organized and active Jewish community concentrated in its capital city.[6]   When the Committee held its first plenary meeting on 2 June, it elected as its chairman, as had been expected, the Swedish judge, Emil Sandström, a former member of the Hague

---

[1] For expressions of appreciation by Zionist leaders, see *Zionist Review*, 23 May, p. 1, 30 May 1947, p. 5; the Arabic press was correspondingly dismayed. Circumstances had indeed changed since the years before the Second World War in which Soviet propaganda had encouraged the Arab Rebellion and denounced Zionism as a weapon of British imperialism; see, generally, Martin Ebon: 'Communist Tactics in Palestine', *Middle East Journal*, July 1948, ii. 255–69.

[2] Considering the circumstances, the number of cases was much smaller than might have been feared. On 31 January Crossman had said that the investigation of many allegations of atrocities committed by the troops, which he had received from Palestine during the previous summer, had convinced him that, while a few cases were authenticated, 'by and large . . . the incredible thing is how little has happened in the last seven months . . . under almost incredible conditions' (H.C.Deb. 5th ser., vol. 432, col. 1323; cf. Trevor: *Under the White Paper*, pp. 249–50, 280). The strain and violence of the next twelve months were to produce a steady lowering of disciplinary standards; but an observer who had commanded a battalion in a United States regular division during the war doubted seriously whether that division, 'disciplined as it was, would have equalled the restraint of the British forces in the face of long harassment' (Kenneth W. Bilby: *New Star in the Near East* (New York, Doubleday, 1950), p. 17).

[3] See above, p. 233.

[4] A regular traffic through the Mediterranean ports of France and Italy, and from the Black Sea, had continued with official connivance, despite British appeals to the governments concerned to co-operate in preventing it; see below, pp. 243, note 3, and 244, note 4.

[5] See *The Times*, 24 April, *New York Times*, 7 June, *New York Herald Tribune*, 10 June 1947.

[6] See M. Z. R. Frank, 'The Jews of the Americas', *Zionist Review*, 2 January 1942, p. 6; A. L. Schusheim: 'Latin-American Jewry', ibid. 6 August 1948, p. 10.

Court; but García-Granados's rival candidature received the votes of a minority, consisting of himself and the delegates of Uruguay and Yugo-slavia.[1] By the time the Committee arrived in Palestine the Arab Higher Committee, dominated by the influence of the Muftī in Cairo, had decided to boycott its proceedings; the more far-seeing members of the Arab community probably realized that their case would suffer, but the very real fear of violent reprisals if they defied the Muftī's command[2] was a powerful deterrent, and the Arab community was solid in this attitude of negation.

The Zionists' approach to the Committee, on the other hand, was positive and opportunist. There were objections from García-Granados and two other members of the Committee when the Palestine Government asked for their spokesman to be heard in closed session on security grounds, and the Jewish Agency protested when its two liaison officers attached to the Committee were excluded from the closed session. The object of these protests was to establish a 'strict parity' of treatment between the Jewish Agency and the Palestine Government;[3] and an opportunity for embarrassing the Government was provided by the coincidence that a military court had just passed death sentences on three I.Z.L. terrorists convicted of taking part on 4 May in a well-organized attack on Palestine's chief prison, the fortress of 'Akka (Acre), which had enabled 41 Jews and 214 Arabs—the latter predominantly common criminals—to escape.[4] The I.Z.L. had declared their readiness to discontinue their terrorist activities during the visit of the United Nations Committee, but only on condition that the British would likewise cease to intercept illegal immigrants, promulgate death sentences, carry out searches, or impose curfews.[5] A Jewish Agency spokesman commented that it was 'very regrettable' that the Committee should begin its work under 'the shadow of the gallows',[6] and this then became a matter of contention in the Committee.

[1] See New York Herald Tribune and The Times, 3 June 1947; García-Granados: The Birth of Israel, pp. 13–15. The Yugoslav representative on the Committee is reported to have 'displayed the keenest interest in all anti-British evidence . . . reminiscent of Gromyko's performance at the special session of the General Assembly', according to Sidney Hertzberg: 'The Month in History', Commentary, August 1947, p. 160. The breach between Yugoslavia and the Soviet Union had not yet occurred.

[2] The murder in the following autumn of the secretary of the Palestine Arab Workers' Society, Sāmī Tāhā, was ascribed to his opposition to the Muftī's leadership (see Richard Graves: Experiment in Anarchy, p. 84; Hurewitz: The Struggle for Palestine, pp. 234, 281, 292–5; and cf. Survey for 1938, i. 418, 421–2, for similar reprisals during the Arab Rebellion of 1938–9).

[3] Zionist Review special correspondent, 27 June 1947, p. 3; García-Granados, op. cit. pp. 43–44.

[4] See Creech Jones's statement in the House of Commons, 7 May 1947, H.C.Deb. 5th ser., vol. 437, coll. 416–17; Wilson: Cordon and Search, pp. 123–7; Begin: The Revolt, pp. 276–9.

[5] See ibid. p. 299.

[6] Zionist Review, 20 June 1947, p. 1. The New Judaea editorial for June 1947, pp. 2–3, commented that 'a measure of generosity might have had a most salutary effect on the country', without reference to the lack of Zionist response to the long series of reprieves terminated only with the executions on 16 April (see above, p. 240).

After nearly two days of discussion, a bare majority of six of its eleven members supported a resolution expressing 'concern as to the possible unfavourable repercussions' of the execution of the sentences. The Government's Chief Secretary replied that the sentences had no legal force unless confirmed by the General Officer Commanding.[1]

Throughout the period of the Committee's inquiry the Zionists retained the initiative in demonstrating their own independence of action and embarrassing the British authorities, who, on their side, were now using sharper language about the Zionists than they had used at the time of the Anglo-American Committee.[2] The atmosphere was also being influenced by current incidents connected with the struggle between the British armed forces in Palestine and the Jewish terrorists. Two members of the United Nations Committee were said to have been present at a 'hero's funeral' given in Tel Aviv to a member of a Palmaḥ detachment who had been killed by a concealed bomb while sealing off a tunnel which the terrorists had excavated with the intention of blowing up the British military head-quarters in Tel Aviv.[3] A very serious incident in which British police were involved was the disappearance on 6 May of Alexander Rubowitz, a sixteen-year-old Jewish youth who had been associated with the terrorist Stern Group;[4] he had evidently been seized by a Palestine Police com-mando unit, which had recently been formed under the command of the twenty-six-year-old Major Roy Farran, D.S.O., M.C., in an attempt to outwit the terrorists.[5] Rubowitz was never found, alive or dead.[6] Farran was never subsequently identified by any of the Jewish witnesses of Rubowitz's abduction, and he claimed to have been elsewhere at the time;[7]

---

[1] See García-Granados: *The Birth of Israel*, pp. 50–62.

[2] See Hurewitz: *The Struggle for Palestine*, p. 292.

[3] See Wilson: *Cordon and Search*, p. 131; *Zionist Review*, 4 July 1947, p. 4; Begin: *The Revolt*, pp. 291–3.

[4] *Daily Telegraph*, 21 June, *The Times*, 26 June 1947.

[5] See Roy Farran: *Winged Dagger* (London, Collins, 1948), p. 351.

[6] His disappearance gave rise to a variety of rumours in the Jewish community. These ranged from the fact of the existence of this autonomous commando unit to the alleged presence of a cell of the British Fascist movement within the police. See *New Judaea*, June 1947, p. 175; *Zionist Review*, 13 June 1947, p. 4; *New York Times*, and *New York Herald Tribune*, 14 June 1947. It was to this alleged 'anti-Semitic fascist gang of police that is known . . . to have formerly been led by Capt. Farran' (*Zionist Review*, 6 February 1948, p. 2; cf. ibid. 13 February, p. 6) that the Zionists afterwards attributed the blowing up of the *Palestine Post* building on 1 February 1948 and a larger explosion in Ben Yehuda St., Jerusalem, on 22 February, in which some fifty Jews were killed. The latter outrage was carried out by a party in British uniform (not in itself conclusive evidence that the wearers were British, in the circumstances obtaining in Palestine at the time) and transported in stolen army and police vehicles, and on 3 March a number of addressees received a circular letter in peculiar English (text in Koestler: *Promise and Fulfilment*, p. 172, note 1) which purported to claim the outrage for the 'British League of Servicemen (Palestine Branch)', i.e. the British Fascists. On 10 March 1948 three British deserters from the police were arrested in a stolen police armoured car while taking part in an Arab attack on a Jewish settlement, for which they received sentences of ten years' imprisonment.

[7] Farran, op. cit. p. 351.

but, being warned by a friend on 2 June that the authorities had decided
to charge him with the youth's murder in order to anticipate Zionist representations to the United Nations Committee, Farran twice escaped from
confinement and twice gave himself up again, and this naturally added
force to Zionist protests. On 7 July a Jewish Agency memorandum, presented to the Committee to illustrate the state of anarchy in Palestine,
charged Farran's commando unit with torturing Rubowitz to death and
said that members of the police were believed to have been responsible
for blowing up the Agency's press office on 16 March.[1]

While the United Nations Committee was in Palestine the British
authorities there were embarrassed by the arrival—which may have been
deliberately timed—of the largest number of illegal immigrants yet carried
in one ship, the *Exodus 1947*. She had been purchased from a United States
shipping line by 'friends of the Haganah' and had been furnished with
a Haganah crew, to sail under a Central American registration from a
United States east coast port. Shadowed and delayed by British interventions with the Portuguese and Italian Governments,[2] she was directed into
the small French port of Sète, 85 miles west of Marseilles, where lorries
organized by Haganah brought from Germany at the end of June a total
of 4,554 Jewish passengers, all provided with passports and visas for the
republic of Colombia. Although, as a result of British representations, a
guard was posted to prevent the ship's departure, she again succeeded in
slipping out of port,[3] and by 17 July was within about sixty miles of the

---

[1] Mrs. Golda Meyerson, still acting head of the Agency's political department, sent to the
High Commissioner on 23 June details of Rubowitz's alleged death by torture, as described in
information submitted to her (*New York Herald Tribune*, 24 June 1947).

Farran came up for trial by general court-martial on 1 October 1947. The Court upheld
the right under English law of his superior officer to decline to disclose a conversation he had had
with Farran on the day after Rubowitz's disappearance, since it might tend to incriminate himself; it also upheld the defence's objection to producing as evidence what Farran had written
in confinement, on the ground that this was privileged as being intended for his defence. In
these circumstances the only evidence that might be held to involve Farran was a felt hat with
a name that looked like his printed on the inside in faded ink, which was produced as having
been left behind by Rubowitz's captors; a Jewish boy aged thirteen, who witnessed the abduction
but afterwards failed at three identification parades to identify Farran or any of his squad of ten,
said that he had taken the hat to a synagogue, and from there it was said to have been handed,
a week later, to Rubowitz's brother, who took it to the police. The evidence at the disposal of
the prosecution under the limitations set by English legal procedure was inconclusive, and
Farran was acquitted.

[2] The chief of Haganah's immigration department had admitted on 15 June that British
diplomatic pressure was seriously interfering with the flow of illegal immigrants from European
displaced persons' camps to Mediterranean ports (*New York Herald Tribune*, 16 June 1947, cf.
New York Times, 2 and 10 July 1947; Mario Rossi, 'Italy: " Viva la Palestina ebraica" ', *Commentary*, July 1947, pp. 23–27).

[3] For details of the escape see Ruth Gruber: *Destination Palestine, the Story of the Haganah Ship
Exodus 1947* (New York, A. A. Wyn, 1948); García-Granados: *The Birth of Israel*, pp. 172–6.
The French attitude to this incident was inspired in part by a desire to retaliate for Britain's
part in France's eviction from the Levant States; cf. an editorial in *Monde*, 24 July 1947;

Palestine coast. 'The Jews here', wrote the *Christian Science Monitor*'s Haifa correspondent, 'believe that one "illegal" ship may be worth ten million words in helping to convince the Committee';[1] and the Haganah 'underground' transmitter began to relay broadcasts from the ship's radio. It was the British procedure to intercept such vessels only within the three-mile limit of Palestinian territorial waters, and this was officially stated to have been done on this occasion;[2] but the ship's radio claimed that she was still fourteen miles outside territorial waters. She adopted 'strong evasive action' in an attempt to pass outside the three-mile limit again, damaging both herself and the British destroyers who were intercepting her. A British naval boarding party was resisted with 'steam jets, oil, smoke bombs, fireworks, the usual missiles of tin cans and bottles, and tear-smoke', and two Jews died from cudgel blows received while the ship was being brought under control.[3] While the *Exodus* was being escorted into Haifa, the Haganah high command in Jerusalem transmitted to UNSCOP a protest against 'the piratical attack committed outside territorial waters in criminal violation of international law', and the Agency took up the complaint against 'a heedless, wanton act . . . an act of senseless cruelty'. The desired effect had in fact been obtained before the Committee left for Beirut on 20 July, the representative of the Yugoslav Communist Government exclaiming: 'It is the best possible evidence we can have.'[4]

'Would it not be strange to make us undertake new responsibilities in the Middle East, when not so long ago every means was set in motion to exclude us from that part of the world?'

[1] 'The length to which the striving for propaganda was carried is illustrated by the example of the exhibition on one occasion of a one-year-old child who had died at sea several days previously, with the statement to the Press: "The dirty Nazi-British assassins suffocated this innocent victim with gas". The *sotto voce* remark, "It's not against you, it's for the Press", made by one of the more moderate passengers to some of the troops, hardly compensated' (Wilson: *Cordon and Search*, p. 110).

[2] Close to the shore, near Rāfa on the Egyptian border; cf. ibid. p. 135.

[3] *The Times* Haifa correspondent, 19 July, *New York Times*, 20 July 1947. Cf. García-Granados: *The Birth of Israel*, pp. 177–82; his informant was a Methodist minister, a member of the pro-Zionist American Christian Palestine Committee, who had embarked in the ship through the good offices of Haganah, at whose New York headquarters he afterwards gave a press interview (*New York Times*, 9 August 1947).

[4] Homer Bigart in *New York Herald Tribune*, 19 and 20 July 1947. The British Foreign Office announced on the 21st that, by a reversion to pre-war practice, in accordance with international procedure and in agreement with the French Government (who had undertaken in March to co-operate in the prevention of illegal immigration to Palestine), the passengers on the *Exodus* were being conveyed back to France in three British transports. 30,000 Jews had now been admitted to Palestine above the White Paper figure and 15,000–16,000 more, or nearly a year's quota, were awaiting their turn in Cyprus (Lord Hall, 13 August 1947, H.L.Deb. 5th ser., vol. 151, col. 1388). The French Government rejoined, however, that they could not be responsible for the passengers' departure from France, since they had had passports with Colombian visas; and, though the Colombian Legation in Paris denied the genuineness of these visas and it appeared that the passports had by this time been destroyed, the French Government stated that the passengers would be given a free choice when they arrived in French waters on 29 July.

The opinion of the British military authorities responsible for the transfer is reported, accord-

When the United Nations Committee, having found the representatives of the Arab League no less uncompromising than they had been at the London conference, began at Geneva to consider its recommendations on 30 July, its members were so much divided on major issues that on 5 August it agreed to adjourn its formal meetings in favour of informal discussions, and these continued until the 27th, only five days before it was due to report to the Secretary-General. There was general agreement that the Mandate had proved unworkable, but the two Muslim representatives of Persia and India and the Communist from Yugoslavia were alone in favouring a bi-national federal state. The majority of eight set themselves to work out a plan for 'partition with economic union', but like their British predecessors in 1938,[1] found that the allocation of western Galilee, the Southern Desert (Negev), and the Jerusalem area presented almost insuperable difficulties. A series of compromises was hastily made, whose effect was to bisect this country, barely larger than Wales or Maryland, longitudinally and then to superimpose a transverse trisection, creating in addition an internationalized enclave of Jerusalem and Bethlehem; 'points of intersection' were contrived for communication between the two northern and the two southern Jewish and Arab areas and their respective

ing to one account, to have been that, 'but for the threats issued by the Jews ashore and the more fanatical ones on board, many of the passengers would undoubtedly have walked willingly off the ships, but, in face of the organized opposition, they faltered and eventually remained' (Wilson: *Cordon and Search*, p. 137). The local French officials allowed Haganah representatives to address the ships through a loud-speaker from a boat; and, during the three weeks that they lay in French waters, only about 130, or 3 per cent., of the passengers, accepted the French invitation to disembark, while a spokesman for the rest declared: 'We shall not land in Europe as long as we are alive.'

Meanwhile, the British official attitude hardened as a result of the discovery in Palestine on 31 July of the bodies of two British sergeants who had been kidnapped and hanged by the I.Z.L. as a reprisal for the recent execution of the death sentences passed on three terrorists on 16 June. In counter-reprisal, members of the British police force murdered a number of Jews in Palestine, and there were anti-Jewish demonstrations with some violence in several British cities, 'not for the first time', as a *Zionist Review* correspondent observed (8 August 1947, pp. 3, 10–11; 15 August 1947, pp. 4, 14; 14 November 1947, p. 6).

The *Exodus* passengers were given a final warning that they would on no account be taken to either Palestine or Cyprus, and a final opportunity to disembark in France, and they were then transported back to the British zone of Germany, 'the only territory under British jurisdiction outside Cyprus where such a large number of people can be adequately housed and fed at short notice' (Foreign Office statement, 21 August 1947). According to one British account of the sequel, 'relations had been so good throughout the voyage that many Jews stated their conviction that these troops would never obey an order to use force on them. In spite of good-humoured attempts by the troops to convince them otherwise, many of the Jews continued with this wishful thinking. Others, who were prepared for the worst, apologized in advance for the resistance which they were determined to put up at Hamburg, and explained that its object would not be directed at the troops, but their Government. However, neither of these approaches, nor any other, made any impression on the troops. When the time came for the disembarkation they were confronted with a hard core of resistance in two of the ships and before the operation was completed a bitter battle had taken place' (Wilson: *Cordon and Search*, pp. 137–8).

[1] Cf. Great Britain, Colonial Office: *Palestine Partition Commission: Report, October 1938*, Cmd. 5854 (London, H.M.S.O., 1938).

central areas.[1] The impracticability of this 'death by a thousand cuts' was emphasized by the provision that the Arab and Jewish states, each consisting of three segments and entwined in an inimical embrace like two fighting serpents, should attain their independence only when they had signed a ten-year treaty of economic union with provision for subsidizing the economically weaker Arab state from the more favoured Jewish state. It was estimated that in the latter no less than 45 per cent. of the population (or, if the Bedouin were reckoned in, 50 per cent. of the population) would originally be non-Jewish, but provision for Jewish immigration in the transitional period would soon rectify this anomaly; the Jewish minority in the proposed Arab state, on the other hand, would be little more than 1 per cent. of its population.[2]

The political commission of the General Zionist Council noted with satisfaction on 2 September the recommendation of the early establishment of a sovereign Jewish state. 'However', its resolution added, 'the territory proposed is a minor part of the territory originally promised to the Jewish people on the basis of its historic rights and does not include areas of the utmost importance.' Weizmann himself had told the United Nations Committee on 8 July: 'I do believe that a great many thoughtful Arabs, if they feel that this project is set into motion with all the authority, dignity, and . . . moral force which the United Nations command . . . will eventually acquiesce. Probably the Mufti will not acquiesce, but I do not think that will present an unsurmountable difficulty.'[3] The 'average Palestinian Jew' was described as 'for the time being essentially optimistic and complacent' about the Report, and this complacency was reflected in an assessment of the probable Arab reaction by a regular correspondent of the *Zionist Review*.[4] Against the inevitable opposition of the Arab states, the United Nations General Assembly set up an *ad hoc* Committee to consider and report on the Palestine proposals. Before the Committee began its work, the decision to transfer the main British Middle East military stores depot from the Canal Zone to Kenya, which had been under consideration for some time, was announced;[5] and Creech Jones opened the Committee's proceedings by saying on 26 September that

[1] See map C at end of volume, which includes the small modifications later adopted by the General Assembly; cf. below p. 249, note 3.

[2] *Report to the General Assembly by the United Nations Special Committee on Palestine* (Official Records of the 2nd session of the General Assembly, 1947, supplement no. 11), with map; cf. García-Granados: *The Birth of Israel*, pp. 233–46.

[3] *Report to the General Assembly by the United Nations Special Committee on Palestine* (Official Records, loc. cit. p. 82). Ben Gurion had told the Committee on 4 July that, if the Zionists received a favourable finding from it, they would go to the Arabs and say: 'Here is a decision in our favour. We are right. We want to sit down with you and settle the question amicably. If your answer is no, then we will use force against you' (ibid. p. 56).

[4] *Zionist Review*, 5 September 1947, p. 1; Major E. Laserson, ibid. 12 September 1947, p. 4.

[5] *The Times*, 13 and 16 September 1947; cf. Attlee, 15 October 1946 and 27 February 1947, H.C.Deb. 5th ser., vol. 427, coll. 791–2; vol. 433, coll. 2275–6.

... the United Kingdom Government was not prepared to undertake the task of imposing a policy in Palestine by force of arms. In considering any proposal that it should participate in the execution of a settlement, it would have to take into account both the inherent justice of the settlement and the extent to which force would be required to give effect to it ... In the absence of a settlement it had to plan for an early withdrawal of British forces and of the British administration from Palestine.[1]

The Zionists originally dismissed this warning of British intentions as 'blackmail', but the *Zionist Review*'s Jerusalem correspondent observed that the High Commissioner's reiteration on 8 October of the intention to withdraw, unless there were Jewish-Arab agreement, 'certainly makes an impression of seriousness'.[2]

The Arab states once again showed their lack of constructive political sense by refusing to offer the slightest concession that might have influenced in their favour some of the many members of the United Nations that were in no way committed to the Zionists.[3] Instead, the Political Committee of the Arab League, meeting at Sawfar (Lebanon) from 16 to 19 September, had determined to resist the implementation of the UNSCOP recommendations by all practical and offensive means; and the Cairo *al-Ahrām* had written that 'the Palestine Arabs will launch a relentless war to repel this attack on their country, especially as they know that all the Arab countries will back and assist them, supplying them with men, money, and ammunition'.[4] The Jewish Elected Assembly forthwith decreed the total mobilization of Jewish man-power, and 'feverish activities' were begun to reorganize the Haganah and convert it from an underground force into a regular army. Haganah forces were deployed along the Syrian frontier, where there were unconfirmed rumours of Arab troop concentrations, and by night they manned pillboxes and watchtowers equipped with searchlights.[5] The *Zionist Review*'s Jerusalem correspondent continued, however, to express scepticism about the likelihood of a conflict with the Arabs;[6] and an anti-Zionist Jewish member of the British Parliament, Daniel

---

[1] U.N. General Assembly, 2nd session, *Ad hoc* Committee on the Palestinian Question, summary records, pp. 3–5. [This will be referred to hereafter as *Ad hoc* Committee.]

[2] *Zionist Review*, 10 October 1947, p. 5, 17 October 1947, p. 6.

[3] See the uncompromising speech by Jamāl al-Husainī (*Ad hoc* Committee, pp. 5–11 and cf. pp. 116–17).

[4] Cf. U.N., Security Council: *Official Records*, 3rd year, supplement for May 1948, p. 4. Two rival paramilitary organizations, al-Futuwwa and an-Najjāda, had grown up among the politically divided Palestine Arabs. Their united strength was estimated at 30,000–40,000, 'with questionable armament and training; they are generally disregarded as a serious military factor. ... The Haganah is altogether a more formidable proposition' (Kevin Hyland, *Scotsman*'s Jerusalem correspondent, 29 August 1947); cf. J. L. Teller: 'Behind Palestine's Arab "Armies"', *Commentary*, March 1947.

[5] *Zionist Review*, 10 October 1947, p. 2; 17 October 1947, p. 5.

[6] Ibid. 10 October 1947, p. 5.

Lipson, met with no success in appealing to Zionists 'not to pursue a policy that would increase the danger of another war'.[1]

In the general debate in the *Ad hoc* Committee both the United States and the Soviet delegates supported the partition proposals, though with reservations about the proposed frontiers between the Jewish and Arab states.[2] The United States delegate noted that the responsibility for the administration of Palestine still rested with the Mandatory Power during the period of transition to independence, after which the maintenance of internal law and order 'might require the establishment of a special constabulary or police force recruited on a volunteer basis by the United Nations'.[3] Creech Jones replied on 16 October with a refusal on the part of the British Government to accept responsibility 'either alone or in the major role'; he deplored Zionist 'rumours and assertions' that the Palestine Government were encouraging an emergence of Arab violence;[4] and he protested against the 'connivance of some Governments in the provision by their nations of ships, arms and money' to promote illegal immigration, 'which greatly influences the feeling of the Arab world and sets irresponsible influences at work which cannot readily be controlled'.[5] The United States delegate, Herschel Johnson, nevertheless continued in sub-committee to try to make the British forces responsible for law and order, under the supervision of a United Nations three-man commission, until 1 July 1948, when the Jewish (and the Arab) state should come to birth.[6] The Soviet delegate, on the other hand, was intent on having the Mandate ended on 1 January 1948, and the British troops withdrawn within three or four months after that date; and on 10 November an American-Soviet compromise was reached for the termination of the Mandate by 1 May and the establishment of the two states by 1 July 1948.

Sir Alexander Cadogan thereupon stated on 13 November that the British Government intended that the withdrawal of their troops from Palestine should be completed by 1 August, although civil administration might be ended at any time after it had become evident that the Assembly had failed to reach a settlement acceptable to both Jews and Arabs. He objected to the proposal, contained in the draft resolution recommended

---

[1] See the attack on him by Hamabit, pseud., *New Judaea*, October–November 1947, p. 6.

[2] See *Ad hoc* Committee, pp. 63, 70.

[3] Ibid. p. 64.

[4] A Haganah spokesman had said that his organization 'had proof that an Arab gang which recently carried out acts of terrorism in various parts of the country had been organized by Government agents, who were also directing its activities' (*Zionist Review*, 12 September 1947, p. 5; cf. J. L. Teller's article, 'Behind Palestine's Arab "Armies" ', *Commentary*, March 1947, pp. 243–5, 249, with its reference to the alleged 'goading' of the Arabs by the 'diversion-hungry British').

[5] See verbatim report in *New Judaea*, October–November 1947, pp. 13–15.

[6] García-Granados (*The Birth of Israel*, pp. 251, 255–6) recorded Johnson's original confidence that the British Government would fall in with this scheme, and his subsequent disillusionment.

by the sub-committee to the *Ad hoc* Committee on 19 November, that, immediately upon the adoption of a resolution by the General Assembly, the administration of Palestine should pass to a commission of five members appointed by the Assembly, while the British mandate might continue until not later than 1 August 1948. The British Government, he said, would insist upon undivided control as long as they continued to hold the Mandate, but would hand over their authority to the proposed commission as and when the territory was evacuated; during their gradual withdrawal British troops would maintain order in the areas that they still occupied, but would not be available as the instrument for enforcing a settlement against either Arabs or Jews, or to maintain order on behalf of the proposed commission, although they would not obstruct it in its work. Cadogan's deputy added that the Mandatory 'could only take note' of a proposal of the sub-committee (originally suggested by the American Zionist, Dr. Emanuel Neumann)[1] that the Mandatory should use its best endeavours to ensure that an area situated in the territory of the Jewish state, including a seaport and hinterland adequate to provide facilities for a substantial immigration, should be evacuated at the earliest possible date and in any event not later than 1 February 1948.[2] The Jewish Agency expressed its readiness, if the sub-committee's proposals were accepted, to abandon its demands for the town of Beersheba, with its population of 6,500 Arabs, an area of 106 square miles extending to the north and north-east of the town, and an area of some 700 square miles in the southern part of the Negev along the Egyptian border; the Arab representatives remained unyielding.[3] The sub-committee's draft resolution called for the fullest possible co-ordination and co-operation between the Mandatory and the commission in the transitional period; but the contingency of having to enforce a United Nations decision on an unwilling Arab community in Palestine had not yet been adequately faced, since no member of the United Nations, other than the Soviet bloc, was anxious to become involved.[4] When the proposals came back to the full *Ad hoc* Committee it first voted on and defeated a proposal, sponsored mainly by the Muslim countries, to create a unitary state in Palestine, and then turned on 25 November to vote on the proposal for partition into a Jewish and an Arab state. A simple majority in Committee would be sufficient for passing on a proposal to the General Assembly, but its final adoption

---

[1] See ibid. p. 261.

[2] See *Ad hoc* Committee, pp. 170, 249, and below, p. 255. Herschel Johnson, for the United States, complained of the lack of co-operation of the British delegation, which was making the Committee's task more difficult (ibid. pp. 169, 180–1).

[3] Ibid. pp. 168, 171; see map C at end of volume. The sub-committee had already proposed that Jaffa, with its 80,000 Arabs, should be an Arab enclave, not part of the Jewish state as suggested by UNSCOP.

[4] See Maurice J. Goldbloom: 'The Month in History', *Commentary*, November 1947, p. 460.

there would require a two-thirds' majority of those voting, abstentions being ignored. The affirmative votes in Committee fell one short of this two-thirds' majority, twenty-five against thirteen (the latter comprising the Muslim and Asiatic states plus Cuba), while there was the large number of nineteen absentees and abstentions.[1]

When the General Assembly began its study of the draft resolution on 26 November, amid a 'great gathering'[2] of New York Jews in the public galleries, Cadogan repeated explicitly, on his Government's instructions, that British troops and administration could not be used to endorse decisions which were not accepted by both parties in Palestine. Herschel Johnson, for the United States, regretted that the British were making this 'impossible condition' for their co-operation; a solution of the Palestine problem, he said, required 'the use of the knife'; but he hoped that the boundaries between the Arab and the Jewish states would be as freely crossed as the boundaries that separated the individual states within the United States, and as friendly as the boundary that ran between Canada and the United States.[3] Some of the delegations who had abstained from voting in the *Ad hoc* Committee now declared their position: the Netherlands, New Zealand, and Belgium in favour of the resolution, since the only alternative to partition was 'still more serious troubles, if not utter chaos'; Greece and Haiti against. The Philippines still wavered, and the Siamese delegate, who had opposed the resolution in the *Ad hoc* Committee, was dismissed by the new Siamese Government which had recently come to power as the result of a *coup d'état*. The Assembly then took a holiday over Thanksgiving Day during which the canvassing for votes continued,[4] and an unofficial estimate now reckoned on thirty-one votes in favour of partition, which would probably give a safe two-thirds' majority. When the Assembly resumed on 28 November, however, France (whose vote had remained uncertain, perhaps because of her millions of Muslim subjects in Africa) proposed a further adjournment of one day in the hope of a last-minute compromise agreement; and, despite the opposition of the United States and Soviet delegations, this proposal was adopted by twenty-

[1] These were Argentina, Belgium, China, Colombia, El Salvador, Ethiopia, France, Greece, Haiti, Honduras, Liberia, Luxembourg, Mexico, Netherlands, New Zealand, Paraguay, Philippines, United Kingdom, Yugoslavia.

[2] Alistair Cooke in *Manchester Guardian*, 28 November 1947.

[3] United Nations: *Official Records of the 2nd session of the General Assembly*, Plenary Meetings, ii. 1324, 1326–7.

[4] According to *The Forrestal Diaries* (pp. 309, 323, 344–6, 348–9, 357–8) President Truman, under pressure from his party advisers, exerted himself to ensure that the votes of states amenable to United States influence or advice should be secured for the partition resolution, and two justices of the Supreme Court made efforts to the same end. This account was corroborated by the former Under-Secretary of State, Sumner Welles (*We Need Not Fail*, p. 63); cf. *Philadelphia Record*, 3 December 1947, quoted in the House of Commons, 11 December 1947, H.C.Deb. 5th ser., vol. 445, col. 1284. García-Granados, on the other hand, claimed to have been personally told by the President that no such pressure had been exerted (*The Birth of Israel*, p. 269).

five votes to fifteen. Earlier attempts in sub-committee to mediate between the Arab and Zionist standpoints had, however, failed,[1] and, despite a new approach by Harold Beeley, who was advising the British delegation,[2] the opening speech of the Lebanese delegate on 29 November revealed no material change of ground on the part of the Arab League. The partition proposal then amply achieved its two-thirds majority, receiving thirty-three votes to thirteen, with ten abstentions.[3]

(e) Guerrilla Warfare in Palestine, and Proclamation of the State of Israel, December 1947 to May 1948

During the four months that had elapsed since the departure of the United Nations Committee from Palestine, there had been sporadic attacks by Arabs on Jews which had been checked by Haganah reprisals;[4] and, as Zionists all over the world celebrated the favourable vote in the United Nations, in the Arab countries—including a place as far away from Palestine as Aden—there were riotous demonstrations (in which there were some foreigners among the victims) against Jews and native Communists (on account of the Soviet bloc's support of partition).[5] While the 'ulamā of the Cairo University of al-Azhar declared a jihād, in Palestine the Arab Higher Committee, directed by the Muftī who was then in Damascus, proclaimed a three-day general strike from 2 to 4 December, to be followed by a demonstration after the midday prayers on Friday the 5th. On the first day of the strike Arab rioters in Jerusalem burnt a Jewish shopping quarter, and on the following day Arab attacks started in the slum area on the borders of Jaffa and Tel Aviv, and in Haifa, the Secretary of the Arab Higher Committee (Dr. Husain al-Khālidī) rejecting the request of

[1] Ad hoc Committee, p. 146.

[2] This was the basis of the Zionist charges against Beeley reported by the Christian Science Monitor and New York Herald Tribune, 29 November 1947.

[3] The following delegations, which had abstained or been absent from the vote in the Ad hoc Committee, were now in favour: France and the three 'Benelux' countries, New Zealand, Haiti, Liberia, Paraguay, and the Philippines. Siam, who had opposed, was now absent; Chile, who had been in favour, now abstained; and Greece, who had abstained, now voted against. None of the delegations from the Middle East and Asia voted in favour of the resolution.

[4] See Richard Graves: Experiment in Anarchy, p. 72; Zionist Review, 15 August–5 September 1947.

[5] In Damascus demonstrators vented their anger on a Soviet institution and on the Syrian Communists, killing several persons. The United States Legations in Damascus and Beirut were attacked, and the U.S. Information Service office in Baghdad was wrecked. At Aleppo 300 Jewish houses and 11 synagogues were burned, and 2,000 of the city's 5,000 Jews were said to have fled (M. Perlmann in Palestine Affairs, January 1948, p. 4). At Aden, where the authorities were taken by surprise, seventy-six Jews and thirty-eight Arabs were officially reported killed. There was considerable criticism of the conduct of the Aden Protectorate [Arab] Levies who constituted the greater part of the security forces available. Cf. Great Britain, Colonial Office: Report of the Commission of Enquiry into the Disturbances at Aden in December 1947 (Colonial, No. 233, London, H.M.S.O., 1948); A. S. Diamond: 'The Aden Disturbances', Jewish Monthly, January 1949, ii. 582–6.

the Palestine Government that the Committee should call off the strike and adding that, while the Committee wished the strike to pass off 'as peaceably as possible', irresponsible elements were 'unavoidably' taking the law into their own hands 'as they do in other places'.[1] The Haganah was mobilized for self-defence, the Zionists complaining that the British security forces were not doing enough to protect Jewish lives and property. Almost certainly they were now doing less than their strict duty in the matter, for the temper of British soldiers in Palestine had been affected by the fact that they had lost 127 killed and 331 wounded at the hands of Jewish terrorists between the end of the Second World War and 20 October 1947, including eight killed and eighty-two injured in the last three months of that period.[2] The British Chairman of the Municipal Commission of Jerusalem recorded his impression that the 'young hooligans' who had begun the Arab rioting in that city had been encouraged by the 'apathy' of the British police.[3] Jewish acts of immediate retaliation in Jerusalem and elsewhere were said, on the Jewish side, to have been instigated by the extremists and against the wish of the Haganah,[4] and from this time onwards the I.Z.L. more or less ceased to attack British installations, except when they wished to seize arms, and directed their attention against the Arabs.

It remained British policy at this stage not willingly to allow the Haganah to come into the open as an armed force,[5] but on 15 December the Palestine Government announced that the policing of the Tel Aviv–Petah Tiqvah area would be turned over entirely to the Jews, and that of Jaffa to the Arabs. As the guerrilla fighting gained momentum the Zionists complained that, while the British forces received orders to observe strict neutrality between the two warring communities, such orders were generally interpreted in a partial fashion prejudicial to themselves; that the British naval patrol of the coast on the watch for illegal immigrants made it more difficult for the Jews to obtain arms from overseas than for the Arabs to equip themselves by land from the neighbouring Arab countries; and that for several weeks the British police authorities refused to allow the Jewish Settlement Police (who were virtually all active members of Palmaḥ) to use the armoured cars which they had acquired during the Arab Rebellion of 1936–9, with the result that a number were killed in Arab ambushes.[6] The Haganah resolutely counter-attacked against points

---

[1] Fitzhugh Turner in *New York Herald Tribune*, 4 December 1947.

[2] 29 July 1947, H.C.Deb. 5th ser., vol. 441, coll. 247–8; 30 July 1947, ibid. *written answers*, col. *50*; 29 October 1947, ibid. vol. 443, *written answers*, coll. *72–73*.

[3] Graves: *Experiment in Anarchy*, pp. 102–3, diary entries of 2–3 December 1947.

[4] Maurice J. Goldbloom, 'The Month in History', *Commentary*, January 1948, p. 60.

[5] See Wilson: *Cordon and Search*, pp. 155–6.

[6] M. Alexander, pseud.: 'Die Gründung des jüdischen Staates Israel', *Europa-Archiv*, 20 September 1949, pp. 2459–60; Sacher: *Israel, the Establishment of a State*, pp. 203–4.

from which they believed that Arab attacks had come, and sought to impress upon the Arab villagers that they had better remain passive because they had more to fear from Jewish reprisals than from the Arab fighting-men.[1] Both sides committed shocking outrages in Haifa and Jerusalem as the new year came in;[2] and in the upper Jordan valley reprisal and counter-reprisal were followed by the first incursion of Arab irregulars over the frontier from Syria to attack two Jewish settlements on 9 January 1948. British armoured cars intervened in this fighting and diplomatic representations were made to the Syrian Government to prevent such incursions.[3] Nevertheless, in the second half of January further bands of trained and well-equipped Syrians, their officers drawn from the Syrian army,[4] entered Palestine to stiffen the less effectual local Arab fighters;[5] on occasion they crossed the Jordan bridges in trucks with the connivance of the Arab Legion,[6] to which the British were leaving the garrisoning of the exclusively Arab parts of Palestine as their own withdrawal proceeded.

---

[1] *Zionist Review* Jerusalem correspondent, 2 January 1948, pp. 4–5.

[2] See Graves: *Experiment in Anarchy*, pp. 120–1, 124; and cf. Maurice J. Goldbloom: 'The Month in History', *Commentary*, February 1948, p. 163.

[3] Wilson: *Cordon and Search*, pp. 159–60; cf. the Jewish Agency's version, in U.N., Security Council: *Official Records*, 3rd year, supplement for May 1948, p. 9.

[4] Among the commanders of these bands were the Syrian Colonel Adīb Shīshaklī and Akram Hawrānī (see *New York Times*, 18 January 1948), who were afterwards to play leading parts in the military *coups d'état* in Syria of 1949–51. Better known was the general commander on this northern front, Fawzī Qāwuqjī, a Muslim from Lebanese Tripoli who had served in the Ottoman army in the First World War and had then had a varied career as intelligence officer under French command in Syria, military adviser to Ibn Saʿūd, and officer in the ʿIrāqī army, and had been 'generalissimo' of the Palestine Arab guerrillas in the 1936 Rebellion (*Survey* for 1936, p. 738). In 1941 he had fought in the abortive ʿIrāqī *putsch* against Britain, and had then escaped to Germany. After the war he had, after a period of detention by the Russians, been released by them and, like the Muftī, found sanctuary in France. Leaving there for Egypt in February 1947 under an assumed name, he had evaded the British passport control at Lydda airport (5 March 1947, H.C.Deb. 5th ser., vol. 434, coll. 468–70, and 3 March 1947, ibid. *written answers*, col. *18*).

[5] An impartial British authority expressed the view to the writer in 1952 that the Arab Higher Committee, directed by the Muftī from outside Palestine, was far better organized during this fighting than it had ever been before, and that the local national committees which it set up in all the Arab towns and some 275 villages (see Hurewitz: *The Struggle for Palestine*, p. 309), with their paramilitary offshoots which were a sort of Home Guard, worked fairly efficiently.

[6] The Jewish Agency complained to the Security Council on 22 February that the British had ignored their warning, forty-eight hours in advance, of such an incursion. The Arab Legion was entirely maintained by a British subsidy provided for in the Anglo-Transjordan Treaty of 1946 and shortly to be confirmed in the revised treaty signed on 15 March 1948 (Great Britain, Foreign Office: *Treaty of Alliance between . . . the United Kingdom . . . and . . . the Hashimite Kingdom of Transjordan, Amman, 15th March, 1948*, Cmd. 7368 (London, H.M.S.O., 1948). Its commander and a substantial number of its officers were British (see below, p. 273, note 2), and it had been used as part of the British garrison of Palestine since the end of the Second World War and the beginning of Jewish 'activism'. For charges against the Arab Legion of 'murderous attacks' and 'unprovoked aggression' against 'peaceful Jewish residents' and traffic see 18 December 1947, H.C.Deb. 5th ser., vol. 445, *written answers*, coll. *418–19*; Shertok, 27 February 1948, in U.N., Security Council: *Official Records*, 3rd year, nos. 16–35, p. 351; Sacher, op. cit. pp. 200, 202; but the Arab Legion had its own account of Zionist provocation: see *Middle East Journal*, Spring 1953, vii. 256.

Despite the serious loss of life and damage to property which Zionist reprisals were inflicting on the exposed fringe of Arab Palestine, the arrival of these reinforcements from outside, who were estimated at the beginning of March to amount to over 5,000 in seven contingents,[1] introduced an element of discipline into the Arab areas of Galilee, Samaria, and the neighbourhood of Jerusalem,[2] and temporarily raised the morale of the *fallāhīn* and the impressionable urban lower classes.[3] Frontal attacks upon Jewish settlements were almost invariably costly failures for the Arabs, but they evolved a more effective, if more protracted strategy of reducing the outlying settlements by attacks upon the road communications by which they were supplied with provisions and munitions; these attacks were bloody affairs in which neither side was accustomed to give quarter or return prisoners,[4] and the Arabs succeeded in destroying a Haganah party of thirty-five men who had been sent to reinforce a Haganah detachment that was manning the Kfar Etsion group of four Jewish settlements isolated in the Judaean hills between Jerusalem and Hebron.[5]

The British Minister of State for Colonial Affairs had stated on 20 January that the policy of allowing both the Jewish and the Arab communities to make arrangements for their own security, in areas where either community was in the great majority, had been carried farther, so that the British police could be concentrated in Jerusalem and other mixed localities; the Jewish Agency had been informed that their defence organizations would not be obstructed if they acted in a purely defensive role, and there would be no searches for arms except in cases of their misuse for offensive purposes. Lord Listowel went on to speak of the violent conflict in recent weeks in the Old City of Jerusalem: much of this had been stimulated by bomb attacks by Jewish terrorist organizations, and the Arabs had retaliated by imposing a blockade on the Jewish quarter of the Old City;

---

[1] See the British Under-Secretary for the Colonies, 3 March 1948, H.C.Deb. 5th ser., vol. 448, *written answers*, coll. 65–66; Shertok, loc. cit.

[2] The Arab commander here was 'Abd ul-Qādir al-Husainī, a cousin of the Muftī who had accompanied him to Baghdād in 1939 and was suspected of having organized the murder there of the Muftī's most active Palestinian opponent, Fakhrī an-Nashāshībī, on 9 November 1941; for the background, see *Survey* for 1938, i. 443–4.

[3] The more moderate and pacific elements of the Arab community were less enthusiastic, however, about the presence of these non-Palestinian Arab troops who attracted Haganah reprisals upon the local population (see Wilson: *Cordon and Search*, pp. 163–4); cf. a Jewish Agency memorandum to the Security Council, dated 13 March 1948, for the alleged indifference of an 'Irāqī commander in Jaffa to the imperilling of the city by his countermanding truce talks between the Arab mayor and the mayor of Tel Aviv (U.N., Security Council: *Official Records*, 3rd year, supplement for May 1948, p. 31).

[4] Wilson, op. cit. pp. 163–4, 184–5; cf. M. Alexander, in *Europa-Archiv*, 20 September 1949, p. 2460.

[5] In refusing to encourage the Arabs by abandoning this precarious position the Jewish Agency were sacrificing strategy to ideology, according to Sacher (*Israel, the Establishment of a State*, pp. 224, 229–30). Heavy losses were incurred in defending the group of settlements until it was finally overrun at the end of the Mandate (see below, p. 271).

food convoys were taken to these Jews under British military escort after the Haganah had threatened to force the blockade.[1] Meanwhile, the five-Power Commission appointed to implement the General Assembly's partition plan (consisting of representatives of Bolivia, Czechoslovakia, Denmark, Panama, and the Philippines), had begun its work at Lake Success on 9 January, but found that the fighting in Palestine had greatly reduced the readiness of the British Government to assist it in carrying into effect the General Assembly's resolution. The British delegation informed the Commission that, in the opinion of the Palestine Government, if the Commission proceeded to Palestine it would be in danger of attack by the Arabs, and could certainly expect no co-operation from the Arab community in general or from those Arab civil servants who constituted some 62 per cent. of the staff of the Administration. The British Government could not be responsible for the Commission's safety or relinquish partial authority to it before the date on which they had determined to end the Mandate (15 May), and were not therefore prepared that the Commission should arrive in Palestine until, say, a fortnight before that time.[2] They could not comply with the Assembly's resolution that they should concede to the Zionists a seaport and hinterland for substantial immigration,[3] since the arrival of large numbers of immigrants and possibly of arms would undoubtedly further inflame the internal conflict, and would make the withdrawal of the British members of the Palestine administration and the evacuation of British troops and stores more hazardous. There were further British objections to allowing the proposed provisional councils of the Jewish and Arab states to exercise legal authority, and to authorizing the formation of armed militias, before the end of the Mandate.[4] In fact, the

[1] H.L.Deb. 5th ser., vol. 153, coll. 487–8, 491–2; cf. Maurice J. Goldbloom: 'The Month in History', *Commentary*, February 1948, p. 163; *New Judaea*, January–February 1948, p. 64; see also below, pp. 264–5.

[2] Creech Jones had already stated this more generally in the House of Commons on 11 December 1947, with the suggestion that officials of the Commission, and perhaps one of its members, might arrive in Palestine earlier (H.C.Deb. 5th ser., vol. 445, coll. 1213, 1227–8). An advance party of four members of the Commission's staff did, in fact, arrive on 22 February 1948, but met with the minimum of co-operation from the British authorities, and in the existing 'chaos' found themselves in practice restricted to the British military zone of Jerusalem (see Jacques de Reynier: *À Jérusalem un drapeau flottait sur la ligne de feu* (Neuchâtel, Éditions de la Baconnière, 1950), pp. 38–39).

[3] Bevin had announced on 12 December 1947 the Government's refusal to relax the immigration restrictions (H.C.Deb. 5th ser., vol. 445, coll. 1374, 1400), and 15,000 Jews had reached Cyprus in the two largest ships which had as yet engaged in the traffic, bringing the total of Jews in the Cyprus camps to over 31,000 (Lord Listowel in the House of Lords, 20 January 1948, H.L.Deb. 5th ser., vol. 153, col. 492).

[4] The Zionists had protested that, whereas the British were supplying to the Arab states with whom they had treaty relations (Egypt, 'Irāq, and Jordan) arms which would find their way to the Palestine Arab guerrillas, Zionist 'implementation' of the United Nations policy was impeded by the ban which the U.S. State Department had imposed on 5 December 1947 on arms shipments to the Middle East and on the issue of passports to United States nationals intending to serve with foreign armed forces (see statement by Shertok, reported by *Zionist Review*,

two warring communities in Palestine were becoming more and more independent of mandatory authority, and though the British desire to maintain at least the vestiges of order until the Mandate expired was probably insufficiently appreciated by the Commission at Lake Success, the United Nations and the world were allowed to form an impression that the British attitude was determined by nothing better than a sulky disinclination to co-operate.[1]

In these circumstances the United Nations Commission on 16 February referred to the Security Council the problem of providing that armed assistance which alone would enable the Commission to carry out its task. The British Colonial Secretary sought on the 24th to justify to the Council his Government's non-compliance with those terms of the General Assembly's resolution which, in their opinion, had unrealistically ignored the difficulties of security and the dangers of divided responsibility. Some of the important administrative services, he said, were now being transferred to the Jewish and Arab authorities; Britain had no wish to wreck what her rule had accomplished in Palestine; but nearly 100 more British servicemen and police had been killed, and some hundreds wounded, in the past three months of guerrilla warfare, and British public opinion would acquiesce no longer in the spending of British life or treasure to impose a policy in Palestine.[2] Shertok, for the Jewish Agency, denounced the British for having adopted a theory of their neutrality and of 'a spurious equality of guilt as between the attackers and the attacked—between those upholding and those defying the authority of the United Nations';[3] he complained that the British were, in fact, discriminating against the Zionists; and, if the 'clearly indicated' international force for Palestine were not established, he called for the raising of embargoes on the supply of arms to 'those ready to assume defence responsibilities in the implementation' of the United Nations proposals (i.e. the Zionists) and the denial of arms to those engaged in resisting it, including all countries of the Arab League.[4]

23 January 1948, p. 4; cf. Bernard Baruch, 3 February 1948, quoted in *The Forrestal Diaries*, p. 364). For the detection of the clandestine loading of explosives purchased by the Jewish Agency in New York see *The Times*, 5, 10, 12 January, and 18 February 1948.

[1] See U.N. Palestine Commission: *First and Second Monthly Progress Reports* (A/AC.21/7, 29 January 1948; S/695, 15 March 1948, containing A/AC.21/14, 12 March 1948). The British Government's general attitude was supported by the Conservative Opposition; see R. A. Butler, 10 March 1948, H.C.Deb. 5th ser., vol. 448, coll. 1262–4.

[2] Creech Jones, 24 February 1948 in U.N., Security Council: *Official Records*, 3rd year, nos. 16–35, pp. 269–73.

[3] The loyal acceptance of United Nations decisions which Shertok claimed for the Jewish community (letter to the Secretary-General, 17 March 1948: U.N., Security Council: *Official Records*, 3rd year, no. 52, p. 11) was to undergo considerable modification as soon as those decisions had served their turn in establishing the Jewish state; cf. Sir Reader Bullard: *Britain and the Middle East* (London, Hutchinson, 1951), p. 156, and below, pp. 277–8.

[4] Shertok, 27 February 1948 in U.N., Security Council: *Official Records*, 3rd year, nos. 16–35, pp. 344–56; and cf. Rabbi Silver, 5 March 1948: ibid. nos. 36–51, pp. 15–16.

The Secretary-General of the United Nations had optimistically told the Palestine Commission at its first meeting on 9 January: 'You are entitled to be confident that, in the event it should prove necessary, the Security Council will assume the full measure of responsibility in implementation of the Assembly's resolution';[1] but the matter was less simple when the Council was faced by the Commission's request for armed assistance. The General Assembly's resolution concerning Palestine was only a recommendation, and therefore not legally binding on any state.[2] The major responsibility for its implementation would rest with the United States, whose planners had a number of difficult considerations to keep in view—among them, the opening that the Soviet Union might find for sending troops or officials to Palestine, as part of a United Nations team,[3] and the effect which the Palestine crisis might have on the United States oil reserves in the Arab countries.[4] These were vital if the oil reserves of the Western Hemisphere were to be in part conserved as a strategic reserve; furthermore Western European needs of fuel oil were expected to be substantially increased by the European Recovery Plan, and an increase in Middle Eastern oil production from 308 million barrels in 1947 to 620 million in 1951 had been postulated. Accordingly, the State and Defence Departments in Washington had reached the conclusion as early as 21 January that the United Nations partition plan was 'not workable' and that the United States was under no obligation to support it if it could not be carried out without the use of force; she had few military forces to spare without a partial mobilization and should therefore take steps to have the plan withdrawn.[5] On 24 February Senator Warren Austin had proposed to the Security Council that its five permanent members should together consider whether there was a threat to international peace and security. His proposal was adopted on 5 March;[6] and, reporting on these delibera-

[1] United Nations Document A/AC.21/SR.1, p. 2.

[2] See Clyde Eagleton: 'Palestine and the Constitutional Law of the United Nations', *American Journal of International Law*, April 1948, pp. 397–9.

[3] Council on Foreign Relations: *The United States in World Affairs, 1947–1948*, p. 339; cf. Hal Lehrman: *Israel, the Beginning and Tomorrow* (New York, Sloane [1952]) p. 271.

[4] The United States share of the oil production of the Arab countries (not Persia) in 1947 had amounted to 72 per cent. of the total. Arab threats to suspend the concessions to United States companies went back to the autumn of 1945 (Hurewitz: *Struggle for Palestine*, p. 231).

[5] *The Forrestal Diaries*, pp. 360, 411. Forrestal's concern for Middle East oil supplies, in his successive appointments as Secretary of the Navy and of Defence, can be traced back to May 1947 (ibid. p. 272). His opposition to indiscriminate United States support of the Zionists brought upon him their hostility; and it is interesting to find James G. McDonald, who besides being an uncritical supporter of Zionism was Forrestal's old friend, going warmly to his posthumous defence: 'The venomous attacks upon him which helped break his mind and body . . . stand out as among the ugliest examples of the willingness of politicians and publicists to use the vilest means—in the name of patriotism—to destroy self-sacrificing and devoted public servants' (McDonald: *My Mission in Israel*, p. 12).

[6] Text in U.N., Security Council: *Official Records*, 3rd year, nos. 36–51, pp. 35–36. A paragraph formally accepting the Assembly's resolution on partition failed to obtain the necessary two-thirds' majority, there being six abstentions.

tions to the Council on the 19th, he declared (against the objections of the Soviet Union, who in the previous December had called on the Council to assume full responsibility for carrying the partition plan into effect) that the Security Council was not prepared to make efforts to implement by force a plan which (as the Palestine Commission, the British, and the Jewish and Arab spokesmen themselves had indicated) could not be carried through peaceably in view of the substantial flow of fighting men and illegal arms to both sides. The United States Government therefore believed that a temporary trusteeship for Palestine should be established under the Trusteeship Council, to give the Jews and Arabs a further opportunity to reach an agreement, without prejudice to the character of that agreement. Such a recommendation from the Security Council would require an immediate special session of the General Assembly, before which the Council should instruct the Palestine Commission to suspend its efforts to implement the proposed partition plan.[1]

The Zionists—who had already expressed indignation at the British Government's announcement on 22 February that, as Palestine's sterling balances (totalling about £100 million) had been rapidly drawn upon in recent months, these would now be blocked and Palestine would forthwith cease to be a member of the sterling area[2]—protested vehemently against

[1] U.N., Security Council: *Official Records*, 3rd year, nos. 36–51, pp. 159–68. The decision to cease supporting partition was said to have been made by the State Department without reference to Truman, who had given a personal assurance of his support to Weizmann on the previous day (J. Daniels: *The Man of Independence* (London, Gollancz, 1950), pp. 318–19); but by 29 March Truman was ready to agree that the United States would take part in implementing a trusteeship 'up to the limit of our ability' (*The Forrestal Diaries*, p. 406). Three months earlier Senator Vandenberg had expressed the view that unilateral United States action in support of partition 'would produce a wave of violent anti-Semitism' (ibid. p. 349); and the Jewish reporter Hal Lehrman remarked that he had 'inspected big batches of pro-partition telegrams to the White House but found only one in about fifty where the sender's name sounded possibly non-Jewish' ('Partition in Washington', *Commentary*, March 1948, p. 213).

[2] £7 million would be released, together with current accessions of sterling, to be used for current expenditure until the expiry of the Mandate, and subsequent policy would be discussed between the British representative at the United Nations and the Commission for Palestine. The Palestine Commission, however, complained that it had not received prior notification of this announcement, although the British Government had kept it informed of the gradual deterioration of the financial position, and it disputed the Palestine Government's charging against current revenue such items as £2 million for the maintenance of Jewish illegal immigrants in Cyprus and compensation payments to Palestine civil servants for the termination of their appointments. It argued that these charges 'should not take precedence over the securing of essential food supplies and the provision of essential working funds for the Commission' (United Nations Palestine Commission: *Report to the General Assembly* (*Official Records of the 2nd special session of the General Assembly*, Supplement no. 1), pp. 30–34; Creech Jones, 23 April 1948: *Official Records of the 2nd special session of the General Assembly*, ii. 61).

The Jewish Agency's Treasurer, Eliezer Kaplan, pointed out that Palestine's sterling balances, unlike those of many other countries, were not merely due to British military spending during the war, but were 'largely due to import of Jewish capital from abroad, totalling over £70 million since the last War'; and he accused the Palestine Government of 'deliberately seeking to impoverish the country' (*Zionist Review*, 27 February 1948, p. 5). On the other hand, there were British eyes in which the Government's action seemed 'well-nigh inescapable' (*The Economist*,

this 'shocking reversal' of United States policy, and in Palestine the Jewish Agency and the Vaad Leumi on 23 March categorically rejected any plan to set up a trusteeship régime, even for a short period.[1] On the 30th, therefore, Warren Austin submitted a new draft resolution which shelved the trusteeship proposal and instead called upon the Zionist and Arab authorities in Palestine to make representatives available to the Council for the purpose of arranging a truce; it emphasized the heavy responsibility which would fall upon any party that failed to comply, called on the Arab and Jewish armed groups to cease acts of violence immediately, and requested the convoking of a special session of the General Assembly.[2] The Syrian delegate welcomed the proposal for a special session, which would have the advantage for the Arabs of tending to delay the implementation of partition, and meanwhile reserved his attitude on the truce proposal. The Jewish Agency Executive qualified its acceptance of an appeal for a truce throughout Palestine, which the British High Commissioner broadcast on 3 April,[3] by insisting on the withdrawal of 'all foreign troops and guerrillas', the removal to Trans-Jordan of all units of the Arab Legion as a British responsibility under the new Anglo-Transjordan Treaty,[4] the prevention of future incursions from Arab countries, and the stipulation that a military truce would not exclude the admission of Jewish immigrants 'whatever their age group or physical condition'. In general, Shertok, the Agency's spokesman at the Security Council, insisted that a truce should not delay the achievement of inde-pendence: the Zionists, he confidently said, had passed the threshold of statehood and refused to be turned back.[5] He charged the British with conniving at the large-scale infiltration of Arab forces across the frontiers, with continuing to arm the Arab states while denying arms to the Zionists, and with allowing the control of the Old City of Jerusalem to be assumed by Arab bands. The Zionist charges[6] that the British were deliberately leaving behind them an 'administrative chaos' in Palestine, were, however, overdrawn; since, although it was true that the British authorities refused to transfer administrative functions to a Zionist or an Arab central govern-ment before the end of the Mandate, they did transfer such functions to

28 February 1948, p. 353), especially in view of the subsequent admission that the Agency had been carrying on surreptitious black-market operations at a rate of $3 to £1 instead of the then official rate of $4.03, 'using the money for purposes [such as illegal immigration and arms-purchases] which . . . helped later in the establishment of the independent State' (*Zion*, October 1949, pp. 4–5).

[1] See Rabbi Silver, 19 and 24 March 1948: U.N., Security Council, *Official Records*, 3rd year, nos. 36–51, pp. 169, 244. Cf. *New Judaea* editorial, March–April 1948, p. 81.
[2] U.N., Security Council: *Official Records*, 3rd year, nos. 36–51, pp. 247–8.
[3] Text ibid. no. 62, pp. 8–9.   [4] See above, p. 253, note 6.
[5] See Shertok's speech to the Security Council, 1 April 1948: *Official Records*, 3rd year, no. 52, pp. 5–23.
[6] Aubrey S. Eban, to the Security Council, 14 October 1948: *Official Records*, 3rd year, no. 116, p. 31; Moshe Pearlman: *The Army of Israel* (New York, Philosophical Library, 1950), p. 126.

local authorities from time to time, and the Zionists had long been preparing the cadres of an administration which progressively assumed
authority as the British withdrew.[1]

Hitherto the Zionists had been prevented from making full use of their
man-power for offensive purposes by the shortage of arms, although they
were helped by the arrival at the end of March of a shipload from Czechoslovakia that was paid for by the dollars contributed by the Jews of the
United States.[2] At the beginning of April the Zionists were still seriously
challenged[3] by the 'Arab Liberation Army', which had by this time
publicly received the blessing of the Governments of the Arab states and
had been reinforced to a strength of between 6,000 and 7,500 men, pre-
ponderantly Syrians and 'Irāqīs with an Egyptian contingent at Gaza.
The Arab forces were based, with a large measure of British tolerance, on
localities within the territory assigned to the Arab state by the resolution
on partition. In the north, by attacking the Jewish settlement of Mishmar
ha-Emeq, twenty-seven miles south-east of Haifa, they threatened the
Jewish communications between Haifa and Tel Aviv, which had had to
be diverted over the Carmel range to avoid hostile Arab villages on the
coast road.[4] In the south, their main attack was against the Jewish 'New
City' of Jerusalem and the main road, dominated by Arab hill villages, by
which it received its essential supplies from the Jewish coastal plain
forty-five miles away. The village of al-Qastal, five miles west of Jerusalem, was a strategic point which was stubbornly contested between the
two armies; and in the early morning of 9 April, while the Haganah were
occupying this stronghold in an engagement in which the Arab commander
of the Jerusalem sector ('Abd ul-Qādir al-Husainī) was killed, two miles
nearer to Jerusalem an I.Z.L. and Stern Group force about 200 strong
attacked the Arab village of Dair Yāsīn, whose inhabitants had the reputation of being peaceable and on good terms with their Jewish neighbours.[5]
On the other hand, it was variously asserted afterwards that an Arab band
had seized the village for an attack on Jerusalem, that it was an important
point in the movements of Arab guerrillas in this sector, or even that the
Haganah regional commander in Jerusalem had authorized the attack in
order to further a plan to establish a Jewish airfield there.[6] The I.Z.L.

[1] Lehrman: *Israel, the Beginning and Tomorrow*, pp. 14, 47; cf. Rabbi Silver, 22 April 1948 in
United Nations: *Official Records of the 2nd special session of the General Assembly*, ii. 46; *New Judaea*,
May 1948, p. 125.
[2] Sacher: *Israel, the Establishment of a State*, pp. 236, 272; Kimche: *Seven Fallen Pillars*, p. 214.
[3] See Sacher, op. cit. pp. 227, 236-7; Pearlman: *The Army of Israel*, p. 99.
[4] See Sacher, op. cit. pp. 234, 236-7.
[5] The Jerusalem correspondent of *New Judaea* (January–February 1948, pp. 64–65) had
reported that they had successfully driven off an Arab band that had entered their village.
Cf. Levin: *Jerusalem Embattled*, p. 57; a correspondent in *Zionist Review*, 25 January 1952, p. 13.
[6] Dana Adams Schmidt in *New York Times*, 10 April 1948, reporting an interview given by
the I.Z.L. immediately after the attack; cf. Begin: *The Revolt*, pp. 162–3.

attackers shouted over a loud-speaker from an armoured car orders in Arabic to the inhabitants to leave their houses and take shelter within fifteen minutes. Some obeyed. The I.Z.L. afterwards claimed to have suffered appreciable casualties in the house-to-house fighting that followed;[1] but of Arabs some 250 were killed, about half of them women and children. When the International Red Cross's chief representative in Palestine visited the village two days later[2] the impression of the I.Z.L. action which he formed was that of a 'deliberate massacre' by a band of young people and adolescents 'admirably disciplined and acting only under orders', but now exulting in having given the Arabs a taste of the atrocities which they had been committing against Jews.[3] On the Red Cross representative's return to Jerusalem the Zionist authorities expressed 'horror and disgust' at his report; but on the same day the Zionist General Council ratified an agreement, concluded before the massacre, for co-operation between the Haganah and the I.Z.L. The Arabs retaliated in their turn by intercepting on the outskirts of Jerusalem a Jewish convoy bound for the isolated Hadassah Hospital and the Hebrew University on the strategic Mount Scopus ridge, and killed some seventy-seven doctors, nurses, and university teachers and students.[4]

In northern Palestine the Haganah successfully repelled the attack on

[1] Four killed and nearly forty wounded, according to Begin (loc. cit.); eight killed and fifty-seven wounded, according to the commander of the attacking force, addressing an audience of New York Jews (*New York Times*, 30 November 1948).

[2] A Jewish police officer who had previously been sent to the scene had reported one Arab killed (Graves: *Experiment in Anarchy*, p. 179), but the Jewish Agency and Haganah had done all they could to prevent the Red Cross representative from investigating (Reynier: *À Jérusalem un drapeau*, pp. 69–70, 77; Levin: *Jerusalem Embattled*, p. 59).

[3] Reynier, op. cit. pp. 71–74. On the same day as the Dair Yāsīn action the *Zionist Review* had published a half-page photograph of Jewish corpses mutilated by Arabs after a battle on the Jerusalem–Hebron road (*Zionist Review*, 9 April 1948, p. 3, and cf. 16 April, p. 7; *New Judaea*, editorial, March–April 1948, p. 83).

[4] The Zionists maintained that the convoy had been marked by the Red Shield (the Jewish equivalent of the Red Cross) and should therefore have been protected by the Geneva Conventions. It was agreed by all parties that the convoy was accompanied by armoured vehicles, and that there were Jews under arms in the Hadassah Hospital and the Hebrew University. Great authority attaches to the account given by Reynier (op. cit. pp. 80–81) since the author was head of the delegation in Palestine of the International Red Cross throughout the period of hostilities, and was called upon by the Jewish Agency to investigate this particular incident on the day on which it occurred (12 April 1948). According to Reynier, the Jews admitted to him, under insistent questioning, that they used the Red Shield convoys for revictualling and relieving their troops in the Hadassah Hospital. They contended that this was justifiable on the ground that their troops were at the hospital only for the purpose of defending it. On this Reynier observes: 'Nous avons maintenu le point de vue qu'une formation sanitaire mobile devait se déplacer sans armes et toujours séparée d'une formation de combat. Il faut choisir si l'on veut avoir recours à une protection armée, ou à celle des Conventions de Genève, donc du drapeau Croix Rouge. Toute la région du Hadassah présente une grande importance stratégique permettant de prendre les lignes arabes à revers. Le maintien d'une troupe et son revitaillement n'a donc rien à voir avec un hôpital.' Next day Reynier put these principles to the proof by travelling to the Hadassah Hospital over the same route with an unarmed party without being attacked either going or returning.

Mishmar ha-Emeq by a numerically superior Arab force commanded by
Fawzī al-Qāwuqjī,[1] and the Zionists were now ready to take the offensive
in this region. It would appear that from about the end of March arms
from Czechoslovakia began to reach the Zionists, evading the British
blockade with the help of dollars and transport furnished by the Jewry
of the United States.[2] Whatever the importance of these new armaments,
the tide of the war now set strongly in the Zionists' favour. At Tiberias
the Arab positions in the lower town were commanded by the Jewish positions higher up on the hillside; truce negotiations under British direction
were allegedly interrupted by the arrival of armed Arabs from outside;
and on 18 April the British forces evacuated the Arab population (which
in normal times was a minority of 47 per cent.) and left the town to the
Jews.[3] At Haifa the Arabs had been enabled by considerable reinforcements (consisting mainly of 'Irāqīs, Syrians, former soldiers of the Trans-
Jordan Frontier Force—a regular force maintained by the Palestine
Government, but recently disbanded—and a few Germans and other
Europeans) to take the offensive and threaten the main Zionist position,
the Hadar ha-Carmel quarter on the slope of the mountain above the
older Arab town. The Zionists also called up reinforcements, and by
19 April an open battle was imminent which the local British forces,
numerically inferior and dispersed, would be unable to control. With less
than a month to go before the end of the British mandate, the British
divisional commander decided to withdraw his force to the port area and
the main roads leading to it, so as to cover the evacuation of British troops
and stores and not to interfere in the Jewish-Arab conflict. He informed
both sides of his plan within an hour of one another on the morning of
21 April;[4] and, as the Jews took the offensive that afternoon, a flight of
the Arab civil population began and was accelerated by a 'psychological
blitz' operated by Haganah loud-speaker vans and leaflets.[5] After a night
of fighting the resistance of the Arab forces ended when their commander

---

[1] al-Qāwuqjī was already having differences with the Muftī, and this defeat was said to have
caused him to put out feelers to the Zionists for a truce, which the latter rejected (see Wilson:
Cordon and Search, p. 182, and cf. pp. 187–8; Levin: *Jerusalem Embattled*, p. 60; Kimche: *Seven
Fallen Pillars*, p. 216). Zionist rumours accused the British of supplying al-Qāwuqjī with ammunition and petrol, and credited him with having British 25-pounder guns of a new type, whereas,
according to later reports, his heavier armament consisted solely of French 75-mm. guns and
mortars (see Begin: *The Revolt*, p. 350; 14 April 1948, H.C.Deb. 5th ser., vol. 449, coll. 953–4;
Pearlman: *The Army of Israel*, p. 109).

[2] See above, p. 260, note 2; Levin, op. cit. p. 208.

[3] See Wilson, op. cit. p. 197; *Zionist Review*, 23 April 1948, p. 1; Shertok, 23 April 1948 in
U.N., Security Council: *Official Records*, 3rd year, no. 62, p. 26.

[4] Wilson, op. cit. pp. 190–2. For Arab charges of collusion between the British military
authorities and the Haganah see Jamāl al-Husainī, 23 April 1948, in U.N., Security Council:
Official Records, no. 62, pp. 13–14; cf. 14 May 1948, H.C.Deb. 5th ser., vol. 450, coll. 2429–36,
and 25 May 1948, vol. 451, col. 3.

[5] Kimche (who was himself present at Haifa), op. cit. p. 219. For similar psychological warfare later at 'Akka, see Sacher: *Israel, the Establishment of a State*, p. 245.

and his staff slipped away. Within a week the normal population of 50,000 had been reduced by flight to a mere 8,000–10,000,[1] and the number fell still further. On 25 April it was the turn of Jaffa and 'Akka to be attacked, by the I.Z.L. and the Haganah respectively, and though there was a temporary cease-fire in Jaffa under threat of R.A.F. intervention, some 30,000 of its Arab population had already fled and more followed.[2] The Zionists now estimated the total number of Arab refugees at more than 150,000, with about thirty Arab villages abandoned in the area of the proposed Jewish state.[3]

The beginnings of the mass Arab flight went back to an early stage of the Arab-Jewish fighting. As early as 27 January the High Commissioner[4] had confirmed a 'steady exodus' of Arab middle-class families who could afford to leave the country, taking with them cars and considerable quantities of household goods. In March Zionist sources estimated that 20,000–25,000 Arabs had already left Haifa and 15,000–20,000 Jaffa; and the Arab irregulars' use of conveniently situated Arab villages as bases for attacks on Jewish localities, and the consequent Jewish reprisals against such villages, had caused a substantial flight of Arabs from villages on the fringes of Jewish territory to safer places.[5] A subsequent Zionist assertion[6] that 'many weeks' before the Dair Yāsīn massacre the Arab Higher Committee had 'called on the Arab population to leave the country en masse' should be treated with reserve in the absence of positive evidence to corroborate it; but there can be no question that the publicity which the Arab press and radio gave to the massacre at Dair Yāsīn for the purpose

---

[1] According to Sacher (op. cit. pp. 243–4) and *The Economist* (2 October 1948, p. 541), on the reported authority of a British eye-witness, the leaders of the Arab civil population of Haifa received instructions from the Arab Higher Committee that they should abandon the city, since the combined armies of the Arab states would soon recover it for them, but this was denied on the Arab side.

[2] It was apparently at Jaffa that Jewish troops first succumbed to the temptation to indulge in wholesale looting (already practised there by Arab irregulars), and within a few days Jewish troops were looting the newly captured Arab suburbs of Jerusalem (see Kimche, op. cit. p. 224; Levin: *Jerusalem Embattled*, pp. 116, 135–6, 226). Ben Gurion himself afterwards admitted that the extent to which respectable Jews of all classes became involved was 'a shameful and distressing spectacle' (*Israel Government Handbook, 5712* (London, Seymour Press, 1951/52)).

[3] Major E. Laserson in *Zionist Review*, 30 April 1948, p. 5; Ben Gurion, ibid. 7 May 1948, p. 1. A later publication spoke of over 130,000 refugees by the beginning of April (Israel Government: *The Arabs in Israel*, 1952, p. 5).

[4] U.N. Palestine Commission: *First Special Report to the Security Council*, A/AC.21/9 (16 February 1948), p. 7. Cf. *Zionist Review*, 26 December 1947, p. 1; and Channing B. Richardson, in 'International Tensions in the Middle East, a Series of Addresses and Papers . . .', *Proceedings of the Academy of Political Science*, January 1952, xxiv. 483.

[5] See *Zionist Review*, 19 March 1948, p. 7, and 2 April 1948, p. 3; Sacher, op. cit. p. 149. That British officials in some cases advised Arabs to seek safety may have been the basis of later Zionist assertions that the British had stimulated the Arab panic and created the refugee problem (see Levin, op. cit. p. 104, reporting the Hebrew press; Begin: *The Revolt*, p. 179).

[6] In a pamphlet published by the American Zionist Council in December 1951, quoted by Edward Latham (ed.) in *Crisis in the Middle East* (New York, H. W. Wilson, 1952), p. 136.

of attracting sympathy greatly accelerated the demoralization and flight
of non-combatant Arabs. At this stage of the fighting the Jewish attitude
to the Arab flight was ambiguous, since, while there is clear evidence that
the civil authorities at Haifa tried to tranquillize the Arab population, the
Jewish combatants there and elsewhere made skilful use of psychological
warfare to break their opponents' morale, and the effect upon the civilians
was only what was to be expected.[1] At a later stage, the Israeli armed
forces did not confine their pressure on the Arab civilian population to
playing upon their fears. They forcibly expelled them: for example, the
population of 'Akka (including refugees from Haifa) in May; the population of Lydda and Ramla (including refugees from Jaffa) in July; and the
population of Beersheba and western Galilee in October.

There were also some Jews who sought to escape the fighting; but those
who tried to leave the country with foreign passports were required by the
Zionist authorities to produce, not merely an exemption from military
service issued by the Haganah, but also 'a receipt for taxes paid to the
Jewish authorities for its military financing and its expenditure for the
saving of Jews in Europe';[2] and these taxes were assessed at a punitive
level where the circumstances seemed appropriate. The movement of
Jews was thus officially controlled and disciplined, and a limited exodus
from Jerusalem to the coastal plain was its principal manifestation.[3]
Jerusalem was, indeed, the locality in which the Zionist cause was now
most immediately endangered, since not only was the Jewish quarter of
the Old City still under Arab blockade, but the Arabs on the heights to the
north had parts of the Jewish New City under fire.[4] Accordingly, when
on 18 April the High Commissioner proposed a local cease-fire the Jewish
Agency indicated its readiness to agree, but the Arab Higher Committee
refused. Negotiations were then begun for a cease-fire limited to the Old
City. They were conducted by a truce commission set up under the auspices of the United Nations Security Council on 23 April and consisting
of the three (United States, French, and Belgian) Consuls-General established in Jerusalem. The Zionists still had no confidence in Arab assurances of the safety and provisioning of the Jewish quarter of the Old City

---

[1] For Haifa, see above, pp. 262–3; and cf. Reynier: À Jérusalem un drapeau, p. 76; Begin: The
Revolt, pp. 164–5; Koestler: Promise and Fulfilment, pp. 207, 215.

[2] Zionist Review special correspondent, 14 May 1948, p. 6.

[3] See U.N., Security Council: Official Records, 3rd year, supplement for May 1948, p. 56,
quoting the New York Times Jerusalem correspondent, Dana Adams Schmidt; Clare Holling-
worth in Observer, 2 May 1948.

[4] It was in the strategic Arab quarter of Shaikh Jarrāh that the Hadassah hospital convoy
had been so disastrously ambushed (see above, p. 261); but when on 25 April the Palmaḥ
seized the locality they were expelled by the British, since it controlled the main road to the
north by which the remnants of the British civil administration were finally withdrawn three
weeks later. The Jews then made a second attempt to seize Shaikh Jarrāh and reopen communications with their positions on Mount Scopus dominating the Arab Old City, but failed.

if the Haganah forces there were withdrawn,[1] but agreement was reached on the 28th for a cease-fire in the Old City. On the night of 29–30 April, however, the Haganah launched an attack on the Arab and European suburb of Qatamon, which had been abandoned by its middle-class residents and which, situated along a ridge, was being used as an Arab strongpoint for firing on the Jewish suburbs which it commanded. The Haganah secured this position and held on to it when complying with a British order of 2 May for a cease-fire to permit negotiations for a wider truce. The chief point now at issue was not so much the position of the 1,700 Jews blockaded in the Old City as the provisioning of the 100,000 Jews in the New City. After the Haganah's capture of al-Qastal on 9 April convoys with much-needed food supplies had reached Jewish Jerusalem from the coast; but on 17 April the Arabs began a desperate effort to block the main road at the defile of Bāb ul-Wād, twelve miles west of the city, and were denying the Jews water as well as food, since the city received most of its water-supply by means of a vulnerable chain of pumping stations from the wells of Rās ul-'Ain, ten miles east of Tel Aviv, and these wells had been occupied by 'Irāqī irregulars, while the pipe-line had been damaged by an explosion. Parleys for a cease-fire continued, and by 9 May the Arabs' military position had so far worsened that they announced their readiness for a cease-fire throughout Jerusalem; but it was now the Jewish Agency's turn not to respond to an invitation from the High Commissioner. Their spokesman at the Security Council (the United States citizen, Emanuel Neumann) explained that, while some of their senior officials in Jerusalem would have met the High Commissioner, the members of the Executive whom he wished to see were in Tel Aviv; and Neumann added:

It is not a simple matter in these days to proceed from Tel Aviv to Jerusalem; there have been certain obstacles and difficulties. The Jewish Agency and the Jews of Palestine generally are now engaged in a serious effort to remove some of these obstacles, and it is hoped that before long it will be possible for people to move back and forth more freely.[2]

---

[1] On 8 March Ben Gurion, discussing a truce plan with the British Chairman of the Jerusalem Municipal Commission, is said to have stigmatized as an insulting suggestion the proposal to withdraw the armed Jews from the Old City and rely on Arab assurances (Graves: *Experiment in Anarchy*, pp. 155–6; cf. Bernard D. Weinryb, 'The Case of Jerusalem', *Palestine Affairs*, May 1948, p. 66: 'The Jewish Agency could not accept an Arab protectorate'). The Haganah themselves were reported to have pressed for the evacuation of the Jewish quarter before the Mandate ended (see Bilby: *New Star in the Near East*, p. 35), but continued to be overruled by the Zionist politicians, whose terms for a truce in Jerusalem were said to be the complete opening of communications 'from Tel Aviv to the Wailing Wall', as well as the withdrawal of all non-Palestinian armed Arabs (Levin: *Jerusalem Embattled*, p. 127, 7 May 1948).

[2] U.N., Security Council: *Official Records*, 3rd year, no. 65, pp. 15–16, 12 May 1948. The Agency's spokesman in Jerusalem (Walter Eytan, afterwards Director-General of the Israeli Foreign Office) had complained that during the cease-fire talks the Agency had received

In this ironical understatement Neumann was referring to a new attack which the Zionist forces had launched on the Arab positions commanding the Bāb ul-Wād road-block;[1] but, though they were initially successful, the Arabs counter-attacked and still prevented them from opening communications with the capital. The large British force in Jerusalem maintained a precarious cease-fire there from 8 to 14 May, but only by opening fire with heavy weapons on both the Arabs and the Jews when they infringed it;[2] and when on 12 May, two days before the termination of the Mandate, the High Commissioner issued new proposals for a truce,[3] the despondent Arab Higher Committee accepted but there was again no response from the Jewish Agency.[4] At 6 a.m. on the 14th the British flags were hauled down from the Government buildings,[5] the last British troops were withdrawn from Jerusalem, and within a few hours both the Haganah and the Jewish 'dissidents' were overcoming Arab resistance in a number of important localities not already occupied by them in the New City.

In the meantime, Senator Warren Austin had informally ventilated to members of the Security Council on 5 April a United States proposal, as an emergency measure to assure public order and the maintenance of public services after the end of the Mandate, that the Trusteeship Council should administer Palestine through a Governor-General until this régime should be superseded by a plan of government approved by a majority of both the Arab and the Jewish communities.[6] When a special session of the General Assembly met at the recommendation of the Security Council to consider further the future of Palestine, the United States proposal was submitted to it on 20 April.[7] Several senior Zionist officials, among whom Shertok's name was included, were said to have been willing to accept it as

off-hand treatment from the British who, he said, were 'trying to save the Arabs from too severe a beating' (*New York Times*, 9 May 1948).

[1] See U.N., Security Council, loc. cit. pp. 2–3.

[2] Truce Commission report to the Security Council: *Official Records*, 3rd year, no. 71, p. 3, document S/762.

[3] These proposals were for a cease-fire with no admission of arms or other fighting equipment; the admission of essential civilian supplies to be subject to checking by an impartial body acceptable to both sides; the routes into Jerusalem to be open for essential supplies and unarmed persons, but without any substantial increase in either the Arab or the Jewish population or in armed strength; in return for free access to the Jewish quarter of the Old City, the Jews should evacuate the Arab suburb of Qatamon.

[4] See 13 May 1948, H.C.Deb. 5th ser., vol. 450, col. 2414, and United Nations: *Official Records of the 2nd special session of the General Assembly*, ii. 268, 13 and 14 May 1948.

[5] For an impression of the final journey of the defunct Administration from Jerusalem to Haifa, see Sir William Fitzgerald, Chief Justice of Palestine: 'The Holy Places of Palestine in History and in Politics', *International Affairs*, January 1950, xxvi. 9–10.

[6] Sacher suggests that this proposal, which he regards as inspired by the British Foreign Office, encouraged the previously hesitant states of the Arab League, whose Council met during the following week, to decide on formal war against the Zionists (*Israel, the Establishment of a State*, pp. 106–8).

[7] United Nations: *Official Records of the 2nd special session of the General Assembly*, Annex to vols. i and ii, pp. 12–31, document A/C.1/277.

a temporary expedient, but to have been overruled by Ben Gurion with support from the militant extremists.[1] Warren Austin was reported to have said that he hoped that the British forces in Palestine, and those of other countries, would be available to enforce law and order under trusteeship;[2] and a vigorous line was taken about this by the Soviet Union and her satellites, whose steadfast purpose it was to destroy British influence, and prevent the growth of United States influence, in the Middle East.[3] While the protracted debate in the General Assembly continued the United States Government opened discussions with the Zionist and Arab delegations to the United Nations, suggesting that the termination of the Mandate should be postponed for ten days to allow representatives to go to Palestine to work out terms for a cessation of hostilities. The suggestion was not acceptable to either of the belligerents, or to the British;[4] and the best that the Assembly could achieve was to appoint, on 14 May, a United Nations Mediator, whose terms of reference significantly did not bind him to the letter of the Assembly's partition resolution of November 1947.[5]

Meanwhile, President Truman had intervened to transfer the supervision of Palestine affairs in the State Department from Loy W. Henderson, who had long been a target for Zionist attacks, to Major-General J. H. Hilldring, who, as alternate United States delegate at the General Assembly in the previous autumn,[6] had ardently supported the establishment of a Jewish state and had confirmed his attitude in an address at the opening rally of the 1948 Jewish Welfare Fund campaign only one day before this latest appointment.[7] As the days passed and it became evident

---

[1] See Bilby: *New Star in the Near East*, p. 260; Begin: *The Revolt*, pp. 246–7.

[2] García-Granados: *The Birth of Israel*, p. 277. Article 7 of the United States proposal had left blank the names of the governments upon whom the proposed Governor-General of Palestine might call for military help. The British Foreign Secretary stated on 4 May that his Government would have to consider most carefully an invitation to collaborate in assisting some kind of interim government in Palestine (H.C.Deb. 5th ser., vol. 450, col. 1117). The sending of British reinforcements to Palestine on 1 May had aroused great interest; but a fortnight later, when the prospects of a truce or an interim government had collapsed, the Minister of Defence declared that their only purpose was to safeguard the British evacuation (14 May 1948, ibid. col. 2439).

[3] See the Ukrainian delegate's speech of 14 May 1948 (United Nations: *Official Records of the 2nd special session of the General Assembly*, ii. 257–8); cf. Joseph Dunner: *The Republic of Israel, its History and its Promise* (New York, Whittlesey House, 1950), p. 89.

[4] See Dr. Philip Jessup, 13 May 1948 (United Nations: *Official Records of the 2nd special session of the General Assembly*, ii. 245). Supporters of Zionism spoke of strong State Department pressure on the Zionist delegates to delay the proclamation of their independence, and of hints in return that this pressure might 'force the Jewish State into the arms of the Soviet' (García-Granados, op. cit. pp. 284–5; Jon Kimche in *Reynolds News*, 9 May 1948, report from Tel Aviv; Lehrman: *Israel, the Beginning and Tomorrow*, p. 282; Dunner, op. cit. p. 96).

[5] See United Nations: *Official Records of the 2nd special session of the General Assembly*, supplement no. 2 (Resolutions), pp. 5–6, no. 186 (S–2).

[6] Carl Levin (*New York Herald Tribune*, 19 September 1947) had reported the Zionist criticisms of Henderson and expectations of 'impartiality' from Hilldring.

[7] See *New York Times*, 29 and 30 April 1948; *Zionist Review*, 7 May 1948, p. 4. The fact that

that, when the Mandate ended on 14 May, there would be neither truce nor interim arrangement to interpose between the new Jewish state and the armies of the Arab League, the difference of views between the State Department and the President's political advisers dwindled to the narrow issue of how soon United States recognition should be extended to the Jewish state. As late as 13 May the President agreed that it should be withheld for the present; the political pressure on him continued, and at midday on the 14th the Secretary of State was asking only for a few days' grace in order to consult the British and French Governments; but one of the President's political advisers, it is said, finally persuaded him to insist that recognition should be immediate.[1] According to one responsible reporter,

nobody in authority denied that a desire to beat the Russians to the punch was one factor. . . If a Jewish state was to be recognized at all, the administration felt it essential that the first government to do so should be a democracy and not a totalitarian power. Soviet Russia hardly deserved such a historic claim on the gratitude of the people of Israel. Further, so I was told, initial recognition by a democracy was necessary not only for Jews in Palestine, but even more for Jews in the United States. There had been enough talk that a Jewish state would be a Kremlin creature.[2]

In the Jewish part of Palestine an ancient people was ready to attend the miraculous rebirth of its independence.

Their faces were alight and shining. They were quiet, very quiet, as if silently praying and thanking God for His mercy that they were alive to see this day. For generation after generation they had prayed, some every day, some once a week and some once a year, for the day of redemption. It had become a routine, meaningless to most Jews—an unattainable prayer, a banished hope. Could it be true? *It was true.*[3]

The hero of the hour was the labour leader, Ben Gurion, whose courage and determination had held firm in the last weeks when his colleagues had been ready to compromise. It was he who, as Prime Minister elect, at a meeting of the Vaad Leumi convened for 4 p.m. on 14 May 1948 in the Tel Aviv Museum of Modern Art, summarized briefly the centuries-long vicissitudes and tragedies of the Jewish people, the rise of political Zionism,

this was once again a major election year in the United States, with the party conventions to nominate the presidential candidates only three months ahead, gave the Zionists a maximum opportunity for bringing Jewish political influence in the United States to bear in favour of their cause. The Government's abandonment in March of the General Assembly's partition plan was reported to have had an unfavourable effect on the Democratic Party's prospects in New York State; and, according to one Zionist source (*Zionist Review*, 7 May 1948, p. 4, despatch from Washington), it was after consultations on this issue that Major-General Hilldring was appointed by the President.

[1] See Daniels: *The Man of Independence*, pp. 319–20; *The Forrestal Diaries*, p. 440.
[2] Lehrman: *Israel, the Beginning and Tomorrow*, pp. 285–6.
[3] Kimche: *Seven Fallen Pillars*, p. 226.

the Nazi holocaust, and the proceedings before the United Nations, and proclaimed in ringing tones 'the establishment of the Jewish state in Palestine, to be called ISRAEL';[1] and, after offering full and equal citizenship to the Arab inhabitants of the state, and peace and amity to all the neighbouring states, and calling on the Jewish people all over the world to rally to Israel, he concluded: 'With trust in the Almighty God, we set our hand on this declaration at this session of the Provisional State Council in the city of Tel Aviv, on this Sabbath eve, the fifth day of Iyar, in the year 5708.'[2] Ben Gurion then read the first decrees passed by the new Government, namely the annulment of the British White Paper of 1939, together with its restrictions on immigration and land-purchase. 'It was', Kimche commented, 'the justification of a man and of an idea; the eternal warrant of the prophet, the extremist, and the agitator against the realists, the moderates, and the statesmen';[3] and, as if to add point to the contrast, the aged and weary Chaim Weizmann[4] was not even present, but was in the United States as Israel's spokesman at the United Nations and to the State Department, and it was only three days later that the Provisional Council at its first meeting elected him as its President.[5]

The immediate *de facto* recognition of Israel by the United States was announced by President Truman's staff sixteen minutes after the proclamation in Tel Aviv; the announcement interrupted the special session of the United Nations General Assembly; and, as García-Granados drove back that evening from Flushing Meadows to New York, he observed the Israeli flag flying proudly from many of its lofty buildings.[6] Indeed, the great metropolis of the United States numbered three times as many Jewish inhabitants as the whole of mandatory Palestine, and the new state—in so far as it owed its birth to the play of power politics—might be said, paradoxical though this might sound, to have been brought to birth in New York.[7] The Guatemalan Government, whose United Nations

[1] The Hebrew name for geographical Palestine was *Eretz Yisrael* ('land of Israel'); but after much discussion this was considered an inappropriate title for the state which had received only a part of Palestine under the United Nations award; and the form *Medinat Yisrael* ('State of Israel') was finally adopted: see Walter Eytan: 'The Search for a Name', *Zionist Review*, 30 January 1948, pp. 5–6.

[2] Text of the proclamation in *Zionist Review*, 21 May 1948, p. 1; *New Judaea*, May 1948, p. 121.

[3] Kimche, op. cit. p. 228.

[4] See McDonald: *My Mission in Israel*, pp. 26–28, 38, for an impression of the Zionist elder statesman at this time. He died in November 1952.

[5] One of the two Revisionist members of the Council objected that Weizmann was a British subject who had never acquired Palestinian nationality, according to Koestler: *Promise and Fulfilment*, p. 202.

[6] García-Granados: *The Birth of Israel*, p. 290. The strain of relations with Britain had its effect on the British Zionists, some of whom afterwards complained that their public rejoicing and enthusiasm, outside their private meetings, 'may have been a little shamefaced' (*Zionist Review* editorial, 30 July 1948, p. 8).

[7] *The Times* correspondent at the General Assembly had reported that, in the general view of delegates, 'regardless of its merits and demerits and the joint support given by the Soviet

delegate was García-Granados, were only one day later than the United States in recognizing Israel, and the next to follow were the Soviet Union (17 May); Poland, Uruguay, and Nicaragua (18 May); Czechoslovakia and Yugoslavia (19 May), the latter not yet being in open breach with the Soviet bloc; South Africa on 24 May, two days before the general election which was to mark the final political eclipse of General Smuts; Hungary, 1 June; Finland and Rumania, 11 and 12 June.

(vi) The Palestine War and its Aftermath, 1948–50

(a) THE PALESTINE WAR, MAY 1948 TO JANUARY 1949

(1) *From the Arab States' Intervention to the First Truce, 15 May to 11 June 1948*

As the Palestine Mandate drew towards its inglorious end the Arabs had temporarily sunk their serious internecine differences to the extent of agreeing on a joint armed intervention against the Zionists; but their preparations for such an intervention were far from complete, and as late as 14 May 1948, the date on which the Mandate expired, the Secretary-General of the Arab League, 'Abd ur-Rahmān 'Azzām, is said to have admitted that he had never expected that the Arab states would actually have to fight. The Arab army comparatively most prepared for war was the Arab Legion of King 'Abdullāh of Jordan; but even this army consisted of only four infantry battalions and one recently formed battery of field artillery, together with an improvised 'home guard', and was seriously under-equipped in important respects. It had received from Britain six 25-pounder guns a few months before, but its gunners had had only three months' training, and the Zionists for their part had manufactured large numbers of mortars and were skilful in their use; the Legion's fifty British armoured cars, though obsolete by British standards in 1941, were superior in quality but greatly outnumbered by the 800 home-made armoured cars of the Zionists; the Legion had only small reserves of ammunition, and a British consignment on its way from the Suez Canal Zone was impounded by the Egyptian army during May and never handed over. A secret Zionist mission to King 'Abdullāh on the eve of the termination of the Mandate failed to dissuade him from taking part in the pan-Arab intervention in Palestine;[1] but the Jordan Government are reliably stated to have agreed with the British Foreign Office that the Arab Legion, in occupying the area of Palestine which the General Assembly resolution of

Union and the United States, the partition scheme would have been carried in no other city than New York' (1 December 1947).

[1] See L. Avigdor in *Zionist Review*, 29 April 1949, p. 4. One of the two members of this mission was the Russian-born woman labour leader, Mrs. Golda Meyerson, acting head of the Jewish Agency's political department.

November 1947 had assigned to the Arabs, should not invade the area assigned to the Zionists.[1]

The Israelis published what purported to be a grandiose Arab plan of combined operations;[2] but, whatever the origin or authenticity of this document, it was certainly not the product of a unified Arab Command, for such a thing did not exist. The Arab armies, except for the Arab Legion, suffered from poor staff-work and organization, and the Egyptians and 'Irāqīs were operating over long lines of communication; the Egyptian combat forces were further handicapped by the corruption or negligence of headquarters staffs that caused grave deficiencies in the supply of arms and ammunition and medical services.[3] In general, moreover, the Arabs lacked the incentive and the discipline to press home their attacks against Israeli resistance that compensated for its material deficiencies[4] by its desperate tenacity in defence and resourcefulness in counter-attack. In the north the Syrian forces were checked in the Jordan valley after severe fighting, and the small Lebanese contingent never offered a serious challenge. The Egyptian army sent forward two columns across the Sinai desert into Palestine. The first advanced along the coast road through predominantly Arab territory to Isdūd (the ancient Philistine city of Ashdod), twenty miles south of Tel Aviv, and came to a halt before the main Israeli defence line; only three small Jewish settlements were abandoned to this advance, while some twenty others went 'underground' and determinedly prepared to resist.[5] The second Egyptian column advanced through entirely Arab territory via Beersheba, Hebron, and Bethlehem to the southern suburbs of Jerusalem. Meanwhile, immediately upon the British evacuation of Jerusalem on 14 May, a determined Israeli offensive was launched to dispose of the irregular Arab forces remaining on the north and south sides of the city and then to relieve the 1,700 Jews besieged in the Jewish quarter of the Old City.[6] The Arab Legion, after taking part in the occupation of the Kfar Etsion group of Jewish settlements, isolated in Arab territory twelve miles south-west of Jerusalem,[7] intervened to defend what remained of Arab Jerusalem, and began shelling the Jewish New City. In the first fortnight of fighting they inflicted upon its 100,000

[1] Bevin afterwards pointed out that the Arab Legion had intervened only 'in territory which the United Nations allocated to the Arabs', not in territory allocated to 'a proposed Jewish state' (26 May and 2 June 1948, H.C.Deb. 5th ser., vol. 451, coll. 187, 999–1000).

[2] See Levin: *Jerusalem Embattled*, p. 170, diary entry of 18 May 1948; Sacher: *Israel, the Establishment of a State*, p. 246, reporting Ben Gurion; and cf. *Zionist Review*, 11 June 1948, p. 5.

[3] These grievances of the combat forces went largely unsatisfied by subsequent inquiries, and were to lead eventually to the Egyptian military *coup d'état* of July 1952.

[4] For details see Sacher, op. cit. pp. 207–17, 272.

[5] See map C at end of volume; cf. Sacher, op. cit. pp. 251–5; Pearlman: *The Army of Israel*, pp. 131–3; Bilby: *New Star in the Near East*, p. 49.

[6] See Levin, op. cit. p. 151; Sacher, op. cit. p. 257.

[7] See above, p. 254. The Legion's intervention saved the Jewish survivors from butchery by the local Arab villagers, according to Levin, op. cit. p. 154.

civilians some 1,200 casualties, of whom 450 were killed; and slow paralysis was threatened by the cutting off of supplies and reinforcements by the road from the coastal plain, which was blocked by the Arab Legion's possession of the police fortress at Latrūn, commanding the approach to the defile of Bāb ul-Wād. Desperate and apparently ill-planned Israeli attempts to seize Latrūn failed,[1] but the Israelis by-passed the position by rapidly and secretly improving a six-mile length of donkey-track into a rough road for vehicles by which a limited amount of relief could be sent to beleaguered Jerusalem.[2] Nothing could save the outpost of traditional Jewish orthodoxy in the Old City, however; despite the Israel Government's desire to retain this ancient symbol,[3] it was compelled to surrender on 28 May, and the dust rising from its bombarded synagogues was an added bitterness for the defenders of the New City. Palestine Arab irregulars who called themselves *al-Jihād al-Muqaddas* (the 'Sacred Army') held the strategic airfield of Lydda, only twelve miles south-east of Tel Aviv; and though the 'Irāqī force sustained a severe defeat in attempting a crossing of the Jordan opposite Baisān—against Arab Legion advice—it occupied after fifteen days the Arab town of Tūl Karm only ten miles from the Mediterranean, and nearly reached the sea in the neighbourhood of the Jewish town of Hadera. The 'Irāqīs had, however, outrun their supply and ammunition columns, and an Israeli counter-offensive from the Vale of Esdraelon against the Arab town of Janīn narrowly failed.

On 17 May, three days after the open intervention of the Arab states, the United States delegation had submitted to the Security Council a resolution, under Article 39 of the Charter, ordering the belligerents to cease fire within thirty-six hours. However, the chief British delegate, Sir Alexander Cadogan, questioned both the desirability of invoking Article 39 (with its attempt to define an aggressor against whom sanctions might be taken) and the practicability of applying a stand-still order in the present fluid situation; he would have liked to see some provision for a thorough study of the juridical status of Palestine after the end of the Mandate; and he suggested that the Council should modestly try for a truce, first perhaps in Jerusalem, in the hope that it might be extended eventually to the whole country. The British Minister of State was afterwards reported to have told a member of the Parliament at Westminster on 21 May that the British diplomatic representatives in all the Arab countries had been

---

[1] See Sacher: *Israel, the Establishment of a State*, p. 261; Pearlman: *The Army of Israel*, pp. 142, 144; Kimche: *Seven Fallen Pillars*, pp. 244–5; Bilby: *New Star in the Near East*, pp. 35–36.

[2] This was the fabled 'Burma Road', afterwards to be superseded by a longer but more manageable 'Road of Courage'; see Levin: *Jerusalem Embattled*, pp. 229, 236; Sacher, loc. cit.

[3] See ibid. pp. 262–3. The French Consul-General, as chairman of the United Nations Truce Commission for Jerusalem, had reported on 17 May 1948 that the Jewish Agency had rejected Arab conditions for the surrender of some 300 combatant and 200 non-combatant Jews besieged in the Great Synagogue (U.N., Security Council: *Official Records*, 3rd year, no. 70, p. 2, document S/758).

instructed to press for a truce on any terms, and that Cadogan had likewise been instructed 'to go as far as possible in order to get a cease-fire, but
not to agree to the imposition of sanctions against the Arabs'.[1] The
intervention in Jerusalem of King 'Abdullāh's Arab Legion directed attention to the fact that British officers serving with it were actually in combat
against the Israelis,[2] and to an announcement that the British Government
would continue to give King 'Abdullāh military and financial aid, within
the terms of their treaty obligations, unless the United Nations found that
Jordan was acting illegally in occupying the areas allotted to the Arabs
by the General Assembly resolution of November 1947.[3] On 22 May
Warren Austin declared that the Arab states' justification of their intervention—that Palestine was a single country whose future, after the end
of the Mandate, should be determined by the will of the Arab majority—
was 'the highest type of evidence of the international violation of the law';
he accused Jordan of contumacy, and invited the Security Council to bind
every member of the United Nations to 'keep Abdullah where he belongs';[4] but the United States proposal to declare a breach of the peace in
Palestine, within the meaning of Article 39 of the Charter, received fewer
than the requisite seven votes.[5] The Council resolved, however, to order
a cease-fire within thirty-six hours; but two days later a majority yielded
to a request of the Arab states, supported by Cadogan, for a two-day extension of the time-limit of the cease-fire order, to enable the Arab League
to consider it. The events of the past ten days had, however, subjected
Anglo-American relations to the worst strain that they had known for
many years. British opinion had long been feeling aggrieved at the prone-
ness, as it appeared in British eyes, of the Administration at Washington
to allow at least its public gestures regarding Palestine to be influenced
too much by its awareness of the power of the Jewish vote in American
domestic politics and too little by consideration for the realities of the
situation in Palestine and for the difficulties of Britain's position there. This
(1948) was again a presidential election year; and the President's immediate
recognition of the State of Israel and the rumours that she might receive
a loan from the United States[6] were received with irritation in London.

[1] Geoffrey D. Goldstein: 'A Talk with Mr. Bevin', *Zionist Review*, 9 February 1951, p. 10.
[2] They numbered thirty-seven, of whom the majority had been seconded from the British
forces, while thirteen were civilians on contract with the Jordan Government, and three (including the Legion's commander, Brigadier J. B. Glubb) had terminated their connexion with the
British Colonial Service at the end of the Palestine Mandate and had entered the Jordan service.
At least one United States officer, Lieut.-Colonel David Marcus, was fighting on the Israeli side.
[3] *The Times* diplomatic correspondent, 19 May 1948; cf. above pp. 270–1.
[4] U.N., Security Council: *Official Records*, 3rd year, no. 72, pp. 42–44.
[5] Colombia, France, the Ukraine, the U.S.A., and the U.S.S.R. in favour; Argentina, Belgium,
Canada, China, Syria, and the United Kingdom abstaining.
[6] President Weizmann was received by President Truman on 25 May, and was reported to
have asked for a loan of $90–100 million, part of which was needed for buying tanks and anti-
tank guns (*The Times* Washington correspondent, 26 and 28 May 1948).

In the United States, on the other hand, the British arguments that the arms which the Arab states were receiving from Britain were supplied as part of her treaty obligations to them and had been ordered 'long before the present fighting',[1] and that some of the British officers serving with the Arab Legion were directly engaged by that force and not therefore subject to British orders, were treated as legalistic quibbles. Senator Brewster found support in the Senate for his suggestion that financial aid to Britain under the European Recovery Programme should be reconsidered 'to determine to what extent the United States is assisting those who both at Lake Success and in the Middle East are apparently so militantly opposing the policy of the United States';[2] and the United States press (which, British observers averred, was under constant pressure from Jewish commercial advertisers to influence its reporting of the Palestine controversy) launched into what a British correspondent in Washington described as the most serious anti-British campaign for twenty years.[3] While the United States Ambassador in London had frequent meetings with Bevin, the Arab spokesmen at the Security Council declared on 26 May that they would accept a cease-fire only on condition that the inflow of Jewish immigrants and arms into Israel ceased. On the following day Cadogan stated that no British officer was taking part in the present fighting in Jerusalem,[4] and that immediate steps were being taken to ensure that those officers seconded to the Legion from the British forces should not serve in Palestine; the obligation to pay the next instalment of the British subsidy to Jordan, which fell due on 12 July, would be reviewed in the light of the United Nations' decisions; the British Government would suspend their present deliveries of arms to Egypt, 'Irāq, and Jordan in completion of existing contracts if the Security Council should decide on a general embargo which would effectively prevent the supply of arms to Arabs and Jews alike. His Government, Cadogan continued, had tried unsuccessfully to persuade the Arab states to accept the Security Council's cease-fire proposal, 'but could not associate itself with a judgment of the situation based

---

[1] *The Times* diplomatic correspondent, 24 May 1948.

[2] *Congressional Record*, 21 May 1948, pp. 6279–81. There had been some Zionist pressure in 1946 to make the United States loan to Britain conditional on Britain's immediate admission of 100,000 Jews to Palestine. Rabbi Stephen Wise, however, had opposed this attempt to impose conditions on the loan.

[3] Frank Oliver in *Sunday Times*, 30 May 1948.

[4] *The Times* correspondent in Jerusalem had, however, reported that British officers had been engaged in the fighting there on the 26th (*Zionist Review*, 28 May 1948, p. 1, quoting the early edition of *The Times* of 27 May; cf. Bevin's equivocal answers to questions on 26 May, H.C.Deb. 5th ser., vol. 451, coll. 187–8). Bevin was afterwards reported to have told a member of Parliament on 20 May that he had ordered all British officers to be withdrawn from the Arab Legion when hostilities began, but also to have remarked that 'the purpose of leaving British officers with the Arab Legion was that it would prevent disintegration of the force, that the Legion would be disciplined, and that they would police the future Arab area' (Geoffrey D. Goldstein: 'A Talk with Mr. Bevin', *Zionist Review*, 9 February 1951, p. 10).

upon the results of that effort alone'. He therefore proposed that the Council should call on both parties to order a cessation of all acts of armed force for a period of four weeks, during which they would not introduce fighting men or men of military age or war material into Palestine; the observance of these conditions should be supervised by a number of military observers directed by the United Nations Mediator in Palestine, Count Folke Bernadotte, who had been appointed in accordance with a General Assembly resolution of 14 May.[1]

When the discussion was resumed on the 28th, the Israeli spokesman (Aubrey S. Eban, afterwards Abba Even, Israeli Ambassador in the United States) declared himself 'aghast at the malice' of the proposals to control Israel's acquisition of arms and admission of immigrants—the latter a 'humiliating limitation' of the new state's sovereignty at 'its most sensitive point of principle and conscience'—while the frontiers of the Arab states lay open for both men and material.[2] A Soviet resolution, which echoed the abortive United States resolution in calling for a cease-fire within thirty-six hours under pain of the application of sanctions under Chapter VII of the Charter, was supported by the United States but received only five votes, the same six representatives abstaining as when the United States resolution had been presented. The British resolution calling for a cessation of hostilities for one month was carried on 29 May, with the abstentions of the Soviet Union and the Ukraine; it included, at the instance of the United States, two concessions to the Israeli protest, namely that the movement of fighting men or war material should be prohibited in or into all the countries involved, instead of merely into Palestine, and that Israel might admit immigrants of military age, but should not mobilize or train them during the truce.[3] A bridge had thus been thrown across the crevasse which had been dangerously widening between the British and the United States attitudes to the Palestine fighting, and the two Governments used the weeks of respite that followed to ensure that their policies in this respect should not again come into such open and serious antagonism.

The application of the truce terms was entrusted to the United Nations Mediator in Palestine, who reported on 4 June that agreement between the parties on its coming into effect was being obstructed by the question of Jewish immigration, since the Arabs persisted in maintaining that the exclusion of all men of military age was implied. The Israeli authorities rejected this interpretation, but were ready to concede to the Mediator the supervision of their immigrants for the period of the truce. Accordingly,

---

[1] See above, p. 267. Count Bernadotte was a member of the Swedish royal family who had been active with the Red Cross during the Second World War.

[2] U.N., Security Council: *Official Records*, 3rd year, no. 76, pp. 6–7, 9.

[3] Ibid. *Official Records*, supplement for May 1948, document S/801.

on 7 June he invited the two parties to agree to a month's truce beginning on the 11th, on condition that he might admit immigrants of military age in such limited numbers as not to give the Israelis a military advantage and that such immigrants would be kept in camps under the supervision of his observers to ensure that they should not be mobilized or trained during the period of the truce.[1] The import of war materials was prohibited on both sides. The disagreement between the two parties whether or not the Arab blockade of supplies of food and water from the coast to the 100,000 Jewish inhabitants of Jerusalem[2] should be lifted was met by the provision that relief should be administered by an International Red Cross committee so as to ensure that stocks of essential supplies should not be substantially increased during the truce, the 'clear intent' being to ensure that no military advantage should accrue to either side.[3] Despite further Israeli reservations concerning the restrictions on immigration both parties accepted the truce, and it duly came into effect on 11 June with only minor infringements during the first few days.

(2) The Operation of the First Truce, 11 June to 7 July 1948

As the Security Council had made no stipulations about the nationalities of the military observers who were to supervise the application of the truce on behalf of the Mediator, the latter had inquired unofficially of the United States, Soviet, British, and French Ambassadors in Cairo on 30 May whether observers from their countries might be available. On 5 June, however, he informed the Soviet chargé d'affaires that, except for the Swedish officers whom the Mediator had himself brought to Palestine, 'it had been decided' to draw military observers only from the three countries (the United States, France, and Belgium) whose Consuls-General in Jerusalem had constituted the Truce Commission there during the past two months;[4] this, Gromyko complained, was a unilateral decision of the United States. Bernadotte afterwards remarked that, despite the enthusiasm which the representatives of the United States had shown in the Security Council for a truce, she was much slower than either France or Belgium in providing her quota of observers, partly (it would seem)

---

[1] The British Government incurred much Zionist criticism for continuing to detain in the Cyprus camps for illegal Jewish immigrants some 7,000–8,000 men of military age until January 1949, the Mediator studiously avoiding either endorsing or condemning this British action.

[2] 'Rations were smaller than in the Nazi concentration camps' (Major E. Laserson in *Zionist Review*, 2 July 1948, p. 3). 'Little over a week ago soldiers in some parts were being fed only on bread and synthetic chocolate spread. The fuel position was catastrophic and the last remnants of oil in central-heating systems throughout the city were requisitioned as fuel for the bakeries. . . . But for the situation in Jerusalem, the Government would not have agreed to the cease-fire' (Levin: *Jerusalem Embattled*, pp. 243–4, diary entry of 10 June 1948).

[3] U.N., Security Council: *Official Records*, 3rd year, supplement for June 1948, pp. 77, 79–84, documents S/823, S/826, S/829.

[4] Bernadotte: *To Jerusalem*, pp. 31, 57.

lest they should suffer casualties which would call down criticism upon the Executive during the impending Presidential election campaign.[1] He admitted that there was some force in the Israeli complaint that the Arab states received inadequate supervision in the earlier stages.[2]

The Israelis disregarded their undertaking not to import war materials during the truce, and took ample advantage of that respite to rectify their almost total lack of combat aircraft, artillery, and heavy armoured vehicles, and their serious limitations in automatic weapons and ammunition.[3] The extent to which the Palestine struggle had cut across the normal frontiers of the cold war was illustrated by the fact that, while the hard currency for these arms transactions was provided largely by the dollar contributions of United States Jewry, one of the most fruitful sources of supply was the state-owned armament factories of Czechoslovakia, where the Communists had seized power in the previous February.[4] The evacuation of the British troops from Palestine was now in its last stages, and, while both Arabs and Israelis were ready with offers of large sums of money to corruptible officers and other ranks, the Israelis in the coastal plain secured the greater part of this illicit traffic in arms and equipment, which even included some tanks.[5] The first bomber aircraft obtained by Israel were smuggled out of the United States and Britain.[6] Italy was another source of supply, in which the Haganah agents were generally successful in outwitting their Arab rivals. Meanwhile, the purchase of a shipload of arms by the militant I.Z.L. which, despite its nominal incorporation in the

---

[1] Ibid. pp. 191–3, 198.

[2] Distribution of observers on

	1 August 1948 (*131 observers*)	8 September 1948 (*315 observers*)
Israel . . .	63 per cent.	40 per cent.
Jerusalem . .	8 ,, ,,	25 ,, ,,
Arab states and Arab Palestine . .	29 ,, ,,	35 ,, ,,

(Source: U.N., General Assembly: *Official Records*, 3rd session, supplement no. 11 (S/648, *Progress Report of the United Nations Mediator*), p. 38; see also McDonald: *My Mission in Israel*, p. 41).

[3] For details see Sacher: *Israel, the Establishment of a State*, p. 272.

[4] Ehud Avriel, who was formally accredited Israeli Minister to Czechoslovakia on 20 June 1948 (*Zionist Review*, 16 July, p. 2, 15 October 1948, p. 6), was afterwards described as Ben Gurion's 'chief agent in the provision of arms in Europe' (Jon Kimche in *Commentary*, September 1952, p. 243; cf. Kimche: *Seven Fallen Pillars*, pp. 249–51; Bilby: *New Star in the Near East*, p. 42). The Israeli Communist leader, Shmuel Mikunis, afterwards claimed to have had Ben Gurion's permission in May 1948 to visit the Cominform countries for the purpose of obtaining arms (*Zionist Review*, 11 May 1951, p. 6).

[5] Two British officers and two staff-sergeants received some £20,000 from Haganah for the sale of arms; see reports of their trial in *The Times*, 21 and 28 October, 13 and 14 December 1951.

[6] The making of a documentary film had been the cover under which the leading Haganah agent in Britain had purchased aircraft for Israel. Two of his British accomplices received terms of imprisonment for their illegal export, and another man pleaded guilty to disposing of the body of a Jewish car-dealer, together with whom he had been associated with a gang engaged in smuggling aircraft and arms to Israel and cars into Britain (ibid. 26 April and 10 October 1948, 24 and 26 January, and 23 December 1950).

Israeli army, still acted with some independence, led to a conflict of policy with the Haganah, whose mortar-fire destroyed the vessel (the *Altalena*) and most of its cargo off Tel Aviv on 22 June.[1]

The General Assembly resolution appointing a Mediator for Palestine[2] had not explicitly bound him to the details of the partition plan of November 1947; and on 27 June 1948 Bernadotte, after consultation with both Jews and Arabs, put forward to them a series of 'suggestions as a possible basis for discussion'.[3] His principle was that mandatory Palestine and Trans-Jordan might together form an economic union in which a Jewish and an Arab state might regulate their common interests through a central council, with the right of appeal to the United Nations in case of disagreement, e.g. on immigration; persons who had been displaced by the fighting should have the right to return home and recover their property. The Mediator also suggested certain territorial adjustments of the November partition plan in order to bring this into conformity with the present military situation. Among the territorial proposals that he now put forward as 'worthy of consideration' were the inclusion of the whole or part of the Negev (southern Palestine) in Arab territory in return for the inclusion of the whole or part of western Galilee in Jewish territory;[4] the inclusion in Arab territory of the city of Jerusalem, with municipal autonomy for the Jewish community (whose communications with the rest of Israel had proved so precarious) and special arrangements for the protection of the Holy Places;[5] and the establishment of a free port at Haifa (to include the oil pipe-line terminals and refineries) and of a free airport at Lydda. While these suggestions had been worked out, according to the Mediator's account,[6] with his personal collaborators (notable among whom was Dr. Ralph Bunche, an official of the United Nations Secretariat who had been

[1] See Begin: *The Revolt*, pp. 154–9, 166–75; Koestler: *Promise and Fulfilment*, pp. 245–52. Some of the illicit arms had already been landed halfway between Tel Aviv and Haifa on the night of 20–21 June, and the United Nations observers failed to secure possession of these from the Israeli authorities; see U.N., Security Council: *Official Records*, supplement for July 1948, pp. 13–17, documents S/862 and S/861/Add. 1, and cf. Bernadotte: *To Jerusalem*, pp. 123–4, 188.

[2] See above, p. 267.

[3] See Bernadotte, op. cit. pp. 126–31.

[4] The provisional Israel Government's representative in London (the moderate Dr. Nahum Goldmann) had told the Mediator on 26 May that the British were considering this exchange of territories, and had commented that 'the Jewish leaders themselves were not in full agreement on the importance of the Southern Negev' (ibid. p. 10). Bevin, in his talks with the Zionist leaders in February 1947, is said to have tried to dissuade them from claiming southern Palestine (Sacher: *Israel, the Establishment of a State*, p. 128).

[5] James G. McDonald 'gathered' from a member of the United States Embassy in London at the end of July that the Mediator's proposal for Jerusalem also was 'substantially' that of the British Government (*My Mission in Israel*, pp. 20, 62, and cf. Jon Kimche in *Zionist Review*, 31 July 1948, p. 3). The Mediator, however, dismissed as irresponsible the allegation of an Israeli newspaper that he had been in direct contact with both the British and United States Governments (Bernadotte, op. cit. p. 107); for his reasons for proposing to include Jerusalem within Arab territory see ibid. pp. 152–3.

[6] Ibid. pp. 118–19.

dealing with the Palestine question since the appointment of the United Nations Special Committee on Palestine a year earlier), they certainly reflected, however indirectly, the desire of the United States and British Governments that the fighting should be ended by an understanding between Israel and Jordan. The Israel Government, however, in their reply of 7 July, not only called the Mediator's suggestion concerning Jerusalem 'disastrous ... encouraging false Arab hopes and wounding Jewish feelings', but submitted that the suggestion to unite Arab Palestine with Trans-Jordan created a new situation fundamentally affecting the territorial provisions of the General Assembly's resolutions of November 1947. Those provisions, they went on to argue, had offered Israel merely an 'irreducible minimum' entailing heavy sacrifices, and now needed improvement both to ensure Israel's security against the perils revealed by Arab aggression and to embody the gains that she had achieved in repelling it.[1]

In the meantime, as the month's truce was approaching its term, the Mediator had appealed to the belligerents on 3 and 5 July to agree to prolong it, and the British delegation moved a resolution to the same effect at the Security Council on the 7th. Israel was prepared for a prolongation, and the British Government, it was reported, 'more or less induced Transjordan, Saudi Arabia, 'Iraq, and Lebanon to agree . . . but Syria and Egypt held out for renewed fighting and eventually forced the other Arab states to come around to their viewpoint'.[2] The Egyptian, Syrian, and 'Irāqī Governments were in fact enmeshed in the web of mendacious propaganda that they had been spinning for their own public opinion during the fighting in May. Both the press accounts of the fighting and the official communiqués had been so wide of the truth that the Egyptian public in particular had been led to expect an early and complete victory —'Tel Aviv in a Week'. The acceptance by the Arab League of the truce order of 11 June therefore came as a surprise and disappointment, and a myth was created that it alone had saved Israel from disaster.[3] The Arab leaders knew that their stocks of military equipment, especially ammunition, had never been adequate for war, and they could not be readily replaced on account of the United Nations embargo. 'The Lebanese

---

[1] U.N., Security Council: *Official Records*, 3rd year, supplement for July 1948, pp. 27–30, document S/870.

[2] *Christian Science Monitor* Lake Success correspondent, 10 July 1948; cf. *The Times*, 10 July 1948. It was charged against King Fārūq, after his enforced abdication in 1952, that he had forced an unwilling Egyptian Government (led by Mahmūd Fahmī an-Nuqrāshī) and army into the war against Israel.

[3] 'Azzām himself, the Secretary-General of the Arab League, had told the Mediator on 30 May that 'the strategic and technical position of the Arab forces was particularly favourable . . . so that they would have no great difficulty in bringing about a military decision to their advantage in a very short time' (Bernadotte: *To Jerusalem*, p. 34). The 'Irāqī delegate to the General Assembly afterwards declared that 'the Arab armies were converging on Tel Aviv and were on the point of liquidating the Zionist threat when the Mediator intervened' (17 November 1948, *Official Records of the 3rd session of the General Assembly*, part I, First Committee, p. 663).

and Syrian armies had shown grave deficiencies, [and] Saudi Arabian
and Yemeni aid other than vocal had been negligible';[1] but in the Arab
countries the drastic application of a censorship, which the authorities had
learnt how to operate in collaboration with the British during the Second
World War, had expunged unfavourable news from both the local and the
foreign press and stifled any criticism of the Arab leadership,[2] with the
result that public opinion, misled into expecting early victory, clamoured
for a renewal of the fighting. Among the adverse factors which had been
concealed from the public was the disintegration, during the month's truce,
of the precarious understanding among the Arab leaders. At the meeting
of the Arab League in April which had determined their intervention in
Palestine when the Mandate expired, they had made a self-denying ordinance not to aim at territorial self-aggrandizement, but only to save Palestine from Zionism and restore the country to its people.[3] However, the
first month of fighting had confirmed King 'Abdullāh, the most realistic
of the heads of the Arab states, in the opinion that Israel was an established
fact that could not be 'driven into the sea' by the weight of Arab arms.
What remained of Arab Palestine was in no sense capable of a healthy
separate existence; and there were several influential Palestine Arab
families, long opposed to the policy of the Muftī of Jerusalem and his Arab
Higher Committee, who favoured the incorporation of Arab Palestine in
'Abdullāh's 'Kingdom of the Jordan'. The British Government and the
Mediator evidently approved;[4] and in the last week of June 'Abdullāh
visited Kings Fārūq[5] and Ibn Sa'ūd—the latter his old opponent whom
he had not seen for twenty-five years—and put his argument to them.
At the time of his intervention in Palestine in mid-May 'Abdullāh had

---

[1] *The Times* Cairo correspondent, 11 February 1949. The following percentages of the proportions of Arab and Israeli prisoners taken on the various fronts illustrate their relative importance:

	Arab prisoners (total, 5,458) per cent.	Israeli prisoners (total, 942) per cent.
Jordan–'Irāq front . .	67·8	77·0
Egyptian front . . .	30·2	16·8
Syrian front . . .	1·4	5·7
Lebanese front . . .	0·6	0·5

(Source: Shabtai Rosenne: *Israel's Armistice Agreements with the Arab States* (Tel Aviv, Blumstein
for the International Law Association, Israel Branch, 1951), p. 64, note 1). The Israelis also
took thirteen British prisoners and two others fighting with the Arabs.

[2] *The Times* Middle East correspondent, 2 August 1948.

[3] Majid Khadduri: 'The Scheme of Fertile Crescent Unity' in *The Near East and the Great
Powers*, ed. Richard N. Frye, pp. 155, 158.

[4] See above, pp. 270–1, and Esmond Wright: 'Abdallah's Jordan: 1947–1951', *Middle East
Journal*, Autumn 1951, v. 445.

[5] Fārūq had informed the Mediator on 7 June that he had just received a complaint from the
Jordan Foreign Minister that the flag used by the Egyptian forces in the Palestine campaign
was four inches larger than the Jordan flag of the Arab Legion; this had led to 'serious com-
plications' (Bernadotte: *To Jerusalem*, p. 69).

declared that the Arab Higher Committee no longer represented the Palestine Arabs, and sought to win over its treasurer, Ahmad Hilmī Pāshā, by nominating him governor of Jerusalem. While in Cairo 'Abdullāh had a meeting with the Muftī, the rival whom he had not seen since the Muftī's flight from Jerusalem to avoid arrest by the British in 1937; but all this was to no purpose. The attitude of the political committee of the Arab League was revealed by its announcement on 9 July of the formation of an 'administrative council' for Palestine under the chairmanship of Ahmad Hilmī, and with the Muftī's relative, Jamāl al-Husainī, as member for internal security[1]—a patent rejection of 'Abdullāh's proposals.

(3) *The Ten Days' Campaign, 8–18 July 1948*

The absence of a common Arab political purpose, and therefore of an agreed military plan, became immediately obvious when, on the expiry of the truce, an Egyptian force went into action in south Palestine in the early morning of 8 July. The Israelis were fully prepared to attack the Arab Legion at their most advanced outposts in the coastal plain, Lydda airport and the neighbouring Arab town of ar-Ramla, only twelve miles south-east of Tel Aviv. The Arab Legion was faced with an imminent Israeli attack on its positions in Jerusalem, which the local Israeli commander was said to have boasted that he could take within four days;[2] the instalment of the vital British financial subsidy to Jordan which was due on 12 July was being withheld pending the Security Council's consideration of the situation, as was the British supply of arms and ammunition. The Legion was thus faced with material paralysis, and its commander, Glubb Pāshā, considered that he must not hazard his force farther west than the strong point of Latrūn commanding the main road between Jerusalem and the coast and must yield Lydda and Ramla to the Israelis. The Israelis were therefore allowed to occupy the two towns.[3] This withdrawal by the Arab Legion appeared to the other Arab states as an unqualified act of desertion, for the Israelis expelled the Arab civilian population of Lydda and Ramla, to the number of 60,000, including Arab civilians from Haifa who were already refugees, and meanwhile the Israelis were occupying virtually the whole of western Galilee, including the Arab town of Nazareth, and were making some gains against the Egyptians on the southern front. In

[1] *New York Times*, 12 July 1948.
[2] Kimche: *Seven Fallen Pillars*, p. 255; and cf. U.N., Security Council: *Official Records*, 3rd year, supplement for July 1948, p. 65, document S/891 (report by the president of the Jerusalem Truce Commission, 11 June 1948).
[3] But see Pearlman: *The Army of Israel*, pp. 151–3; Sacher: *Israel, the Establishment of a State*, pp. 278–81. The Israelis were helped by the use of two Cromwell tanks which they had acquired by corrupting some British soldiers immediately before the final British withdrawal from Haifa (Bilby: *New Light in the Near East*, p. 43; Gershon Agronsky in *Zionist Review*, 10 September 1948, p. 7).

Jerusalem they were checked, and they failed also to cut the Arab Legion's communications with Latrūn. After the United Nations Mediator had flown to Lake Success to report in person to the Security Council, Philip C. Jessup, who had taken the place of Warren Austin as chief United States delegate, had moved a resolution on 13 July ordering a cease-fire within three days, on pain of sanctions under Chapter VII of the Charter. It was stated that the young Israeli chief of military operations and his military colleagues urged their Government 'not to accept the cease-fire but to drive on to victory', and in Israel Cadogan's immediate support for the United States resolution was sarcastically compared with the stubborn opposition to sanctions against the Arabs which he had maintained in May.[1] However, even if the second truce, adopted by the Security Council on 15 July and coming into force on the 18th, denied the Israelis further successes, they had good reasons for satisfaction, for during the ten days' fighting between the two truces they had won from the Arabs some three times the amount of territory that they had gained during the fighting of the first month; and the disunity of the Arab states had been greatly aggravated by Jordan's failure to defend Lydda and Ramla.[2]

(4) The Second Truce, and the Murder of the United Nations Mediator, 17 September 1948

The observance of the second truce was chequered by numerous failures by both sides to comply with its terms, so that desultory warfare continued, notably in Jerusalem. The Israelis, flushed by their recent successes, were inclined to deal summarily with localities from which Arab irregulars had attacked their communications.[3] The Egyptians in the south refused to allow Israeli road convoys to provision the twenty-five Negev settlements until the Israelis ceased to supply them by air, while the Israelis refused to discontinue this means of supplying them or submit it to United Nations supervision until the Egyptians allowed the road convoys to pass. Similarly, as the Arab Legion still held the Latrūn pumping-station on the water pipe-line from the coast to Jerusalem, the Jordan Government refused to allow pumping to be resumed to the 100,000 Jews in the New City, on the ground (which did not satisfy the Mediator) that the Israelis had

[1] See Zionist Review, 30 July 1948, p. 5, 20 August 1948, p. 1; Kimche: Seven Fallen Pillars, pp. 252–5.

[2] The £500,000 instalment of the British subsidy to Jordan, which had been withheld on 12 July, was paid on the 28th in recognition of Jordan's acceptance of the new truce.

[3] United Nations observers established that 'less than 130' villagers were killed or missing as the result of an Israeli 'police raid' against three Arab villages in the foothills of the Carmel range during the week after the coming into force of the second truce; the remainder of the inhabitants were expelled and two of the villages destroyed. The Secretary-General of the Arab League and some Arab states had complained that those captured and massacred amounted to tens of thousands (Progress Report of the United Nations Mediator: General Assembly, Official Records, 3rd session, supplement no. 11 (A/648), p. 40).

not complied with the truce clause providing for the demilitarization of Jerusalem.[1]

Antagonism between the Mediator and the Israel Government can be traced back to within ten days of his arrival in Palestine, when he took such exception to Shertok's 'highly irritated' criticisms of his truce proposals as to threaten him 'without mincing matters' with the disapproval of the Security Council and world opinion.[2] The tension was, however, greatly increased by Bernadotte's putting forward on 27 June, as 'worthy of consideration', the suggestion that Jerusalem should be included within Arab territory.[3] The majority of the Arab states (probably on account of their growing disagreement with King 'Abdullāh) were prepared at the end of July to consider the demilitarization of Jerusalem, which they had found wholly unacceptable a month before; it was now the Israel Government's turn to make this demilitarization conditional on the withdrawal of the Mediator's suggestion to place Jerusalem under Arab rule;[4] and meanwhile the extremists of the I.Z.L. and the Stern Group, who were determined to resist the Mediator's proposal, had concentrated their forces in Jerusalem.[5] The Stern Group, under the direction of their leader Nathan Friedman-Yellin, had recently taken on an extreme Left-wing character.[6] From the very beginning of the first truce the Stern Group had adopted a threatening attitude towards the Mediator and his United Nations observers,[7] and openly demonstrated against him when he visited Jerusalem

[1] See Bernadotte: *To Jerusalem*, pp. 141, 145, 203. The Mediator eventually ruled that, in return for the Israelis' withdrawal from two Arab villages which they had occupied after the truce, the Latrūn pumping-station should be placed under the control of a United Nations observer, and he hoped that pumping to Jerusalem could be resumed in a couple of days; but before the armed United Nations guards had been sent in answer to his request, Arabs (possibly irregulars) completely demolished the pumping-station with explosive charges on the night of 11/12 August. The Israelis then brought into use a pipe-line of their own and held on to the two villages.

[2] Ibid. p. 60.   [3] See above, p. 278.

[4] Statements by Shertok (28 July) and Bernard Joseph (3 August 1948): *Progress Report of the United Nations Mediator*, pp. 12–13.

[5] The Irgun were induced to hand over to the Haganah for trial five British officials of the Jerusalem Electric Corporation whom they had arrested on 6 July 1948 on suspicion of espionage; but a British Jewess has described how in August she and Jews of her acquaintance were interrogated under torture by the Stern Group on a similar charge (see Pauline Rose: *The Siege of Jerusalem* (London, Patmos Publishers, 1949), pp. 74–85). The significant feature is the independence of action of the extremist groups.

[6] Martin Ebon: 'Communist Tactics in Palestine', *Middle East Journal*, July 1948, ii. 265, n. 17. When Henry Wallace opened the convention of his party in the United States presidential campaign of 1948, 'the only literature distributed at Mr. Wallace's press conference was that of . . . the Stern group who have set up offices here for Wallace delegates' (*The Times* Philadelphia correspondent, 25 July 1948). The former Haganah commander-in-chief, Moshe Sneh (for whom see above, pp. 194 and 221, note 5), had also, after revisiting his native Poland under its Communist régime in 1947, decided that 'the young Jewish state could gain more by orienting itself toward the Soviet Union than it had achieved by attachment to London and Washington' (Ebon, loc. cit. pp. 266–7).

[7] The Soviet bloc had protested vigorously at the Security Council against the non-admission

from 9 to 11 August.[1] Significantly, a section of the Israeli press accused the Mediator of having, as representative of the International Red Cross, had dubious dealings with Himmler during the last stages of the Second World War[2] and of being now an agent of 'Anglo-American imperialism' and of the 'oil interests'. Apart from these extravagant charges, the Israel Government and virtually the whole of the press were hostile to the Mediator and his United Nations observers, charging them with partiality in favour of the Arabs or with ineffectiveness.[3] Early in September the Mediator was greatly concerned by the tense situation in Jerusalem, and was considering transferring to that city his own headquarters (then on the island of Rhodes, whose air communications with Palestine would be affected by the winter storms) and the headquarters of his observers, then at Haifa. The leader of the Stern Group, without presumably knowing of the Mediator's intention at this stage, had concluded an article in his Tel Aviv news-sheet on 6 September with the words: 'The task of the moment is to oust Bernadotte and his observers. Blessed be the hand that does it.'[4] When, however, reports of the threatening attitude of the Jewish extremist organizations in Jerusalem were brought to the attention of the Israeli authorities, they did not appear to be alarmed. Their military governor in Jerusalem, Bernard Joseph, was against the Mediator's establishing himself in the city; and Shertok stated on 14 September that the Cabinet had postponed taking a decision to dissolve the extremist organizations because some Ministers hoped to persuade them to disband peacefully.[5] Two days later, on the eve of the Mediator's arrival, Shertok himself and the director of military operations were reported to have criticized the United Nations observers publicly at a press conference in Tel Aviv.[6] The Mediator, visiting the Jewish-occupied part of Jerusalem on 17 September for the first time since the Stern Group demonstration against him in August, was accompanied by an Israeli liaison officer but had no armed escort.[7] His car was obstructed by a jeep, and one of a group of four men

of Soviet observers into Palestine (see above, p. 276), and maintained a consistent attitude of criticism of Count Bernadotte, who was accused of having recruited volunteers for Finland when she was attacked by the Soviet Union in 1939 (cf. V. Berezhkov: 'The Assassination of Count Bernadotte', *New Times*, 29 September 1948, p. 30, reprinted in *Daily Worker*, 19 October).

[1] U.N., Security Council: *Official Records*, 3rd year, no. 116 (14 October 1948), p. 15.

[2] Bernadotte: *To Jerusalem*, p. 158.

[3] Ibid. p. 222; cf. McDonald: *My Mission in Israel*, p. 47.

[4] U.N., Security Council: *Official Records*, 3rd year, supplement for October 1948, p. 5 (report from the Acting Mediator, Ralph J. Bunche, document S/1018, 27 September 1948).

[5] McDonald, op. cit. pp. 62–65.

[6] *New York Times* Jerusalem correspondent, 19 September 1948.

[7] The absence of an escort gave rise to a variety of explanations. The United States special envoy to Israel understood that the Mediator had been 'unwilling to enlarge Israel's authority' by accepting an escort (McDonald, op. cit. p. 85, diary entry of 25 September 1948), and an Israel Government statement of 3 May 1949 commented that he 'took the view that owing to his position an armed escort was unnecessary and . . . undesirable. . . . It was for this reason that no armed protection was accorded him' (Security Council document, S/1315, p. 1, paragraph 3).

in Israeli army uniform shot him and a French observer dead at point-blank range. The perpetrators were alleged to have been immediately smuggled by air to Czechoslovakia; they were subsequently stated to belong to an organization called Hazit ha-Moledeth or 'Fatherland Front', ostensibly an offshoot of the Stern Group which was repudiated by the main body.[1]

After the murder more than twenty hours were allowed to elapse before Bernard Joseph ordered a curfew in Jerusalem, during which time members of the Stern Group were still moving freely there, while its 'official spokesman' issued a statement accusing British intelligence officers of having committed the crime.[2] The excuse offered for the delay was that the Israeli military authorities had been reluctant to move troops from their defence positions in Jerusalem because they expected Arab attacks;[3] but those Stern Group members who were arrested by the Israeli police were allowed to escape[4] or were gradually released. Friedman-Yellin and his operations commander were sentenced on 10 February 1949 to eight and five years' imprisonment respectively for membership of a terrorist

Ralph Bunche had, however, reported that, while the Mediator never requested an armed escort, whenever local authorities saw fit to provide one 'it was accepted by him without question . . . as it had been on some of his earlier visits to territory under Israel control' (U.N., Security Council: *Official Records*, 3rd year, supplement for October 1948, pp. 6–7, document S/1018, 27 September 1948); and the *Manchester Guardian*'s Tel Aviv correspondent finally reported the Israel Government as admitting, in a memorandum to the Swedish Government, that the Mediator 'was not provided with an escort because it was thought he would not like one' (*Manchester Guardian*, 20 June 1950).

On 28 August Sa'ūdī Arabian irregulars serving with the Egyptian forces murdered two United Nations observers whose aircraft had landed at Gaza airfield without advance warning (*Progress Report of the United Nations Mediator*: General Assembly, *Official Records*, 3rd session, supplement no. 11 (A/648), p. 40, paragraph 16).

[1] An Israeli military court expressed its conviction that the actual murderers and the 'Fatherland Front' organization, if it actually existed, came from the ranks of the Stern Group, but that there was no proof that they had acted by order of the Group (Security Council document S/1315, 3 May 1949, annex, pp. 3–5. The letters LHY in this document were the abbreviation of the Stern Group's official Hebrew title, *Lohmei Herut Yisrael*, 'Fighters for the Freedom of Israel').

[2] See *The Times* Tel Aviv correspondent, 19 October 1948; the Israeli representative to the United Nations, 5 May 1949: *Official Records of the 3rd session of the General Assembly*, part II, *Ad hoc* Political Committee, Summary Records, p. 244.

The Israeli police afterwards arrested two South African Jews who had formerly moved in British circles in Jerusalem, alleging them to be agents of both the Stern Group and the British Intelligence (see Bilby: *New Star in the Near East*, p. 134). Soviet propaganda rapidly seized on the insinuation that the British had organized the crime (see V. Berezhkov: 'The Assassination of Count Bernadotte', *New Times*, 29 September 1948, p. 31; G. Osipov: 'The Palestine Doings of Charles Clayton', ibid. 22 December 1948, p. 11.)

[3] See McDonald: *My Mission in Israel*, pp. 70–74.

[4] 'When the Stern Group prisoners at Jaffa turned their jail into a Gilbertian satire by disarming their guards, taking over the prison and giving a party to their friends, with police sergeants acting as bar-tenders, most people felt that a heroic joke had been played—that here was an exploit no Jew could fail to admire. "You've got to hand it to those boys" was the attitude even of the staidest legalists' (Michael Davidson in *Observer*, 24 October 1948, after a visit to Israel; cf. Sacher: *Israel, the Establishment of a State*, p. 132) and *Survey* for 1939–46: *The Middle East in the War*, p. 321, note 3.

organization, but were released under the simultaneous proclamation of a general amnesty, and Friedman-Yellin took his seat in the Israeli Parliament to which he had just been elected. The Swedish Government complained of the serious negligence of the Government of Israel in investigating Count Bernadotte's murder, and nearly two years passed before the breach was closed by an Israeli admission of 'organizational deficiencies and inexperience'.[1]

(5) *Israel's Offensives of October 1948*

Meanwhile, the imposition of the second truce had left the leaders of the Arab states to their manœuvres, during the summer of 1948, over the political status of a Palestine in which they were still so far from achieving their military objectives. An 'Arab Government of All Palestine' under the presidency of the Muftī was proclaimed on 20 September, and received the recognition of all the Arab states except Jordan during October. Installed in Gaza, it exercised a temporary, shadowy authority in that part of south Palestine occupied by the Egyptian forces; but King 'Abdullāh's supporters had meanwhile been organizing a 'National Palestine Congress'; and on 1 October 5,000 notables, claiming to represent the Palestine Arabs and the people of Trans-Jordan, met at 'Ammān to denounce the Gaza Government and call on 'Abdullāh to take Palestine under his protection.[2] The Israeli forces, which had meanwhile been receiving a steady supply of war material by means of the surreptitious supply line from Czechoslovakia and other sources,[3] thus had reason to believe that if they refrained from attacking the Arab Legion on the Jerusalem–Latrūn front, the Legion might remain indifferent to an Israeli offensive on the Egyptian front. The Mediator's progress report (published in mid-September) recommended[4] that, in return for Israel's retaining western Galilee, now occupied by her but awarded to the Arabs by the General Assembly's resolution of November 1947, she should yield to the Arabs all that part of Palestine south of a line from Majdal to Fallūja which the General Assembly had awarded to Israel. The Israelis refused, however, to abandon the twenty-five settlements in the Negev south of that line[5] or the possibility of finding mineral resources in the remoter desert; and the continuing dispute with the Egyptian forces occupying south Palestine concerning the provisioning of those beleaguered settlements[6] gave them

[1] See *New York Times*, 10 March, 20 June, 6 July 1950.

[2] Esmond Wright: 'Abdallah's Jordan, 1947–1951', *Middle East Journal*, Autumn 1951, v. 445–6; *New York Times*, 2 October 1948.

[3] The British Foreign Office estimated that the Israeli air force, after deducting losses in combat, increased from 40 to 114 machines between the first truce and the end of 1948 (*The Times* diplomatic correspondent, 6 January 1949).

[4] See U.N., General Assembly: *Official Records*, 3rd session, supplement no. 11 (A/648), p. 18.

[5] See map C at end of volume, and McDonald: *My Mission in Israel*, pp. 48–49, 80.

[6] See above, pp. 271–2 and 282.

a pretext for direct action in this sector. Early in October the Israeli General Staff, insisting on Egyptian satisfaction of their claim to send road convoys to the settlements, obstructed the posting of a permanent United Nations observer to this area and at the same time systematically trans-ferred to it troops and equipment from all the other fronts.[1] On 14 October they informed the United Nations Chief of Staff that they would dispatch a road convoy on the following morning, and later declared that the Egyptians had attacked it; the Egyptian army commander counter-charged that an Israeli armoured-car attack had been launched in the vicinity during the night, and that this became part of a general offensive in the morning of the 15th.[2] The Israelis, now enjoying for the first time a superiority in the air, made substantial gains of territory against stiff Egyptian resistance,[3] capturing Beersheba on the 21st, Bait Hanūn (only five miles north-east of Gaza) on the 22nd, and Bait Jibrīn (in the direction of Hebron)[4] soon afterwards; an Egyptian brigade in the area of al-Fallūja was isolated, but held out under its Sudanese commander for another three months.[5]

While both sides accepted a cease-fire with effect from 22 October, the Israel Government strongly resisted a proposal, suggested by Ralph Bunche as Acting Mediator and supported in the Security Council by the British and Chinese delegations, that, in return for satisfaction in the matter of the sending of convoys to the Negev settlements, they should withdraw their forces to the positions from which they had advanced on the 14th. The Israeli delegate objected that part of the territory occupied since that date had been awarded to Israel by the General Assembly's resolution of November 1947, and declared that it was deliberate British policy to detach it from Israel, although the processes of 'settlement,

---

[1] U.N., Security Council: *Official Records*, 3rd year, supplement for October 1948, document S/1042 with Annex I, pp. 58–60, 62–63; cf. the Israeli delegate, Aubrey S. Eban, and the Acting Mediator, Ralph Bunche, 19 October, ibid. no. 118, pp. 7–17; Bilby: *New Star in the Near East*, pp. 49–50.

[2] U.N., Security Council: *Official Records*, 3rd year, no. 118, p. 4, and supplement for October 1948, pp. 55–56. The Israeli army claimed that the Egyptians had already attacked Israeli positions on 6 and 9 October (Pearlman: *The Army of Israel*, pp. 173, 176; McDonald: *My Mission in Israel*, p. 59); but Sacher writes candidly that he finds the question 'rather academic . . . The Egyptians by blundering managed to shoulder most of the blame' (*Israel, the Establishment of a State*, p. 295).

[3] See Pearlman, op. cit. pp. 188, 215; Sacher, op. cit. p. 299.

[4] The Israeli force that captured Bait Jibrīn advanced eastwards in the direction of Hebron, but was driven from the hills by the Arab Legion (the Egyptian forces having already been with-drawn from their Hebron–Bethlehem salient). According to Sacher (op. cit. p. 263) Ben Gurion about this time contemplated an attack on the Arab Legion position at Rāmallāh, north of Jerusalem, with the intention of advancing to the River Jordan, but was overruled by his Cabinet colleagues.

[5] Egyptian propagandists compared this exploit with that of the defence of Stalingrad. See Ahmad Husain (president of the extremist Young Egypt party): *The Defence of El Faluje* (London, published by the author, pamphlet no. 6, 1949).

construction, and development' were already going on there.[1] By way of counter-attack, Israel Government spokesmen asked the United Nations to investigate reports that a British battalion had recently entered Palestine from Trans-Jordan and was concentrated near Jerusalem, and accused Britain of violating the truce by supplying arms to 'Irāq and possibly other Arab countries; but these allegations were not pressed when the British Foreign and War Offices categorically denied them.[2] The Security Council adopted on 16 November a compromise resolution instructing the Acting Mediator to call upon the belligerents to negotiate for an armistice which would define permanent demarcation lines and enable a withdrawal and reduction of armed forces; and Israel found fine-drawn arguments for retaining her recent conquests.[3]

Fighting had also broken out on 22 October on the north-eastern frontier of Palestine, where the truce lines had left part of northern Galilee under the occupation of the 'National Liberation Army' commanded by Fawzī al-Qāwuqjī and based on Lebanon (whose own forces had ceased to play any significant part in the war). Both the Israelis and al-Qāwuqjī's forces appear to have transgressed the truce lines, and the former refused to allow investigation by the United Nations observers on the ground that the observers had 'already interfered . . . beyond their authority'. After al-Qāwuqjī's forces had refused to withdraw from hill positions which they had reoccupied within the Israeli truce lines, the Israelis defied a warning by the United Nations Chiefs of Staff and launched a large-scale attack which by 31 October had entirely cleared Palestinian territory of al-Qāwuqjī's forces and had occupied some fifteen villages situated two to six miles within Lebanese territory at its south-east corner.[4]

---

[1] See U.N., Security Council: *Official Records*, 3rd year, no. 122, pp. 17–21, and no. 124, pp. 13–18, 28 October and 4 November 1948. All the settlements in this region had in fact been established since the issue of the 1939 White Paper, with the primary purpose of establishing a claim to possession; and their total population was only some 2,000 (see Sacher: *Israel, the Establishment of a State*, p. 251).

[2] Hal Lehrman, indeed, admits that the arms embargo had operated as a 'strictly one-way affair . . . against the Arabs. Everybody knew how weapons had flowed to Israel from Czechoslovakia. United Nations observers had stood by in comic helplessness while Haifa stevedores unloaded guns for Israel' (*Israel, the Beginning and Tomorrow*, p. 290).

[3] The Israel Government informed the Security Council on 19 November that they had withdrawn all the forces that had advanced into newly won territory since 14 October (Security Council document S/1051, 19 November 1948); but they sought to reconcile this statement with their actual retention of the newly occupied area by claiming that Israeli mobile forces had previously been operating there behind the Egyptian lines and that therefore this was not territory that had been newly won by them.

[4] Report by the Acting Mediator, 6 November 1948: U.N., Security Council: *Official Records*, 3rd year, supplement for November 1948, document S/1071; cf. Sacher, op. cit. pp. 300–2.

The *Zionist Review* had already reported the existence of a 'Free Lebanese movement' in Israel (15 October 1948, p. 5), and the Israeli delegate afterwards informed the Security Council that some southern Lebanese (Shi'ī) villages had asked to be taken under Israeli military

(6) *Stalemate at the United Nations, October to December 1948*

Meanwhile, the first committee of the United Nations General Assembly had begun to debate the territorial and other recommendations of the late Mediator's progress report,[1] which were unreservedly supported by Britain, while the United States more tepidly accepted them as a basis for the peaceful adjustment of differences. In drawing up these recommendations shortly before his murder in September, Bernadotte had discarded his suggestion of 27 June to include the Jerusalem area in Arab territory, and had proposed instead that Jerusalem should be placed under effective United Nations control with the maximum possible local autonomy for its Arab and Jewish communities. The late Mediator had, however, retained the proposal that Israel should relinquish the greater part of south Palestine, which at that time she had not yet occupied, in return for regularizing her *de facto* occupation of western Galilee. The Israeli spokesmen, Shertok and Eban, uncompromisingly claimed both the whole of south Palestine to the Gulf of 'Aqaba, in accordance with the General Assembly's resolution of November 1947, and the entire area of Galilee as now being 'in the hands of Israel because of successful defence'. They asserted that the Jewish New City of Jerusalem must be an integral part of Israel, while favouring United Nations control of the Arab-held Old City as containing the great majority of the Holy Places; and, recalling that the General Assembly's resolution of November 1947 had envisaged an independent status for Arab Palestine, they opposed the late Mediator's more practical recommendation to combine what remained of it with Trans-Jordan. While the United States delegation argued that if Israel claimed territory in addition to the General Assembly's partition award (e.g. western Galilee) she must offer the Arabs an appropriate exchange through negotiations, representatives of the Soviet bloc accused Britain and the United States of having influenced the late Mediator's recommendations in order to satisfy their own strategic and oil interests in south Palestine.[2] The Soviet bloc continued to insist that Arab Palestine should be an independent state, and strongly opposed the British support of the late Mediator's recommendation

---

authority (16 November 1948, U.N., Security Council: *Official Records*, 3rd year, no. 126, p. 26; cf. Roy Alan: 'Lebanon, Israel's Friendliest Neighbour', *Commentary*, June 1952, xiii. 556–7). The Israelis raised small detachments for their army from the Durūz and Circassian minorities in northern Palestine, and already before the end of the British mandate the terrorist Stern Group had enlisted the support of the Abū Ghawsh (Ghosh) family, which was of Bosniak origin and which from its village stronghold had exacted safe-passage money from travellers between Jaffa and Jerusalem from an early date in the nineteenth century down to the establishment of a British administration in Palestine (see *Zionist Review*, 27 August 1948, p. 9; *Israel Economist*, July 1952, viii. 144).

[1] U.N., General Assembly: *Official Records*, 3rd session, supplement no. 11 (A/648), p. 18.

[2] Petroleum Development (Palestine) Ltd., a subsidiary of the Anglo-American-French Iraq Petroleum Co., had in fact done some test drilling and prospecting in this area; see *Petroleum Times: Review of Middle East Oil* (London, June 1948), pp. 64–65.

to combine Arab Palestine with Trans-Jordan, with rectifications in favour of other Arab states where desirable. The other Arab states led by Egypt not only rejected any acknowledgement of Israel's *de facto* existence but, having recognized the Muftī's shadowy 'Government of All Palestine', strongly objected to the proposal to award Arab Palestine to King 'Abdullāh, the friend of Britain who, they declared, had 'deserted' the Arab cause in July and had kept his Arab Legion strictly on the defensive while Israel was making her gains on the Egyptian and Lebanese fronts in October.[1] The *New York Herald Tribune*'s correspondent in Israel had travelled to 'Ammān and back as a personal intermediary between Ben Gurion and 'Abdullāh,[2] and negotiations between the Israeli army and Arab Legion for a cease-fire in the Jerusalem sector were concluded on 30 November, while on the following day a congress of 2,000 Palestine Arab delegates at Jericho acclaimed 'Abdullāh as 'King of All Palestine'. In reaction against this the other Arab states, and a number of Asian and Latin American states at the General Assembly, combined with the Soviet bloc on 3 December to defeat the paragraph in the late Mediator's recommendations, now embodied in a British resolution, to combine Arab Palestine with Trans-Jordan.[3] The principal outcome of the protracted debate was that Israel was left in *de facto* occupation of her recent territorial gains, and that a Conciliation Commission of three members was set up to take over the late Mediator's functions and seek a final settlement in Palestine. A large majority agreed that the Commission should consist of representatives of the United States, France, and Turkey, to the exclusion of a representative of the Soviet bloc.

Meanwhile, the Security Council had begun on 2 December to consider an application by the Israel Government for admission to the United Nations. The United States delegate, Dr. Philip Jessup, asked the Council to treat the application with special urgency, in order that Israel might take her place in the General Assembly before the end of the present session. Observing that Article 4 of the Charter offered membership to all peace-loving states, he declared that the Council would recall the degree to which the Israel Government had 'extended its co-operation in the implementation of proposals made by the Security Council or by the Mediator'. Anticipating Cadogan's objection that Israel's frontiers were still quite unsettled, not only in detail but in large and important areas

---

[1] But cf. above, p. 286.

[2] See Bilby: *New Star in the Near East*, pp. 53–58.

[3] For the voting, see U.N.: *Official Records of the 3rd session of the General Assembly, 1948*, part I, First Committee, pp. 887–90. Despite recrimination from the other Arab capitals the Trans-Jordan Parliament on 13 December unanimously adopted a resolution to incorporate what remained of Arab Palestine, and on the 20th 'Abdullāh announced the appointment of one of his supporters as Muftī of Jerusalem to replace his uncompromising opponent, Hājj Muhammad Amīn al-Husainī (see Esmond Wright: 'Abdallah's Jordan', *Middle East Journal*, Autumn 1951, v. 446–7).

(notably Galilee and south Palestine), Jessup observed that when the
United States of America first came into existence the land 'had not even
been explored, and no one knew just where the American claims ended
and where French and British and Spanish claims began'.[1] While the
Soviet Union supported Israel's application, Cadogan called for its indefinite postponement, since the Conciliation Commission needed some time
to get to work and the General Assembly would be unable to act on a
recommendation from the Security Council until the session beginning on
1 April 1949.[2] The French delegate could not accept Jessup's comparison
between the Palestine situation and that of the infant United States:
Israel's frontiers would not depend on clearing virgin forest or a struggle
against savage tribes, but on agreement with existing states. He proposed
a postponement for one month; but neither this, nor the British proposal,
nor Israel's substantive application, was able on 17 December to secure
the necessary seven votes, and the matter was automatically deferred for
the time being.[3]

(7) *Israel 'spoils the Egyptians' and forces Bevin's hand, December 1948 to*
January 1949

On 22 December the Israeli forces on the Egyptian front, claiming their
freedom of action to defend their territory, attacked the Egyptian brigade
which had been encircled since October at al-Fallūja, while Israeli aircraft
bombed Gaza and villages to the south of it. The grounds for the renewal
of this offensive, as later given by Israeli spokesmen and writers,[4] were
that the Egyptians had been trying to relieve their encircled garrison at
al-Fallūja by moving up considerable reinforcements, and had made continuous attacks on Israeli settlements close to the frontier, while Egyptian
aircraft had raided Haifa, Tel Aviv, and the outskirts of Nazareth. Proposals made by the Acting Mediator, to couple the gradual return to
Egypt of the al-Fallūja garrison with the opening of armistice negotiations
between Israel and Egypt, had encountered (according to these Israeli
sources) the same Egyptian quibbling as Bernadotte's attempt in the
summer to regulate the provisioning of the then encircled Israeli settle-

[1] U.N., Security Council: *Official Records*, 3rd year, no. 128, pp. 11–12.
[2] The French and Canadian delegates had agreed that Israel's standing as a peace-loving
nation could be judged only by her compliance with the recommendations which would emerge
from the General Assembly's debate on the late Mediator's progress report. The United States'
wish to see Israel admitted to the Assembly during its present session had thereby been disappointed.
[3] Israel's application received the votes of the United States, the Soviet Union, the Ukraine,
Argentina, and Colombia; Belgium, Canada, China, France, and the United Kingdom abstained,
and Syria opposed.
[4] See Maurice Fisher, at the U.N. Security Council, 28 December 1948: *Official Records*,
3rd year, no. 136, pp. 14–22; Pearlman: *The Army of Israel*, pp. 221, 224, 226; Sacher: *Israel,
the Establishment of a State*, pp. 304–5.

ments in the same region. The Israeli offensive, they continued, had been precipitated by official information (conveyed by the Chief of the United Nations truce supervision staff, the American General Riley) that the Egyptians had rejected the proposal to open negotiations;[1] and the Israelis also claimed that their action had merely anticipated an Egyptian offensive timed for the 27th, according to the alleged statements of Egyptian officers captured between those two dates. On the other hand, General Riley's report to the Acting Mediator[2] disclosed systematic evasions by the Israelis of the terms on which a truce had been reimposed after the October fighting—notably their refusal to allow United Nations observer posts to be set up in this region; and the Israeli spokesman's attempt to make compliance with those terms dependent on the Security Council's later resolution concerning the negotiation of an armistice was considered clever but unacceptable by the Belgian and French representatives on the Security Council. A British resolution of 29 December calling for an immediate cease-fire, withdrawal to the positions occupied before the October fighting, and effective supervision by the United Nations observers, accordingly received a two-thirds' majority, with the United States, the Soviet Union, and the Ukraine abstaining.[3]

The resolution was no more effective than its predecessors, however. While the Egyptian brigade at al-Fallūja still held out, the Egyptian right flank, based on the motor-road running south-west from Beersheba through Hafīr al-'Awja towards the Suez Canal, had been rolled up by a surprise attack and their main body was hemmed into the Gaza area, while the Israeli forces made substantial penetrations into Egyptian territory in Sinai. Meanwhile, in Cairo, the inglorious course of the war, which could not be entirely concealed by the censorship, had unleashed the hostility of the extremist militant bodies, and notably of the powerfully organized Ikhwān al-Muslimūn (Muslim Brotherhood), against the Government of Mahmūd Fahmī an-Nuqrāshī; and while the campaign of street terrorism had in the earlier months of the war vented itself upon Jews and Europeans,[4] the belated attempts of the Government in October and November to curb what seemed like an extremist bid for political power led to the murder of the Prime Minister himself by a member of the Ikhwān al-Muslimūn on 28 December.[5] In these circumstances of military confusion on

---

[1] Insisting, as a pre-condition, on the immediate and total evacuation of the al-Fallūja garrison, according to Fisher, loc. cit.; but Sacher represents the Egyptians as demanding the withdrawal of the Israeli forces to the positions from which they had advanced in October.

[2] U.N., Security Council: *Official Records*, 3rd year, supplement for December 1948, document S/1152, pp. 300-4.

[3] Ibid. 3rd year, no. 137, pp. 23-25.

[4] See S. Landshut: *Jewish Communities in the Muslim Countries of the Middle East* (London, the *Jewish Chronicle*, 1950), pp. 33-38; and for reprisals against Jews in the other Arab countries, ibid. pp. 47-50, 55-56, 59-60.

[5] The Government had ordered the dissolution of the Ikhwān on 8 December, after the killing

Egypt's frontiers and the danger of political chaos in her capital, the British Government threatened on 31 December to invoke their 1936 treaty with Egypt (regardless of the fact that Egypt had sought in 1947 to have it set aside by the Security Council)[1] and intervene against the Israeli forces unless they were promptly withdrawn from Egyptian territory. The United States Government, in transmitting this British warning to the Israel Government, deplored the reports at this time of Israeli troop movements threatening Jordan,[2] and added their own warning that United States policy towards Israel might have to be reviewed unless her forces were withdrawn.[3] However, the Egyptian Government, now led by Ibrāhīm 'Abd ul-Hādī, had no wish to have the 1936 treaty invoked by Britain, and, feeling themselves deserted by their former Arab allies,[4] informed the Acting Mediator's staff that they were willing to enter into negotiations for an armistice if Israel would agree to a cease-fire. The Israelis claimed to have withdrawn their forces from Egyptian territory by 2 January 1949; but their accounts speak of the continued presence of Israeli forces south of the frontier village of Rafah as late as the 7th;[5] and British air reconnaissances, which were being flown from the R.A.F. bases in the Canal Zone, were stated to have revealed a fresh Israeli incursion in strength into Egyptian territory on the 6th. Another reconnaissance by four Spitfires was ordered for the following morning (7 January), with orders to spend the minimum time over the battle area and not to cross the Egypt–Palestine frontier. The Egyptian Air Force had, however, been appearing over the battle area more frequently in the last few days, and Israeli aircraft intercepted and shot down the whole of the British reconnaissance flight. The Egyptians had accepted a cease-fire, to become effective at 2 p.m. G.M.T. that day, but confirmation of this was slow to reach the British in the Canal Zone. Local Israeli-Egyptian fighting continued at Rafah for another three hours, and during that time Israeli aircraft had shot down another British aircraft[6] which crashed on the Palestine side

of the Chief of Police by a student of Cairo University during demonstrations. The murder of the Prime Minister was the retaliation for this, and on 13 February 1949 persons unknown shot dead the leader of the Ikhwān, the once insignificant schoolmaster Hasan al-Banna, in whom the war-fever was thought to have aroused the ambition for seizing political power independently of the conventional parties (see J. Heyworth-Dunne: *Religious and Political Trends in Modern Egypt* (Washington, published by the author, 1950), pp. 48, 74–76).

[1] See above, pp. 130–6.   [2] Cf. below, p. 310.

[3] McDonald: *My Mission in Israel*, pp. 107–8; cf. *The Forrestal Diaries*, p. 542; Bilby: *New Star in the Near East*, p. 59; Sacher: *Israel, the Establishment of a State*, p. 307.

[4] See the complaint of the Government newspaper *al-'Assās*, reported by *The Times*, 5 January 1949. The *New York Times* of 6 January contained a good example of Arab anti-'Abdullāh and anti-British propaganda, reported from Beirut.

[5] Pearlman: *The Army of Israel*, p. 241; Sacher op. cit. p. 306.

[6] According to Pearlman (op. cit. pp. 241, 243) the Israeli air force had not identified the British aircraft as such before shooting them down; but one of the British pilots who was temporarily a prisoner of the Israelis reported afterwards that they were greatly elated over the incident, perhaps as enhancing the prestige of the Haganah *vis-à-vis* the I.Z.L. The Israeli

of the frontier; it was part of another reconnaissance sent to search for the British aircraft lost that morning. These incidents caused considerable tension between Britain and Israel. President Truman rejected a request from the British Ambassador in Washington for United States support, while the Israel Government accused Britain of organizing an 'imposing display of military and political activity' against them on the eve of the armistice negotiations, including 'large-scale naval manœuvres in the East Mediterranean' and manœuvres 'based on simulated landings on the coast of Israel'; the Israelis also repeated the false charge that Britain was secretly supplying war material to the Arab countries in alliance with her.[1] The opening of armistice negotiations between Israel and Arab states, together with the shock given by the incidents to British parliamentary and public opinion, brought about a change in Bevin's hitherto unyielding attitude towards Israel. On 18 January he stated that the Government were prepared to allow the release of the Jewish immigrants of military age who had been hitherto detained in Cyprus,[2] and Britain's *de facto* recognition of Israel was announced on 29 January. The United States announced her *de jure* recognition of both Israel and Jordan two days later.

(b) The Aftermath of the War, 1949–50

(1) *The Israeli-Arab Armistices, January to July 1949*[3]

Representations by the United States Government were believed to have played an important part in bringing about the opening of armistice talks between Israel and Egypt on 13 January. Held at Rhodes under the auspices of the Acting Mediator,[4] they soon encountered difficulties, since the Egyptians, in spite of their recent defeat, still demanded a return to the military positions occupied before the Israeli October offensive,[5] while the Israelis countered with a demand for the Egyptian evacuation of the coastal strip between Gaza and the Egyptian frontier, and withheld their agreement to the evacuation of the Egyptian forces isolated at al-Fallūja. Relenting on these two points, Israel still insisted on retaining the frontier locality of al-'Awja, strategically situated at a junction on the inland road between Egypt and Beersheba by which the Egyptian right-hand column had entered Palestine in May 1948; the Egyptians still refused to admit the

civil authorities, on the other hand, were greatly concerned over the incident, according to a responsible British civilian source.

[1] Cf. above, p.288, and see McDonald: *My Mission in Israel*, pp. 115–16; U.N., Security Council document S/1201, 11 January 1949. Sacher also claims knowledge of British orders to prepare a commando force for a projected landing at Gaza (*Israel, the Establishment of a State*, p. 141) and cf. ibid. pp. 304–5 for the alleged British supply of tanks to Egypt during the truce.

[2] H.C.Deb. 5th ser., vol. 460, coll. 36–37.   [3] See map D at end of volume.

[4] He was continuing to act, pending his replacement by the Conciliation Commission that the United Nations General Assembly had appointed (see p. 290 above).

[5] Cf. above, pp. 287–8.

legitimacy of the Israeli occupation of Beersheba. A compromise Armistice Agreement was, however, signed on 24 February. The demarcation
lines which this and later agreements laid down were 'delineated without
prejudice to the rights, claims and positions of either Party . . . as regards
ultimate settlement of the Palestine question', and were 'not to be con-
strued in any sense as a political or territorial boundary'. The Gaza
strip, left under Egyptian military occupation, was defined as being of
twenty-five miles in length to the mouth of the Wādi al-Hāsī, and of three
and a half to five and a half miles in depth from the coast; its population
of about 70,000 before the outbreak of the Palestine war had been swelled
by the advent of some 200,000 refugees, and the armistice line separated
many villages from their farmlands, which were left to be tilled by the
Israelis.[1] The strategic area of al-'Awja on the Palestine side of the frontier
was demilitarized, and the Egyptians on their side of the frontier were to
have no defensive positions nearer to al-'Awja than a distance of fourteen
to seventeen miles.[2]

The participation of Lebanon in the war against Israel had always been
half-hearted;[3] and on 16 January, the fourth day of the Israeli-Egyptian
negotiations, representatives of Israel and Lebanon had met at Ras an-
Naqūra on the Lebanon–Palestine frontier to initiate exploratory talks,
and the Israeli troops had been withdrawn from four Lebanese villages
which they had occupied in the previous October. These negotiations also
were protracted owing to Israel's unwillingness to evacuate strategic positions on Lebanese territory near the Syrian-Lebanese frontier until the
Syrians had shown readiness to evacuate positions which they held on
neighbouring territory on the Palestine side of the frontier; but on 21 March
the Acting Mediator could report that Syria was willing to negotiate,
and the armistice with Lebanon was accordingly signed on the 23rd. It
adopted the Palestine–Lebanon frontier as the demarcation line, with demilitarized zones on either side of it in which neither party was to maintain
more than 1,500 men.[4]

---

[1] See United Nations Conciliation Commission for Palestine: *Final Report of the United Nations
Economic Survey Mission for the Middle East* (1949), part I, p. 19.

[2] Text of Armistice in U.N., Security Council: *Official Records*, 4th year, special supplement
no. 3, with maps annexed to special supplement no. 1.

[3] Lebanese regular army casualties were reported to amount to under ten killed and twenty
wounded, according to Kenneth Bilby (*New York Herald Tribune*, 25 April 1949); cf. the Israeli
Chief of Operations in *Zionist Review*, 30 July 1948, p. 5. This half-heartedness was due at least
in part to the religious disunity of the population of Lebanon. Among the non-Muslim half,
there were elements that did not feel at home in the Arab League. At the same time, there was
a large section of the Orthodox Christian community, and a smaller section of the Catholic
Christian community, that did believe fully in the Arab League, and, even among those Lebanese
who were not Arab nationalists, there were many who saw in Zionism a direct political and
economic threat to Lebanon—e.g. the Catholic and Lebanese nationalist newspaper *Le Jour*
was as strongly anti-Zionist as it was anti-Arab.

[4] Text in U.N., Security Council: *Official Records*, 4th year, special supplement no. 4.

Although the General Assembly resolution of November 1947 had recommended that the long southern extension of Palestine to the Gulf of 'Aqaba should go to Israel, that region had still been void of Jewish settlers or troops when in June 1948 the Arab Legion had occupied two former Palestine Police posts within some twenty miles of the southern end of the Dead Sea. It will be recalled that the British Government, and the late Mediator, had proposed during the summer that Jordan should retain this region in exchange for Israel's acquisition of western Galilee.[1] The Israelis, however, were determined to secure an outlet on the Gulf of 'Aqaba, and thus to the Red Sea and the Indian Ocean without using the Suez Canal, and they hoped to develop the mineral resources of the extreme south of Palestine which had been exploited as early as the time of King Solomon. Once they had thrust back the Egyptians in the coastal plain by means of their October offensive they advanced down the Wādī 'Araba during November to a position forty-five miles south of the Dead Sea, and on 1 December (one day after the cease-fire agreement with the Arab Legion at Jerusalem) they fought a skirmish with troops of that force in this remote southern sector. The defeat of the Egyptians in December left the Israelis free to pursue this southward advance; but King 'Abdullāh was reported to have invoked the Anglo-Transjordan Treaty on 2 January 1949, with the result that a small British force was established at 'Aqaba.[2] The military situation remained unchanged until the last week in February, when armistice negotiations between Jordan and Israel were about to begin in Rhodes. On 24 February, however, an Israeli patrol (advancing southward through Egyptian Sinai in violation of the Israeli-Egyptian armistice) appeared at the head of the precipitous pass ten miles north-west of 'Aqaba, withdrawing four days later. When the armistice negotiations opened on 2 March, the Israelis denied having been in the locality; but when the Jordan Government claimed to be in effective occupation of the Wādī 'Araba to a distance of sixty miles north of 'Aqaba, the Israelis accused them of attempting to prejudice the negotiations by a *fait*

---

[1] See above, p. 278 and note 4.

[2] Bevin intimated to the House of Commons on 26 January 1949 that the initiative had come from 'Abdullāh, with the remark, however, that 'previous Jewish patrols had crossed the frontier of Transjordan, and following the reports at that time I began to wonder whether, in the exuberance of victory, things were not getting a little out of hand' (H.C.Deb. 5th ser., vol. 460, col. 939). For reports that the successful young Israeli commanders had to be restrained by their Government from continuing their advance indefinitely into Arab territory see McDonald: *My Mission in Israel*, p. 105; Kimche: *Seven Fallen Pillars*, pp. 266–7; R. H. S. Crossman in *New Statesman and Nation*, 10 February 1951, p. 149.

The Israel Government protested to the Security Council against the British Government's 'menacing attitude' and denied that they were threatening the territorial integrity of Trans-Jordan (United Nations document S/1201, 11 January 1949); and it was alleged in Israel that, in a secret meeting with an Israeli representative at 'Ammān on 31 January, 'Abdullah gave him a 'categorical denial that he knew in advance—or had even been asked—about sending British troops to 'Aqaba' (McDonald, op. cit. p. 124).

accompli,[1] and riposted with complaints of incidents in that part of central Palestine held by the 'Irāqī and Jordan forces, which constricted the Israeli-held coastal plain to a width of a mere eight miles at its narrowest. The armistice negotiations came to a standstill on 7 March, and early that morning two Israeli columns thrust southwards down the Wādī 'Araba towards the Gulf of 'Aqaba. Meanwhile the 'Irāqī Government, which had refused to negotiate an armistice of their own with Israel but had agreed to be bound by an armistice signed by Jordan, had decided to withdraw their forces from central Palestine before Israel attacked them. The Arab Legion, whose thinly held line already extended over 130 miles from the Gulf of 'Aqaba to north of Jerusalem, thus had also to cover its exposed northern flank and could not risk a conflict in the extreme south. Early on 10 March the withdrawal of the small Arab Legion force there allowed the Israelis to reach the Gulf, five miles west of 'Aqaba, at the former Palestine Police post of Umm Rashrash which they afterwards renamed Elath.[2] A cease-fire arranged by the Acting Mediator was signed on the 11th, but when, two days later, the British garrison at 'Aqaba was reinforced to brigade strength the Israelis protested that this action was holding up a settlement with Jordan, while the latter asked for British patrols to be sent northwards as far as the Dead Sea to check Israeli incursions across the former Palestine–Trans-Jordan boundary. While in the United States the Acting Mediator criticized the British reinforcement of 'Aqaba as being contrary to the truce,[3] the British Under-Secretary for Foreign Affairs expressed his Government's conviction that it was the presence of this force that had stabilized the situation and allowed the Israeli-Jordan negotiations to continue.[4] Assurances had been given to Israel that the purpose of the force was defensive only, and it did not interfere with Israel's occupation of former Palestinian territory in the south. In the north, however, the Israelis threatened Jordan with the non-recognition of the Arab Legion's taking over the former 'Irāqī sector, and, in a secret meeting with King 'Abdullāh at his winter palace at Shūna, Reuven Shiloah, formerly Zaslani (in charge of 'special services' at the Israeli Foreign Ministry), and Colonel Moshe Dayan compelled him, on pain of

[1] *'Fait Accompli'* seems in fact to have been the Israeli army's code-name for the operation, according to an unpublished source.

[2] Six months later, Kenneth Bilby was told by the commander of the Israeli forces in the region: 'Assuredly . . . we violated the truce. . . . It was one of those calculated violations which we had to carefully weigh against political risks' (*New Star in the East*, pp. 103–5); see also *The Times* 'Ammān correspondent, 15 March 1949, after an interview with Glubb Pāshā; U.N. Security Council document S/1295, 23 March 1949; Pearlman: *The Army of Israel*, pp. 245, 247.

[3] See *Manchester Guardian*, 24 March 1949, but cf. the anodyne character of Bunche's report of 23 March (U.N. Security Council document S/1295). Sacher derides the British reinforcement of 'Aqaba as 'the last splutter of Mr. Bevin's sterile and ridiculous bellicosity' (*Israel, the Establishment of a State*, p. 145).

[4] 28 March 1949, H.C.Deb. 5th ser., vol. 463, col. 846; cf. Dunner: *The Republic of Israel*, pp. 183–4; *The Times* diplomatic correspondent, 22 March 1949.

resuming hostilities, to accept a withdrawal of the Arab Legion for an
average depth of two miles along this fifty-five mile front. This relieved
the constriction of the Israeli-held coastal plain east of Tel Aviv and

The Shūna Agreement of March 1949

——— Armistice Line imposed by Israel
- - - - Cease-fire Line, as claimed by Jordan

Miles
0   20

Sea of Galilee

•Affūla

Beth Sh'an

Hadera•

•Janīn

ISRAEL

Nathanya•

•Tūlkarm

JORDAN

•Nablus

•Qalqīlīya

Petah Tiqvah•

•Tel Aviv

Hadera, and gave Israel unimpeded control of the strategic main road
over the Carmel range to the Vale of Esdraelon and Galilee;[1] it also
separated a considerable number of Arab villagers from the greater part of
their lands, leaving the inhabitants destitute (as in the Gaza strip);[2] and
it was afterwards used by 'Abdullāh's Arab enemies as a new propaganda
weapon against him.[3] In return, in the Armistice Agreement signed on

[1] At the defile of Megiddo, where the road descends from Carmel into Esdraelon, Thothmes
III of Egypt had routed the Prince of Qadesh and his Palestinian allies early in the fifteenth
century B.C.; a pharaoh of the 26th Egyptian dynasty had defeated and killed Josiah, king of
Judah, in 608 B.C.; and Allenby had routed the Seventh and Eighth Ottoman Armies in September, A.D. 1918.   [2] See above, p. 295.
[3] See below, p. 310 and p. 315, note 2 ('economic refugees'). One false allegation, still
current in London in 1953, was that the Jordan delegates to the Rhodes Armistice Commission
were given a faked 1:250,000 map to sign; but the writer has a photostat of a composite 1:100,000

3 April, Jordan received very minor territorial concessions in the Hebron area. The demarcation line left the city of Jerusalem divided from south-west to north-east by the barbed-wire defences of the two armies, and referred to a special committee such outstanding questions—covered in the Armistice by an agreement in principle—as the isolation of the Hebrew University and the Hadassah hospital from the Israeli New City, the isolation of the Arab Old City from the Jerusalem power-station, and the general right of access to the Holy Places.[1]

The opening of negotiations between Israel and Syria had been delayed by the internal instability of the latter country. The Government of the National Bloc, elected in 1943 and enabled by British intervention to rid itself of French military control in 1945,[2] had had its mandate renewed in a reasonably free election in 1947, but had proved incapable of the efficient prosecution of the war against Israel in 1948. Military humiliation and increasing economic hardship had combined with the usual rumours of official profiteering and corruption[3] to cause student demonstrations and a general strike which forced the resignation of Jamīl Mardam's Government on 1 December 1948. After an interregnum of more than a fortnight, a Government largely composed of non-party personalities had been formed by an independent statesman and former Prime Minister, Khālid al-'Azm. This Government had brought to a successful conclusion negotiations with France, on currency questions outstanding from the Mandate, which the previous Government had broken off in January 1948;[4] they had ratified an agreement with the United States Trans-Arabian Pipeline Company for an oil-pipe to connect the Sa'ūdī Arabian oilfields with a new Mediterranean port at Saida (Sidon);[5] and they had at length consented to open armistice negotiations with Israel. In their efforts to check the continuing financial deterioration, however, they had proposed to cut the pay of the army, and this was a factor in what followed. Colonel Husnī az-Za'īm, an officer of Kurdish origin who had been trained in the Ottoman army and had served both King Faisal in 1919–20 and afterwards the French, had been promoted to the position of Chief of Staff in the reshuffle of senior appointments which had followed the

---

map of the Shūna concessions complete with the Jordanian signatures. It is true that there were afterwards some minor disputes at Rhodes, and again when the demarcation line was surveyed on the ground.

[1] Text in U.N., Security Council: *Official Records*, 4th year, special supplement no. 1.

[2] See *Survey* for 1939–46: *The Middle East in the War*, pp. 272–306, and above, pp. 106–13.

[3] Notable among these was the allegation that the Prime Minister's nephew, Captain Fu'ād Mardam, sent to Italy to buy a consignment of arms, had misappropriated his funds and allowed the arms to be acquired by Israel (*Cahiers de l'Orient Contemporain*, 1er trimestre 1949, xvii. 50, and 2me et 3me trimestres 1949, xviii–xix. 157).

[4] See above, pp. 114–15.

[5] The previous Government had likewise withheld their ratification of this agreement because of the United States Government's support of Israel.

disclosure of the incompetence of the Syrian army within ten days of the Arab League's intervention in Palestine in May 1948.[1] After the fall of Jamīl Mardam's Government in December, a personal tour of the country which az-Zaʿīm had made had restored a measure of public confidence and had probably awakened in him a conviction that the security and welfare of the country were henceforward his responsibility.[2] It was afterwards reported that in February 1949 he had made tentative preparations, perhaps in collusion with some members of Khālid al-ʿAzm's Government, to overthrow that Government by a military *coup d'état*, and that President Shukrī al-Quwwatlī, the leader of the National Bloc, had accordingly intended to dismiss him from his post of Acting Chief of Staff.[3] Az-Zaʿīm, however, struck first. Early in the morning of 30 March troops occupied the telephone exchange and other key buildings in Damascus and without bloodshed arrested the President, the Prime Minister, and other Ministers. A special meeting of the Chamber on 1 April gave a vote of confidence, but only by a slight majority, to az-Zaʿīm and to an all-embracing programme of 'democratic' reforms which he presented to it; but the politicians were in general reluctant to commit themselves to the support of the military *coup d'état*, and on the following day az-Zaʿīm announced the dissolution of the Chamber and the appointment of a commission to draft a new Constitution 'guaranteeing the aspirations of the people and the restoration of their violated rights and liberties'.[4] Formal negotiations for an armistice between Syria and Israel were begun on 12 April, but there was a protracted stalemate when the Syrians insisted on retaining three small areas, of which they were still in military occupation, on the Palestine side of the frontier. The Anglo-French Agreement of 23 December 1920[5] had drawn that frontier so as to place the whole of the upper Jordan valley for twenty-five miles north of the Sea of Galilee within Palestine; and the largest of the areas now claimed by Syria consisted of sparsely settled land, much of it infested with malaria, on both banks of the Jordan below Lake Hūla. To relieve the deadlock the Acting Mediator recommended that these areas, together with some adjacent areas controlled by Israel, should be made a demilitarized zone supervised, like those provided for in the other armistice agreements, by a Mixed Armistice Commission with a chairman appointed by the United Nations. The Armistice Agreement signed on 20 July 1949[6] duly embodied this proposal

[1] The resignation of the Minister of Defence, Ahmad Sharabātī, had been announced on 24 May 1948.

[2] Dr. Alford Carleton, President of Aleppo College: 'The Syrian Coups d'État of 1949', *Middle East Journal*, January 1950, iv. 3–4.

[3] *The Times* special correspondent in Damascus, 15 August 1949.

[4] *The Times* special correspondent in Beirut, 4 April 1949.

[5] Great Britain, Foreign Office: *Franco-British Convention of December 23, 1920 on . . . the Mandates for Syria and the Lebanon, Palestine and Mesopotamia*, Cmd. 1195 (London, H.M.S.O., 1921).

[6] U.N., Security Council: *Official Records*, 4th year, special supplement no. 2, with map.

in its Article V, with special provision for the 'gradual restoration of normal civilian life' in the demilitarized zone and 'without prejudice to the ultimate settlement'; but there were seeds of conflict in the subsequent Syrian and Israeli interpretations of this article. The Syrians wished to restore the conditions which had existed in the zone when the British mandate ended, with the further contention that the demarcation of the Palestine-Syrian frontier by the Anglo-French Agreement of 1920 was not binding upon the Syrian Republic. The Israelis could show that the whole region had been awarded to them by the General Assembly's resolution of November 1947, and were determined to proceed with their long-established plans for draining the malarial Hūla basin and for the agricultural utilization of its alluvial soil for the settlement of thousands of immigrants in this strategic area. Israel's persistence in pursuing these plans within the demilitarized zone was to lead to a serious local conflict with Syria in the spring of 1951.[1]

(2) Israel's Admission to the United Nations, May 1949

Meanwhile, at the Security Council on 3 March 1949 the French delegate, recalling that his Government had in the previous December proposed the adjournment of Israel's request for admission to the United Nations,[2] remarked that, through the conclusion of the armistice with Egypt and the progress of the negotiations with Lebanon and Trans-Jordan, Israel now showed every sign of being a peace-loving state, and his delegation would vote for her admission. The United States and the Soviet Union, consistently with their former attitude, supported this, while Egypt, with equal consistency, opposed it and tried to initiate a procedural wrangle. The British representative, Sir Terence Shone, observed that his Government, while satisfied with the improvement in the Palestine situation and sympathizing generally with Israel's desire for admission to the United Nations, were nevertheless disturbed by statements made by Ben Gurion and other responsible Israelis that the internationalization of Jerusalem, which the last session of the General Assembly had, on 11 December 1948, reaffirmed as United Nations policy,[3] should apply only to the Arab-held Old City, and that the Jewish New City must be incorporated in Israel; it was also, Shone continued, not sufficiently clear whether Israel was prepared to honour the General Assembly's resolution of the same date that the Palestine Arab refugees, now estimated at more than half a million, should either be allowed to return to their homes on

---

[1] See Jacob C. Hurewitz: 'The Israeli-Syrian Crisis in the Light of the Arab–Israel Armistice System', *International Organization*, August 1951, v. 459–79.

[2] See above, pp. 290–1.

[3] See U.N.: *Official Records of the 3rd session of the General Assembly*, Resolutions, no. 194 (III), paragraph 8, p. 23.

territory now held by Israel or receive compensation.[1] The Council's recommendation to the General Assembly that Israel should be admitted was carried by nine votes against the negative vote of Egypt and the abstention of the United Kingdom.[2] When the matter came before the *ad hoc* Political Committee of the General Assembly on 3 May the question of Israel's attitude to the internationalization of Jerusalem and to the Arab refugee problem was raised by various Roman Catholic states, a recent Papal encyclical[3] having placed great emphasis on the internationalization of Jerusalem and thereby attracted much criticism from Zionists throughout the world. The Danish representative was not satisfied that Israel had yet taken effective measures to bring Count Bernadotte's murderers to justice,[4] and was supported in this by the British delegate. Israel's spokesman, Abba Even (formerly Aubrey Eban), now contended that his countrymen's defence of Jerusalem had been favourable to Christian interests in the Holy City, which would otherwise have been irrevocably incorporated in a Muslim state, and he represented that his Government's recent transfer of five Ministries from Tel Aviv to Jerusalem was not intended to create a new political or juridical situation, but merely to stimulate the economic recovery of Jewish Jerusalem; Israel's contribution to the resettlement of the Arab refugees would depend entirely on the establishment of peace and good relations between her and the Arab states. A Lebanese resolution to defer until the autumn a decision on admitting Israel to the United Nations was defeated by 25 votes to 19, and the *Ad hoc* Committee then recommended her admission by 33 votes to 11, with 13 abstentions;[5] it became effective on 11 May.

(3) *The United Nations Conciliation Commission, 1949*

Meanwhile, on 27 April the three members (United States, French, and Turkish) of the United Nations Conciliation Commission for Palestine had begun a series of meetings at Lausanne with representatives of Israel and the Arab states, and on 12 May invited them to consider the Arab refugee problem and territorial adjustments, using the partition of Palestine proposed by the General Assembly in November 1947 as a basis. The Arab states continued to argue that the first step towards the rehabilitation of the refugees must be Israel's accepting back those who wished to return to their homes, as prescribed in the General Assembly's resolution of

[1] See U.N.: *Official Records of the 3rd session of the General Assembly*, Resolutions, no. 194 (III), paragraph 11, p. 24.
[2] U.N., Security Council: *Official Records*, 4th year, nos. 16–17, 3 and 4 March 1949.
[3] Text in *Osservatore Romano*, 15 April 1949; *Oriente Moderno*, April–June 1949, pp. 52–53.
[4] For the Swedish Government's continued complaints see above, p. 286.
[5] The United Kingdom, Sweden and Denmark, Greece and Turkey, were among those who supported the Lebanese proposal for deferring a decision; and in abstaining on the substantive motion they were joined by France, Belgium, and South Africa, who had abstained on the Lebanese proposal.

11 December 1948; the Arabs further proposed the immediate return of those refugees who had left areas which had been assigned to the Arab state by the General Assembly's recommendation of November 1947 but which had been occupied by Israel during the subsequent fighting. Israel, on the other hand, stated that if she were allowed to incorporate the Gaza area she would be prepared to accept as Israeli citizens its present Arab population, both original inhabitants and refugees, on the understanding that the resettlement of the refugees on Israeli territory would be subject to international aid; if, however, the Gaza area were not ceded to Israel, the Israeli delegation was not in a position to submit proposals concerning the number of refugees that their Government could accept.[1] On 28 July, after some indecisive pressure from the United States,[2] the Israeli delegation offered the apparent concession that the refugee problem might be given first place on the agenda of joint discussion of a general peace settlement, and on 3 August advanced its own proposals. These were that Israel would be ready to accept the return of 100,000 refugees on condition that she had the right to resettle them where they would fit into the general plan of Israel's economic development and where they could not be used as a fifth column against her. The Commission considered these proposals unsatisfactory, and the Arab states rejected the suggestion that the resettlement of the refugees should be thus subordinated to the economic and strategic convenience of Israel. The Arabs continued to seek to base the discussion of boundaries upon the November 1947 partition plan which they had so vehemently opposed when it was first adopted, even as they had condemned the British White Paper of May 1939 at the time of its publication, only to invoke it from 1945 onwards as the palladium of Arab political rights when the passage of time was already consigning it to a dusty place on the shelves of history. On 23 August the Conciliation Commission decided to set up an Economic Mission subsidiary to itself, and consisting of a United States chairman (Gordon R. Clapp)[3] with British, French, and Turkish members, to examine the economic situation in the countries affected by the Palestine War and to make recommendations for the repatriation, resettlement, and economic and social rehabilitation of the refugees, in order to reintegrate them into the region's economic life

---

[1] United Nations Conciliation Commission for Palestine: *3rd Progress Report*, document A/927, 21 June 1949, p. 4. It had previously been reported from Lausanne that the Egyptian delegation had intimated its Government's readiness to give up the Gaza strip and its refugees; and that Jordan, whose physical communications with the West were dependent on the uncertain good will of Syria and Lebanon and were in any case cumbersome and costly, had sought a direct access to the Mediterranean by means of a 'corridor' from the Hebron area to Gaza (see *Observer*, 1 May, C. L. Sulzberger in *New York Times*, 7 May 1949, and below, p. 309).

[2] See McDonald: *My Mission in Israel*, pp. 165–8; Sacher: *Israel, the Establishment of a State*, pp. 147–8.

[3] The chairman's name involved the inconvenience that in Arabic the Clapp Commission immediately became known as Lajnat ul-Kilāb ('The Commission of Dogs').

on a self-sustaining basis within a minimum period of time and to promote economic conditions conducive to the maintenance of peace and stability. The Economic Mission produced proposals for a number of 'pilot demonstration' schemes to provide both immediate work for the refugees and useful experience for those administering them; the estimated cost of these over the eighteen months beginning 1 January 1950 would be $35 million (of which some $6 million would be made available in kind by the local Governments), plus the expenditure of $19 million on direct relief for those eligible for it, whose legitimate number was estimated at 652,000, although the voluntary relief agencies (whose efforts were being co-ordinated by a United Nations Relief for Palestine Refugees organization, with funds amounting to $32 million contributed voluntarily by thirty-three Governments) were at present distributing as many as 940,000 rations.[1]

(4) Stalemate over Jerusalem, 1949

In setting up the Conciliation Commission, the General Assembly had instructed it to prepare detailed proposals, consequent upon the recommendations of the previous year,[2] for a permanent international régime for the Jerusalem area which would guarantee each distinctive group the maximum local autonomy compatible with the special international régime. When this resolution of December 1948 was carried the Israeli and Jordan armies had already agreed to a cease-fire on a line which divided the city of Jerusalem into two unequal portions, the larger western portion held by the Israelis and the smaller eastern portion (including the whole of the Old City with the majority of the Holy Places) held by Jordan.[3] The Conciliation Commission recommended on 1 September 1949 the recognition of a Jewish zone and an Arab zone (the demarcation

---

[1] See *Final Report of the United Nations Economic Survey Mission for the Middle East*, 28 December 1949, part I, pp. 18–19, 22–23. The relative burden of the refugees upon each country or administrative area is approximately shown by the proportion of their estimated numbers to the previous population, as follows:

				per cent.
Gaza strip .	.	.	.	280
Arab Palestine	.	.	.	60
Trans-Jordan	.	.	.	15
Lebanon	.	.	.	9
Israel	.	.	.	4
Syria	.	.	.	2
'Irāq	.	.	.	negligible

[2] See above, pp. 245–6 and 289.

[3] See above, p. 290. When the Arabs and Jews in 1944–5 could not agree on the succession to the Mayoralty of Jerusalem, a commission had officially recommended to the mandatory Government of Palestine that the city should be divided into Jewish and Arab areas for purposes of local administration (see *Survey* for 1939–46: *The Middle East in the War*, pp. 319–20, note 4, and Sir William Fitzgerald: *Report on the Local Administration of Jerusalem*, 28 August 1945 (Jerusalem, 1946)). Since that time the Israelis had overrun the Arab south-western suburbs, but the small Jewish community within the Old City had been evicted in the fighting of April–May 1948.

line between them to be determined later), whose 'present demographic equilibrium' was not to be altered by immigration into either zone and whose respective local authorities should be given full powers over the residents of each zone for such matters as would not be reserved to the international administration. This would consist of (1) a neutral Commissioner appointed by the United Nations, who would ensure the protection of the Holy Places and free access to them, would supervise the permanent demobilization and neutralization of the Jerusalem area, and would protect the individual and group rights of its inhabitants; (2) a Council of fourteen members, of whom five each would be appointed by the responsible authorities of the two zones, while the Commissioner would appoint two from distinctive minority groups in each zone. The Council would co-ordinate and operate the main public services of interest to both zones, and would recommend to their respective local authorities measures for promoting the economic development of the Jerusalem area and its trade with the world in general; (3) a Mixed Tribunal for hearing cases whose principals were not all residents of one zone; and an International Tribune for hearing cases within the competence of the Commissioner, or involving the responsible authorities of the two zones and/or the Commissioner, and for reviewing the decisions of the Mixed Tribunal.[1]

It is stated by a well-placed authority[2] that

there were some important Israel leaders who considered the strategic vulnerability of Jerusalem and the economic advantages of its internationalization more important than its historical and religious appeal. These 'realists' would, had they dared, have favoured a compromise or at any rate a less unyielding attitude than that adopted by Ben Gurion and his Cabinet. But none of them spoke out, because Israel public opinion was simply adamant against any form of internationalization of the New City.

Within a week of the publication of the Conciliation Commission's proposals, the Israeli Foreign Minister (Moshe Sharett, formerly Shertok) had attacked their proposals as 'anachronistic and incongruous', rejecting the plan for equal Jewish and Arab representation on the Council, and describing the ban on immigration into Jerusalem as unenforceable besides being a menace to the city's economic future. Complete demilitarization, he said, ignored the fact that the Jewish zone was surrounded on three sides by Arab territory, making formal equality in demilitarization a sham; the future for Jewish Jerusalem was as a part of the State of Israel; and international responsibility need not go beyond supervision of the Holy Places, unless it were confined to the Old City, where most of them were situated.[3]

[1] United Nations document A/973, 12 September 1949.
[2] McDonald: *My Mission in Israel*, p. 189.
[3] *New York Times*, 17 September 1949. At the United Nations General Assembly the Israeli spokesman, Abba Even, assailed the Conciliation Commission's proposals (see *Official Records of*

The general policy of the Arab states, including Jordan, was to admit the principle of an internationalized Jerusalem in its original context of the United Nations General Assembly's partition recommendation of November 1947; but the Egyptian Government, in particular, were still opposed to any accession of territory to the pro-British King 'Abdullāh,[1] and were therefore ready to press for the internationalization of Jerusalem on its own merits; and 'Abdullāh insisted that he could relinquish possession of the Arab half of the city, which was strategically 'the key to Jordan',[2] only if the Israelis withdrew to the areas allotted to them in November 1947. On such terms he was prepared to negotiate a peace settlement with Israel, either through the good offices of the Conciliation Commission or directly.[3]

When the Conciliation Commission's proposals came before the *Ad hoc* Committee of the General Assembly on 24 November the United States delegate thought them a 'moderate, practical and common-sense course', which would cost the United Nations less than $1 million per year to implement, compared with an annual cost of $30 million for establishing Jerusalem as a *corpus separatum*, as proposed in 1947; moreover, the present proposals took account of the political developments since that time. His Government were firmly convinced that the Jerusalem area should be demilitarized under international supervision, but dissociated themselves from the proposal that the United Nations Commission should be able to limit or prohibit the settlement of Jews (or Arabs) in Jerusalem, except in an emergency. The French delegation regarded the proposals as a valuable basis for discussion and would support them subject to any later amendments. The delegation of the Australian Government, however, which two years before had supported the establishment of the State of Israel, now proposed that the Conciliation Commission should be enlarged and given a year in which to produce a plan for the complete internationalization of the Jerusalem area as a *corpus separatum*.[4] After Cadogan

the *4th session of the General Assembly*, Plenary Meetings, pp. 93–94); and in Jerusalem members of the Herut Party, the political embodiment of the terrorist I.Z.L., threatened to reorganize themselves to remove any United Nations commissioner who might seek to play the part of Count Bernadotte (see *The Times*, 22 September 1949; Pierre Rondot: 'Le Problème des Lieux Saints', *L'Afrique et l'Asie*, 1er trimestre 1950, p. 14).

[1] According to *Bourse Égyptienne*, 27 October 1949, the Egyptian Government's motive, in proposing to the autumn 1949 meeting of the Arab League a collective security pact, was not merely to meet the risk of aggression by Israel, but also to forestall any such 'sectional groupings' of Arab states as the union of Arab Palestine with Jordan, or the union of Syria with Jordan or 'Irāq. There had been a strong movement for Syrian-'Irāqī *rapprochement* in the second half of 1949, until it was checked by the December *coup d'état* of Colonel Adīb Shīshaklī; see below, p. 312 and note 2, and p. 314, note 1.

[2] Rondot, op. cit. p. 13.

[3] See *The Times*, 21 November 1949, reporting its 'Ammān correspondent's interview with King 'Abdullāh.

[4] It was significant that a general election was impending in Australia, and that 20·7 per cent. of the population at the 1947 census were Roman Catholics who might, in view of the recent Papal encyclical (see above, p. 302), be expected to have views favourable to the internationalization

had declared the British Government's general support of the Conciliation Commission's draft statute, it was strongly attacked by Moshe Sharett on behalf of Israel. 'The exigencies of religious symbolism', he said, were being given 'gratuitous predominance over the needs of life' of the New City, with its industry and commerce, education and culture. He recommended that the United Nations should retain only a functional authority for the supervision of the Holy Places:

The Old City, which contained the chief sanctuaries of the three faiths, all the Christian patriarchates, a number of monasteries, the Moslem ecclesiastical foundations and a Jewish quarter, with all the ancient synagogues, covered only 6·5 per cent. of the municipal territory of Jerusalem and only 2 per cent. of its town planning area; it was for the most part a maze of narrow, winding, vaulted alleys flanked by old and insanitary buildings . . . in Arab hands. Its Jewish synagogues . . . had been practically razed to the ground since the fighting had ended. The Arab authorities had refused the Jews access to the Wailing Wall. . . .

If the Arab inhabitants of the Walled City could be induced, by the offer of better housing facilities, to move of their own free will out of the congested quarters and settle in the free space outside the walls, then the Walled City could be converted into a site containing only Holy Places and religious foundations, consecrated to religious worship and pilgrimage by members of all faiths, under the aegis of the United Nations.[1]

It was already clear that many votes would be swayed by the thought that Jerusalem was no ordinary city whose future was to be decided by political and pragmatic considerations only, but one whose varied spiritual associations remained for many paramount. Support for full internationalization came from the Roman Catholic and Orthodox Churches, from the Arab and Muslim bloc (except Jordan), and from the Soviet bloc, which ascribed to imperialist motives the preference of the United States and British Governments for a compromise with the present *de facto* situation. Those two Governments, and the French, were more concerned, however, lest the United Nations might once again, as two years earlier, make recommendations that they lacked the authority or the power to implement. When at the end of November the *Ad hoc* Committee appointed a sub-committee of seventeen members to examine the various proposals and produce a draft resolution, there was an expectation in Israel that the necessary two-thirds' majority would not be found either

of Jerusalem (cf. *Official Yearbook of the Commonwealth of Australia, 1946–1947*, xxxvii. 1286, and Lillie Shultz: 'The Jerusalem Story', *The Nation* (New York), 17 December 1949).

[1] U.N.: *Official Records of the 4th session of the General Assembly, Ad hoc* Political Committee, Summary Records, pp. 261–4. The Israel Government afterwards unofficially suggested that, in the event of peace with Jordan, Israeli money might be available, as compensation for Arab property expropriated in the Jewish New City, for resettling expropriated Arabs in 'an Arab New City east and south of the Old City' (McDonald: *My Mission in Israel*, p. 192).

for complete internationalization or for the Conciliation Commission's compromise.[1] However, the sub-committee reported back on 2 December with a draft recommendation for full internationalization under a statute to be drawn up by the Trusteeship Council.[2] The United States delegate criticized it in much the same terms[3] that the British Government had used of the recommendation for the partition of Palestine two years before, namely that it proposed a solution that might involve the use of force which the United Nations would not be ready to apply. The United States delegation supported a compromise moved by the Netherlands and Swedish delegations, whereby the powers of the United Nations commissioner would be limited to the protection of the Holy Places; but this belated action did not exempt the United States Government from Zionist recrimination for not exerting their powerful influence on doubtful delegations to counteract the 'direct intervention of the Vatican'.[4] In the *Ad hoc* Committee on 7 December the resolution for complete internationalization was carried by a heterogeneous majority[5] of more than the requisite two-thirds, and was carried in the plenary meeting of the Assembly on the 9th with an increased majority.

While the Trusteeship Council on 19 December instructed its French president, Roger Garreau, to prepare a working paper as the basis of a draft statute for the internationalization of Jerusalem, the United Nations and the United States warned both Israel and Jordan to do nothing which would prejudice the resolution in favour of internationalization. Nevertheless, the Israeli Parliament met in Jerusalem instead of Tel Aviv on 26 December; most of the Ministries which had not already been transferred to Jerusalem now moved there, with the exception of the Foreign Ministry, which remained in Tel Aviv to be in touch with the foreign diplomatic missions; and on 23 January 1950 the Parliament approved a proclamation that Jerusalem had been the capital of Israel since the declaration of independence nearly two years before. While it was reported that the

---

[1] See McDonald: *My Mission in Israel*, pp. 186–7; Lehrman: *Israel, the Beginning and Tomorrow*, pp. 239–40.

[2] United Nations document A/AC.31/11, 2 December 1949; and cf. Lehrman, op. cit. p. 237.

[3] See U.N.: *Official Records of the 4th session of the General Assembly, Ad hoc* Political Committee, Summary Records, p. 344.

[4] Lillie Shultz: 'The Jerusalem Story', *The Nation*, 17 December 1949, pp. 589–91. Hal Lehrman (op. cit. pp. 238, 247) states that the Vatican had ordered its diplomatic representatives to call on the Foreign Ministers of the Governments to which they were accredited, with 'instantaneous and startling' effects on the voting in the General Assembly; and he adds that the probable explanation of the 'vacillating policy' of the United States Government was the 'formidable consideration' that their country contained 25 million Roman Catholics.

[5] The majority of thirty-eight for internationalization at the final vote in the plenary meeting consisted of seventeen Roman Catholic states, twelve Arab and Asian states, five states of the Soviet bloc, Australia, Ethiopia, Greece, and Liberia. Among those who opposed it were Israel, the United States, the United Kingdom, Canada, South Africa, Turkey, Yugoslavia, and the Scandinavian countries.

Israel and Jordan Governments were discussing an agreement that would (among other things) settle their respective zones of authority in Jerusalem, Roger Garreau on 30 January recommended to the Trusteeship Council a compromise between the General Assembly's resolution for full internationalization and the Conciliation Commission's recommendations. His suggestion was that, whereas the entire Jerusalem territory should be a demilitarized *corpus separatum*, the Jewish and Muslim zones should remain under the sovereignty of Israel and Jordan respectively; and the Christian and Jewish quarters of the Old City, together with those few Holy Places that lay outside the Old City walls, should be placed under the collective sovereignty of the United Nations as an 'international city' whose inhabitants would be free either to opt for citizenship of it or to retain their present nationality.[1] This suggestion was, however, rejected by all concerned as an unacceptable compromise; Israel would not modify her intention to incorporate the Jewish New City, and Jordan would not even discuss internationalization; and the Trusteeship Council turned to the academic task of revising the draft statute already prepared by it in 1948, a protracted operation which was not completed until 4 April.[2]

(5) *King 'Abdullāh between Israel and the Arab League, 1950*

Meanwhile, Israel and Jordan, having in common their opposition to the internationalization proposals and to the Arab League's support of them, had been negotiating for a settlement between them. The United States Ambassador in Israel understood that before the General Assembly's debate on Jerusalem 'Abdullāh had renewed his request for an outlet to the Mediterranean through Beersheba and Gaza, had claimed the return of the lost Arab suburbs of Jerusalem, and had sought the facilities of a free port at Haifa, in return for which he made Israel the modest offer of free port facilities at 'Aqaba and access to the site of the potash works at the northern end of the Dead Sea which had been abandoned and fired by the Jews, and looted by Arabs, in May 1948.[3] Such terms were naturally not acceptable to Israel. Early in 1950, however, as a consequence of the General Assembly's resolution to internationalize Jerusalem, the Israel Government were understood to have accepted as a basis for negotiations a proposal made by 'Abdullāh for a five-year non-aggression pact, under which trade and travel would be freely allowed across the existing armistice

---

[1] U.N., Trusteeship Council: *Official Records*, 4th year, 6th session, pp. 49–50, and 52, paragraphs 36–37.

[2] At the 1950 General Assembly neither a Swedish nor a Belgian resolution concerning Jerusalem obtained the necessary two-thirds' majority (see U.N., General Assembly, 5th session: *Official Records*, Annexes, agenda item no. 20, pp. 7–8 (document A/1724, report of the *Ad hoc* Political Committee) and 326th plenary meeting, 15 December 1950, p. 684).

[3] The Zionist allegation that the Arab Legion was responsible for the looting has been denied to the writer.

line, while a free port zone at Haifa would give Jordan her much-needed Mediterranean outlet.[1] Ben Gurion and the Israeli military authorities, however, are said to have disagreed with their Foreign Ministry on the advisability of showing some generosity, and contradictory reports emanating from Israeli sources about the prospects of reaching an agreement[2] precipitated the opposition to 'Abdullāh, both from his enemies in Egypt and Syria and within Jordan itself. At the beginning of March 1950 the Jordan Government of Tawfīq Abū'l-Hudā, which was opposed to a settlement with Israel, resigned but was re-formed after Samīr ar-Rifā'ī had failed to form a government more compliant with 'Abdullāh's wishes. In Egypt the Wafdist Government, which had been returned by the general election of January 1950, opened a violent press campaign against 'Abdullāh as part of its general anti-British policy, and did not hesitate to invent a story that 'Abdullāh and Ben Gurion had secretly signed an agreement aboard a British warship at 'Aqaba, in the presence of the British and United States Ministers.[3] 'Abdullāh at-Tall, a young ex-officer of the Arab Legion who had won his King's favour during the defence of Jerusalem in 1948 but had afterwards, when his overweening ambition was not satisfied, resigned his commission and withdrawn to Cairo, now opportunely furnished the newspaper *Akhbār ul-Yawm* with copies of the Shūna agreement which the Israelis had extorted from King 'Abdullāh in March 1949,[4] and suggested that the Arab League should call on him to abdicate. The Jordan Minister to Sa'ūdī Arabia also resigned his post and moved to Cairo, and when the spring session of the Council of the Arab League opened on 25 March there was a move led by Egypt to exclude Jordan from membership on the ground of 'Abdullāh's negotiations with Israel.[5] These negotiations had, however, been abruptly suspended,[6] and on 1 April (after British mediation between Egypt and Jordan, it was said) the Jordan Minister in Cairo signed on behalf of his Government an Arab

---

[1] See McDonald: *My Mission in Israel*, pp. 193–4.

[2] See *New York Times*, 1 March 1950 (Jerusalem correspondent reporting a 'highly-placed Israeli source'); *The Times* Tel Aviv correspondent, 2 March 1950; Jon Kimche in *Jewish Observer and Middle East Review*, 29 February 1952, pp. 10–11.

[3] See A special correspondent in Geneva, *Observer*, 5 March, *Bourse Égyptienne*, 14 March, and *Monde*, 15 March 1950, citing, as source, the Lebanese Minister in 'Ammān, reported by the Damascus correspondent of the Agence France-Presse; cf. the Communist *Moyen-Orient*, May 1950, p. 5.

[4] See above, pp. 297–8; tendentious extracts republished in *Progrès Égyptien*, 27 March 1950. The murder of King 'Abdullāh in Jerusalem on 20 July 1951 was believed to have been organized by 'Abdullāh at-Tall and the ex-Muftī jointly; see S.G.T.: 'King Abdullah's Assassins', *The World Today*, October 1951, vii. 416–17.

[5] See *Bourse Égyptienne*, 28 March 1950, 'Vers l'exclusion de la Jordanie'. The technique adopted was an Egyptian proposal that the ex-Muftī's phantom 'Government of All-Palestine' should be invited to send a representative to the League Council, a direct challenge to 'Abdullāh's claim to the remnant of Arab Palestine.

[6] *New York Times* Tel Aviv correspondent, 25 March 1950.

League resolution that forfeiture of membership should be the penalty for the making of a separate treaty or agreement with Israel.

The holding of a general election in both Trans-Jordan and the remnant of Arab Palestine had already been announced in December 1949 and took place on 11 April 1950, 'Abdullāh having declared that the Jordan Government would henceforth be responsible to the Chamber so elected, instead of to the Crown, as formerly. The ex-Muftī called for a boycott. 'There were some disturbances in Hebron, Nablus, and the Old City [of Jerusalem], and there were some accusations of forged ballot papers: the voting in one area was said to be well over 100 per cent.' Some prominent critics of 'Abdullāh's policy were elected, and five of the eleven members of the new Cabinet were Palestinians.[1] The new Prime Minister, Sa'īd al-Muftī, announced on 24 April the formal incorporation of Arab Palestine (excepting the Gaza strip, occupied by Egypt) in Jordan, despite a warning issued two days earlier by the Secretary-General of the Arab League; and the Senate and Chamber of Deputies, sitting together, gave their approval.[2] The Israel Government refused to recognize this 'unilateral' act of incorporation and declared that the status of 'the Arab areas west of the Jordan' remained an open question for them.[3] The British Government's formal recognition was coupled with their *de jure* recognition of Israel, in an announcement by the Minister of State on 27 April.[4] The Anglo-Jordan Treaty of 1948 would be held to apply to the whole territory east of the Israel–Jordan armistice line or any modification of it upon which the two parties might agree, but Britain would not seek military bases west of the river Jordan in peace-time; the partition of the Jerusalem area between Israel and Jordan would be recognized only *de facto*, in view of the General Assembly's vote for internationalization in the previous December. The Minister associated himself with a question put by Churchill on the possibility of bringing King 'Abdullāh and President Weizmann 'into the closest harmonious contact'; but the extension of the Anglo-Jordan Treaty to Arab Palestine was ill received by the Israel Government, who in their negotiations with 'Abdullāh had always insisted that its application should be confined to Trans-Jordan.[5] Egypt now

---

[1] Esmond Wright, 'Abdallah's Jordan', *Middle East Journal*, Autumn 1951, v. 457; and see *Figaro*, 13 April 1950, reporting the Agence France-Presse correspondent in 'Ammān.

[2] Contrary to Egyptian and Syrian propaganda at the time, it is stated on good authority that the great majority of the ex-Palestinians favoured the union as giving them the support of a stable government and army, while some Trans-Jordanians were more doubtful because they feared the encroachments of the better-educated Palestinians.

[3] *New York Times*, 25 April 1950, from its Tel Aviv correspondent.

[4] H.C.Deb. 5th ser., vol. 474, coll. 1137–9. For an Anglo-Israeli financial agreement of 30 March 1950 see Great Britain, Foreign Office: *Agreement . . . for the settlement of financial matters outstanding as a result of the termination of the Mandate for Palestine, London, 30th March 1950*, Cmd. 7941 (London, H.M.S.O., 1950).

[5] *The Times* Tel Aviv correspondent, 29 April 1950.

proposed to the political committee of the Arab League that Jordan should be expelled for her contumacy in incorporating Arab Palestine, but failed on 15 May to obtain a unanimous vote, owing to the abstention of 'Irāq and the Yaman. At a resumed meeting in June Egypt had the support of only Sa'ūdī Arabia in demanding Jordan's expulsion, and had to be content with a face-saving resolution (which 'Abdullāh had rejected when 'Irāq had proposed it as a compromise in May) 'to treat the Arab part of Palestine annexed by Jordan as a trust in its hands until the Palestine case is finally solved in the interest of its inhabitants'.[1]

(6) *The Three Western Powers' Declaration of May 1950*

In the meantime the United States, British, and French Foreign Ministers, meeting in London from 11 to 13 May, had sought to harmonize their Middle East policies. One of the matters at issue was the supply of arms to the Middle Eastern countries. The United Nations embargo on the supply of arms to the belligerents in the Palestine War had been lifted when, in August 1949, the Security Council had ruled that the conclusion of the Arab armistices with Israel had superseded the truce and the accompanying arms embargo.[2] Britain had thereupon resumed the supply of arms under the treaty undertakings to Egypt, 'Irāq, and Jordan, and France was reported to have furnished considerable quantities of arms to her protégé, the Syrian dictator Husnī az-Za'īm.[3] Although the arms supplied by Britain were officially described as 'limited quantities' only,[4] it was pointed out that they included jet-aircraft, tanks, and artillery which might be used not merely for the defence of the Middle East in a third world war, but more immediately in an Arab 'second round' against Israel; and that that country was thus forced to buy arms 'through devious channels at greatly inflated costs', since supplies from Britain and the United States were still denied her. The official British view was stated to be that Israel still had a preponderance of military strength which stiffened her attitude towards any settlement with her Arab neighbours;[5] but it was reported that the United States Government had objected to

---

[1] *Egyptian Gazette*, quoting *al-Ahrām*, 22 June 1950.

[2] For the views of Israel, Britain, the Acting Mediator, the United States, and France, see respectively U.N., Security Council, *Official Records*, 4th year, no. 36 (4 August 1949), pp. 15, 21, 22, 27; and no. 38 (11 August 1949), p. 2.

[3] See *Observer*, 18 June 1949, *Scotsman*, 2 December 1949.

[4] The British Under-Secretary for Foreign Affairs, 19 April 1950, H.C.Deb. 5th ser., vol. 474, col. 114.

[5] See William Clark: 'Arms Tension in Middle East', *Observer*, 5 March 1950, with the indication from the Israeli side that the Anglo-American embargo might once again force Israel to buy arms behind the Iron Curtain. Israel had 'sufficient war material for her internal security and defence', according to the British Under-Secretary for Foreign Affairs (loc. cit.); one responsible estimate was that her military strength equalled, and that her strength in aircraft was double, that of all the Arab states together.

the scale of British military supplies to the Arab states, and had taken the lead in holding the tripartite talks on this subject.[1] Another question for consideration by the Foreign Ministers was the obvious opposition of France, and of some quarters in the United States, to what was alleged to be British encouragement for the schemes of the 'Irāqī and Jordan Governments to bring the Syrian Republic into some kind of 'Fertile Crescent Unity'.[2] On 25 May, accordingly, the United States, British, and French Governments issued a joint declaration confirming their opposition to the development of an arms race between the Arab states and Israel, and stating that all applications for arms or war material from these countries would be considered in the light of their legitimate self-defence and their part in the defence of the area as a whole. They declared

their desire to promote the establishment and maintenance of peace and stability in the area, and their unalterable opposition to the use of force or threat of force between any of the States in that area. The three Governments, should they find that any of these States was preparing to violate frontiers or armistice lines, would, consistently with their obligations as members of the United Nations, immediately take action, both within and outside the United Nations, to prevent such violation.[3]

The Arabs objected to the declaration because, as they saw it, it pledged the support of the three Powers for the maintenance of armistice lines which the Israelis had secured by breaking the truce with the acquiescence of the United States, and also because the Arabs doubted, in view of the American attitude, whether the three Powers would in fact intervene effectively to prevent the further expansion of Israel by force of arms. In a long reply, the political committee of the Arab League declared that, 'notwithstanding their sincere desire for peace, they could not permit any action calculated to affect their sovereignty or independence'.[4]

(7) Conclusions
(a) Arab Defeat and the Refugees

The United Nations in 1949, and the more reluctant British Government in 1950, had thus set their seal on the successive failures of the Arab

[1] New York Times Washington correspondent, 25 May 1950; Hal Lehrman: Israel, the Beginning and Tomorrow, p. 292.
[2] See Lenczowski: The Middle East in World Affairs, p. 254, and Majid Khadduri: 'The Scheme of Fertile Crescent Unity', in The Near East and the Great Powers, ed. by Richard N. Frye, especially p. 171. The French Legation in Damascus was believed to have encouraged the Syrian dictator, Husnî az-Za'im, in his opposition to these schemes (see Alford Carleton: 'The Syrian Coups d'État of 1949', Middle East Journal, January 1950, iv. 7–8); and when he was shot by a rival Syrian military junta on 14 August 1949 the Monde (16 August), departing from its usual standard, laid the responsibility upon 'the clan Sterling, Frere, Spears, Glubb, and Company' (see above, p. 115).
[3] Text in New York Times, The Times, and Figaro, 26 May 1950.
[4] Bourse Égyptienne, 22 June 1950.

League, first to prevent by force of arms the birth of the State of Israel, and then to contain it within the areas proposed by the General Assembly in November 1947 or to bring about a fair exchange of territories. The disturbance of the already precarious political balance within the Arab countries was manifested, as we have seen, in the murders of Nuqrāshī Pashā in Egypt and of King 'Abdullāh, and in a series of military *coups d'état* in Syria involving the shooting of two successive colonel-dictators;[1] but, much more fundamentally, the severe shock to the Arabs' pride and sense of justice gave a powerful impetus to that reaction against the authority and prestige of the West which was already inherent in the national movements for independence. The original British sponsoring in the Balfour Declaration of the establishment of a Jewish national home, and its subsequent defence by British arms, notably against the Palestine Arab Rebellion of 1936–9, could not be effaced from Arab memories by the British effort from 1939 onwards to curb the Zionist bid for supremacy in Palestine; for in Arab eyes that British effort seemed irresolute and half-hearted in comparison with the decisive steps taken to quell the Palestine Arabs in 1938–9;[2] and Britain's yielding to the forward movement of Zionism in 1947, and her abdication of the Mandate in 1948, were regarded as a greater betrayal than the active support given to Israel by the United States. For most Arabs the partial responsibility of the West for their defeat in the Palestine War largely overshadowed their own failure to achieve political unity and military cohesion, although two distinguished Arab thinkers did venture to analyse, frankly and in writing, the causes of that failure. Mūsā al-'Alamī (a former Palestine Government civil servant who had resigned in 1937 at the time of the Palestine Arab Rebellion, had afterwards dissociated himself from the extremism of the Muftī, had officially represented the Palestine Arabs at the conferences in 1944–5 which had brought the Arab League into being,[3] and in 1946 with the help of the 'Irāqī Government had organized Arab Offices in the United States, London, and Paris for the purpose of countering Zionist propaganda there) admitted that first the Palestine Arabs, and then the Arab

---

[1] Za'īm's supplanter, Sāmī al-Hinnāwī, who favoured a dual monarchy union with 'Irāq, was arrested on 19 December 1949 in a third military coup led by Adīb Shīshaklī, and after being released was shot dead in Beirut on 30 October 1950 by a cousin of Husnī az-Za'īm's Prime Minister, who had been shot with his leader. For two years Shīshaklī was content to be the power behind the scenes while Syria was governed under a new Constitution of 5 September 1950 (see Majid Khadduri: 'Constitutional Development in Syria', *Middle East Journal*, April 1951, v. 149–60); but on 29 November 1951 he led a fourth *coup d'état* against the Government of the Hizb ush-Sha'b (People's Party), and was elected President without effective opposition in a plebiscite conducted in July 1953. He resigned, after an army revolt, on 25 February 1954.

[2] An account of the Arab rising against the British Administration in Palestine (which was only put down after strong British reinforcements had been drafted into the country and drastic counter-measures, including collective punishments of suspect Arab villages, had been taken against the rebels) will be found in the *Survey* for 1938, i. 414–22.

[3] See *Survey* for 1939–46: *The Middle East in the War*, p. 340.

states, had totally failed to match the organization, discipline, and single-
ness of purpose of the Zionists, and had been betrayed by their own divisions and slackness:

> In the face of the enemy the Arabs were not a state, but petty states; groups,
> not a nation; each fearing and anxiously watching the other and intriguing
> against it. What concerned them most and guided their policy was not to win
> the war and save Palestine from the enemy, but what would happen after the
> struggle, who would be predominant in Palestine, or annex it to themselves,
> and how they could achieve their own ambitions. Their announced aim was the
> salvation of Palestine, and they said that afterward its destiny should be left to
> its people. This was said with the tongue only. In their hearts all wished it for
> themselves; and most of them were hurrying to prevent their neighbors from
> being predominant, even though nothing remained except the offal and bones.[1]

On the other hand, the great majority of politically minded Arabs were
inclined to throw the larger part of the responsibility for their defeat upon
Israel, the West, and the United Nations; and this refusal of theirs to face
all the facts found expression most harmfully in respect of the practical
measures proposed for dealing with the problem of the Arab refugees,
whose numbers an Economic Survey Mission of the United Nations estimated in November 1949 at 757,000, plus many thousands who remained
in their villages but had been separated from the lands that previously
maintained them by the demarcation lines drawn in the armistices with
Israel.[2] Of this total number it was estimated that less than one-fifth were
temporarily self-supporting or otherwise provided for, while the remainder
were destitute. The refugees naturally demanded to be reinstated in their
homes and property, and the political leaders of the Arab World had not
the courage to tell them that they were asking for the impossible. It remained a stubbornly maintained Arab political principle (from which it
might be physically dangerous for an Arab statesman to express public
dissent, whatever he might do privately) that Israel must make full restitution of their homes and lands to this unhappy multitude; the refugees
were encouraged by irresponsible political mentors to insist on receiving
nothing less, and to reject proposals made by the United Nations Relief and

---

[1] Musa Alami: 'The Lesson of Palestine', *Middle East Journal*, October 1949, iii. 385. This
article was a partially summarized translation of his Arabic essay *Ibrat Filastīn* (Beirut, 1949);
for another English version see *Arab News Bulletin* (London), 13 April 1949. Another analysis
of the subject was by a future President of the Syrian University, Dr. Constantine Zuraiq:
Ma'nā un-Nakba ['The Meaning of the Disaster'] (Beirut, Kashaf Press, 1948), reviewed in
Middle East Journal, October 1949, iii. 469–70.

[2] The number of these 'economic and psychological refugees' had previously been estimated at
some 60,000; but the latest studies of the problem at the time of writing placed the number as
high as 130,000–150,000, over and above a total of 867,000 displaced refugees eligible for United
Nations aid (see Georgiana G. Stevens: 'Arab Refugees: 1948–1952', *Middle East Journal*,
Summer 1952, vi. 281–98; Lord Kinross: 'The Maturing State of Jordan', *Listener*, 28 August
1952, p. 326).

Works Agency (set up early in 1950 to supersede the purely relief organization) for their resettlement and reintegration in appropriate Arab territories; and the Arab Governments themselves (except that of King 'Abdullāh, in his desire to consolidate his enlarged Kingdom of the Jordan) gave little encouragement to the resettlement proposals.[1] The cost of resettlement schemes proposed in 1949 by the United Nations Economic Survey Mission was inflated by rising world prices, and far outstripped the sums obtained by the voluntary subscriptions of member states of the United Nations. The Korean War created a new refugee problem which took precedence over the existing Arab problem in the eyes of most nations; and in 1952 a traveller found the great majority of the Arab refugees subsisting on bare relief in conditions of the most deplorable frustration and apathy.[2]

(β) Israel's Economic Problem

A particular grievance of the Arabs was that £4 to £5 million, standing to Arabs' accounts in banks which had become subject to Israel in the partitioning of Palestine, had been sequestrated by Israel as enemy property. The Israel Government had consistently announced that they would consider releasing these sums, and receiving back a stipulated number of Arab refugees or contributing in other ways to the alleviation of their position, only as part of a negotiated general peace settlement with the Arab states which would include a cessation of the Arab economic boycott of Israel. There were, indeed, serious limits to what Israel was materially able to offer, for she too had not won her independence and her victory over the Arabs cheaply. Besides the casualties among the most vigorous of her manhood,[3] the cost in money was put at about £100 million, the loss to civilian property being more than £10 million.[4] As in the case of the Arab states, however, the immediate material losses due to the war were of less consequence than delayed effects on the national psychology. The objective for which, more than any other, the Zionists had undermined the authority of the British mandate and fought the Arabs was freedom of immigration. It was politically inevitable, and

---

[1] Even in Jordan in 1952 only some 500 families of refugees had been integrated, or were in process of integration, into the economy of the country (Lord Kinross, loc. cit.). For the demonstration project of the Arab Development Society organized by Mūsā al-'Alamī, see Cecil A. Hourani: 'Experimental Village in the Jordan Valley', Middle East Journal, Autumn 1951, v. 497–501.

[2] See Owen Tweedy: 'The Arab Refugees', International Affairs, July 1952, xxviii. 338–43.

[3] Casualties in the armed forces were stated to be four times as heavy proportionately as those of the United States army in the Second World War (see Hon. Edwin Samuel in Jewish Monthly, December 1949, p. 548). They included 6,000 killed, according to Jon Kimche (Commentary, September 1952, p. 243).

[4] Zionist Review, 7 October 1949, p. 13; 17 March 1950, p. 18. The war directly cost Jordan £6·5 million; the Egyptian Government claimed to have spent £120 million.

also, no doubt, militarily advantageous, that, once independence had been proclaimed, the gates of Israel should be thrown open to an unrestricted flow of immigrants,[1] of whom half a million had arrived by the end of 1950, an addition of some 70 per cent. to the Jewish population of Palestine as it stood at the time when the Mandate expired. Israel entered upon her peace-time existence under the leadership of Ben Gurion, who continued to display admirable energy and resourcefulness and was filled with a sublime confidence.[2] There was a tendency to believe that the miracle of political success in out-manœuvring the British Government and of military victory over the Arabs would be followed by some equally miraculous solution of the economic problem of a country whose principal export products were citrus fruit and potash, but which lacked adequate sources of power (especially since the 'Irāqīs had closed the oil pipe-line from the Kirkūk fields to the Haifa refinery), the essential raw materials for most branches of heavy and light industry, and the basic foodstuffs for both man and beast. All this had to be built up on the Zionist Movement's foundations of exceptional ingenuity and resource, reinforced by continuing financial aid from world Jewry. In 1948, the year of the Palestine War, private donations from the United States through the United Jewish appeal produced $150 million (declining to $86 million by 1950), and at the beginning of 1949 the Export-Import Bank extended a credit to Israel of $100 million, which was later augmented by $35 million. It was estimated that during the first three years the sums raised for Israel in the United States—as gifts, credits, or investments—exceeded $400 million.[3] However, the careful selection and training to which the immigrant 'pioneers' (halutzim) had before 1939 been subjected, in order to make them economically useful almost from the time of their arrival in Palestine, could not be applied to the main inflow of immigrants in the years of independence. Their numbers rapidly outstripped the available housing, even allowing for that abandoned by the Arab refugees,[4] and also the available resources for putting the immigrants to productive employment. Moreover, the new immigrants were of uneven quality, since previous immigration had already absorbed the majority of those inspired by a creative zeal for Zionism. Those who were allowed to leave the Eastern European

---

[1] Ben Gurion admitted in April 1949 that many of them were living in conditions of 'frightful overcrowding' and presenting 'grave economic problems', but 'the maximum increase of the Jewish population was vital to the security of Israel' (Sacher: *Israel, the Establishment of a State*, p. 146).

[2] See Lehrman: *Israel, the Beginning and Tomorrow*, p. 195.

[3] Ibid. p. 299.

[4] Many abandoned Arab villages were blown up by the Israelis for tactical reasons during the fighting, without foreseeing that they would be needed to accommodate immigrants, according to Lehrman (ibid. pp. 224–5) 'The rate of annual building, three years after [the] creation of the state, produced scarcely half of the structures which would have been required to house just the immigrants who arrived that same year' (ibid. p. 61).

countries were rather, for the most part, *petits bourgeois* escaping from the Communist régimes behind the Iron Curtain, and an appreciable number of these sought to follow their traditional pursuit of small trading and went to swell the population of the already overcrowded cities, Tel Aviv, Haifa, and Jerusalem. A different problem of social and economic assimilation was presented by the Oriental Jews from the Yaman, 'Irāq, and Libya,[1] for whose rescue from the risk of Arab reprisals and from medieval ghetto conditions there were successive organized air-lifts. The inflow of investment capital from the United States and elsewhere was intended to be directed to projects which would increase exports, replace imports, or satisfy essential needs; but serious doubt was expressed whether these objects were being achieved.[2] The fundamental problem was how a country whose exports (in a very limited range of commodities, because of lack of raw materials) amounted in 1950 to only one-eighth of its imports was to contain the simultaneous inflationary pressures of immigration at an annual rate of more than 20 per cent. of the existing population; the maintenance of a proportionately large and well-equipped army which would deter the Arab states from venturing on a 'second round'; and the aspiration to a Central European standard of living for organized labour, whose political influence was paramount in the government Mapai party (led by Ben Gurion) and in the all-pervading Histadruth federation of trade unions, but whose actual productive efficiency could not yet support such a standard.[3] Already in 1950 a policy had been adopted of moving new immigrants directly to working-camps (*ma'abaroth*), particularly in the less densely settled frontier districts, where they might be put to agricultural work, road-making, or tree-planting, or find regular or casual employment in industry. This was, however, only a palliative, for the rise in world prices that followed the outbreak of the Korean War was to increase the Finance Minister's difficulties; the attempt to impose on the consumer a régime of austerity in the most essential foodstuffs and clothing was largely

[1] See Lehrman, op. cit. p. 62. The inflow of nearly 42,000 Yamanī Jews in 1949–50 was immediately followed by the 'Irāqī Government's permission to the Jews of 'Irāq to leave, so that over 100,000 had availed themselves of the opportunity by the end of 1951. When at that time the state of Libya became independent, the removal of its ancient Jewish community to Israel was virtually complete. Immigration from French North Africa had been subordinated to these more urgent operations, but the trend of Muslim nationalism in the protectorates of Morocco and Tunisia, and the French attitude towards it, were carefully watched in Israel.

[2] 'There is every indication that many of these newly established industries have used their limited raw materials for producing non-essential goods for the local market, thus raising living standards beyond what our means justify. . . . It seems that the character of foreign investments has been conditioned more by the traditional habits and propensities of Jews abroad than by the needs of the Israel economy' (*Israel Economist*, June 1952, viii. 137; cf. 'Lean Years for Israel', *The Economist*, 28 June 1952, pp. 893–4, and 5 July 1952, pp. 30–32; and, generally, Gerald de Gaury: *The New State of Israel* (London, Verschoyle, 1952), chapter viii).

[3] 'The public was for a year or so allowed to live in a sort of cloud cuckoo land of "All this and Heaven too!" ' (S. Hoofien: *Israel To-day and To-morrow* (an address at the inaugural meeting of the Anglo-Israel Chamber of Commerce, London, 18 October 1950), p. 10).

circumvented by recourse to the black market in goods and foreign currencies, which had a most depressive effect on the free value of the Israeli
pound. From a nominal value of $2.80 or £1 sterling, it was unofficially
quoted at as little as U.S. 60 cents. In an attempt to provide a turning-
point in 'the tortuous struggle for economic survival', therefore, a so-called
New Economic Policy was initiated on 13 February 1952. The exchange
value of the Israeli pound was progressively reduced from $2.80 to the
still unrealistic figure of $1, and immigration during 1952 was cut to only
13·5 per cent. of the 1951 figure. Currency exchange and a compulsory
loan in June 1952 effected a temporary 15 per cent. reduction in the banknote circulation; but by December the figure was again above the previous
maximum of 1 May, and was still rising in February 1953. The proportion
of imports covered by exports had fallen from 16·7 per cent. in the first
seven months of 1951 to only 13 per cent. in the same period of 1952. The
glamorous prognostications of previous years were accordingly abandoned.
It was admitted, for example, that the ambitious afforestation schemes
which Ben Gurion had proclaimed were 'investments on such long terms
and without immediate help to production that the result was a heavy
drain on our money resources';[1] and in a retrospect of one year's operation
of the New Economic Policy the former Director-General of the Ministry
of Finance was reduced to describing Israel as 'a poor and undeveloped
country' with a 'lack of values and assets which would warrant the expansion of purchasing power': the New Economic Policy was not 'and was
not intended to be a panacea which would cure all the ills of our economic
life caused by a disparity between needs and possibilities, aims and means'.[2]

[1] Gerda Luft, in *Jerusalem Post*, 12 February 1953, p. 7.
[2] David Horowitz, ibid. pp. 5–6.

INDEX[1]

'Abd ul-Hādī, Ibrāhīm, Egyptian politician, 125, 293.

'Abd ul-Husain Hazhīr, *see* HAZHĪR.

'Abd ul-Ilāh, the Amīr, Regent of 'Irāq: and Anglo-'Irāqī Treaty, 149; opposes ratification of new treaty, 156; announces resignation of Sālih Jabr, 157.

'Abd ul-Karīm (Abdel Krim), 134–5.

'Abdullāh, King of Trans-Jordan (later of the Hashimite Kingdom of the Jordan):
Anglo-Transjordan Treaty invoked by, 296.
Arab Higher Committee, attitude to, 280–1.
British financial and military aid to, 273.
Fārūq, visit to, 280.
Israel: territorial demands on, 309; five-year non-aggression pact with, proposed, 309–10.
Jerusalem, internationalization of, 306.
'King of All Palestine', acclaimed as, by Palestinian Arabs, 290.
Muftī of Jerusalem, replaces, 290 n.
murder of, 13, 310 n., 314.
opposition to: in Egypt, 144, 310; in Jordan, 310; in Syria, 310.
Sa'ūd, Ibn, visit to, 280.
Shūna Agreement, 297–8.
Turkey, visit to, 30.

Abū'l-Hudā, Tawfīq, Jordan politician, 310.

Acheson, Dean, U.S. Acting Secretary of State, 217, 226.

Ad hoc Committee, *see under* UNITED NATIONS: Palestine.

Adamantos, AKEL Mayor of Famagusta, 183.

Ağri Dağ (Mount Ararat), abortive U.S. expedition to, 49.

AKEL, *see under* CYPRUS: Political parties.

Akka (Acre), terrorist attack on prison at, 241.

'Alā, Husain, Persian Ambassador in Washington, 59; brings Soviet-Persian dispute before Security Council, 68–69, 70; reports on evacuation of Soviet troops, 72; instructed to make no further statements on Soviet-Persian dispute, 73.

'Alamī, Mūsā al-, on causes of Arab defeat, 314–15.

Aleppo, 21, 22.

Alexandretta (Iskenderun), strategic importance of, to Turkey, 39–40.

Alexandretta, Sanjaq of (Hatay), 22, 30.

Allen, George V., U.S. Ambassador to Persia, and military supervision during elections, 80.

All-Persian Supreme Planning Board, and Seven-Year Plan, 98.

Alsop, Stewart, U.S. commentator, 35, 36.

Altrincham, Lord (formerly Sir Edward Grigg), advises withdrawal of British troops from Egypt, 116.

al-Wafd al-Misrī (Wafd Party newspaper), editor of, arrested, 123.

American Political Action Committee for Palestine, 200.

Anatolia, north-east, 26.

Anglo-Iranian Oil Company, *see under* OIL.

Ankara University, anti-Communist demonstration in, 50.

Aqaba, Gulf of, 13, 296–7.

Arab Government of All Palestine: proclaimed 20 Sept. 1948, 286; recognized by Egypt, 290.

Arab Higher Committee: and London conference on Palestine, 228; boycotts UNSCOP proceedings, 241; calls for anti-Jewish demonstrations, 251; and guerrilla warfare against Jews, 253 n.; and High Commissioner's truce proposals, 264, 265, 266.

Arab League:
'administrative council' for Palestine formed by, 281.
conference with British Government, 228–9, 236.
Egypt uses as instrument of anti-British policy, 144.
equipment, inadequacy of, 279–80.
formation of (1945), 3, 189.
Jordan, attempts to exclude from, 310, 311–12.
lack of cohesion in, 6, 19, 53, 280.
Palestine, proposals for unitary state in, 228 and n.

---

[1] In the cross-references in this Index references in capitals and small capitals are to other main headings, while those in ordinary type are to subdivisions of the same main heading. For the explanation of Abbreviations see also list on p. vii.

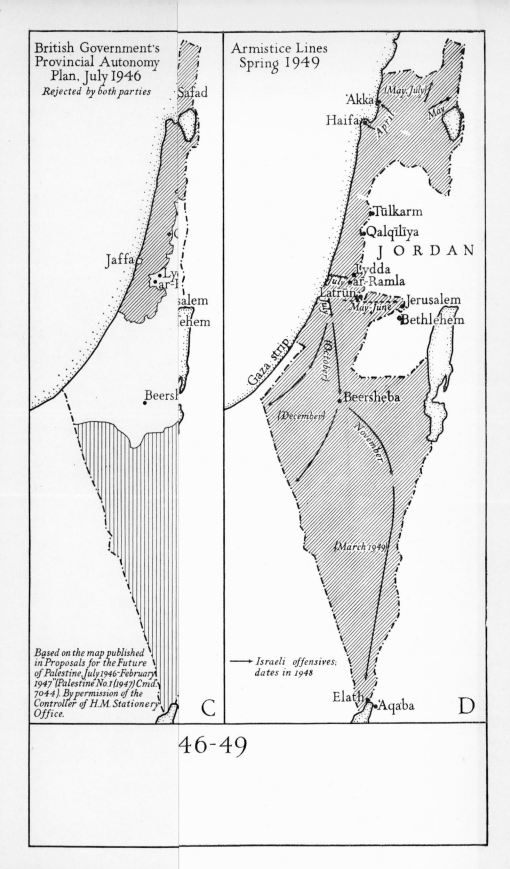

British Government's Provincial Autonomy Plan, July 1946
Rejected by both parties

Safad

Jaffa

Ly
ar-I

salem

ehem

Beersh

Based on the map published in Proposals for the Future of Palestine, July 1946-February 1947 (Palestine No.1 (1947) Cmd. 7044). By permission of the Controller of H.M. Stationery Office.

C

Armistice Lines Spring 1949

'Akka   *(May, July)*

Haifa   April   May

Tulkarm
Qalqīlīya
J O R D A N
Lydda
ar-Ramla
July
Latrun
May-June   Jerusalem
July   Bethlehem
(October)

Gaza strip

Beersheba
(December)
November

(March 1949)

→ *Israeli offensives; dates in 1948*

Elath   Aqaba

D

46-49